MOTOCOURSE™

THE WORLD'S LEADING GRAND PRIX & SUPERBIKE ANNUAL

icon
PUBLISHING LIMITED

RIDE
WITH US !

FIM-LIVE.com   FIM-STORE.com   FIM-TV.com

FÉDÉRATION INTERNATIONALE
DE MOTOCYCLISME

CONTENTS

MOTOCOURSE 2011–2012

is published by:
Icon Publishing Limited
Regent Lodge
4 Hanley Road
Malvern
Worcestershire
WR14 4PQ
United Kingdom

Tel: +44 (0)1684 564511

Email: info@motocourse.com
Website: www.motocourse.com

Printed in the United Kingdom by
Butler Tanner and Dennis Ltd
Caxton Road, Frome
Somerset BA11 1NF

ISBN: 978-1905334-62-9

DISTRIBUTORS

Gardners Books
1 Whittle Drive, Eastbourne
East Sussex BN23 6QH
Tel: +44 (0)1323 521555
email: sales@gardners.com

Chaters Wholesale Ltd
25/26 Murrell Green Business Park
Hook, Hampshire RG27 9GR
Telephone: +44 (0) 1256 765 443
Fax: +44 (0)1256 769 900
email: books@chaters.co.uk

NORTH AMERICA
Quayside Distribution Services
400 First Avenue North, Suite 300
Minneapolis, MN 55401, USA
Telephone: 612 344 8100
Fax: 612 344 8691

Dust jacket: Repsol Honda's Casey
Stoner, who won ten races on his
way to the 2011 MotoGP World
Championship.

Title page: Carlos Checa took the
Superbike World Championship on
his Ducati.
Photos: Gold & Goose

Acknowledgements

The Editor and staff of MOTOCOURSE wish to thank the following for their assistance in compiling the 2011–12
edition: Henny Ray Abrams, Majo Botella, Alex Briggs, Jerry Burgess, Paul Butler, Peter Clifford, Rhys Edwards, William
Favero, Aldo Gandolfo, Maria Guidotti, Chris Jonnum, Isabelle Lariviere, Hector Martin, Gavin Matheson, Elisa Pavan,
David Pato, Judith Pieper-Koehler, Ignacio Sagnier, Mike Trimby, Frine Vellila, Mike Webb and Günther Wiesinger, as
well as the riders and technicians who helped with inside information for this book. A special thanks to Marlboro,
Repsol and Honda hospitality staff for lunch, and numerous colleagues and friends for their always helpful advice.

Photographs published in MOTOCOURSE 2011–2012 have been contributed by:
Chief photographers: Gold& Goose.

Other photographs contributed by: AMA Pro Series, Bauer, Gavan Caldwell, Clive Challinor, Dave Collister, Dave
Ducati, Tom Hnatiw, Mortons, Dave Purves, Neil Spalding, Mark Walters, Yamaha Classic Racing Team

publisher
STEVE SMALL

steve.small@iconpublishinglimited.com

commercial director
BRYN WILLIAMS

bryn.williams@iconpublishinglimited.com

editor
MICHAEL SCOTT

text editor
IAN PENBERTHY

results and statistics
PETER McLAREN

chief photographers
GOLD & GOOSE
David Goldman
Gareth Harford
Patrik Lundin

www.gngpix.com

tel +44 (0)20 8444 2448

MotoGP and circuit illustrations
ADRIAN DEAN

f1artwork@blueyonder.co.uk

www.motocourse.com

FOREWORD by CASEY STONER

MY 26th birthday was an incredible day. I won my fifth straight home GP at Phillip Island and my second world championship. We've had some tough years since the first one; 2011 could not have gone any better.

Moving to the Repsol Honda team was my dream as a kid, when the whole family would be around the TV to watch Mick Doohan piling up the wins and titles on those beautiful Repsol Honda 500 two-strokes.

Today's four-stroke bikes are different, but the dream came true from the first time I rode the RC212V. The motorcycle and the team were everything I could have expected.

Many people have asked if the year has been easy, straightforward. Not so. We – myself and the crew I was fortunate to bring with me from Ducati – may have had a really good bike, but we still had to work hard to get the best out of it, week in week out.

For one thing, I had to beat all the other guys on Hondas. And Jorge was also riding really well, all year long. Thanks to my guys, to Honda and to all the other people supporting us: winning championships really is a team effort.

I was sorry to see my old team Ducati struggling so soon after my last wins on the bike. Rossi is one of my greatest rivals, and I was looking forward to the chance of trying to beat him again on my new bike. It never came.

But I'm pleased that it is me on the cover of *MOTOCOURSE* again. It's been the most important record of racing since before I was born.

I was the first and the last 800cc champion, and I won more 800cc races than anybody. But I'm not sorry to see them go in favour of 1000cc in 2012. I'm hoping the extra capacity and greater torque will make racing more exciting and enjoyable for everybody, by giving the rider more possibilities. I'd rather we were still racing 500 two-strokes with no electronics, but going to 1000cc is definitely a step in the right direction.

I can hardly wait.

THE SPIRIT LIVES ON

Above: The loss of Marco Simoncelli cast a long shadow.

Right: Just so much expensive scrap. The 800s are off to the museum.

Far right: MotoGP's commercial face is always smiling. Tissot provide the official timing, a watch for every pole position, and here for Nicky Hayden a limited-edition special. He's flanked by Dorna's Ezpeleta (*left*) and Tissot president Francois Thiebaud.

Photos: Gold & Goose

SOME very fundamental questions were being addressed at the end of 2011. The first was posed by the tragic loss of young lion Marco Simoncelli at the 17th of 18 rounds. The shock resounded far and wide. It made everyone, from riders to fans, think deeply about the meaning, and the spirit, of racing.

Nobody answered better than Casey Stoner at the last grand prix of the year. "I hadn't taken any risks all year. I decided to take one now," he said after winning his tenth race by inches.

Another queried the role of the factories in racing, and the role of racing as a development tool for technology.

That answer will come in 2013 and beyond, when Dorna's proposed programme of dumbing down – principally a control ECU and a rev limit – is due to take effect. Racing will become slower and humbler. But, if the example of Moto2 means anything, it might get significantly more exciting than through most of the five-year 800cc era.

Two-strokes have gone from the GPs now, although perhaps not forever. Significant research work continues elsewhere, and the light and simple strokers remain in so many ways the ideal motorcycle engine.

But the current New Dawn is all four-stroke, downbeat and low cost. The response has been encouraging. The Moto3 250 four-strokes will replace the 125s in 2012, and production-based CRT bikes will swell the MotoGP grid back to respectable numbers. Interest from independent manufacturers has been lively in both categories.

The sound will be different. I fear that the distant purring of the new Moto3 machines might prove to be slightly soporific, while the identical *vuvuzela* chorus of Moto2 never fails to irritate.

The spirit remains strong, as it was in the late Marco Simoncelli. Let us honour it.

MICHAEL SCOTT – Wimbledon, November 2011

FIM WORLD CHAMPIONSHIP 2011

TOP TEN RIDERS

THE EDITOR'S CHOICE

Rider Portraits by Gold & Goose

1 CASEY STONER

TWO aspects served to throw the spotlight on the sheer talent that powered Stoner to a second world championship year. The first was his near-flawless performance: ten wins, a four-stroke record for 12 poles, rising above the other Honda riders who shared the best bike of the year. He was on every rostrum except when Rossi knocked him off. The other aspect was the dire performance of the Ducati. Stoner had won three races on basically the same bike at the end of 2010.

For the 26-year-old Australian, joining the Repsol squad fulfilled a childhood dream. He got on with the bike from the very start, but never slackened his work rate, even when leading the times. The result was a show of superiority that swamped the bad years of physical injury and weakness since his first title in 2007.

No one has won more 800cc races than Stoner, and nobody has won more 800cc titles. He looks as though he'll be even better on a 1000.

2 JORGE LORENZO

NOBODY could have got more out of the Yamaha than the defending world champion. His season was an almost year-long display of on-the-limit riding and high corner speed, and all with the utmost consistency.

In this way, he won three races, and won every time he raced in Italy – something of a sweetener after the sour atmosphere in which Rossi had left the Yamaha team the year before. But, quite simply, the Hondas were too much better than his M1.

His rostrum record was not as good as Stoner's, and he crashed out of an important Silverstone Grand Prix. Even so, he kept his title challenge at least mathematically alive to the third-last round in Australia. There he finally payed the price for his year on the edge, falling in practice and sustaining a nasty finger injury that sidelined him for the rest of the season.

Lorenzo's stature grew in 2011 in spite of the bad ending. He matured as a racer and will be formidable again in 2012.

3 DANI PEDROSA

THINGS didn't really go Dani's way in 2011. Quite apart from the arrival of a vexingly fast new team-mate. He'd barely got over one collarbone injury before the other one was broken in the notorious incident with Simoncelli at Le Mans. The Italian took the official blame, but some (including Kevin Schwantz) thought Pedrosa as much responsible, for trying too hard to defend the indefensible.

This was a new accusation for Pedrosa, hitherto criticised for being too unwilling to engage in close combat. It reflected, after a long wait for his supporters, the arrival of a more effective racer.

Dani fought hard for position on several occasions, and on his day he was the class of the field.

He won three races, adding six more top-three finishes. He also was absent from three races, in the early part of the season, and was still riding hurt when he came back.

But for his injuries, without doubt he would have made Stoner's campaign more difficult.

4 ANDREA DOVIZIOSO

DOVI spent the year under a cloud. He'd retained his Repsol Honda contract only by hard-nosed negotiating. Thus HRC had an unique three-rider team, and he was very much number three. This left him radiating an air of some dudgeon.

It got worse through the year, as he was passed over for tests of the new 1000cc machine. Instead Simoncelli was given a chance (at Motegi). It was another blow to Dovi's self-esteem just a couple of weeks before the same rider defeated him for second in a fierce last-lap battle in Australia, as he had done at Misano. In fact, it would be Dovizioso's great rival from childhood here on this list, were it not open only to still-active riders.

Gloomy or not, Dovizioso rode better than ever in 2011. Although he never did get a win, he did beat Pedrosa to claim third overall at the last race.

Dovi has turned his back on Honda, in the hope that Yamaha's satellite team might offer a route into the factory team. Desperate times.

5 MARC MARQUEZ

WHAT 18-year-old Marquez achieved in his maiden Moto2 season, his fourth in GPs, was really remarkable. He had marched to an imperious 125 title the year before, and now he almost did the same in his first experience of racing a four-stroke.

Marquez has the best possible backing: financially from Repsol (intent on making him part of the family) and otherwise from former 125 champion Emilio Alzamora. Technically also: his team can afford the highest level of support from Suter, which included extensive testing and an exclusive improved 2012 chassis by round 14.

He deserved it. He crashed out early on, but once he found his feet he started to win with monotonous regularity, cutting back an 82-point deficit at round six to take the lead from eventual champion Bradl at Motegi, round 15. Things went wrong after that with two crashes, only one of them his fault.

Marquez combines cool-headed tactics with a merciless streak: he is not afraid of racing as a contact sport. He is being groomed for superstardom and seems to have all the right ingredients.

6 BEN SPIES

BEN'S second MotoGP season, his first in a factory team, was not flashy. He still seemed to suffer in the first few laps, and (as in 2010) then show his pace as he made up places later in the race. It showed he was good at overtaking, but cost him results.

But he won his first GP, and paid three more visits to the rostrum in a year when the Yamaha was not well favoured. In general, he was a better rider than the year before.

Various things conspired against him, ranging from a fuel overflow clip left on his bike in Portugal to innocent involvement in Rossi's crash at Motegi, but he was still best of the rest overall, behind the Hondas and his senior team-mate.

In the end, a battering injury made the last part of the season difficult – until he came within inches of a second win at Valencia.

Ben still needs to prove he can step up to the next level, but he's on the top rung of the ladder.

THE cheerful Spaniard made a good fist of his first MotoGP season in 2010, but the shortcomings of his Rizla Suzuki kept him mainly near the back of the secondary mid-field battle. Things changed in 2011. By the latter half of the season, the British team had finally unlocked the secret of how to match their bike to the control Bridgestone tyres. All of a sudden Bautista was to be seen fighting with the factory Ducatis or better – he even managed a (slightly fortuitous) first front-row start in Australia.

For improvement alone, he and his team deserve a gold star.

The better handling of the bike showed both engine and rider to advantage. Had it come earlier, the whole attitude of the Suzuki factory to MotoGP might have been more positive, for they clearly also had a rider ready to make the most of it.

At season's end, Bautista finally abandoned hope of a Suzuki return, moving to the Gresini team and a Honda. He deserves a decent ride, but must stop falling off in so many races.

THE results sheet doesn't back it up, but it proved unthinkable to have a *MOTOCOURSE* Top Ten without Rossi. He hadn't forgotten how to ride, after all. Just how to win.

But we did see a new Rossi: unable or unwilling to adapt his style to the very particular Ducati, and furthermore unable so far to find the right development direction to change the bike to suit him.

The more the changes came, the worse things got, until his sole rostrum at Le Mans was a distant memory. He became a regular at the wrong end of the grid.

When the flag dropped, he'd put a race on; and there were glimpses of the old inspirational Rossi at Jerez and Phillip Island when the conditions became tricky. Each time, however, he fell off. He had a total of 12 accidents recorded in the season, exactly double the number of any previous year in MotoGP.

He remained stoically cheerful throughout, however, and is still the greatest figurehead of the sport. How could he not be in the Top Ten?

9 MAVERICK VINALES

THE most exciting racing debut for years came from a taciturn and tough-looking teenager from Catalunya. Vinales was racing on a number of new tracks against seasoned competitors. It took him four races to qualify on the front row, and win.

He did so thrice more and stood on the rostrum a total of nine times. All at the age of 16.

Riding in the improbably Paris Hilton-backed Blusens team, he quickly outpaced his experienced team-mate Sergio Gadea, a three-time winner. Confronted on the grid at Catalunya by his sponsor, he merely looked embarrassed.

His style was distinctive and inspiring: tucked right in and hard on the gas. Nor were his tactics wanting, comprising mainly an overwhelming urge to overtake anybody and everybody.

It may seem premature to put such a callow youth, a teenage rookie, in this sort of elevated company. But Vinales is that special. Who could deny the feeling that we were watching the beginning of something very big?

10 JOHANN ZARCO

THE title may have gone to Terol, after an almost immaculate season on a bike that clearly had a few horses more than anyone else's, but the excitement came from young Frenchman Zarco, another fighter who has given up a lot to race.

In his third season, Zarco certainly had a penchant for second place. Once it was so close that a photo-finish couldn't determine the winner. Zarco lost it because of a slower race lap time. More often, it was because the experienced Terol was faster in the dash to the line.

For a 20-year-old with one hand on a first win, sometimes the frustration was too much to bear, hence his dangerous barge on to the grass in Catalunya, and his desperate waving and swerving at Misano. The win finally came at Motegi, and it was convincing.

Using corner speed and inspiration, Zarco made what otherwise would have been a dull runaway championship into a serious fight. The real thing, or another French flash in the pan? Either way, he was always exciting to watch.

MARCO SIMONCELLI

By Michael Scott

THE impact made by Marco Simoncelli's death was astonishing. It went far beyond motorbike racing – an outpouring of respect, affection and grief that spilled over to F1 and far beyond to the world at large, with Italy approaching national mourning..

The reasons are many. He was a big presence: natural charisma, still a little gauche at 24, and a reputation for hard riding were wrapped in a 183cm frame with a booming voice. But it was more than that. Racing lost so much potential in that freakish moment. Simoncelli was a growing force of real power.

He was from that crucible of talent that stretches up and down the Adriatic Riviera: a string of holiday towns with a go-kart track every mile or two. Here the pre-teens race mini-motos, and the list of GP and world championship winners to come from around about Rimini is long and impressive. Rossi is one. Also Dovizioso, and Melandri, Pasini, de Angelis and many more.

Marco's motorcycling was sparked when he accompanied his father, Paolo, to a motorcycle showroom. He spotted a minibike, fell for it, got it for Christmas. He was seven; two years later, he was racing on the go-kart tracks and already building a reputation as fearless. "I don't give presents to the other riders," he told me back in 2008.

He'd just won the 250 title on a Gilera, in bruising style, after moving up through the Italian and European championships (he won the latter) on a 125. He came to GPs in the same class in 2002 and won twice before moving to 250s in 2006. There he would take 12 more GPs.

Dani Pedrosa was a year or two ahead, and watching. "He was a bit strange to understand for me, because normally the first year he was in 125, 250 and MotoGP he was not so good, but suddenly from one year to another, he would make a jump from being 10th or 12th to being in the top group. That was pretty interesting. He didn't move progressively."

Exactly so in 2011: his second MotoGP year followed a flawed, but interesting 2010 debut. And it was Pedrosa who made the greatest contribution to Simoncelli's increasingly threatening bad reputation, when he blasted him verbally after they'd collided at Le Mans. The crash came after a spat with Lorenzo the race before, at Estoril, where the world champion had accused him of dangerous riding.

"I do not agree," boomed the Italian rider. "Your example is wrong."

Nor was he happy to accept the blame for the Pedrosa incident, and his side of the argument was supported by, among others, Kevin Schwantz. And by Rossi: the two lived close to each other, and would train and talk together, becoming firm friends over the years.

Asked by *MOTOCOURSE* for a happy memory of Marco two weeks after his death, Rossi smiled broadly and recalled the French race. "That weekend, we had a lot of problems in the Safety Commission from Stoner and Lorenzo. They were very hard on Simoncelli. He said: 'I don't agree.' I also said I did not agree. Later I was speaking with Marco, and I said, 'Just for tomorrow, keep some attention for the other guys, because everyone is looking at you.' He looked at me and said, 'I agree.' The next day, he crashed with Pedrosa.

"That was Marco."

Simoncelli was a motorbike racer to the very core. A breed of competitor to gladden the heart of every fan. An attacking rider, who had started to match and even improve upon the lap times of the MotoGP superstar 'Aliens'. And potentially he was their nemesis. He had a factory-bike contract for 2012. Surely it would not be too long before his first win.

He also crashed a lot. But that is not why he died.

It could have been anyone. It was one of those rare events where physics, momentum and chance combined in a particular way, to prove a truth that we all prefer to forget. Motorcycle racing is still dangerous.

Most conspicuous after his death were the dignity and spirit of his father, Paolo. It was he who requested "a minute of chaos" at the last race at Valencia. And he who said, with a courageous honesty that honoured his son's memory, "We taught him to be a warrior, to never give up. I do not know if we did right or wrong."

A big future was snuffed out in that moment. The loss to racing is enormous, and it will be felt for years to come. So too will Simoncelli be remembered, as an icon of real racing.

Big people cast long shadows.

Left: Marco Simoncelli as we remember him best.

Below: Near the end of his journey. On the Gresini Honda during qualifying in Malyasia, 2011.

Photos: Gold & Goose

CLAUDIO CASTIGLIONI

By Paolo Scalera *Corriere dello Sport*/GPOne.com

CLAUDIO Castiglioni is gone. It's hard for an old journalist to explain just how much he meant to motorcycling. A captain of industry, passionate fan, enthusiast, gentleman. A friend. Someone with whom we shared a love of racing, in our respective roles, without respecting our roles. From the circuits of the Grand Prix World Championship to the sands of Dakar, he made us forget that he was the one responsible for Cagiva's presence there, coloured red because he was already thinking of MV Agusta.

And he won with Cagiva, both on-road and off. Because *il Signor Claudio* was a dreamer who had the ability to realise his dreams and was capable of transmitting his enthusiasm to others, making them part of his adventure.

That is why we were never surprised by his early-morning telephone calls, when he wanted to tell us that Cagiva had set a record time in some other part of the world. Quite the opposite, we were proud that it was the man himself, Claudio, who was telling us.

There was no such thing as a press release with him, just as there were no low-key celebrations. Instead we would be preparing to leave together, at an hour's notice. Like the time he took half the Italian press corps to Paris to celebrate Hubert Auriol, who had just lost the Paris-Dakar, injuring himself when the race win was already in the bag.

But his biggest accomplishment came in 1991, when he convinced Eddie Lawson to race for him, to reinvent a bike, the Cagiva 500, which had never won. It was an adventure even greater than Valentino Rossi's with Ducati today.

Claudio entered Lawson's motorhome at the 1990 French Grand Prix; he was barely able to speak English, but it was his smile that convinced Eddie.

Then, when 'Awesome Lawson' got to know him better, he fell in love. Repayment came in 1992, with that incredible win in the Hungarian Grand Prix that made Castiglioni cry like a baby. Because Claudio would cry when he achieved success, making all of us cry, too. Like we are now.

Steady Eddie would tell you, "God speed", Claudio. We can't find the words.

Above: Claudio Castiglioni with son and successor Giovanni *(left)*, in 2010 after they had bought MV Agusta back from Harley-Davidson.
Photo: MV Augusta

GARY NIXON

By Steve McLaughlin Former US road racer/founder World Superbike Championship

GARY Nixon was the American benchmark, standard-bearer and trailblazer for my generation, and some would say until his death.

Gary started as a motorbike-mad kid, then got into competition: first local American dirt-track events, then professional AMA racing, which required he learn to road race. This, in turn, brought him to the world stage, worldwide renown, and his loving and patient British wife, Mary.

Gary was one of the few two-time AMA Grand National champions, which at that time required someone to ride in five disciplines: mile, half-mile, short-track and TT on dirt circuits and road races in a gruelling annual calendar, normally in excess of 25 events. If today's racers think 25 events are too many, they should know that in the summer Nixon and his colleagues raced what was called 'the county fair circuit', adding 30–60 extra races, and they loved every minute of it!

The 1960s brought the Japanese to the forefront in the largest expansion of motorcycle production and sales in motorcycling history, and Nixon was there to ride the wave. He rode for Yamaha, Kawasaki and Suzuki, setting records, winning races and almost a world championship that is still disputed to this day.

Gary the racer was a man of those times: he rode hard, gave no quarter, expected no quarter. He partied hard and was quick with the one-liners – but Nixon was different in that he wasn't unkind and for the most part was usually instructive. Once, at a 1970s post-Daytona 200 party, several of the riders who had led the race said they couldn't believe Don Emde had won. Nixon said, "Next year, the record book will read Don Emde, not whose bike failed. And remember Emde's bike seized in turn one and he got it going again."

Nixon was the first AMA rider to make $50,000 the first year he won the AMA Grand National championship, and although small potatoes by today's standards, in 1967 it was big bucks.

Nixon was the first person to make himself a brand. Barry Sheene, one of the greatest 'rider brands' the sport has ever had, picked up on it immediately and was quick to learn from the legend as well as become his friend. Gary branded his name, his number and the hippy peace symbol with the Stars and Stripes, selling merchandise and image long be-

fore it was the mega-business of today. He understood the need to communicate and develop a fan base, but he also loved talking racing, so it came naturally to him.

When vintage events first got going, Gary was right there, although a few European promoters were less than happy when he demanded an appearance fee. One promoter

wrote to him, saying that he was "a typical American only interested in money". He was many things, but never typical. He asked the promoter if the spectator entry was free. They paid him.

Nixon was the complete motorcyclist, who wanted to race or had raced in just about every discipline, although he said he didn't think free-style would have worked for him. He loved racing, motorcycle riding, motorcyclists and the fact that he spent his life doing the thing he loved most with the people he loved most.

In racing, we get to meet many people, but as in life we have few friends; I was lucky that Gary was my friend.

Above: Gary Nixon with the winner's trophy after the 1976 Venezuelan 750cc Grand Prix. Steve Baker *(left)* was later declared the winner, Nixon being demoted to second place
Photo: Motocourse Archive

RACING AT THE CROSSROADS... AGAIN

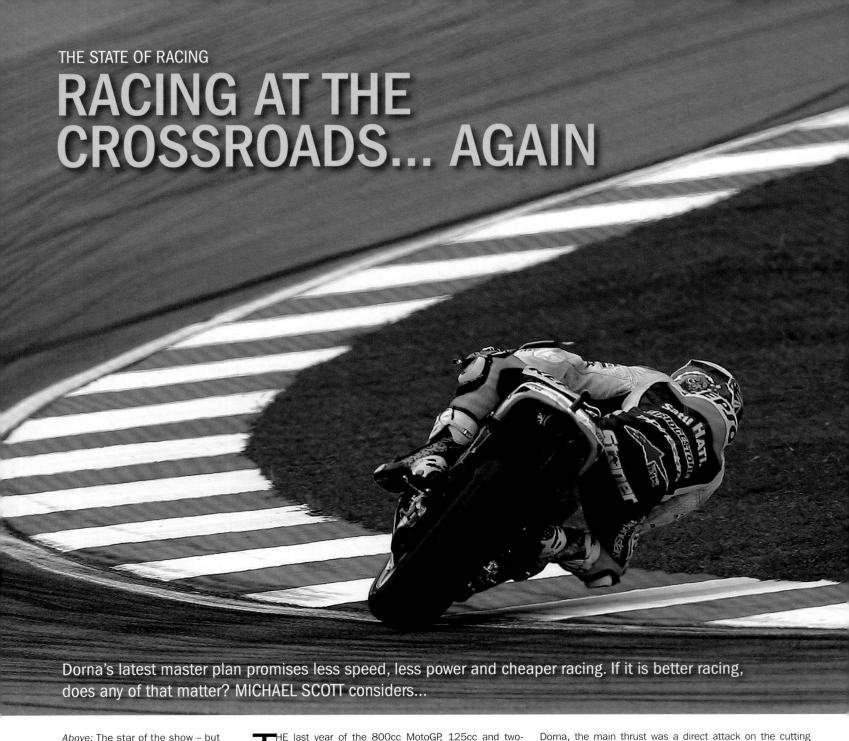

Dorna's latest master plan promises less speed, less power and cheaper racing. If it is better racing, does any of that matter? MICHAEL SCOTT considers...

Above: The star of the show – but not even Stoner's brilliant brinkmanship could mask a weak supporting cast.

Right: Carmelo Ezpeleta – the man who wants to "dumb-down" racing?

Below right: The lone Suzuki improved dramatically in 2011, but the factory withdrew days after the last race.

Photos: Gold & Goose

THE last year of the 800cc MotoGP, 125cc and two-strokes was momentous for grand prix racing, in these and in many other ways. At the final round at Valencia, in the wake of the sobering tragedy of Simoncelli's death, Dorna chief Carmelo Ezpeleta made it crystal clear that even more fundamental changes were coming, fast.

MotoGP was struggling to flourish in an economic environment where the news just seemed to keep getting worse. The rising costs, especially of electronics, were set against dwindling sponsorship income (Yamaha was unable to find a naming-rights backer in spite of winning the 2010 triple crown). Then, just ten days before the first race, came the shocking impact to Japan of the catastrophic 11th March earthquake and tsunami.

Squeezed from all sides, Ezpeleta found himself at the crossroads. And the turning he proposed to take led not only to reduced costs, but also to reduced performance, and a technologically controlled future where the role of the factories would become increasingly irrelevant.

In short, he laid down new battle lines.

Next year, 2012, would be transitional – the first fielding of the fledgling production-based CRT bikes (the original Claiming Rule Teams name is veering towards Constructor Racing Teams), and potentially the last in which factories would hold sway over the technical rules.

The threat came in the form of a radical proposal to the Saturday GP Commission. Put forward jointly by the FIM and Dorna, the main thrust was a direct attack on the cutting edge of MotoGP technology. In place of free development in electronics, so crucial to success, MotoGP should adopt a control ECU, incorporating a rev limiter.

In this way, Ezpeleta told *MOTOCOURSE*, not only would safety be protected by a reduction in straight-line speed, but also it would serve the all-important element of show – "spectacularity", as he called it. "For me, an ideal championship would be … all the engines with more or less the same possibility, and it is the chassis, the set-up, the visibility [appearance] that makes the difference one to another."

His strong stance came in the light of world economic circumstances, and in the wake of long-standing and ultimately unsuccessful attempts to force the factories to cut costs. Prime among these had been the request years ago to make engines available to lease, for independent constructor teams. "They said, 'Here, 1.5 million euros lease for one year.' It's unfeasible."

Instead, and particularly Honda over the last year, the factories were locked into a mode where costs continued to rise. In pursuit, said Ezpeleta, of "a technological battle which is going nowhere. Okay, we are a technology business … this is the world championship for riders *and* bikes. But technology is not the main issue: that is the races and the battles between the riders."

Ezpeleta was anxious to mollify any opinion that he had declared war on the factories. They understood the finan-

cial constraints and were themselves suffering under them, he said. He also firmly refused to envisage a future without factory participation, or where the factory teams would not have a stranglehold on the championship. "No matter what, always they will have the best technology ... and the best riders," he said. At the same time, he pledged that in 2013 he would switch the under-the-counter financial backing from Dorna from needy satellite teams to be shared instead among the CRT teams. "Perhaps in 2013, the factory bikes will be just two each."

More than that, in a much more direct attack, he hinted that he would continue to amend the technical rules to narrow the performance gap between factory and CRT. Would he give them extra fuel, for example? "Maybe, maybe."

But if Ezpeleta hoped to pacify the individual manufacturers, there was less comfort for the hitherto almost all-powerful MSMA, their joint Motor Sport Manufacturers Association. For one thing, Dorna had always contracted with the MSMA to get the bikes on the grid. In 2011, for the first time, he was signing contracts with them factory by factory. Divide and conquer?

Ezpeleta also made it clear that while this was still only a proposal, he believed he had the muscle to sweep aside any opposition. The MSMA, he confirmed, still retained its crucial power of veto over the technical rules – but that only applied with the GP Commission. If unanimous agreement was not forthcoming within that commission, the decision would pass to the higher authority, the Permanent Bureau. This ultimate authority has never had to be invoked, said Ezpeleta, because until now unanimous decisions have always been forthcoming. But the power is there.

The Permanent Bureau is composed of Carmelo Ezpeleta and FIM president Vito Ippolito, the same pair that put in the proposal in the first place.

On the one hand, this technical dumbing down is not only a logical step towards reducing costs at a time when this has become urgent, but also it follows trends set by F1 and other sports. However, it finally kills off any lingering notion that MotoGP has any value for research and development, or that it is a sport on the cutting edge of technology.

The reaction from the factories is not yet known, with only guarded comments from sundry spokesmen, pending high-level factory discussions. Although in an informal moment, a Yamaha engineer with some previous F1 experience, when asked what he thought about a control ECU, responded with a laugh: "Very easy to cheat."

Ezpeleta had demanded a decision by May, 2013. There can be little doubt about the way the decision will go. But how will the factories respond?

When a similarly stringent technical restriction was announced by the FIM in the late 1960s, led by Honda, they voted with their feet.

SUZUKI PULLS THE PLUG

Among all the ends of era, one went unheralded and uncelebrated. In fact, it only came to fruition in the darkening November days after the last race of the season.

It was the end of an era that had begun in 1960, when Suzuki followed Honda one year after their 1959 world debut in the Isle of Man TT.

Suzuki's first faltering steps had been boosted just two years later, when the factory acquired the technical knowledge and skills of defector and ex-MZ rider/engineer Ernst Degner. Using the secrets developed in East Germany, Suzuki and Degner won the first ever two-stroke world title in 1962 (50cc), and the Japanese manufacturer went on to become a leading light in the invasion of two-strokes all the way to the 500 class.

The decision did not come as a great surprise, although it was a great disappointment. At the end of 2010, Suzuki had halved its team establishment, but while the only England-based team in the paddock clung to hopes of an about-face, at the same time at last finding some improving results, others feared that the cuts had simply been the first step towards withdrawal.

So it proved, but the decision was far from clear-cut, with rival factions within the factory pulling different ways and no decision forthcoming even as riders and sponsorship opportunities melted away. In the end, it came down to a deadline from Dorna: the Friday after Valencia. Backed against the wall, the Suzuki board said, "No."

It is not the first time that this has happened. Circumstances influencing a potential return are rather different nowadays, however.

Suzuki had continued in the smaller classes with some adventurous designs, backed off after the 1960s technical embargo, but soon moved into the 500 class. Yamaha won the first two-stroke 500 title in 1975, but Suzuki's square-four RG500 was a design classic, and the compact and powerful disc-valve took Barry Sheene's consecutive championships in 1976 and 1977. The same basic design was good enough to win again in 1981 and 1982, and at the same time had become the privateer's must-have, selling in large numbers and helping to put a stranglehold on the constructors' championship from 1976 to 1982.

Then Honda joined the class, the stakes got higher and Suzuki withdrew. As now, the English-based team members were left aghast by the news. Then manager Garry Taylor, with key backing from the British Suzuki importer, Heron, decided to carry on regardless. In two-stroke days, engine costs were paltry by today's standards. The team embarked on a series of far-sighted chassis developments, including honeycomb-sandwich and carbon-fibre construction. While embarrassed Suzuki management turned a blind eye, the highly partisan racing department continued to provide engine developments. It was only when the factory had a change of heart and returned in 1987 with a full V4 that the same team reassumed full official factory status. Meantime, Suzuki had continued to compete without a break.

History is not likely to repeat itself. Neither the technology nor the business model would allow it. At the same time, Suzuki had already been testing two 1000cc prototypes, one V4 and one in-line four. There might be another change of heart in the future, when the financial situation is different.

Would there be space for a returned factory Suzuki on a grid full of CRT teams? Suzuki's withdrawal could prove another nail in the coffin of the factory-bike grand prix era.

NEW RULES, SAME GAME

The grids had a different look in 2011. For the first time, all classes followed the lead set by MotoGP – three instead of four per row for Moto2 and 125s.

One benefit for the middle class was in spacing the field out a bit more, making the crush into the first corner a little less crowded. By the same token, however, the riders at the back had ridden further and thus were travelling faster when they arrived at the braking zone. However, there were fewer such accidents in the class in 2011 compared with the previous season, and generally they involved fewer riders.

Moto2 had a stay of execution, or at least a deferral of a decision, when it was decided late in the year that the contract to supply a Honda control engine to all should be extended from the end of 2012 to the end of 2014. According to Dorna's Ezpeleta, "Our intention was to go to multi-brand, but that would increase the cost a little, or possibly a lot. For the moment, we decided to keep it as it is."

A significant rule change for MotoGP was hurriedly passed at the last race, as officials turned their attention to the more important control-ECU proposal. It completely reversed a situation whereby factory riders hardly got a chance to ride their bikes, except at the races.

Above: Honda's half-dozen. Their six bikes made up more than a third of the grid. There were also six Ducatis.

Top: The future? The CRT Suter-BMW unveiled at Estoril.

Opposite: Paul Butler, who stepped down after 12 years at the helm.

Photos: Gold & Goose

two laps behind after falling and remounting, but it's still in the books as a top-ten finish for Karel Abraham.

In 2012, the Czech rider will run a leased Ducati once again. He is one of a dwindling number: Pramac is to cut team strength from two to one (Barbera); while the Aspar team is to switch to a CRT bike, after sponsorship fell short of the necessary budget. That's four Ducatis, against six in 2011. Yamaha's establishment will stay at four – two factory, two satellite. Hondas presence will shrink: the three-rider factory team becomes two; the Gresini team will put its second rider on a CRT machine; LCR will stay at one. And no Suzuki.

The CRT rules were still being fine-tuned during the season. Particularly the Claiming Rule that gave rise to the initials. By mid-year, this had been honed down: only factory teams would have the right to claim an engine for a set fee of 25,000 euros, and only once from each team. By now, it was little more than window dressing: the likelihood of a Japanese factory losing face by claiming a privately developed engine was thought to be negligible.

In other respects, the rules remained substantially as set out in 2010:

Capacity: up to 1000cc	
Maximum number of cylinders: four	
Maximum bore: 81mm	
Minimum weight: 150kg (up to 800cc) or 153kg (over 800cc)	
Maximum number of engines per rider: six (Claiming Rule Teams, 12)	
Fuel tank capacity: 21 litres (Claiming Rule Teams, 24)	

There was a rush of enthusiasm for CRT at first, but numbers contracted during the year as deposits fell due. Another worry was the performance of the sole prototype, a BMW in a Suter chassis, which joined post-race tests at Mugello, ridden by Kallio: dismally, it was six seconds off the pace.

Things had changed by year's end, and a key moment came when Jorge Martinez, owner of the Aspar team, announced in Australia that he would be switching from Ducati to CRT, possibly even running two riders for the cost of one lease-bike rider. His stature in the paddock reinforced the credibility of the future of CRT. At the same time, new interest had emerged to replace those who had faded away, including former Kawasaki World Superbike team owner Paul Bird among many others. By then, veteran rider Colin Edwards had thrown in his lot with the new class, joining the Forward Racing team on what eventually would turn out to be a Suter BMW.

Engine power chosen (and in some cases already under test) included BMW, Aprilia, Honda CRR1000RR and Kawasaki. Chassis were being developed by Suter, FTR, Moriwaki and others. There were fewer than five months to go before the first race, but the prospect was looking brighter.

In 2012, they will be B-team racers. The future is less clear. With Ezpeleta's plans to speed up the CRT bikes and slow down the factory entries, the future for MotoGP will have more in common with Moto2's unseemly brawl than the more usual careful processions of the 800cc era.

As for Moto3, much remains to be seen in the new beginner class. Observers noted that in terms of power output, the 250cc four-stroke singles are comparable to the Manx Norton: a machine that won the 500 class championship in 1951 and was for years the backbone of the premier class. They are, however, considerably lighter.

They are also likely to be slower than the 125 machines they replace.

As with CRT, however, there was a growing flurry of interest by season's end, with new engines from Oral and Ioda, Mahindra confirming participation with its own chassis, and production racers from Honda and KTM already on the market.

Since 2008, not only had the number of official tests been cut back, but also full-time riders had been forbidden from taking part in private tests. The result, rather than cutting costs, was to direct the budgets towards factory test teams, which now became essential. Their only restriction was a ban on pre-testing at GP circuits, other than a single nominated track. It allowed the miles to be put in for engineering developments, but one weakness remained. Test riders are not as fast as the real racers, putting a serious limit on the value of the information they obtain.

For 2012, another factor came into play: CRT teams. With all-new motorcycles to develop, they would need as much testing as possible, but they lacked the budgets for private test teams.

It was mainly to suit them that the restriction on active riders testing was overturned at Valencia, with the only limitation being a restricted allocation of tyres during the course of the year. It also suited one MotoGP manufacturer more than the others: Ducati, which had sorely missed the chance of Rossi getting extra test time in his troubled first development year.

CRT AND MOTO3: NEW BEGINNINGS

Whatever the future will bring for the premier class, the CRT bikes could hardly have come soon enough. At the time of going to press, racing can currently count on a maximum of 12 factory MotoGP bikes for 2012.

The grid was 17-strong in 2011, compared with the 22–24 envisaged as ideal by Dorna and IRTA, and the weakness showed increasingly towards the end of the season as injuries took their toll. At the Australian GP at Phillip Island, there were only 14 starters and ten finishers. The last of them was

THE 'FAT CONTROLLER' BOWS OUT

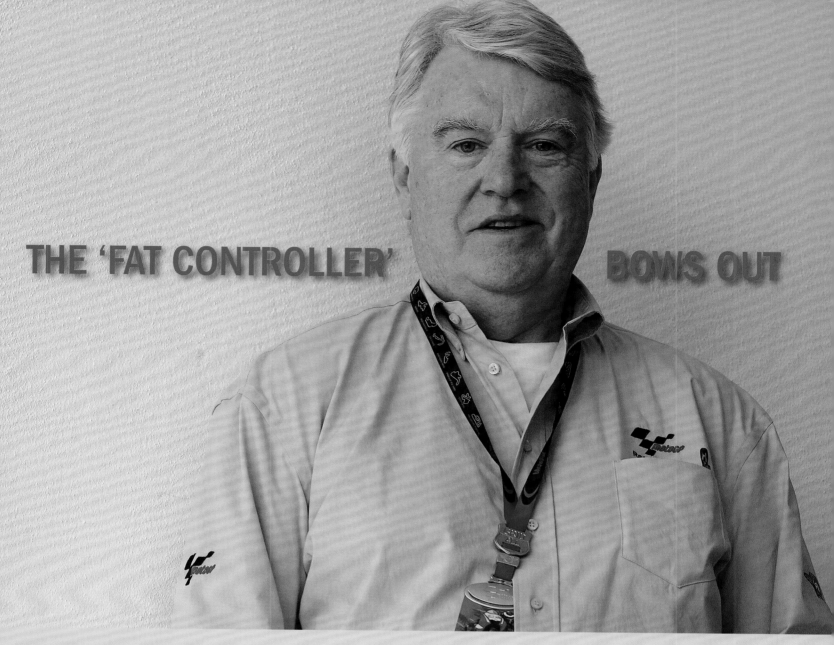

AT the end of 2011, along with 125s, two-strokes and the 800cc class, Race Director Paul Butler retired, after 12 years in control of everything from starts to punishment of wayward riders.

His career in motorcycle racing had begun in the 1970s, working with Dunlop. In the interim, the Englishman had been team manager for the retired Kenny Roberts. It was then that he became a founder member of teams' association IRTA, which gave the final impetus to change GP racing from an all-amateur show, where all but the top riders were at the bottom of the food chain, to a modern professional sporting business.

The job of race director is among the innovations. Before that, "more or less forever," there were no permanent officials, and races were overseen by a changing panel of FIM representatives, "tourists from all the federations under the sun, who would probably only do two or three races a year. They made it up as they went along," said Butler.

A rain-hit Belgian GP at Spa in 1989 was "one of the critical events. We had three races. Claude Danis [now FIM representative in Race Direction and the GP Commission] was clerk of the course and took the decision that under the rules there was nothing to prevent a race being restarted twice. His judgement was based on giving the punters something to watch.

"The FIM jury met hours afterwards, after all the pots had been presented, decided it was illegal and nullified the result. This goes back to the motivation for IRTA to create a professional series."

In 1980, an attempted racing coup by the Roberts-inspired World Series had failed to take over the FIM's prize championship only at the last hurdle. IRTA wanted similar changes, but went about it in a more gradual and business-like way.

"I was involved at the beginning. Exciting times. Our first president, Michel Metraux, and Serge Rosset were the French part of the axis, and on the other side the fat controllers: me [Team Roberts manager], Garry Taylor [Suzuki manager], Steve Whitelock [Honda co-ordinator] and Mike Trimby [IRTA founder]. And we thrashed it all out. There was a tremendous spirit, because there was a lot of stuff to get our teeth into. A lot of stuff needed changing and improving. It was exciting, because we got results."

Matters in hand ranged from safety to rates of pay, based on a system where the teams had a responsibility to IRTA, and IRTA to the organisers and the FIM. Progress was often bumpy, but importantly IRTA remained a stable entity while the FIM was engaged in a complex series of stop-start deals concerning TV and commercial rights, first with Bernie Ecclestone and the short-lived Two Wheel Promotions, and subsequently with Dorna.

Now, more than two decades later, Butler praises Dorna chief Ezpeleta's efforts to achieve the current state of consensus and co-operation between the various interested parties.

The first race director was appointed in 1992; Butler took over in 1999. At the same time, the Race Direction committee was formed, sharing the director's previously exclusive powers with delegates from Dorna and the FIM. Decisions have to be unanimous. "Actually it works very well. You have to reach a reasonable consensus, and we've all been around long enough," said Butler.

In that time, there have been several radical changes, including the switch to MotoGP four-strokes and the "unstoppable" electronics revolution.

"I've also seen tremendous swings in horsepower, in relation to chassis capacity and tyre performance. It made me think there's a very strong argument for having more horsepower than you need, because it gives flexibility in the racing. There's more sliding, it's more spectacular, and it should be less expensive and more attainable.

"I feel we're coming back to that now with 1000cc, because street-derived engines are putting out plenty of power. I'm very optimistic that once the constructor teams get going, they will be there or thereabouts. Top six ... why not?"

Does he see a viable future without factory teams?

"Well, I've seen it before. I certainly could see it happening again. The beautiful thing about motorcycles ... there are no cars out there on the streets you could convert to go and run a Formula One race. But you'll see an armload of motorcycles that, with the right kind of investment, you could convert into grand prix motorcycles. When Honda pulled out in the late 1960s, we had a period of seriously good racing.

"I think the potential for motorcycle racing to ride the storm, however severe, is massive, because of the wonderful road-going machinery that's out there."

TWIST AND SHOUT

The need for controlled chassis flex is well known, but development has never stopped. The latest work concerns the relationship between torsional and lateral stiffness, and new swing-arm designs show that engineers are understanding more about the effects of the Axis of Twist. As NEIL SPALDING reveals, the concept has been around for years...

"THE rider first tried the new bike out in pre-season testing: it was horrible, he couldn't feel the front. Everyone knew there was a problem, but what to do about it? By the first race, there was a second frame, but it still wasn't right. The bike was difficult to set up and seemed to react inconsistently to changes.

"By the time the season started, the team were beginning to understand and an experiment with an old frame design was tried. The rider liked the feel; he could slide and float the bike as he wished; all the confidence he needed was straight back."

The year was 1993, the rider was Wayne Rainey, and he was with Team Roberts on factory Yamahas.

There was a sense of incredulity about both the problem and the cure. The new frame had been a lot stiffer than the previous year; it was a natural extension of the previous decade of development: the stiffer the chassis, the better the bike worked. Now it seemed you could make something too stiff. Some sort of limit had been breached. That decade had seen the coming of the aluminium beam frame, and the steel tubes that had ruled the roost since motorcycling began faded into obscurity.

Warren Willing was one of the senior engineers at Team Roberts at that time. He continued, "Basically, we had been watching what was happening in the car world at the time. The advances in car chassis were in making them ever stiffer and stiffer, taking the suspension to where it had a more stable platform. We, that is myself, Mike Sinclair, Tom O'Kane, we thought this was the way to go and then to focus on making the suspension more compliant. We had been nagging for over a season. The Japanese put one of their more junior engineers at the time on it, Nakajima san, so he went through this learning experience with the rest of us.

"They came up with a chassis that was 100 per cent stiffer in torsional stiffness and substantially stiffer in lateral stiffness. Wayne went out for the first test on it, at Phillip Island, just to do a couple of slow laps, an installation lap. He came back in, saying it was fantastic, it feels like a 250, it changes direction so easy, it's so nimble, it feels light. Then he went out and tried to go fast, and he couldn't. The more lean angle he put on, the less feel he had. Then at Siberia, it tried to chatter him off the track.

"For the next few months of testing, we tried everything we could imagine to make the suspension work. We tested in Eastern Creek, we went to Laguna Seca. By then, things were starting to get a bit restless; we ended camping in California, testing every lunchtime for the next month. We tried everything we could think of: weaker yokes, different yokes, stronger ones, weaker forks, anything. In the end, we got to a point where the racing was coming up, and we were in trouble. Wayne and Kenny met with Yamaha and said, 'Have you got any of last year's frames?' They said, 'We can't. We haven't got the materials, and we haven't built anything.'

"That was a period when Kenny had persuaded Yamaha to release plans of their bikes and engines to Harris and ROC, and we got hold of an ROC chassis, and Wayne tested it and said yup, that would do. That's what we started the season on. By Assen, Yamaha had a chassis that looked like an F2, but which was designed to have a similar stiffness to the older ones. Wayne tried it in practice and said, 'It feels like last year's. Lets race it.'

"The chassis was a deltabox, spar frames with a front engine hanger. You can control your bending stiffness, but you are always talking bending stiffness, total stiffness, lateral stiffness, torsional stiffness versus something else. Nothing works in isolation. You want to reduce the twisting, but you want to control some lateral stiffness. In a perfect world, as I understand it, if you grabbed the bike by its axle and held it at 90 degrees, the bike would bend in a long uniform manner. You don't want any pinch points, you don't want any inconsistencies.'"

MOTOGP: THE FOUR-STROKE ERA

At the start of MotoGP, all the factories concerned built bikes based on the chassis dimensions of their 500s, except Honda. They built something different: the RC211V had a V5 engine in an aluminium beam frame, equipped with a long swing-arm and long front engine mounts.

Over the next three years, as the other factories struggled to compete, the secrets of the RC211V were slowly revealed and understood. What was surprising was that while Honda had stayed true to quite a lot of the secrets of their 500 experience, several other factories hadn't. Yamaha's first three years of MotoGP competition saw an overly rigid M-1 with a low centre of gravity. The arrival of Masao Furusawa in mid-2003 led to things changing rapidly, while the subsequent recruitment of Rossi prompted a new, much stronger effort from Yamaha.

Chassis flex development seems to come in fits and starts. The first big change occurred with Yamaha's preparations for the arrival of Rossi, when a new bike was used at Valencia in 2003 for just one race. This was at a time when the Yamaha had a reputation for losing the front end all the time, and most certainly didn't have the most predictable handling.

Norick Abe and Carlos Checa were the official team runners and they had one each for the last GP of the year. These bikes had modified cylinders with mounting lugs on them, extended front engine mounts and 'upside-down' swing-arm bracing, beneath rather than above. The riders liked them a lot, declining to go back to the old ones.

Rossi arrived straight after New Year 2004. His first test entailed choosing an engine configuration, and shortly thereafter setting up the chassis. Yamaha had further extended the front engine mounts, allowing the entire headstock to flex as necessary; mounts were attached to the frame above the clutch, allowing the team to adjust rigidity, too. Rossi and Burgess raised and lengthened the bike, introducing more pitch, improving braking and acceleration grip. By the start of the season, it looked strange – very high and pointy – but it worked. The rest, as they say, is history.

Rossi rode a bike that was a bodge for the whole year and snatched the championship from under the nose of a very surprised Honda. For 2005, Yamaha corrected all the basic geometry points. They kept the new centre of gravity height, but redesigned the engine to put the swing-arm back where they felt it should have been – and won again.

So what have we learned?

At full lean – and these days, that's over 60 degrees – there are a lot of forces at play. The bike is subject to 2g acting down through its centre axis, in the same manner as an aircraft at that angle of bank. The forks are compressed almost completely by that force, and in any case are at the wrong angle to react to any small bumps as the bike rolls through the corner. Therefore, any suspension movement comes from the bike's designed-in 'controlled flex'.

As Warren Willing observed, it's difficult to separate the various forces, so you have to play a balancing act with the basic frame and swing-arm design to obtain the effects you want in the right proportions. The flex has to be spread right through the bike: the tyre sidewalls, the design of the wheels, and the size and shape of the axles and spacers all make a difference. So do the forks and their triple clamps – all that before you get to the frame itself.

Chassis-wise, ignoring Ducati's current experi-

THE TWIST AXIS

A motorcycle frame and its swing-arm have to resist bending from braking forces and then provide a seamless lateral flex over their entire length, all the while keeping the torsional flex under control. These are not large movements: by most measures, MotoGP machines would be considered very stiff. However, they cannot be too stiff: there has to be some movement, and it has to be the right amount in the right place.

The snag is that we are trying to achieve all the aforementioned with one basic structure: the relationships between the various rigidities overlap. You might want a lot of torsional stiffness at the end of the swing-arm, but a lot of lateral flex. The same piece of metal is trying to do both jobs. Likewise the chassis. This means that some careful design is needed to get the right combinations of flex from the frame and swing-arm

The level required is set by the construction of the tyres, the weight distribution and the rider's riding style. It matters not only where and how the parts flex, but also, and equally crucially, in what plane they flex. Different constructions can cause different directions of flex, and reinforcing a construction to make it stiffer in one direction can cause it to become weaker in another.

The definitive text on the subject was a paper written 25 years ago by British academic Dr Martin Raines (who has stayed close to his first love, motorcycles, as Dorna's official statistician). His work was titled *The theory of the relationship between twist axis and effective torsional stiffness of the frame* and was included in his PhD thesis.

The twist axis is defined both by geometry and structure. The term is self-explanatory. Dr Raines' thesis examined the relationships and explained that for a given angle of twist, the frame needs to increase in torsional stiffness in direct proportion to the distance of the twist axis from where the force is applied: the force input points.

A swing-arm gives an example, measuring the twist between the wheel axle and the swing-arm pivot. Dr Raines: "If the reinforcing material is above the swing-arm centre line, the twist axis will be higher than if the swing-arm is braced below the centre line. If the twist axis is lower and closer to the contact patch, then the

ments, all the rest have aluminium beam frames with long front engine mounts. Front engine mountings are right down at the crankshaft, and the rear mounting at the top of the gearbox. The whole frame structure passes above these two mountings, gaining no support from them. Although several bikes have the mountings available to bolt up the frame between those two points, it is very unusual to see them being used.

It's difficult to obtain hard numbers for how much chassis flex is desirable: it's the holy grail of chassis design right now, and no one is giving anything away. But there are some ways in which we can at least visualise the way the bike has to operate.

First consider the way a bike works. Approaching a right-hand corner braking hard, the brakes (via the forks) are holding the mass of the bike. The load transfers to the front of the bike as the front suspension compresses and the rider starts to turn in. First a flick to the left, then the bike trips over itself to the right. The forks are still trying to buckle back under the engine, and as the bike rolls into the corner, the frame has to keep them in line while also stopping them from flexing too far back

The bike 'falls' into the corner and the rider uses

the throttle to modulate power to balance it. At the same time, the suspension is being compressed by the loading straight down through the bike. The normal suspension is now at about 60 degrees to the vertical; any bumps are pushing the wheels sideways. Bump absorption is by chassis flex.

As the bike completes the corner, the rider gently applies power and the bike starts to stand up. As it rises, the load transfers back to the rear, twisting the swing-arm and compressing the suspension The linkage works with the shock absorber/spring to support the rear, and chain force likewise. All the while, the bike is trying to twist and bend.

The roles played by tyres, forks, frame and swing-arm geometry, weight distribution, suspension linkages and spring rates are fairly well understood. It's the frame itself and the way it should act that aren't really talked about. We know it should bend and flex a little, but where? And how?

Herein lies the current most significant strand of development, as engineers begin to understand how to reduce torsional flex (stop the wheels from twisting out of plane with one another) while offering the right kind of lateral flex for the bike to cope better with bumpy corners.

Above: In early 2003, the works Yamaha had a swing-arm braced at the top and the cylinder head bolted directly to the frame.

Above right: After Furusawa was put in charge, Yamaha fielded two bikes at the end-of-season Valencia race with longer front engine mounts and an 'upside-down' swing-arm.
Photos: Neil Spalding

Right: 'A bit pointy' – Rossi's 2004 bike was a further development, set up to run longer and higher.

Far right: It would be 2008 before Honda tried the underslung bracing.
Photos: Gold & Goose

Below: Imagine this bike is leaned hard right. This is how a bike should bend: evenly over its entire length, while resisting torsional twist. The challenge is to achieve both conditions simultaneously.
Photos: Neil Spalding

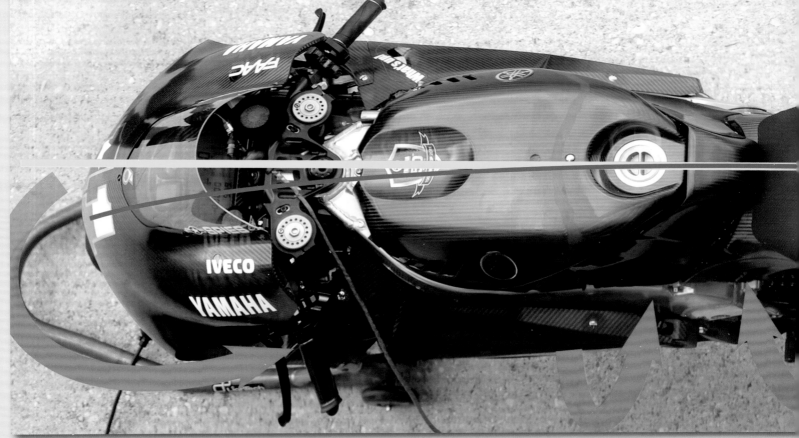

twisting will not be as great as it would have been had the twist axis been further away."

In other words, the swing-arm can be a lighter and less-rigid structure for the same effect, introducing further possibilities for controlling lateral flex.

Martin Raines' original research was in how to stiffen frames for road use, but he is quite clear that the same rules mean you can manage the combination of lateral stiffness and torsional stiffness for modern day racing: "This means that something can be made to move only laterally at high angles of lean. That in turn means that the wheel doesn't go out of plane; it means you have achieved better control of the torsional flex. We carried out additional research, and it soon became obvious to us that a swing-arm assembly that had its twist axis very low, and which as a result allowed very little camber twist, gave the rider a much greater feeling of security and confidence."

In Superbike racing, the swing-arm is the most important element, as it's the only part that can

be modified. Marco Bertolatti of Aprilia: "The biggest thing is that you want the right torsional stiffness from the swing-arm pivot to the contact patch. With a standard old reinforced-at-the-top swing-arm, you can imagine the plane the swing-arm is twisting through. If you build the swing-arm with the reinforcement nearer to the ground, you can have the same rigidity as with the old structure, but you can do it with less material.

"If you do it right, the less-rigid structure can be designed to give you the torsional stiffness you need, but with more lateral flex. The lower design means that you can have greater latitude between torsional and lateral stiffness; one will always influence the other. None of this makes a difference to other things like linkage design. It's simply a question of managing the flex."

In MotoGP, the swing-arm matters just as much, but the main frame is also custom built. Back to Warren Willing: "The twist axis is important. There is one

through the main chassis from the swing-arm pivot, and another from the swing-arm pivot to the tyre contact patch. The twist axis runs through the swing-arm pivot, and the neutral point is the line where, were you to push on it, the bike would simply bend laterally. Above that point, the frame would also twist torsionally away from you; below that, it would twist the other way. Bikes always seem to work better if that neutral point runs very close to the lower front steering bearing mount."

So we now have some idea of the manner in which the frame and swing-arms must flex. We can measure the result of small changes – like the way a small piece of additional material welded on can modify not just the rigidity of the part, but also the plane in which the twist occurs. The trick now is to quantify the precise amounts of flex required for each application and to work out the best material from which to make it, then how to make the structure in an accurate and repeatable fashion.

THE HISTORIAN ENGINEER

MARTIN Raines has been a regular at MotoGP events for years, compiling a database of results and statistics of GP racing to give historians and researchers an accurate method of reporting both historic and current events. It's a hobby, one he is very good at. Twenty-five years ago, however, he was a research student doing postgraduate work in the engineering department of Manchester University, in a department that was doing world-leading research into motorcycle chassis construction and pioneering the use of computer analysis in motorcycle frame design.

"I was one of the very first to use finite element analysis on motorcycle frames. To do any finite element analysis at the time was incredibly time consuming and laborious. We had some of the best computing facilities in the world: every element and every node had to be defined by a punch card; the pile would be about nine inches high. I would take them across to the computer centre, and if just one was wrong, the results just wouldn't make sense. There were no graphic read-outs, just a list of stresses and deflections. No one else was doing motorcycle frames at the time. Now the graphic packages make that sort of thing a lot easier. Things I did then that took two years could be done in a week now.

"We went to Japan in 1986, to the International Conference on Computational Mechanics in Tokyo. The trip included a day-long visit with Yamaha. We gave a talk to 20 or 25 of their engineers about this, then they gave us a full tour of the Yamaha factory.

"We did a lot of work for BMW at the university.

"To be honest, we stumbled across the concept of a twist axis as a result of trying to determine what torsional stiffness of chassis was appropriate. I came to the conclusion that we couldn't measure the twist unless you could define where the centre of stiffness was. We needed to know which axis we were going to twist everything in. I hung loads off a bar mounted at the swing-arm pivot point of a frame. I twisted things about different points and I was getting different answers. What I was actually doing was twisting and bending it, but by plotting some graphs of the deflections, you could actually find the centre of twist. It became part of my PhD; the twist axis was just one part.

"We did this work originally as a way of making bikes more stable. The reason this is important again now is because the bikes are operating at extreme lean angles. They need some flexibility, and the axis matters. Now it's not just the rigidities that matter, it is the plane of the rigidities."

2011 MOTOGP BIKE BY BIKE

DUCATI

CASEY Stoner's skills made up for the Ducati's failings over the last four years; unfortunately, his ability also hid from Ducati the need for change. First with the steel tube trellis, then the carbon stressed airbox, Casey's ability to ride around issues gave Ducati success they could only have dreamed of before.

The arrival of Valentino Rossi was supposed to create an Italian dream team; instead it became a nightmare. Initially, little was done to the bike; it was Estoril (the third race of the season), fully six months after Rossi had first sat on the bike, before Ducati turned up with a carbon airbox with a different rigidity for him to try.

The test after that same meeting brought a high-inertia-crankshaft engine to allow Rossi to control the bike's erratic throttle response. This trait had proved particularly unhelpful when he was trying to gently dial on power while still keeping the front brake on, a tactic he uses to keep the bike's suspension as he wants it mid-corner.

Several new carbon airbox/frames, each 'softer' than its predecessor, were tried, but the front-end feel that Rossi, the Doctor, needs above everything else simply never came.

Ducati had a second bike under wraps, their new-for-2012 1000cc V4, the GP12. Development was fast-forwarded: a short-stroke crankshaft and matching long conrods were made, and the now 800cc bike, renamed the GP11.1, made its debut at Assen.

The new bike had the same stressed-airbox frame concept at the front as the GP11, but the swing-arm and rear linkage were similar in design to the successful Yamaha. It was better; the savage pumping action from the rear had gone, but the bike still felt inert to Rossi's inputs and he had great difficulty holding a line in corners.

The GP12 design also had a seamless gearbox to counter Honda's new transmission; that, too, went across to the new 800.

Belatedly, Ducati realised that they had to completely redevelop their bike for Rossi. A new aluminium frame was built in only eight weeks and tested at Mugello by their star rider in the bike's 1000cc guise. The increased testing allowed for the development of the 2012 1000cc bikes permitted rapid redevelopment of Ducati's 800 as well.

The next chassis arrived at Aragón, made not of carbon, but aluminium, once more for Rossi only at first. It employed the same carbon rear sub-frame mountings at the rear of the rear cylinder head; at the front, those from the old steel-tube frame were resurrected, but the swing-arm pivot remained on the engine casings. Effectively, it was an abbreviated beam frame built around the airbox, with a risk of some heat transfer to intake air, resulting in a drop in peak power.

Ducati engineers had also been seen with CAD drawings for a more conventional, full beam aluminium frame, a deltabox to use Yamaha's preferred name, but it needed new crankcases with new mounting points. Rossi tested such a bike as a 1000 at Jerez in late September, but it never turned up as an 800.

Above: Karel Abraham's satellite Ducati at pre-season tests.
Photo: Gold & Goose

Right: Forks protruding: Hayden's Ducati always ran the front end lower than Rossi's.
Photo: Neil Spalding

Opposite: The nerve centre: Rossi's Ducati shows its electronics at Indianapolis.
Photo: Gold & Goose

Above: A new underslung swing-arm arrived for Rossi at Assen, along with a third carbon chassis revision.

Left: By Aragon, Rossi had an aluminium GP11.1.
Photos: Gold & Goose

Right: The Ducati GP9/GP10 and GP11 were structurally virtually identical. Note how the airbox/mini-chassis bolts to the inlet-cam area of each cylinder. You can also see the vestigial mounts for the original steel frame on the cam-drive cover.
Photo: Neil Spalding

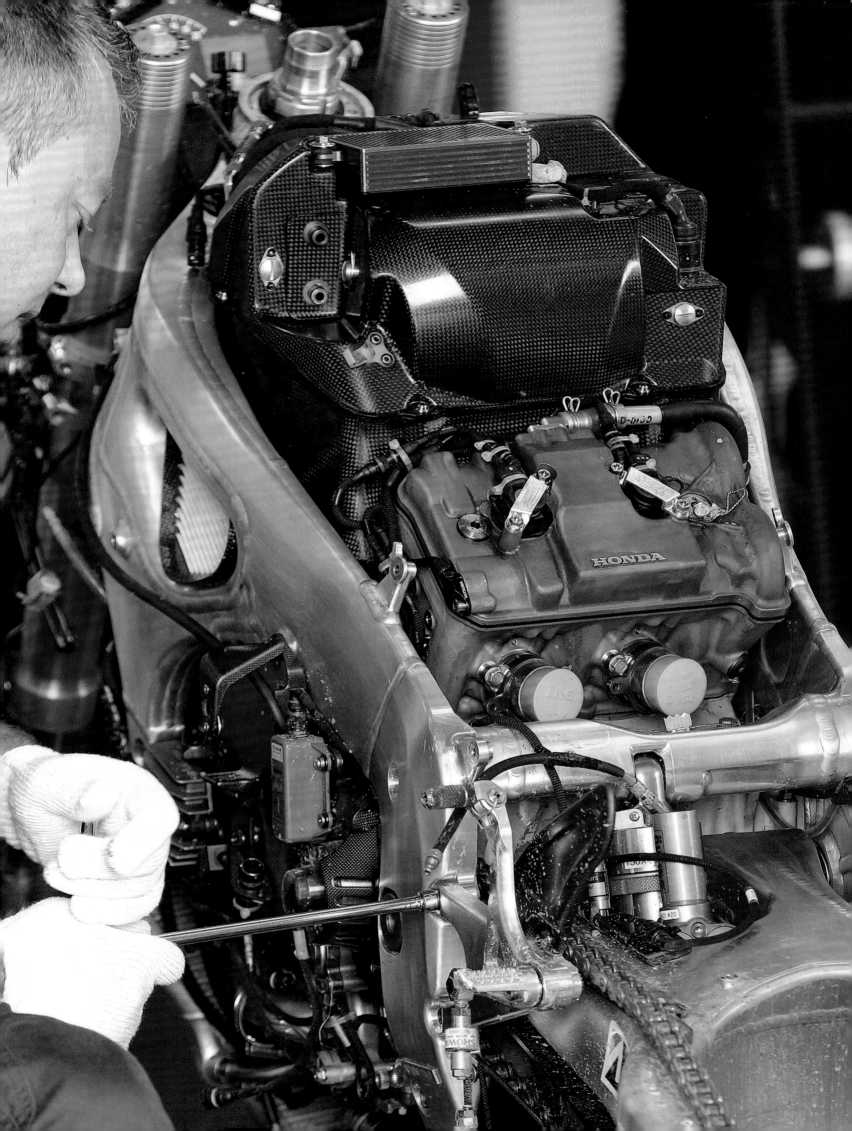

Above: Honda's final 800cc RC212V was the most thoroughly developed bike on the grid.

Photo: Neil Spalding

Right: Electronic sensors on Pedrosa's Honda were part of the seamless gearshift arrangement.

Left: Close-up of Stoner's machine at Brno shows top rear suspension mount; typical high standard of finish.

Photos: Gold & Goose

HONDA

FOUR years of intensive work and a complete reconstruction of their MotoGP race effort were needed to put Honda back on top, after their first 800 spectacularly failed to make an impression. Honda had tried to make a delicate bike with a high centre of gravity to suit Pedrosa, but it was promptly destroyed by the Ducati/Stoner combination.

The following year, a new bike arrived, but finding the right combination of power and power delivery to suit Pedrosa proved difficult. It took most of a year to persuade him to swap to the more powerful pneumatic-valve-spring bike. Then came the Bridgestone switch, and Honda had to start on the long path of re-engineering their entire motorcycle, in public, to work with the new tyres.

Once Shuhei Nakamoto arrived in early 2009, however, things moved up a gear. Technical progress was faster and there were many personnel. Within months, Öhlins suspension was being tested on full Repsol works bikes; two of Yamaha's top electronics technicians and Ducati team manager Livio Suppo were hired.

That winter, the bike appeared with a Torducter device on the gearbox output shaft, but the new 'wobbly' frames were the talking point. Honda had grown tired of waiting for guidance from its riders and had taken a big step in one direction, that of flexibility, to force the issue. Early 2010 became a race to see how fast the frame could be stiffened correctly to obtain the right combination of lateral and torsional flex to maximise the pressure they were able to exert on the tyres.

By the end of 2010, Honda clearly had an impressive bike. Pedrosa had won several races, and would have had a shot at the title if not for a mechanical mistake that hospitalised him at Motegi. For 2011, Nakamoto put two final pieces in place. Technically, he fitted a seamless-shift gearbox, a development first started while Honda were in Formula 1. This allows a new gear to be selected (up or down) while the current gear is still operating. The selector mechanism then automatically disengages the current gear as the newly selected one changes the speed of the gear shaft. One would expect a considerable jerk to be felt through the bike at such a sudden change of crankshaft speed, but this has been managed away by a sophisticated throttle dip system.

Honda would not discuss the arrangement, but it is very likely that the whole Torducter system is used to provide vital information to the ECU on the output torque, so assisting it in managing the precise timing and size of the throttle dip. The benefit of this design is that there is no break in the acceleration curve; constructors of similar gearboxes claim that a seven-per-cent improvement in acceleration is possible, and if the advantage isn't taken by actual acceleration, it is realised as an improvement in fuel consumption.

The final piece was getting Casey Stoner into the team. Stoner's ability to ride around handling issues on bikes is becoming legendary, but with the Honda there weren't that many issues. Nevertheless, he managed the bike's occasionally wayward corner entry better than anyone else. His style was very aggressive, and mid-season he appeared to go through a period when he was destroying his rear tyre more rapidly than his team-mates, which certainly cost him the Mugello and Sachsenring races. Overall, though, Stoner and the Honda were an unbeatable combination.

Above: Suzuki's new frame was far more effective than the old one, especially when they shortened it at the rear.

Below: Made by hand for racing: exhaust system shows comforting race-shop touches.

Photos: Gold & Goose

SUZUKI

SUZUKI took two giant leaps forward in 2010, one planned and the other not. The bike started out looking pretty much unchanged. There had been rigidity experiments certainly, but from the outside it didn't look so different.

There were some electronics improvements – the traction control system on the Mitsubishi ECU had been uprated – but that was all. Unfortunately, sole rider Alvaro Bautista crashed heavily at Qatar in practice, so the team missed the first race.

For the test in Estoril, however, a new frame, in CNC-machined aluminium, was ready – the first complete redesign for several years, and clearly it helped. By Silverstone and Assen, Bautista was fit again, but the weather intervened.

The very cold temperatures suffered in late June in northern Europe brought Suzuki's cold-weather problems to a head. The bike hadn't ever worked in really cold conditions, and at Assen it was no different. It had difficulty in getting the Bridgestones to operating temperature and keeping them there. In a desperate attempt to solve this, the bike was raised dramatically and also shortened as much as possible. This gave better weight transfer front and rear, under braking and acceleration. The improvement was sufficient to avoid being lapped. It wasn't a good race, but the extreme settings had focused everyone on a new development direction.

By Brno, there was a new shorter swing-arm to test, curved and almost organic in appearance. With the right flexibility to work at the shorter length, better performances came almost immediately. By Aragón, there were two swing-arms, and the improvements kept coming. By mid-October, on a cold day at Phillip Island, a circuit that previously had been Suzuki's *bête noire*, Bautista started from the front row, an achievement that would have been inconceivable just three months earlier.

Suzuki's future in MotoGP is in some doubt: their sport bike sales continue to lag well behind their developing-world commuter bikes, and there is a serious legal argument going on with Volkswagen about the terms of a cross shareholding that was only created two years ago. If Suzuki don't see a connection (as Yamaha can) between their third-world sales and MotoGP, or if they have to buy back 20 per cent of their shares from Volkswagen, their MotoGP adventure may be over. It would be a real shame, because on the evidence of the end of the 2011 season, they have finally cracked it.

Above: Tech 3 Yamaha at Silverstone. The satellite team used the highly-effective 2010 chassis all year.

Right: Factory bike has newer, more flexible chassis. By Assen, the 2010 frames were back.

Photos: Neil Spalding

Below: The devil in the detail: method of front axle mounting is an important element of controlled flex.

Photo: Gold & Goose

YAMAHA

THE 2011 Yamaha wasn't a success initially. The first version was criticised for being too slow and lacking in rear grip. By Assen, there were frame changes, while engine development went on all year. Jorge Lorenzo was critical throughout the season of the bike's performance, but the results showed that when he was riding at his best, and that best was very good indeed, it was only beaten by the combination of Stoner and the Honda.

To enhance handling, a 'softer' main frame was developed during winter testing; it was supposed to help at high lean angles, but it didn't really work. Like all good things, there was a limit, and this derivation of the superb-handling Yamaha frame was just a little too flexible.

The changes were very slight and quite difficult to see: the most identifiable part was a smaller section around the swing-arm pivot. It took until Assen for the final decision to be made, and then both works bikes went back to the 2010 frames – luckily for Ben Spies, who promptly took one to victory.

One new feature that did seem to work was the very wide seat pad. This changed the way the rider sat on the bike at lean: it was intended to help the rider to move his weight over the rear tyre for maximum grip during acceleration.

The Yamaha had always been good into and through the corners, but there is no doubt that in 2011 the Hondas ruled on the way out. They tested a longer wheelbase in an attempt to increase the speed at which the bike would wheelie, but in the end it remained short and agile, and slightly compromised on exit. In turn, that meant that the twisty tracks were where it would do business best, and so it proved.

One aspect of the 2011 engine was a crankshaft with slightly higher inertia. This allowed more accurate throttle control, but didn't give the bike a feeling of urgency out of the corners. Yamaha also stuck with their relatively conventional floating-dog-ring gearbox. This is capable of very quick gearshifts, but not as quick as the seamless-shift boxes, so Yamaha riders were denied the benefit their Honda rivals enjoyed.

One senses that Yamaha had decided to put what little budget they had into their new 1000 for 2012, which leaves several 'ifs'. If Yamaha had reverted to the earlier chassis sooner, and if Honda had not secured the services of Casey Stoner, they might well have got away with another championship. Despite being beaten in its last year, the Yamaha M-1 is the definitive 800cc MotoGP bike – fast and accessible. Yamaha's redesign after 2007 was stunningly effective, and it took Honda three long years to catch up.

THE HIGH NOTES

In 2011, Yamaha celebrated its 50th year in grand prix racing. MICHAEL SCOTT charts the events that brought the Japanese musical instrument maker 36 rider titles and more than 450 race wins...

Yamaha men past and present at the US GP 18 titles between them. *From left:* Cal Crutchlow, Colin Edwards, Kenny Roberts, Jorge Lorenzo, Ben Spies, Eddie Lawson, Kel Carruthers, and Wayne Rainey.
Photo: Gold & Goose

決勝点

Above: On the flanks of Mount Fuji – scene of Yamaha's first race, 1955.

Inset, above right: Yamaha's first ever factory team, Mount Fuji, 1955.

Right: Takehiko Hasegawa poses on the Isle of Man with Yamaha's influential first 250, the RD48.

Below right: The same model in action at Assen in 1961.

Photos: Yamaha Classic Racing Team

Above: The TT adventure. Fumio Ito took sixth place on a 250 RD48.

Above right: The TT team: Fumio Ito, Hideo Ohishi, Taneharu Noguchi, Hiroshi Hasegawa.

Below right: Phil Read was Yamaha's first champion. Here he is in action in 1966.

Below: Yamaha's first GP winner was Fumio Ito, in 1963.

Photos: Yamaha Classic Racing Team

MANY Japanese racing stories start on the rough, half-paved half-cinder tracks on the flanks of a volcano. So too with Yamaha in July, 1955, on the sacred slopes of Fuji-San himself. The nascent factory team entered three of the company's first motorcycle, a DKW-based 125 two-stroke only in production for six months. The Yamahas finished first and second. Later that same year, the same machine took the first four places in the gruelling Asama race, humbling all rivals.

For this and other reasons, when the company brochures assert that racing is part of Yamaha's genetic make-up, the statement can be taken at face value.

Motorcycles were a new venture for a company that hitherto produced musical instruments: hence the crossed tuning forks on the tank badge. It was a momentous time for the Japanese industry, when numerous small manufacturers were going out of business or being swallowed up, and the modern dynasties of Honda, Suzuki and Yamaha were still at the fledgling stage. Racing success played a big part in making sure they didn't follow other motorcycle names like Tohatsu, Showa, Monarch and Cabton into oblivion.

Honda was first into the world championship in 1959; Suzuki followed a year later. Yamaha had other things to worry about, after some commercial difficulties. And they were doing things a little differently: the very first foreign racing venture actually preceded Honda's TT debut by a year, and was to the USA. The factory entered the annual Catalina Island road race, off-shore from Los Angeles and the focus of a huge motorcycle market. The Yamaha two-strokes fared well.

Grand prix participation came in 1961, at the French GP at Clermont Ferrand. Yamaha entered two air-cooled, twin-cylinder 250 two-strokes in a class dominated by Honda. Rider Fumio Ito would eventually finish a distant ninth overall, but importantly the name Yamaha was on the world championship roster for the first time. It's been there ever since.

Yamaha's five decades in racing span several sweeps of history. Technically, the bikes cover the gamut: large and small, two-stroke and four-stroke, simple and complex. Not all have been successful, but all share a common thread. Yamahas, by and large, have seldom been the fastest through the speed traps. But, again by and large, they have often offered the sweetest handling and the most predictable roadholding. Yamahas were rider-friendly long before the term was coined.

The machines

That first RD56 twin was a defining model. The same basic design would last for many generations, and give rise to the hosts of production-racer 250 and 350 Yamahas that were the backbone of grand prix and most other forms of racing for more than two decades. But the early 1960s were a time of vaulting ambition and technical high adventure as the Japanese factories strove for ascendancy.

Honda raced four-strokes, Yamaha and Suzuki two-strokes. And Honda was a step ahead. Feeling the hot breath of the strokers, especially in the smallest classes, the company had already embarked on a series of increasingly ambitious and complex designs that culminated mid-decade in a five-cylinder 125 and a six-cylinder 250.

Suzuki had been campaigning a water-cooled square-four two-stroke since 1963. Yamaha played the game slightly differently, also marrying a pair of 125 twins with their crankshafts geared together, but with the cylinder pairs splayed outwards. It was the RD05, the first two-stroke V4 – yet another piece of engine architecture that would prove influential and longevitous, in a forthcoming generation of V4 500 racers by Yamaha and others.

In 1965, it was at the cutting edge, with an eight-speed gearbox and 65 horsepower at 13,500rpm, even in its earliest form.

The on-track battles are the stuff of legend. Jim Redman and Mike Hailwood on the Hondas, Phil Read and Bill Ivy on the Yamahas. The honours were evenly divided only after Honda withdrew in 1968. Yamaha secured a second 125 and a third 250 crown to match Honda's tally. But it was oh so close: in 1967, Hailwood and Read were equal on points, and judges had to resort to a time aggregate to award the title to the Honda rider.

And still the technical elaborations continued to appear – Yamaha's next V4 was half the size and twice as complex:

the 125 required an extra gear to make use of its narrow rev range.

Action to halt the runaway engineering costs came at the end of 1969, with new regulations limiting the numbers of cylinders (two in the 125 and 250 classes) and the number of gears (six).

The restrictions killed the multi-cylinder factory bikes, but offered new opportunities for Yamaha's production racers, already successful clubman's machines. Ideally suited to the new regulations, the TD/TR2 (250/350) Yamahas and the later water-cooled TZ developments became the choice of the vast majority of privateers. Relatively simple, reliable and rider-friendly, and also amenable to further development, they became the backbone of racing. Between 1970 and 1984, these workmanlike, but well-developed parallel twins took seven of the 15 available titles, far more than any rival. More importantly, Yamahas filled most of the other positions as well. In 1976, as a random example, Walter Villa won the title on a Harley-Davidson; but Takazumi Katayama's Yamaha was second, and of 37 riders to score points, all but four of them rode Yamahas.

By now, Yamaha's factory engineers had embarked on the next target. Hitherto, two-strokes had been considered suitable only for small-capacity engines. But the 500 class was there to be conquered, and it was only a matter of time. Already nominally over-bored 350 Yamaha twins were heading up the championship charts: in 1972, Giacomo Agostini and Alberto Pagani won the title on their factory MV Agustas, but third and fourth went to '351' production-racer Yamahas, ridden by Brno Kneubuhler and Rod Gould.

Suzuki came close, but it was Yamaha that finally broke the 17-year stranglehold of the MV Agustas, when Giacomo Agostini won the first ever two-stroke 500 title, on an in-line four-cylinder Yamaha in 1975.

It might have happened two years earlier, but for the tragic accident at Monza that had claimed the life of Yamaha's new

Above: Four-stroke generation: the Yamaha M1s of Rossi and Edwards wear 'bee-sting' anniversary livery in 2005.

Above left: Yamaha's disc-valve RD56 was successful and influential. Here a 1965 version takes centre stage at Assen in 2011.
Photos: Gold & Goose

Top left: Yamaha's first international venture was to Catalina in 1958, with this on/off-road 250 twin.

Top centre: The RA97 was Yamaha's first twin-cylinder 125. Water-cooled, the engine formed the basis of the later 250 V4.
Photos: Yamaha Classic Racing Team

Above: Jarno Saarinen en route to the 250cc title in 1972.

Left: Bill Ivy leads Phil Read on their way to a 1-2 finish in the 1967 French 250 GP at Clermont Ferrand.
Photos: Yamaha Classic Racing Team

Below: Rossi's new Yamaha M1 at pre-season tests in 2005. He would win his second title on it.
Photo: Gold & Goose

star, Jarno Saarinen. The Finn had won two of the first three races from Read's MV Agusta, and had seized a commanding early world championship lead. The grief-stricken Yamaha team withdrew for the rest of the season.

There were to be more glory years for the in-line two-stroke Yamaha, principally powered by maverick US invader Kenny Roberts; but the ultimate 500 two-stroke design harked back to the 1960s and the full-factory 250: it was a twin-crank V4, the YZR500, which saw Yamaha through to the end of the two-stroke days, when MotoGP four-strokes were introduced in 2002.

Yamaha had been among the prime movers in changing the premier racing category from two-stroke to four-stroke. The two-stroke engine had fallen from fashion, and Yamaha's range of fast sports bikes now used typical high-performance, four-cylinder four-stroke engines. MotoGP brought grand prix racing back hand in hand with their high-street showrooms.

While their main rival, Honda, went for a dedicated racing design in an innovative V5 format, Yamaha kept a much closer link. The M1 was an in-line engine like those of their road bikes. Another decision proved even more counter-productive: believing that a smaller engine could provide more effective racing performance than the full 990cc of the regulations, the bikes came undersize. It was not until both these aspects had been attended to that the Yamaha M1 began to assume its true stature.

The engine size was easy, but it took a stroke of engineering genius to overcome problems endemic with the in-line engine. It was a subtle matter, involving a sort of flutter in the power transmission that worked against the tyre's ability to grip. This stemmed from inertia effects on the crankshaft at the points of top- and bottom-dead-centre, when the pistons stop and reverse direction. In a conventional two-up/two-down in-line four, these impulses were large and awkwardly timed, compared with the rival vee engines.

Above: Phil Read on the RD05 – the first V4 two-stroke – at the 1968 TT. Team-mate Ivy won after Read suffered a puncture.

Above right: Ivy and his Japanese mechanics with the victorious machine.

Above far right: Jarno Saarinen, one of the sport's great lost talents.

Top: The majestic Wayne Rainey took three consecutive titles for Yamaha.

Top, inset: Rainey's predecessor was Eddie Lawson, champion for Yamaha in 1984, 1986 and 1988. He won a fourth title on a Honda.

Photos: Yamaha Classic Racing Team

It was senior management figure and engineer, Masao Furusawa, who devised a solution. He changed the cylinder timing away from two-up/two-down, arranging the cylinder pairs 90 rather than 180 degrees apart. An improved balance shaft contained the consequent vibration, and the in-line engine had become a virtual V4, without gaining the extra bulk and weight of that configuration.

The cross-plane crank combined with the arrival of Valentino Rossi was the crucial point in turning the M1 into a bike that would win five of the seven titles on offer between 2004 and 2010. It did so in 990 and 800cc form, and Honda had to expend a huge and expensive effort to oust the M1 from the top of the tree in 2011.

The cross-plane crank migrated to Yamaha's sporting street bikes – a case of racing informing road-bike engineering. Funnily enough, when they started out, it was the other way around.

The men

A great number of great riders have played their part in Yamaha's half-century of grand prix racing – from serial 1980s/90s champions Eddie Lawson and Wayne Rainey to privateer champions like Jon Ekerold and Rodney Gould, and

to the super-professional 2010 winner, Jorge Lorenzo. Some have been pivotal, both in racing and in Yamaha's history.

The first was Phil Read. Canny as well as fast, the Englishman could see the potential of the Yamahas and managed to secure himself a seat in the factory squad. Phil went on to win Yamaha's first world championship in 1964 in the 250 class. He would win it again in 1965 and 1968, the last year of the factory machine. Then once more, as a privateer, in 1971. Read also took the 125 crown in 1968, a year when he and compatriot Bill Ivy gave a new meaning to the concept of rivalry between team-mates.

The next giant was Saarinen. An innovative rider/engineer with an exciting style and a blistering turn of speed, Jarno rode a semi-private Yamaha to the 250 title in 1972. So highly was he regarded that he was clear favourite to take a double 250/500 title (he'd also won the first three 250 rounds). It was at the fourth round at Monza that he and Italian Renzo Pasolini fell together at the head of the pack. Both were killed instantly. Notoriously, spilled oil was blamed, with no warning flags shown.

As happens in racing, the next pivotal figure was waiting to arrive. When Yamaha returned the following season, it was with none other than Giacomo Agostini, already (and still) the most successful rider in the history of the sport, with

Above: King Kenny. Roberts took control for Yamaha in the 500cc class from 1978 to 1980.

Above right: Roberts on his iconic 1978 Yamaha. The American was a grand prix rookie.

Above far right: Matinee idol and multi-champion Agostini.

Right: Ago, here winning the French GP at Le Castellet, went on to take the 1975 title, the first ever for a two-stroke.

Photos: Yamaha Classic Racing Team

Below: Valentino Rossi helped revive Yamaha's fortunes with four titles between 2004 and 2009.

Photo: Gold & Goose

Top left: The master. Valentino Rossi won a symbolic 46 races on the M1 in his six years leading the team.

Top right: The pupil. Jorge Lorenzo joined Rossi in 2009 and beat him in 2010. Rossi left directly.

Above: Lorenzo on the gas on his way to taking the 2010 championship in Malaysia.

Photos: Gold & Goose

seven 500-class titles to his name on the MV Agusta. Some feared that Ago might be a spent force. Far from it. He won only two races in his first year, 1974, but in 1975 he doubled that number and pushed the top MV Agusta rider to an unaccustomed second. Funnily enough, it was Phil Read, the lynchpin of Yamaha's early success.

Ago remained with Yamaha after retirement to manage the factory team, fielding Eddie Lawson, who won the championship three times for Yamaha, and then once more on a Honda. (Yamaha has since forgiven him, and he played a role of honour during the 50-year celebrations at the US GP. Rossi, now actively riding for a rival company, has yet to be forgiven.)

King Kenny Roberts was Yamaha's next giant. Already double AMA Grand National champion on the Japanese machines, he burst on to the European scene as a bumptious rookie in 1978 and overturned the status quo with a debut-season world championship. He won it for the next two years straight, and remained a dominant figure not only when he stopped winning it, but also after he stopped racing. Like

Ago, Kenny went on to manage the factory Yamaha team, through a purple patch, when his protégé, Wayne Rainey, became the new star on Yamaha's list.

Rainey repeated Kenny's feat of three wins in a row, and was leading on points for a fourth when he crashed at Misano, suffering back injuries that ended his career.

There was one more to come – Valentino Rossi. Disillusioned by Honda's lack of personal appreciation for winning two titles in a row, he took a gamble by switching to then-underdog Yamaha. It was perfectly timed to coincide with the arrival of the cross-plane crankshaft. This gave Rossi the basis upon which he and Yamaha could build the bike that became the envy of the paddock.

Valentino won four of the next six titles on the bike he and his crew had developed, hand in hand with Yamaha's race department. The seventh went to Jorge Lorenzo, riding the same motorcycle.

In its 50 years of grand prix racing, Yamaha has won 36 rider world championships and more than 450 grands prix. And more besides.

50th Anniversary 1961 World GP 2011

PASS ON THE SPIRIT

RD56
1964 - Phil Read

YZR-M1
2011 - Jorge Lorenzo

2011 is a landmark for Yamaha. Fifty years ago we were making our first bold steps in Grand Prix racing and the sport has been part of our spirit ever since. Aside from all the excitement that can be found on the track, our desire to succeed and entertain has helped us fine-tune new technologies to be placed directly into your hands for the road. With 37 Grand Prix titles and over 450 victories during the past 50 years, our desire to be the best is still fiercely strong which is reflected in our entire model range, from 50cc up to 1900cc.

With great offers available making our quality range of Yamaha motorcycles and scooters more affordable, we really are able to pass on the spirit!

Visit our website for more on racing, our offers and our bikes and to find your nearest authorised Yamaha dealer.

www.yamaha-motor.co.uk

YAMAHA

BREAKING THE LINK

After 63 years, the last of the original classes has been axed – the last also of a two-stroke generation. The 125 class gave us more world champions than any other and introduced grand prix racing's two greatest engineers. Mat Oxley pays tribute...

Above: Last ever 125cc World Champion Nico Terol leads the swarm into the first turn at Aragon, 2011.
Photo: Gold & Goose

Insets, clockwise from top left: Battle of the streamliners – Werner Haas (NSU) leads Carlo Ubbiali (MV) at the Nürburging in 1955; inaugural 125 World Champion Nello Pagani in 1949; 1954 champ Rupert Hollaus (NSU) negotiates Governor's Bridge at the 1953 TT.

Right: Before the ban, the dustbins of history. The factory Ducatis wear stripes and the prancing-horse logo in 1957 in Italy.
Photo: Ducati

DURING the last 20 odd years of its 63-year existence, the 125s were little more than a feeder class, preparing young talent for 250s and then 500s, and more recently for Moto2 and then MotoGP.

It wasn't always so. For four decades, the 125 world title wasn't merely an apprentice-of-the-year prize, it was a world championship in its own right, to which many riders dedicated the majority of their careers. The category even had its own superstars – most successfully Carlo Ubbiali and Angel Nieto – who achieved greatness through their pursuit of the smaller classes.

Of course, the class was always a good place for apprentices, for riders working their way into the world championships, learning the tracks and acquiring the skills. Both Mike Hailwood and Valentino Rossi won their first grand prix victories on 125 machinery. They, like many others, were just passing through on their way to bigger and better things, which is why the class has given us more world champions than any other – 44 different riders, compared to just 25 in the premier class.

Over the years, the eighth-litre division also proved itself a wonderful training ground for aspiring engineers and ambitious new brands. Two-stroke genius Walter Kaaden and four-stroke mastermind Soichiro Honda – arguably the greatest brains to have worked in the sport – both took their first tentative steps into the pit lane with 125 machinery, if only because it saved them from having to compete with the bigger factories in the glamour classes. Thus two of the biggest transformations ever to hit the sport – the Japanese invasion and two-stroke domination – both began in 125s. MV Agusta and Ducati may now be synonymous with exotic

high-performance motorcycles, but both of these legendary Italian marques enjoyed their first world-class successes with 125 bikes.

Ironically, Kaaden and Honda transformed what had been a fairly simple and straightforward category into something far more complicated. But for most of its life, 125 was the real class for the *garagiste* – little teams with humble resources who otherwise might never have had a chance to go grand prix racing. It was also the class for little people – riders of smaller stature who could squeeze the maximum from smaller, lower-powered machinery. In every sense, the 125 class gave the little man more of a chance.

When the FIM announced the inaugural 1949 motorcycle world championship line-up, the 125 class was the only real surprise of the four solo divisions. The 250, 350 and 500 categories were already well established through the European championships that had been contested annually since 1924. The one-two-fives (or one-twenty-fives, as they say in the States) were not. An ultra-light class for 175cc machines had been added to the European series in 1925, only to be dropped after 1934.

The 125 World Championship owed its creation to the post-war boom in 125cc machines – usually cheap and very basic two-strokes that helped put Europe back on the road. Nowhere was this trend more marked than in Italy, which explains why the inaugural 125 World Championship was a very partisan affair, with only Italian riders on Italian machines scoring points.

The main players in the 1949 series were three brand-new motorcycle marques trying to cash in on this boom. Two of them – MV Agusta and Morini – went to the very first 125

grand prix grid at Berne on 2nd July, 1949, with plain little two-stroke singles, because those were the machines that they sold in the shops.

Mondial, however, arrived with a dohc four-stroke single with shaft-and-bevel cam drive, a design so advanced that it went on to win every race in the first three years of the championship.

Count Domenico Agusta didn't take that long to realise that he also needed a four-stroke. After watching Nello Pagani win the first 125 crown, he acquired a Mondial for his engineering team. He wasn't the only boss of a legendary motorcycle brand to do so. At the same time, Agusta knew he needed a good four-stroke engineer, so he headhunted Piero Remor from Gilera. Like most people, Agusta was convinced that the two-stroke had been killed as a viable racing engine by the post-war ban on supercharging.

Mondial continued its domination for another two years. Bruno Ruffo took the 1950 crown (probably a doddle after surviving the Russian front during World War 2), the following year's title going to Ubbiali, who had started racing MV scooters. By 1952, the new MV – a dohc all-alloy unit-construction engine making 14hp at 10,800rpm – was fully up to speed. Cecil Sandford scored the marque's first world-class race win at the TT and went on to win MV's first world title later that year. The Briton's success was the start of something very big.

But if the count expected to rule the 125 world for a while, he was in for a nasty shock. Just one month after Sandford's historic TT win, a new grand prix outfit turned out for the West German GP at Solitude. The NSU squad was something else. Backed by the world's biggest motorcycle factory, it took scientific professionalism to a new level. NSU boffin Dr Walter Froede created the Rennfox four-stroke 125 single (and Rennmax 250 twin), following his studies into reducing internal friction and improving gas flow. The engine made extensive use of magnesium, featured a very narrow valve angle and developed 18hp at 11,500rpm: too much for the MVs and Mondials.

At Solitude, Werner Haas won first time out on the Rennfox – the first non-Italian machine to win a 125 GP – and

Photo: Bauer

Top left: Ernst Degner (*right*) discusses two-stroke trickery with MZ wizard Walter Kaaden. Months later, Degner defected from East Germany and sold Kaaden's secrets to Suzuki.

Above: The world is about to change – Naomi Taniguchi leads Honda's 1959 TT debut.
Photos: Mortons

Above right: Phil Read and Bill Ivy aboard their 336bhp-per-litre, nine-speed Yamaha V4s in 1968. New rules outlawed such elaboration.
Photo: Bauer

Right: Two new forces in grand prix racing at the 1959 TT – Degner's pioneering MZ two-stroke leads the young Mike Hailwood's Ducati. Further behind, Honda made its debut.
Photo: Mick Wollett

returned for a full season in 1953, when he dominated the series. The following year, it was NSU team-mate Rupert Hollaus' turn to rule, thrashing Ubbiali, now back at MV.

Sadly, Hollaus didn't get long to celebrate. After securing the title, he lost his life during practice at Monza. The next day, riders honoured their fallen rival by riding the opening lap of the race in formation and at low speed. To this day, the Austrian is the sport's only posthumous world champion.

Things were starting to move faster now. In June 1954, the son of a Japanese blacksmith flew halfway around the world to a small island in the Irish Sea. His name was Soichiro Honda and he was there to witness the world's biggest motorcycle races. Just weeks earlier, he had announced Honda's ambition to contest the TT, a declaration that attracted some derision.

After watching the 125 race – won by Hollaus – he began to wonder if indeed he had spoken too soon. The NSU made almost twice as much horsepower as his own 125 single, prompting his despairing admission that "we had never seen or dreamed of machines like that".

NSU believed it had proved its point with its 125 and 250 title double, so the factory quit at the end of 1954 to focus on its car business. And so began Ubbiali's great era of domination on the MV. He wasn't your typical Italian racer: he was sombre and thoughtful, a disciplined perfectionist who never had a serious crash. His cool, calculating approach won him 26 victories and six world titles in the class.

Ubbiali's reign took 125s into and out of the dustbin-fairing era. These all-enclosing streamliners cut through the air with slippery efficiency, but were the cause of many an accident – including several fatalities – so they were banned after 1957.

Honda failed to turn up at the 1955 TT and neither did it make the '56, '57 or '58 races. But Honda-san was still working towards his big ambition, and in 1956 he bought a Mondial 125 as part of his research.

"We stripped the engine and got a lot of data about materials," said Honda, a metallurgist who made his name making piston rings for the Japanese military during World War 2. "The aluminium was especially good, of a quality unobtainable in Japan."

In some ways, Honda was well behind its European counterparts – it was still casting engine parts instead of forging them – but in other ways, it was about to move ahead. While the motorcycle business boomed in Japan, it was collapsing in Europe due to a new wave of cheap 'mini' cars, like Fiat's 500. As a result, Mondial, Gilera and Moto Guzzi all withdrew from racing at the end of 1957.

Ducati, on the other hand, was only just joining the fun. Fabio Taglioni's first desmodromic engine – a twin-plug 125 single – came close to winning the 1958 title. Taglioni was in a rich vein of creativity at the time: he also had a desmo 125 twin and a non-desmo 125 four under development. The gear-driven dohc four was never raced, because Ducati's race department also fell victim to market decline at the end of 1958, but its existence belies the myth that the Japanese pioneered cylinder miniaturisation and multiplication in the smaller classes.

At the same time as Taglioni was drawing his 125 four, two other game-changing forces were under way. In Tokyo, Honda-san resolved to build a twin-cylinder 125 because his single was getting badly beaten by its two-stroke rivals in Japan. A short-stroke twin made a lot of sense – the wider bores comfortably accommodated four smaller, lighter valves, which solved the high-rpm problems associated with bigger valves in two-valve heads.

Meanwhile in Zschopau, East Germany, former Nazi rocket scientist Kaaden was starting to obtain serious horsepower from his MZ two-stroke 125. By combining new-fangled expansion-chamber technology with rotary-valve induction and a third transfer port, he had unlocked the secrets of the two-stroke.

In 1959, Ernst Degner scored MZ's first 125 win at Monza, where he beat Ubbiali's MV by a few feet, sending the count into an incandescent rage. From this moment on, the writing was on the wall for the four-stroke – over the following years, every grand prix class would fall to bikes that employed Kaaden's know-how in one way or another.

Three months before Degner's historic win, Honda had finally got around to making its TT debut. The RC142 twins ran well enough, Naomi Taniguchi taking the last world championship point in sixth place, albeit seven minutes behind Tarquino Provini's winning MV.

Australian privateer Tom Phillis was one of the first to guess the potential of the Oriental machines. He wrote to Honda, asking for a ride, and at Barcelona in April, 1961, he became Honda's first grand prix winner. The '61 season developed into a duel between Phillis on his 23bhp 2RC143 twin and Degner on his MZ single, the world's first normally-aspirated engine to make 200bhp per litre. Honda won the title after Degner had made a cloak-and-dagger defection to the West, where he sold Kaaden's secrets to Suzuki.

Suzuki's 125 two-stroke singles had been woefully uncompetitive, so the company turned to industrial espionage to get on the pace. Kaaden's stolen know-how won the factory's (and the two-stroke's) first world title the very next year, in the brand-new 50cc class.

With the burgeoning might of Japanese industry behind it, the two-stroke quickly changed everything. When Hugh Anderson and Suzuki's new 125 – a 26bhp, eight-speed twin – beat Luigi Taveri and Honda's twin to the 1963 title, things started becoming gloriously silly. Honda knew there was only one way to keep the dastardly two-stroke at bay: more revs, which meant more cylinders.

In 1964, Honda regained the title with a 17,000rpm four, but Suzuki upped its game for 1965 and successfully came back at Honda with 31bhp, so Honda went away and built an eight-speed five. The 34x27.5mm engine – which made 32bhp at 20,000rpm – put Taveri back on top in 1966. The bike was a pig to ride – it would barely run below 18,000rpm – and maintenance was no easier. Mechanics reckoned they could rebuild five Manx Norton engines in the time it took to rebuild one RC148.

Life wasn't about to get any easier for Honda. Yamaha became serious about winning the 125 title in 1967, unleashing the highly-complex, nine-speed two-stroke RA31 V4, which made usable power on a knife edge between 15,500 and 17,000rpm. Where would it all end?

Disappointingly, there was no clash of the titans that year between the RC148 and RA31, because Honda withdrew from the smaller classes, perhaps aware that it was running out of options against the ever-improving two-stroke.

Yamaha monopolised the 1967 and 1968 campaigns with its 336bhp-per-litre V4. Bill Ivy was the company's first 125 champ, then Phil Read, who went on to become the first man to complete the triple crown – the 125, 250 and 500 titles. Only one other has managed it since – Rossi.

The ear-splitting shriek of the RA31 was the last hurrah of what many consider to be bike racing's golden age, when technology was moving ahead at a stratospheric rate. Perhaps there was something in the air at the time; after all, mankind was only months away from landing on the moon.

But the factories didn't have NASA budgets. By the end of 1968, all three Japanese manufacturers had quit the grand prix circuit because they were feeling the pain of developing increasingly complex machinery during a period of decreasing sales.

At the same time, the FIM stepped in to put the brake on runaway technology, fully aware that soon there would be no factories left if development continued apace. Fabulous exotica was banned: from now on, the 125 class would be limited to six-speed twins. The restrictions instantly wiped

Above: Fausto Gresini leads team mate Casanova in the 1987 Austrian Grand Prix. The Garelli pair scored a 1-2 in both this race and the championship that year.
Photo: Gold & Goose

Top left: Kent Andersson tuned his Yamaha twins to take back-to-back titles in 1973 and 1974.
Photo: Bauer

Above centre: Pierpaolo Bianchi flat out on his Morbidelli in 1977, when the Italian machines were ridden by 18 of the top 20 scorers in the World Championship.

Above right: Angel Nieto (Minarelli) heads Guy Bertin (Sanvenero) at Imatra, 1981. This was one of the Spaniard's record 62 125 victories.

Inset top right: Tough little Spaniard Nieto won seven 125 World Championships between 1971 and 1984.
Photos: Motocourse Archive

Inset above right: Loris Capirossi is the youngest ever 125 World Champion – he won the 1990 crown aged 17 years and 165 days.
Photo: Gold & Goose

four-strokes from the class, and the next two years were dominated by what had only recently been obsolete twin-cylinder two-strokes. Briton Dave Simmonds won the 1969 title on an ex-factory Kawasaki two-stroke twin, built in 1966. The following year, it was the turn of German Dieter Braun, riding an ex-factory Suzuki twin of 1967 vintage.

The Japanese factories now had little interest in the smaller classes, preferring to focus their attention on the championships that attracted more media attention, which gave smaller European concerns a chance to shine once again.

Derbi was the first, the company's brilliant engineer Francisco Tombas building a 40bhp twin that took Angel Nieto to the 1971 and '72 titles. Nieto had already won the 1969 and '70 50cc crowns for Derbi, so this was the start of Spain's huge push into the world championships. The Spanish industry – Derbi, Bultaco, Ossa, Montesa and others – flourished at the time, thanks to General Franco's policy of protectionism, which prevented a Japanese invasion. Yamaha did buck the trend briefly, supplying Swede Kent Andersson with twins on which he won the 1973 and '74 titles, but this was not the start of a Japanese counterattack.

If great things were happening in Spain, these were fascinating times in Italy, too, with a new generation of motorcycle-mad businessmen making its mark in grand prix racing. A few years after Count Agusta's death, Giancarlo Morbidelli's machines won the 125 world title in 1975, '76 and '77. Morbidelli used his woodworking machinery business to bankroll his racing department, just as Agusta had spent the profits of his helicopter business on bikes. Then there was construction magnate Emilio Sanvenero, who built grand prix winning 125s, and furniture manufacturer Egido Piovaticci, whose 125s would also prove victorious, if only after he had run out of money and sold his race department to Bultaco.

But the most important man in 125 GPs at the time was German boffin Jorg Muller. He was the brains behind the Morbidelli twin that came to utterly dominate the class, filling 25 of the top 30 places in 1977. Bikes or engines created or tuned by Muller – Morbidelli, MBA (Morbidelli Benelli Armi), Minarelli and Garelli – won 13 straight 125 titles from 1975 to 1987.

Muller's Morbidelli was the first of a new breed of GP machine, a product that used the best parts from all over the world, not solely from the bike's country of origin. The disc-valve twin employed German-made Mahle pistons and Hoekle crank, Japanese Mikuni carburettors, Italian Brembo brakes, Campagnolo wheels and Marzocchi suspension. Meanwhile, two-stroke technology continued apace, the machines becoming faster and more rideable with each passing year. Instead of the three transfer ports used in the 1960s, the 125s had five and even six transfer ports, making for very holey cylinder walls. By the mid-1980s, some 125s were running eight transfers!

Nieto enjoyed arguably the best years of his career on Muller-designed machines. After winning several GPs on the ex-Piovaticci Bultaco in 1976 and 1977, he joined Muller in 1978 and won five world 125 titles over seven seasons, the first two with Minarelli and the next three with Garelli, which bought the Minarelli race department at the end of 1981.

Fausto Gresini and Luca Cadalora also won titles for Garelli, but the company's run of success ended abruptly when the technical regulations were rewritten for the 1988 season, restricting the class to single-cylinder machines.

It took a few years for the single-cylinder status quo to be established. Jorge Martinez won the first single title with Derbi, then Alex Crivillé took the 1989 title with Antonio Cobas' JJ Cobas Rotax, but from the early 1990s the class

125cc MILESTONES

1949	Nello Pagani wins first title on 11bhp Mondial four-stroke single.
1952	MV scores first GP win and first world title with dohc 125.
1953	NSU dominates with 18bhp single.
1956	Fabio Taglioni builds first desmo Ducati, a 125 single.
1958	Ducati (*below right*) unleashes desmo twin making 22.5bhp at 14,000rpm.
1959	Honda makes TT debut with 125 twin.
1960	Suzuki makes woeful TT debut with 13bhp two-stroke.
1961	Tom Phillis scores Honda's first GP win, which is also the first 125 success by a twin.
1963	Hugh Anderson and 25.5bhp, eight-speed Suzuki dominate series.
1964	Honda and Luigi Taveri regain title with 125 four, making 28bhp at 18,000rpm.
1965	Taveri and Honda champions again with 125 five.
1968	Yamaha wins second straight 125 title with nine-speed, V4 two-stroke, making 42bhp at 16,500rpm.
1969	New rules restrict 125 class to two cylinders and six gears.
1971	Angel Nieto takes Derbi's first 125 crown on 125 twin.
1974	Giancarlo Morbidelli signs engineer Jorg Muller. Fritz Reitmaier wins strike-hit Nürburgring GP on Maico, the last victory by a single until 1988.
1977	Twenty-five of the top 30 in 125 championship ride Morbidellis.
1978	Eugenio Lazzarini champion on MBA and self-made monocoque chassis.
1981	Vittorio Minarelli dies; the company sells its racing department to Garelli.
1988	Class restricted to single-cylinder machines. Jorge Martinez and Derbi are champions. Minimum age for 125 class reduced from 17 to 16.
1990	Loris Capirossi wins Honda's first 125 crown since 1966. The Italian will go down in history as the youngest-ever 125 world champ
1991	Noboru Ueda wins Suzuka, kick-starting the Japanese rider invasion.
1992	Alessandro Gramigni wins Aprilia's first world title.
1996	Combined minimum weight rule introduced – bike and rider must weight no less than 130kg. Max Sabbatani (at 39kg and 1.5m tall) holds the ballast record, at 12kg.

Photo: Ducati

became a two-way duel between Honda and Aprilia, headed by Dutch engineer Jan Witteveen. During their rivalry, which lasted a decade and a half, only one title went to another manufacturer – Gilera in 2001.

When Loris Capirossi won the 1990 title, he became Honda's first 125 world champion for 24 years, and it would be hard to imagine two more different race bikes than Taveri's madly exotic five-cylinder four-stroke and Capirossi's beautifully simple, reed-valve two-stroke single. In many ways, the rule change had taken the 125 class back to where it started – relatively simple machines put together by small teams.

Honda never ran a factory 125 effort. The RS125, its engine originally derived from a CR motocrosser, was a very affordable production bike manufactured in its thousands, which became the backbone of the class, not only at world level, but also in national and even club events. HRC did supply 'A' or 'B' kits to favoured grand prix riders, but usually team tuners found the best way to extract maximum performance was to do their own development work.

Hans Spaan, Capirossi's greatest rival in 1990, was one such man. He tuned his own RS125s and later fettled the Hondas that took Haruchika Aoki to the 1995 and 1996 world titles. The Dutchman was still tuning 125s in 2011, working on the Aprilias of Luis Salom, still entranced by the two-stroke's nebulous nature.

In 1992, Aprilia won its first world championship with its disc-valve 125 engine, originally engineered by Rotax. After that, the championship swung between Aprilia and Honda until the Japanese company stopped RS125 production as part of its plan to terminate manufacture of all two-stroke motorcycles.

The move to single-cylinder machines certainly created closer racing, and soon the 125 class became renowned for

Photo: Gold & Goose

Photo: Gold & Goose

1997	Valentino Rossi secures his first world title, in the 125 class.
2004	Maximum age limit introduced – no rider over 28 can race in 125s.
2010	The minimum age is returned to 16.
2011	Nico Terol (*above left*) and 54bhp Aprilia win final title. A new economic force arrives in 125 GP racing – Mahindra (*left*) is the first Indian factory in grand prix racing.

125cc WINS
(races/titles)

RIDERS	
Nieto	62/7
Ubbiali	26/6
PP Bianchi	24/3
Taveri	22/3
Gresini	21/2
Anderson	17/2
Martinez	15/1
Andersson	14/2
Ivy	14/1
Raudies	14/1
Ueda	13/0

CONSTRUCTORS	
Honda	164/15
Aprilia	136/10
Derbi	63/4
Yamaha	47/4
Garelli	44/4
Suzuki	35/3
MV Agusta	34/7
Minarelli	32/4
Morbidelli	30/3
MBA	20/2
Mondial	14/4

Right: The 125 class was renowned for coaching new talent. Marc Marquez (93), 2010 World Champion, shown here leading Bradley Smith at Assen, is the latest potential future superstar.

Below: Valentino Rossi (46) won his first GP on 125s and went on to become only the second rider (after Phil Read) to win championships on 125s, 250s and 500s.
Photos: Gold & Goose

Below right: More future MotoGP heroes learning how it's done on 125s: Dani Pedrosa heads Casey Stoner (27) and Jorge Lorenzo (48) at Motegi, 2003.
Photos: Gold & Goose

Right: End of an era. Retiring Race Director Paul Butler flags final 125cc champion Nico Terol over the finish line at Valencia.
Photo: Gold & Goose

providing the most thrilling race of the day. Rijeka in 1989 was a particularly memorable encounter – the first nine riders to cross the line separated by just eight-tenths of a second. Over the years, the 125 class saw 70 races won by less than a second, most of those in the last two decades.

Capirossi's 1990 success (he retained the title the following year) was the start of a new era in grand prix racing. The minimum age limit had recently been lowered to 16 years, and in 1996 it was lowered again, to 15, which brought a new younger generation of racers into the paddock. These teenagers – many of whom had started road racing before they went to school – became regulars on 125 podiums. Capirossi will go down in history as the youngest 125 world champion – at 17 years and 165 days old – but there have been seven other teenage 125 champions since: Aoki, Dani Pedrosa, Rossi, Manuel Poggiali, Andrea Dovizioso, Thomas Luthi and Marc Marquez. Pagani, incidentally, is the oldest 125 champ at 37 years and 241 days.

Not only were younger and younger riders welcomed in recent years, but older riders were actually barred, to reinforce the category's status as a feeder class. From 2004, no rider older than 28 was allowed to enter a 125 GP.

Honda's withdrawal was perhaps the beginning of the end for 125s. Only one other manufacturer seemed prepared to build bikes in any quantity, so the class became something

of an Aprilia monopoly. Austrian brand KTM contested the championship from 2004 to 2007, but with only a handful of machines.

One man was determined to end the Aprilia domination: Piaggio race boss Giampiero Sacchi, who hired another Dutch two-stroke genius to build a 125 engine for Derbi, recently bought by Piaggio. Jan Thiel (who was responsible for the Piovaticci/Bultaco bikes, had taken over from Muller at Minarelli and Garelli, and later had a major hand in Aprilia's success) created the Derbi RE-VE, which gained extra performance from positioning the rotary valve above the crankshaft instead of at its side. But no sooner had Thiel completed his masterpiece than Piaggio bought the better-known Aprilia brand, so his engine became the Aprilia RSA. The RSA was good for 54bhp (or 432bhp per litre) and won the last four 125 crowns, two for Derbi and two for Aprilia.

When the 125s ran their last grand prix race at Valencia on 6th November, 2011, it was also the end of the line for two-strokes in world championship road racing; an emotional moment for dozens of engineers in the paddock, who had dedicated much of their careers to this endlessly fascinating engine. Rightly or wrongly, the three-class MotoGP series is now exclusively four-stroke. Now it is the turn of Moto3 – the 250cc four-stroke series that replaced the 125s – to make its own history.

125cc WORLD CHAMPIONS

1949 Nello Pagani (Mondial)
1950 Bruno Ruffo (Mondial)
1951 Carlo Ubbiali (Mondial)
1952 Cecil Sandford (MV Agusta)
1953 Werner Haas (NSU)
1954 Rupert Hollaus (NSU)
1955 Carlo Ubbiali (MV Agusta)
1956 Carlo Ubbiali (MV Agusta)
1957 Tarquinio Provini (Mondial)
1958 Carlo Ubbiali (MV Agusta)
1959 Carlo Ubbiali (MV Agusta)
1960 Carlo Ubbiali (MV Agusta)
1961 Tom Phillis (Honda)
1962 Luigi Taveri (Honda)
1963 Hugh Anderson (Suzuki)
1964 Luigi Taveri (Honda)
1965 Hugh Anderson (Suzuki)
1966 Luigi Taveri (Honda)
1967 Bill Ivy (Yamaha)
1968 Phil Read (Yamaha)
1969 Dave Simmonds (Kawasaki)
1970 Dieter Braun (Suzuki)
1971 Angel Nieto (Derbi)
1972 Angel Nieto (Derbi)
1973 Kent Anderson (Yamaha)
1974 Kent Anderson (Yamaha)
1975 Paolo Pileri (Morbidelli)
1976 Pierpaolo Bianchi (Morbidelli)
1977 Pierpaolo Bianchi (Morbidelli)
1978 Eugenio Lazzarini (MBA)
1979 Angel Nieto (Minarelli)
1980 Pierpaolo Bianchi (MBA)
1981 Angel Nieto (Minarelli)
1982 Angel Nieto (Garelli)
1983 Angel Nieto (Garelli)
1984 Angel Nieto (Garelli)
1985 Fausto Gresini (Garelli)
1986 Luca Cadalora (Garelli)
1987 Fausto Gresini (Garelli)
1988 Jorge Martinez (Derbi)
1989 Alex Crivillé (JJ Cobas)
1990 Loris Capirossi (Honda)
1991 Loris Capirossi (Honda)
1992 Alessandro Gramigni (Aprilia)
1993 Dirk Raudies (Honda)
1994 Kazuto Sakata (Aprilia)
1995 Haruchika Aoki (Honda)
1996 Haruchika Aoki (Honda)
1997 Valentino Rossi (Aprilia)
1998 Kazuto Sakata (Aprilia)
1999 Emilio Alzamora (Honda)
2000 Roberto Locatelli (Aprilia)
2001 Manuel Poggiali (Gilera)
2002 Arnaud Vincent (Aprilia)
2003 Dani Pedrosa (Honda)
2004 Andrea Dovizioso (Honda)
2005 Thomas Luthi (Honda)
2006 Alvaro Bautista (Aprilia)
2007 Gabor Talmacsi (Aprilia)
2008 Mike di Meglio (Derbi)
2009 Julian Simon (Aprilia)
2010 Marc Marquez (Derbi)
2011 Nico Terol (Aprilia)

TECHNICAL ESSAY
TYRE TALK

Control tyres have changed the racing landscape. This is not the first time that the rubber has played such a role. KEVIN CAMERON presents a brief history of the continuous development of the Black Art...

THE corner speeds and spectacular angles of lean we see in MotoGP are a direct result of otherwise invisible advances in tyre technology. Without tyre grip, engine power and rider brilliance are nothing. Tyre technology advances continually, so tyre revolutions periodically reshape racing. Results are sometimes dramatic, as at present, but can also be subtle.

The introduction of synthetic tread rubber in the late 1950s dramatically increased wet grip. In 1964, Dunlop's famous 'Trigonal' tyre displaced round-section tyres with its broad and flat cornering footprint. The first 100-horsepower 750s from Japan destroyed the best available tyres at 170mph speeds in the 1972 Daytona event, forcing drastic change. That change was the super-wide, round-profile tyre, developed at Dunlop by Tony Mills. Its very large footprint controlled wear and reduced operating temperature – rubber's great enemy. Dunlop launched this tyre in 1974, its smooth tread interrupted by only a few vestigial water drainage grooves. At Goodyear, racing manager Mike Babich asked, "Why can't we use slicks?" Slick tyres, by placing a maximum amount of rubber in contact with the pavement, and by eliminating the constant bending and heat generation of freestanding tread elements, greatly increased grip and the ability of motorcycle tyres to survive high speed and power.

The focus of racing motorcycle development soon shifted to the 500 Grand Prix. By 1981, 135hp 500s had used up the new capabilities of slick tyres. Now a race tyre lost its peak properties after only seven to ten laps, forcing riders to come to the start with shiny, unscuffed tyres. Tyre conservation was the only race strategy. A rider might lead for five laps, then have to fall back, saying afterwards, "My tyres went off."

The grip of rubber increases with its softness, for softer rubber more closely fills the texture of the pavement, generating an increased area of true contact, rather than simply touching the pavement at its high points. In the area of true contact, short-range forces momentarily bind the rubber to the pave-ment. But typically, the softer the rubber, the lower its tensile strength. The development of racing tread rubber compounds has been a constant struggle to combine greater softness with the high tensile strength needed for it to remain in one piece rather than begin to tear.

In school, we learn a simple law of friction – that if we double the load pressing two surfaces together, we double the friction that results from sliding one against the other. Rubber behaves in this way only initially. As we increase the load on a tyre, its grip increases in proportion for a time, but if we plot the grip versus load on a graph, we see a rising slope that eventually softens, peaks, and curves back downwards. What is happening here is that in the initial rising slope, each increase of load is pressing the rubber deeper and deeper into the texture of the pavement, increasing its true area of contact – and increasing the grip. But at some point, the rubber's tensile strength is no longer sufficient to transmit so large a grip force. It begins to tear here and there, so the curve ceases to rise smoothly as before. As the tearing becomes more general, the curve flattens, then heads downwards.

Rubber begins life as liquid polymer – a gooey mass of long molecular chains, conceptually like a pot of boiling spaghetti. It is transformed into a visco-elastic solid by the process of vulcanisation, which uses heat and the presence of sulphur to link the molecular chains to each other in many places. The elasticity of rubber arises from the whirling of the molecular chains between sulphur bonds. It is temperature – the measure of molecular activity – that whirls the molecular chains, generating a tension that resists any pulling apart of their ends. As we stretch a bit of rubber, we can feel that stretching is a limited process – it doesn't go on forever. At some percentage of stretch, the rubber stiffens and its resistance increases; all its molecular chains have been pulled straight.

To further increase the durability of rubber, finely divided carbon black is added (this makes tyres black, but in the Edwardian era, when tyres were reinforced with zinc oxide, they

Left: Black Magic, and you can take your pick.

Below: A fresh Bridgestone rear for the Repsol Honda. The white line indicates the softer of two available compounds.

Photos: Gold & Goose

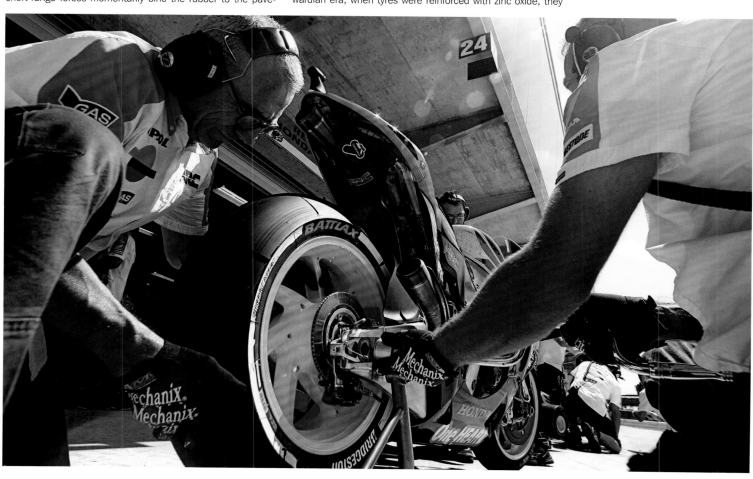

51

Above: Three decades ago and Giacomo Agostini is taking his MV's tyres to the limit. Looks rather sedate by today's 60-degree-lean standards.
Photo: Motocourse archive

Top: 2011-style grip lets Stoner lean his Honda almost to the ground.

Top right: Tyre management still matters. This is Stoner's rear Bridgestone after his win in Aragon.

Above right: Unsung heroes. Dunlop fitters are faced with supplying an array of tyres for all conditions.

Right: Dunlop supplied tyres to all the riders in the Moto2 and 125cc fields.
Photos: Gold & Goose

were white). Carbon is 'sticky' in a molecular sense, which explains its use in cigarette filters, where it attracts active chemicals to its surface. The presence of myriad tiny carbon particles in the rubber adds to the cohesion of the rubber chains, much as little magnets would bind a mass of thin steel fibres together. Individual bonds might break and reform elsewhere, but there is an overall binding effect.

Over many years, the process of improving racing rubber depended upon producing finer and finer carbon particles that could generate cohesive effect without making the rubber too hard to grip well. Finer carbon made it more difficult to fully mix the viscous mass, just as it is real work to incorporate dry flour into cookie dough. Giant mixers, called Banbury machines, driven by 50,000hp electric motors, attempted to achieve full mixing before the mass of uncured rubber became so hot that it began to vulcanise prematurely. Oils and waxes, termed 'mixing agents' or 'extender oils', were added to the rubber to both ease mixing and make the resulting product softer. Some kinds of racing rubber have been seen to 'sweat', tiny droplets of this oil separating and rising to the tread surface.

In the late 1950s, it was discovered that best grip – especially in the wet – required less-than-complete vulcanisation. Tyres are vulcanised (cured) at just under 160°C in steam-heated metal moulds, while race tyres operated at around 100°C. That meant that on the track, the hot rubber would resume curing, but at a reduced rate, slowly becoming harder. When the tyres cooled after use, they were found to be useless for racing, as the chemical change that had taken place in them was irreversible. This is what riders called "going off".

Racing tread rubber compounds have a limited range of useful operating temperature. At room temperature, they lack the softness to generate grip by closely filling the pavement texture. At excessive temperatures, they begin to lose their optimum mix of properties. One of these is the viscosity necessary for another aspect of grip – hysteresis. Rubber hysteresis – or internal friction – became important after about 1958 with the adoption of synthetic rubbers. It was promoted as 'Cling' or 'Road-Hug' rubber. Think of a single nub in the pavement surface as the hull of a tiny boat being pushed through the sea of rubber as the tyre slides against the surface. Drag in this case is the pressure of the rubber against the upstream surface of the nub. If the rubber is highly elastic, it will quickly snap back as the nub passes, thereby also exerting some force on its *downstream* side. This pressure on the downstream side opposes the drag force; in other words, it reduces grip. But if we make the rubber a bit less elastic, its recovery of shape as the nub passes will be slowed by its internal friction, and there

will be *no pressure* on the downstream side of the nub. This maximises the drag force produced against the nub, thereby generating the *hysteretic component of traction*. In the early days of high-hysteresis rubber in racing tyres, top speeds were reduced by a few miles per hour by the material's low elasticity (that is, it displayed higher rolling resistance), but the gain in cornering grip more than compensated, resulting in faster lap times.

Riders on the new slick tyres of the mid-1970s often fell shortly after the start of a race because their tyres were not yet warm enough to grip. Slicks, lacking the heat-generating flexing of individual tread elements, heated up less quickly than treaded tyres. In time, this led to the provision of a warm-up lap before the start, and in the late 1980s to the practice of pre-heating tyres in electric tyre warmers. Even with these measures, the first three laps of today's races are tricky – an aggressive rider pushes hard for position, trying both to stay upright and to get his tyres quickly to operating temperature.

By 1981, the compromises in rubber compounding and tyre construction had resulted in a tyre life at peak properties of as little as seven to ten laps. The 1981 world champion, Marco Lucchinelli, adopted the strategy of riding the early laps at the tail end of the lead group, conserving tyre properties for a late push to the front. If timed right, this push would succeed just as the leaders' tyres were nearing the end of their usefulness. The harder they rode to stay with Lucchinelli, the faster their tyres 'went off', causing them to lose position or even to fall.

The radial tyre revolution, initiated by Michelin in 1984, reset all compromises. Previously, a tyre carcass consisted of multiple plies, each made of parallel, uni-directional textile fibres (nylon, rayon, aramid) in a thin skim of rubber, applied at alternating angles – on the bias – to the tyre's central plane. These bias-ply (cross-ply) tyres flexed in rolling and the multiple plies scissored against each other, generating rubber-destroying heat. In the simplest radial carcass, a single ply is orientated at 90 degrees to the tyre's central plane, reducing the generation of heat by eliminating ply-to-ply motions. Radials, being thinner, were also more flexible and therefore laid down a larger footprint. This allowed use of softer tread rubber, increasing grip and shortening lap times.

Radial construction sounds like a wonderfully simple solution, but in fact practical radial motorcycle tyres are complicated by the need for tread-stiffening reinforcing belts, sidewall stiffeners and other modifications. Tyre engineering is extremely complex because every variable affects every other variable. The path to improvement is never easy or direct.

The cooler running of radial construction allowed tyres to catch up in some degree to the ever-rising power of 500cc two-strokes. But as power swelled from 135 to 190hp, tyre distress returned. Mick Doohan, 500 champion from 1995 to 1999 inclusive, described spending "the last ten laps sliding around." Fastest race laps were set as soon as tyres reached operating temperature, but tyre properties still declined after 10–15 laps.

In the late 1990s, Michelin's automated C3M tyre building system, using a multi-segmented mould, greatly improved quality control. As a result, less extra rubber was necessary to guarantee necessary minimum thicknesses at all points. Less rubber again meant cooler running. Any time operating temperature can be reduced, softer rubber compounds may become usable, offering increased grip. Lap times took another three-quarter-second drop. An onlooker could identify the new tyres by their many visible radial mould lines.

C3M's fast production cycle allowed Michelin engineers to match Sunday's tyres to actual weekend weather and track conditions. Tyres were made overnight and whisked to the track. This allowed their tyres to be closely matched to race-day temperature, within a range of 5°C. Remarkable performance was the immediate result.

A subsequent rule change stopped such overnight production. Michelin, finding itself far up an avenue of development based upon a very close match of tyre and track conditions,

had to go back to the beginning and start over in new directions to comply with the new regulations. If there is any field in which 'scheduled breakthroughs' are impossible, it is tyre technology. A company can pour money into research, but physics and chemistry set the pace of progress.

Meanwhile, the world became concerned about vehicle fuel economy as oil prices and climate concerns rose. Intensive research sought the causes of tyre rolling resistance. Rubber hysteresis, for so long the basis of wet grip, became a villain to be eliminated. In the late 1980s, rubber companies found a new source of wet grip – rubber reinforced by ultra-fine silica (its coarse cousin is ordinary quartz sand). Initial research around 1990 found ways to use silica to make rubber softer at rainy-day temperatures, but silica-to-rubber bonds fell apart at the elevated temperatures of racing use.

Since then, continuous research has rapidly developed the chemistry of silica reinforcement. It was found possible to combine low rolling resistance with wet grip by developing rubber with frequency-sensitive hysteresis. At present, silica-reinforced rubber can display very low hysteresis at the frequency of a rolling tyre (15 cycles per second at motorway speed), but usefully high, traction-boosting hysteresis at the much higher frequencies (hundreds of cycles) of rubber gripping, releasing and gripping again over fine pavement projections. As with any new technology, it takes time to exploit new possibilities. Grip-enhancing hysteresis in race tyres no longer depended upon incomplete curing, so rubber retained optimum properties longer.

When Bridgestone prepared to enter MotoGP, its early test tyres often worked best at cool temperatures, such that in the 2003 race season cool mornings were called 'Bridgestone weather'. Bridgestone worked hardest to broaden tyre operating temperature range – with its factory in Japan, there could be no last-minute manufacture of bespoke tyres to compensate for the sun having gone behind a cloud.

When MotoGP was made a single-tyre series, Bridgestone was designated the sole supplier. Many first-time users commented that Bridgestones behaved very differently from their previous experience. Colin Edwards Jr said, "Load 'em up. The more load you put on 'em, the better they grip." Paddock pundits, knowing Bridgestones had heavy, stiff carcasses, somehow translated this into a novel ability to spread out under load. This is the opposite of fact: the softer the carcass, the larger its footprint and the greater its ability to increase that footprint under load.

So what *is* different about recent Bridgestone tyres? The difference is new tread rubber technology that has allowed a dramatic increase in tensile strength while retaining the softness that generates high grip. Nuggets of information appear on the Internet – that Bridgestone has developed 'bi-functional silane coupling agents', which allow rubber chains to bind specifically to a silica surface.

In conventional rubbers reinforced only by carbon black, the carbon particles have affinity for the rubber chains, but do not form actual chemical bonds with them. In Bridgestone's new carbon-plus-silica scheme, rubber chains are *chemically* bonded to silica particles by strong covalent bonds – bonds based upon the sharing of electrons. Without actual explanations from Bridgestone chemists, we can only speculate that this bonding creates an unusually strong, yet open network within the rubber, greatly increasing its tear resistance, but not increasing hardness. The strength of the bonds enables such rubber to resist the fatigue that could otherwise break bonds and cause tearing to occur at lower stress.

As a rider brakes for a turn, weight transfers to the front tyre, forcing its soft rubber deeply into the texture of the pavement, which generates an increasingly larger area of true contact. With the increased tensile strength given by the new silica technology, this rubber does not begin to tear at the usual stress level, but continues to hang on. What our eyes see of this latest tyre revolution are today's amazing angles of lean, and riders setting their fastest laps very near the finish.

TEAM-BY-TEAM

2011 MOTOGP REVIEW

Teams and Riders

MATTHEW BIRT

Bike Specifications

NEIL SPALDING

Bike Illustrations

ADRIAN DEAN

ANDREA DOVIZIOSO
Born: 23 March, 1986 – Forli, Italy

GP Starts: 169 (71 MotoGP, 49 250cc, 49 125cc)

GP Wins: 10 (1 MotoGP, 4 250cc, 5 125cc)

World Championships: 1 125cc

DANI PEDROSA
Born: 29 September, 1985 – Sabadell, Spain

GP Starts: 176 (98 MotoGP, 32 250cc, 46 125cc)

GP Wins: 38 (15 MotoGP, 15 250cc, 8 125cc)

World Championships: 3 (2 250cc, 1 125cc)

CASEY STONER
Born: 16 October, 1985 – Southport, Australia

GP Starts: 161 (100 MotoGP, 31 250cc, 30 125cc)

GP Wins: 40 (33 MotoGP, 5 250cc, 2 125cc)

World Championships: 2 MotoGP

IF Repsol Honda had been a sleeping giant throughout the 800cc era, it roused from its slumber in spectacular fashion in 2011 as HRC restored its reputation as the undisputed powerhouse in MotoGP.

Not since 2003 had Honda ruled MotoGP with such domination, the Japanese factory bouncing back to prominence with 13 victories to inflict humiliation on Yamaha and Ducati, which had dominated the 800cc era from 2007 to 2010.

HRC took a clean sweep of rider, team and constructor titles, and the catalyst for dragging the be-leaguered factory out of the doldrums was the signing of Casey Stoner.

The 2010 season was barely under way when Stoner was snared from Ducati, with HRC Communication and Marketing Director Livio Suppo heavily influential in the deal. Suppo had signed Stoner for Ducati at the end of 2006 and he knew better than anybody that with him on board, if Honda delivered a competitive bike, the fearsomely fast Australian would do the rest.

HRC Vice-President Shuhei Nakamoto also played a pivotal role in the capture of Stoner. Nakamoto was in his third season at the helm, and the changes he implemented on his arrival from Honda's defunct Formula One team in 2009 reaped huge dividends in 2011.

One key decision was to install Shinichi Kokubu as technical director for 2010, and he remained the engineering brains behind the RC212V, transforming the bike into one that every rider wanted to be on.

But the role Stoner played in ending Honda's embarrassing lack of success can't be underestimated. He was already the most successful rider in 800s in terms of race wins, having wrestled Ducati's

HONDA RC212V

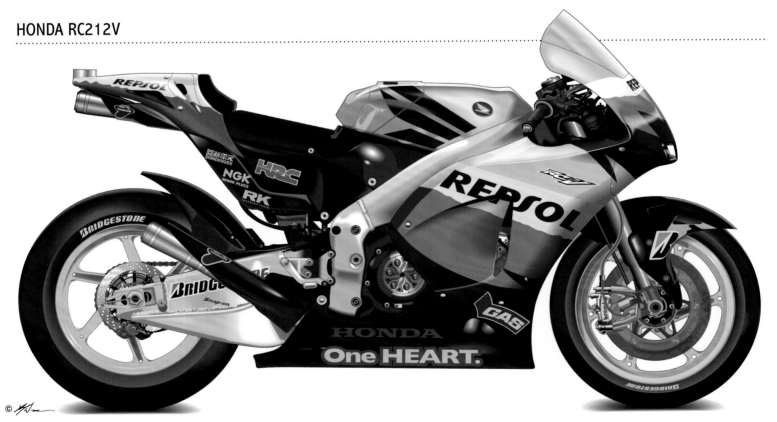

Sponsors and Technical Suppliers: Repsol · One HEART · GAS · Bridgestone · NGK · RK Chains · Shindengen · Snap-on · Termignoni · Yutaka

Engine: 800cc, 76-degree V4, 360-degree crank (tbc), PVRS. *Power:* More than 225ps

Ancillaries: HRC electronics, ride-by-wire throttle and fuel injection system with torducter; NGK sparking plugs

Lubrication: Repsol · *Fuel:* 21 litres, Repsol

Transmission: Gear primary drive, multi-plate dry slipper clutch, six-speed seamless-shift cassette-style gearbox; RK chain

Suspension: Front, Öhlins TRSP25 48mm 'Through Rod' forks · Rear, TRSP44 gas shock with linkage

Wheels: Front, 16.5in Marchesini · Rear, 16.5in Marchesini · *Tyres:* Bridgestone

Brakes: Front, Brembo carbon-carbon 314/320mm · Rear, Yutaka steel 218mm

HIROSHI AOYAMA

Born: 25 October, 1981 – Chiba, Japan

GP Starts: 116 (12 MotoGP 104 250cc)
GP Wins: 9 250cc
World Championships: 1 250cc

brutal Desmosedici to 23 in four years. His blistering speed, combined with Honda's phenomenal RC212V machine, was a potent combination, and by the end of the season he'd won another ten races to take his second world title.

The signs were ominous from the off when he won on his Honda debut in Qatar. The only blemish on an outstandingly consistent season came at the next race at a rain-lashed Jerez. Stoner was battling for the podium when he was innocently wiped out by bitter rival Valentino Rossi. It was the only time he failed to finish, and in every other race he was on the podium.

Sharing in Stoner's glory was the loyal crew who had followed him out of the exit door at Ducati. His crew chief remained Cristian Gabbarini and chief mechanic was Bruno Leoni. Roberto Clerici, Andrea Brunetti, Lorenzo Gagni and Filippo Brunetti all moved to HRC in Stoner's wake, and the only major change to his crew was Carlo Luzzi. The electronics engineer had worked previously with Jorge Lorenzo at Yamaha before switching to Honda in 2010.

Stoner's stunning arrival in the team put previous Honda and Repsol favourite Dani Pedrosa firmly in the shadows.

The Spaniard was in his sixth season with the official factory team, but once again the year proved to be one dominated by pain and disappointment.

Manager and mentor Alberto Puig once again spearheaded his crew. Officially he was listed on the HRC organogram as advisor, but his influence extended across all aspects of Pedrosa's racing life, both on and off the track.

Mike Leitner once again served as his crew chief, and Pedrosa was actually leading the early title chase when he was involved in one of the major controversies of the year at the French round in Le Mans. Battling for second with Simoncelli, the pair tangled, with Pedrosa once again proving to be as fragile as a china doll. He broke his left collarbone and missed the next three races to see his world title hopes vanish for another season.

Honda only ran a replacement for Pedrosa once, when Hiroshi Aoyama was promoted from the San Carlo Gresini squad in Assen, where the Japanese rider was eighth.

Dani still showed his class with a victory in only his second comeback race in Germany and he won again in Japan, but critics pointed to the fact that when fully fit, he still couldn't win with the regularity of Stoner.

Honda reluctantly fielded its strongest line-up since 2000, as it had three Repsol-sponsored bikes on the grid. The third was for Italian Andrea Dovizioso, whose stubbornness forced Honda to expand to a three-rider effort. HRC had already signed Stoner and Pedrosa in 2010 when Dovizioso invoked a

clause in his contract that assured him a factory ride in 2011.

He had to be in the top five in the championship by the end of July, and despite repeated attempts to find an alternative solution, HRC had to bite the bullet and honour its contract, keeping Dovizioso in the Repsol squad for a third successive season.

Dovizioso's team remained the same and once again he worked with Ramon Aurin as crew chief. He enjoyed his best ever season in MotoGP and he finished third in the final rankings after defeating Pedrosa in the final race in Valencia. Only once in 17 starts did he finish outside the top five. But with HRC making it clear that it would revert to a two-rider factory squad for 2012, Dovizioso was the odd man out. He talked at length with Lucio Cecchinello's LCR Honda squad, with HRC offering him factory support for the satellite entry, but finally opted to join Hervé Poncharal's Tech 3 Yamaha squad prior to the Australian Grand Prix at Phillip Island.

HRC also ran veteran rider Shinichi Ito during the re-scheduled Japanese Grand Prix at the Twin Ring Motegi. The 44-year-old, who had stepped out of retirement to win the Suzuka 8-Hours earlier in the season, raced in HRC colours to show support to East Japan following the devastating earthquake and tsunami that struck in March. Ito resides in Miyagi Prefecture, which was one of the worst affected areas, and he finished 13th.

REPSOL HONDA TEAM

TEAM STAFF

Shuhei NAKAMOTO: HRC Vice President
Shinichi KOKUBU: HRC Technical Director
Livio SUPPO: HRC Communications and Marketing Director
Gianni BERTI: Technical Co-ordinator
Roger VAN DER BORGHT: Co-ordinator
Katsura SHIBASAKI: Spare Parts Control

ANDREA DOVIZIOSO PIT CREW

Ramon AURIN: Chief Engineer
Mark LLOYD: Chief Mechanic
Mechanics
Katsuhiko IMAI
David GUTIERREZ
Yuji KIKUCHI
Fabio RAVELLI
Francesco FAVA: Electronics Engineer
Andrea ZUGNA: Data Analyst
Teruaki MATSUBARA: HRC Engineer
Pete BERGVALL: Öhlins Technician

DANI PEDROSA PIT CREW

Mike LEITNER: Chief Engineer
Alberto PUIG: Advisor
Christophe LEONCE: Chief Mechanic
Mechanics
Mark BARNETT: Engine Technician
Emanuel BUCHNER
Masashi OGO
John EYRE
Toshio ISHIKURA: Electronics Engineer
Jose Manuel ALLENDE: Data Analyst
Takeo YOKOYAMA: HRC Engineer

CASEY STONER PIT CREW

Cristian GABARRINI: Chief Engineer
Bruno LEONI: Chief Mechanic
Mechanics
Roberto CLERICI
Andrea BRUNETTI
Lorenzo GAGNI
Filippo BRUNETTI
Carlo LUZZI: Electronics Engineer
Giulio NAVA: Data Analyst

Top: Repsol Honda's three-bike MotoGP team.

Above left, centre: Shuhei Nakamoto was in charge.

Above left: Cristian Gabbarini, Stoner's crew chief.

Above far left: Livio Suppo.
Photos: Gold & Goose

YAMAHA TEAM

TEAM STAFF

Masahiko NAKAJIMA: General Manager, Yamaha Motorsport Development
Kouichi TSUJI: MotoGP Group Leader
Lin JARVIS: Managing Director, Yamaha Motor Racing
Massimo MEREGALLI: Team Director
Wilco ZEELENBERG: Team Manager
William FAVERO: Communications Manager
Laura MOTTA: Race Events Co-ordinator
Gavin MATHESON: Press Officer

JORGE LORENZO PIT CREW

Ramon FORCADA: Crew Chief
Mechanics
Walter CRIPPA
Javier ULLATE
Valentino NEGRI
Juan Llansa HERNANDEZ (assistant/logistics)
Takashi MORIYAMA: Yamaha Engineer
Davide MARELLI: Data Engineer

BEN SPIES PIT CREW

Tom HOUSEWORTH: Crew Chief
Mechanics
Gregory WOOD
Jurij PELLEGRINI
Ian GILPIN
Olivier BOUTRON
Hiroya ATSUMI: Yamaha Engineer
Erkki SIUKOLA: Data Engineer

JORGE LORENZO
Born: 4 May, 1987 – Palma de Mallorca, Spain
GP Starts: 161 (67 MotoGP, 48 250cc, 46 125cc)
GP Wins: 38 (17 MotoGP, 17 250cc, 4 125cc)
World Championships: 3 (1 MotoGP, 2 250cc)

BEN SPIES
Born: 11 July, 1984 – Memphis, Tennessee, USA
GP Starts: 37 MotoGP
MotoGP Wins: 1
World Championships: 1 World Superbike

YAMAHA'S Milan-based official factory MotoGP squad lost a lot in the 12 months since it swept to a historic third successive triple crown at the end of 2010.

One of the biggest losses was the departure of talismanic Italian Valentino Rossi who, after four world titles and 46 race wins, ended his seven-year association with the Japanese factory to try to resurrect the flagging fortunes of rivals Ducati.

Inevitably, Rossi left en masse with his entire trusted and loyal crew, led by pragmatic Aussie Jerry Burgess. The crew was a non-negotiable element of any transfer deal involving the nine-times world champion, and even some Yamaha hospitality staff defected to the red side with Rossi at Ducati.

Also missing from Yamaha was the understated influence of Masao Furusawa. As executive officer, engineering operations, he single handedly re-modelled Yamaha's race department in readiness for Rossi's arrival back in 2004. Furusawa was the technical genius and driving force behind the most successful period in Yamaha's history, but he was unashamedly a loyal admirer of The Doctor.

Due to retire just before the first race in Qatar, Furusawa made it clear that had Rossi been persuaded to stay, he would have postponed his departure.

YAMAHA M1

Sponsors and Technical Suppliers: Petronas · Semakin Di Depan · Yamalube · Bridgestone · FAAK · Akrapovic · Iveco · 2D · NGK · DID · Exedy Magneti Marelli · Alpinestars · Beta · Eastpak · Flex · Adidas · Dspace

Engine: 800cc, across-the-frame in-line 4; reverse-rotating cross-plane crankshaft, DOHC, 4 valves per cylinder, Pneumatic Valve Return System
       Power: Around 220bhp at approx 18,000rpm

Ancillaries: Magneti Marelli electronics, NGK sparking plugs, full electronic ride-by-wire · *Lubrication:* Yamalube · *Fuel:* 21 litres, Petronas

Transmission: Gear primary drive, multi-plate dry slipper clutch, six-speed constant-mesh floating-dog-ring cassette-style gearbox; DID chain

Suspension: Front, Öhlins TRSP25 48mm 'Through Rod' forks · Rear, Öhlins TRSP44 shock with linkage

Wheels: Front, 16.5in Marchesini · Rear, 16.5in Marchesini · *Tyres:* Bridgestone

Brakes: Front, Brembo carbon-carbon 320mm · Rear, Yamaha steel

KATSUYUKI NAKASUGA

Born: 9 August, 1981 – Shizuoka, Japan

GP Starts: 4 (1 MotoGP, 3 250cc)

Left: Ben Spies scored his maiden MotGP win at Assen.

Below centre: Lorenzo and Spies at Brno.

Bottom: Masao Furusawa *(right)* relinquished his position in favour of Masahiko Nakajima.

Photos: Gold & Goose

LIN JARVIS   MASSIMO MEREGALI   WILCO ZEELENBERG   RAMON FORCADA

Yamaha without Rossi just didn't have the same appeal and he passed control to Masahiko Nakajima, whose previous role was as team director. A much more regimented figure, who appeared less in the public eye than when Furusawa was at the helm, he became general manager of Yamaha's motorsport development division.

Other senior management figures included President Shigeto Kitagawa, while Lin Jarvis continued as managing director of Yamaha Motor Racing.

Kouichi Tsuji took on the role of MotoGP group leader as well as YZR-M1 project leader.

There was one other strikingly obvious difference to Yamaha's factory effort in 2011. Gone was title sponsor Fiat as the global economic crisis continued to ravage the automotive industry.

Indicative of the severity of the financial meltdown, Yamaha was unable to find a replacement naming-rights sponsor, despite dominating MotoGP for three successive seasons with an unprecedented clean sweep of rider, team and constructor titles. Air Asia and Petronas had both been tempted, but without signing the cheque.

The lack of a title sponsor at least gave Yamaha the freedom to run a stunning red and white livery to mark its 50th anniversary in grand prix racing at selected races. But emulating the unrivalled success of the previous three seasons to celebrate the half-century milestone was always going to be a big task. Since 2008, the YZR-M1 had a winning tally in double figures, but at the end of 2011 Jorge Lorenzo and Ben Spies had amassed just four victories between them.

Lorenzo found defending the title a much sterner test than winning it in 2010, largely because of the inspired Casey Stoner at Honda.

After a stellar 2010 season had seen him win nine races, there was no tinkering with a winning format, and his crew remained completely unchanged, with Wilco Zeelenberg at the helm. The Dutchman's experience had proved an invaluable asset in 2010; Spaniard Ramon Forcada remained crew chief.

Lorenzo kept his nerve in a deluge at Jerez to win, but he would only add two more victories in Mugello and Misano, although they were two of the standout rides of a Honda-dominated campaign.

Ten podiums in 14 races had kept his title hopes alive, but an uncharacteristic mistake in a cold and wet British Grand Prix badly dented his prospects before his challenge unravelled in Australia. He surrendered his title on an operating table in Melbourne after a warm-up crash in Phillip Island wore 8mm from the tip of the ring finger on his left hand.

The injury also ruled him out of the Sepang and Valencia races, his place being taken by little-known Japanese test rider Katsuyuki Nakasuga.

Spies arrived in the factory team on the back of

an outstanding rookie campaign for the Monster Yamaha Tech 3 Team, and great things were expected with the full weight of Yamaha support behind him. He surrounded himself with familiar faces: Tom Houseworth remained as his trusted crew chief, while long-time mechanic Gregory Wood also graduated from the Tech 3 squad.

Data technician Erkki Siukola and mechanic Jurij Pellegrini had both worked previously with Spies in either the American or World Superbike series, while his former Yamaha World Superbike boss, Massimo Meregalli, headed the Texan's operation. Meregalli actually filled a dual role, as he also took on the job of team director, meaning he reported directly to Jarvis and Tsuji while also overseeing Spies.

Another big bonus for the 2009 World Superbike champion was Yamaha-assigned Hiroya Atsumi as his Japanese race engineer. Atsumi had the ear of Rossi and Burgess during their glory years at Yamaha, and what he didn't know about the YZR-M1 wasn't worth knowing.

Spies, though, largely underachieved in 2011. He did score a breakthrough win in Assen that was helped immeasurably by a first-lap collision between Marco Simoncelli and Lorenzo. He scored two more podiums, in Barcelona and Indianapolis, but his year was also dominated by costly errors on his own part and a calamitous mistake by his crew.

He'd already crashed out of a podium place in

the rain in Jerez, then his Estoril race turned into a farce when a mechanic mistakenly left a surgical clamp blocking the fuel overflow pipe on his bike. He was battling for the podium in the rain at Silverstone when he crashed, then a horrific 170mph qualifying crash at Phillip Island forced him to withdraw from the Australian Grand Prix with a severe concussion. Finally, he withdrew from the Sepang race after two further heavy crashes.

But there was a happy ending, when he was only denied victory in the final race of the season at Valencia by inches.

DUCATI MARLBORO TEAM

TEAM STAFF

Alessandro CICOGNANI: MotoGP Project Director
Vittoriano GUARESCHI: Team Manager
Massimo BARTOLINI: Technical Manager
Francesco RAPISARDA: Communications Director
Federica DE ZOTTIS: Press Manager
Chris JONNUM: Press Officer
Amedeo COSTA: Team Co-ordinator
Paola BRAIATO: Administration, Logistics & Hospitality
Mauro GRASSILLI: Sponsor Account
Luigi MITOLO: MotoGP Reliability Manager
Davide BARALDINI: Warehouse and Components

VALENTINO ROSSI PIT CREW

Jeremy BURGESS: Crew Chief
Matteo FLAMMINI: Track Engineer
Mechanics
Alex BRIGGS · Bernard ANSIAU · Brent STEVENS
Gary COLEMAN · Mark ELDER
Gabriele CONTI: Electronics Engineer
Roberto BRIVIO: Crew Co-ordinator

NICKY HAYDEN PIT CREW

Juan MARTINEZ: Race Engineer
Roberto BONAZZI: Track Engineer
Davide MANFREDI: Chief Mechanic
Mechanics
Massimo MIRANO · Pedro Calvet CARAL · Lorenzo
CANESTRARI · Luca ROMANO
Jose Manuel CASEAUX: Electronics Engineer
Emanuele MAZZINI: Crew Co-ordinator

VALENTINO ROSSI
Born: 16 February, 1979 – Urbino, Italy
GP Starts: 258 (198 MotoGP/500cc, 30 250cc, 30 125cc)
GP Wins: 105 (79 MotoGP/500cc, 14 250cc, 12 125cc)
World Championships: 9 (6 MotoGP, 1 500cc, 1 250cc, 1 125cc)

NICKY HAYDEN
Born: 30 July, 1981 – Owensboro, Kentucky, USA
GP Starts: 151 MotoGP
GP Wins: 3 MotoGP
World Championships: 1 MotoGP

EVER since Ducati's factory squad dominated the first season of the 800cc era, back in 2007, its success rate has shrunk dramatically. Casey Stoner won ten races in 2007 to humiliate Honda and Yamaha, but as each year passed, the wins became fewer and fewer, and the Aussie left for Repsol Honda at the end of 2010 with just three victories from that season.

The fortunes of Ducati's official squad plummeted to an all-time low in 2011, though, and the embarrassing slump came at a time when most least expected it. After years of flirting with the idea of combining two Italian racing icons together, Valentino Rossi was finally tempted by the challenge of trying to prove that the blood-red and brutal Desmosedici was not a bike that only Stoner could master.

But by the end of the last 800cc campaign, Rossi had been thrashed and his legacy unquestionably tainted after he failed miserably to get even close to replicating the heroics Stoner performed for the Bologna factory.

The wins that had become scarce in 2010 dried up completely, and Rossi endured the most humbling experience of his distinguished career. The numbers didn't lie. He scored just a solitary podium in fortuitous circumstances at Le Mans, and for the

DUCATI Desmosedici GP11

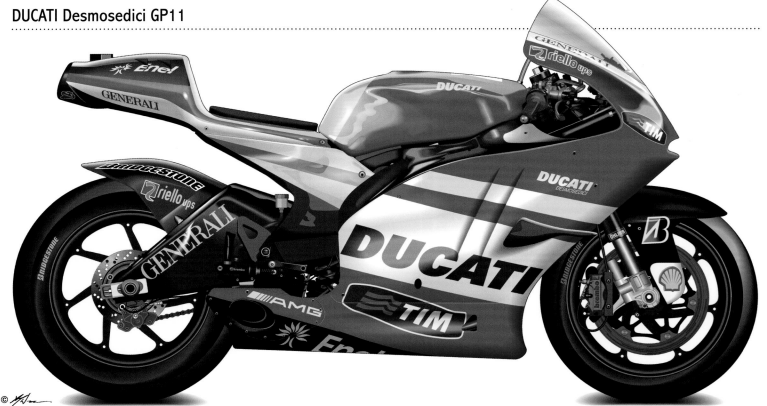

Sponsors and Technical Suppliers: Philip Morris (Marlboro) · TIM (Telecom Italia) · Generali Insurance · Enel · AMG · Riello · Bridgestone · Shell Advance · Diesel
Acer · Bosch · Ditech Entrematic · Guabello · Inver · Lampo · Puma · SuperEnalotto · Tata Consultancy · Tudor Watches
Capit · CM Composit · DID · Fiamm · Magneti Marelli · Mechanix · NGK · SKF · Termignoni · USAG

Engine: 800cc, 90-degree V4; irregular-fire crank, DOHC, 4 valves per cylinder, Desmodromic valve gear, variable-length inlet tracts
Power: Around 225bhp, revs up to 18,500rpm

Ancillaries: Magneti Marelli electronics, NGK sparking plugs, full electronic ride-by-wire · *Lubrication:* Shell Advance · *Fuel:* 21 litres; Shell

Transmission: Cassette Xtrac seamless-shift gearbox

Suspension: Front, Öhlins TRSP25 48mm 'Through Rod' forks · Rear, Öhlins TRSP44 shock with linkage

Wheels: Front, 16.5in Marchesini · Rear, 16.5in Marchesini · *Tyres:* Bridgestone *Brakes:* Front, Brembo carbon-carbon 320mm · Rear, steel 200mm

first time in his 16-year career he didn't win a race. He never qualified higher than sixth, and nine times he started outside of the top ten. And he crashed out of the last four races, including being involved in three early multi-rider collisions in Japan, Malaysia and Valencia. The second and most devastating of these, both on a personal and professional level, resulted in the tragic death of Rossi's bosom buddy, Marco Simoncelli.

Simoncelli's passing certainly put Rossi's woeful season into perspective, but there was no disguising the fact that the Italian had seriously misjudged just how bad the Ducati was and what a phenomenal job Stoner had done.

The realisation of the size of the hole Rossi had dug for himself hit around mid-season, when a radical redesign of the GP11 – badged the GP11.1 – failed to spark any revival in fortunes. In fact, results were so dire at that stage that rumours started to emerge in Laguna Seca that Rossi was trying to buy himself out his two-year contract to run his own private Honda team in 2012.

The downbeat mood was in stark contrast to the copious optimism and expectation when Rossi attended his first official Ducati engagement in early January. Ducati's annual team launch is shared with Ferrari's Formula One team and is a lavish, no-expense-spared affair in the stunning Madonna di Campiglio ski resort, nestled in the heart of the Dolomites. The event is bankrolled by Marlboro, who once again remained Ducati's title sponsor, the tobacco giant eager to cash in on the overwhelming popularity of Rossi, who indisputably remained bike racing's box-office attraction.

All of Ducati's senior management attended, including Gabriele del Torchio, who continued as president and CEO of Ducati Motor Holding. Ducati Corse CEO Claudio Domenicali remained a hugely influential figure, while popular Filippo Preziosi continued as the engineering mastermind behind the Desmosedici project.

Preziosi had a demanding time, rolling out four major modifications to the Desmosedici in less than a year, and by the post-race tests in Valencia, the new prototype 1000cc GP12 marked another major philosophy shift when a twin-spar aluminium frame was unveiled. Its introduction was in response to Rossi and team-mate Nicky Hayden's incessant complaints of a vague front-end feeling and chronic understeer. The severity of the problem was perfectly illustrated by the fact that Rossi had never crashed so much in a single MotoGP season.

Management on the shop floor at every race was unchanged, too. Alessandro Cicognani was MotoGP project director and former test rider Vittoriano Guareschi was team manager.

Rossi's on-track struggles also dented the reputa-tion of his tight-knit crew, who walked out on Yamaha mob-handed at the end of 2010. Jerry Burgess was crew chief, while Alex Briggs, Brent Stephens, Matteo Flamigni, Bernard Ansiau and Gary Coleman all remained loyal to Rossi.

The only new face was electronics engineer Gabriele Conti. He had intimate knowledge of the Desmosedici and was the only member of Stoner's old team who didn't transfer with the Aussie.

American mechanic Mark Elder, who had previously worked with Hayden and most recently Aleix Espargaro in the satellite Pramac squad, was also integrated into Rossi's crew. He was a long-serving Ducati crew member who would help Rossi's crew become familiar with the idiosyncrasies of the bike quicker. And he was fluent in Italian, assisting in the communication between factory staff and the predominantly English-speaking crew.

American Hayden was in his third year at Ducati, but he too struggled to match his previous form on the finicky GP11. His solitary podium also arrived in somewhat fortuitous circumstances when he lucked into third at the end of a crash-strewn race at rain-hit Jerez. He made just two other visits to the top six, at Silverstone and Assen, though he only had two DNFs, in Misano and Valencia.

The 2006 world champion once again worked under crew chief Juan Martinez, while key members of his operation were track engineer Roberto Bonazzi, electronics engineer Jose Manuel Caseaux and chief mechanic Davide Manfredi.

Above: Project director Alessandro Cicognani and team manager Vito Guareschi.

Top: Influential figure: Ducati Corse CEO Claudio Domenicali.

Top left: Mechanics fettle Hayden's bike in the team garage.

Left: Jerry Burgess, Rossi's crew chief.

Below left: Engineering mastermind: Filippo Preziosi.

Bottom: The dream that turned into a nightmare. Rossi struggled on the Ducati in 2011.

Photos: Gold & Goose

MONSTER YAMAHA TECH 3

TEAM STAFF

Hervé PONCHARAL: Team Manager

Gérard VALLEE: Team Co-ordinator

Laurence LASSERRE: Team Assistant

Eric REBMANN: Parts Manager

Benjamin BOUVIER: Fuel/Tyres

Judith PIEPER-KOEHLER: Press and Communications

COLIN EDWARDS PIT CREW

Guy COULON: Crew Chief

Mechanics

Laurent DUCLOYER · Jerômé PONCHARAL

Josian RUSTIQUE

Andrew GRIFFITH: Telemetry

Youichi NAKAMAYA: Yamaha Motor Company Engineer

CAL CRUTCHLOW PIT CREW

Daniele ROMAGNOLI: Crew Chief

Mechanics

Steve BLACKBURN · Julien LAJUNIE

Sebastien LATORT

Nicolas GOYON: Telemetry

Masahiko IWATA: Yamaha Motor Company Engineer

COLIN EDWARDS
Born: 27 February, 1974 – Houston, Texas, USA
GP Starts: 152 MotoGP
World Championships: 2 World Superbike

CAL CRUTCHLOW
Born: 29 October, 1985 – Coventry, England
GP Starts: 15 MotoGP
World Championships: 1 World Supersport

HERVÉ Poncharal's highly-respected independent Yamaha squad marked its tenth year in the MotoGP class by adopting a tried-and-tested formula that married the vast experience of Colin Edwards with the potential of an emerging talent plucked from World Superbikes.

Cal Crutchlow followed compatriot James Toseland and Ben Spies from World Superbikes into the French-based squad on a two-year contract. But the British rider and the team experienced a season of rollercoaster emotions.

Edwards was in his fourth season with Tech 3, and once again he worked closely with renowned crew chief Guy Coulon. The outspoken American, though, proved why, at the age of 37, he still had one of the most coveted seats on the grid.

Starting the season on the final version of the previous year's factory YZR-M1, Edwards was still undoubtedly fast and he was cruelly denied a rare podium finish in only the second race of the season at a rain-lashed Jerez. His experience at knowing where and when it was safe to push in appalling conditions seemed certain to secure him the position when he started the final lap in third. But he only made it to the first corner, where his bike juddered to a halt with a faulty fuel pump.

YAMAHA M1 YZR

Sponsors and Technical Suppliers: Monster · Leon Vince · Motul · DeWalt · Bridgestone · Antonio Lupi · LightTech · Stanley

Engine: 800cc, across-the-frame in-line 4; reverse-rotating cross-plane crankshaft, DOHC, 4 valves per cylinder, Pneumatic Valve Return System
Power: Around 220bhp at approx 18,000rpm

Ancillaries: Magneti Marelli electronics, NGK sparking plugs, full electronic ride-by-wire · *Lubrication:* Yamalube · *Fuel:* 21 litres

Transmission: Gear primary drive, multi-plate dry slipper clutch, six-speed constant-mesh floating-dog-ring cassette-style gearbox; DID chain

Suspension: Front, Öhlins TTxTR25 48mm forks · Rear, Öhlins TRSP44 shock with linkage

Wheels: Front, 16.5in Marchesini · Rear, 16.5in Marchesini · *Tyres:* Bridgestone

Brakes: Front, Brembo carbon-carbon 320mm · Rear, Yamaha steel

JOSH HAYES

Born: 4 April, 1975 – Gulfport, Mississippi, USA

GP Starts: 1 (MotoGP)

His luck deserted him again in Spain when, just three races later, his proud record of never having missed a MotoGP round since his debut for Aprilia back in 2003 ended at Catalunya. A Friday practice high-side smashed his right collarbone into seven pieces, but having undergone surgery, he returned to the paddock on Sunday morning determined to race. He wanted to do two laps to keep his appearance record intact, but failed a medical.

Defying the pain from severe muscle damage around the right side of his ribcage, Edwards was back in action less than a week later at Silverstone, and in monsoon conditions that placed less physical stress on his battered upper body, he splashed his way to his 12th career podium.

He was only out of the top ten twice in the next ten races before his long and distinguished Yamaha career was ended prematurely and tragically.

The immensely popular Edwards was involved in the incident on the second lap of the Malaysian Grand Prix that left rising Italian star Marco Simoncelli fatally injured. Edwards suffered multiple small fractures to the top of his left humerus, and surgery required to re-attach cartilage torn off the bone meant he was unable to participate in the season finale at Valencia.

Double American Superbike champion Josh Hayes was drafted in to replace Edwards for the final race of the frequently dull 800cc era, and he finished a very worthy seventh.

The Sepang tragedy was the second of the season for Edwards and his crew. Crew chief Coulon

fatally injured a motorcyclist when he reversed the team's Moto2 truck out of a motorway toll en route to Le Mans in May.

Rookie Crutchlow had a thankless task following Spies, who was fast-tracked into Yamaha's factory team after a hugely successful learning year with Tech 3 in 2010.

The 2009 World Supersport champion had pushed Poncharal to bring his Yamaha World Superbike crew chief, Marcus Eschenbacher, with him to MotoGP, but he was paired with vastly experienced Italian Daniele Romagnoli, who was crew chief to Edwards during the Texan's spell in Yamaha's factory squad between 2005 and '07. Then he managed Jorge Lorenzo's factory Yamaha squad before moving to the Tech 3 Moto2 team in 2010 as crew chief to Italian Raffaele de Rosa.

Crutchlow impressed during an eye-catching start to the season. Three top-eight finishes in the opening five races silenced many critics who feared he'd be a regular backmarker while he adjusted his riding style to suit the high-cornering-speed 800s and the specific technique required to master the Bridgestone tyres.

His early progression stalled, however, in painful fashion in front of his home fans at Silverstone. He fell heavily in the early stages of qualifying and suffered multiple fractures to his left collarbone. The injury had a profound effect on his confidence, and in the 11 races that followed he only managed another three top-ten places.

Despite the endless stories of independent

teams being under threat from the lingering global financial crisis, the future of Tech 3 at least seemed reasonably secure. Monster Energy reinforced its commitment by signing a three-year extension to its deal that had begun in 2009, and a new two-year collaboration with Yamaha (until the end of 2014) was also agreed.

The only significant future change to Tech 3 was the departure of Edwards. He announced in Misano that he'd agreed a deal with the Forward Racing squad to ride a CRT machine in 2012. His initial intention was to run Yamaha's R1 World Superbike-spec engines in a chassis built by Tech 3. Coulon and Crutchlow's data engineer, Nicolas Goyon, had experience of designing and developing a frame for Tech 3 Racing's MotoGP project, and Edwards wanted to tap into that expertise, while also retaining some association with the team and Yamaha.

That concept never came close to materialising, however, and instead he will campaign a tuned BMW S1000RR motor housed in a chassis designed and built by Swiss specialist Eskil Suter.

Edward's pace couldn't detract from his advancing years, and keen to invest in younger talent, Poncharal strongly courted German Stefan Bradl in the first half of the season. When that trail went cold, he focussed on Andrea Dovizioso and Alvaro Bautista, offering both identical deals during the Motorland Aragón weekend. It was on a first-come, first-served basis, and Dovizioso agreed terms between the Japanese and Australian rounds, ending a career-long association with Honda.

Top: Colin Edwards splashed his way to a podium at Silverstone.

Far left: Crutchlow with crew chief Romagnoli.

Left: Team principal Hervé Poncharal.

Below left: Guy Coulon, crew chief again for Edwards

Photos: Gold & Goose

SAN CARLO HONDA GRESINI

TEAM STAFF

Fausto GRESINI: Team Manager
Carlo MERLINI: Sales and Marketing Manager
Ivo TAMBURRINI: Marketing
Aldo GANDOLFO: Press and Media Relations
Fulvia CASTELLI: Logistics

HIROSHI AOYAMA PIT CREW

Antonio JIMINEZ: Chief Mechanic
Mechanics
Daniele GRELLI
Ryoichi MORI
Alberto PRESUTTI
Diego GUBELLINI: Telemetry

MARCO SIMONCELLI PIT CREW

Aligi DEGANELLO: Chief Mechanic
Mechanics
Ivan BRANDI
Federico VICINO
Marco Rosa GASTALDO
Elvio DEGANELLO: Telemetry
Michel MASINI: Spare Parts
Renzo PINI: Pit Assistant

MARCO SIMONCELLI
20 January, 1987 – -23 October, 2011
GP Starts: 148 (34 MotoGP, 64 250cc, 50 125cc)
GP Wins: 14 (12 250cc, 2 125cc)
World Championships: 1 250cc

HIROSHI AOYAMA
Born: 25 October, 1981 – Chiba, Japan
GP Starts: 133 (29 MotoGP, 104 250cc)
GP Wins: 9 250cc
World Championships: 1 250cc

FATE conspired cruelly against Fausto Gresini's satellite Honda squad for the second time in less than a decade in 2011.

A season that had started full of hope and expectation after Marco Simoncelli starred during the winter testing programme ended in tragedy when the charismatic and much-loved Italian succumbed to multiple injuries sustained in a freak accident during the Malaysian Grand Prix.

Simoncelli's death robbed MotoGP of one of its great future hopes and plunged Gresini's squad into mourning once again, eight years after team rider Daijiro Kato had died in a horrific crash during the first race of 2003 at Suzuka. Like Simoncelli, he had passed away right at the time when he seemed destined to move on to great things.

After a tough rookie season in 2010, Simoncelli matured rapidly in the closed season and his confidence soared after a series of eye-catching performances in winter testing. He had a greater understanding of what it took to race at the front in MotoGP, and so did his crew. Aligi Deganello remained as his crew chief, having graduated from the Gilera 250cc squad with Simoncelli for 2010. Elvio Deganello was his telemetry engineer. Crucially in 2011, Simoncelli was elevated to full factory-rider status.

HONDA RC212V

Sponsors and Technical Suppliers: San Carlo · Agos Ducato · Airdale · Berner · BigMat · Cotton Joy · Domino · Pascucoi · Prink · Rifle · Rizoma · SAG Group ZeroRH · Castrol · Bridgestone · Termignoni · Bike Lift · Nissin · Thermal Technology · Dread · Honda Italia

Engine: 800cc, 76-degree V4; 360-degree crank (tbc), PVRS. *Power:* More than 210ps

Ancillaries: HRC electronics, ride-by-wire throttle and fuel injection system; NGK sparking plugs · *Lubrication:* Castrol · *Fuel:* 21 litres

Dimensions: 2050mm long, 1440mm wheelbase, 1130mm high, 645mm wide; weight, 148kg

Transmission: Gear primary drive, multi-plate dry slipper clutch, six-speed constant-mesh cassette-style gearbox; RK chain

Suspension: Front, Öhlins TRSP25 48mm forks · Rear, Öhlins TRSP44 gas shock with linkage

Wheels: Front, 16.5in Marchesini. · Rear, 16.5in Marchesini · *Tyres:* Bridgestone

Brakes: Front, Nissin carbon-carbon 320mm · Rear, HRC steel 218mm

KOUSUKE AKIYOSHI

Born: 12 January, 1975 – Kurume, Japan

GP Starts: 8 MotoGP

Signs of his burgeoning confidence and self-belief began to appear in Estoril, where he claimed his first front-row start. He crashed on the first lap. Then he qualified on the front row in each of the next five races without ever being able to convert the advantage into a first podium.

A combination of rotten luck, over-exuberance, and his robust and aggressive riding constantly being examined in microscopic detail prolonged the wait for his maiden top-three until Brno, where he scored a brilliant third.

Not only was Simoncelli's stock rising on the track, but also his fun-loving personality and instantly-recognisable mop of hair made him an attractive proposition for sponsors. Ducati monitored his contract renewal negotiations with HRC with some interest, but he penned a new one-year deal with the latter and Gresini shortly before the Japanese GP.

The contract talks demonstrated further evidence of Simoncelli's growing stature. HRC Vice-President Shuhei Nakamoto had wanted to replace his entire crew with Repsol Honda rider Andrea Dovizioso's team, led by Ramon Aurin. He vehemently resisted, and succeeded in keeping Deganello and the rest of his pit at his side for 2012.

San Carlo were aware of Simoncelli's attraction to the paying public, and less than a week after he'd re-signed, the Italian snack-food giant agreed a new one-year contract with Gresini in the build-up to the Australian Grand Prix. There, the Italian took a career-best second, but just one week later he forfeited his life on the second lap at Sepang. He lost control at turn 11, but veered back across the racing line, where he was struck by a helpless Colin Edwards and Valentino Rossi.

Results on the other side of the garage illustrated how vital Simoncelli had become to the squad.

Hiroshi Aoyama was a darling of HRC, having clinched the final 250cc two-stroke title in 2009, ironically beating Simoncelli in a last-round decider at Valencia. The Japanese rider had suffered a torrid rookie MotoGP campaign in 2010 after breaking his back in a sickening high-side at the British Grand Prix. Then his Interwetten Honda squad folded, before Gresini offered him a chance to work with experienced crew chief Antonio Jimenez.

It was another tough season, though, and long after scoring a solitary top six in Jerez, he confirmed he was quitting MotoGP to move to the Ten Kate Honda World Superbike squad. He did at least get to ride a factory RC212V, however, when he replaced injured Pedrosa in the Repsol squad to finish a respectable eighth at Assen.

Aoyama's seat went to test and development rider Kousuke Akiyoshi, who finished 13th.

The overwhelming emotion at Simoncelli's loss was still raw when Gresini had to quickly contem-

plate finding a replacement. Italian Moto2 rider and emerging star Andrea Iannone was the first to be linked with the one RC213V 1000cc Honda that Gresini had been allocated. But Spaniard Alvaro Bautista eventually signed a deal immediately after the final round in Valencia. The former 125cc world champion had finally given up waiting on clarification of Suzuki's future plans.

Unable to find the budget to lease a second RC213V bike, Gresini planned to run a CRT machine with an Aprilia RSV4 motor housed in either a Japanese-built Moriwaki or British-designed and developed FTR chassis.

Honda vetoed that, so Gresini confirmed in Japan he would base his CRT racer on a tuned Honda CBR1000RR production motor.

Above: Marco Simoncelli – a great loss.

Top: Aoyama – another tough season.

Left: Team boss Gresini.

Below: Simoncellli's bike in the pit at Valencia.

Photos: Gold & Goose

RIZLA SUZUKI MOTOGP

TEAM STAFF

Shinichi SAHARA: Project Manager
Paul DENNING: Team Manager
Takayuki NAKAMOTO: Engine Development & Control
Tetsuya SASAKI: Chassis Development
Tex GEISSLER: ECU Control Assistance
Russell JORDAN: Parts and Logistics
Charlie MOODY: Operations Manager
Tim WALPOLE: Press and PR Manager
Helen TAYLOR: Team Administrator
Dirk DEBUS: 2D Electronics
Yukihiko KUBO: Bridgestone Tyres
Graeme IRVINE: Öhlins Suspension
Eugenio GANDOLFI: Brembo Brakes
Paul SENIOR: IT Consultant

ALVARO BAUTISTA PIT CREW

Tom O'KANE: Crew Chief
Simon WESTWOOD: Crew Leader
Mechanics
Ray HUGHES
Mark FLEMING (driver/mechanic)
George DZIEDZIC
Jez WILSON (driver/mechanic)
Gary McLAREN: Telemetry

ALVARO BAUTISTA
Born: 21 November, 1984 – Talavera de la Reina, Spain
GP Starts: 148 (32 MotoGP, 49 250cc, 67 125cc)
GP Wins: 16 (8 250cc, 8 125cc)
World Championships: 1 125cc

JOHN HOPKINS
Born: 22 May, 1983 – Ramona, California, USA
GP Starts: 112 MotoGP/500cc

SUZUKI'S factory squad raced with a large cloud looming overhead for almost the entire season. The future of the British-based squad hung in the balance until days after the season finale in Valencia.

The question of whether Suzuki would continue racing in 2012 was a hot topic before the season began, after management dropped the bombshell at the end of 2010 that its involvement would be slashed from a two-rider factory effort to just one.

Suzuki blamed the ongoing impact of the global financial crisis for its decision, which angered Dorna CEO Carmelo Ezpeleta to the point where he in-structed his legal team to investigate the possibility of court action.

It was Ezpeleta's belief that Suzuki was obliged to field a two-rider team in 2011 under a participation agreement with the Motorcycle Sport Manufacturers Association. Suzuki, though, stood firm. Its understanding was that while participation was required, there was no stipulation concerning the number of bikes. Entering one rider – contracted Spaniard Alvaro Bautista – honoured its obligation, and the threat of a lawsuit remained only a threat, as Ezpeleta abandoned plans for a courtroom battle.

Many felt that the cutback was the first step to-

SUZUKI GSV-R

Sponsors and Technical Suppliers: Rizla · Bridgestone · Motul · 2D · Akrapovic · Marchesini · Troy Lee Designs · Draggin Jeans · Beta · DC Shoes · Dread · DAF
Puig Racing Screens · Blue Chip · Big Rock Holidays · Caffe Monforte · Arushi · RK · NGK · T.Rad · Mitsubishi · Tras

Engine: 800cc, 75-degree V4; 360-degree crank, Pneumatic Valve Return System · *Power:* Around 220bhp

Ancillaries: Mitsubishi electronics, NGK sparking plugs, electronic ride-by-wire · *Fuel:* 21 litres

Transmission: Constant-mesh cassette-style gearbox

Suspension: Front, Öhlins TRSP25 48mm forks · Rear, Öhlins TRSP44 shock with linkage

Wheels: Front, 16.5in Marchesini · Rear, 16.5in Marchesini · *Tyres:* Bridgestone

Brakes: Front, Brembo carbon-carbon 320mm · Rear, steel

Above: Rizla Suzuki at the Italian GP.

Left: Paul Denning was manager for a sixth successive season.

Far left: Sole entry for Alvaro Bautista.

Left: Project manager Shinichi Sahara.

Photos: Gold & Goose

wards a complete withdrawal, however, as Suzuki ended the 800cc era with a solitary victory. As the season wore on with no official decision on whether or not it would race on in 2012, speculation became increasingly intense.

One week the news was positive, and the next bleak. Dithering Suzuki management in Japan had still not delivered a decision when the season drew to a close in Valencia in early November.

Project manager Shinichi Sahara and team manager Paul Denning were anxious for Suzuki to continue, and they had the support of the global dealership network. Suzuki's results were certainly nothing to write home about, but the brand exposure of MotoGP on TV meant it was still a valuable marketing tool.

Denning was at the helm again for a sixth season, and the squad managed to retain its investment from Rizla, despite only fielding one bike.

It was clear from the outset that if Suzuki did agree to race in 2012 it would certainly start with its existing 800cc GSV-R. The uncertainty over the future of the team inevitably meant development on a new 1000cc project had virtually ground to a halt in Hamamatsu.

Behind the scenes, though, Ezpeleta had grown weary of Suzuki's indecision, and the day after the Valencia race he issued an ultimatum. If there was no agreement in place on the Friday after the race (11th November), he would offer the grid slot to somebody else.

Suzuki's baffling hesitation had a great impact on the team's ability to carry out any forward planning. Rider negotiation became an impossible task, and the dilly-dallying meant former 125cc World Cham-

pion Bautista eventually quit.

Despite Bautista's reluctance to start the inaugural 1000cc campaign on the current 800cc GSV-R, he was equally reluctant to relinquish his factory rider status. He repeatedly withheld confirmation of his own plans while awaiting Suzuki's decision, and it seemed certain he would join Lucio Cecchinello's satellite Honda squad as his patience evaporated. But there was another twist, as he turned towards a different Honda RC213V for 2012 with Fausto Gresini's effort. Gresini had been forced back into the rider market in the most heartbreaking circumstances following the death of Simoncelli.

The best-case scenario for Sahara and Denning was to have a two-rider effort in 2012 with Bautista and John Hopkins.

Hopkins was a reformed character in 2011, having gone from wild party animal to teetotaller as he sought to resurrect a career that had been in freefall since he had quit Suzuki to make an ill-fated switch to Kawasaki at the end of 2007.

He was back in the frame after he'd signed a deal with the Samsung Crescent Suzuki squad to contest the British Superbike Championship. The team was owned by Denning and the intention was to offer Hopkins a route back to the premier class if the BSB assault went well.

Suzuki's MotoGP campaign started off in the worst fashion imaginable when Bautista broke his left femur in practice for the opening race in Qatar on Friday night. His injury immediately exposed Suzuki's decision to run only one rider, with the marque unrepresented in the showpiece curtain raiser. A deal to put MZ Moto2 rider Anthony West on the bike collapsed. Ironically, Hopkins had been in Doha

to help Suzuki with filming promotional videos, but had not stayed for the race.

The American replaced Bautista in Jerez, and in treacherously wet conditions he scored a creditable tenth in his first MotoGP outing since 2008. But injury wrecked two golden opportunities to put himself back in the shop window for 2012, as he failed to start in two further wild-card appearances.

He fell heavily in a wet final practice in Brno and badly damaged his right hand. And when he returned for a second chance in Sepang, he withdrew on Saturday morning, having aggravated the injury.

Hopkins' return also saw Suzuki stalwart Stuart Shenton back in the paddock. He had been a loyal and long-serving crew chief who had been the highest-profile casualty of the reduction of the team.

When Bautista was fit, he was certainly fast. He was under the stewardship of crew chief Tom O'Kane again, and the team that remained had a familiar look, with Simon Westwood crew leader and Gary McLaren data analyst.

His best result was fifth in the Silverstone monsoon, but a lowly 13th overall could and should have been significantly better had he not crashed out in five of the last eight races. He fell while in the top six at Laguna Seca and Brno, then again while in a career-best fourth in Japan. A top five beckoned again in Phillip Island until he crashed, and finally he was culpable for the four-rider pile-up in Valencia that wiped out Ducati trio Valentino Rossi, Nicky Hayden and Randy de Puniet at the first corner.

Randy De Puniet tested the GSV-R at Valencia, but hopes of a ride collapsed when final news of Suzuki's withdrawal broke as *MOTOCOURSE* was going to press.

PRAMAC RACING TEAM

TEAM STAFF

Paolo CAMPINOTI: Team Principal
Fabiano STERLACCHINI: Technical Director
Felix RODRIGUEZ: Team Co-ordinator
Matteo VITELLO: Communication Manager
Sara TICCI: PR and Travel Co-ordinator
Alex GHINI: Hospitality Manager
Vincenzo CAPUANO: Catering Manager

LORIS CAPIROSSI PIT CREW

Fabiano STERLACCHINI: Track Engineer
Michele ANDREINI: Chief Technician
Mechanics
Guglielmo ANDREINI
Pedro RIVERA
Davide CAPIROSSI (tyres and fuel)
Cristian BATAGLIA: Electronics Engineer

RANDY DE PUNIET PIT CREW

Marco RIGAMONTI: Track Engineer
Michele PERUGINI: Chief Technician
Mechanics
Cristian AIELLO
Raul RUIZ
Francesco GALINDA (tyres and fuel)
Alberto GIRIBUOLA: Electronics Engineer

LORIS CAPIROSSI

Born: 4 April, 1973 – Bologna, Italy
GP Starts: 328 (217 MotoGP/500cc, 84 250cc, 27 125cc)
GP Wins: 29 (9 MotoGP/500cc, 12 250cc, 8 125cc)
World Championships: 3 (1 250cc, 2 125cc)

RANDY DE PUNIET

Born: 14 February, 1981 – Maisons Laffitte, France
GP Starts: 216 (103 MotoGP, 80 250cc, 33 125cc)
GP Wins: 5 250cc

No other team in MotoGP could boast the wealth of experience the Pramac Ducati squad enjoyed in 2011, as Loris Capirossi and Randy de Puniet had joined the Italian squad.

Paolo Campinoti's team had tried to invest in younger talent in the previous couple of seasons, but that policy had backfired, with Niccolo Canepa, Mika Kallio and Aleix Espargaro all failing to grasp their big chance in the elite class. So Pramac CEO Campinoti abandoned that strategy to sign proven MotoGP talent, hoping for a drastic change in the fortunes of his under-achieving outfit.

Capirossi was back at Ducati for the first time since 2007, and despite racing in grands prix for over two decades, with more than 300 appearances to his name, he showed no signs of wanting to hang up his leathers when the season kicked off in Doha.

As in previous years, Fabiano Sterlacchini served a dual purpose in 2011. Not only was he Capirossi's track engineer, but also technical director of the squad. Working directly under Sterlacchini on Capirossi's side of the garage was electronics engineer Cristian Battaglia and crew chief Michele Andreini.

Capirossi's final season turned out to be a disaster, however, and he quickly abandoned aspirations of having another shot at riding a 1000cc MotoGP bike in 2012.

The season wasn't even a lap old when both

DUCATI Desmosedici GP11

Sponsors and Technical Suppliers: Pramac · ENI · Riello · Bridgestone · Lifter · Boxeur des Rues · Valmy · FAAM · IVECO · Erba Vita · SC · Puma · Flex · Beta
CHT Chiaravalli · Termo Race · Meco Alto Spa · AMG · Gefco · Cima · Speedfiber · Deltacom · Chicco Doro · Age Consulting

Engine: 800cc, 90-degree V4; 360-degree crank, DOHC, 4 valves per cylinder, Desmodromic valve gear, variable-length inlet tracts
Power: Around 225bhp, revs up to 18,500rpm

Ancillaries: Magneti Marelli electronics, NGK sparking plugs, full electronic ride-by-wire · *Lubrication:* Shell · *Fuel:* 21 litres, Shell

Transmission: Constant-mesh cassette gearbox

Suspension: Front, Öhlins TRSP25 48mm forks · Rear, Öhlins TRSP44mm shock with linkage

Wheels: Front, 16.5in Marchesini · Rear, 16.5in Marchesini · *Tyres:* Bridgestone

Brakes: Front, Brembo carbon-carbon 320mm · Rear, steel 200mm

SYLVAN GUINTOLI
Born: June 24, 1982 – Montelimar, France
GP Starts: 118 (38 MotoGP/500cc, 80 250cc)

DAMIAN CUDLIN
Born: 19 October, 1982 – Sydney, Australia
GP Starts: 1 MotoGP

Pramac bikes were on the ground in Qatar, after a high-side by de Puniet had also taken out innocent team-mate Capirossi.

The pattern had been set for a painful season for both riders, Capirossi claiming distant top-ten finishes in Catalunya and Silverstone before he dislocated his right shoulder and suffered rib cartilage damage after being hit by his own GP11 in a qualifying crash at Assen. He missed his home race in Mugello, and the team gave a post-race test to rising Italian Moto2 star Andrea Iannone, but it was Sylvain Guintoli who replaced him for the Sachsenring round.

The British-based Frenchman was no stranger to the Pramac squad, having ridden for the team when it was backed by Italian telecommunications giant Alice in 2008. But he was only 17th in Germany.

Capirossi returned with a 12th in Laguna Seca and 13th in Brno, but in the final seven races he would only finish twice. A front tyre issue in Indianapolis and then a rear sprocket problem in Misano forced him to retire from both races.

Retirement had become a buzzword for Capirossi during the weeks leading up to Misano. His nightmare struggle to make Ducati's disastrous GP11 competitive had drastically altered his future ambitions. It was during an emotional pre-event Press conference in Misano that he tearfully announced his retirement after 22 years in the world championship arena.

More disaster struck during the Motorland Aragón race, when he fell heavily while pursuing Toni Elias and subsequently aggravated the right shoulder injury first sustained in Assen.

Capirossi's place in Japan's Twin Ring Motegi race went to 28-year-old Australian Damian Cudlin, whose only other MotoGP experience was a handful of test days on the BMW S1000-powered Suter CRT machine. He had been on his way to a rock festival in Germany when he got the call to fly to Japan, and he acquitted himself superbly before crashing out of 12th.

Capirossi bowed out of racing with ninth in an emotionally charged Valencia race, the triple world champion ditching his famous number 65 to run the 58 plate in memory of close friend Marco Simoncelli. Remarkably, it was the 38-year-old's 328th appearance, but agonisingly he bowed out on 99 career podiums.

Experienced French rider de Puniet also had a torrid year, and he managed to finish only twice in the opening seven races. Marco Rigamonti worked as his track engineer and Michele Perugini as chief technician, but injury played a part in de Puniet's campaign, too. He suffered back and pelvis injuries in a heavy qualifying fall at Laguna Seca that ruled him out of the Californian race.

His best result was sixth in a crash-strewn Phillip

Island race, and his season finished as it started, with a crash on the first lap at Valencia. He was caught up along with Rossi and Hayden in a first-turn incident triggered by Alvaro Bautista.

It was well known before the end of the season that the Pramac squad, which continued its environmentally friendly ethos by being the self-styled Green Energy Team, would be reducing its involvement in 2012. Campinoti's team certainly wasn't immune from the global economic crisis and will only lease one GP12 from Ducati, having briefly flirted with the idea of using an Aprilia RSV4 motor for a CRT project to retain its two-rider status. Spaniard Hector Barbera was confirmed as the lone rider on the Monday after Valencia.

Above: Randy de Puniet suffered his fair share of crashes.

Above left: Damian Cudlin made a brief appearance, but crashed out.

Above centre: Loris Capirossi wound down his career with an injury-interrupted season.

Top right: Paolo Campinoti, team principal.

Photos: Gold & Goose

CARDION AB DUCATI

TEAM STAFF

Karel ABRAHAM Sr: Team Manager
Jiri SMETANA: Communications

KAREL ABRAHAM PIT CREW

Christian PUPULIN: Track Engineer
Dario MASSARIN: Telemetry
Michele BUBBOLINI: Logistics
Marco GRANA: Chief Mechanic

Mechanics
Yannis MAIGRET
Martin HAVLICEK
Martin NESVADBA
Pietro BERTI (tyres and transport)

KAREL ABRAHAM

Born: 2 January, 1990 – Brno, Czech Republic
GP Starts:109 (16 MotoGP 14 Moto2, 48 250cc, 31 125cc)
GP Wins: 1 Moto2

Photos: Gold & Goose

THE Czech Republic-based Cardion AB squad completed a meteoric rise to prominence in 2011 by becoming the only new entry on another threadbare MotoGP grid of just 17 bikes. The team only entered the world championship arena in the 125cc class in 2006, but funded by Czech medical supplies company Cardion AB, its aspirations to become a big-time player in the paddock were realised by collaboration with Ducati for the lease of a single GP11 Desmosedici for Karel Abraham.

The team is a family affair, since Abraham's father, also named Karel, an astute and wealthy entrepreneur, owns the Cardion AB company and a substantial part of the Brno circuit.

Ducati devoted its best possible support when Christian Pupulin was appointed Abraham's factory track engineer. Pupulin was a former crew chief who

had worked with Loris Capirossi, Marco Melandri and Nicky Hayden; he'd also been technical director for Ducati's official factory team. In addition, he was a data analyst guru, and his main role was to liaise with Abraham's chief mechanic, Marco Grana. The Italian had worked with Abraham right from the start of his grand prix career in 2006. Ducati also dispatched telemetry specialist Dario Massarin to lessen Abraham's steep learning curve.

Family nepotism was clearly at the forefront, and when Abraham's MotoGP switch was confirmed, many felt that it was money and not talent talking. His claim to fame prior to his MotoGP move was a brilliant victory in the final Moto2 race of 2010 at Valencia. Previously, he had never scored a podium in his grand prix career, and he was expected to be a lamb to the slaughter in such elite company.

Yet Abraham acquitted himself superbly in trying circumstances, the 2011 Ducati arguably being the Bologna factory's most finicky and non-compliant Desmosedici of the 800cc era. Six times he finished inside the top ten, and four times he out-qualified Italian legend Valentino Rossi.

The low point was a sickening second-corner crash at the state-of-the-art Motorland Aragón track that left him hospitalised for a night with a severe concussion. He flew to Japan for the Twin Ring Motegi race, but withdrew after the warm-up because of concentration issues resulting from the head blow he had suffered in Spain.

Abraham's performances were so impressive that the season hadn't even reached the halfway stage before he and the team had signed a contract extension with Ducati for 2012 at the Dutch TT in June.

DUCATI Desmosedici GP11

Major Sponsors and Technical Suppliers: Cardion AB Moto Racing · Brno Circuit · KAPE · ABR Invest · ASV · Arai · Dunlop · PSI Racing · IFL
ENI · IG · Motomo · Racestyl

Engine: 800cc, 90-degree V4; 360-degree crank, DOHC, 4 valves per cylinder, Desmodromic valve gear, variable-length inlet tracts
        Power: Around 225bhp, revs up to 18,500rpm
Ancillaries: Magneti Marelli electronics, NGK sparking plugs, full electronic ride-by-wire · *Fuel:* 21 litres
Transmission: Constant-mesh cassette-style gearbox
Suspension: Front, Öhlins TRSP25 48mm forks · Rear, Öhlins TRSP44 shock with linkage
Wheels: Front, 16.5in Marchesini · Rear, 16.5in Marchesini · *Tyres:* Bridgestone
Brakes: Front, Brembo carbon-carbon 320mm · Rear, steel 200mm

MAPFRE ASPAR DUCATI

TEAM STAFF

Jorge MARTINEZ: Team Manager
Facundo GARCIA: General Manager
Sylvia PELUFO: Administration Manager
Gino BORSOI: Sporting Manager
Maria-Jose BOTELLA: Media and Logistics Manager
Ricardo PEDROS: Media Officer

HECTOR BARBERA PIT CREW

Luca GASBARRO: Track Engineer
Andrea ORLANDI: Technical Manager
Mechanics
Miguel Angel GALLEGO · Juan-Manuel ALCANIZ
Ignacio CABEZA · Salvador MORALEDA
Maurizio CASARIL: Spare Parts
Tommaso PAGANO: Electronics Engineer

HECTOR BARBERA
Born: 2 November, 1986 – Dos Aguas, Spain
GP Starts: 156 (34 MotoGP 75 250cc, 47 125cc)
GP Wins: 10 (4 250cc, 6 125cc)

DAMIAN CUDLIN
Born: 19 October, 1982 – Sydney, Australia
GP Starts: 1 MotoGP

WHEN legendary Spaniard Jorge Martinez moved into MotoGP in 2010, he did so with bold ambitions of further expanding what was already the biggest outfit in the GP paddock.

It was no different in 2011, when Aspar entered a three-rider squad in the last ever 125cc series. He also ran a two-rider effort in Moto2 with Mapfre, and Spain's leading insurance company took over the naming rights of the MotoGP squad.

Martinez was team manager, and he kept Facundo Garcia as general manager. Sporting manager Gino Borsoi was the public voice of the squad.

Spanish rider Barbera retained an identical crew for his second premier-class campaign. Luca Gasbarro was his track engineer, having a long employment history at Ducati. Tommaso Pagano was his electronics engineer, and Andrea Orlandi technical manager.

Even before a wheel was turned in anger, talks were well advanced between Martinez and Ducati about an expansion deal that would see the team lease two bikes in 2012. Agreement was reached early in the season, and Martinez began talking to the likes of Dovizioso and his former rider, Bautista, about a deal to partner Barbera.

However, a funding crisis was bubbling under the surface that eventually would scupper the project. After numerous meetings, Bankia and Mapfre made it clear: they wouldn't desert him, but there would be no additional funding.

With the same budget as in 2011, Martinez continued talks over remaining with the existing set-up. But further meetings with Ducati management at the Japanese Grand Prix in early October signalled the end of their brief collaboration.

Martinez and Borsoi were immediately galvanised into action, and the alternative was to form a CRT 1000cc project. Negotiations took place with Aprilia, and they also considered running the Suter/BMW.

Martinez's desire for expansion also wasn't helped by a lacklustre season on track. Barbera scored just one top six in a crash-strewn home race at Jerez in treacherous conditions, and was forced to miss the Australian round at Phillip Island after breaking his right collarbone in a second-lap fall in Japan.

Having impressed during a replacement ride for the Pramac Ducati squad in Japan, Damian Cudlin was signed for the Phillip Island race. But he didn't get to start in front of his home crowd after suffering a left hip injury following a monstrous high-side in final practice. He withdrew after completing one painful lap in the warm-up.

DUCATI Desmosedici GP11

Major Sponsors and Technical Suppliers: Mapfre Insurance · Bridgestone · IVECO · Northgate · NH Hotels · Flex · Air Nostrum · Circuit de Valencia
Grupo Molca · Giannelli · Beta · BG Bikes · Coca-Cola · Casa Ricardo · Avant Pro · Kyocera · Vincente Gandia

Engine: 800cc, 90-degree V4; 360-degree crank, DOHC, 4 valves per cylinder, Desmodromic valve gear, variable-length inlet tracts
　　　　Power: Around 225bhp, revs up to 18,500rpm

Ancillaries: Magneti Marelli electronics, NGK sparking plugs, full electronic ride-by-wire · *Lubrication:* Shell · *Fuel:* 21 litres, Shell

Transmission: Constant-mesh cassette-style gearbox

Suspension: Front, Öhlins TRSP25 48mm forks · Rear; Öhlins TRSP44 shock with linkage

Wheels: Front, 16.5in Marchesini · Rear, 16.5in Marchesini · *Tyres:* Bridgestone

Brakes: Front, Brembo carbon-carbon 320mm · Rear, steel 200mm

HONDA LCR

TEAM STAFF

Lucio CECCHINELLO: Team Owner and Manager

Martine FELLONI: Administration and Legal

Oscar HARO: Public Relations

Elisa PAVAN: Press Officer

TONI ELIAS PIT CREW

Christophe BOURGIGNON: Chief Engineer

Mechanics

Joan CASAS

Xavier CASANOVAS

Chris RICHARDSON

Brian HARDEN: Telemetry

Tomonori SATO: HRC engineer

Ugo GELMI: Tyres

Steve JENKNER: Bridgestone Tyres

TONI ELIAS

Born: 26 March, 1983 – Manresa, Spain

GP Starts: 196 (96 MotoGP, 17 Moto2, 48 250cc, 35 125cc)

GP Wins: 17 (1 MotoGP, 7 Moto2, 17 250cc, 2 125cc)

World Championships: 1 Moto2

KOUSUKE AKIYOSHI

Born: 12 January, 1975 – Kurume, Japan

GP Starts: 8 MotoGP

LUCIO Ceccinello's sixth season as one of the leading private enterprises in MotoGP was definitely his most difficult and disappointing. The Monaco-based squad hired experienced Spaniard Toni Elias after his class shone through to win the inaugural Moto2 championship in 2010. Being Spanish helped, as he was viewed as a much more commercially viable option than Frenchman Randy de Puniet, who had occupied the seat at LCR for the previous three seasons.

There was Dorna influence, too, with Carmelo Ezpeleta pivotal. He felt it essential that the Moto2 world champion be rewarded with a place on the MotoGP grid. He was concerned about the effect on young aspiring riders if winning Moto2 didn't open (or in this case re-open) doors to MotoGP.

The arrival of Elias was the only notable change to the LCR Honda squad, with respected former 125cc racer Cecchinello sticking with Christophe Bourguignon as crew chief and Brian Harden as data technician. Xavier Casanovas, Joan Casas and Chris Richardson were all long-serving crew members.

Hopes that Elias would be riding the crest of a wave from his Moto2 success were extinguished before the first race of the season in Doha. Elias struggled woefully to make the transition back to MotoGP, and he had to wait until the fifth round in Catalunya just to qualify inside the top 15. He only scored five top-ten finishes, with a best of eighth in rain-hit races at Silverstone and Phillip Island.

The awful results placed an immediate strain on the relationship between Elias and Bourguignon.

HONDA RCV212V

Major Sponsors and Technical Suppliers: Playboy · Eurobet · Givi · TS Vision · Elettronica Discount · Effenberg · Dinamica · Elf · VIAR

Engine: 800cc, 76-degree V4; 360-degree crank (tbc), PVRS · *Power:* More than 210ps

Ancillaries: HRC electronics, ride-by-wire throttle and fuel injection system, Denso sparking plugs · *Fuel:* 21 litres

Dimensions: 2050mm long, 1440mm wheelbase, 1130mm high, 645mm wide; weight, 148kg

Transmission: Gear primary drive, multi-plate dry slipper clutch, six-speed constant-mesh cassette-style gearbox, RK chain

Suspension: Front, Öhlins TRSP25 48mm forks · Rear, Öhlins TRSP 44 shock with linkage

Wheels: Front, 16in Marchesini · Rear, 16.5in Marchesini · *Tyres:* Bridgestone

Brakes: Front, Nissin carbon-carbon 314mm · Rear, HRC steel 218mm

BEN BOSTROM

Born: 7 May, 1974 – Redding, California, USA

GP Starts: 1 MotoGP

SHINICHI ITO

Born: 7 December, 1956 – Miyagi, Japan

GP Starts: 67 MotoGP/500cc

Above: Team principal Luchio Chechinello.

Left: Toni Elias returned to MotoGP as the Moto2 champion, but endured a torrid time aboard the LCR Honda.

Below: Crew engineer Christophe Bourguignon.

Photos: Gold & Goose

HONDA RACING TEAM

As part of its efforts to boost the grid at the re-scheduled Japanese GP, which at one stage was under threat of a boycott by leading riders, Honda supported a special one-rider wild card entry for veteran Shinichi Ito. Aged 44, he was the oldest on the grid by seven years.

It was also a gesture of support to the tsunami victims of East Japan: Ito hails from the Miyagi Pre-fecture, which was badly hit. And a reward to the former team-mate to Doohan in the 500cc Repsol Honda team, the first rider to record more than 200 mph on a grand prix bike. At the end of July, Ito had won the prestigious Suzuka 8-Hour race, partnered by Ryuichi Kiyonari and Kousuke Akiyoshi.

He promised to keep out of the way of the regulars, and finished 13th and last after a popular if short-lived GP career revival.

The season had barely started when rumours emerged that Cecchinello wanted to hire a second rider for selected races, with Californian John Hop-kins approached about a handful of wild-card rides.

Another American rider joined Elias for a one-off appearance at Laguna Seca. Motorcycle accesso-ries manufacturer Rizoma was embarking on a pro-motional drive in America and part of its sponsor-ship deal saw 37-year-old Ben Bostrom ride one of the team's RC212V bikes.

The transition to Bridgestone tyres, carbon brakes and sophisticated electronics on the RC212V meant it was a mentally and physically demanding experi-ence, and Elias only had one bike at his disposal again at the Twin Ring Motegi, where Honda test rider Kousuke Akiyoshi joined the team to show sup-port to the Japanese people following the devastat-ing earthquake and tsunami. He finished 12th.

Elias' results were certainly damaging to his per-sonal prospects, but his dismal performance also threatened Cecchinello's ability to retain or attract investors. LCR once again remained one of the few teams in the paddock to grasp the value of localis-ing its sponsorship focus. Without a naming rights backer, Cecchinello funded his project by selling space on his RC212V to sponsors interested in maximising exposure in their prominent markets.

Cecchinello used numerous single-event title sponsors, like Elf, Givi, Effenberg, Linear and Play-boy, during the season.

Some were surprised that Elias survived the sea-son without being axed, but it was apparent early on that he stood little chance of remaining at LCR.

Cecchinello was strongly linked to German Stefan Bradl during the mid-season phase. Bradl's Viess-mann Kiefer Moto2 team had MotoGP aspirations, but was struggling to meet the extortionate costs of leasing a Honda and eventually had to abandon its plans.

He then focused his attention on Dovizioso, who was surplus to requirements at Repsol Honda. But after receiving an offer at the Twin Ring Motegi, which included continued factory support from HRC, the rider declined and accepted a rival bid by Mon-ster Yamaha Tech 3.

Cecchinello was still talking to Hopkins, de Pu-niet and Alvaro Bautista at that stage. The Spaniard appeared the favourite, but then he agreed a deal with the Gresini Honda squad two days after the last race to take the place of the late Marco Simoncelli.

Last-minute talks then began again with Bradl, who was the overwhelming favourite after he tested an RC212V 800cc machine over two days at the traditional post-race Valencia test.

MARC MARQUEZ

FIM MOTO2
WORLD CHAMPIONSHIP

2011 TEAMS AND RIDERS

By PETER McLAREN

THE second season of the all-action Moto2 World Championship saw higher performance, lower diversity and the crowning of the first German world champion since Dirk Raudies in 1993.

Again, the class featured identical 600cc four-stroke Honda-built engines, while Dunlop was the exclusive tyre supplier. The grid remained jam-packed, the year beginning with a full-time entry of 38 riders. However, a market-driven chassis cull meant that seven of the 15 manufacturers present at the beginning of the previous season – I.C.P, BQR, Bimota, Promoharris, Force GP210, ADV and early-casualty RSV – were absent from year two. The eight that remained were Suter, Kalex, FTR, Motobi, Tech 3, Moriwaki, Pons Kalex and MZ-RE Honda. Seven of them scored at least one podium finish, just one fewer than in 2010.

A growing elitism meant that six riders won a Moto2 race in 2011 (on four types of bike), compared with nine different winners (on six different bikes) in 2010.

The 2011 grid included two riders – Mika Kallio and Aleix Espargaro – who were looking to follow in the footsteps of inaugural champion Toni Elias by stepping down from MotoGP. Four out of the top six from 2010's 125cc championship, including title winner Marc Marquez, entered from the opposite direction.

Elias, Karel Abraham and Roberto Rolfo were the only 2010 winners to leave the class, while full-time arrivals from beyond the GP arena included World Superbike race winner Max Neukirchner and World Supersport champion Kenan Sofuoglu.

The entry list contained eight riders from Spain,

seven from Italy, three each from Great Britain, France and Switzerland, and two each from Germany and Colombia. Australia, Belgium, Finland, Japan, Qatar, San Marino, Thailand, Turkey, the USA and Venezuela were each represented by a single rider.

The chassis choice at the start of year was split 13 for Suter, ten for FTR, five for Moriwaki, three for Tech 3, two each for Kalex, Pons Kalex and MZ, plus one for Motobi.

Six of the 17 rounds saw victories of less than one second (compared with seven in 2010), with five dominant wins of over four seconds (four in 2010). The smallest margin of victory was 0.071 second for Marquez at Mugello, and the largest 7.850 seconds for Andrea Iannone at a wet Jerez. Sixteen different riders (one less than 2010) finished on the Moto2 podium.

The rate of development meant that lap records dropped significantly in 2011, with gains of over one second commonplace in dry conditions.

Suter

As in 2010, the Suter was the most popular chassis on the grid, growing from 11 to 13 entries over the winter. Winner of the inaugural Moto2 constructors' title, the Swiss firm continued its partnerships with the Aspar, Technomag-CIP, Marc VDS, Forward Racing and Italtrans teams, while adding single-rider Speed Master, Interwetten and Catalunya Caixa Repsol entries.

The Repsol bike was for reigning 125cc champion

THOMAS LUTHI

SCOTT REDDING

MIKA KALLIO

JULIAN SIMON

ANDREA IANNONE

Marc Marquez, and his team became viewed as an unofficial factory entry, due to priority given to technical developments and an extensive testing programme.

Most notably, the young Spaniard was the first to debut a 2012 chassis and swing-arm at round 13 (Aragon). But while other teams looked on with envy, few could argue that the exciting 18-year-old didn't deserve maximum support.

After no-scores in the first three rounds, Marquez won next time at Le Mans, before a further no-score at round six (Silverstone) left him a massive 82 points behind title leader Stefan Bradl (Kalex). Then he beat Bradl in the next eight races, six of which he won, and completed an incredible recovery by taking the title lead by a single point at round 14 in Japan.

Just when the hardest work looked to be over, Marquez's title hopes were put in peril by a dangerous mistake in practice for the following Phillip Island round – when he slammed into the back of Ratthapark Wilairot – resulting in a last-place grid penalty. However, he defied the odds to reach third in the race, directly behind a dejected Bradl, but another Friday practice incident in Malaysia proved insurmountable.

Marquez – who had announced he would stay in Moto2 for 2012 the previous evening – was one of several riders to fall when marshals failed to warn of a wet section of track, leaving him battered, bruised and dizzy. He sat out all of practice, then rode for two laps in qualifying. However, he was unfit to race and had to watch from the pits as Bradl claimed 20 points, with second going to Thomas Luthi.

Continued vision problems kept Marquez sidelined for Valencia, ending any chance of the crown, although second place in the championship was already secure. Also, he had won most of the season's races.

Having scored three wins (an amount exceeded only by Elias) on his way to third overall in 2010, Andrea Iannone made the winter switch from Speed Up to Suter, by joining the Speed Master team. The 22-year-old began the season strongly with a second place and a win, his Jerez victory also making him the only rider other than Bradl and Marquez to lead the championship standings. But then he seemed to lose his way, being absent from the podium for the following seven rounds and slipping to seventh in the championship.

The Italian's fight back began in perfect style with victory after the summer break at Brno; three further podiums followed from the next four races, including a third victory of the season in Japan, where Suter clinched the 2011 constructors' title. The last part of the season saw Iannone locked in a battle for third in the championship with Alex de Angelis (Motobi), which went in the former's favour by just three points.

Fifth in the final standings was Interwetten rider Luthi, whose narrow victory in the red-flagged Sepang race marked his first win since 2006 in the 125cc class, the year after he won the title.

Fourth with five podiums on a Moriwaki during the 2010 Moto2 season, Luthi and Interwetten began their Suter association in style with podiums in the first two rounds. Like Iannone, however, the 25-year-

old Swiss rider suffered a slump in form, before finally returning to the podium at Motegi. Luthi received the latest swing-arm for the following Australian round, then claimed victory in Malaysia.

Unlike the Repsol, Speed Master and Interwetten teams, Marc VDS already had a year of Suter experience under their belts and, having enjoyed a strong end to the 2010 season with Scott Redding, had high hopes for a 2011 title attack. Everything looked in place on paper, especially with former MotoGP rider – and 125 and 250cc title contender – Mika Kallio signed to partner Redding. However, neither rider scored in the first four rounds, fifth place for Redding in his wet home British Grand Prix marking the team's only top six in the opening ten events.

The frustration was barely disguised, although the second half of the season proved more profitable, culminating in a debut podium for Kallio at the Valencia finale. Even so, the pair were only 15th (Redding) and 16th (Kallio) in the championship.

The Marc VDS and Suter partnership extended beyond Moto2, the Belgian team helping in the development of the Suter MotoGP bike. With that in mind, they were somewhat disappointed by the delay in receiving the latest Moto2 parts. "I'm a little disappointed that Marc Marquez was the only rider to test the 2012 Suter chassis [before Aragon], as there was ample opportunity for Scott to ride the bike during the Valencia test," said team manager Michael Bartholemy. "We will get the new parts in Japan."

Redding duly received the 2012 chassis at

Motegi, but chose to race the 2011 bike due to a lack of set-up time, with the new swing-arm then arriving for Australia. Kallio remained on the 2011 chassis, but received the new swing-arm at Valencia. Marc VDS will switch to Kalex for 2012.

The Mapfre Aspar team, which had moved to Suter from RSV early in 2010, also had big aspirations, having retained the previous year's title runner-up Julian Simon to spearhead its challenge. The Spaniard lost out on a debut Moto2 victory by just 0.147 second to Bradl at round three in Portugal, his first podium of the year, then rose to second in the standings with fourth at the following Le Mans round.

But disaster struck next time in Catalunya, when the home star was flicked into a leg-breaking high-side by unintentional contact from Kenan Sofuoglu. Forced to sit out the next three rounds, Simon returned in Germany, where he tumbled off at the first turn, fortunately without further harm. The 24-year-old former 125cc world champion then suffered another heavy fall at Brno, prompting him to withdraw from the race, before making a comeback for the Indianapolis, Misano and Aragón rounds.

Simon was still struggling with braking issues, however, caused by his healing right leg and, after a 17th place at Aragon, underwent further surgery that saw him sidelined until Valencia, where he finished the season with a tenth place. He scored 68 points, 49 of which came in the first four rounds.

A revolving door of replacements had taken over Simon's Suter, starting with Jordi Torres at Silverstone, then woman racer Elena Rosell at Assen and Italian Raffaele de Rosa at Mugello (after planned replacement WSS rider David Salom dropped out). There was no replacement for Motegi, before another Spaniard, Ivan Moreno, was selected as stand-in for the Australian and Malaysian rounds. None scored points.

Torres was promoted to a full-time race seat at the expense of countryman Javier Fores from round eight (Mugello) onwards. Spanish Formula Extreme champion Fores had failed to score.

After a nightmare debut at Assen, which saw her miss the race, Rosell returned at Aragon, where she became the first Spanish female rider to finish a grand prix, in 33rd place. A further appearance followed at Valencia, where she finished 25th.

Technomag-CIP, which had won the first ever Moto2 grand prix with the late Shoya Tomizawa, looked to have found an able replacement for the much-missed Japanese rider in the form of reigning double WSS champion Kenan Sofuoglu. He had impressed during two end-of-season rides for the team in 2010, but 2011 would prove far more challenging. The Turkish star failed to score in the first five rounds, before opening his account with eighth in the wet British GP.

A debut Moto2 rostrum with second place in the damp Dutch TT followed, but proved to be a false dawn, as Sofuoglu dropped to the tail end of the top ten in the following rounds. A spectacular high-side in practice at Indianapolis left him with a broken right foot, forcing him out of three events, before a return to action in Japan. The 27-year-old concluded his first grand prix season in 17th position and will return to WSS in 2012.

Alongside Sofuoglu was Dominique Aegerter, who had kept his seat with Technomag-CIP. The 21-year-old Swiss delivered by far his best grand prix season, scoring in all but four rounds and claiming a debut podium at Valencia. Aegerter finished eighth in the championship.

While Sofuoglu was injured, the team called upon the services of former 125cc race winner Tomoyoshi Koyama at Misano and Aragón. Koyama made a further Moto2 appearance as a wild-card on a TSR, but wasn't able to score.

Forward Racing retained Jules Cluzel for 2011, pairing the frantic Frenchman with new signing 26-year-old Alex Baldolini, who had scored a shock podium with the I.C.P. chassis at Estoril in 2010. A debut race winner that year, Cluzel was unable to build on what had been his best grand prix season, slipping from seventh in the inaugural Moto2 championship to 21st in 2011. Cluzel scored on seven occasions, the best of which was a fourth at Silverstone.

Baldolini took points in four races before being replaced by Raffaele de Rosa from Indianapolis. The latter, who had begun the year on a G22 Moriwaki, didn't score.

Forward Racing will graduate to MotoGP in 2012, running the Suter-BMW CRT bike for Colin Edwards, and have signed Alex de Angelis for Moto2.

Claudio Corti, who had raced for Forward in 2010, moved sideways to the Italtrans Racing Team, alongside Venezuelan Robertino Pietri. The highlight of Corti's 2010 season, his first in grand prix, had been pole at Silverstone. The 24-year-old couldn't repeat

STEFAN BRADL

DOMINIQUE AEGERTER

AXEL PONS

CLAUDIO CORTI

SIMONE CORSI

that feat, but did repeat 25th place in the championship. Pietri, who scored one point during his debut grand prix season, didn't crack the top 15.

The most frequent of the Suter wild-card entries was for South African rookie Steven Odendaal, who made six appearances for MS Racing, the best of which resulted in a 27th place. Italian Mattia Tarozzi (Faenza Racing) and Australian Kris McLaren (BRP Racing) also rode as Suter wild-cards in front of their home fans.

Thanks to Marquez and Iannone, the Suter chassis won more races than any other, claiming 11 victories, compared with four during 2010.

Kalex/Pons Kalex

Having joined forces with Sito Pons' team for the inaugural Moto2 season, German manufacturer Kalex Engineering also produced a fully in-house design for 2011, resulting in both Pons Kalex and Kalex being listed as constructors.

Again, the Pons team consisted of two bikes, while Kiefer Racing swam against the tide by leaving Suter to operate the new Kalex entries. Kiefer retained Stefan Bradl for the Viessmann-backed bike and ran rookie Randy Krummenacher under the GP Team Switzerland banner.

Bradl, whose only podium of 2010 had been a victory at Estoril, enjoyed instant success with Kalex by winning from pole in Qatar. The German went on to win four of the opening six rounds – plus one further podium – to build a title lead of 62 points by Silver-

stone. Amazingly, that was the 21-year-old's final victory of the year.

The first chink in Bradl's armour appeared in the form of a crash in the following Dutch round, which coincided with the rise of Marquez. Initially, Bradl looked able to contain the young Spaniard through consistent podium finishes, but bad races at Indianapolis (ill-suited to the Kalex) and Aragon (tyre problems) helped Marquez snatch the title advantage with four rounds to go.

Although unable to capitalise fully on Marquez's grid penalty at Phillip Island, Bradl kept his focus to put the title all but out of reach with a runner-up finish in the Spaniard's absence at Sepang.

Stefan, the son of 1991 250cc championship runner-up, Helmut Bradl, was confirmed as champion when Marquez was unfit to ride in the Valencia finale. He had claimed 11 podiums and seven poles during his fourth full GP season.

Krummenacher, who had claimed one podium during four years in the 125cc class, made a promising start in Moto2 with points in seven out of the first nine rounds, including fourth place in Germany. But the 21-year-old failed to score in the remaining eight races, leaving him 18th in the standings and perhaps underlining the ground gained by rival machines.

The Pons team had taken one podium in 2010, a feat repeated in 2011 thanks to former MotoGP rider Aleix Espargaro, signed to ride alongside Sito's son, Axel. Espargaro claimed his rostrum at Catalunya (round five) and finished the season in 12th, just ahead of younger brother Pol.

Injuries once again blighted Axel Pons' campaign. The 20-year-old missed Indianapolis, Misano and Aragon after surgery on a hand injury from Mugello. He was replaced by Alex Baldolini, who had begun the year with Forward Racing.

After returning for Motegi and Phillip Island, Pons was hospitalised following a race-stopping fall at Sepang; he finished the year with just a single point.

Bradl's efforts carried Kalex to second in the constructors' championship, while Pons Kalex repeated its seventh place from 2010.

FTR

After winning four races in 2010 – three with Iannone in modified Speed Up form and another as an official FTR entry for Karel Abraham – the British manufacturer made the greatest gains in terms of machine numbers for 2011: ten full-time riders, plus unofficial bike(s) at MZ. Two of those additions were due to the Speed Up bikes being officially classified as FTRs, while the single-rider Aeroport de Castello squad also continued its association for a second season.

New FTR converts came in the form of the SAG team (which made the switch from Bimota), Blusens/Avintia-STX (formerly with BQR) and the new Ioda Racing Project, run by Giampiero Sacchi.

A podium finisher on a JiR-Motobi in 2010, Ioda rider Simone Corsi proved the most successful FTR competitor. The Italian repeated his podium tally from the previous season and was ranked as high as second in the championship, on his way to an eventual sixth.

Following a disjointed debut Moto2 campaign, Corsi's team-mate and fellow Italian, Mattia Pasini, completed his first full season of 600cc racing in 2011, but could only manage occasional points finishes (a best of sixth) as he struggled to replicate his two-stroke success. By contrast, former 125cc star Esteve Rabat (Blusens-STX) was quick to adapt, the Moto2 rookie scoring points in 11 rounds – highlighted by third place at Indianapolis – on his way to tenth in the standings.

Speed Up signing Pol Espargaro was another Moto2 rookie to stand on the podium for FTR. The former 125cc title contender took rostrums at Indianapolis and Sepang, although a lack of points in the first half of the season limited the 20-year-old to 13th in the championship.

Yonny Hernandez (Blusens-STX) scored just over half the points of Espargaro on his way to 19th place. The Colombian's second season in GPs was hindered by injury at Brno, which saw him skip the Indianapolis, Misano and Aragon races, although he did score his first top-six finishes in Germany and Valencia.

Thai Honda Singha rider Ratthapark Wilairot suffered a drama-filled year. The 23-year-old had been left fighting for his life after a road traffic accident in December, but took his place for round one in Qatar and scored his only points of the year with 12th next time in Jerez. He missed the Catalan round after a heavy fall in warm-up, and was sidelined from the Australian and Malaysia races after the Marquez collision at Phillip Island.

Aeroport de Castello's 2010 rider, Alex Debon, moved into a management role with the team for 2011, handing his FTR ride to British rookie Kev Coghlan. Coghlan rode from 24th to eighth in the wet Jerez race, missed Estoril through injury, then scored further points in Britain before splitting with the team after round seven (Assen).

Italian Tommaso Lorenzetti took over the seat for the next three events, before American JD Beach got the ride at Indianapolis. Countryman Jacob Gagne, who rode as a GP Tech-FTR wild-card at Indy, then joined the squad for the following Misano round.

Some stability returned when experienced Spaniard Joan Olive, who stood in at Blusens for the injured Yonny Hernandez at Misano, joined the Aeroport de Castello team from Aragón onwards. However, Coghlan remained their only rider to score.

Kenny Noyes had planned to remain with the Jack&Jones/Antonio Banderas team for 2011, and switch from Promoharris to Suter, but the squad's collapse left the American's young GP career in jeopardy. A subsequent rescue deal saw Noyes race an FTR under the Avintia-STX banner, with support from GP Tech and FOGI Racing, which had dipped a toe into Moto2 with wild-card entries in 2010. He looked in danger of finishing the season without a point, however, until he rode from 23rd to fifth in the Valencia finale.

Failing to score were Espargaro's Speed Up team-mate, Valentin Debise, who had raced the ADV chassis in 2010, plus Wilairot's rookie SAG team-mate, Santiago Hernandez (brother of Yonny).

In addition to Gagne, other short-term FTR appearances came in the form of Raffaele de Rosa, who stood in for Santiago Hernandez at Silverstone, and former 250cc privateer Martin Cardenas, who replaced Yonny Hernandez at Indianapolis.

Alessandro Andreozzi (Andreozzi Reparto Corse) rode as a wild-card at Misano, while Blake Leigh-Smith (BRP Racing) did likewise at Phillip Island. Apiwat Wongthananon replaced injured countryman Wilairot at Sepang.

Although FTR didn't win a race in 2011, it climbed from fifth to third in the constructors' championship.

Motobi

Having run a two-rider team in 2010, the Motobi project – combining Japanese chassis specialist TSR and former MotoGP team JiR – was reduced to a single rider for 2011.

Former MotoGP podium finisher Alex de Angelis remained on board for a full season, but hopes of a title attack soon faded as the Sammarinese took until round nine to claim a rostrum. A repeat of his 2010 victory from pole at Phillip Island followed, while a strong end to the season saw the 27-year-old reach fourth in the standings. He also scored enough points for Motobi to repeat its fourth place in the constructors' championship.

During the year, JiR team principal Gianluca Montiron led calls for a combined weight limit: "Between [Marquez] and our rider, we are at least 11kg to the

BRADLEY SMITH

MIKE DI MEGLIO

ANTHONY WEST

MAX NEUKIRCHNER

Photos: Gold & Goose

disadvantage... Establishing a combined weight of bike and rider is crucial if Moto2 is to be a training class for future MotoGP riders, where the power of machines makes weight and body shape irrelevant."

Johann Zarco, 125cc title runner-up, will spearhead the JiR challenge in 2012.

Tech 3

Tech 3 had an all-new line-up for 2011, with Mike di Meglio moving from the Aspar team and being joined by 125cc front-runner 20-year-old Bradley Smith. A new 'B-team' bike was run for Belgian Xavier Simeon.

Smith quickly formed an effective working relationship with his team – led by Hiroshi Aoyama's 2010 MotoGP crew chief, Tom Jojic – and defied his lack of four-stroke experience with a fourth place in round two at Jerez. His season reached its peak with consecutive podiums at Silverstone, Assen and Mugello. The second half of the year was tougher, though, and included a shoulder injury in the same accident as Marquez at Sepang, but he racked up three further top-six finishes to end an impressive debut Moto2 season seventh in the championship.

The Englishman's form saw him considered for a Tech 3 MotoGP ride. Smith subsequently re-signed for another year in Moto2, then MotoGP in 2013.

Former 125cc world champion di Meglio again struggled to replicate his two-stroke success. The Frenchman scored points on six occasions (best of seventh place) and finished 23rd in the standings.

Simeon, who had raced a Moriwaki in 2010, concluded his first full grand prix season in 26th place. He finished a best of eighth, at Valencia.

Although a repeat of Yuki Takahashi's 2010 victory eluded Tech 3, the team increased its constructors' championship haul by 50 points relative to the previous year and rose from sixth to fifth.

Moriwaki

Moriwaki may have won seven races and the Moto2 riders' title with Toni Elias in 2010, but full-time chassis numbers decreased from six to five for the new season. With Elias moving back to MotoGP, Gresini fielded a new line-up of Yuki Takahashi (from Tech 3) and Michele Pirro (from World Supersport).

Podiums for Takahashi at rounds three and four put the experienced Japanese fourth in the championship, but his season went largely downhill thereafter. Like Suter, Moriwaki introduced a new chassis for Aragon, but Takahashi scored points in only five of the final 13 rounds – and crashed out of the lead in Valencia – to finish 11th in the championship.

Pirro took his first grand prix podium in the wet British race, then finished the season with a fairytale victory (from pole) at Valencia.

Two other full-season Moriwakis were in the hands of the QMMF Racing Team. Mashel Al Naimi (Qatar) completed his second season without a point, while Spaniard Ricard Cardus claimed two points from 13 starts. The team also ran Qatari Nasser Hasan Al

Malki at his home round, Silverstone and Valencia, with Australian Alexander Cudlin riding at Le Mans.

The Desguaces La Torre G22 team swapped Raffaele de Rosa for Carmelo Morales after Le Mans, then at Aragon replaced Morales with Sergio Gadea, who began the season with Paris Hilton Racing in 125cc. But he was injured next time at Motegi, forcing the team to miss the following flyaway events in Australia and Malaysia. Alex Baldolini stepped in for Valencia. G22 also ran Polish rookie Lukasz Wargala as a wild-card at Jerez. None scored.

The Sepang round saw a double wild-card Moriwaki entry by Petronas Malaysia for local riders Hafizh Syahrin and Mohamad Zamri Baba.

MZ-RE Honda

MZ Racing returned with an expanded line-up for 2011, with German Max Neukirchner joining the team alongside the retained Anthony West. Although the team continued to be officially listed as using an MZ-RE Honda chassis, in reality the squad switched both riders to FTRs.

Neukirchner had an M210 from the start of the season, while West made his FTR debut at Le Mans. Use of the latest M211 model, with its distinctive circular air intake, followed.

West scored the team's best Moto2 finish with a fourth in the slippery Dutch TT, a feat he repeated in similar conditions at Valencia. Neukirchner rode from 39th to tenth in Holland for his best finish of the year.

NICOLAS TEROL

MIGUEL OLIVEIRA

MAVERICK VINALES

JOHANN ZARCO

ALEXIS MASBOU

DANNY KENT

MARCEL SCHROTTER

HECTOR FAUBEL

LUIS SALOM

SANDRO CORTESE

FIM 125cc WORLD CHAMPIONSHIP

2011 TEAMS AND RIDERS

THE final 125cc World Championship drew to a close at Valencia, ending the longest running chapter in grand prix motorcycle racing. It had been the only class remaining from the inaugural 1949 World Championship, and fittingly the last title was decided at the final round, after a season in which six riders won races, four of them for the first time.

Four different manufacturers scored points, although the championship was dominated again by the Piaggio-owned Aprilia and Derbi brands, using close variations of the same motorcycles (in RSA or lower RSW spec).

Twenty-four places on the start-of-season entry list were for Aprilia riders (12 on RSA bikes), with Derbi's presence limited to three riders (two RSAs). There were no full-time Japanese machines, but two unofficial KTMs were enrolled. Lambretta, new in 2010, had departed, but the team (nee Malaguti, nee Loncin) was back with upgraded machinery and much more serious backing from Indian brand Mahindra.

Of the 31 full-time riders (five more than 2010), nine were from Spain; four each from Italy, Germany and Great Britain; two from France; and one each from Switzerland, Portugal, The Netherlands, Malaysia, Japan, India, Finland and the Czech Republic.

There were 14 official rookies, and some rounds saw five additional wild-card entries. Thirty-four different riders scored a point during the 17 rounds.

Fans watching 125cc in 2011 saw six races won by less than a second (seven if you count Catalunya), including a perfect photo-finish at Sachsenring. The new Moto3 class will have a lot to live up to.

Derbi/Aprilia

The 2010 Championship runner-up Nicolas Terol remained for one last shot at the title with the Bankia Aspar Aprilia team. The 22-year-old won the first three rounds, before resistance arrived in the unexpected shape of a last-gasp defeat at the hands of 16-year-old rookie Maverick Vinales at Le Mans.

Vinales – the reigning Spanish and European champion – had been thrust into the limelight even before the season began, when the Blusens Aprilia team secured backing linked to socialite Paris Hilton. She visited Catalunya (round five), where she saw Vinales finish second to Terol after a post-race penalty had been given to first-over-the-line Johann Zarco.

Twenty-one-year-old Zarco had switched from WTR Aprilia to reigning champions Ajo Derbi for his third season in the 125cc championship, and took his first two podiums at Jerez and Estoril. Catalunya was the first of several near misses.

After being handed his fourth victory of the season by Zarco's penalty, Terol's luck took a turn for the worse when he suffered a finger tendon injury during qualifying for the Dutch TT, which forced him to miss the race. A victorious return at Mugello followed, rebuilding his lead to 39 points. But two races later, it had dropped to just 12, with a fourth in Germany followed by a mechanical DNF in Brno.

Zarco again came agonisingly close to victory in both those events, losing a tie-break to Terol's teammate, Hector Faubel, at the Sachsenring, then being narrowly beaten by Cortese in the Czech Republic.

Terol reacted firmly to the title threat, winning the

next three rounds at Indianapolis, Misano and Aragon (where Aprilia clinched the constructors' crown), before Zarco took a long-overdue first victory at Motegi. This was the first – and last – non-Aprilia win of the season, although the French rider clawed a further 11 points from Terol over the next two rounds.

Zarco was still 20-points behind, however, heading into the Valencia finale, where an early crash confirmed Terol as champion. The Spaniard, who won eight races during the season, had raced in 125cc since 2004.

Third in the standings was Vinales, who followed his Le Mans victory with wins at Assen, Sepang and Valencia. Five further podiums and three poles completed a dream debut year, in which he was also voted winner of the Michel Metraux Trophy by fellow riders.

Although Zarco proved to be Terol's nearest championship challenger, the first half of the season saw the runner-up position alternate between Germans Sandro Cortese and Jonas Folger.

Third in 2010, Cortese moved from Ajo Derbi to Racing Team Germany Aprilia for his seventh season in the class and started strongly with two podiums from three rounds. He experienced a podium drought leading up to the summer break, however, then retaliated with a debut victory at Brno and a second win at Phillip Island. Those successes, combined with four further podiums, propelled him to a best ever fourth in the championship.

Folger's career was in need of a kick-start, and the 18-year-old's switch to Red Bull Ajo Aprilia produced the desired effect, with three podiums in the first six races, including a debut victory in the wet British GP.

EFREN VAZQUEZ · JAKUB KORNFEIL · JONAS FOLGER · ALBERTO MONCAYO · JASPER IWEMA · ZULFAHMI KHAIRUDDIN · SIMONE GROTZKYJ · LOUIS ROSSI · SERGIO GADEA · ADRIAN MARTIN · DANNY WEBB

By PETER McLAREN

That win put him back ahead of Cortese for second, but it was his last podium of the season and he dropped to sixth in the championship. Folger missed Brno due to illness and spent several races on an RSW before prising his RSA away from team-mate Danny Kent.

Faubel had returned to 125cc for the first time since finishing runner-up in 2007, but was unable to mount a consistent challenge against team-mate Terol. As well as his German win, the 28-year-old took three further podiums for fifth overall.

Zarco's Ajo Derbi team-mate, Efren Vazquez, claimed two podiums and seventh in the championship, two places lower than 2010. Luis Salom (RW Racing Aprilia) took his first two podiums, in his third year of grands prix, for a career-best eighth overall, despite missing Brno and Indianapolis due to injury.

Spanish veteran Sergio Gadea rode as team-mate to Vinales for the first 12 rounds, achieving two third places before an ill-fated switch to Moto2. Classified ninth in the final 125cc standings, he was replaced by Spanish rookie Josep Rodriguez, who scored a best of 14th.

Alberto Moncayo completed the championship top ten. The 20-year-old Andalucia Banca Civica Aprilia rider made solid progress during his second season, highlighted by a debut podium at Brno.

The top RSW regular was Folger's team-mate, Danny Kent, in 11th. The 17-year-old had joined Red Bull Ajo Aprilia after some impressive appearances for Lambretta in 2010 and developed his talent with four top-six finishes in 2011, including fourth in the slippery Jerez race.

Twelfth overall, Jakub Kornfeil (Ongetta Aprilia) was the highest rider without a top-six finish. Two riders below him claimed a better race result: 13th overall Adrian Martin (Aspar Aprilia) was sixth at Silverstone, while British rookie Taylor Mackenzie (Phonica Aprilia) claimed most of his 2011 points with fifth at Jerez.

Sixteen-year-old rookie Miguel Oliveira, team-mate to Moncayo, couldn't match the heroics of former Spanish championship rival Vinales, but did score on six occasions (from eleven starts) for 14th.

Two Aprilia riders scored more often than Oliveira, but with a lower total: Phonica's Simone Grotzkyj took points in seven of his 11 races (before being injured) for 16th in the championship, while Matteoni's Louis Rossi scored nine times on his way to 17th.

The third Derbi was in the hands of Zulfahmi Khairuddin, who moved to the Ajo team for his second year in the class. The 20-year-old steered his RSW to a best of seventh, in front of his home fans in Malaysia, and finished 18th in the championship.

Riding in his first full season, Team Italia FMI's Luigi Morciano failed to score until round ten, then collected points in six of the last eight races, including a ninth place at Valencia. He was 20th overall.

Seventeen-year-old Niklas Ajo, son of team manager Aki Ajo, saved his best until last with eighth at Valencia for TT Motions Aprilia. Ajo finished his rookie season in 21st.

Other Aprilia point scorers were Dutchman Jasper Iwema (Ongetta-Abbink Metaal), Italians Alessandro Tonucci (Team Italia FMI) and Manuel Tatasciore (Phonica), Britons Harry Stafford (Ongetta) and John McPhee (Racing Steps), Czech Miroslav Popov (Ellegi

Racing), Swiss Giulian Pedone (Phonica) and Norwegian Sturla Fagerhaug (WTR).

Mahindra

Mahindra became the first Indian manufacturer to enter grands prix in 2011, using the acquisition of Italian firm Engines Engineering to construct its own motorcycles and run a two-rider team.

Eighteen-year-old German Marcel Schrotter (second year of grands prix) and 20-year-old Briton Danny Webb (fifth year) scored regular points on their way to 15th and 19th respectively in the championship.

The team's best result was ninth for Schrotter at Assen, but the most memorable moment came in qualifying for Valencia, when Webb defied spots of rain to take his and Mahindra's first ever pole.

Mahindra will continue in grands prix with a Moto3 project in 2012.

KTM

Caretta Technology was the only team to use KTM motorcycles throughout the season. They began the year with Japanese Hiroki Ono and German Daniel Kartheininger, but that lasted just two rounds before Hungarian Peter Sebestyen replaced the latter.

Ono, eighth at Jerez, then left the team after round four and was replaced by French veteran Alexis Masbou. He remained for the rest of the year, scoring six times, plus once for WTR Aprilia, for 22nd overall.

Sebestyen left after Indianapolis, his seat going to young Australian Jack Miller.

MOTOGP · MOTO2 · 125cc

GRANDS PRIX 2011

Reports by MICHAEL SCOTT

Statistics compiled by PETER McLAREN

Inset right: Back with Honda, winner Stoner waves his new flag of allegiance.

Inset, far right top: Lorenzo was overjoyed with second.

Inset, far right bottom: Pedrosa looked spent after the race. There was worse to come.

Main photo: A show of solidarity from riders and officials for the victims of the Japanese earthquake.

Photos: Gold & Goose

FIM WORLD CHAMPIONSHIP · ROUND 1

QATAR GRAND PRIX

LOSAIL CIRCUIT

Left: In the battle for supremacy at HRC, Pedrosa is about to be overhauled by Stoner.
Photo: Gold & Goose

THE long awaited moment – Rossi's debut on a Ducati – had been trailed through the compressed season of testing. It took place at night in Qatar, and perhaps contributed to the increased crowd figure – 8,501 fans this year, 1,200 up on 2010. They were lost in the vast grandstands, but the world watched the TV feed with bated breath.

So far, his progress had been slow: two runs at Sepang and one at Qatar had seen him struggling with his shoulder and the motorcycle. He was nowhere near the top of the time sheets. But Rossi is Rossi, and hopes lingered on. Even when he qualified only ninth, not even the best Ducati (Hector Barbera's satellite bike was sixth in the official figures, a frequent factor that factory riders tend to ascribe to his eagerness to follow them in practice, then get a good tow down the straight).

Stoner and his fellow Honda riders were at the sharp end now, as he had been when he had made his own Ducati debut at the same track in 2007. He had won that race and gone on to take the championship. Stoner won the next two races at the desert track, day and night; and fell off while leading in 2010. The omens for 2011 were clear, as he dominated all three free practices and qualifying. The race would prove to have few surprises.

The message from the tests had been obvious enough: look out for Honda. The improvement to its machine had already begun in the previous season. Now, with a last chance to win the company's first 800cc title, the team hadn't stopped over the winter. The final iteration of the RC212C was gilded still further with the latest instant-change gearbox, giving audibly seamless upshifts. More important than the few tenths this might save over a lap compared with bikes with the usual discernible pause between gears was that the smoother power flow meant the bike stayed settled under acceleration. The Honda riders could power out of Qatar's last corner on to the kilometre-long straight conspicuously better than all the other bikes, and then enjoy the further advantage of plentiful top speed (although, oddly, Barbera's Ducati was fastest of all).

On top of all that, Honda had three factory riders – although one of them, Pedrosa, would run into previously unsuspected physical problems, the aftermath of his broken collarbone at Motegi in 2010. Pain and stiffness intervened

to help the latter stages of what otherwise might not have been such an easy win for his new and potentially troublesome team-mate. It would be a few weeks yet before the reasons were diagnosed and repaired. Meantime, having a trio instead of the usual pair complicated scoring for the teams' championship, where two riders' points count. The solution applied to Honda would be to take the points of the best and worst scoring rider at each race: the best possible result would be a clean sweep of the rostrum, scoring first and third, while rivals might enjoy the scores of first and second.

As well as those who had changed classes (including Abraham up to MotoGP, Aleix Espargaro and Kallio down to Moto2, and a rash of 125 stars like Marquez, Pol Espargaro and Bradley Smith up to Moto2), there were all-new rookies to watch in all classes, notably (as it would transpire) Cal Crutchlow in MotoGP and Maverick Vinales in 125. The latter was a 16-year-old who would soon be winning races; Crutchlow the latest British ex-Superbike hope. His first race would be tricky, as he'd damaged his left little finger badly in a high-side crash during testing on the Monday night.

Mistrust of the desert night's potential for cold track temperatures and heavy dew in 2010 saw the riders requesting earlier race times, which were granted: everything was an hour earlier, the main race starting at 10pm. To make sure nobody would be riding in daylight, the schedule was expanded by an extra day and, rather bizarrely, race-day warm-up was run on the previous evening for Moto2 and 125. Proceedings opened on Thursday with the smaller classes taking their first two sessions, MotoGP only one, and so on. Only the big class had the chance to run warm-up tests on the same day as the race.

Bautista, Suzuki's sole rider (the Yang to HRC's three-rider Ying), didn't get that far. A high-sider in Friday's final free practice session snapped his femur, leaving the team frantically searching the almost-overflowing Moto2 paddock for a warm body to put in his place. Anthony West's team owner, Martin Wimmer, declined to release his rider; Sito Pons ramped the price of Aleix Espargaro out of reach, and no one else was available, so the first race of the year had only 16 starters.

Back in 1992, the first round in Japan had 23 500s on the

Above: You tell me. Burgess and Rossi discuss the Ducati's handling.

Top left: Damage limitation for Lorenzo as he overhauls the fading Pedrosa.

Top right: HRC president Tetsuo Suzuki watches over his three-man Repsol team.

Top right centre: Finger trouble. New boy Cal Crutchlow was patched up after a high-side in practice.

Right: Marco Simoncelli lays rubber as he fends off Dovizioso.

Photos: Gold & Goose

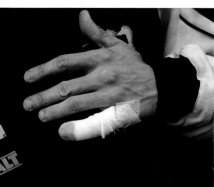

grid. That was when Dorna took over. Now this was the Spanish company's 300th GP, and they had planned to celebrate it. In the wake of the earthquake and tsunami in north-east Japan, however, this was replaced by one minute's silence on the grid and banners proclaiming (only slightly confusingly) "We X Japan"; while riders wore special stickers with a message of support. Obviously the Japanese GP, due to take place a month later, was not going to happen, and there was concern throughout the paddock, with its several Japanese members.

Bridgestone was confirmed as control tyre supplier for MotoGP for three more years, until 2014, which was welcomed in a paddock that generally appreciated that the company's tyres and support had been consistently good over the previous two seasons. Michelin and Pirelli had been interested, the former on condition that tyre competition would be opened up again in the future. Dorna went for Bridgestone's revised plan, where instead of charging for tyres as expected, the company instead traded more liberal advertising rights to MotoGP riders' images.

All classes adopted the MotoGP grid pattern, three riders to each row. In the case of Moto2, with 39 starters, this meant 13 rows stretching a long way back down the straight, but as the year wore on, it would prove effective at reducing the number of first-corner pile-ups..

MOTOGP RACE – 22 laps

Practice was clear cut: the Hondas were flying with Stoner leading the way, Pedrosa alongside him; but the Yamahas were capable of a fast lap too, in spite of Lorenzo's complaints of a lack of acceleration and speed. He completed the front row.

New team-mate Spies was fifth, behind Simoncelli; Barbera was a surprise sixth on the best Ducati. And Rossi was on the far end of row three, behind Dovizioso and rookie Crutchlow (suffering hand injuries from a testing prang) and exactly 1.5 seconds slower than Stoner. Hayden was 13th, while Moto2 champion Elias began his MotoGP revival qualified last.

The winner may have been predictable, but the race was close down the field, with plenty of stirring battles.

Pedrosa led away from Stoner and Lorenzo, with Simoncelli and Dovizioso next, then Rossi. Lorenzo was pushing hard and by the end of the lap was ahead of both Hondas. De Puniet had already crashed midfield, his bike striking and crushing new team-mate Capirossi's left hand, while Hayden dropped almost to last avoiding it. Capirossi retired two laps later.

Stoner moved past Pedrosa the second time through turn one, and then inside Lorenzo into the three right-handers.

His lead would last slightly longer, but Pedrosa was also past the Yamaha by the end of lap two and was riding with a point to prove. At the same time, Stoner was locked into tactics that would serve him well into the season – relatively cautious in the early laps, but knowing his settings and speed would become better when the fuel went down and the tyres wore in.

So it was that Dani took over at the start of lap six. The two Hondas already had a full second over Lorenzo, and they continued in commanding formation. Both looked strong; it was hard to know who was playing with whom. Until the race approached the halfway point.

Stoner struggled to pass Pedrosa, whose corner exit on to the front straight made him impregnable into turn one. But the Australian was faster on the middle part of the track, and a move that took three corners to develop was clean and successful on lap 12. Now Stoner showed just how he and his Honda could work together. He set fastest lap next time around, taking 1.3 seconds out of Pedrosa, a gap that would almost treble by race end.

Pedrosa had not run out of his new-found pluck. Unbeknown to his deriders and unexpected by the rider, his left arm had gone weak and numb. Lorenzo was past him four laps later, but he used his Honda's exit and straight-line speed advantage to put up a spirited defence, until Lorenzo finally made it stick on lap 19. Only then did Pedrosa's pace ease, and his rostrum was well deserved. "At the end, I was hanging on. I couldn't use the clutch," he said.

Lorenzo's second had him celebrating over the line and afterwards as if he had won. Since his was the only bike in the top five not to be a Honda, it was almost as if he had. But he sounded an ominous note, saying, "If I go like today in other races this year, I will crash for sure."

Fourth was hotly disputed throughout by Simoncelli and Dovizioso, the former incurring Dovi's wrath and a post-race complaint (a hint of what was to come) when he slammed past into the left-hand hairpin on lap eight. Nine laps later, the factory rider made his own decisive manoeuvre, although this time avoiding collision. Simoncelli continued to loom until Dovi outdistanced him with a sizzling final lap.

Further back (16 seconds by the end, or almost three-quarters of a second each lap), all eyes had been on Rossi in the midfield, awaiting the miracle.

He'd started well, but had lost sixth to Barbera by the end of lap one. It took until lap three before he could resume the position, by which time Spies, slow off the line on Rossi's old bike, had caught them. By lap six, the factory-bike first-timer had dispensed with Barbera, and now began a long spell of wondering how to get past a rider whose bike was slower, but whose skill and determination meant late braking in spite of his corner-entry difficulties.

Right: Bradl escaped the crush for a convincing maiden Moto2 victory.

Below: New boy, new bike: the Stoner/Honda combination began the season in dominant form.

Photos: Gold & Goose

The first attempt at turn one failed when Spies ran wide; a couple of laps later, on the 16th, he succeeded through the next corners, and after feeling Rossi's hot breath for a couple of laps managed to get away. Rossi's condition had prevailed at the end. "I am too slow in the change of direction and I don't have enough power to stop the bike, so I arrive always wide," he said.

Colin Edwards was another ten seconds away after coming through from tenth; Hayden, 13th on lap one, had gained places steadily, achieving a close ninth, having finally shaken off Aoyama.

Another five seconds down, Crutchlow got the best of a lively spat with Barbera, with fellow rookie Abraham only three seconds behind. Elias had dropped to the back, then crashed out on lap 19.

MOTO2 RACE – 20 laps

The second race of the evening, at 8.15pm, would turn out to be the start of something big, as Bradl had dominated free practice and claimed the first pole in his career – by two-tenths from class rookie Marquez, with Luthi alongside on the new three-strong front row. The fastest man's Kalex chassis was laying down a marker ahead of the two Suters.

Takahashi led row two, new boy Bradley Smith the third; Iannone was fast in free practice, but was one to stumble when the wind changed in qualifying, down in 19th.

Redding was tenth; ex-MotoGP men Aleix Espargaro and Mika Kallio, 14th and 25th; Pol Espargaro and Krummenacher (like Marquez and Smith up from 125) were 24th and 29th. Ex-Superbike racer Neukirchner (on an FTR in MZ colours) did rather better in 12th. There were 16 GP winners on the 39-strong grid, including four world champions.

There was never much doubt about Bradl's second Moto2 victory, the first for the Kalex – he had been on a Suter in 2010. The white bike led into the first corner, quickly broke the draught and then eased away, his lead growing slowly, but steadily, to an eventual 4.330 seconds.

Marquez was smothered back in the pack, 29th after the first lap, but Iannone had made a strong start, crossing the line ninth and still moving. The pursuit gang was led by Luthi from Cluzel, Takahashi, Simon, Corsi and Smith.

Redding's race was over on lap two: he crashed out of 12th place.

The pursuit formed into two groups: Luthi, Takahashi and Cluzel chasing the leader, then a little gap to the next five

Above right: Making night into day: the moon couldn't compete with Losail's floodlights.

Left: Sefan Bradl started his season a step ahead.

Centre left: The man who fell to earth. 125cc champion Marquez bows out gracefully on his Moto2 debut.

Below: Terol had a lonely 125cc race, in a class of his own.

Photos: Gold & Goose

comprising Corsi, Iannone, Simon, Smith and Marquez, now up to ninth.

As Bradl drew away, they closed up, with Marquez following Iannone forward. Then it was over for the rookie, who high-sided out on lap five.

Now followed a typical Moto2 battle of wits and elbows. By the mid-point, Iannone led the gang narrowly, from Takahashi and Luthi. Cluzel had lost touch and now was behind a charging de Angelis, who set a new record on lap nine and soon joined the trio ahead.

Takahashi started the last lap with a desperate bid for second into the first corner, but ran wide, giving Iannone a small, but important cushion that he would carry to the end, and also letting Luthi escape. By the end of the lap, he had lost another place to de Angelis in turn ten.

Corsi took sixth from Cluzel on the run to the line; Pirro was two-tenths behind in a strong class debut.

It was a good start also for Smith, ninth and holding at bay a pair of fast men: Simon and Aleix Espargaro. Neukirchner just made the points; Sofuoglu was 18th and Kallio two places down. Pasini, West, Santi Hernandez, Coghlan and Wilairot swelled the crash list, along with home hope Mashel Al Naimi, on the first lap – wild-card Nasser Hasan Al Malki survived, finishing 32nd and last, one place down on the remounted Redding.

125cc RACE – 18 laps

Nico Terol's margin of pole was a narrow one: less than a tenth over Cortese. His margin of victory by contrast was ominously large.

Vazquez completed the front row; Gadea led the second from Faubel and Folger. They were left to play among themselves as the first race of the evening kicked off at 7pm. Terol's lead from a standing start was less than half a second after the first lap, but 1.76 seconds next time, and so on. On lap 13, before he slackened his pace to enjoy his sixth win, it was up to more than 14.

The battle was for second. In the early stages, it was between Cortese, Vazquez and Faubel, joined after half-distance by Gadea and Folger.

Cortese was in control until lap 13. Then Faubel took over, but as he ran into the first corner, he sat up and slowed – his engine had gone sick, and from then on he dropped to an eventual 11th, 40 seconds behind the leader and still falling back.

Over the last two laps, Cortese put his head down and gained a little space: the other three fought to the end. Vazquez did get ahead in the last corners, but Gadea won the drag to the distant finish line by three-tenths; Folger was even closer, in fifth.

Sixth to ninth was covered by 0.690 second. Zarco held off Moncaya, Salom and hot rookie Vinales. Rookie Oliveira was a lone tenth; Iwema, Kent and Grotzkyj narrowly failed to pass Faubel, while Webb was 16th, behind Rossi, narrowly missing a debut point for the new-old Mahindra team.

LOSAIL INTERNATIONAL CIRCUIT

22 laps
Length: 5.380 km. / 3.343 miles
Width: 12m

Key
96/60 kph/mph
⚙ Gear

Photos: Gold & Goose

MotoGP	RACE DISTANCE: 22 laps, 73.545 miles/118.360km · RACE WEATHER: Dry (air 19°C, humidity 31%, track 20°C)

Pos.	Rider	Nat.	No.	Entrant	Machine	Tyres	Laps	Time & speed
1	**Casey Stoner**	AUS	27	Repsol Honda Team	Honda	B	22	42m 38.569s 103.480mph/ 166.536km/h
2	**Jorge Lorenzo**	SPA	1	Yamaha Factory Racing	Yamaha	B	22	42m 42.009s
3	**Dani Pedrosa**	SPA	26	Repsol Honda Team	Honda	B	22	42m 43.620s
4	**Andrea Dovizioso**	ITA	4	Repsol Honda Team	Honda	B	22	42m 44.511s
5	**Marco Simoncelli**	ITA	58	San Carlo Honda Gresini	Honda	B	22	42m 45.927s
6	**Ben Spies**	USA	11	Yamaha Factory Racing	Yamaha	B	22	42m 49.037s
7	**Valentino Rossi**	ITA	46	Ducati Team	Ducati	B	22	42m 55.000s
8	**Colin Edwards**	USA	5	Monster Yamaha Tech 3	Yamaha	B	22	43m 04.862s
9	**Nicky Hayden**	USA	69	Ducati Team	Ducati	B	22	43m 05.985s
10	**Hiroshi Aoyama**	JPN	7	San Carlo Honda Gresini	Honda	B	22	43m 07.489s
11	**Cal Crutchlow**	GBR	35	Monster Yamaha Tech 3	Yamaha	B	22	43m 13.108s
12	**Hector Barbera**	SPA	8	Mapfre Aspar Team MotoGP	Ducati	B	22	43m 13.398s
13	**Karel Abraham**	CZE	17	Cardion AB Motoracing	Ducati	B	22	43m 16.526s
	Toni Elias	SPA	24	LCR Honda MotoGP	Honda	B	18	DNF
	Loris Capirossi	ITA	65	Pramac Racing Team	Ducati	B	1	DNF
	Randy de Puniet	FRA	14	Pramac Racing Team	Ducati	B	0	DNF

Fastest lap: Casey Stoner, on lap 13, 1m 55.366s, 104.318mph/167.883km/h.

Lap record: Casey Stoner, AUS (Ducati), 1m 55.153s, 104.510mph/168.193km/h (2008).

Event best maximum speed: Hector Barbera, 205.200mph/330.200km/h (race).

Qualifying

Weather: Dry
Air Temp: 22° Humidity: 31%
Track Temp: 24°

1	Stoner	1m 54.137s
2	Pedrosa	1m 54.342s
3	Lorenzo	1m 54.947s
4	Simoncelli	1m 54.988s
5	Spies	1m 55.095s
6	Barbera	1m 55.223s
7	Dovizioso	1m 55.229s
8	Crutchlow	1m 55.578s
9	Rossi	1m 55.637s
10	Edwards	1m 55.647s
11	De Puniet	1m 55.656s
12	Aoyama	1m 55.724s
13	Hayden	1m 55.881s
14	Capirossi	1m 56.323s
15	Abraham	1m 56.665s
16	Elias	1m 57.992s

Fastest race laps

1	Stoner	1m 55.366s
2	Pedrosa	1m 55.392s
3	Lorenzo	1m 55.730s
4	Spies	1m 55.812s
5	Dovizioso	1m 55.837s
6	Simoncelli	1m 55.871s
7	Rossi	1m 56.053s
8	Aoyama	1m 56.493s
9	Hayden	1m 56.600s
10	Edwards	1m 56.615s
11	Barbera	1m 56.663s
12	Abraham	1m 56.680s
13	Crutchlow	1m 56.828s
14	Elias	1m 57.957s
15	Capirossi	2m 16.031s

Championship Points

1	Stoner	25
2	Lorenzo	20
3	Pedrosa	16
4	Dovizioso	13
5	Simoncelli	11
6	Spies	10
7	Rossi	9
8	Edwards	8
9	Hayden	7
10	Aoyama	6
11	Crutchlow	5
12	Barbera	4
13	Abraham	3

Team Points

1	Repsol Honda Team	38
2	Yamaha Factory Racing	30
3	San Carlo Honda Gresini	17
4	Ducati Team	16
5	Monster Yamaha Tech 3	13
6	Mapfre Aspar Team MotoGP	4
7	Cardion AB Motoracing	3

Constructor Points

1	Honda	25
2	Yamaha	20
3	Ducati	9

Grid order	1	2	3	4	5	6	7	8	9	10	11	12	13	14	15	16	17	18	19	20	21	22	
27 STONER	1	27	27	27	27	26	26	26	26	26	26	27	27	27	27	27	27	27	27	27	27	27	1
26 PEDROSA	27	26	26	26	26	27	27	27	27	27	27	26	26	26	1	1	26	26	1	1	1	1	2
1 LORENZO	26	1	1	1	1	1	1	1	1	1	1	1	1	1	26	26	1	1	26	26	26	26	3
58 SIMONCELLI	4	4	4	4	4	4	4	58	58	58	58	58	58	58	58	58	4	4	4	4	4	4	4
11 SPIES	58	58	58	58	58	58	58	4	4	4	4	4	4	4	4	58	58	58	58	58	58	5
8 BARBERA	8	8	46	46	46	46	46	46	46	46	46	46	46	46	46	11	11	11	11	11	11	11	6
4 DOVIZIOSO	46	46	8	8	8	11	11	11	11	11	11	11	11	11	11	46	46	46	46	46	46	46	7
35 CRUTCHLOW	11	11	11	11	11	8	8	5	5	5	5	5	5	5	5	5	5	5	5	5	5	8
46 ROSSI	35	5	5	5	5	5	5	8	8	8	7	7	7	69	69	69	69	69	69	69	9
5 EDWARDS	5	35	35	35	35	7	7	7	7	7	8	7	69	69	7	7	7	7	7	7	10
14 DE PUNIET	24	7	7	7	7	35	35	35	69	69	69	69	8	8	8	8	8	35	8	8	35	11
7 AOYAMA	7	69	69	69	69	69	69	69	35	35	35	35	35	35	35	35	35	8	35	35	8	12
69 HAYDEN	69	24	24	17	17	17	17	17	17	17	17	17	17	17	17	17	17	17	17	17	13
65 CAPIROSSI	17	17	17	24	24	24	24	24	24	24	24	24	24	24	24	24						
17 ABRAHAM	65																					
24 ELIAS																						

65 Pit stop

Moto2

RACE DISTANCE: 20 laps, 66.860 miles/107.600km · RACE WEATHER: Dry (air 20°C, humidity 23%, track 21°C)

Pos.	Rider	Nat.	No.	Entrant	Machine	Laps	Time & Speed
1	**Stefan Bradl**	GER	65	Viessmann Kiefer Racing	Kalex	20	40m 38.549s 98.704mph/ 158.848km/h
2	**Andrea Iannone**	ITA	29	Speed Master	Suter	20	40m 42.879s
3	**Thomas Luthi**	SWI	12	Interwetten Paddock Moto2	Suter	20	40m 43.686s
4	**Alex de Angelis**	RSM	15	JIR Moto2	Motobi	20	40m 44.474s
5	**Yuki Takahashi**	JPN	72	Gresini Racing Moto2	Moriwaki	20	40m 45.170s
6	**Simone Corsi**	ITA	3	Ioda Racing Project	FTR	20	40m 52.766s
7	**Jules Cluzel**	FRA	16	Forward Racing	Suter	20	40m 52.806s
8	**Michele Pirro**	ITA	51	Gresini Racing Moto2	Moriwaki	20	40m 53.050s
9	**Bradley Smith**	GBR	38	Tech 3 Racing	Tech 3	20	40m 57.459s
10	**Julian Simon**	SPA	60	Mapfre Aspar Team Moto2	Suter	20	40m 57.723s
11	**Aleix Espargaro**	SPA	40	Pons HP 40	Pons Kalex	20	40m 57.991s
12	**Yonny Hernandez**	COL	68	Blusens-STX	FTR	20	40m 59.379s
13	**Dominique Aegerter**	SWI	77	Technomag-CIP	Suter	20	40m 59.386s
14	**Esteve Rabat**	SPA	34	Blusens-STX	FTR	20	40m 59.404s
15	**Max Neukirchner**	GER	76	MZ Racing Team	MZ-RE Honda	20	41m 05.352s
16	Axel Pons	SPA	80	Pons HP 40	Pons Kalex	20	41m 05.844s
17	Ricard Cardus	SPA	88	QMMF Racing Team	Moriwaki	20	41m 06.629s
18	Kenan Sofuoglu	TUR	54	Technomag-CIP	Suter	20	41m 06.761s
19	Mike di Meglio	FRA	63	Tech 3 Racing	Tech 3	20	41m 13.488s
20	Mika Kallio	FIN	36	Marc VDS Racing Team	Suter	20	41m 13.511s
21	Claudio Corti	ITA	71	Italtrans Racing Team	Suter	20	41m 16.531s
22	Pol Espargaro	SPA	44	HP Tuenti Speed Up	FTR	20	41m 22.040s
23	Valentin Debise	FRA	53	Speed Up	FTR	20	41m 22.208s
24	Kenny Noyes	USA	9	Avintia-STX	FTR	20	41m 26.025s
25	Xavier Simeon	BEL	19	Tech 3 B	Tech 3	20	41m 26.304s
26	Javier Fores	SPA	21	Mapfre Aspar Team Moto2	Suter	20	41m 28.904s
27	Randy Krummenacher	SWI	4	GP Team Switzerland Kiefer Racing	Kalex	20	41m 29.093s
28	Alex Baldolini	ITA	25	Forward Racing	Suter	20	41m 43.428s
29	Robertino Pietri	VEN	39	Italtrans Racing Team	Suter	20	41m 48.221s
30	Raffaele de Rosa	ITA	35	Desguaces La Torre G22	Moriwaki	20	41m 48.330s
31	Scott Redding	GBR	45	Marc VDS Racing Team	Suter	20	42m 02.292s
32	Nasser Hasan Al Malki	QAT	96	QMMF Racing Team	Moriwaki	20	42m 17.654s
	Ratthapark Wilairot	THA	14	Thai Honda Singha SAG	FTR	10	DNF
	Kev Coghlan	GBR	49	Aeroport de Castello	FTR	6	DNF
	Marc Marquez	SPA	93	Team CatalunyaCaixa Repsol	Suter	4	DNF
	Santiago Hernandez	COL	64	SAG Team	FTR	4	DNF
	Anthony West	AUS	13	MZ Racing Team	MZ-RE Honda	4	DNF
	Mattia Pasini	ITA	75	Ioda Racing Project	FTR	3	DNF
	Mashel Al Naimi	QAT	95	QMMF Racing Team	Moriwaki	0	DNF

Fastest lap: Alex de Angelis, on lap 9, 2m 01.003s, 99.458mph/160.062km/h (record).
Previous lap record: Thomas Luthi, SWI (Moriwaki), 2m 02.537s, 98.213mph/158.058km/h (2010).
Event best maximum speed: Bradley Smith, 173.900mph/279.900km/h (free practice 3).

Qualifying: Dry
Air: 22° Humidity: 14% Ground: 24°

1	Bradl	2m 00.168s
2	Marquez	2m 00.375s
3	Luthi	2m 00.996s
4	Takahashi	2m 01.179s
5	Cluzel	2m 01.408s
6	Simon	2m 01.430s
7	Smith	2m 01.442s
8	De Angelis	2m 01.465s
9	Pirro	2m 01.479s
10	Redding	2m 01.564s
11	Corsi	2m 01.574s
12	Neukirchner	2m 01.741s
13	Pasini	2m 01.893s
14	A. Espargaro	2m 01.895s
15	Aegerter	2m 01.895s
16	Iannone	2m 01.903s
17	Rabat	2m 02.154s
18	Corti	2m 02.237s
19	Di Meglio	2m 02.352s
20	Y. Hernandez	2m 02.392s
21	Fores	2m 02.397s
22	Cardus	2m 02.505s
23	Pons	2m 02.529s
24	P. Espargaro	2m 02.536s
25	Kallio	2m 02.549s
26	Debise	2m 02.828s
27	Wilairot	2m 02.838s
28	Sofuoglu	2m 02.847s
29	Krummenacher	2m 02.897s
30	Pietri	2m 03.151s
31	Baldolini	2m 03.246s
32	S. Hernandez	2m 03.264s
33	Coghlan	2m 03.276s
34	Noyes	2m 03.461s
35	Simeon	2m 03.657s
36	De Rosa	2m 03.684s
37	West	2m 04.043s
38	Al Naimi	2m 04.875s
39	Al Malki	2m 05.299s

Fastest race laps

1	De Angelis	2m 01.003s
2	Bradl	2m 01.038s
3	Takahashi	2m 01.039s
4	Iannone	2m 01.170s
5	Marquez	2m 01.216s
6	Luthi	2m 01.353s
7	Corsi	2m 01.394s
8	Cluzel	2m 01.398s
9	Simon	2m 01.774s
10	Pirro	2m 01.782s
11	Y. Hernandez	2m 01.808s
12	Rabat	2m 01.873s
13	A. Espargaro	2m 01.902s
14	Aegerter	2m 01.927s
15	Sofuoglu	2m 01.969s
16	Neukirchner	2m 02.073s
17	Pons	2m 02.115s
18	Smith	2m 02.126s
19	Kallio	2m 02.174s
20	Cardus	2m 02.248s
21	Corti	2m 02.667s
22	Di Meglio	2m 02.712s
23	Fores	2m 02.726s
24	Debise	2m 02.768s
25	P. Espargaro	2m 02.933s
26	Coghlan	2m 03.029s
27	Wilairot	2m 03.099s
28	Noyes	2m 03.226s
29	Krummenacher	2m 03.250s
30	Simeon	2m 03.358s
31	Redding	2m 03.537s
32	Pasini	2m 03.562s
33	Baldolini	2m 03.729s
34	De Rosa	2m 04.249s
35	Pietri	2m 04.290s
36	S. Hernandez	2m 04.415s
37	West	2m 04.893s
38	Al Malki	2m 05.107s

Championship Points

1	Bradl	25
2	Iannone	20
3	Luthi	16
4	De Angelis	13
5	Takahashi	11
6	Corsi	10
7	Cluzel	9
8	Pirro	8
9	Smith	7
10	Simon	6
11	A. Espargaro	5
12	Y. Hernandez	4
13	Aegerter	3
14	Rabat	2
15	Neukirchner	1

Constructor Points

1	Kalex	25
2	Suter	20
3	Motobi	13
4	Moriwaki	11
5	FTR	10
6	Tech 3	7
7	Pons Kalex	5
8	MZ-RE Honda	1

125cc

RACE DISTANCE: 18 laps, 60.174 miles/96.840km · RACE WEATHER: Dry (air 23°C, humidity 11%, track 25°C)

Pos.	Rider	Nat.	No.	Entrant	Machine	Laps	Time & Speed
1	**Nicolas Terol**	SPA	18	Bankia Aspar Team 125cc	Aprilia	18	38m 28.687s 93.830mph/ 151.005km/h
2	**Sandro Cortese**	GER	11	Intact-Racing Team Germany	Aprilia	18	38m 36.397s
3	**Sergio Gadea**	SPA	33	Pev-Blusens-SMX-Paris Hilton	Aprilia	18	38m 37.834s
4	**Efren Vazquez**	SPA	7	Avant-AirAsia-Ajo	Derbi	18	38m 38.201s
5	**Jonas Folger**	GER	94	Red Bull Ajo MotorSport	Aprilia	18	38m 38.385s
6	**Johann Zarco**	FRA	5	Avant-AirAsia-Ajo	Derbi	18	38m 43.947s
7	**Alberto Moncayo**	SPA	23	Andalucia Banca Civica	Aprilia	18	38m 44.039s
8	**Luis Salom**	SPA	39	RW Racing GP	Aprilia	18	38m 44.383s
9	**Maverick Vinales**	SPA	25	Pev-Blusens-SMX-Paris Hilton	Aprilia	18	38m 44.597s
10	**Miguel Oliveira**	POR	44	Andalucia Banca Civica	Aprilia	18	38m 56.083s
11	**Hector Faubel**	SPA	55	Bankia Aspar Team 125cc	Aprilia	18	39m 11.250s
12	**Jasper Iwema**	NED	53	Ongetta-Abbink Metaal	Aprilia	18	39m 12.459s
13	**Danny Kent**	GBR	52	Red Bull Ajo MotorSport	Aprilia	18	39m 12.688s
14	**Simone Grotzkyj**	ITA	15	Phonica Racing	Aprilia	18	39m 12.959s
15	**Louis Rossi**	FRA	96	Matteoni Racing	Aprilia	18	39m 18.717s
16	Danny Webb	GBR	99	Mahindra Racing	Mahindra	18	39m 19.111s
17	Niklas Ajo	FIN	31	TT Motion Events Racing	Aprilia	18	39m 30.232s
18	Taylor Mackenzie	GBR	17	Phonica Racing	Aprilia	18	39m 31.618s
19	Zulfahmi Khairuddin	MAL	63	Airasia-Sic-Ajo	Derbi	18	39m 33.879s
20	Luigi Morciano	ITA	3	Team Italia FMI	Aprilia	18	39m 33.960s
21	Marcel Schrotter	GER	77	Mahindra Racing	Mahindra	18	39m 34.083s
22	Alessandro Tonucci	ITA	19	Team Italia FMI	Aprilia	18	39m 41.145s
23	Jakub Kornfeil	CZE	84	Ongetta-Centro Seta	Aprilia	18	39m 59.316s
24	Daniel Kartheininger	GER	12	Caretta Technology Forward Team	KTM	18	39m 59.479s
25	Harry Stafford	GBR	21	Ongetta-Centro Seta	Aprilia	18	39m 59.485s
26	Giulian Pedone	SWI	30	Phonica Racing	Aprilia	18	40m 23.074s
27	Francesco Mauriello	ITA	43	WTR-Ten10 Racing	Aprilia	18	40m 23.235s
28	Adrian Martin	SPA	26	Bankia Aspar Team 125cc	Aprilia	14	39m 57.832s
	Joan Perello	SPA	36	Matteoni Racing	Aprilia	9	DNF
	Hiroki Ono	JPN	76	Caretta Technology Forward Team	KTM	7	DNF

Fastest lap: Nicolas Terol, on lap 3, 2m 06.463s, 95.164mph/153.151km/h.
Lap record: Scott Redding, GBR (Aprilia), 2m 05.695s, 95.745mph/154.087km/h (2008).
Event best maximum speed: Sergio Gadea, 144.000mph/231.800km/h (race).

Qualifying: Dry
Air: 24° Humidity: 10% Ground: 26°

1	Terol	2m 06.605s
2	Cortese	2m 06.695s
3	Vazquez	2m 07.651s
4	Gadea	2m 07.857s
5	Faubel	2m 08.062s
6	Folger	2m 08.298s
7	Zarco	2m 08.582s
8	Moncayo	2m 08.683s
9	Vinales	2m 09.218s
10	Salom	2m 09.331s
11	Rossi	2m 09.466s
12	Oliveira	2m 09.487s
13	Kent	2m 09.705s
14	Grotzkyj	2m 09.835s
15	Martin	2m 09.859s
16	Ajo	2m 10.091s
17	Khairuddin	2m 10.161s
18	Ono	2m 10.223s
19	Morciano	2m 10.269s
20	Mackenzie	2m 10.373s
21	Iwema	2m 10.559s
22	Schrotter	2m 10.602s
23	Webb	2m 10.608s
24	Tonucci	2m 11.335s
25	Perello	2m 11.699s
26	Kornfeil	2m 12.180s
27	Pedone	2m 12.341s
28	Stafford	2m 13.379s
29	Kartheininger	2m 13.769s
30	Mauriello	2m 14.994s

Outside 107%

Kumar	2m 15.620s

Fastest race laps

1	Terol	2m 06.463s
2	Faubel	2m 07.313s
3	Cortese	2m 07.332s
4	Vazquez	2m 07.490s
5	Zarco	2m 07.658s
6	Folger	2m 07.806s
7	Salom	2m 07.947s
8	Gadea	2m 07.951s
9	Vinales	2m 08.029s
10	Moncayo	2m 08.070s
11	Oliveira	2m 08.522s
12	Iwema	2m 08.805s
13	Grotzkyj	2m 08.988s
14	Kent	2m 09.190s
15	Martin	2m 09.253s
16	Mackenzie	2m 09.342s
17	Ono	2m 09.644s
18	Rossi	2m 09.715s
19	Webb	2m 09.783s
20	Ajo	2m 10.010s
21	Morciano	2m 10.462s
22	Schrotter	2m 10.575s
23	Khairuddin	2m 10.691s
24	Tonucci	2m 11.086s
25	Kartheininger	2m 11.879s
26	Stafford	2m 11.900s
27	Kornfeil	2m 12.065s
28	Perello	2m 12.481s
29	Pedone	2m 12.712s
30	Mauriello	2m 12.934s

Championship Points

1	Terol	25
2	Cortese	20
3	Gadea	16
4	Vazquez	13
5	Folger	11
6	Zarco	10
7	Moncayo	9
8	Salom	8
9	Vinales	7
10	Oliveira	6
11	Faubel	5
12	Iwema	4
13	Kent	3
14	Grotzkyj	2
15	Rossi	1

Constructor Points

1	Aprilia	25
2	Derbi	13

FIM WORLD CHAMPIONSHIP · ROUND 2

SPANISH
GRAND PRIX

JEREZ CIRCUIT

Spear tackle, but no red card! Stoner
eyes the apex he will never reach,
while Rossi's "ambition outweighs
his talent".
Photo: Gold & Goose

Above: Rossi, his engine still running, is helped by a host of marshals; Stoner struggles to restart his bike with just one.

Photo: Gold & Goose

"DID your ambition outweigh your talent?" Casey Stoner's response to Rossi's post-race apology left the Italian rider (still with his helmet on) wondering what "outweigh" meant, and listening TV viewers laughing at the impudence. But Rossi had deserved it.

The key moment of what otherwise might have been a fascinating second race, on a damp, but drying track, came on the eighth of 27 laps. Rossi had qualified badly after crashing in the crucial hour (one of seven to fall on the quirky and temperature-sensitive Jerez surface), but the rain had changed everything, and he had come bounding through to the leading group with his tail high. Now he was third, and looking for a way past Stoner to chase down Simoncelli. Then, at the first corner, he blundered. Too fast, he swerved inside Stoner, lost the front wheel and slid low-side down into the side of the Honda.

What followed was almost operatic. Stoner was left tumbling on the track, but before he had parted company with his Honda, he'd flicked the kill-switch, to protect the precious engine. Rossi was half-trapped under both bikes, but crucially kept his engine going. A small crowd of white-clad marshals rushed to help him, and patted him on the back as he found first gear and took off, now second from last. Only one attended Stoner, frantically trying to restart his undamaged Honda; the rest joined him only after Rossi had gone. But while they tried for a bit, push starting the RS212V was never going to work. Not uphill, and not without the locking pins needed to bypass the slipper clutch. Most especially on Stoner's bike, for HRC confirmed to *MOTOCOURSE* that he uses the lightest slipper spring loading of all three riders. The Australian was left to shake his fist as Rossi came flying by again, recovering a gap of just under 30 seconds to pull through once more to a fifth he hardly deserved.

The recriminations were widespread. After lambasting Rossi, Stoner included race management and the federation in his wide-ranging condemnation of what he saw as blatant favouritism by the marshals. "It was completely unfair, but riders up against Rossi have to deal with this," he said. The incident was formally investigated at Estoril, and the marshals exonerated, while a debate within Race Direction concluded that bike racing's unique rules allowing marshals to help a rider get going again should not be changed, but reminded all that the safety of the marshals was paramount. At the same time, with four-strokes in all three classes for 2012, the restart problem would need more study – perhaps self-starters would be an answer?

And Honda modified the clutch so that the slipper mechanism would automatically disengage for push starts in future.

The postponement of the Japanese GP meant that there was a long break between this first European GP and the next, almost a full month away. It was a blessing for anyone in any kind of trouble.

Like Pedrosa, whose arm and shoulder problems at first had been diagnosed as a pinching of a nerve junction, but who since had been given a different medical answer (constriction to the artery in certain positions), with the hope that it might be relieved by surgery. Now he also had the time to have the operation.

Pedrosa was the butt of another argument, whereby Rossi had proposed to the Safety Commission that MotoGP should adopt a 125-class rule with a minimum weight for both bike and rider. Rossi had watched tiny Dani (160cm, 51kg) accelerate away from the start line often enough to resent the Spaniard's power-to-weight advantage, but this call was prompted by his pal Simoncelli (183/72), who argued the case strongly. His extra size and weight cost him not only acceleration and top speed, but more seriously also fuel consumption. At the end of the race at Qatar, he explained, his fuel saving program had turned his performance right down, while other Honda riders had been able to enjoy full power.

Various points of view were aired, some arguing that any performance advantage a light rider might enjoy was negated by a bigger rider's ability to muscle the bike around more. The idea would die away over the coming weeks, but not before Pedrosa had his say: "This question has followed me throughout my career. But when I came to MotoGP, many said I wouldn't be able to manage a big bike. Now it's the other way. Maybe I should take some medicine to make my-

self bigger. Or maybe bigger riders should try what it is like to be small."

Rossi and Hayden, against the improved Japanese rivals, were still struggling with poor steering due to a lack of feel and grip. Hayden was particularly downcast when his qualifying time was slower than it had been the year before. Ducati used the forthcoming break for both riders to test the 2012 machine – with unexpected results, when a small-engine version of the bike surfaced later in the year as their handling problems continued.

There was a familiar grin back in the Suzuki garage, where Bautista's place had been taken by former factory rider John Hopkins. The American had been with Suzuki from 2003 to 2007, then had switched to Kawasaki for a career meltdown. He had been hurt in a bad crash mid-2008, then had been left jobless when Kawasaki withdrew. A mid-grid Superbike ride had been the best he could muster, and further injuries had followed. He told a 'to-hell-and-back' story of how his life had descended into angry drunkenness, and how he had quit drinking and turned it all around again. Now he had a ride in BSB with the Suzuki team run by the same dealership as the MotoGP team, and one condition was that he should race the GP bike if at all possible. His chance had come, and gamely he made the most of it.

Jerez set another kind of pattern for the forthcoming races: bad weather. The first two days were dry and fine, but race day was cold, wet and difficult – the first wet race since Malaysia, 2009. The wet tyres were getting ripped to bits on the drying track. Dovizioso even pitted for a tyre change.

The riders would have to get used to bad weather after a mercifully dry 2010. As for the 123,750 fans, their discomfort was alleviated by a most varied and unpredictable race.

MOTOGP RACE – 27 laps

It looked like Stoner's race as he dominated practice, then took his first pole at what has always been a bogey track. He led warm-up as well. It was the first time he had ridden his new Honda in the wet.

Above: Hayden, here heading Edwards and co, was fast, then slow, but on the rostrum anyway.

Above top left: One more lap and it would have been Aoyama in third.

Above left: Simoncelli led comfortably – until disaster struck.

Left: Jorge Lorenzo scored an important win as the 'Stoner Steamroller' failed to score.

Photos: Gold & Goose

Pedrosa and Lorenzo were alongside; Spies, Simoncelli and Dovizioso next; with Crutchlow flanking team-mate Edwards on a third row led by de Puniet's private Ducati; both factory Ducatis were on row four.

To be fair, Rossi had been near the front in free practice, but had lost his chance when he fell. Stoner, Aoyama, Spies, Edwards, Abraham and (inevitably) de Puniet also crashed in qualifying.

Stoner took the early lead, with Lorenzo following and Simoncelli third. Pedrosa was fourth through the first timing stage, but had dropped to ninth by the end of lap one. He was sliding badly and feeling cautious: it would take five or six laps before he would assume his proper speed.

Rossi was eighth and on the charge, up to fourth and within two seconds by the time Simoncelli had closed on the leaders on lap three. "I was really excited because of the chances of the wet: the bike works well and it is less strain on my shoulder." Too excited, as he later admitted.

Simoncelli overtook Lorenzo at the first corner and Stoner at the Dry Sack hairpin at the end of the back straight, all on lap six. He was leading a MotoGP race for the first time and soon was opening up a gap as his rivals chose a more cautious approach.

At the start of lap eight came the Rossi/Stoner incident, which promoted Hayden to third. He'd started well, then got ahead of Spies and the already troubled Dovizioso, following Rossi through. Spies was three seconds behind, with Pedrosa on his back wheel, but finding no way past.

Now Simoncelli was seriously pushing ahead, by 2.6 seconds as they started lap 12 – only to go flying at the first corner. He had shown his speed, and now also his headstrong nature.

This handed the lead to Lorenzo for the first time, and he was never to lose it in an exemplary ride. But by this stage, Pedrosa had come through to second and closed to within 1.1 seconds on lap 15. Lorenzo picked up his pace slightly and pulled steadily clear to the end.

At the same time, Pedrosa was starting to slow, with a combination of sliding tyres and failing arm strength. Spies had caught and passed Hayden, and over the next five or six laps he closed rapidly on the Spaniard. He was on him by lap

22, ahead by lap 24 and on the ground before he finished lap 25. "I think the tyres were the biggest factor," was his understated explanation.

That left Pedrosa alone and unmolested to the end.

Crutchlow had followed Pedrosa up, become stuck behind Dovizioso for a short time, then had found himself within sight of Hayden and promoted to fifth. On lap 19, Hayden ran into serious grip problems as his tyres gave up, and he slowed by a second or more per lap. The British rookie closed to within less than two seconds, a possible rostrum in sight, then slid off. His have-a-go attitude meant he got straight back on.

Hayden was in serious trouble, while Edwards had been carrying a steady pace midfield, and his tyres were stronger. He easily caught and passed the Ducati on lap 25, pulling clear by better than two seconds – only to stop at the first corner of the last lap. "It felt strange coming out of the last corner, then it just died," he said. His fuel pump had failed.

Aoyama had come through the midfield pack convincingly and was closing rapidly. With one more lap, he would have claimed the last rostrum spot.

Rossi was next, a long way back; then came Barbera, alone ahead of Abraham. Crutchlow was next, five seconds away. A long way back came Elias, who had managed to pass and then leave trailing Hopkins, who pleased his old team by both outqualifying and out-racing ex-Suzuki incumbent Capirossi. Dovizioso was a lap down, but got four points anyway in the depleted field. De Puniet had crashed out after dropping back within a lively mid-race battle involving Abraham, Barbera, de Puniet, Capirossi and Hopkins, broken up only when Rossi came through.

MOTO2 RACE – 26 laps

Stefan Bradl's early strength remained impressive with a second successive pole position, displacing Takahashi and Luthi. Rookies Marquez (of whom much was expected at home) and Smith led row two from the doughty de Angelis. Iannone, still adapting to his chassis change from FTR to the tricky new Suter, was 11th, on row four. Redding, also struggling with the new chassis, was one row behind.

Above: Suzuki substitute John Hopkins battles with Karel Abraham.

Above right: Iannone took Moto2 honours, his last win for a long spell.

Right: Corsi (3) Luthi (12) and Smith (38) fight for second place. In the end, Luthi prevailed.

Far right: Rookies in the rain: Britons Danny Kent (top) and Taylor Mackenzie (bottom) took fourth and fifth in the 125cc race.

Below right: A home win for Terol strengthened his early grip on the championship lead.

Photos: Gold & Goose

Former Jerez winner Smith got the jump, chased by Luthi and Takahashi, with Iannone back in eighth. Then Corsi pushed through to the front for four laps, only to be displaced by Luthi, who opened up a small, but handy gap.

By now, however, Takahashi had crashed out and Iannone was up to second. He rapidly closed up the 1.3 seconds and was leaning on the Swiss rider by lap 13. Next time around, Luthi slid on the exit from the final hairpin, giving the Italian the chance to move cleanly past on the pit straight.

The pair pulled away to the end, with Corsi hanging on to third, while Smith lost touch slightly.

Bradl had made a mediocre start, finishing lap one in sixth, but by half-distance, he was closing steadily. He caught Smith on lap 16 and went straight past; the issue seemed resolved. But the Briton stayed close and was pushing harder as the end approached. On the penultimate lap, Bradl touched a white line at the apex of the corner before the back straight, giving Smith the chance to get ahead. Head down, he stayed there.

Simon had been alone in sixth for much of the race, and stayed that way to the end.

The ride of the day came from de Angelis. He'd jumped forward on the line, stopped again, but had been penalised. He was tenth on lap three and rejoined after his ride-through penalty in 32nd. Then he gave a demonstration to most of the Moto2 grid, passing one or two riders every lap, up to 15th by half-distance. Not finished yet, he carried on sweeping through and was up to seventh by the end, by now well clear of the next pair: GP rookie Coghlan impressively leading class rookie Pirro. Their group had been broken up by the

Cortese had taken pole, ahead of team-mates Terol and Faubel; Vazquez headed row two.

It was Terol who ran away from the start, better than two seconds clear after two laps. Vazquez led the next group from rookie Oliveira and Faubel.

Oliveira crashed out spectacularly at the end of lap six; by now, Faubel had got ahead and closed up on Terol. The two team-mates soon began to pull well clear, in a class of their own.

Their battle was absorbing. Faubel took the lead from laps eight to ten, then again from laps 17 to 21. But Terol was right with him and biding his time. As they started the 22nd, he dived past into the first corner, opening up a small, but telling lead. Faubel crashed on the last lap trying to get back at him, but scrambled back on board to finish 11th.

Behind them, Zarco had got to the front of the next tight quartet, only to be displaced first by Cortese and then by Vazquez, with Folger in close attendance.

The 18th lap was crucial. First Vazquez slipped off and then Cortese, leaving the youngsters alone for their rostrum finish.

Young British rookies Danny Kent and Taylor Mackenzie behind them got their reward for being steadfast throughout, almost ten seconds adrift and two seconds apart. The re-mounted Cortese was sixth; then came Kornfeil, five seconds ahead of Ono's KTM. Vazquez was back on board and on his tail, with tenth going to Malaysia's Khairuddin. The Mahindra (née Malaguti/Loncin/Vespa) took its first points in its latest guise, with Schrotter 13th; team-mate Danny Webb had crashed out while lying 11th.

arrival from behind of another GP new boy, Max Neukirchner, 31st on lap one.

West was behind him, the Australian disappointed after running a strong seventh in the middle part of the race, his legendary wet-weather skills overcoming the usual problems of his overweight MZ chassis. But his team had elected to run without a front mudguard, and by the end he was unsighted by the amount of spray misting up his visor.

Marquez's race lasted for only ten laps. Until then, it had progressed well enough as he climbed through the field to fifth place and set his sights on Smith. But the last man he'd passed had been the enthusiastic Frenchman Cluzel, who, in trying to redeem his position, had knocked both of them down.

125cc RACE – 23 laps

. . . .

The first race of the day got the worst of the conditions, turning into an attenuate battle of attrition, with a lengthy and distinguished crash list, several of whom remounted.

CIRCUITO DE JEREZ

27 laps
Length: 4.423 km. / 2.748 miles
Width: 11m

Expo '92 100/62
265/165
Alex Criville 160/99
Ferrari 180/112
Michelin 75/47
Peluqui 115/72
Jorge Martinez Aspar 130/81
Turn 4 160/99
Angel Nieto 100/62
Turn 7 155/96
Ducados 75/47
Dry Sack 75/47
Sito Pons 130/81
275/171

Key
96/60 kph/mph
Gear

MotoGP

RACE DISTANCE: 27 laps, 74.205 miles/119.421km · RACE WEATHER: Dry (air 17°C, humidity 90%, track 15°C)

Pos.	Rider	Nat.	No.	Entrant	Machine	Tyres	Laps	Time & speed
1	**Jorge Lorenzo**	SPA	1	Yamaha Factory Racing	Yamaha	B	27	50m 49.046s 87.613mph/ 141.000km/h
2	**Dani Pedrosa**	SPA	26	Repsol Honda Team	Honda	B	27	51m 08.385s
3	**Nicky Hayden**	USA	69	Ducati Team	Ducati	B	27	51m 18.131s
4	**Hiroshi Aoyama**	JPN	7	San Carlo Honda Gresini	Honda	B	27	51m 18.597s
5	**Valentino Rossi**	ITA	46	Ducati Team	Ducati	B	27	51m 51.273s
6	**Hector Barbera**	SPA	8	Mapfre Aspar Team MotoGP	Ducati	B	27	51m 57.486s
7	**Karel Abraham**	CZE	17	Cardion AB Motoracing	Ducati	B	27	52m 03.166s
8	**Cal Crutchlow**	GBR	35	Monster Yamaha Tech 3	Yamaha	B	27	52m 08.156s
9	**Toni Elias**	SPA	24	LCR Honda MotoGP	Honda	B	27	52m 31.952s
10	**John Hopkins**	USA	21	Rizla Suzuki MotoGP	Suzuki	B	27	52m 37.441s
11	**Loris Capirossi**	ITA	65	Pramac Racing Team	Ducati	B	27	52m 40.922s
12	**Andrea Dovizioso**	ITA	4	Repsol Honda Team	Honda	B	26	51m 39.633s
	Colin Edwards	USA	5	Monster Yamaha Tech 3	Yamaha	B	26	DNF
	Ben Spies	USA	11	Yamaha Factory Racing	Yamaha	B	24	DNF
	Randy de Puniet	FRA	14	Pramac Racing Team	Ducati	B	16	DNF
	Marco Simoncelli	ITA	58	San Carlo Honda Gresini	Honda	B	11	DNF
	Casey Stoner	AUS	27	Repsol Honda Team	Honda	B	7	DNF

Fastest lap: Valentino Rossi, on lap 4, 1m 48.753s, 90.976mph/146.412km/h.

Lap record: Dani Pedrosa, SPA (Honda), 1m 39.731s, 99.206mph/159.657km/h (2010).

Event best maximum speed: Dani Pedrosa, 174.900mph/281.500km/h (qualifying practice).

Qualifying

Weather: Dry
Air Temp: 22° Humidity: 31%
Track Temp: 30°

1	Stoner	1m 38.757s
2	Pedrosa	1m 38.915s
3	Lorenzo	1m 38.918s
4	Spies	1m 39.390s
5	Simoncelli	1m 39.486s
6	Dovizioso	1m 39.709s
7	De Puniet	1m 39.892s
8	Edwards	1m 39.895s
9	Crutchlow	1m 40.019s
10	Aoyama	1m 40.168s
11	Hayden	1m 40.175s
12	Rossi	1m 40.185s
13	Barbera	1m 40.217s
14	Hopkins	1m 40.310s
15	Capirossi	1m 40.523s
16	Abraham	1m 40.601s
17	Elias	1m 41.114s

Fastest race laps

1	Rossi	1m 48.753s
2	Simoncelli	1m 48.780s
3	Lorenzo	1m 48.871s
4	Stoner	1m 49.010s
5	Pedrosa	1m 49.177s
6	Hayden	1m 49.434s
7	Crutchlow	1m 49.581s
8	Dovizioso	1m 49.619s
9	Spies	1m 49.864s
10	Edwards	1m 49.959s
11	Hopkins	1m 50.540s
12	De Puniet	1m 50.553s
13	Barbera	1m 50.581s
14	Capirossi	1m 50.652s
15	Aoyama	1m 50.812s
16	Abraham	1m 51.065s
17	Elias	1m 52.897s

Championship Points

1	Lorenzo	45
2	Pedrosa	36
3	Stoner	25
4	Hayden	23
5	Rossi	20
6	Aoyama	19
7	Dovizioso	17
8	Barbera	14
9	Crutchlow	13
10	Abraham	12
11	Simoncelli	11
12	Spies	10
13	Edwards	8
14	Elias	7
15	Hopkins	6
16	Capirossi	5

Team Points

1	Repsol Honda Team	58
2	Yamaha Factory Racing	55
3	Ducati Team	43
4	San Carlo Honda Gresini	30
5	Monster Yamaha Tech 3	21
6	Mapfre Aspar Team MotoGP	14
7	Cardion AB Motoracing	12
8	LCR Honda MotoGP	7
9	Rizla Suzuki MotoGP	6
10	Pramac Racing Team	5

Constructor Points

1	Yamaha	45
2	Honda	45
3	Ducati	25
4	Suzuki	6

Grid order	1	2	3	4	5	6	7	8	9	10	11	12	13	14	15	16	17	18	19	20	21	22	23	24	25	26	27	
27 STONER	27	27	27	27	27	58	58	58	58	58	58	1	1	1	1	1	1	1	1	1	1	1	1	1	1	1	1	1
26 PEDROSA	1	1	1	1	1	27	27	1	1	1	1	26	26	26	26	26	26	26	26	26	26	26	11	26	26	26		2
1 LORENZO	58	58	58	58	58	1	46	69	69	69	26	11	11	11	11	11	11	11	11	11	11	11	26	5	5	69		3
11 SPIES	4	4	46	46	46	46	1	11	11	26	69	69	69	69	69	69	69	69	69	69	69	69	69	69	7			4
58 SIMONCELLI	11	11	4	4	4	69	69	26	26	11	11	35	35	35	35	35	35	35	5	5	5	5	5	7	7	46		5
4 DOVIZIOSO	69	46	69	69	69	4	4	4	35	35	5	5	5	5	5	5	5	7	7	7	7	7	46	46	8			6
14 DE PUNIET	5	69	11	11	11	11	11	35	35	5	14	14	17	17	17	17	7	8	46	46	46	46	8	8	17			7
5 EDWARDS	46	5	5	26	26	26	5	14	14	8	17	8	7	7	7	7	8	46	8	8	8	17	17	35				8
35 CRUTCHLOW	26	26	26	5	5	35	35	14	14	65	65	17	7	7	8	8	46	35	17	17	17	35	35	24				9
7 AOYAMA	35	35	35	35	35	5	8	65	65	8	8	14	14	14	46	46	21	21	35	35	35	24	24	21				10
69 HAYDEN	8	8	8	8	8	65	14	65	65	17	7	21	21	21	21	21	17	17	21	21	21	21	21	65				11
46 ROSSI	21	21	21	14	65	14	8	7	7	7	21	65	65	46	46	65	65	65	65	24	24	65	65					12
8 BARBERA	14	14	14	65	14	8	65	21	17	4	21	4	46	46	65	65	24	24	24	65	65	65	4	4				
21 HOPKINS	24	65	65	21	7	7	7	17	21	21	4	46	4	4	4	4	4	4	4	4	4	4						
65 CAPIROSSI	65	7	7	7	21	21	21	46	46	46	46	24	24	24	24	24												
17 ABRAHAM	7	17	17	17	17	17	17	24	24	24	24																	
24 ELIAS	17	24	24	24	24	24	24																					

4 Pit stop   4 Lapped rider

Moto2

RACE DISTANCE: 26 laps, 71.456 miles/114.998km · RACE WEATHER: Wet (air 17°C, humidity 89%, track 18°C)

Pos.	Rider	Nat.	No.	Entrant	Machine	Laps	Time & Speed
1	**Andrea Iannone**	ITA	29	Speed Master	Suter	26	49m 56.423s 85.850mph/ 138.162km/h
2	**Thomas Luthi**	SWI	12	Interwetten Paddock Moto2	Suter	26	50m 04.273s
3	**Simone Corsi**	ITA	3	Ioda Racing Project	FTR	26	50m 09.048s
4	**Bradley Smith**	GBR	38	Tech 3 Racing	Tech 3	26	50m 11.778s
5	**Stefan Bradl**	GER	65	Viessmann Kiefer Racing	Kalex	26	50m 14.273s
6	**Julian Simon**	SPA	60	Mapfre Aspar Team Moto2	Suter	26	50m 20.670s
7	**Alex de Angelis**	RSM	15	JIR Moto2	Motobi	26	50m 24.414s
8	**Kev Coghlan**	GBR	49	Aeroport de Castello	FTR	26	50m 32.604s
9	**Michele Pirro**	ITA	51	Gresini Racing Moto2	Moriwaki	26	50m 33.198s
10	**Max Neukirchner**	GER	76	MZ Racing Team	MZ-RE Honda	26	50m 37.830s
11	**Anthony West**	AUS	13	MZ Racing Team	MZ-RE Honda	26	50m 38.134s
12	**Ratthapark Wilairot**	THA	14	Thai Honda Singha SAG	FTR	26	50m 38.293s
13	**Mattia Pasini**	ITA	75	Ioda Racing Project	FTR	26	50m 38.736s
14	**Yonny Hernandez**	COL	68	Blusens-STX	FTR	26	50m 41.807s
15	**Esteve Rabat**	SPA	34	Blusens-STX	FTR	26	50m 43.616s
16	Kenan Sofuoglu	TUR	54	Technomag-CIP	Suter	26	50m 43.627s
17	Mika Kallio	FIN	36	Marc VDS Racing Team	Suter	26	50m 43.739s
18	Javier Fores	SPA	21	Mapfre Aspar Team Moto2	Suter	26	50m 47.100s
19	Xavier Simeon	BEL	19	Tech 3 B	Tech 3	26	50m 54.381s
20	Pol Espargaro	SPA	44	HP Tuenti Speed Up	FTR	26	50m 54.977s
21	Claudio Corti	ITA	71	Italtrans Racing Team	Suter	26	51m 03.890s
22	Ricard Cardus	SPA	88	QMMF Racing Team	Moriwaki	26	51m 07.348s
23	Scott Redding	GBR	45	Marc VDS Racing Team	Suter	26	51m 12.572s
24	Aleix Espargaro	SPA	40	Pons HP 40	Pons Kalex	26	51m 15.935s
25	Raffaele De Rosa	ITA	35	Desguaces La Torre G22	Moriwaki	26	51m 18.882s
26	Mike di Meglio	FRA	63	Tech 3 Racing	Tech 3	26	51m 23.176s
27	Randy Krummenacher	SWI	4	GP Team Switzerland Kiefer Racing	Kalex	26	51m 33.649s
28	Dominique Aegerter	SWI	77	Technomag-CIP	Suter	26	51m 39.261s
29	Kenny Noyes	USA	9	Avintia-STX	FTR	26	51m 50.955s
30	Valentin Debise	FRA	53	Speed Up	FTR	26	51m 53.543s
31	Santiago Hernandez	COL	64	SAG Team	FTR	25	50m 32.370s
32	Steven Odendaal	RSA	97	MS Racing	Suter	25	50m 32.815s
33	Mashel Al Naimi	QAT	95	QMMF Racing Team	Moriwaki	23	50m 30.878s
	Alex Baldolini	ITA	5	Forward Racing	Suter	12	DNF
	Marc Marquez	SPA	93	Team CatalunyaCaixa Repsol	Suter	10	DNF
	Jules Cluzel	FRA	16	Forward Racing	Suter	10	DNF
	Yuki Takahashi	JPN	72	Gresini Racing Moto2	Moriwaki	9	DNF
	Robertino Pietri	VEN	39	Italtrans Racing Team	Suter	4	DNF
	Lukasz Wargala	POL	99	Desguaces La Torre G22	Moriwaki	1	DNF

Fastest lap: Andrea Iannone, on lap 10, 1m 53.893s, 86.870mph/139.804km/h.
Lap record: Toni Elias, SPA (Moriwaki), 1m 44.710s, 94.489mph/152.065km/h (2010).
Event best maximum speed: Stefan Bradl, 157.500mph/253.500km/h (free practice 1).

Qualifying: Dry
Air: 26° Humidity: 25% Ground: 33°

1	Bradl	1m 42.706s
2	Takahashi	1m 42.988s
3	Luthi	1m 43.288s
4	Marquez	1m 43.332s
5	Smith	1m 43.500s
6	De Angelis	1m 43.613s
7	Pirro	1m 43.615s
8	A. Espargaro	1m 43.676s
9	Corti	1m 43.687s
10	Simon	1m 43.766s
11	Iannone	1m 43.782s
12	Sofuoglu	1m 43.860s
13	Redding	1m 43.897s
14	Kallio	1m 43.935s
15	Aegerter	1m 44.024s
16	Cluzel	1m 44.054s
17	Debise	1m 44.087s
18	Corsi	1m 44.188s
19	Cardus	1m 44.375s
20	Pons	1m 44.478s
21	Rabat	1m 44.521s
22	Y. Hernandez	1m 44.532s
23	Baldolini	1m 44.593s
24	Coghlan	1m 44.637s
25	Noyes	1m 44.648s
26	Fores	1m 44.692s
27	P. Espargaro	1m 44.722s
28	Krummenacher	1m 44.755s
29	Di Meglio	1m 44.921s
30	West	1m 45.037s
31	Wilairot	1m 45.103s
32	Simeon	1m 45.158s
33	De Rosa	1m 45.170s
34	Pasini	1m 45.184s
35	Pietri	1m 45.314s
36	Neukirchner	1m 45.578s
37	S. Hernandez	1m 45.613s
38	Odendaal	1m 46.342s
39	Al Naimi	1m 46.896s
40	Wargala	1m 48.892s

Fastest race laps

1	Iannone	1m 53.893s
2	Corsi	1m 53.997s
3	De Angelis	1m 54.291s
4	Wilairot	1m 54.365s
5	Marquez	1m 54.496s
6	Luthi	1m 54.517s
7	Takahashi	1m 54.745s
8	Smith	1m 54.773s
9	Coghlan	1m 54.894s
10	Simon	1m 54.910s
11	Pirro	1m 54.965s
12	Bradl	1m 55.000s
13	Neukirchner	1m 55.194s
14	Cluzel	1m 55.248s
15	Y. Hernandez	1m 55.356s
16	Pasini	1m 55.441s
17	De Rosa	1m 55.520s
18	West	1m 55.532s
19	Cardus	1m 55.581s
20	Rabat	1m 55.612s
21	Corti	1m 55.760s
22	P. Espargaro	1m 55.770s
23	Fores	1m 55.817s
24	Sofuoglu	1m 55.854s
25	Kallio	1m 55.971s
26	Noyes	1m 56.160s
27	Simeon	1m 56.242s
28	A. Espargaro	1m 56.335s
29	Redding	1m 56.519s
30	Di Meglio	1m 56.978s
31	Krummenacher	1m 57.739s
32	Baldolini	1m 57.964s
33	Debise	1m 58.023s
34	Aegerter	1m 58.030s
35	S. Hernandez	1m 58.496s
36	Pietri	1m 58.587s
37	Odendaal	1m 58.588s
38	Al Naimi	1m 58.783s
39	Wargala	2m 13.932s

Championship Points

1	Iannone	45
2	Bradl	36
3	Luthi	36
4	Corsi	26
5	De Angelis	22
6	Smith	20
7	Simon	16
8	Pirro	15
9	Takahashi	11
10	Cluzel	9
11	Coghlan	8
12	Neukirchner	7
13	Y. Hernandez	6
14	West	5
15	A. Espargaro	5
16	Wilairot	4
17	Pasini	3
18	Aegerter	3
19	Rabat	3

Constructor Points

1	Suter	45
2	Kalex	36
3	FTR	26
4	Motobi	22
5	Tech 3	20
6	Moriwaki	18
7	MZ-RE Honda	7
8	Pons Kalex	5

125cc

RACE DISTANCE: 23 laps, 63.211 miles/101.729km · RACE WEATHER: Wet (air 17°C, humidity 90%, track 20°C)

Pos.	Rider	Nat.	No.	Entrant	Machine	Laps	Time & Speed
1	**Nicolas Terol**	SPA	18	Bankia Aspar Team 125cc	Aprilia	23	44m 50.646s 84.575mph/ 136.110km/h
2	**Jonas Folger**	GER	94	Red Bull Ajo MotorSport	Aprilia	23	45m 08.092s
3	**Johann Zarco**	FRA	5	Avant-AirAsia-Ajo	Derbi	23	45m 14.601s
4	**Danny Kent**	GBR	52	Red Bull Ajo MotorSport	Aprilia	23	45m 23.529s
5	**Taylor Mackenzie**	GBR	17	Phonica Racing	Aprilia	23	45m 25.359s
6	**Sandro Cortese**	GER	11	Intact-Racing Team Germany	Aprilia	23	45m 42.161s
7	**Jakub Kornfeil**	CZE	84	Ongetta-Centro Seta	Aprilia	23	45m 45.566s
8	**Hiroki Ono**	JPN	76	Caretta Technology Forward Team	KTM	23	45m 50.810s
9	**Efren Vazquez**	SPA	7	Avant-AirAsia-Ajo	Derbi	23	45m 50.932s
10	**Zulfahmi Khairuddin**	MAL	63	Airasia-Sic-Ajo	Derbi	23	45m 51.045s
11	**Hector Faubel**	SPA	55	Bankia Aspar Team 125cc	Aprilia	23	45m 51.406s
12	**Adrian Martin**	SPA	26	Bankia Aspar Team 125cc	Aprilia	23	45m 58.385s
13	**Marcel Schrotter**	GER	77	Mahindra Racing	Mahindra	23	46m 10.356s
14	**Louis Rossi**	FRA	96	Matteoni Racing	Aprilia	23	46m 12.458s
15	**Josep Rodriguez**	SPA	28	Wild Wolf-Racc-MS	Aprilia	23	46m 13.764s
16	Alberto Moncayo	SPA	23	Andalucia Banca Civica	Aprilia	23	46m 14.686s
17	Simone Grotzkyj	ITA	15	Phonica Racing	Aprilia	23	46m 21.256s
18	Harry Stafford	GBR	21	Ongetta-Centro Seta	Aprilia	23	46m 21.598s
19	Alessandro Tonucci	ITA	19	Team Italia FMI	Aprilia	23	46m 46.000s
20	Luigi Morciano	ITA	3	Team Italia FMI	Aprilia	22	45m 03.283s
21	Daniel Ruiz	SPA	34	Larresport	Honda	22	45m 04.752s
22	Daniel Kartheininger	GER	12	Caretta Technology Forward Team	KTM	22	45m 18.245s
23	Joan Perello	SPA	36	Matteoni Racing	Aprilia	22	45m 28.547s
24	Kevin Hanus	GER	86	Team Hanusch	Honda	21	45m 07.173s
	Maverick Vinales	SPA	25	Pev-Blusens-SMX-Paris Hilton	Aprilia	15	DNF
	Sergio Gadea	SPA	33	Pev-Blusens-SMX-Paris Hilton	Aprilia	15	DNF
	Jasper Iwema	NED	53	Ongetta-Abbink Metaal	Aprilia	15	DNF
	Francesco Mauriello	ITA	43	WTR-Ten10 Racing	Aprilia	13	DNF
	Danny Webb	GBR	99	Mahindra Racing	Mahindra	10	DNF
	Luis Salom	SPA	39	RW Racing GP	Aprilia	9	DNF
	Giulian Pedone	SWI	30	Phonica Racing	Aprilia	8	DNF
	Miguel Oliveira	POR	44	Andalucia Banca Civica	Aprilia	5	DNF
	Niklas Ajo	FIN	31	TT Motion Events Racing	Aprilia	2	DNF

Fastest lap: Hector Faubel, on lap 13, 1m 55.605s, 85.584mph/137.734km/h.
Lap record: Julian Simon, SPA (Aprilia), 1m 47.057s, 92.417mph/148.731km/h (2009).
Event best maximum speed: Jasper Iwema, 134.700mph/216.800km/h (free practice 1).

Qualifying: Dry
Air: 24° Humidity: 32% Ground: 31°

1	Cortese	1m 47.399s
2	Terol	1m 47.608s
3	Faubel	1m 47.969s
4	Vazquez	1m 48.413s
5	Zarco	1m 48.601s
6	Salom	1m 48.791s
7	Folger	1m 48.799s
8	Oliveira	1m 48.825s
9	Kent	1m 49.181s
10	Moncayo	1m 49.247s
11	Gadea	1m 49.416s
12	Vinales	1m 49.463s
13	Rossi	1m 49.682s
14	Martin	1m 49.785s
15	Iwema	1m 49.975s
16	Mackenzie	1m 49.977s
17	Kornfeil	1m 50.025s
18	Khairuddin	1m 50.082s
19	Webb	1m 50.169s
20	Rodriguez	1m 50.258s
21	Ono	1m 50.276s
22	Grotzkyj	1m 50.367s
23	Schrotter	1m 50.465s
24	Ajo	1m 50.492s
25	Morciano	1m 50.611s
26	Tonucci	1m 50.971s
27	Stafford	1m 51.192s
28	Pedone	1m 51.687s
29	Kartheininger	1m 51.714s
30	Perello	1m 52.262s
31	Ruiz	1m 52.417s
32	Hanus	1m 53.236s
33	Mauriello	1m 54.097s
Outside 107%		
	Kumar	1m 55.366s

Fastest race laps

1	Faubel	1m 55.605s
2	Terol	1m 55.624s
3	Vinales	1m 55.742s
4	Folger	1m 55.975s
5	Cortese	1m 55.991s
6	Vazquez	1m 56.197s
7	Zarco	1m 56.319s
8	Oliveira	1m 56.422s
9	Salom	1m 56.474s
10	Kent	1m 56.676s
11	Gadea	1m 56.896s
12	Mackenzie	1m 56.968s
13	Kornfeil	1m 57.037s
14	Ono	1m 57.681s
15	Khairuddin	1m 57.768s
16	Martin	1m 58.184s
17	Schrotter	1m 58.576s
18	Rodriguez	1m 58.670s
19	Webb	1m 58.703s
20	Moncayo	1m 58.857s
21	Iwema	1m 58.957s
22	Rossi	1m 58.995s
23	Grotzkyj	1m 59.089s
24	Stafford	1m 59.145s
25	Mauriello	1m 59.743s
26	Tonucci	1m 59.946s
27	Morciano	1m 59.991s
28	Kartheininger	2m 00.821s
29	Perello	2m 00.954s
30	Ruiz	2m 01.360s
31	Ajo	2m 01.388s
32	Hanus	2m 03.382s
33	Pedone	2m 10.225s

Championship Points

1	Terol	50
2	Folger	31
3	Cortese	30
4	Zarco	26
5	Vazquez	20
6	Gadea	16
7	Kent	16
8	Mackenzie	11
9	Faubel	10
10	Kornfeil	9
11	Moncayo	9
12	Ono	8
13	Salom	8
14	Vinales	7
15	Khairuddin	6
16	Oliveira	6
17	Martin	4
18	Iwema	4
19	Schrotter	3
20	Rossi	3
21	Grotzkyj	2
22	Rodriguez	1

Constructor Points

1	Aprilia	50
2	Derbi	29
3	KTM	8
4	Mahindra	3

PORTUGUESE GRAND PRIX

ESTORIL CIRCUIT

First corner, and Lorenzo takes an early lead from Pedrosa; Stoner has been bullied out by Simoncelli. Behind Spies, Rossi muscles inside Dovizioso. There were few in the stands to see the action.
Photo: Gold & Goose

RIDER feuds are part of the psychological warfare intrinsic to any successful world championship. Estoril saw a flowering of them, which would bloom on through the races to come.

One was between Stoner and Rossi, the Australian expressing surprise at Rossi's difficulties in being competitive on the Ducati, casting aspersions on his riding manners and wondering pointedly why he was still complaining about his shoulder. For good measure, he gestured at him in free practice when he thought he was being followed, patting his leg as if to call a dog to heel.

Rossi responded in his own Press briefing. The Australian was unable to get over being beaten back at Laguna in 2008 and spoke too freely on topics he knew nothing about, he said: "He talks about my injury like he is the first doctor at the Melbourne Hospital of Shoulders." If anyone knows how to play the psycho game, it is Rossi, and he would soon find ways to benefit also from the other great war.

This was conducted face to face between champion Lorenzo and pretender Simoncelli. The Spaniard had given an interview criticising Simoncelli's gung-ho style, referring not only to the pass on Dovi at Qatar, but more to their clash at Valencia at the end of the 2010 season, when Simoncelli had swooped back across in front of his attempted inside pass, and they had collided.

The riposte came at the pre-event Press conference. "Your example was wrong," Simoncelli thundered repeatedly, looming large over the table as he leaned towards his critic. Lorenzo was trying to be reasonable, saying there would be no problem if it didn't happen again. And if it did, wondered Simoncelli, to great hilarity, "I will be arrested?"

The Italian emerged the hero of the confrontation, and Lorenzo (chastising the audience for laughing when "we are risking our lives") somehow was diminished, even though he had right on his side. Future events would prove that, starting with Sunday's race, when Simoncelli would crash out for a second race in succession and a third time that weekend. Rossi obviously would take any side that wasn't Lorenzo's, and a few days later he referred to the newest generation of MotoGP riders as "pussies" compared with his heroes from the golden age of the 500 two-strokes. He would discover different methods of exploiting the divisions in the coming races, but would his Ducati have the speed to make the most of them?

Ducati had brought a new electronics package for the factory riders, which both liked: it softened the savage throttle responses in the lower reaches and offered a more sophisticated traction control system. A setback for Hayden came on day one, with "a pretty big bang" indicating a major engine failure. He became the first to pull out a third engine from his year's allocation of six.

But Ducati's main problem remained handling, and Rossi and Hayden were looking forward to the post-race tests, the first of the season, when they would have a revised front chassis to evaluate. There was also a revised engine with a heavier crankshaft, to further soften response at the bottom. Yamaha had a new electronics package and a minor engine change to test, Honda nothing much at all – reflecting their various states of readiness.

Pedrosa was on tenterhooks following surgery to his left shoulder. The plate had been taken from his collarbone and tissue removed to ease the space for the crucial artery, but he explained there was no guarantee that the remedy would be successful. The injury had left the bone straight rather than the slight ess-shape it should be: "We will have to wait and see." His caution was rewarded with a complete cure, which he proved by taking a clear first win of the year.

Bautista was back, still on crutches, but passed fit to ride barely six weeks after his broken femur had been pinned. He deferred his own decision on racing until after first free practice, when he found that though weak in direction changes and two seconds off the pace, he was enjoying himself enough to carry on.

Ben Spies had a most unusual problem. With the bikes standing more than ten minutes on the grid – warm engines, brimmed fuel tanks – there is the risk of losing fuel due to expansion. To prevent this, Yamaha clamps off the overflow tube with a device that looks slightly medical, which is removed as mechanics depart before the warm-up lap. The forceps even have a big red tag dangling below the right clip-on to make them hard to miss. Somehow, though, they were overlooked by mechanics and only came to the rider's attention when the tag flapped up between the throttle and brake lever. "I almost hit Casey," he revealed. It took a couple of

Above: "I will be arrested?" Simoncelli and Lorenzo have a heated exchange.

Top left: Déjà vu: Rossi battled all race with Dovizioso, only to lose by inches.

Top right: IRTA chief Mike Trimby was delighted with 16 proposals to join MotoGP's B-class in 2012.

Top right centre: Rossi was developing a pensive look.

Right: Rookie Crutchlow menaced 250 champion Aoyama throughout.

Photos: Gold & Goose

laps to remove the clamp, but that left him worried about the function of the overflow pipe he'd ripped free. By then, he'd dropped back to tenth, his confidence and his race ruined.

Estoril marked the first stage of the rather rushed process of lining up new teams for MotoGP in 2012, under new and not yet defined 'Claiming Rule Team' regulations. Applications from interested teams had to be in by Friday, and IRTA general secretary Mike Trimby was cheered by a total of 16 applications, all from teams already within the paddock. Two of them had been discarded at once, leaving 14 teams and 21 riders. They would receive a full briefing detailing financial terms and have to start digging for deposits by the Catalunyan GP in five weeks' time.

In Moto2, away from the limelight of the front-runners, MZ was continuing its lone attempt to use a steel chassis. Although new rider Neukirchner had insisted on an FTR chassis for his effort, West had been given another different frame, made of steel tubes by a new German firm, IAMT. With each rider also on different suspension and brakes, the direction of the effort seemed confused. Then it went badly wrong when Neukirchner crashed in qualifying, flying directly home for an operation on a badly lacerated finger.

MOTOGP RACE – 28 laps

Changeable weather and track conditions complicated practice and qualifying, but Simoncelli was on top no matter what – until Lorenzo, winner at Estoril for the previous three years, shaded him by two-tenths at the end of the hour. The Italian had one more go, and was three-tenths inside Lorenzo's pole when he slipped off. Pedrosa was alongside – shrugging off the shoulder problems as "so far so good".

Stoner was a little out of sorts heading row two from Spies and Dovizioso; the satellite Yamahas – Edwards and track first-timer Crutchlow – were next. Only then came Rossi, with team-mate Hayden two rows further back. The front-end problems were proving resistant to setting changes and alterations to ride height: both had been quick in the first outings, but then had failed to improve along with the rest.

Lorenzo got a flying start, chased down the hill by Pedrosa and Simoncelli, with Stoner baulked by Pedrosa off the line and fourth into the first corner. He and Simoncelli tangled on the way out, and by the end of the lap, he was 1.8 seconds adrift of the two leaders.

Simoncelli had only got a couple of corners further before high-siding out alone; a little further around, Barbera did the same thing in the middle of the pack.

Rossi had a storming first lap, bullying his way ahead of Dovizioso and the troubled Spies, dropping out of the picture.

Stoner never would get closer to the pair up front, losing one- or two-tenths on most laps. Rossi was doing the same behind him, with Dovizioso his constant companion and Edwards close behind.

That was the order for 24 processional laps. Without Simoncelli to provide drama, the race up front became a waiting game. All the gaps kept stretching , except that between Pedrosa and Lorenzo.

At some points, the Yamaha was faster, but every time down the straight Pedrosa would close right up again, several times looking as though he might pass under braking.

When the pass did come, as they started lap 25, it was earlier on the straight and as clean as a whistle. And Dani drew away steadily – a second clear two laps later, and three seconds by the finish. The race up front had been tense and exemplary from both riders, but not especially exciting.

Increasingly far behind – nine seconds at half-distance and 16 by the end – Rossi and Dovizioso were glued together. Rossi was riding more like his old self, not giving Dovi any chance to attack – until the very last corner: "I tried to be a little faster and I had a slide, so I had to close the throttle, and that gave him the chance." The Honda pulled alongside and fractionally ahead over the stripe. For Rossi, it was a replay of 2006, when he lost the race to Toni Elias by two-thousandths.

Edwards had a good race to sixth, trying at first "to reel in Valentino and Andrea, but I was pushing so hard just to stay in touch."

The action came behind him, and there was some fair variety to it. Hayden had run off the track at the end of the back straight on lap one: he had back-shifting problems that would trouble him all race. He kept running wide, and on lap six, eager charger Crutchlow was ahead. Three laps later, Aoyama also got by, and he and Crutchlow battled from there to the end. Aoyama was ahead on lap 20; Crutchlow got him back on lap 25, but an error going out of the last corner slowed his penultimate run down the straight, and Aoyama got to the first corner ahead of him. One last effort from Crutchlow at the slow esses nearly took both of them down, he said, and the fast and forceful rookie settled for eighth, for a second race in a row.

Hayden fell back into the clutches of Spies, who had never really settled down after his early problems, and they had a big battle with plenty of near contact, Hayden doggedly declining to give way. Then Spies crashed out on lap 13, leaving the Ducati alone in ninth to the finish.

Behind them, de Puniet had finally disposed of the fading Capirossi by lap eight for his own lonely tenth, leaving the Italian to the mercy of Elias' Honda. They went to and fro

almost to the end, Elias finally breaking clear by better than a second.

Bautista was alone throughout, holding station some 20 seconds adrift of the pair after having been pushed off the track when Abraham crashed out on lap two. It was an impressive comeback all the same.

MOTO2 RACE – 26 laps

Bradl started from pole again and led almost from start to finish, but the pressure was constant and immense: it was an impressive second win.

His first attacker was Luthi, catching up from a second behind and forcing past into the lead as they started lap four. But he never led over the line, sliding out into the gravel on the last corner.

Now Bradl had Takahashi behind him, looking threatening, but not dangerous. Rookie Sofuoglu was coming up fast from sixth on lap one, however, and he looked set to make a bid to lead as well. But before half-distance, he was losing ground and would drop to fifth before crashing out on lap 17.

After lap ten, Simon was settled in second, holding station a second adrift, and not to be ruled out.

Two more potential threats had long gone. On lap eight, Marquez was pushing his way rapidly through a big gang disputing what was then third place, when he braked too late for the corner at the end of the back straight. He tried to dive underneath Redding, lost the front, and took both of them down and out in an echo of the infamous double Repsol crash when Pedrosa had knocked Hayden down at the same spot in 2006.

The real danger man, as so often, was Jerez winner Iannone. Qualified 14th, he'd finished lap one two places lower, but soon was carving through the packed midfield. By half-distance, he was up to fifth and about to grab fourth from Sofuoglu. It took him another lap to pass Takahashi; now he set about Simon, taking another six laps before he managed to make a passing move that stuck.

The gap to Bradl was less than a second: he was on his tail by lap 21, and ahead of him by the end of the next one,

after running wide in his first attempt at outbraking at the first corner.

It was all too much. Next time into the slow uphill ess-bend, he lost the front and went down, although he remounted to save three points in 13th.

It still wasn't over for Bradl, as Simon started to attack with vigour over the final laps. Bradl repulsed every attempt to win by 0.147 second.

Takahashi was six seconds down in third. Ten seconds away, Aegerter had been holding off Corsi for much of the race, and to the flag, by two-tenths.

Pol Espargaro came through in the closing stages to lead the next close quintet over the line for sixth, from Krummenacher, Baldolini, di Meglio and Rabat.

Pirro crashed out of the lead group on the first lap; Cluzel, Kallio and West swelled the crash list, West rejoining for 27th. Smith qualified 15th, then suffered a puncture, pitting for a replacement and rejoining to finish last, two laps adrift.

Above: Victory is ... painful. Pedrosa looks pale, but his winning comeback showed this particular injury was mending.

Top: Dani skips the light fandango. He had the upper hand all weekend.

Photos: Gold & Goose

Left: Simon shadows Bradl in the battle for Moto2 victory.

Below left: It's tough midfield in Moto2. American Kenny Noyes leads Aleix Espargaro and Pasini, finishing just out of the points.

Below: Yuki Takahashi took the final podium step. In tribute, he holds a photo of a fallen Japanese comrade.
Photos: Gold & Goose

125cc RACE – 23 laps

Terol's second pole was by a demoralising margin – seven-tenths ahead of Cortese. Rookie Oliveira satisfied home-country ambitions in third; Faubel led row two from Moncayo and Zarco, but Moncayo would miss the start with last-minute bike problems.

Terol's third win was similarly demoralising. He led into the first corner and never saw another motorcycle, winning by a comfortable 3.6 seconds. At half-distance, he had been 7.2 seconds clear and gaining, but at that point he switched to cruise control.

The battle for second was distant, but good. Cortese made the early running, from Oliveira, who would lose touch gradually, with Faubel closing. By lap 12, the Spaniard was in front.

Vinales, ninth on lap one, was cutting through fast, Zarco tagging on behind as he broke free to close on the battle for second. Faubel got ahead for a spell after half-distance, but

there was never anything in it, and Cortese would lead over the line again, and then, just once, Vinales, having no trouble at all among the more experienced riders in only his third GP.

In fact, it was Faubel, the most seasoned rider in the class (this was his 151st start) who tumbled, coming out of the loop after the back straight on lap 19 while fighting off the rookie.

The last lap was everything. Cortese managed to fend off Vinales at the first corner, and then gain just enough air as Zarco pushed inside Vinales at the uphill ess-bend. The rookie fought back, faster through the final corner. A photo-finish gave third to Zarco by two-thousandths.

Folger had been left behind after half-distance, but stayed clear of Vazquez, with Oliveira dropping away behind.

Salom narrowly won a race-long battle with Martin; Grotzkyj was tenth. Webb only just missed his first Mahindra points, caught and passed in the closing stages by rookie compatriot and namesake Danny Kent, on a charge after a ride-through for a jumped start.

Above: Three in a row for Terol and his pals.

Above left: Local boy Oliveira took seventh in the 125cc race.
Photos: Gold & Goose

bwin GRANDE PREMIO DE PORTUGAL

29 April–1 May, 2011 · FIM WORLD CHAMPIONSHIP ROUND 3

OFFICIAL TIMEKEEPER

CIRCUITO DO ESTORIL

28 laps
Length: 4.182 km / 2.598 miles
Width: 14m

Key
96/60 kph/mph
2 Gear

Turn 8 145/90
Variante 58/36
Turn 3 74/46
Esses 105/65
Turn 2 131/81
Orelha 87/54
VIP 81/50
Recta da Meta 250/155
Turn 1 76/47
312/194
Parabolica Interior 95/59
Parabolica 210/130

MotoGP

RACE DISTANCE: 28 laps, 72.760 miles/117.096km · **RACE WEATHER:** Dry (air 20°C, humidity 38%, track 38°C)

Pos.	Rider	Nat.	No.	Entrant	Machine	Tyres	Laps	Time & speed
1	**Dani Pedrosa**	SPA	26	Repsol Honda Team	Honda	B	28	45m 51.483s 95.198mph/ 153.206km/h
2	**Jorge Lorenzo**	SPA	1	Yamaha Factory Racing	Yamaha	B	28	45m 54.534s
3	**Casey Stoner**	AUS	27	Repsol Honda Team	Honda	B	28	45m 59.141s
4	**Andrea Dovizioso**	ITA	4	Repsol Honda Team	Honda	B	28	46m 08.013s
5	**Valentino Rossi**	ITA	46	Ducati Team	Ducati	B	28	46m 08.038s
6	**Colin Edwards**	USA	5	Monster Yamaha Tech 3	Yamaha	B	28	46m 24.058s
7	**Hiroshi Aoyama**	JPN	7	San Carlo Honda Gresini	Honda	B	28	46m 30.232s
8	**Cal Crutchlow**	GBR	35	Monster Yamaha Tech 3	Yamaha	B	28	46m 32.395s
9	**Nicky Hayden**	USA	69	Ducati Team	Ducati	B	28	46m 46.370s
10	**Randy de Puniet**	FRA	14	Pramac Racing Team	Ducati	B	28	46m 51.180s
11	**Toni Elias**	SPA	24	LCR Honda MotoGP	Honda	B	28	46m 51.857s
12	**Loris Capirossi**	ITA	65	Pramac Racing Team	Ducati	B	28	46m 53.276s
13	**Alvaro Bautista**	SPA	19	Rizla Suzuki MotoGP	Suzuki	B	28	47m 15.853s
	Ben Spies	USA	11	Yamaha Factory Racing	Yamaha	B	12	DNF
	Karel Abraham	CZE	17	Cardion AB Motoracing	Ducati	B	1	DNF
	Marco Simoncelli	ITA	58	San Carlo Honda Gresini	Honda	B	0	DNF
	Hector Barbera	SPA	8	Mapfre Aspar Team MotoGP	Ducati	B	0	DNF

Fastest lap: Dani Pedrosa, on lap 27, 1m 37.629s, 95.820mph/154.208km/h.

Lap record: Dani Pedrosa, SPA (Honda), 1m 36.937s, 99.505mph/155.309km/h (2009).

Event best maximum speed: Marco Simoncelli, 202.200mph/325.400km/h (free practice 2).

Qualifying

Weather: Dry
Air Temp: 18° Humidity: 53%
Track Temp: 26°

1	Lorenzo	1m 37.161s
2	Simoncelli	1m 37.294s
3	Pedrosa	1m 37.324s
4	Stoner	1m 37.384s
5	Spies	1m 37.866s
6	Dovizioso	1m 38.073s
7	Edwards	1m 38.080s
8	Crutchlow	1m 38.189s
9	Rossi	1m 38.271s
10	Barbera	1m 38.363s
11	Aoyama	1m 38.497s
12	Abraham	1m 38.786s
13	Hayden	1m 38.922s
14	Capirossi	1m 38.934s
15	Bautista	1m 39.172s
16	De Puniet	1m 39.378s
17	Elias	1m 39.894s

Fastest race laps

1	Pedrosa	1m 37.629s
2	Stoner	1m 37.853s
3	Lorenzo	1m 37.865s
4	Dovizioso	1m 38.263s
5	Rossi	1m 38.318s
6	Edwards	1m 38.489s
7	Crutchlow	1m 38.736s
8	Aoyama	1m 38.783s
9	Hayden	1m 38.877s
10	Spies	1m 39.078s
11	De Puniet	1m 39.131s
12	Elias	1m 39.648s
13	Capirossi	1m 39.720s
14	Bautista	1m 39.888s
15	Abraham	1m 50.239s

Championship Points

1	Lorenzo	65
2	Pedrosa	61
3	Stoner	41
4	Rossi	31
5	Hayden	30
6	Dovizioso	30
7	Aoyama	28
8	Crutchlow	21
9	Edwards	18
10	Barbera	14
11	Abraham	12
12	Elias	12
13	Simoncelli	11
14	Spies	10
15	Capirossi	9
16	De Puniet	6
17	Hopkins	6
18	Bautista	3

Team Points

1	Repsol Honda Team	96
2	Yamaha Factory Racing	75
3	Ducati Team	61
4	Monster Yamaha Tech 3	39
5	San Carlo Honda Gresini	39
6	Pramac Racing Team	15
7	Mapfre Aspar Team MotoGP	14
8	Cardion AB Motoracing	12
9	LCR Honda MotoGP	12
10	Rizla Suzuki MotoGP	9

Constructor Points

1	Honda	70
2	Yamaha	65
3	Ducati	36
4	Suzuki	9

Grid order	1	2	3	4	5	6	7	8	9	10	11	12	13	14	15	16	17	18	19	20	21	22	23	24	25	26	27	28	
1 LORENZO	1	1	1	1	1	1	1	1	1	1	1	1	1	1	1	1	1	1	1	1	1	1	1	1	26	26	26	26	1
58 SIMONCELLI	26	26	26	26	26	26	26	26	26	26	26	26	26	26	26	26	26	26	26	26	26	26	1	1	1	1	1	1	2
26 PEDROSA	27	27	27	27	27	27	27	27	27	27	27	27	27	27	27	27	27	27	27	27	27	27	27	27	27	27	27	27	3
27 STONER	46	46	46	46	46	46	46	46	46	46	46	46	46	46	46	46	46	46	46	46	46	46	46	46	46	46	46	4	4
11 SPIES	4	4	4	4	4	4	4	4	4	4	4	4	4	4	4	4	4	4	4	4	4	4	4	4	4	4	46	46	5
4 DOVIZIOSO	11	5	5	5	5	5	5	5	5	5	5	5	5	5	5	5	5	5	5	5	5	5	5	5	5	5	5	5	6
5 EDWARDS	65	65	69	69	69	69	35	35	35	35	35	35	35	35	35	35	35	35	7	7	7	7	7	7	35	35	35	7	7
35 CRUTCHLOW	5	69	35	35	35	69	69	69	7	7	7	7	7	7	7	7	7	7	35	35	35	35	35	35	7	7	7	35	8
46 ROSSI	69	35	65	11	7	7	7	7	69	69	69	69	69	69	69	69	69	69	69	69	69	69	69	69	69	69	69	69	9
8 BARBERA	35	11	11	65	11	11	11	11	11	11	11	11	14	14	14	14	14	14	14	14	14	14	14	14	14	14	14	14	10
7 AOYAMA	7	7	7	7	65	14	14	14	14	14	14	24	24	24	24	24	24	65	65	65	65	65	24	24	24	24	24	24	11
17 ABRAHAM	19	14	14	14	14	65	14	65	65	65	65	24	65	65	65	65	65	65	24	24	24	24	65	65	65	65	65	65	12
69 HAYDEN	17	24	24	24	24	24	24	24	24	24	65	19	19	19	19	19	19	19	19	19	19	19	19	19	19	19	19	19	13
65 CAPIROSSI	14	19	19	19	19	19	19	19	19	19	19	19																	
19 BAUTISTA	24																												
14 DE PUNIET																													
24 ELIAS																													

Moto2

RACE DISTANCE: 26 laps, 67.563 miles/108.732km · RACE WEATHER: Dry (air 18°C, humidity 58%, track 25°C)

Pos.	Rider	Nat.	No.	Entrant	Machine	Laps	Time & Speed
1	**Stefan Bradl**	GER	65	Viessmann Kiefer Racing	Kalex	26	44m 40.765s 90.730mph/ 146.016km/h
2	**Julian Simon**	SPA	60	Mapfre Aspar Team Moto2	Suter	26	44m 40.912s
3	**Yuki Takahashi**	JPN	72	Gresini Racing Moto2	Moriwaki	26	44m 46.953s
4	**Dominique Aegerter**	SWI	77	Technomag-CIP	Suter	26	44m 57.587s
5	**Simone Corsi**	ITA	3	Ioda Racing Project	FTR	26	44m 57.841s
6	**Pol Espargaro**	SPA	44	HP Tuenti Speed Up	FTR	26	45m 06.721s
7	**Randy Krummenacher**	SWI	4	GP Team Switzerland Kiefer Racing	Kalex	26	45m 06.867s
8	**Alex Baldolini**	ITA	25	NGM Forward Racing	Suter	26	45m 07.098s
9	**Mike di Meglio**	FRA	63	Tech 3 Racing	Tech 3	26	45m 07.401s
10	**Esteve Rabat**	SPA	34	Blusens-STX	FTR	26	45m 09.842s
11	**Claudio Corti**	ITA	71	Italtrans Racing Team	Suter	26	45m 20.402s
12	**Alex de Angelis**	RSM	15	JIR Moto2	Motobi	26	45m 20.678s
13	**Andrea Iannone**	ITA	29	Speed Master	Suter	26	45m 23.231s
14	**Ricard Cardus**	SPA	88	QMMF Racing Team	Moriwaki	26	45m 28.147s
15	**Axel Pons**	SPA	80	Pons HP 40	Pons Kalex	26	45m 28.171s
16	Raffaele de Rosa	ITA	35	Desguaces La Torre G22	Moriwaki	26	45m 28.790s
17	Kenny Noyes	USA	9	Avintia-STX	FTR	26	45m 33.303s
18	Yonny Hernandez	COL	68	Blusens-STX	FTR	26	45m 34.243s
19	Javier Fores	SPA	21	Mapfre Aspar Team Moto2	Suter	26	45m 34.703s
20	Mattia Pasini	ITA	75	Ioda Racing Project	FTR	26	45m 36.854s
21	Marc Marquez	SPA	93	Team CatalunyaCaixa Repsol	Suter	26	45m 45.462s
22	Michele Pirro	ITA	51	Gresini Racing Moto2	Moriwaki	26	45m 45.655s
23	Robertino Pietri	VEN	39	Italtrans Racing Team	Suter	26	45m 57.866s
24	Santiago Hernandez	COL	64	SAG Team	FTR	26	45m 58.875s
25	Scott Redding	GBR	45	Marc VDS Racing Team	Suter	26	46m 06.955s
26	Xavier Simeon	BEL	19	Tech 3 B	Tech 3	26	46m 08.365s
27	Anthony West	AUS	13	MZ Racing Team	MZ-RE Honda	26	46m 17.305s
28	Mashel Al Naimi	QAT	95	QMMF Racing Team	Moriwaki	25	45m 43.284s
29	Bradley Smith	GBR	38	Tech 3 Racing	Tech 3	24	44m 44.650s
	Valentin Debise	FRA	53	Speed Up	FTR	23	DNF
	Ratthapark Wilairot	THA	14	Thai Honda Singha SAG	FTR	21	DNF
	Mika Kallio	FIN	36	Marc VDS Racing Team	Suter	18	DNF
	Aleix Espargaro	SPA	40	Pons HP 40	Pons Kalex	18	DNF
	Kenan Sofuoglu	TUR	54	Technomag-CIP	Suter	17	DNF
	Jules Cluzel	FRA	16	NGM Forward Racing	Suter	11	DNF
	Steven Odendaal	RSA	97	MS Racing	Suter	7	DNF
	Thomas Luthi	SWI	12	Interwetten Paddock Moto2	Suter	4	DNF

Fastest lap: Andrea Iannone, on lap 14, 1m 42.026s, 91.691mph/147.562km/h (record).
Previous lap record: Scott Redding, GBR (Suter), 1m 45.456s, 88.708mph/142.762km/h (2010).
Event best maximum speed: Marc Marquez, 179.300mph/288.500km/h (free practice 1).

Qualifying: Dry
Air: 19° Humidity 50% Ground: 24°

1	Bradl	1m 41.591s
2	Luthi	1m 41.754s
3	Simon	1m 41.905s
4	Marquez	1m 42.073s
5	Aegerter	1m 42.143s
6	Pirro	1m 42.219s
7	Takahashi	1m 42.259s
8	Sofuoglu	1m 42.307s
9	Cluzel	1m 42.400s
10	P. Espargaro	1m 42.456s
11	A. Espargaro	1m 42.493s
12	Baldolini	1m 42.546s
13	Redding	1m 42.563s
14	Iannone	1m 42.591s
15	Smith	1m 42.743s
16	Pons	1m 42.746s
17	Corsi	1m 42.844s
18	De Rosa	1m 42.953s
19	Pasini	1m 42.996s
20	Cardus	1m 43.080s
21	Simeon	1m 43.120s
22	Kallio	1m 43.140s
23	Rabat	1m 43.189s
24	Wilairot	1m 43.286s
25	Krummenacher	1m 43.346s
26	Di Meglio	1m 43.366s
27	Noyes	1m 43.399s
28	De Angelis	1m 43.472s
29	West	1m 43.660s
30	Corti	1m 43.674s
31	Fores	1m 43.710s
32	Debise	1m 44.010s
33	Y. Hernandez	1m 44.090s
34	S. Hernandez	1m 44.355s
35	Pietri	1m 44.835s
36	Al Naimi	1m 45.100s
37	Coghlan	1m 45.380s
38	Odendaal	1m 46.555s

Fastest race laps

1	Iannone	1m 42.026s
2	Simon	1m 42.259s
3	Bradl	1m 42.420s
4	Takahashi	1m 42.457s
5	Cluzel	1m 42.578s
6	Sofuoglu	1m 42.613s
7	Redding	1m 42.873s
8	P. Espargaro	1m 42.877s
9	Marquez	1m 42.903s
10	Aegerter	1m 42.956s
11	Di Meglio	1m 42.976s
12	Baldolini	1m 42.991s
13	Corsi	1m 43.010s
14	Rabat	1m 43.147s
15	Pirro	1m 43.162s
16	Smith	1m 43.170s
17	Luthi	1m 43.176s
18	Krummenacher	1m 43.289s
19	De Angelis	1m 43.403s
20	Simeon	1m 43.421s
21	Cardus	1m 43.485s
22	Corti	1m 43.551s
23	Pons	1m 43.604s
24	Y. Hernandez	1m 43.628s
25	Wilairot	1m 43.634s
26	Debise	1m 43.670s
27	Kallio	1m 43.685s
28	De Rosa	1m 43.803s
29	Fores	1m 43.837s
30	Pasini	1m 43.925s
31	West	1m 43.936s
32	Noyes	1m 43.978s
33	A. Espargaro	1m 43.985s
34	S. Hernandez	1m 44.516s
35	Pietri	1m 44.622s
36	Al Naimi	1m 46.668s
37	Odendaal	1m 49.092s

Championship Points

1	Bradl	61
2	Iannone	48
3	Corsi	37
4	Luthi	36
5	Simon	36
6	Takahashi	27
7	De Angelis	26
8	Smith	20
9	Aegerter	16
10	Pirro	15
11	P. Espargaro	10
12	Krummenacher	9
13	Cluzel	9
14	Rabat	9
15	Baldolini	8
16	Coghlan	8
17	Di	7
18	Neukirchner	7
19	Y. Hernandez	6
20	Corti	5
21	West	5
22	A. Espargaro	5
23	Wilairot	4
24	Pasini	3
25	Cardus	2
26	Pons	1

Constructor Points

1	Suter	65
2	Kalex	61
3	FTR	37
4	Moriwaki	34
5	Tech 3	27
6	Motobi	26
7	MZ-RE Honda	7
8	Pons Kalex	6

125cc

RACE DISTANCE: 23 laps, 59.767 miles/96.186km · RACE WEATHER: Dry (air 20°C, humidity 44%, track 40°C)

Pos.	Rider	Nat.	No.	Entrant	Machine	Laps	Time & Speed
1	**Nicolas Terol**	SPA	18	Bankia Aspar Team 125cc	Aprilia	23	41m 21.986s 86.689mph/ 139.513km/h
2	**Sandro Cortese**	GER	11	Intact-Racing Team Germany	Aprilia	23	41m 25.657s
3	**Johann Zarco**	FRA	5	Avant-AirAsia-Ajo	Derbi	23	41m 26.452s
4	**Maverick Vinales**	SPA	25	Blusens by Paris Hilton Racing	Aprilia	23	41m 26.454s
5	**Jonas Folger**	GER	94	Red Bull Ajo MotorSport	Aprilia	23	41m 34.126s
6	**Efren Vazquez**	SPA	7	Avant-AirAsia-Ajo	Derbi	23	41m 42.290s
7	**Miguel Oliveira**	POR	44	Andalucia Banca Civica	Aprilia	23	41m 47.891s
8	**Luis Salom**	SPA	39	RW Racing GP	Aprilia	23	42m 08.302s
9	**Adrian Martin**	SPA	26	Bankia Aspar Team 125cc	Aprilia	23	42m 08.381s
10	**Simone Grotzkyj**	ITA	15	Phonica Racing	Aprilia	23	42m 11.433s
11	**Zulfahmi Khairuddin**	MAL	63	Airasia-Sic-Ajo	Derbi	23	42m 13.057s
12	**Sergio Gadea**	SPA	33	Blusens by Paris Hilton Racing	Aprilia	23	42m 22.351s
13	**Jakub Kornfeil**	CZE	84	Ongetta-Centro Seta	Aprilia	23	42m 22.465s
14	**Niklas Ajo**	FIN	31	TT Motion Events Racing	Aprilia	23	42m 33.724s
15	**Danny Kent**	GBR	52	Red Bull Ajo MotorSport	Aprilia	23	42m 35.738s
16	Danny Webb	GBR	99	Mahindra Racing	Mahindra	23	42m 37.343s
17	Hiroki Ono	JPN	76	Caretta Technology	KTM	23	42m 40.141s
18	Marcel Schrotter	GER	77	Mahindra Racing	Mahindra	23	42m 49.886s
19	Giulian Pedone	SWI	30	Phonica Racing	Aprilia	23	42m 54.609s
20	Joan Perello	SPA	36	Matteoni Racing	Aprilia	23	42m 57.074s
21	Luigi Morciano	ITA	3	Team Italia FMI	Aprilia	22	41m 23.149s
22	Kevin Hanus	GER	86	Team Hanusch	Honda	22	42m 31.114s
23	Peter Sebestyen	HUN	56	Caretta Technology	KTM	22	42m 42.777s
24	Sarath Kumar	IND	69	WTR-Ten10 Racing	Aprilia	21	41m 28.969s
	Hector Faubel	SPA	55	Bankia Aspar Team 125cc	Aprilia	19	DNF
	Harry Stafford	GBR	21	Ongetta-Centro Seta	Aprilia	18	DNF
	Jasper Iwema	NED	53	Ongetta-Abbink Metaal	Aprilia	12	DNF
	Francesco Mauriello	ITA	43	WTR-Ten10 Racing	Aprilia	8	DNF
	Louis Rossi	FRA	96	Matteoni Racing	Aprilia	6	DNF
	Alberto Moncayo	SPA	23	Andalucia Banca Civica	Aprilia	4	DNF

Fastest lap: Nicolas Terol, on lap 4, 1m 46.815s, 87.580mph/140.946km/h.
Lap record: Gabor Talmacsi, HUN (Aprilia), 1m 45.027s, 89.070mph/143.345km/h (2007).
Event best maximum speed: Nicolas Terol, 153.200mph/246.600km/h (qualifying).

Qualifying: Dry
Air: 18° Humidity 53% Ground: 26°

1	Terol	1m 46.556s
2	Cortese	1m 47.270s
3	Oliveira	1m 47.405s
4	Faubel	1m 47.600s
5	Moncayo	1m 47.750s
6	Zarco	1m 48.353s
7	Salom	1m 48.498s
8	Folger	1m 48.557s
9	Vazquez	1m 48.594s
10	Martin	1m 48.639s
11	Vinales	1m 48.673s
12	Gadea	1m 48.936s
13	Rossi	1m 48.959s
14	Grotzkyj	1m 49.237s
15	Khairuddin	1m 49.607s
16	Kornfeil	1m 49.638s
17	Stafford	1m 50.090s
18	Webb	1m 50.167s
19	Ajo	1m 50.195s
20	Iwema	1m 50.197s
21	Ono	1m 50.433s
22	Morciano	1m 50.559s
23	Kent	1m 50.587s
24	Pedone	1m 50.875s
25	Perello	1m 51.608s
26	Mackenzie	1m 51.803s
27	Schrotter	1m 52.280s
28	Sebestyen	1m 53.508s
29	Mauriello	1m 53.740s
Outside 107%		
31	Hanus	1m 54.875s
32	Kumar	1m 55.530s

Fastest race laps

1	Terol	1m 46.815s
2	Vinales	1m 47.118s
3	Faubel	1m 47.123s
4	Cortese	1m 47.146s
5	Zarco	1m 47.298s
6	Folger	1m 47.451s
7	Vazquez	1m 47.808s
8	Oliveira	1m 47.854s
9	Salom	1m 48.622s
10	Kent	1m 48.623s
11	Martin	1m 48.688s
12	Grotzkyj	1m 48.947s
13	Khairuddin	1m 49.013s
14	Gadea	1m 49.173s
15	Kornfeil	1m 49.371s
16	Ono	1m 49.953s
17	Stafford	1m 50.022s
18	Webb	1m 50.040s
19	Ajo	1m 50.085s
20	Rossi	1m 50.176s
21	Iwema	1m 50.194s
22	Pedone	1m 50.244s
23	Schrotter	1m 50.338s
24	Morciano	1m 50.546s
25	Moncayo	1m 50.609s
26	Perello	1m 50.814s
27	Sebestyen	1m 53.291s
28	Mauriello	1m 54.362s
29	Hanus	1m 54.420s
30	Kumar	1m 56.288s

Championship Points

1	Terol	75
2	Cortese	50
3	Folger	42
4	Zarco	42
5	Vazquez	30
6	Gadea	20
7	Vinales	20
8	Kent	17
9	Salom	16
10	Oliveira	15
11	Kornfeil	12
12	Mackenzie	11
13	Martin	11
14	Khairuddin	11
15	Faubel	10
16	Moncayo	9
17	Ono	8
18	Grotzkyj	8
19	Iwema	4
20	Schrotter	3
21	Rossi	3
22	Ajo	2
23	Rodriguez	1

Constructor Points

1	Aprilia	75
2	Derbi	45
3	KTM	8
4	Mahindra	3

Main photo: Casey Stoner was in runaway good form.

Below: Disaster for Pedrosa as he clips Simoncelli's back wheel. And the consequences…

Below right: …For Dani, how his other collarbone was broken.

Bottom: …For Simoncelli, a ride-through that cost him the rostrum – and lasting opprobrium from other riders.

Photos: Gold & Goose

FRENCH GRAND PRIX

LE MANS CIRCUIT

Above: It might not be a win, but for Rossi on the podium, it felt like one.

Above right: Stoner and the Repsol team's Livio Suppo head to Race Direction to face the music after his on-track punch-up.

Right: Serial crasher Randy de Puniet about to taste tarmac once more for a traditional home-race nightmare.

Photos: Gold & Goose

THE early title chase got a major reshuffle at Le Mans, in front of an unexpectedly sun-soaked crowd of 88,400. It was all thanks to racing's villain of the moment, Marco Simoncelli. In one fell swoop, literally, he dismantled Dani Pedrosa's chances, and his right collarbone, just days after the little Spaniard had recovered from problems with his left.

It was the most controversial moment of a race that supplied controversy aplenty.

The incident, on the 18th of 28 laps, was examined over and over in slow motion during the three-week break that followed. Race Direction hadn't needed that long to decide that it was a punishable offence, and to call Simoncelli (narrow survivor of the collision) in for a ride-through penalty, which cost him his first MotoGP rostrum. After the race, he insisted that the move had been fair, and that the punishment was more the result of accumulated complaints and polemic in the preceding weeks.

Was he right? Certainly there had been plenty of verbal accusations. The crash happened like this.

Dani had chased leader Stoner for a while, but was losing pace. Simoncelli had been a couple of seconds behind, but was closing rapidly. He caught up on the run down the hill and outbraked the Spaniard into Garage Vert to take second place. Lightweight Pedrosa was faster on the back straight,

however, and marginally ahead and inside as they started braking. The looming Simoncelli braked later ("at my normal point," he insisted later) and dived for the left-hander.

Simoncelli did leave a little room, but it was barely enough for another motorcycle. Pedrosa didn't even try for it, picking up the bike instead and clipping Simoncelli's rear wheel in the process. That sent the Italian careering across inside the kerb of the following right-hander, though he did regain control, and Dani cartwheeling into the gravel. He stood up and clutched at his right collarbone. Nightmare time.

Harsh words were spoken, especially by Dani's manager, Alberto Puig (he dubbed Simoncelli "criminal"), but Simoncelli did have a few supporters, notably Kevin Schwantz, who thought the mistake had been Dani's in trying too hard to defend against a firm, but fair pass. Most of the current riders thought that Simoncelli had stepped a bit too far over the line. Most notably Rossi, who this time sided with, rather than against Lorenzo. If nothing else, it meant his friend was now too much of a rival for comfort. (Lorenzo, meanwhile, asked by *MOTOCOURSE* how he responded to Rossi's description of MotoGP riders as "pussies", replied, "It must be a shame to get beaten by kids every weekend.")

Simoncelli's penalty (nobody could remember one such previously in the premier class) was not the only official flex-

ing of muscles. A potentially nasty incident during morning warm-up also invoked official sanction. Stoner had come out on to the back straight on a fast lap, only to find Randy de Puniet on a very slow lap, veering to and fro across the racing line. The Australian had swerved and braked hard, then pulled alongside the Frenchman to give him a hearty punch on the arm, followed by a familiar display of gesture and head shaking. Both were summoned to Race Direction, Stoner being fined 5,000 euros. "It's good to see Race Direction actually doing something," he said. "For them to make a judgement is quite rare." Many felt that de Puniet equally deserved a fine.

The Hondas were rampant again. Hoped-for engine upgrades for the Yamaha hadn't materialised at Estoril tests, while the Hondas' seamless acceleration out of the trademark Le Mans U-turns was just formidable. Two of the three factory riders were due also to test the 2013 prototype during the break after the race. Stoner wondered whether he "might not want to get back on the 800". Dovizioso was not invited – even after Pedrosa's injury ruled him out, Stoner getting two days to himself on the bike.

The upgrades had come at Ducati, but problems continued. The new heavier-crank engine had met with approval, but stayed on the back burner for now. More crucial was the revised chassis (later dubbed Step Two), with more flex built into the tiny carbon front air-box/chassis. But not enough. Rossi: "It is better, but we expected more. I am entering the

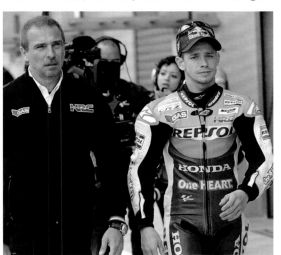

corners like an old lady with a big bag of shopping in the supermarket." Hayden was at pains to point out that he'd been asking for more flex long before Rossi's arrival, since the first time he'd tested the carbon monocoque in 2010: "I wish they'd made a bigger change." It didn't stop Rossi getting his first rostrum on the bike, which helped disguise the fact that he was still about 15 seconds behind the winner, the same as at Qatar.

There'd been a rash of crashes in 2010 on the left-hand side of cold tyres: for the first time, Bridgestone brought asymmetric compounds for the soft option as well as the hard, to universal acclaim. Not as much acclaim, however, as for a prototype 2012 tyre available at the Estoril test, which had significantly better warm-up performance. The riders wanted it now, but knew they couldn't have it. With this in mind, tyre issues would foment in the coming weeks.

Lorenzo lost an engine in a warm-up crash in full view of the pits. The ignition cut-out hadn't worked soon enough to stop the engine – jammed on full throttle – from blowing itself to bits in a fiery display. He was consigned to his spare for the race.

The paddock was becoming occupied with the question of the Japanese GP, rescheduled for 2nd October, with fears of nuclear contamination spreading among riders and other paddock folk, in spite of reassurances from official sources. Although slightly incongruous among professional daredevils, these fears would grow, likewise the controversy in weeks to come.

Le Mans may also have marked the start of something big down at the small end. The 125 race was a first win for Maverick Vinales. The 16-year-old had outraced and outfumbled Nico Terol to do it, bringing to an end a series of runaway wins for his fellow Spaniard. Vinales was in his fourth GP, Terol in his hundredth.

MOTOGP RACE – 28 laps

The front row looked like a Honda showroom: Stoner on pole for a third time, emerging victor by six-hundredths, by far his smallest margin of the weekend. He'd won an end-of-session joust with Simoncelli; while Dovizioso had shaded Pedrosa, who led row two. Only then came the rather discomfited Yamahas – Lorenzo (first time off the front row since Japan, 2010) and surprise track first-timer Crutchlow.

Rossi was at the far end of row three, behind Edwards and Spies; Hayden one place lower.

With unexpected sun on the grid, Pedrosa was back on

fast-starting form, leading through the chicane and under the Dunlop Bridge. Stoner had pushed back up to second by that point, from Dovizioso, Simoncelli, Lorenzo, Edwards and Rossi.

By the end of the lap, Simoncelli was ahead of Dovi, while Stoner was already starting to look for a way past Pedrosa. He found it next time around, at the last left-hander, but his planned escape was a long time coming. The gap stayed at a couple of tenths until lap ten, when it was up to half a second. From then on, it would grow – more than a second on lap 12, and up to two seconds three laps later.

Stoner explained how trouble finding neutral on the grid had left his clutch overheated and led to "a terrible start. But I was pretty aggressive in the first turns."

Lorenzo was in bullish mood too, mounting a very rough attack on Dovizioso into the turn two/three chicane at the start of lap two (enough, some thought, to merit a penalty for the rider who had been most vocal about safe and polite overtaking). It took a few goes to get past Simoncelli, and that didn't last even one lap. Simoncelli passed him back, cleanly, at the end of the back straight and immediately began to pull clear.

He didn't close on Pedrosa, the gap being more than two seconds on lap 11. But the tide was about to turn, with Pedrosa's lap times becoming slightly slower as the opposite happened to Simoncelli.

Soon he was catching him hand over fist, and at the end of lap 17 was just seven-tenths behind and clearly faster. He attacked at Garage Vert, losing the place again on the back straight – and then came the incident that caused all the trouble.

Behind them, Lorenzo had fallen into the hands of Dovizioso and Rossi by lap five. They kept station for the next five, Rossi not close enough to attack. Dovizioso did get past the Yamaha at Garage Vert on lap 11, but Lorenzo was in front again from laps 15 to 23, by which time Rossi had gained momentum. He passed the Honda on lap 18, and the Yamaha as well on lap 24. That was, he said later, the sweetest moment of the whole race.

The issue was resolved when Lorenzo ran wide at the first looping right-hander on lap 25, losing more than two seconds. The Italians continued scrapping to the end.

Rossi thought that lap 27 was the last and attacked hard in the last corners, but Dovi stayed narrowly ahead, and managed it even better next time around. It was for each the best result of the year.

Edwards had held a strong seventh in the early stages, while Spies, Crutchlow and Hayden had been scrapping a couple of seconds behind. Crutchlow slid off on lap six, and the two Americans gradually closed on their older compatriot, Spies ahead.

Then Edwards slid off, Spies had to slow and Hayden caught up again, ahead from laps 17 to 21. Spies was in close attendance, in front at the chicane on lap 22 and able to pull a little gap.

Simoncelli had taken his penalty at the end of lap 24 and rejoined close behind Hayden. By lap 26, he was past the Ducati and closing on Spies; he took him also to regain fifth on the last lap.

Aoyama had been alone behind them almost all race long, after escaping from a five-bike battle at the very back. There was more chopping and changing among this group than even in Moto2.

Capirossi had dropped to the back by half-distance, eventually crashing out; then Elias, heading the gang, had a huge wobble on lap 13, strong enough to trigger the airbags in his leathers. He dropped to the back as they deflated again, while Barbera, Abraham and Bautista each took a turn or two to lead the group over the line.

They finished Barbera, Abraham, Elias, Bautista, the quartet within less than half a second over the line.

Edwards, 13th, was two laps down. De Puniet had yet another dire home GP, finishing lap one where he'd qualified, 11th, and crashing out on the second lap.

MOTO2 RACE – 26 laps

Bradl took a fourth successive pole on a very close Moto2 grid, with 34 of 40 qualifiers within 2.28 seconds, the time frame that covered 17 MotoGP bikes. The German narrowly shaded Luthi and Takahashi, with Aleix Espargaro leading the second row from Redding and Marquez. Favourite Iannone was eighth.

Amazingly, all 40 riders made it unscathed through the first chicane under the Dunlop bridge, but Jerez winner Iannone didn't get much further, sliding out before the first half-lap was done.

Bradl led away, with Luthi, Takahashi, Simon and Aleix Espargaro in pursuit, and the whole field packed up close. Marquez was ninth at the end of lap one, but already picking up places – seventh on lap three, sixth on lap six and fifth, ahead of Espargaro, on the 11th.

Left: Marc Marquez celebrates his maiden Moto2 victory.

Far left: Elias leads Barbera, Abraham and Bautista in the battle at the back of the pack.

Below left: Ben Spies played himself back into form with sixth.

Bottom left: Dunlop-clad grid girls are as much part of Le Mans as the Dunlop Bridge.

Below: Spanish teen sensation Maverick Vinales pips Terol for a first win in only his fourth GP.

Photos: Gold & Goose

Over the next three laps, Espargaro would lose touch, although he was far enough ahead of the pursuit not to be caught; the others kept the same order ahead of him.

The lead changed hands on lap 16, when Luthi passed Bradl on the first corner, then Takahashi and Marquez over the next couple of corners. His different tyre choice had played him foul, he said.

Marquez was now third and looking for more after his deeply disappointing start to the season. He passed Takashi on lap 20 and immediately started to attack Luthi. Two laps later, it was over – Marquez was in front and going away for his first victory in the class. Next time around, he was better than a second ahead, and almost two at the end. An impressive display, reminiscent of his technique in the 125 class during 2010.

Bradl now revived somewhat and played a strong part in a lively battle for second. By the finish, Takahashi just managed to fend him off, with Simon and Luthi right behind. The quartet was covered by eight-tenths of a second.

Espargaro was a lone sixth and Corsi a lone seventh for most of the race, while a couple of seconds behind, Smith had his hands full with a brawling gang on his back wheel. By lap 21, the Briton had got clear, with only Aegerter able to go with him. By the finish, Aegerter had got ahead and pulled clear, right on Corsi's back wheel at the flag.

In the closing stages, de Angelis escaped from the group as well to close on Smith. The rookie just managed to hold him at bay over the line.

Almost three seconds behind, Cluzel, Krummenacher and Pol Espargaro were scrapping to the end. Di Meglio had crashed out of this gang on the penultimate lap; Pirro was a couple of seconds off it by the end, with Neukirchner on his back wheel for the last point. The returned German's MZ team-mate, West, now also on an FTR chassis, was 25th.

Kallio, Baldolini and wild-card Steve Odendaal retired; Cardus and Pons also crashed out.

125cc RACE – 24 laps

The first race began just like all the other 125 races so far in the season – Terol leaping into the lead from his fourth pole and sailing off into the distance, almost a second clear by the end of the second lap.

There was a difference. Leading the chase was rookie Vinales, and next time around he'd halved the gap, Cortese and Faubel at full stretch to stay with him.

Cortese nearly fell in the attempt, and by the end of lap four, Vinales was right with Terol, Faubel heading Vazquez, Cortese and Folger three seconds adrift.

Unable to make his usual escape, Terol ceded the lead on lap 12 for two laps before moving ahead again. But Vinales had the taste now, and as they fought he led six of the last ten laps.

Terol led on to the last one and all the way around. But somehow in the final tight corner, he let his guard down and ran wide. Vinales was through, to win by 0.048 second.

By the end, Vazquez had escaped from the chasers by better than a second, while Faubel had his hands full with Zarco, who had come through from the next group.

Folger was right behind, Cortese less than half a second behind him. Eighth-placed Gadea was comfortably clear of Oliveira, Salom tenth.

Terol's title lead grew still more massive in spite of the defeat, now a massive 95 points.

MONSTER ENERGY GRAND PRIX DE FRANCE

13–15 MAY, 2011 · FIM WORLD CHAMPIONSHIP ROUND 4

OFFICIAL TIMEKEEPER

LE MANS – BUGATTI

28 laps
Length: 4.185 km / 2.600 miles
Width: 13m

Key
96/60 kph/mph
⚙ Gear

Garage Vert 80/50
275/171
Chemin aux Boeufs 115/71
La Chappelle 105/65
Le Musée 90/56
"S" du Garage Bleu 105/65
95/59
Chicane Dunlop 80/50
Courbe Dunlop 266/166
Raccordement 90/56

MotoGP

RACE DISTANCE: 28 laps, 74.812 miles/117.180km · RACE WEATHER: Dry (air 17°C, humidity 35%, track 29°C)

Pos.	Rider	Nat.	No.	Entrant	Machine	Tyres	Laps	Time & speed
1	**Casey Stoner**	AUS	27	Repsol Honda Team	Honda	B	28	44m 03.955s / 99.140mph / 159.551km/h
2	**Andrea Dovizioso**	ITA	4	Repsol Honda Team	Honda	B	28	44m 18.169s
3	**Valentino Rossi**	ITA	46	Ducati Team	Ducati	B	28	44m 18.519s
4	**Jorge Lorenzo**	SPA	1	Yamaha Factory Racing	Yamaha	B	28	44m 25.030s
5	**Marco Simoncelli**	ITA	58	San Carlo Honda Gresini	Honda	B	28	44m 35.200s
6	**Ben Spies**	USA	11	Yamaha Factory Racing	Yamaha	B	28	44m 35.564s
7	**Nicky Hayden**	USA	69	Ducati Team	Ducati	B	28	44m 39.521s
8	**Hiroshi Aoyama**	JPN	7	San Carlo Honda Gresini	Honda	B	28	44m 55.457s
9	**Hector Barbera**	SPA	8	Mapfre Aspar Team MotoGP	Ducati	B	28	45m 07.686s
10	**Karel Abraham**	CZE	17	Cardion AB Motoracing	Ducati	B	28	45m 07.840s
11	**Toni Elias**	SPA	24	LCR Honda MotoGP	Honda	B	28	45m 08.023s
12	**Alvaro Bautista**	SPA	19	Rizla Suzuki MotoGP	Suzuki	B	28	45m 08.147s
13	**Colin Edwards**	USA	5	Monster Yamaha Tech 3	Yamaha	B	26	45m 03.007s
	Loris Capirossi	ITA	65	Pramac Racing Team	Ducati	B	21	DNF
	Dani Pedrosa	SPA	26	Repsol Honda Team	Honda	B	17	DNF
	Cal Crutchlow	GBR	35	Monster Yamaha Tech 3	Yamaha	B	6	DNF
	Randy de Puniet	FRA	14	Pramac Racing Team	Ducati	B	1	DNF

Fastest lap: Dani Pedrosa, on lap 9, 1m 33.617s, 99.999mph/160.932km/h (record).
Previous lap record: Valentino Rossi, ITA (Yamaha), 1m 34.215s, 99.363mph/159.910km/h (2008).
Event best maximum speed: Casey Stoner, 182.200mph/293.200km/h (qualifying practice).

Qualifying

Weather: Dry
Air Temp: 18° Humidity: 31%
Track Temp: 33°

1	Stoner	1m 33.153s
2	Simoncelli	1m 33.212s
3	Dovizioso	1m 33.621s
4	Pedrosa	1m 33.683s
5	Lorenzo	1m 33.706s
6	Crutchlow	1m 33.804s
7	Edwards	1m 34.063s
8	Spies	1m 34.206s
9	Rossi	1m 34.206s
10	Hayden	1m 34.277s
11	De Puniet	1m 34.351s
12	Bautista	1m 34.513s
13	Aoyama	1m 34.612s
14	Barbera	1m 34.650s
15	Capirossi	1m 34.866s
16	Abraham	1m 35.010s
17	Elias	1m 35.433s

Fastest race laps

1	Pedrosa	1m 33.617s
2	Stoner	1m 33.671s
3	Simoncelli	1m 33.840s
4	Lorenzo	1m 34.269s
5	Rossi	1m 34.273s
6	Dovizioso	1m 34.304s
7	Spies	1m 34.462s
8	Edwards	1m 34.529s
9	Hayden	1m 34.730s
10	Crutchlow	1m 34.805s
11	Aoyama	1m 35.400s
12	Abraham	1m 35.604s
13	Bautista	1m 35.699s
14	Barbera	1m 35.736s
15	Elias	1m 35.740s
16	Capirossi	1m 35.828s
17	De Puniet	1m 43.987s

Championship Points

1	Lorenzo	78
2	Stoner	66
3	Pedrosa	61
4	Dovizioso	50
5	Rossi	47
6	Hayden	39
7	Aoyama	36
8	Simoncelli	22
9	Edwards	21
10	Barbera	21
11	Crutchlow	21
12	Spies	20
13	Abraham	18
14	Elias	17
15	Capirossi	9
16	Bautista	7
17	De Puniet	6
18	Hopkins	6

Team Points

1	Repsol Honda Team	121
2	Yamaha Factory Racing	98
3	Ducati Team	86
4	San Carlo Honda Gresini	58
5	Monster Yamaha Tech 3	42
6	Mapfre Aspar Team MotoGP	21
7	Cardion AB Motoracing	18
8	LCR Honda MotoGP	17
9	Pramac Racing Team	15
10	Rizla Suzuki MotoGP	13

Constructor Points

1	Honda	95
2	Yamaha	78
3	Ducati	52
4	Suzuki	13

Lap chart

Grid order	1	2	3	4	5	6	7	8	9	10	11	12	13	14	15	16	17	18	19	20	21	22	23	24	25	26	27	28	
27 STONER	26	27	27	27	27	27	27	27	27	27	27	27	27	27	27	27	27	27	27	27	27	27	27	27	27	27	27	27	1
58 SIMONCELLI	27	26	26	26	26	26	26	26	26	26	26	26	26	26	26	26	26	58	58	58	58	58	58	58	46	4	4	4	2
4 DOVIZIOSO	58	58	1	58	58	58	58	58	58	58	58	58	58	58	58	58	58	1	1	1	1	1	1	46	4	46	46	46	3
26 PEDROSA	4	1	58	1	1	1	1	1	1	1	1	4	4	4	4	1	1	1	46	46	46	46	46	46	4	1	1	1	4
1 LORENZO	1	4	4	4	4	4	4	4	4	4	1	1	1	4	4	4	4	4	4	4	4	4	1	11	11	11	58		5
35 CRUTCHLOW	46	46	46	46	46	46	46	46	46	46	46	46	46	46	46	46	69	69	69	69	11	11	11	69	58	58	11		6
5 EDWARDS	5	5	5	5	5	5	5	5	5	5	5	11	11	11	69	11	11	11	69	69	69	69	58	69	69	69			7
11 SPIES	11	11	11	11	11	11	11	11	11	11	11	69	69	69	7	7	7	7	7	7	7	7	24	24	8	8	8	7	8
46 ROSSI	35	35	35	35	35	69	69	69	69	69	69	69	7	7	7	7	19	8	8	8	8	8	8	8	24	24	24	8	9
69 HAYDEN	69	69	69	69	69	7	7	7	7	7	7	7	19	19	19	19	8	17	17	17	17	24	24	8	8	24	17		10
14 DE PUNIET	14	65	7	7	65	65	8	24	24	24	24	19	8	8	19	8	17	17	17	24	8	8	17	17	19	19	24		11
19 BAUTISTA	65	7	65	65	65	8	24	19	19	19	19	8	17	17	17	24	24	24	19	19	19	19	19	19					12
7 AOYAMA	7	17	17	17	24	24	65	8	8	8	17	65	65	65	24	65	65	65	65	5	5	5	5	5					13
8 BARBERA	17	24	24	8	8	17	19	19	65	17	17	17	65	24	24	24	65	5	5	5	5								
65 CAPIROSSI	8	8	8	24	24	19	17	17	65	65	65	24	5	5	5	5													
17 ABRAHAM	24	19	19	19	19	35																							
24 ELIAS	19																												

5/35 Pit stop   5 Lapped rider
58 Ride-through penalty

Moto2

RACE DISTANCE: 26 laps, 67.611 miles/108.810km · RACE WEATHER: Dry (air 16°C, humidity 43%, track 20°C)

Pos.Rider	Nat.	No.	Entrant	Machine	Laps	Time & Speed
1 Marc Marquez	SPA	93	Team CatalunyaCaixa Repsol	Suter	26	43m 03.308s 94.220mph/ 151.633km/h
2 Yuki Takahashi	JPN	72	Gresini Racing Moto2	Moriwaki	26	43m 05.290s
3 Stefan Bradl	GER	65	Viessmann Kiefer Racing	Kalex	26	43m 05.545s
4 Julian Simon	SPA	60	Mapfre Aspar Team Moto2	Suter	26	43m 05.657s
5 Thomas Luthi	SWI	12	Interwetten Paddock Moto2	Suter	26	43m 05.917s
6 Aleix Espargaro	SPA	40	Pons HP 40	Pons Kalex	26	43m 15.603s
7 Simone Corsi	ITA	3	Ioda Racing Project	FTR	26	43m 22.047s
8 Dominique Aegerter	SWI	77	Technomag-CIP	Suter	26	43m 22.226s
9 Bradley Smith	GBR	38	Tech 3 Racing	Tech 3	26	43m 23.716s
10 Alex de Angelis	RSM	15	JIR Moto2	Motobi	26	43m 23.874s
11 Jules Cluzel	FRA	16	NGM Forward Racing	Suter	26	43m 26.533s
12 Randy Krummenacher	SWI	4	GP Team Switzerland Kiefer Racing	Kalex	26	43m 26.667s
13 Pol Espargaro	SPA	44	HP Tuenti Speed Up	FTR	26	43m 26.984s
14 Michele Pirro	ITA	51	Gresini Racing Moto2	Moriwaki	26	43m 28.064s
15 Max Neukirchner	GER	76	MZ Racing Team	MZ-RE Honda	26	43m 28.371s
16 Scott Redding	GBR	45	Marc VDS Racing Team	Suter	26	43m 32.895s
17 Kenny Noyes	USA	9	Avintia-STX	FTR	26	43m 36.111s
18 Xavier Simeon	BEL	19	Tech 3 B	Tech 3	26	43m 36.305s
19 Raffaele de Rosa	ITA	35	Desguaces La Torre G22	Moriwaki	26	43m 36.581s
20 Yonny Hernandez	COL	68	Blusens-STX	FTR	26	43m 38.145s
21 Esteve Rabat	SPA	34	Blusens-STX	FTR	26	43m 39.073s
22 Claudio Corti	ITA	71	Italtrans Racing Team	Suter	26	43m 44.810s
23 Mattia Pasini	ITA	75	Ioda Racing Project	FTR	26	43m 53.010s
24 Ratthapark Wilairot	THA	14	Thai Honda Singha SAG	FTR	26	43m 53.506s
25 Anthony West	AUS	13	MZ Racing Team	MZ-RE Honda	26	43m 54.097s
26 Kenan Sofuoglu	TUR	54	Technomag-CIP	Suter	26	43m 54.670s
27 Kev Coghlan	GBR	49	Aeroport de Castello	FTR	26	43m 54.779s
28 Valentin Debise	FRA	53	Speed Up	FTR	26	44m 05.212s
29 Javier Fores	SPA	21	Mapfre Aspar Team Moto2	Suter	26	44m 17.347s
30 Robertino Pietri	VEN	39	Italtrans Racing Team	Suter	26	44m 17.646s
31 Mashel Al Naimi	QAT	95	QMMF Racing Team	Moriwaki	26	44m 32.135s
32 Alexander Cudlin	AUS	8	QMMF Racing Team	Moriwaki	26	44m 33.197s
Mike di Meglio	FRA	63	Tech 3 Racing	Tech 3	24	DNF
Axel Pons	SPA	80	Pons HP 40	Pons Kalex	23	DNF
Ricard Cardus	SPA	88	QMMF Racing Team	Moriwaki	19	DNF
Steven Odendaal	RSA	97	MS Racing	Suter	14	DNF
Alex Baldolini	ITA	25	NGM Forward Racing	Suter	9	DNF
Mika Kallio	FIN	36	Marc VDS Racing Team	Suter	4	DNF
Andrea Iannone	ITA	29	Speed Master	Suter	0	DNF
Santiago Hernandez	COL	64	SAG Team	FTR	0	DNF

Fastest lap: Marc Marquez, on lap 7, 1m 38.533s, 95.010mph/152.903km/h (record).
Previous lap record: Jules Cluzel, FRA (Suter), 1m 39.169s, 94.400mph/151.922km/h (2010).
Event best maximum speed: Aleix Espargaro, 162.900mph/262.100km/h (warm-up).

Qualifying: Dry
Air: 19° Humidity 25% Ground: 33°

1	Bradl	1m 38.357s
2	Luthi	1m 38.402s
3	Takahashi	1m 38.540s
4	A. Espargaro	1m 38.560s
5	Redding	1m 38.655s
6	Marquez	1m 38.679s
7	Corsi	1m 38.706s
8	Iannone	1m 38.799s
9	Simon	1m 38.819s
10	Aegerter	1m 38.849s
11	Cluzel	1m 39.005s
12	De Angelis	1m 39.031s
13	Pirro	1m 39.064s
14	Pons	1m 39.122s
15	Pasini	1m 39.138s
16	Krummenacher	1m 39.221s
17	Smith	1m 39.223s
18	Wilairot	1m 39.394s
19	P. Espargaro	1m 39.481s
20	Neukirchner	1m 39.485s
21	De Rosa	1m 39.491s
22	Rabat	1m 39.542s
23	Kallio	1m 39.561s
24	Fores	1m 39.576s
25	Sofuoglu	1m 39.655s
26	Baldolini	1m 39.689s
27	Di Meglio	1m 39.809s
28	Corti	1m 39.849s
29	Cardus	1m 39.916s
30	Y. Hernandez	1m 39.917s
31	Simeon	1m 39.949s
32	Pietri	1m 39.987s
33	West	1m 40.016s
34	Noyes	1m 40.361s
35	Coghlan	1m 40.639s
36	S. Hernandez	1m 40.641s
37	Debise	1m 40.774s
38	Cudlin	1m 41.666s
39	Al Naimi	1m 41.875s
40	Odendaal	1m 41.897s

Fastest race laps

1	Marquez	1m 38.533s
2	Bradl	1m 38.650s
3	Takahashi	1m 38.679s
4	Luthi	1m 38.722s
5	Simon	1m 38.738s
6	A. Espargaro	1m 38.779s
7	De Angelis	1m 39.010s
8	Aegerter	1m 39.062s
9	Pirro	1m 39.153s
10	Di Meglio	1m 39.162s
11	Corsi	1m 39.198s
12	Cluzel	1m 39.243s
13	P. Espargaro	1m 39.253s
14	Rabat	1m 39.304s
15	Neukirchner	1m 39.362s
16	Pons	1m 39.374s
17	Noyes	1m 39.387s
18	Baldolini	1m 39.389s
19	Smith	1m 39.390s
20	Krummenacher	1m 39.407s
21	Redding	1m 39.425s
22	Corti	1m 39.570s
23	Cardus	1m 39.588s
24	De Rosa	1m 39.650s
25	Simeon	1m 39.656s
26	Y. Hernandez	1m 39.683s
27	Wilairot	1m 39.750s
28	West	1m 39.876s
29	Sofuoglu	1m 39.922s
30	Coghlan	1m 39.967s
31	Pasini	1m 40.033s
32	Debise	1m 40.440s
33	Pietri	1m 40.659s
34	Fores	1m 40.804s
35	Al Naimi	1m 41.116s
36	Cudlin	1m 41.435s
37	Kallio	1m 41.820s
38	Odendaal	1m 42.474s

Championship Points

1	Bradl	77
2	Simon	49
3	Iannone	48
4	Takahashi	47
5	Luthi	47
6	Corsi	46
7	De Angelis	32
8	Smith	27
9	Marquez	25
10	Aegerter	24
11	Pirro	17
12	A. Espargaro	15
13	Cluzel	14
14	Espargaro	13
15	Krummenacher	13
16	Rabat	9
17	Baldolini	8
18	Coghlan	8
19	Neukirchner	8
20	Di Meglio	7
21	Y. Hernandez	6
22	Corti	5
23	West	5
24	Wilairot	4
25	Pasini	3
26	Cardus	2
27	Pons	1

Constructor Points

1	Suter	90
2	Kalex	77
3	Moriwaki	54
4	FTR	46
5	Tech 3	34
6	Motobi	32
7	Pons Kalex	16
8	MZ-RE Honda	8

125cc

RACE DISTANCE: 24 laps, 62.411 miles/100.440km · RACE WEATHER: Dry (air 14°C, humidity 51%, track 22°C)

Pos.Rider	Nat.	No.	Entrant	Machine	Laps	Time & Speed
1 Maverick Vinales	SPA	25	Blusens by Paris Hilton Racing	Aprilia	24	42m 00.505s 89.139mph/ 143.456km/h
2 Nicolas Terol	SPA	18	Bankia Aspar Team 125cc	Aprilia	24	42m 00.553s
3 Efren Vazquez	SPA	7	Avant-AirAsia-Ajo	Derbi	24	42m 07.341s
4 Hector Faubel	SPA	55	Bankia Aspar Team 125cc	Aprilia	24	42m 08.803s
5 Johann Zarco	FRA	5	Avant-AirAsia-Ajo	Derbi	24	42m 09.095s
6 Jonas Folger	GER	94	Red Bull Ajo MotorSport	Aprilia	24	42m 10.741s
7 Sandro Cortese	GER	11	Intact-Racing Team Germany	Aprilia	24	42m 11.172s
8 Sergio Gadea	SPA	33	Blusens by Paris Hilton Racing	Aprilia	24	42m 16.147s
9 Miguel Oliveira	POR	44	Andalucia Banca Civica	Aprilia	24	42m 23.343s
10 Luis Salom	SPA	39	RW Racing GP	Aprilia	24	42m 31.406s
11 Alberto Moncayo	SPA	23	Andalucia Banca Civica	Aprilia	24	42m 34.301s
12 Simone Grotzkyj	ITA	15	Phonica Racing	Aprilia	24	42m 34.918s
13 Louis Rossi	FRA	96	Matteoni Racing	Aprilia	24	42m 35.201s
14 Adrian Martin	SPA	26	Bankia Aspar Team 125cc	Aprilia	24	42m 41.741s
15 Alexis Masbou	FRA	10	WTR-Ten10 Racing	Aprilia	24	42m 57.448s
16 Hiroki Ono	JPN	76	Caretta Technology	KTM	24	42m 57.914s
17 Danny Kent	GBR	52	Red Bull Ajo MotorSport	Aprilia	24	42m 58.268s
18 Jasper Iwema	NED	53	Ongetta-Abbink Metaal	Aprilia	24	42m 58.328s
19 Zulfahmi Khairuddin	MAL	63	Airasia-Sic-Ajo	Derbi	24	42m 58.389s
20 Luigi Morciano	ITA	3	Team Italia FMI	Aprilia	24	43m 02.594s
21 Jakub Kornfeil	CZE	84	Ongetta-Centro Seta	Aprilia	24	43m 03.218s
22 Taylor Mackenzie	GBR	17	Phonica Racing	Aprilia	24	43m 25.923s
23 Giulian Pedone	SWI	30	Phonica Racing	Aprilia	24	43m 43.003s
24 Francesco Mauriello	ITA	43	WTR-Ten10 Racing	Aprilia	24	43m 44.390s
25 Peter Sebestyen	HUN	56	Caretta Technology	KTM	24	43m 45.408s
26 Alessandro Tonucci	ITA	19	Team Italia FMI	Aprilia	24	43m 45.861s
27 Kevin Szalai	FRA	91	Maxiscoot MVT Racing	Aprilia	23	42m 23.829s
28 Kevin Thobois	FRA	92	Team RMS	Honda	23	43m 28.245s
Joan Perello	SPA	36	Matteoni Racing	Aprilia	20	DNF
Danny Webb	GBR	99	Mahindra Racing	Mahindra	17	DNF
Marcel Schrotter	GER	77	Mahindra Racing	Mahindra	17	DNF
Harry Stafford	GBR	21	Ongetta-Centro Seta	Aprilia	13	DNF
Niklas Ajo	FIN	31	TT Motion Events Racing	Aprilia	3	DNF

Fastest lap: Nicolas Terol, on lap 9, 1m 44.083s, 89.943mph/144.749km/h.
Lap record: Marc Marquez, SPA (Derbi), 1m 43.787s, 90.199mph/145.162km/h (2010).
Event best maximum speed: Jasper Iwema, 138.000mph/222.100km/h (free practice 2).

Qualifying: Dry
Air: 17° Humidity 35% Ground: 29°

1	Terol	1m 43.578s
2	Faubel	1m 43.967s
3	Vinales	1m 44.315s
4	Cortese	1m 44.355s
5	Folger	1m 44.497s
6	Zarco	1m 44.592s
7	Martin	1m 44.726s
8	Gadea	1m 44.755s
9	Vazquez	1m 44.776s
10	Salom	1m 45.347s
11	Grotzkyj	1m 45.423s
12	Oliveira	1m 45.593s
13	Khairuddin	1m 45.629s
14	Kornfeil	1m 45.682s
15	Moncayo	1m 45.697s
16	Iwema	1m 45.720s
17	Rossi	1m 45.746s
18	Kent	1m 45.965s
19	Masbou	1m 46.230s
20	Webb	1m 46.381s
21	Morciano	1m 46.473s
22	Stafford	1m 46.477s
23	Ono	1m 46.531s
24	Schrotter	1m 47.364s
25	Mauriello	1m 47.533s
26	Mackenzie	1m 47.540s
27	Ajo	1m 47.563s
28	Pedone	1m 48.027s
29	Sebestyen	1m 48.127s
30	Szalai	1m 48.607s
31	Tonucci	1m 48.825s
32	Perello	1m 48.987s
33	Thobois	1m 50.591s

Fastest race laps

1	Terol	1m 44.083s
2	Vinales	1m 44.094s
3	Vazquez	1m 44.340s
4	Cortese	1m 44.392s
5	Faubel	1m 44.437s
6	Folger	1m 44.527s
7	Zarco	1m 44.555s
8	Gadea	1m 44.594s
9	Oliveira	1m 44.600s
10	Salom	1m 44.879s
11	Grotzkyj	1m 45.107s
12	Moncayo	1m 45.537s
13	Rossi	1m 45.566s
14	Martin	1m 45.766s
15	Kent	1m 45.846s
16	Iwema	1m 45.917s
17	Khairuddin	1m 45.987s
18	Morciano	1m 46.135s
19	Webb	1m 46.404s
20	Ono	1m 46.419s
21	Masbou	1m 46.431s
22	Kornfeil	1m 46.650s
23	Mackenzie	1m 47.519s
24	Stafford	1m 47.530s
25	Mauriello	1m 47.581s
26	Ajo	1m 47.618s
27	Pedone	1m 47.671s
28	Perello	1m 47.755s
29	Schrotter	1m 47.903s
30	Tonucci	1m 48.034s
31	Sebestyen	1m 48.336s
32	Szalai	1m 48.672s
33	Thobois	1m 51.875s

Championship Points

1	Terol	95
2	Cortese	59
3	Zarco	53
4	Folger	52
5	Vazquez	46
6	Vinales	45
7	Gadea	28
8	Faubel	23
9	Oliveira	22
10	Salom	22
11	Kent	17
12	Moncayo	14
13	Martin	13
14	Kornfeil	12
15	Grotzkyj	12
16	Mackenzie	11
17	Khairuddin	11
18	Ono	8
19	Rossi	6
20	Iwema	4
21	Schrotter	3
22	Ajo	2
23	Masbou	1
24	Rodriguez	1

Constructor Points

1	Aprilia	100
2	Derbi	61
3	KTM	8
4	Mahindra	3

FIM WORLD CHAMPIONSHIP · ROUND 5

CATALUNYA GRAND PRIX

CATALUNYA CIRCUIT

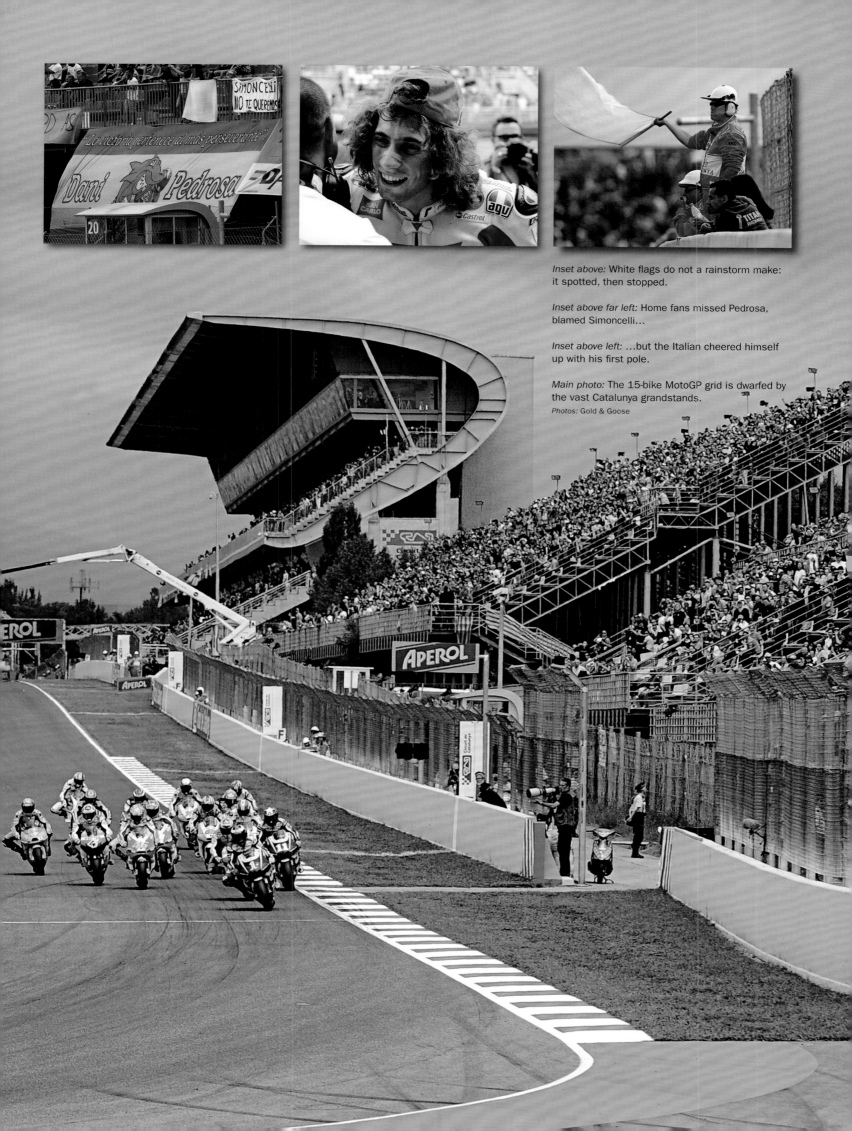

Inset above: White flags do not a rainstorm make: it spotted, then stopped.

Inset above far left: Home fans missed Pedrosa, blamed Simoncelli…

Inset above left: …but the Italian cheered himself up with his first pole.

Main photo: The 15-bike MotoGP grid is dwarfed by the vast Catalunya grandstands.

Photos: Gold & Goose

Above: Knee and elbow skimming the paint, Stoner didn't waste an inch.

Above right: Back to the future? Alex Criville takes over Pedrosa's empty pit as he prepares to give the Moto3 Honda an underwhelming debut.

Above far right: Track first-timer Crutchlow looks apprehensive on the grid – he raced to a strong seventh.

Right: Another good race to not come last: Capirossi leads Abraham, Barbera and Bautista in a tight battle for ninth. The veteran Italian held off the Czech rookie by inches.

Photos: Gold & Goose

THE news from Pedrosa was not good. Although the collarbone, broken three weekends before, had been screwed and plated directly thereafter, he would not be taking part in his home race. By racing convention, this fix for the injury generally entails a rapid return, as demonstrated by Tech 3 team-mates Edwards, this race, and Crutchlow after the next – with a rostrum finish in the former's case nine days after the injury. So where was Dani?

In the fevered world of the Spanish Press, this was enough to start a turmoil of rumours that would grow in the weeks to come. Dani, it was whispered, had injured himself again falling off a motorbike while training. Or perhaps a bicycle. Or was it a ladder? Neither Repsol nor Honda had any firm answers, and it was the start of a strange spell in the wannabe top Spaniard's fretful premier-class career.

Who to blame? Easy. Marco Simoncelli was Public Enemy Number One, and in recognition of this, the local Granoliers police provided 24-hour armed guards: two by day free of charge, one by night for a fee. To avoid drawing attention, the burly pair were dressed in San Carlo team uniforms, and even accompanied Simoncelli to the Press conference after he'd qualified on pole for the first time.

The worst he got from the crowd was a hearty booing whenever he showed his curly head; he and team boss Fausto Gresini also got a wigging from Race Direction, which then announced on his behalf that he felt properly chastened. *"Simoncelli responded that in the interval after the French Grand Prix he had had time for reflection and regretted the statements he had made in the heat of the moment immediately after the Grand Prix. He also recognized that he had made an error of judgment and stated that in future he would try to evaluate situations better and be a little more cautious,"* read the document.

The fast and flowing circuit's notorious bumps prompted

a smart-Alec response from Stoner, when asked whether the recent Formula One race had made them any worse: "It hasn't been resurfaced, but they seem to have taken some of the bumps out. Maybe it's because I'm on a Honda now that it feels smoother." Repayment in advance for his third win in five races.

Back in the red pit that he had left behind, bumps weren't the issue. That remained front-end feel. But there was the comfort of a new engine. Both riders received the heavier-crank unit, which did little more (said Hayden) than "smooth things out a little; same lap time". (It was his fourth engine, out of six, in just five races.) But Rossi had a couple of cheerier milestones: his first race when his shoulder had not required him to take pain-killers, and a result that (at 7.3 seconds) had more than halved his gap to the winner.

Edwards broke his right collarbone. It happened on Friday afternoon, when a cold left side of the tyre caught him out at the downhill hairpin following the long opening series of right-handers. His first broken bone since starting MotoGP in 2003 was badly smashed, and promptly put together again with seven screws and a plate, at the nearby Dexeus clinic, popular with Spanish riders. By Sunday morning, Edwards was back at the track and wanting to ride – if only to do a few laps. He hadn't missed a race in 141 consecutive GPs. The doctors, however, said no.

That left a depleted grid of just 15 – on a weekend that the promised announcement of 2011's 'Claiming Rule Teams' was deferred for the first time – meaning points for all, and a sparse and processional race for a crowd of 81,838. They had braved rain that was troublesome almost all weekend, and that further spoiled the MotoGP race with a sprinkling in the middle of it. Once again, the best entertainment came from the lively battle not to come last.

The smaller classes compensated, at least in terms of

controversy. The Moto2 chances of local hero Julian Simon were well scuppered by the impetuous Turk Sofuoglo. Attacking him for second place with eight laps to go, he first knocked him flying, then ran him over in the gravel. Simon would be out for ten weeks and effectively longer, with a double fracture in his right leg. The incident was investigated by a busy Race Direction at the next race and accepted as a racing incident.

Not so the gripping finale to the 125 race. Once again, Terol's runaway habit was put on hold: his rival this time was Frenchman Johann Zarco, still seeking his first win. A desperate attack in the last corner put him alongside, and then he used his elbow to push Terol on to the grass. Zarco crossed the line first, but was promptly demoted to sixth by a well-earned 20-second penalty.

News from the Safety Commission (the nearest thing there is to a riders' briefing, although only voluntary) alarmed some riders, whose radiation fears were growing. Told that Motegi was definitely to go ahead as planned, Lorenzo once again lead the chorus of trepidation, fending off probing questions

at a lively pre-race Press conference with an insistence that fear of the unknown was an entirely justifiable reason.

A gentle purring noise that was almost drowned out by the motor for the starter-roller announced the first public airing of a Moto3 steed. With former 125 and 500 champion Alex Criville on board, the new Honda NSF250R made demonstration laps and was also on display in the paddock. With 47 horsepower and a backward-leaning cylinder, which had the induction up front and the exhaust snaking out the rear, the bike was simple, but thorough, and surprisingly cheap – just 23,600 euros from your local (Spanish) Honda dealer. It was potentially undercut by another offering, from Spain – the BeOn, currently with a Honda motocross engine, but ready to be adapted for come what may.

MOTOGP RACE – 25 laps

Simoncelli's first pole was, he said, the perfect riposte to "all the polemic" since Le Mans. He had narrowly knocked Stoner off his perch; Lorenzo scraped in next. Spies led row two,

Dovizioso alongside and then remarkable rookie Crutchlow sixth, ahead of Rossi, as at every other race so far. "But I haven't beaten him in a race yet," he pointed out. Rossi led row three after just getting ahead of Hayden at the last: his best grid with Ducati.

The story of the race could be told by a list of names. That's how it went up front, with only three changes of position among the top eight all race long.

Simoncelli, swamped off the line, had messed up his pole. "Maybe I held the clutch too long, but it slipped and a lot of riders passed me. After that, it was hard to get back into my rhythm," he explained.

The first pass was for the lead, and on lap two. Lorenzo had shot off the line, from Stoner, Spies, Rossi and Dovizioso, and they finished the first lap with Dovi ahead of Rossi.

Stoner lined up Lorenzo as expected into the first corner at the end of the long straight, slipped cleanly past and proceeded to ride away. Lorenzo stayed close for a couple of laps, but it was a losing battle, even if slightly protracted. The gap was up to a second by lap six, and double that by lap 11, and any lingering hopes that he might be able to attack had long faded away.

Then the rain came – just spots, mid-way through and only on parts of the track. The white flags were shown ("They were waving them like there was a monsoon," said Crutchlow) to signify a flag-to-flag race, allowing riders to change bikes. But while it was a worry to all, it came to nothing.

Stoner slowed cautiously and Lorenzo closed to within 1.7 seconds at the end of lap 14.

But the leader got the message and started to stretch away again. It had been a flawless riding display from both of them, but Stoner's bike was faster, and that was that.

They had quickly gapped Spies, busy coming to terms with front forks he'd never used before – plans to test them in morning warm-up had been foiled when it was wet. After six laps, he was two seconds adrift, and Dovizioso and Rossi were right with him.

The trio stayed right up close, but stagnant until the white flags at half-distance, but with no attacks. At that point, Simoncelli had closed to within eight-tenths, and by the 15th lap he was right with Rossi. Again, he was never quite close

enough to attack, and when discretion overcame him after lap 20, he started to drop away again.

Simoncelli had passed Hayden on lap four, and it quickly became clear that the American was in trouble. He was losing ground, while Crutchlow was steadily closing up. By lap eight, he was on him, and two laps later he slipped past easily in the first corner, to pull away steadily.

Neither would see another bike for the rest of the race; by the finish, Nicky was seven seconds down on the rookie, but comfortably clear of the pursuit.

This had been thinned at the start of lap four, when Aoyama crashed at the first corner, taking out the unfortunate de Puniet with him.

As in France, the quartet at the back gave the crowd something to watch. Bautista led the gang until half-distance; then Capirossi took over. The Suzuki would keep on losing positions at the end, without losing touch.

Abraham took over behind Capirossi, with Barbera well in the mix, and they were swapping back and forth over the rest of the distance. Abraham was in front for laps 22 and 23, then Capirossi got him back. The Czech rookie seemed to have timed it right when he pulled alongside over the finish line, and if it had been a hundred yards later probably would have been ahead. Then came Barbera, with Bautista a little off the back.

Elias had never been part of the group and was almost 15 seconds adrift at the end.

The championship was taking a different shape without Pedrosa. Consistent Lorenzo still led, but Stoner was closing fast, seven points behind and on blazing form.

MOTO2 RACE – 23 laps

Bradl preserved his full house of pole positions, overcoming unexpected handling problems to consign front-row first-timer Aleix Espargaro to second. Takahashi rounded out the top three; Thomas Luthi led row two. Iannone was 21st, after crashing out on only his second lap. The bike was patched up just in time for him to run three more; Simone Corsi was in similar circumstances, qualified 15th.

The race was frighteningly close through the field and in-

cluded a couple of potentially very bad crashes. Bradl managed to stay clear of it all, and to stretch his lead at the end for his third win of the season.

He led every lap except the second, when Simon nosed in front. It was the safest place to be.

For the first ten laps, he was closely pursued, but with problems within the group. The first came near the back of the front pack after five laps, and was triggered when Luthi had a near high-side, regaining traction only to fall off the inside of his bike. Takahashi couldn't avoid colliding with him; Smith also was involved. The Briton stayed on, but dropped right back to midfield before climbing back to eighth, only to run on at the end of the back straight on the final lap after touching a wet white line under braking. He finished an eventual 19th.

The next incident came on lap 16. Bradl was already better than a second clear of Simon, who had seen off a challenge from Espargaro. Sofuoglu had picked his way through from 11th on lap one, however, and had just passed Espargaro to attack Simon.

He did so with way too much enthusiasm and went piling into the back of him going into the right-hander in the final stadium section. Simon went flying, Sofuoglu following on to run over the fallen rider in the gravel. Simon got to his feet and stood by the barrier in spite of his broken right leg, lucky not to be more severely hurt.

Marquez had been seventh at the end of lap one, but was picking up places gradually. With these two gone and Aegerter also crashing earlier on the same lap, he was now third. He promptly passed Espargaro for second.

The chasers were still close. Corsi was ahead of Krummenacher, who had pulled through from tenth. De Angelis, Rabat and Kallio finished in that order, after battling hard over the closing laps.

Hernandez was ninth, narrowly ahead of Neukirchner and Redding, with Pirro close behind. Iannone never quite overcame his disastrous qualifying position and finished 15th.

Bradl's points lead stretched further still: 102 to Corsi's 59. Iannone and Simon had 49, then came Takahashi and Luthi with 47 each; Marquez was closing on 45.

125cc RACE – 22 laps

Points leader Nico Terol took his fourth pole in five races in the 125 class, with team-mate Gadea four-tenths slower and rookie Vinales a similar distance behind. Zarco ominously led row two.

Terol took his fourth win of the year, but he didn't cross the line first. He'd played it cool all race long and taken a convincing lead on the last lap, only to be pushed on to the grass on the exit from the last corner by Zarco.

The track was still slightly damp for the first race of the day and a handful of riders gambled on wet tyres. They were never part of the race – one was Grotzkyj, who pitted for slicks.

It was all action up front, Terol passed on lap two by Le Mans winner and home boy Vinales. The older rider took over again on lap eight as Zarco caught up. Two laps later, the Frenchman nipped into second. Soon afterwards, Vinales lost touch.

Now it was a tactical game to the end, with Terol letting Zarco ahead with four laps to go. He swept past under braking as they started the last lap and stretched away convincingly. It looked like he had it won, until Zarco's final attack.

Vinales was ten seconds adrift at the end, but inherited second.

Folger and Cortese came through to catch a battle between Vazquez and Faubel. Faubel was pushed out; Folger narrowly defeated Cortese for third, with Vazquez next, the trio covered by seven-tenths.

Zarco was dropped to sixth; then Faubel was just ahead of Gadea; Martin narrowly defeated Kornfeil for ninth. Britons Webb and Stafford crashed out together in the first corner.

OFFICIAL TIMEKEEPER

CIRCUIT DE CATALUNYA

25 laps
Length: 4.727km / 2.892 miles
Width: 12m

Renault 145/90
Repsol 100/62
Seat 80/50
Campsa 150/87
Europcar 145/90
Abolaño 175/109
Banc Sabadell 100/62
Elf 130/81
Würth 105/65
319/198
La Caixa 100/62
Tourisme de Catalunya 145/90

Key
96/60 kph/mph
Gear

MotoGP — RACE DISTANCE: 25 laps, 73.431 miles/118.175km · RACE WEATHER: Dry (air 20°C, humidity 49%, track 25°C)

Pos.	Rider	Nat.	No.	Entrant	Machine	Tyres	Laps	Time & speed
1	**Casey Stoner**	AUS	27	Repsol Honda Team	Honda	B	25	43m 19.779s
								101.681mph/
								163.640km/h
2	**Jorge Lorenzo**	SPA	1	Yamaha Factory Racing	Yamaha	B	25	43m 22.182s
3	**Ben Spies**	USA	11	Yamaha Factory Racing	Yamaha	B	25	43m 24.070s
4	**Andrea Dovizioso**	ITA	4	Repsol Honda Team	Honda	B	25	43m 25.034s
5	**Valentino Rossi**	ITA	46	Ducati Team	Ducati	B	25	43m 27.150s
6	**Marco Simoncelli**	ITA	58	San Carlo Honda Gresini	Honda	B	25	43m 31.610s
7	**Cal Crutchlow**	GBR	35	Monster Yamaha Tech 3	Yamaha	B	25	43m 46.262s
8	**Nicky Hayden**	USA	69	Ducati Team	Ducati	B	25	43m 53.022s
9	**Loris Capirossi**	ITA	65	Pramac Racing Team	Ducati	B	25	44m 02.871s
10	**Karel Abraham**	CZE	17	Cardion AB Motoracing	Ducati	B	25	44m 02.892s
11	**Hector Barbera**	SPA	8	Mapfre Aspar Team MotoGP	Ducati	B	25	44m 04.003s
12	**Alvaro Bautista**	SPA	19	Rizla Suzuki MotoGP	Suzuki	B	25	44m 05.018s
13	**Toni Elias**	SPA	24	LCR Honda MotoGP	Honda	B	25	44m 18.047s
	Randy de Puniet	FRA	14	Pramac Racing Team	Ducati	B	3	DNF
	Hiroshi Aoyama	JPN	7	San Carlo Honda Gresini	Honda	B	3	DNF

Fastest lap: Casey Stoner, on lap 5, 1m 43.084s, 102.576mph/165.080km/h.

Lap record: Dani Pedrosa, SPA (Honda), 1m 42.358s, 103.304mph/166.251km/h (2008).

Event best maximum speed: Hiroshi Aoyama, 205.100mph/330.000km/h (race).

Qualifying

Weather: Dry
Air Temp: 25° Humidity: 44%
Track Temp: 37°

1	Simoncelli	1m 42.413s
2	Stoner	1m 42.429s
3	Lorenzo	1m 42.728s
4	Spies	1m 42.742s
5	Dovizioso	1m 42.749s
6	Crutchlow	1m 43.202s
7	Rossi	1m 43.223s
8	Hayden	1m 43.228s
9	Bautista	1m 43.447s
10	Barbera	1m 43.656s
11	Aoyama	1m 43.734s
12	De Puniet	1m 43.764s
13	Capirossi	1m 44.068s
14	Elias	1m 44.510s
15	Abraham	1m 45.661s

Fastest race laps

1	Stoner	1m 43.084s
2	Lorenzo	1m 43.416s
3	Dovizioso	1m 43.506s
4	Spies	1m 43.637s
5	Simoncelli	1m 43.684s
6	Rossi	1m 43.709s
7	Crutchlow	1m 44.049s
8	Hayden	1m 44.263s
9	Abraham	1m 44.453s
10	Barbera	1m 44.505s
11	Bautista	1m 44.653s
12	Capirossi	1m 44.723s
13	Elias	1m 45.011s
14	De Puniet	1m 45.317s
15	Aoyama	1m 45.626s

Championship Points

1	Lorenzo	98
2	Stoner	91
3	Dovizioso	63
4	Pedrosa	61
5	Rossi	58
6	Hayden	47
7	Spies	36
8	Aoyama	36
9	Simoncelli	32
10	Crutchlow	30
11	Barbera	26
12	Abraham	24
13	Edwards	21
14	Elias	20
15	Capirossi	16
16	Bautista	11
17	De Puniet	6
18	Hopkins	6

Team Points

1	Repsol Honda Team	146
2	Yamaha Factory Racing	134
3	Ducati Team	105
4	San Carlo Honda Gresini	68
5	Monster Yamaha Tech 3	51
6	Mapfre Aspar Team MotoGP	26
7	Cardion AB Motoracing	24
8	Pramac Racing Team	22
9	LCR Honda MotoGP	20
10	Rizla Suzuki MotoGP	17

Constructor Points

1	Honda	120
2	Yamaha	98
3	Ducati	63
4	Suzuki	17

Grid order	1	2	3	4	5	6	7	8	9	10	11	12	13	14	15	16	17	18	19	20	21	22	23	24	25	
58 SIMONCELLI	1	27	27	27	27	27	27	27	27	27	27	27	27	27	27	27	27	27	27	27	27	27	27	27	27	1
27 STONER	27	1	1	1	1	1	1	1	1	1	1	1	1	1	1	1	1	1	1	1	1	1	1	1	1	2
1 LORENZO	11	11	11	11	11	11	11	11	11	11	11	11	11	11	11	11	11	11	11	11	11	11	11	11	11	3
11 SPIES	4	46	4	4	4	4	4	4	4	4	4	4	4	4	4	4	4	4	4	4	4	4	4	4	4	4
4 DOVIZIOSO	46	4	46	46	46	46	46	46	46	46	46	46	46	46	46	46	46	46	46	46	46	46	46	46	46	5
35 CRUTCHLOW	69	69	69	58	58	58	58	58	58	58	58	58	58	58	58	58	58	58	58	58	58	58	58	58	58	6
46 ROSSI	58	58	58	69	69	69	69	69	69	35	35	35	35	35	35	35	35	35	35	35	35	35	35	35	35	7
69 HAYDEN	65	35	35	35	35	35	35	35	35	69	69	69	69	69	69	69	69	69	69	69	69	69	69	69	69	8
19 BAUTISTA	35	65	65	19	19	19	19	19	19	19	19	19	19	65	65	65	65	65	65	65	17	17	65	65		9
8 BARBERA	19	19	19	65	8	8	8	8	8	8	8	65	19	19	17	17	8	17	17	17	17	65	65	17	17	10
7 AOYAMA	24	8	8	8	65	65	65	65	65	65	65	8	17	19	8	17	8	8	8	8	8	8	8	8		11
14 DE PUNIET	8	24	14	17	17	17	17	17	17	17	17	17	8	8	19	19	19	19	19	19	19	19	19	19		12
65 CAPIROSSI	14	14	24	24	24	24	24	24	24	24	24	24	24	24	24	24	24	24	24	24	24	24	24	24		13
24 ELIAS	17	17	17																							
17 ABRAHAM	7	7	7																							

Moto2

RACE DISTANCE: 23 laps, 67.556 miles/108.721km · RACE WEATHER: Dry (air 22°C, humidity 49%, track 32°C)

Pos.	Rider	Nat.	No.	Entrant	Machine	Laps	Time & Speed
1	**Stefan Bradl**	GER	65	Viessmann Kiefer Racing	Kalex	23	41m 38.888s 97.324mph/ 156.627km/h
2	**Marc Marquez**	SPA	93	Team CatalunyaCaixa Repsol	Suter	23	41m 43.029s
3	**Aleix Espargaro**	SPA	40	Pons HP 40	Pons Kalex	23	41m 47.297s
4	**Simone Corsi**	ITA	3	Ioda Racing Project	FTR	23	41m 49.219s
5	**Randy Krummenacher**	SWI	4	GP Team Switzerland Kiefer Racing	Kalex	23	41m 50.549s
6	**Alex de Angelis**	RSM	15	JIR Moto2	Motobi	23	41m 51.271s
7	**Esteve Rabat**	SPA	34	Blusens-STX	FTR	23	41m 51.490s
8	**Mika Kallio**	FIN	36	Marc VDS Racing Team	Suter	23	41m 52.355s
9	**Yonny Hernandez**	COL	68	Blusens-STX	FTR	23	41m 55.500s
10	**Max Neukirchner**	GER	76	MZ Racing Team	MZ-RE Honda	23	41m 55.623s
11	**Scott Redding**	GBR	45	Marc VDS Racing Team	Suter	23	41m 55.919s
12	**Michele Pirro**	ITA	51	Gresini Racing Moto2	Moriwaki	23	41m 57.348s
13	**Alex Baldolini**	ITA	25	NGM Forward Racing	Suter	23	42m 01.821s
14	**Xavier Simeon**	BEL	19	Tech 3 B	Tech 3	23	42m 02.304s
15	**Andrea Iannone**	ITA	29	Speed Master	Suter	23	42m 02.337s
16	Pol Espargaro	SPA	44	HP Tuenti Speed Up	FTR	23	42m 02.958s
17	Claudio Corti	ITA	71	Italtrans Racing Team	Suter	23	42m 02.999s
18	Carmelo Morales	SPA	31	Desguaces La Torre G22	Moriwaki	23	42m 04.239s
19	Bradley Smith	GBR	38	Tech 3 Racing	Tech 3	23	42m 08.137s
20	Valentin Debise	FRA	53	Speed Up	FTR	23	42m 13.965s
21	Santiago Hernandez	COL	64	SAG Team	FTR	23	42m 20.554s
22	Anthony West	AUS	13	MZ Racing Team	MZ-RE Honda	23	42m 30.991s
23	Jules Cluzel	FRA	16	NGM Forward Racing	Suter	23	42m 41.380s
24	Kev Coghlan	GBR	49	Aeroport de Castello	FTR	23	42m 55.182s
	Axel Pons	SPA	80	Pons HP 40	Pons Kalex	18	DNF
	Julian Simon	SPA	60	Mapfre Aspar Team Moto2	Suter	15	DNF
	Kenan Sofuoglu	TUR	54	Technomag-CIP	Suter	15	DNF
	Dominique Aegerter	SWI	77	Technomag-CIP	Suter	15	DNF
	Javier Fores	SPA	21	Mapfre Aspar Team Moto2	Suter	13	DNF
	Mattia Pasini	ITA	75	Ioda Racing Project	FTR	7	DNF
	Thomas Luthi	SWI	12	Interwetten Paddock Moto2	Suter	5	DNF
	Yuki Takahashi	JPN	72	Gresini Racing Moto2	Moriwaki	5	DNF
	Mike di Meglio	FRA	63	Tech 3 Racing	Tech 3	5	DNF
	Robertino Pietri	VEN	39	Italtrans Racing Team	Suter	3	DNF
	Mashel Al Naimi	QAT	95	QMMF Racing Team	Moriwaki	2	DNF
	Kenny Noyes	USA	9	Avintia-STX	FTR	0	DNF

Fastest lap: Bradley Smith, on lap 5, 1m 47.762s, 98.123mph/157.914km/h.
Lap record: Andrea Iannone, ITA (Speed Up), 1m 47.543s, 98.323mph/158.236km/h (2010).
Event best maximum speed: Stefan Bradl, 176.700mph/284.300km/h (free practice 3).

Qualifying: Dry
Air: 23° Humidity: 45% Ground: 34°

1	Bradl	1m 46.753s
2	A. Espargaro	1m 46.867s
3	Takahashi	1m 46.978s
4	Luthi	1m 47.068s
5	Marquez	1m 47.154s
6	Smith	1m 47.207s
7	Kallio	1m 47.226s
8	Simon	1m 47.355s
9	Rabat	1m 47.426s
10	Cluzel	1m 47.456s
11	Redding	1m 47.527s
12	Aegerter	1m 47.558s
13	Fores	1m 47.741s
14	Pirro	1m 47.765s
15	Corsi	1m 47.781s
16	Pons	1m 47.817s
17	Sofuoglu	1m 47.846s
18	Corti	1m 47.861s
19	Krummenacher	1m 47.937s
20	De Angelis	1m 47.954s
21	Y. Hernandez	1m 47.988s
22	Iannone	1m 48.005s
23	Morales	1m 48.068s
24	Neukirchner	1m 48.081s
25	P. Espargaro	1m 48.087s
26	Debise	1m 48.156s
27	Baldolini	1m 48.179s
28	Pietri	1m 48.213s
29	Wilairot	1m 48.234s
30	Di Meglio	1m 48.282s
31	Simeon	1m 48.331s
32	West	1m 48.487s
33	Coghlan	1m 48.631s
34	Pasini	1m 48.755s
35	S. Hernandez	1m 48.841s
36	Noyes	1m 49.048s
37	Al Naimi	1m 49.926s

Fastest race laps

1	Smith	1m 47.762s
2	A. Espargaro	1m 47.819s
3	Sofuoglu	1m 47.932s
4	Bradl	1m 47.944s
5	Marquez	1m 47.989s
6	Corsi	1m 47.994s
7	Luthi	1m 48.001s
8	Simon	1m 48.010s
9	Aegerter	1m 48.014s
10	Pons	1m 48.086s
11	Krummenacher	1m 48.146s
12	Rabat	1m 48.149s
13	Takahashi	1m 48.159s
14	De Angelis	1m 48.183s
15	Kallio	1m 48.274s
16	Redding	1m 48.369s
17	Pirro	1m 48.383s
18	Iannone	1m 48.444s
19	Y. Hernandez	1m 48.535s
20	Fores	1m 48.540s
21	P. Espargaro	1m 48.597s
22	Cluzel	1m 48.609s
23	Morales	1m 48.609s
24	Neukirchner	1m 48.630s
25	Corti	1m 48.667s
26	Di Meglio	1m 48.690s
27	Baldolini	1m 48.780s
28	Simeon	1m 48.860s
29	Pasini	1m 48.946s
30	Coghlan	1m 49.081s
31	Debise	1m 49.159s
32	S. Hernandez	1m 49.361s
33	West	1m 49.556s
34	Pietri	1m 49.635s
35	Al Naimi	1m 59.797s

Championship Points

1	Bradl	102
2	Corsi	59
3	Iannone	49
4	Simon	49
5	Takahashi	47
6	Luthi	47
7	Marquez	45
8	De Angelis	42
9	A. Espargaro	31
10	Smith	27
11	Aegerter	24
12	Krummenacher	24
13	Pirro	21
14	Rabat	18
15	Cluzel	14
16	Neukirchner	14
17	P. Espargaro	13
18	Y. Hernandez	13
19	Baldolini	11
20	Kallio	8
21	Coghlan	8
22	Di Meglio	7
23	Redding	5
24	Corti	5
25	West	5
26	Wilairot	4
27	Pasini	3
28	Simeon	2
29	Cardus	2
30	Pons	1

Constructor Points

1	Suter	110
2	Kalex	102
3	FTR	59
4	Moriwaki	58
5	Motobi	42
6	Tech 3	36
7	Pons Kalex	32
8	MZ-RE Honda	14

125cc

RACE DISTANCE: 22 laps, 64.619 miles/103.994km · RACE WEATHER: Dry (air 19°C, humidity 68%, track 25°C)

Pos.	Rider	Nat.	No.	Entrant	Machine	Laps	Time & Speed
1	**Nicolas Terol**	SPA	18	Bankia Aspar Team 125cc	Aprilia	22	42m 29.647s 91.239mph/ 146.835km/h
2	**Maverick Vinales**	SPA	25	Blusens by Paris Hilton Racing	Aprilia	22	42m 40.003s
3	**Jonas Folger**	GER	94	Red Bull Ajo MotorSport	Aprilia	22	42m 44.907s
4	**Sandro Cortese**	GER	11	Intact-Racing Team Germany	Aprilia	22	42m 45.317s
5	**Efren Vazquez**	SPA	7	Avant-AirAsia-Ajo	Derbi	22	42m 45.589s
6	**Johann Zarco**	FRA	5	Avant-AirAsia-Ajo	Derbi	22	42m 49.405s
7	**Hector Faubel**	SPA	55	Bankia Aspar Team 125cc	Aprilia	22	42m 56.137s
8	**Sergio Gadea**	SPA	33	Blusens by Paris Hilton Racing	Aprilia	22	42m 56.328s
9	**Adrian Martin**	SPA	26	Bankia Aspar Team 125cc	Aprilia	22	43m 05.781s
10	**Jakub Kornfeil**	CZE	84	Ongetta-Centro Seta	Aprilia	22	43m 06.423s
11	**Danny Kent**	GBR	52	Red Bull Ajo MotorSport	Aprilia	22	43m 07.583s
12	**Louis Rossi**	FRA	96	Matteoni Racing	Aprilia	22	43m 40.487s
13	**Niklas Ajo**	FIN	31	TT Motion Events Racing	Aprilia	22	43m 41.351s
14	**Alexis Masbou**	FRA	10	Caretta Technology	KTM	22	43m 41.445s
15	**Alberto Moncayo**	SPA	23	Andalucia Banca Civica	Aprilia	22	43m 45.356s
16	Marcel Schrotter	GER	77	Mahindra Racing	Mahindra	22	43m 51.652s
17	Jasper Iwema	NED	53	Ongetta-Abbink Metaal	Aprilia	22	43m 55.104s
18	Luigi Morciano	ITA	3	Team Italia FMI	Aprilia	22	43m 55.275s
19	Sturla Fagerhaug	NOR	50	WTR-Ten10 Racing	Aprilia	22	44m 24.943s
20	Francesco Mauriello	ITA	43	WTR-Ten10 Racing	Aprilia	22	44m 25.029s
21	Giulian Pedone	SWI	30	Phonica Racing	Aprilia	22	44m 25.135s
22	Peter Sebestyen	HUN	56	Caretta Technology	KTM	21	42m 33.113s
23	Josep Rodriguez	SPA	28	Wild Wolf-Racc-MS	Aprilia	21	43m 53.121s
24	Kevin Hanus	GER	86	Team Hanush	Honda	21	43m 55.815s
25	Simone Grotzkyj	ITA	15	Phonica Racing	Aprilia	21	44m 24.811s
26	John McPhee	GBR	71	Racing Steps Foundation KRP	Aprilia	20	43m 42.078s
27	Joan Perello	SPA	36	Matteoni Racing	Aprilia	20	43m 47.681s
28	Taylor Mackenzie	GBR	17	Phonica Racing	Aprilia	20	43m 47.798s
29	Alessandro Tonucci	ITA	19	Team Italia FMI	Aprilia	20	44m 05.548s
	Luis Salom	SPA	39	RW Racing GP	Aprilia	16	DNF
	Danny Webb	GBR	99	Mahindra Racing	Mahindra	0	DNF
	Miguel Oliveira	POR	44	Andalucia Banca Civica	Aprilia	0	DNF
	Zulfahmi Khairuddin	MAL	63	Airasia-Sic-Ajo	Derbi	0	DNF
	Harry Stafford	GBR	21	Ongetta-Centro Seta	Aprilia	0	DNF

Fastest lap: Johann Zarco, on lap 18, 1m 52.621s, 93.890mph/151.101km/h.
Lap record: Pol Espargaro, SPA (Derbi), 1m 50.590s, 95.614mph/153.876km/h (2010).
Event best maximum speed: Luis Salom, 147.900mph/238.000km/h (qualifying practice).

Qualifying: Dry
Air: 20° Humidity: 53% Ground: 26°

1	Terol	1m 51.281s
2	Faubel	1m 51.683s
3	Vinales	1m 52.099s
4	Zarco	1m 52.135s
5	Vazquez	1m 52.288s
6	Cortese	1m 52.449s
7	Folger	1m 52.476s
8	Salom	1m 52.629s
9	Gadea	1m 52.635s
10	Martin	1m 52.747s
11	Kent	1m 52.859s
12	Moncayo	1m 53.224s
13	Iwema	1m 53.607s
14	Webb	1m 53.640s
15	Kornfeil	1m 53.706s
16	Oliveira	1m 53.801s
17	Masbou	1m 53.804s
18	Grotzkyj	1m 54.044s
19	Khairuddin	1m 54.122s
20	Schrotter	1m 54.126s
21	Rossi	1m 54.197s
22	Morciano	1m 54.422s
23	Ajo	1m 54.682s
24	Stafford	1m 55.115s
25	Rodriguez	1m 55.159s
26	McPhee	1m 55.486s
27	Mauriello	1m 55.596s
28	Pedone	1m 55.895s
29	Fagerhaug	1m 56.384s
30	Sebestyen	1m 56.431s
31	Perello	1m 56.533s
32	Tonucci	1m 56.982s
33	Hanus	1m 57.975s
34	Mackenzie	1m 58.533s

Fastest race laps

1	Zarco	1m 52.621s
2	Terol	1m 52.664s
3	Vinales	1m 53.025s
4	Cortese	1m 53.184s
5	Vazquez	1m 53.748s
6	Folger	1m 53.828s
7	Gadea	1m 54.253s
8	Faubel	1m 54.309s
9	Salom	1m 54.522s
10	Kornfeil	1m 54.553s
11	Martin	1m 54.659s
12	Kent	1m 54.805s
13	Rossi	1m 55.243s
14	Masbou	1m 55.331s
15	Pedone	1m 55.884s
16	Morciano	1m 55.995s
17	Iwema	1m 56.017s
18	Grotzkyj	1m 56.088s
19	Ajo	1m 56.267s
20	Moncayo	1m 56.468s
21	McPhee	1m 56.535s
22	Schrotter	1m 56.666s
23	Sebestyen	1m 57.590s
24	Fagerhaug	1m 58.071s
25	Mauriello	1m 58.219s
26	Tonucci	1m 58.220s
27	Mackenzie	1m 58.454s
28	Perello	2m 00.140s
29	Hanus	2m 01.803s
30	Rodriguez	2m 02.835s

Championship Points

1	Terol	120
2	Cortese	72
3	Folger	68
4	Vinales	65
5	Zarco	63
6	Vazquez	57
7	Gadea	36
8	Faubel	32
9	Kent	22
10	Oliveira	22
11	Salom	22
12	Martin	20
13	Kornfeil	18
14	Moncayo	15
15	Grotzkyj	12
16	Mackenzie	11
17	Khairuddin	11
18	Rossi	10
19	Ono	8
20	Ajo	5
21	Iwema	4
22	Schrotter	3
23	Masbou	3
24	Rodriguez	1

Constructor Points

1	Aprilia	125
2	Derbi	72
3	KTM	10
4	Mahindra	3

BRITISH GRAND PRIX

SILVERSTONE CIRCUIT

Welcome back to the revamped
Silverstone – all changed,
except for the weather.
Photo: Gold & Goose

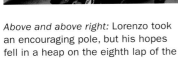

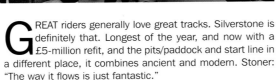

Above and above right: Lorenzo took an encouraging pole, but his hopes fell in a heap on the eighth lap of the wet race.

Photo: Gold & Goose

Top: Intense concentration from the Honda pair: Stoner and Dovizioso conquer treacherous conditions.

Photo: Gavan Caldwell

Centre, from top: The dramatic new pit complex; Rossi shivers on the grid; from hospital to rostrum: Edwards was third only days after smashing his collarbone.

Right: Bautista and Edwards on the first lap – the American would soon be past.

Photos: Gold & Goose

GREAT riders generally love great tracks. Silverstone is definitely that. Longest of the year, and now with a £5-million refit, and the pits/paddock and start line in a different place, it combines ancient and modern. Stoner: "The way it flows is just fantastic."

Rossi also loved it, on his first visit (he had missed 2010's inaugural return with a broken leg). Unfortunately, the love is not always reciprocated, and that was especially the case when the great rider's bike served only to sap his confidence. The hard yards of the classic British airfield circuit brought out the worst in his Ducati, and Rossi had "the worst weekend of my career".

The Ducati circus was surrounded by contradictions. Specifically, Hayden spoke of expecting a revised chassis at the next race, while Rossi insisted the opposite: "I don't expect another new front chassis this year." Hayden was right, also Rossi, but disingenuously so. He wouldn't get a new chassis. He would get a whole new motorbike.

This was in the future; the present was depressing. Although Hayden was up to third in wet practice (Rossi a downbeat ninth), they qualified with Hayden leading row three, but Rossi down in 13th. Capirossi's was the only Ducati behind the marque's new figurehead. "If it's wet, I can be a little less slow," Rossi promised before the race.

It was wet, and he got a lucky sixth. He also recorded an uncomfortable milestone, having been outqualified and outraced by team-mate Hayden all weekend. It had happened before with Lorenzo, but never to this extent, and after the race he acknowledged the fact: "We have two problems: the Yamaha and Honda are faster than us, and secondly my team-mate was faster than me all weekend. His side of the garage worked better than ours."

To long-time followers of British weather forecasts, the rain had seemed inevitable ever since an official drought had been declared in East Anglia, not too far away, on the eve of the race. Ditto to Silverstone old hands, and to those who had come for the first time in 2010. Sure enough, the question was not would it rain, but how often and for how long? Even when it wasn't raining, a biting wind turned the long walk up and down the half-mile paddock into an ordeal. The new buildings were impressively jagged, more impressive in their sheer scale. Pit boxes were cavernous all the way to the (very) far end, where 125 teams were four to a box and still had masses of space. Accustomed to cosier surroundings, many felt the atmosphere was lacking.

The biggest change for the riders was the new location of the pit lane and start-finish straight: a layout that worked well, though the weather was not conducive to last-corner battles. Familiar from 2010, but no less tricky for it, was the mix of surfaces. Parts of the old track, such as the former first corner, Copse, not only had a different tar finish, but also were bumpier and tended to puddle worse. It made every lap potentially different from the last, and it caught out some big names. Not only did Rossi fall in practice, but also Lorenzo and Simoncelli in the race; and Spies – victim of the Copse puddles at such speed that he slid all the way to the con-

crete barrier and hit it back-first with a mighty thump. "My back protector did its job," he commented gratefully.

No protective measure could have saved Cal Crutchlow, whose crash had come in the dry and for different reasons. After a highly impressive start in MotoGP, this was his big chance: a familiar track with all close-to-home comforts. He'd won the double on the Superbike here in the previous year – and now the weather was bad. It was all to his advantage. Cal was fourth fastest in the wet free practice, behind only Stoner, Simoncelli and Hayden; and a close fifth among the fast guys in the dry.

Then on only his third full lap in qualifying, he fell victim to the cold-side tyre syndrome. On the first left-hander for some time, the back stepped out on entry, gripped and tossed him. He landed heavily, smashing his left collarbone. He was also concussed, and surgery had to be postponed for a few days until that had cleared – but like team-mate, Edwards, he would be back at the next race.

It was actually a fairy-tale return for the American, who rode heroically to claim his first rostrum since 2009. It showed what is expected of a bike racer. Once again, however, Pedrosa cloaked his aura in mystery by doing the opposite. HRC still had no firm explanation, but said they would defer as long as possible the entry of a replacement for Assen a fortnight later.

Deferred also, for a second race running, was the list of new teams for MotoGP. "As far as we're concerned, it's ready," said IRTA's Mike Trimby, but Dorna put the brakes on until later in the week while they counted up how many factory entries they could expect. At this stage, nobody knew whether Suzuki would be among them.

Moto2 was busy, with Marquez taking his first pole only to crash spectacularly at the end of morning warm-up on the puddled last corner. The bike stayed upright and veered back across the track to hit the pit wall very hard, leaving his team with a major rebuild job with less than two hours to the race.

Smith had a torrid time in qualifying, his Tech 3 dying over and over. Towards the end and getting panicky, when it died again he turned around and pushed it down the pit lane. Against the flow of the traffic, this incurred a fine of 1,000 euros. He managed only seven laps and was 28th on the grid, but next day proceeded on a heroic ride through blinding spray to end up on the rostrum.

A little landmark in the 125 class for Vinales: his first pole position. The 16-year-old with the tucked-in style and searing speed already had his first win, and was well and truly on the map.

MOTOGP RACE – 20 laps

Stoner's fourth pole in six races came after assured domination in practice. When Simoncelli nosed ahead now and then, the Australian could always respond. Lorenzo was third, welcoming a track where the slower acceleration and top speed mattered less than smoothness and aggression. Spies led row two, from Dovi and the surprise rookie Abraham, top Ducati rider and grinning from ear to ear.

Hayden glumly led row three from Edwards and Bautista; Rossi was an astonishing 13th, almost four seconds off pole. Only Elias and Capirossi were behind the grand master.

It was raining steadily with a biting cold wind as the big bikes assembled in front of a crowd of 72,544 hardy fans. Dovizioso and Hayden both managed two sighting laps on the well-wetted track, but the quest to put more heat in the tyres worked only for the former. He got away well as Lorenzo led into the first corner, moved past Stoner into second after the halfway point of lap one, and led Stoner, Simoncelli and Lorenzo over the line at the end of it.

Stoner was already worried about being unsighted in the spray and pushed past into the lead on the second lap. He was seven-tenths ahead of the two Hondas next time around, but the gap grew only slowly as he battled with vision problems. "I copped a lot of water in my face, and some got behind my visor. I started to panic a bit," he said.

By lap seven, the droplets were clearing, and now he took 1.4 seconds out of Dovizioso to build the lead to almost three, adding another second a lap over the next two. The race was as good as won. All he had to do was keep going and brave the conditions, but that was far from easy. "Every time I tried to ease the pace, the tyre temperature would drop off, so I had to speed up again. It was a vicious circle," he said.

At the start of lap four, Simoncelli suffered a near crash into the first corner and Lorenzo took third. He could still see Stoner tantalisingly close, and rapidly closed a second's gap to Dovizioso and started attacking fiercely. Dovi kept him

Above: Beaming Bradley Smith rode from 28th on the grid all the way to second.

Photo: Gold & Goose

Top: Smith's inch-close dive inside countryman Scott Redding was no closer than the other 26.

Photo: Gavan Caldwell

behind as best he could, but Lorenzo wouldn't take no for an answer – until he slipped, flicked and fell at the first corner at the start of lap eight. He was unhurt, but disgruntled: "I think I could have fought with Casey for victory, but I had to overtake Andrea because he was getting away."

Simoncelli was right behind again at this point and took over the task of hassling the factory Honda. He did get ahead of Dovizioso on lap ten, but only briefly; at the start of lap 11, he also lost the front under brakes at the same corner and crashed out of yet another race. "I am distraught," he said later.

At this point, Dovizioso was more than five seconds behind Stoner, and the gap would grow to more than 15 by lap 16. But with no further threat from behind, Dovizioso's second was perfectly safe; it was a second well-judged wet British GP rostrum – the time before, he had won at Donington.

Hayden had been the early leader of the pursuit, but lost two places when he ran off on lap three, and first Spies and then Edwards came past. He would almost lose another place to Bautista over the following laps as he struggled to gain pace.

Edwards, smooth as ever, was now well up to speed, and quickly caught and passed Spies for fifth. Soon he saw P3 on his board, as the two leaders crashed out. "Nine days ago, I was going home, flights booked. All I can say is: good doctor," he beamed.

The younger Texan dropped back, and was about to fall into the clutches of Hayden and the pursuing Bautista when he crashed out on lap eight.

There were no further changes among the first six. The only rider doing any overtaking was Rossi, and it was at a desultory pace compared with his usual. He'd got away 12th, passed Aoyama for 11th on lap three, and then took another five to close on Elias and slip by.

His next victim, on lap nine, was Abraham, but he would get no further. Only attrition promoted him to sixth.

The only other change came when Aoyama, stuck inches behind Capirossi for most of the race, finally pounced on lap 18. He rapidly rode away to close right up on Elias at the flag.

Stoner took over the title lead in style: it looked ominous for the rest. But the struggle wasn't over yet.

MOTO2 RACE – 18 laps

Conditions were dire for the first race of the day, with Hernandez crashing on the sighting lap and mechanics making hasty repairs on the grid to get him away just in time. Marquez likewise had mechanics fussing around his hastily-built new bike, setting it as best they could.

The Spaniard had Redding and Bradl alongside; Cluzel, Corsi and Pirro behind. Fast men were spread all the way back, caught out by the conditions: de Angelis tenth, Luthi 15th, Smith 28th and Iannone in 33rd. There would be more than the usual overtaking going on, but in the spray kicked up by 38 bikes, it wasn't going to be easy for the spectators to follow, let alone the riders.

Those fans were rewarded when Redding led away, with Bradl, Krummenacher and Sofuoglu in pursuit. By the end of lap one, Marquez had already dropped to ninth, and he would fall further back before crashing out on lap seven.

Redding's run lasted just three laps, until Bradl slipped cleanly past at Copse. By now, Pasini, who had qualified 22nd, but finished lap one sixth, was past Sofuoglu, and made short work of Redding to take second on lap five. He was in the mood for overtaking and flew straight past Bradl as well. By the end of lap six, he was a full second ahead. He didn't make the end of the next lap, however, sliding down and out in the wet grass with a certain inevitability.

Bradl was now three seconds clear of Sofuoglu, with Redding falling further back.

The Briton thrilling the crowd was Smith. He'd gained 15 places on the first lap alone, riding almost completely blind and trusting in fate. He carried on gaining three or four places a lap until he arrived behind Redding at the end of lap seven.

Smith was straight past him, too, and then began hunting down Sofuoglu when the Turk fell at the last corner at the end of lap ten. Bradl by now was out of reach, more than five seconds away; Smith, in turn, was comfortably clear of what had become a three-way battle between Pirro, Redding and Cluzel. By the end, Pirro was well ahead, and Redding more than five seconds down on Cluzel in fifth.

The rest of the top ten were spaced out behind – Rabat sixth; then Takahashi getting ahead of the remounted

Sofuoglu, and Hernandez, with Corsi taking tenth narrowly ahead of Krummenacher. Iannone was a pointless 16th after another dire weekend.

Not surprisingly, there were crashers galore, including (as well as those named above) Pons, Jordi Torres (substituting for the injured Simon), Morales, Simeon and de Rosa, who was back with a new team, SAG, in place of Colombian Santiago Hernandez, supposedly because he had visa problems, but in fact he wouldn't be back.

Bradl's fourth win in six races meant that he had almost double the points of the next man: 127 to Corsi on 65. He was making it look easy.

125cc RACE – 17 laps

It was still raining for the 125s, though not as hard as earlier. Vinales was narrowly ahead of Terol on the front row, with Zarco alongside.

The race for the lead was absorbing and long lasting. Folger was first, Terol heading the pursuit. But the points leader was dropping back rapidly, and by the end of lap two, Zarco was on the German's back wheel and the pair were well ahead of the pursuit.

They needed no help to make a race of it. Zarco led laps seven and eight, then again 11 and 12. Next time around, Folger was in front again and intent on breaking away. Riding with a maturity beyond his 17 years, he gained almost a second on the following lap and was 3.8 ahead at the finish.

Terol had quickly dropped to the back of the pursuing group, with Vinales taking over – until he crashed out on lap 12. He had dragged Faubel clear of the pack, and he was left in a safe third.

Martin had a spell leading the chase, but by the end Salom and Vazquez had got past him. Cortese was next, Terol dropping off the back.

Kornfeil was ninth and Kent tenth, but only after Schrotter had crashed the independent Mahindra in front of them with three laps to go. Danny Webb was 11th on the second Mahindra, his first points for the improving Indian-owned team.

Folger's third podium brought him within sight of Terol on points. The championship was hotting up here as well.

Above: Bradl won masterfully in the wet, but it was the start of a long drought for the German.

Left: Fausto Gresini congratulates his rider, Michele Pirro, on gaining his first Moto2 rostrum.

Below: Johan Folger (94) escaped this attack to deny Zarco that elusive win.

Photos: Gold & Goose

AIRASIA BRITISH GRAND PRIX

10–12 JUNE, 2011 · FIM WORLD CHAMPIONSHIP ROUND 6

OFFICIAL TIMEKEEPER

SILVERSTONE GRAND PRIX CIRCUIT

20 laps
Length: 5.902km / 3.667 miles
Width: 17m

Key
96/60 kph/mph
⚙ Gear

Club 130/81
Vale 78/48
Luffield 75/47
Woodcot 160/99
Abbey 160/99
Brooklands 75/47
Stowe 160/99
Farm 160/99
Wellington Straight
Hangar straight 312/194
The Loop 87/54
Copse 95/59
Chapel 140/87
Becketts 150/93
Maggotts 160/99

MotoGP · RACE DISTANCE: 20 laps, 73.347 miles/118.040km · RACE WEATHER: Wet (air 11°C, humidity 85%, track 10°C)

Pos.	Rider	Nat.	No.	Entrant	Machine	Tyres	Laps	Time & speed
1	**Casey Stoner**	AUS	27	Repsol Honda Team	Honda	B	20	47m 53.459s 91.891mph/ 147.885km/h
2	**Andrea Dovizioso**	ITA	4	Repsol Honda Team	Honda	B	20	48m 08.618s
3	**Colin Edwards**	USA	5	Monster Yamaha Tech 3	Yamaha	B	20	48m 14.939s
4	**Nicky Hayden**	USA	69	Ducati Team	Ducati	B	20	48m 20.443s
5	**Alvaro Bautista**	SPA	19	Rizla Suzuki MotoGP	Suzuki	B	20	48m 29.028s
6	**Valentino Rossi**	ITA	46	Ducati Team	Ducati	B	20	48m 57.985s
7	**Karel Abraham**	CZE	17	Cardion AB Motoracing	Ducati	B	20	49m 26.109s
8	**Toni Elias**	SPA	24	LCR Honda MotoGP	Honda	B	20	49m 45.397s
9	**Hiroshi Aoyama**	JPN	7	San Carlo Honda Gresini	Honda	B	20	49m 45.809s
10	**Loris Capirossi**	ITA	65	Pramac Racing Team	Ducati	B	20	49m 56.771s
11	**Hector Barbera**	SPA	8	Mapfre Aspar Team MotoGP	Ducati	B	19	48m 10.582s
12	**Randy de Puniet**	FRA	14	Pramac Racing Team	Ducati	B	19	48m 13.094s
	Marco Simoncelli	ITA	58	San Carlo Honda Gresini	Honda	B	10	DNF
	Jorge Lorenzo	SPA	1	Yamaha Factory Racing	Yamaha	B	8	DNF
	Ben Spies	USA	11	Yamaha Factory Racing	Yamaha	B	7	DNF

Fastest lap: Nicky Hayden, on lap 17, 2m 21.432s, 93.348mph/150.229km/h.
Lap record: Jorge Lorenzo, SPA (Yamaha), 2m 03.526s, 106.879mph/172.005km/h (2010).
Event best maximum speed: Casey Stoner, 193.500mph/311.400km/h (free practice 1).

Qualifying

Weather: Dry
Air Temp: 17° Humidity: 25%
Track Temp: 32°

1	Stoner	2m 02.020s
2	Simoncelli	2m 02.208s
3	Lorenzo	2m 02.237s
4	Spies	2m 02.677s
5	Dovizioso	2m 03.212s
6	Abraham	2m 04.151s
7	Hayden	2m 04.304s
8	Edwards	2m 04.508s
9	Bautista	2m 04.520s
10	De Puniet	2m 04.589s
11	Aoyama	2m 04.919s
12	Barbera	2m 05.164s
13	Rossi	2m 05.781s
14	Elias	2m 05.862s
15	Capirossi	2m 06.256s
16	Crutchlow	2m 07.911s

Fastest race laps

1	Hayden	2m 21.432s
2	Stoner	2m 21.723s
3	Edwards	2m 21.823s
4	Simoncelli	2m 22.189s
5	Dovizioso	2m 22.723s
6	Lorenzo	2m 22.752s
7	Bautista	2m 23.025s
8	Rossi	2m 24.421s
9	Abraham	2m 25.182s
10	Aoyama	2m 25.287s
11	Spies	2m 25.292s
12	Elias	2m 26.302s
13	Barbera	2m 27.485s
14	Capirossi	2m 27.843s
15	De Puniet	2m 29.065s

Championship Points

1	Stoner	116
2	Lorenzo	98
3	Dovizioso	83
4	Rossi	68
5	Pedrosa	61
6	Hayden	60
7	Aoyama	43
8	Edwards	37
9	Spies	36
10	Abraham	33
11	Simoncelli	32
12	Barbera	31
13	Crutchlow	30
14	Elias	28
15	Bautista	22
16	Capirossi	22
17	De Puniet	10
18	Hopkins	6

Team Points

1	Repsol Honda Team	171
2	Yamaha Factory Racing	134
3	Ducati Team	128
4	San Carlo Honda Gresini	75
5	Monster Yamaha Tech 3	67
6	Cardion AB Motoracing	33
7	Pramac Racing Team	32
8	Mapfre Aspar Team MotoGP	31
9	Rizla Suzuki MotoGP	28
10	LCR Honda MotoGP	28

Constructor Points

1	Honda	145
2	Yamaha	114
3	Ducati	76
4	Suzuki	28

Grid order	1	2	3	4	5	6	7	8	9	10	11	12	13	14	15	16	17	18	19	20	
27 STONER	4	27	27	27	27	27	27	27	27	27	27	27	27	27	27	27	27	27	27	27	1
58 SIMONCELLI	27	4	4	4	4	4	4	4	4	4	4	4	4	4	4	4	4	4	4	4	2
1 LORENZO	58	58	58	1	1	1	1	1	58	58	5	5	5	5	5	5	5	5	5	5	3
11 SPIES	1	1	1	58	58	58	58	58	5	5	69	69	69	69	69	69	69	69	69	69	4
4 DOVIZIOSO	69	69	11	11	5	5	5	5	69	69	19	19	19	19	19	19	19	19	19	19	5
17 ABRAHAM	11	11	5	5	11	11	11	69	19	19	46	46	46	46	46	46	46	46	46	46	6
69 HAYDEN	5	5	69	69	69	69	69	19	46	46	17	17	17	17	17	17	17	17	17	17	7
5 EDWARDS	24	24	24	19	19	19	19	17	17	17	24	24	24	24	24	24	24	24	24		8
19 BAUTISTA	19	19	19	24	24	17	17	46	24	24	65	65	65	65	65	65	65	7	7	7	9
14 DE PUNIET	17	17	17	17	17	24	24	24	65	65	7	7	7	7	7	65	65	65		10
7 AOYAMA	7	7	46	46	46	46	46	65	7	7	14	14	14	14	14	14	8	8		11
8 BARBERA	46	46	7	7	7	65	65	7	8	14	8	8	8	8	8	8	14	14		12
46 ROSSI	8	65	65	65	65	7	7	8	14	14										
24 ELIAS	65	8	8	8	8	8	8	14												
65 CAPIROSSI	14	14	14	14	14	14	14													

8/14 Lapped rider

Moto2 — RACE DISTANCE: 18 laps, 66.012 miles/106.236km · RACE WEATHER: Wet (air 11°C, humidity 82%, track 12°C)

Pos.	Rider	Nat.	No.	Entrant	Machine	Laps	Time & Speed
1	**Stefan Bradl**	GER	65	Viessmann Kiefer Racing	Kalex	18	44m 10.236s 89.668mph/ 144.307km/h
2	**Bradley Smith**	GBR	38	Tech 3 Racing	Tech 3	18	44m 17.837s
3	**Michele Pirro**	ITA	51	Gresini Racing Moto2	Moriwaki	18	44m 22.477s
4	**Jules Cluzel**	FRA	16	NGM Forward Racing	Suter	18	44m 27.507s
5	**Scott Redding**	GBR	45	Marc VDS Racing Team	Suter	18	44m 33.767s
6	**Esteve Rabat**	SPA	34	Blusens-STX	FTR	18	44m 38.897s
7	**Yuki Takahashi**	JPN	72	Gresini Racing Moto2	Moriwaki	18	44m 42.627s
8	**Kenan Sofuoglu**	TUR	54	Technomag-CIP	Suter	18	44m 44.898s
9	**Yonny Hernandez**	COL	68	Blusens-STX	FTR	18	44m 47.417s
10	**Simone Corsi**	ITA	3	Ioda Racing Project	FTR	18	44m 49.217s
11	**Randy Krummenacher**	SWI	4	GP Team Switzerland Kiefer Racing	Kalex	18	44m 49.893s
12	**Max Neukirchner**	GER	76	MZ Racing Team	MZ-RE Honda	18	45m 01.858s
13	**Kev Coghlan**	GBR	49	Aeroport de Castello	FTR	18	45m 05.046s
14	**Alex Baldolini**	ITA	25	NGM Forward Racing	Suter	18	45m 06.478s
15	**Thomas Luthi**	SWI	12	Interwetten Paddock Moto2	Suter	18	45m 11.005s
16	Andrea Iannone	ITA	29	Speed Master	Suter	18	45m 16.434s
17	Mike di Meglio	FRA	63	Tech 3 Racing	Tech 3	18	45m 29.766s
18	Aleix Espargaro	SPA	40	Pons HP 40	Pons Kalex	18	45m 37.328s
19	Javier Fores	SPA	21	Mapfre Aspar Team Moto2	Suter	18	45m 40.085s
20	Dominique Aegerter	SWI	77	Technomag-CIP	Suter	18	45m 40.574s
21	Raffaele de Rosa	ITA	35	SAG Team	FTR	18	46m 08.028s
22	Valentin Debise	FRA	53	Speed Up	FTR	18	46m 21.340s
23	Robertino Pietri	VEN	39	Italtrans Racing Team	Suter	18	46m 39.404s
24	Mashel Al Naimi	QAT	95	QMMF Racing Team	Moriwaki	17	46m 17.686s
25	Nasser Hasan Al Malki	QAT	96	QMMF Racing Team	Moriwaki	17	46m 17.874s
	Pol Espargaro	SPA	44	HP Tuenti Speed Up	FTR	15	DNF
	Anthony West	AUS	13	MZ Racing Team	MZ-RE Honda	14	DNF
	Kenny Noyes	USA	9	Avintia-STX	FTR	14	DNF
	Claudio Corti	ITA	71	Italtrans Racing Team	Suter	13	DNF
	Alex de Angelis	RSM	15	JIR Moto2	Motobi	11	DNF
	Xavier Simeon	BEL	19	Tech 3 B	Tech 3	10	DNF
	Carmelo Morales	SPA	31	Desguaces La Torre G22	Moriwaki	8	DNF
	Ratthapark Wilairot	THA	14	Thai Honda Singha SAG	FTR	8	DNF
	Marc Marquez	SPA	93	Team CatalunyaCaixa Repsol	Suter	7	DNF
	Mattia Pasini	ITA	75	Ioda Racing Project	FTR	6	DNF
	Mika Kallio	FIN	36	Marc VDS Racing Team	Suter	6	DNF
	Jordi Torres	SPA	18	Mapfre Aspar Team Moto2	Suter	3	DNF
	Axel Pons	SPA	80	Pons HP 40	Pons Kalex	0	DNF

Fastest lap: Stefan Bradl, on lap 16, 2m 25.096s, 90.990mph/146.435km/h.

Lap record: Thomas Luthi, SWI (Moriwaki), 2m 09.886s, 101.646mph/163.583km/h (2010).

Event best maximum speed: Stefan Bradl, 167.500mph/269.500km/h (free practice 3).

Qualifying: Dry

Air: 14° Humidity: 37% Ground: 23°

1	Marquez	2m 08.101s
2	Redding	2m 08.598s
3	Bradl	2m 08.618s
4	Cluzel	2m 08.923s
5	Corsi	2m 08.976s
6	Pirro	2m 09.021s
7	A. Espargaro	2m 09.216s
8	Krummenacher	2m 09.415s
9	Di Meglio	2m 09.527s
10	De Angelis	2m 09.646s
11	Corti	2m 09.656s
12	Takahashi	2m 09.679s
13	Sofuoglu	2m 09.711s
14	Luthi	2m 09.725s
15	De Rosa	2m 09.803s
16	Pons	2m 09.994s
17	Neukirchner	2m 10.069s
18	Simeon	2m 10.077s
19	Torres	2m 10.122s
20	Rabat	2m 10.220s
21	Y. Hernandez	2m 10.262s
22	Pasini	2m 10.312s
23	P. Espargaro	2m 10.514s
24	Coghlan	2m 10.551s
25	Morales	2m 10.565s
26	Kallio	2m 10.744s
27	Noyes	2m 10.765s
28	Smith	2m 10.804s
29	Debise	2m 10.920s
30	Fores	2m 10.968s
31	Aegerter	2m 11.057s
32	Wilairot	2m 11.085s
33	Iannone	2m 11.335s
34	Baldolini	2m 11.399s
35	Pietri	2m 11.562s
36	West	2m 13.483s
37	Al Naimi	2m 13.935s
38	Al Malki	2m 15.869s

Fastest race laps

1	Bradl	2m 25.096s
2	Smith	2m 25.425s
3	Pirro	2m 25.676s
4	Sofuoglu	2m 25.697s
5	Pasini	2m 25.741s
6	Takahashi	2m 26.238s
7	Cluzel	2m 26.415s
8	Rabat	2m 26.426s
9	Redding	2m 26.973s
10	Simeon	2m 27.050s
11	Y. Hernandez	2m 27.223s
12	Neukirchner	2m 27.271s
13	West	2m 27.405s
14	Krummenacher	2m 27.501s
15	Baldolini	2m 27.574s
16	Kallio	2m 27.799s
17	Corsi	2m 27.934s
18	De Rosa	2m 28.106s
19	Coghlan	2m 28.163s
20	Iannone	2m 28.166s
21	Marquez	2m 28.170s
22	Luthi	2m 28.596s
23	A. Espargaro	2m 29.523s
24	Di Meglio	2m 29.550s
25	Fores	2m 29.873s
26	Morales	2m 29.934s
27	P. Espargaro	2m 30.237s
28	Aegerter	2m 30.326s
29	Torres	2m 30.730s
30	De Angelis	2m 31.426s
31	Debise	2m 31.885s
32	Wilairot	2m 31.905s
33	Corti	2m 32.252s
34	Pietri	2m 32.688s
35	Noyes	2m 32.815s
36	Al Naimi	2m 37.646s
37	Al Malki	2m 38.690s

Championship Points

1	Bradl	127
2	Corsi	65
3	Takahashi	56
4	Iannone	49
5	Simon	49
6	Luthi	48
7	Smith	47
8	Marquez	45
9	De Angelis	42
10	Pirro	37
11	A. Espargaro	31
12	Krummenacher	29
13	Rabat	28
14	Cluzel	27
15	Aegerter	24
16	Y. Hernandez	20
17	Neukirchner	18
18	Redding	16
19	P. Espargaro	13
20	Baldolini	13
21	Coghlan	11
22	Sofuoglu	8
23	Kallio	8
24	Di Meglio	7
25	Corti	5
26	West	5
27	Wilairot	4
28	Pasini	3
29	Simeon	2
30	Cardus	2
31	Pons	1

Constructor Points

1	Kalex	127
2	Suter	123
3	Moriwaki	74
4	FTR	69
5	Tech 3	56
6	Motobi	42
7	Pons Kalex	32
8	MZ-RE Honda	18

125cc — RACE DISTANCE: 17 laps, 62.345 miles/100.334km · RACE WEATHER: Wet (air 11°C, humidity 79%, track 11°C)

Pos.	Rider	Nat.	No.	Entrant	Machine	Laps	Time & Speed
1	**Jonas Folger**	GER	94	Red Bull Ajo MotorSport	Aprilia	17	43m 48.862s 85.375mph/ 137.398km/h
2	**Johann Zarco**	FRA	5	Avant-AirAsia-Ajo	Derbi	17	43m 52.747s
3	**Hector Faubel**	SPA	55	Bankia Aspar Team 125cc	Aprilia	17	44m 03.813s
4	**Luis Salom**	SPA	39	RW Racing GP	Aprilia	17	44m 06.026s
5	**Efren Vazquez**	SPA	7	Avant-AirAsia-Ajo	Derbi	17	44m 06.265s
6	**Adrian Martin**	SPA	26	Bankia Aspar Team 125cc	Aprilia	17	44m 08.098s
7	**Sandro Cortese**	GER	11	Intact-Racing Team Germany	Aprilia	17	44m 10.471s
8	**Nicolas Terol**	SPA	18	Bankia Aspar Team 125cc	Aprilia	17	44m 14.029s
9	**Jakub Kornfeil**	CZE	84	Ongetta-Centro Seta	Aprilia	17	44m 21.207s
10	**Danny Kent**	GBR	52	Red Bull Ajo MotorSport	Aprilia	17	44m 21.833s
11	**Danny Webb**	GBR	99	Mahindra Racing	Mahindra	17	44m 43.566s
12	**Taylor Mackenzie**	GBR	17	Phonica Racing	Aprilia	17	44m 52.831s
13	**Louis Rossi**	FRA	96	Matteoni Racing	Aprilia	17	45m 24.178s
14	**Alexis Masbou**	FRA	10	Caretta Technology	KTM	17	45m 32.245s
15	**John McPhee**	GBR	71	Racing Steps Foundation KRP	Aprilia	17	45m 34.835s
16	Niklas Ajo	FIN	31	TT Motion Events Racing	Aprilia	17	45m 35.201s
17	Alberto Moncayo	SPA	23	Andalucia Banca Civica	Aprilia	17	45m 41.698s
18	Zulfahmi Khairuddin	MAL	63	Airasia-Sic-Ajo	Derbi	17	46m 14.831s
19	Joan Perello	SPA	36	Matteoni Racing	Aprilia	17	46m 25.594s
20	Alessandro Tonucci	ITA	19	Team Italia FMI	Aprilia	16	45m 25.571s
	Marcel Schrotter	GER	77	Mahindra Racing	Mahindra	14	DNF
	Sergio Gadea	SPA	33	Blusens by Paris Hilton Racing	Aprilia	12	DNF
	Maverick Vinales	SPA	25	Blusens by Paris Hilton Racing	Aprilia	11	DNF
	Peter Sebestyen	HUN	56	Caretta Technology	KTM	11	DNF
	Giulian Pedone	SWI	30	Phonica Racing	Aprilia	11	DNF
	Simone Grotzkyj	ITA	15	Phonica Racing	Aprilia	10	DNF
	Jasper Iwema	NED	53	Ongetta-Abbink Metaal	Aprilia	10	DNF
	Francesco Mauriello	ITA	43	WTR-Ten10 Racing	Aprilia	9	DNF
	Sturla Fagerhaug	NOR	50	WTR-Ten10 Racing	Aprilia	0	DNF
	Harry Stafford	GBR	21	Ongetta-Centro Seta	Aprilia	0	DNS

Fastest lap: Adrian Martin, on lap 8, 2m 32.946s, 86.320mph/138.919km/h.

Lap record: Pol Espargaro, SPA (Derbi), 2m 13.781s, 98.686mph/158.820km/h (2010).

Event best maximum speed: Nicolas Terol, 139.600mph/224.700km/h (qualifying practice).

Qualifying: Dry

Air: 17° Humidity: 26% Ground: 33°

1	Vinales	2m 14.684s
2	Terol	2m 14.720s
3	Zarco	2m 15.266s
4	Vazquez	2m 15.284s
5	Cortese	2m 15.589s
6	Salom	2m 15.713s
7	Faubel	2m 15.747s
8	Folger	2m 16.073s
9	Moncayo	2m 16.250s
10	Gadea	2m 16.274s
11	Martin	2m 16.743s
12	Kent	2m 17.038s
13	Grotzkyj	2m 17.298s
14	Khairuddin	2m 17.468s
15	Webb	2m 17.677s
16	Kornfeil	2m 17.751s
17	Fagerhaug	2m 17.766s
18	Iwema	2m 17.784s
19	Rossi	2m 18.001s
20	Masbou	2m 18.076s
21	Ajo	2m 18.259s
22	Schrotter	2m 18.674s
23	Stafford	2m 18.906s
24	Pedone	2m 19.421s
25	Sebestyen	2m 19.539s
26	Mackenzie	2m 19.619s
27	Tonucci	2m 19.875s
28	Morciano	2m 20.308s
29	Perello	2m 20.879s
30	McPhee	2m 21.235s
31	Mauriello	2m 22.012s

Fastest race laps

1	Martin	2m 32.946s
2	Zarco	2m 33.010s
3	Folger	2m 33.045s
4	Vazquez	2m 33.084s
5	Vinales	2m 33.245s
6	Faubel	2m 33.444s
7	Kent	2m 33.567s
8	Grotzkyj	2m 33.866s
9	Terol	2m 33.914s
10	Cortese	2m 33.920s
11	Salom	2m 33.969s
12	Gadea	2m 34.190s
13	Schrotter	2m 34.200s
14	Kornfeil	2m 34.256s
15	Mackenzie	2m 35.477s
16	Webb	2m 35.981s
17	Rossi	2m 36.617s
18	Iwema	2m 36.664s
19	Masbou	2m 36.960s
20	Pedone	2m 38.067s
21	Moncayo	2m 38.638s
22	Ajo	2m 38.657s
23	McPhee	2m 38.863s
24	Khairuddin	2m 38.913s
25	Perello	2m 40.099s
26	Sebestyen	2m 40.335s
27	Tonucci	2m 47.948s
28	Mauriello	2m 50.237s

Championship Points

1	Terol	128
2	Folger	93
3	Zarco	83
4	Cortese	81
5	Vazquez	68
6	Vinales	65
7	Faubel	48
8	Gadea	36
9	Salom	35
10	Martin	30
11	Kent	28
12	Kornfeil	25
13	Oliveira	22
14	Mackenzie	15
15	Moncayo	15
16	Rossi	13
17	Grotzkyj	12
18	Khairuddin	11
19	Ono	8
20	Webb	5
21	Ajo	5
22	Masbou	5
23	Iwema	4
24	Schrotter	3
25	McPhee	1
26	Rodriguez	1

Constructor Points

1	Aprilia	150
2	Derbi	92
3	KTM	12
4	Mahindra	8

DUTCH TT
ASSEN CIRCUIT

Ben Spies was the unexpected winner,
riding clear of the field after the tangle
(inset) between Simoncelli and Lorenzo.
Photos: Gold & Goose

BEN Spies greeted his first GP win with the hint of a grin, but no more animation in his voice than usual. "I'm still pumped up with adrenalin. It'll take a while to sink in," he droned at the post-race conference.

"Jeez," commented Stoner alongside. "If this is what you're like when you're pumped up, I'd hate to see you when you're not."

Spies's win was, in its way, as monotonous as his account of it, in that he'd led from the first lap to the last and had made it look straightforward to 92,150 race-day fans. His main excitement came as he swooped inside fast-starting team-mate Lorenzo on the way out of the first corner. He anticipated trouble three corners later, on the first left-hander. And he was right.

Immediately behind him, Simoncelli in third got caught out by the notorious cold-tyre snap and took Lorenzo down with him. Spies spotted it all on the big screen by the track on the back straight and set off to motor home. All he had to do was wait to see what the Hondas might do. Even with Stoner on board, that wasn't enough.

Spies had regularly shown the speed for top finishes, but tended to take time to get going. Not this time, and it was a fine way for Yamaha to crown the weekend's 50th-anniversary celebrations that had seen proud past relics, both human and mechanical, parade around the classic venue. All in the same red-and-white retro factory livery from the 1960s and 1970s.

Simoncelli may have been one among several fresh victims of the cold-side tyre syndrome, but if he had been hoping to retrieve his reputation somewhat after his second pole in three races, it could hardly have gone more wrong. Although both he and Lorenzo remounted, by knocking the Spaniard down, he had given the fullest justification to his greatest critic. Jorge was voluble, recalling how a one-race suspension had calmed him down: "He is faithful to his style. He consistently crashes in every race. He was rid-

ing like he was playing the PlayStation, just like we are all indestructible."

Others to fall victim to the cold-side tyre problem had been Stoner and Dovizioso, within minutes of each other on Friday morning's free practice. Both got away with it, not so Capirossi in qualifying, who fell at the fast Ramshoek before the chicane and was chased by his bike. He suffered broken ribs and a shoulder injury that would keep him out for two races to come.

The pre-race safety briefing had been another lively meeting, with control tyres top of the agenda. In practice, Bridgestone's pre-season predictions had been undermined again by cold weather, and the crashes underlined the complaints. Response was prompt: Bridgestone offered to ship in a fresh consignment of softer rear tyres – those used at Silverstone – overnight from their depot in Germany. This deviation from the regulations would require the agreement of all teams, but even as the truck was being loaded, one rogue team (thought to be Simoncelli's Gresini squad) said no, and that for the moment was the end of that.

Riders were short of practice anyway, because one of those problems of four-strokes struck with two fists in the Moto2 first free practice, forcing serial postponement and eventually cancellation of all afternoon proceedings. In tricky wet conditions, Marquez had slipped off, but got back on to return to the pits, unaware that he had holed the engine case. Almost simultaneously, Baldolini's motor blew. Again he was unaware that he was laying a stream of oil. A huge section of track was involved, and a number fell on the oil. Herculean efforts were made to clean up, until eventually the scrubbing trucks ran out of water. Hence cancellation, with extended sessions on Friday morning.

Four-strokes are always prone to laying a lethal trail and the likelihood will increase still further with Moto3 in 2012. Do riders need re-educating to get them off the track quicker? Stoner would not condemn Baldolini. With spray behind,

Above left: Try as they might, they couldn't clear the oil. Friday afternoon practice had to be cancelled.

Left: Giacomo Agostini was one of many old heroes who helped celebrate Yamaha's 50 years of grand prix racing.

Below left: New bike, but not much new joy for Rossi. This was 2012's prototype, with a shrunken engine.

Far left: Stoner goes rolling. Dovizioso and temporary Repsol team-mate Aoyama all crashed in the same Saturday morning session.

Below: From pole to the dog-box – a wild-eyed Simoncelli before the start.
Photos: Gold & Goose

oil smoke is not easy to see, and an engine misfire could be for all sorts of reasons. His answer was simple: "We should all go back to two-strokes."

The latest chapter in the Rossi-Ducati saga came in the form of a new bike. Dubbed GP11.1, this was a hybrid version of the GP12 that both riders had already tested. The main difference was a totally different rear suspension arrangement, which appeared to solve the pumping problem – at least with the full-size 1000cc-rules engine fitted. Ducati guru Filippo Preziosi had the idea of installing the 800cc engine, but differences in the 2012 unit meant that 2011's wouldn't fit. The solution was to reduce the capacity of the GP12 engine to 800cc. It was effectively a new bike, but Rossi's bright hopes were played foul by the restricted practice and the bad weather: in terms of lap times, he was no better off than before.

Hayden meanwhile received a new front chassis, dubbed GP11 Step Two, but given the conditions it stayed in the truck. "I don't believe qualifying is the right time to be testing a new bike," he commented.

Crutchlow was back, screwed together and strapped up, ready to race at another track where he had prior knowledge. Pedrosa was not, in spite of the two-weekend break, and the rumours were growing wilder and wilder while his team still had no firm information. Aoyama took his place on the Repsol factory bike, with tubby tester Kousuke Akiyoshi standing in for him on the San Carlo Honda.

A rare appearance by a girl GP racer ended badly for Spanish national campaigner Elena Rosell, the latest replacement for Simon in the Aspar team. She was one of the victims of the oil and had two more crashes that left her badly knocked about. She did not get as far as the qualifying session.

MOTOGP RACE – 26 laps

A return to 2010's three sessions meant the new routine of practice and qualifying was disrupted, while the wet first session further stole away set-up time. This was especially costly for Rossi, who was second fastest in the first wet session on his new bike, but fell away thereafter to qualify 11th; Abraham was the top Ducati rider in seventh.

Up front, it was Simoncelli fastest in every session and all conditions, although Spies allowed that he might have tipped him off pole had he not been baulked by Capirossi's crash while on his best lap. He was still very close, with Stoner fully three-tenths off, unsettled if unhurt by his morning high-sider.

Lorenzo led row two from Dovizioso and the returned Crutchlow; Hayden was at the far end of the row behind.

Morning warm-up was wet, spoiling chances to test set-up changes, but giving Rossi his first chance all year to top the time sheet. But it was hardly relevant: second place went to an unenthusiastic Lorenzo, splashing around for only four laps, while Stoner did a mere three and was fourth from last.

Thirty minutes before the race start, it was still raining. Ben Spies went out for the sighting lap on wet tyres. When he saw how it was drying, he pitted for a hasty bike change and just made it to the grid in time.

Lorenzo took a blazing start from row two to lead into the first corner, Spies pushing past immediately: a wise move. The crash behind him gave a little breathing space and he made the most of it. "In some ways, it was an easy race; in some ways, hard," he said. "It's been a while since I've led a race, and when you see your pit board saying 'Plus 3.5', but the name underneath is 'Stoner', you don't rest easy."

Those following avoided the debris, with Dovizioso heading the pursuit from Stoner and Crutchlow. Rossi had got through the first-corners scramble well and was right behind, but he would take five to pass the English rider. Even so, Crutchlow stayed with him until he pitted on lap 11. His front tyre was ruined, along with his hopes of a good result on his comeback from injury.

Up front, Stoner passed Dovi on lap two, and they stayed close for the first half of the race. The Australian was unsure of his potential after his morning crash: "After that, we couldn't get grip in the rear. We tried a different setting to test in warm-up, but it was wet, so taking it into the race was a bit of a gamble."

This made him tentative in the early laps as Spies sped away, and the gap was more than four seconds by lap three. He did close it down to just under 3.5 before half-distance, but then it opened up again when he decided that second was enough for his championship chances. Dovi had dropped a long way back by the end, battling with a soft front tyre he felt obliged to choose because of the conditions, but didn't like. "But Valentino was not so fast, so I could control the gap," he said.

Rossi had never been close enough to challenge and was alone after passing Crutchlow. But he took some positives. After problems setting up his new GP11.1 in practice, they'd made a change overnight that improved the feeling at the rear. "In some corners, I was 15km/h faster than yesterday," he said. "I am a lot more optimistic today, but we still lose a lot of time [a second a lap] on the leaders."

Hayden was another 12 seconds adrift in fifth, having lost time running across the chicane on the first lap. He'd been passed by Edwards in the early stages, but the Texan faded with tyre problems as the race wore on, and Nicky was ahead again with nine laps to go. But at the end, he was only two seconds away from being caught by Lorenzo, charging up from the back.

The champion had lost only 30 seconds through his tumble, while Simoncelli was a bit more battered and another half-minute behind him. The Spaniard cut steadily through from then to the end of the race, intent on salvaging what he could.

This put Edwards seventh, with Pedrosa replacement Aoyama eighth. Then came the remounted Simoncelli, who passed Elias on the last lap. Bautista was the last rider on the same lap as the leader. Barbera and Akiyoshi trailed in behind, Crutchlow another lap down, but still in the points.

Abraham crashed out on the first lap, de Puniet on the second.

MOTO2 RACE – 24 laps

Hitherto, Bradl's domination of the class seemed to have been easy. Even now, he was being courted by MotoGP teams – by Honda for a learning year with LCR, and Yamaha to join Tech 3, with a further offer of a CRT ride for his current team. Did all this mean he took his eye of the ball?

He was still on pole, his sixth in seven races, but Marquez was second and ready to suggest imminent regime change. So far, the young Spaniard had only finished two of his first six races, but with a win and a second place. Assen brought a third finish and a second win, and he moved up to second in the championship.

Corsi completed the front row; Luthi, Takahashi and Aleix Espargaro formed the second. Redding and Smith were on rows three and four; Iannone again way back in 25th.

The race was wet at the start, gradually drying.

Corsi led away, but by the third lap he'd been swallowed and was dropping back. Smith was the new leader and he hung on until lap ten, by which time he, Sofuoglu and Marquez were clear of the rest, Takahashi hanging on behind.

Sofuoglu took over for the next six laps, while Marquez firmly grabbed second from Smith on the 14th. Three laps later, he did the same to Sofuoglu. It was Takahashi who followed on, and they stayed close until the Japanese rider slid off on lap 20, giving Marquez the breathing space he needed to pull away by better than two seconds.

There was one more change, when Sofuoglu made a daring pass on Smith; then they all settled where they were and finished quite spaced out.

Wet specialist and 2003 Assen winner Anthony West had come through from 13th on the first lap to fourth, enjoying

Above: "He stays faithful to his style … like he was playing the PlayStation." Simoncelli skittles Lorenzo at the first left-hand corner.

Top right: Eventual winner Marquez (93) trails Sofuoglu (54) and rostrum-bound Smith.

Above right: Just to be sure, Moto2 was declared a wet race.

Above far right: Conditions gave rain-master West the chance to show his talent on the MZ.

Above right: Esteve Rabat presses on as Moto2 points leader Bradl slides to earth.

Right: Maverick Vinales and his Blusens crew celebrate another 125cc win.

Photos: Gold & Goose

the conditions and a rare chance to shine on the struggling MZ: he now had a third (or was it fourth?) new chassis, this time an FTR like team-mate Neukirchner's. It was his best result since 2005, after years of mainly very unequal struggles. He was 16 seconds down on Smith and three clear of the next battle.

Here de Angelis reclaimed fifth from Pasini on the last lap: the latter had charged through the midfield pack. Rabat also took Luthi on a busy last lap, with Krummenacher less than a second adrift. Pirro had been involved in the battle, but slipped off and remounted, finishing out of the points.

Neukirchner was another ten seconds away in tenth.

Bradl had been in the front group early on, finishing lap one fifth, but had fallen back two places to the next group, never looking confident and dropping to 13th when he ran wide. He was back up to seventh when he crashed out on lap 21. Iannone moved unspectacularly through to 12th; Corsi fell back to an eventual 14th.

Cluzel was first of a number to slip off – on the warm-up lap. He made the start, then crashed again on lap two, by which time countryman di Meglio had also tumbled out. They were followed by Hernandez, Wilairot, Debise, Pons, Simeon, Takahashi, Pol Espargaro, Noyes, Bradl, Odendaal and Pirro. Kallio retired to the pits.

125cc RACE – 14 laps (shortened from 22)

The crucial title moment came in qualifying, when Terol fell and sustained hand injuries that put him out of the race. The crucial race moment was on lap 15 of 22, marking two-thirds distance. In worsening conditions, it meant the race could be stopped. That gave dazzling rookie Vinales a fine second win, after a second successive pole start.

Conditions were tricky and the race tooth-and-nail.

Gadea led at first, a huge gang inches behind. Vazquez and team-mate Zarco each took a turn, then Cortese, who took Zarco and Gadea with him as he opened a little gap by lap seven. Then rain started spotting here and there, and they closed up again – and Vinales started to move forwards from the back of the group.

He took over on lap ten. Two laps later, he was still only narrowly ahead when the rain became heavier. Those in pursuit slowed down, Cortese actually raising his hand. But Vinales took no notice, and his lead was up to 3.6 seconds at the end of lap 15, when the race was stopped.

Salom moved to the front of the group as conditions deteriorated to take second, Gadea a close third.

Zarco and British rookie Kent were both ahead of cautious Cortese; Vazquez behind lost touch in the rain, and was all but swallowed up by Folger and Schrotter, the Mahindra's best result so far (team-mate Webb was 13th, the team's first double points). Substitute Fagerhaug crashed out, then Martin and Iwema together. The Dutchman remounted only to crash again; Stafford and Rossi also crashed, but both managed to rejoin.

motoGP | **TISSOT** SWISS WATCHES SINCE 1853

OFFICIAL TIMEKEEPER

TT ASSEN

26 laps
Length: 4.542km / 2.822 miles
Width: 13m

Haarbocht 115/71
Geert Timmer Bocht 100/62
Strubben 75/47
Duikersloot 105/65
Meeuwenmeer 265/165
Ramshoek 186/116
Ossebroeken
Asfalt Surf 275/178
Madijk
Ruskenhoek 110/68
De Bult 115/71
Stekkenwal 130/81
Mandeveen 105/65

Key
96/60 kph/mph
Gear

MotoGP

RACE DISTANCE: 26 laps, 73.379 miles/118.092km · RACE WEATHER: Dry (air 14°C, humidity 82%, track 16°C)

Pos.	Rider	Nat.	No.	Entrant	Machine	Tyres	Laps	Time & speed
1	**Ben Spies**	USA	11	Yamaha Factory Racing	Yamaha	B	26	41m 44.659s
								105.469mph/
								169.736km/h
2	**Casey Stoner**	AUS	27	Repsol Honda Team	Honda	B	26	41m 52.356s
3	**Andrea Dovizioso**	ITA	4	Repsol Honda Team	Honda	B	26	42m 12.165s
4	**Valentino Rossi**	ITA	46	Ducati Team	Ducati	B	26	42m 15.343s
5	**Nicky Hayden**	USA	69	Ducati Team	Ducati	B	26	42m 27.831s
6	**Jorge Lorenzo**	SPA	1	Yamaha Factory Racing	Yamaha	B	26	42m 29.195s
7	**Colin Edwards**	USA	5	Monster Yamaha Tech 3	Yamaha	B	26	42m 52.771s
8	**Hiroshi Aoyama**	JPN	7	Repsol Honda Team	Honda	B	26	42m 55.412s
9	**Marco Simoncelli**	ITA	58	San Carlo Honda Gresini	Honda	B	26	43m 09.584s
10	**Toni Elias**	SPA	24	LCR Honda MotoGP	Honda	B	26	43m 10.875s
11	**Alvaro Bautista**	SPA	19	Rizla Suzuki MotoGP	Suzuki	B	26	43m 23.125s
12	**Hector Barbera**	SPA	8	Mapfre Aspar Team MotoGP	Ducati	B	25	42m 11.017s
13	**Kousuke Akiyoshi**	JPN	64	San Carlo Honda Gresini	Honda	B	25	42m 58.437s
14	**Cal Crutchlow**	GBR	35	Monster Yamaha Tech 3	Yamaha	B	24	43m 07.755s
	Randy de Puniet	FRA	14	Pramac Racing Team	Ducati	B	1	DNF
	Karel Abraham	CZE	17	Cardion AB Motoracing	Ducati	B	0	DNF

Fastest lap: Ben Spies, on lap 12, 1m 35.240s, 106.679mph/171.684km/h.

Lap record: Dani Pedrosa, SPA (Honda), 1m 34.525s, 107.486mph/172.982km/h (2010).

Event best maximum speed: Nicky Hayden, 187.700mph/302.100km/h (qualifying).

Qualifying

Weather: Dry
Air Temp: 17° Humidity: 47%
Track Temp: 23°

1	Simoncelli	1m 34.718s
2	Spies	1m 34.727s
3	Stoner	1m 35.008s
4	Lorenzo	1m 35.143s
5	Dovizioso	1m 35.244s
6	Crutchlow	1m 35.329s
7	Abraham	1m 35.742s
8	Edwards	1m 35.818s
9	Hayden	1m 35.866s
10	De Puniet	1m 36.435s
11	Rossi	1m 36.564s
12	Aoyama	1m 36.580s
13	Barbera	1m 36.590s
14	Bautista	1m 36.820s
15	Capirossi	1m 37.130s
16	Elias	1m 37.651s
17	Akiyoshi	1m 39.006s

Fastest race laps

1	Spies	1m 35.240s
2	Stoner	1m 35.422s
3	Lorenzo	1m 35.641s
4	Dovizioso	1m 35.673s
5	Simoncelli	1m 35.962s
6	Edwards	1m 36.320s
7	Rossi	1m 36.700s
8	Crutchlow	1m 36.727s
9	Hayden	1m 36.764s
10	Aoyama	1m 37.561s
11	Elias	1m 38.516s
12	Bautista	1m 38.567s
13	Barbera	1m 39.040s
14	Akiyoshi	1m 40.512s

Championship Points

1	Stoner	136
2	Lorenzo	108
3	Dovizioso	99
4	Rossi	81
5	Hayden	71
6	Pedrosa	61
7	Spies	61
8	Aoyama	51
9	Edwards	46
10	Simoncelli	39
11	Barbera	35
12	Elias	34
13	Abraham	33
14	Crutchlow	32
15	Bautista	27
16	Capirossi	22
17	De Puniet	10
18	Hopkins	6
19	Akiyoshi	3

Team Points

1	Repsol Honda Team	199
2	Yamaha Factory Racing	169
3	Ducati Team	152
4	San Carlo Honda Gresini	85
5	Monster Yamaha Tech 3	78
6	Mapfre Aspar Team MotoGP	35
7	LCR Honda MotoGP	34
8	Rizla Suzuki MotoGP	33
9	Cardion AB Motoracing	33
10	Pramac Racing Team	32

Constructor Points

1	Honda	165
2	Yamaha	139
3	Ducati	89
4	Suzuki	33

Grid order	1	2	3	4	5	6	7	8	9	10	11	12	13	14	15	16	17	18	19	20	21	22	23	24	25	26	
58 SIMONCELLI	11	11	11	11	11	11	11	11	11	11	11	11	11	11	11	11	11	11	11	11	11	11	11	11	11	11	1
11 SPIES	4	27	27	27	27	27	27	27	27	27	27	27	27	27	27	27	27	27	27	27	27	27	27	27	27	27	2
27 STONER	27	4	4	4	4	4	4	4	4	4	4	4	4	4	4	4	4	4	4	4	4	4	4	4	4	4	3
1 LORENZO	35	35	35	35	46	46	46	46	46	46	46	46	46	46	46	46	46	46	46	46	46	46	46	46	46	46	4
4 DOVIZIOSO	46	46	46	46	35	35	35	35	35	35	5	5	5	5	5	5	5	69	69	69	69	69	69	69	69	69	5
35 CRUTCHLOW	5	69	69	69	5	5	5	5	5	69	69	69	69	69	69	69	5	5	5	5	1	1	1	1	1	1	6
17 ABRAHAM	69	5	5	69	69	69	69	69	69	35	7	7	1	1	1	1	1	1	1	1	5	5	5	5	5		7
5 EDWARDS	7	7	7	7	7	7	7	7	7	7	24	1	7	7	7	7	7	7	7	7	7	7	7	7			8
69 HAYDEN	24	24	24	24	24	24	24	24	24	24	1	24	24	24	24	24	24	24	24	24	24	24	24	58			9
14 DE PUNIET	14	19	19	19	19	19	19	19	19	1	19	19	19	19	19	19	19	19	19	58	58	58	24				10
46 ROSSI	19	8	8	8	8	1	1	1	1	19	19	8	58	58	58	58	58	58	58	19	19	19	19				11
7 AOYAMA	8	64	64	64	64	8	8	8	8	8	64	58	8	8	8	8	8	8	8	8	8	8					12
8 BARBERA	64	1	1	1	1	64	64	64	64	64	58	64	64	64	64	64	64	64	64	64	64	64					13
19 BAUTISTA	1	58	58	58	58	58	58	58	58	58	35	35	35	35	35	35	35	35	35	35	35						14
24 ELIAS	58																										
64 AKIYOSHI																											

35 Pit stop   8/35/64 Lapped rider

Moto2 — RACE DISTANCE: 24 laps, 67.734 miles/109.008km · RACE WEATHER: Wet (air 13°C, humidity 84%, track 13°C)

Pos.	Rider	Nat.	No.	Entrant	Machine	Laps	Time & Speed
1	**Marc Marquez**	SPA	93	Team CatalunyaCaixa Repsol	Suter	24	44m 30.409s 91.313mph/ 146.954km/h
2	**Kenan Sofuoglu**	TUR	54	Technomag-CIP	Suter	24	44m 32.806s
3	**Bradley Smith**	GBR	38	Tech 3 Racing	Tech 3	24	44m 36.827s
4	**Anthony West**	AUS	13	MZ Racing Team	MZ-RE Honda	24	44m 53.212s
5	**Alex de Angelis**	RSM	15	JIR Moto2	Motobi	24	44m 56.291s
6	**Mattia Pasini**	ITA	75	Ioda Racing Project	FTR	24	44m 57.260s
7	**Esteve Rabat**	SPA	34	Blusens-STX	FTR	24	44m 58.534s
8	**Thomas Luthi**	SWI	12	Interwetten Paddock Moto2	Suter	24	44m 59.121s
9	**Randy Krummenacher**	SWI	4	GP Team Switzerland Kiefer Racing	Kalex	24	45m 00.153s
10	**Max Neukirchner**	GER	76	MZ Racing Team	MZ-RE Honda	24	45m 10.176s
11	**Alex Baldolini**	ITA	25	NGM Forward Racing	Suter	24	45m 17.567s
12	**Andrea Iannone**	ITA	29	Speed Master	Suter	24	45m 21.255s
13	**Yonny Hernandez**	COL	68	Blusens-STX	FTR	24	45m 27.527s
14	**Simone Corsi**	ITA	3	Ioda Racing Project	FTR	24	45m 31.184s
15	**Claudio Corti**	ITA	71	Italtrans Racing Team	Suter	24	45m 36.719s
16	Aleix Espargaro	SPA	40	Pons HP 40	Pons Kalex	24	45m 37.173s
17	Michele Pirro	ITA	51	Gresini Racing Moto2	Moriwaki	24	45m 37.232s
18	Dominique Aegerter	SWI	77	Technomag-CIP	Suter	24	45m 46.705s
19	Ricard Cardus	SPA	88	QMMF Racing Team	Moriwaki	24	45m 51.933s
20	Carmelo Morales	SPA	31	Desguaces La Torre G22	Moriwaki	24	45m 52.698s
21	Kev Coghlan	GBR	49	Aeroport de Castello	FTR	24	46m 08.570s
22	Michael van der Mark	NED	66	EAB Racing	Ten Kate	24	46m 12.297s
23	Javier Fores	SPA	21	Mapfre Aspar Team Moto2	Suter	24	46m 12.598s
24	Scott Redding	GBR	45	Marc VDS Racing Team	Suter	23	44m 33.423s
25	Mashel Al Naimi	QAT	95	QMMF Racing Team	Moriwaki	23	44m 35.214s
26	Robertino Pietri	VEN	39	Italtrans Racing Team	Suter	23	44m 43.949s
	Stefan Bradl	GER	65	Viessmann Kiefer Racing	Kalex	20	DNF
	Steven Odendaal	RSA	97	MS Racing	Suter	20	DNF
	Yuki Takahashi	JPN	72	Gresini Racing Moto2	Moriwaki	19	DNF
	Pol Espargaro	SPA	44	HP Tuenti Speed Up	FTR	19	DNF
	Kenny Noyes	USA	9	Avintia-STX	FTR	19	DNF
	Xavier Simeon	BEL	19	Tech 3 B	Tech 3	18	DNF
	Mika Kallio	FIN	36	Marc VDS Racing Team	Suter	23	DNF
	Axel Pons	SPA	80	Pons HP 40	Pons Kalex	7	DNF
	Ratthapark Wilairot	THA	14	Thai Honda Singha SAG	FTR	5	DNF
	Valentin Debise	FRA	53	Speed Up	FTR	5	DNF
	Santiago Hernandez	COL	64	SAG Team	FTR	3	DNF
	Mike di Meglio	FRA	63	Tech 3 Racing	Tech 3	2	DNF
	Jules Cluzel	FRA	16	NGM Forward Racing	Suter	2	DNF

Fastest lap: Pol Espargaro, on lap 15, 1m 47.615s, 94.412mph/151.941km/h.
Lap record: Andrea Iannone, ITA (Speed Up), 1m 38.917s, 102.714mph/165.302km/h (2010).
Event best maximum speed: Thomas Luthi, 164.100mph/264.100km/h (qualifying).

Qualifying: Dry
Air: 17° Humidity: 43% Ground: 22°

1	Bradl	1m 39.305s
2	Marquez	1m 39.600s
3	Corsi	1m 39.700s
4	Luthi	1m 39.844s
5	Takahashi	1m 39.890s
6	A. Espargaro	1m 39.962s
7	Sofuoglu	1m 40.123s
8	Redding	1m 40.149s
9	Pirro	1m 40.234s
10	Smith	1m 40.238s
11	P. Espargaro	1m 40.469s
12	Di Meglio	1m 40.550s
13	Aegerter	1m 40.647s
14	Simeon	1m 40.726s
15	Corti	1m 40.744s
16	Kallio	1m 40.804s
17	Krummenacher	1m 40.925s
18	Pasini	1m 40.985s
19	Rabat	1m 41.036s
20	West	1m 41.068s
21	Y. Hernandez	1m 41.211s
22	De Angelis	1m 41.364s
23	Cluzel	1m 41.536s
24	Fores	1m 41.564s
25	Iannone	1m 41.642s
26	Noyes	1m 41.732s
27	Wilairot	1m 41.739s
28	Baldolini	1m 41.908s
29	S. Hernandez	1m 41.931s
30	Coghlan	1m 42.077s
31	Cardus	1m 42.160s
32	Morales	1m 42.308s
33	Van der Mark	1m 42.565s
34	Pons	1m 42.682s
35	Debise	1m 42.908s
36	Pietri	1m 43.200s
37	Odendaal	1m 44.240s
38	Al Naimi	1m 44.282s

Outside 107%

Neukirchner	1m 53.043s
Rosell	No Time

Fastest race laps

1	P. Espargaro	1m 47.615s
2	Marquez	1m 47.746s
3	Smith	1m 47.851s
4	Takahashi	1m 47.925s
5	Bradl	1m 48.024s
6	De Angelis	1m 48.070s
7	West	1m 48.108s
8	Simeon	1m 48.115s
9	Neukirchner	1m 48.123s
10	Krummenacher	1m 48.157s
11	Rabat	1m 48.165s
12	Sofuoglu	1m 48.176s
13	Pirro	1m 48.238s
14	Baldolini	1m 48.310s
15	Pasini	1m 48.523s
16	Luthi	1m 48.660s
17	Y. Hernandez	1m 48.764s
18	Iannone	1m 49.315s
19	Morales	1m 49.622s
20	Aegerter	1m 49.704s
21	Corti	1m 49.742s
22	Corsi	1m 50.176s
23	A. Espargaro	1m 50.760s
24	Cardus	1m 50.848s
25	Van der Mark	1m 50.999s
26	Coghlan	1m 51.339s
27	Odendaal	1m 51.458s
28	Al Naimi	1m 51.478s
29	Redding	1m 51.590s
30	Noyes	1m 51.633s
31	Pietri	1m 51.757s
32	Fores	1m 51.777s
33	Kallio	1m 53.058s
34	Di Meglio	1m 54.206s
35	Pons	1m 55.386s
36	Wilairot	1m 56.026s
37	Cluzel	1m 57.047s
38	Debise	1m 57.080s
39	S. Hernandez	1m 57.146s

Championship Points

1	Bradl	127
2	Marquez	70
3	Corsi	67
4	Smith	63
5	Takahashi	56
6	Luthi	56
7	Iannone	53
8	De Angelis	53
9	Simon	49
10	Pirro	37
11	Rabat	37
12	Krummenacher	36
13	A. Espargaro	31
14	Sofuoglu	28
15	Cluzel	27
16	Aegerter	24
17	Neukirchner	24
18	Y. Hernandez	23
19	West	18
20	Baldolini	18
21	Redding	16
22	Pasini	13
23	P. Espargaro	13
24	Coghlan	11
25	Kallio	8
26	Di Meglio	7
27	Corti	6
28	Wilairot	4
29	Simeon	2
30	Cardus	2
31	Pons	1

Constructor Points

1	Suter	148
2	Kalex	134
3	FTR	79
4	Moriwaki	74
5	Tech 3	72
6	Motobi	53
7	Pons Kalex	32
8	MZ-RE Honda	31

125cc — RACE DISTANCE: 14 laps, 39.512 miles/63.588km · RACE WEATHER: Dry (air 15°C, humidity 58%, track 17°C)

Pos.	Rider	Nat.	No.	Entrant	Machine	Laps	Time & Speed
1	**Maverick Vinales**	SPA	25	Blusens by Paris Hilton Racing	Aprilia	14	25m 04.147s 94.566mph/ 152.190km/h
2	**Luis Salom**	SPA	39	RW Racing GP	Aprilia	14	25m 06.702s
3	**Sergio Gadea**	SPA	33	Blusens by Paris Hilton Racing	Aprilia	14	25m 06.802s
4	**Sandro Cortese**	GER	11	Intact-Racing Team Germany	Aprilia	14	25m 07.817s
5	**Johann Zarco**	FRA	5	Avant-AirAsia-Ajo	Derbi	14	25m 08.050s
6	**Danny Kent**	GBR	52	Red Bull Ajo MotorSport	Aprilia	14	25m 08.616s
7	**Efren Vazquez**	SPA	7	Avant-AirAsia-Ajo	Derbi	14	25m 12.975s
8	**Jonas Folger**	GER	94	Red Bull Ajo MotorSport	Aprilia	14	25m 14.563s
9	**Marcel Schrotter**	GER	77	Mahindra Racing	Mahindra	14	25m 14.938s
10	**Hector Faubel**	SPA	55	Bankia Aspar Team 125cc	Aprilia	14	25m 17.385s
11	**Alexis Masbou**	FRA	10	Caretta Technology	KTM	14	25m 19.402s
12	**Simone Grotzkyj**	ITA	15	Phonica Racing	Aprilia	14	25m 20.208s
13	**Danny Webb**	GBR	99	Mahindra Racing	Mahindra	14	25m 29.567s
14	**Zulfahmi Khairuddin**	MAL	63	Airasia-Sic-Ajo	Derbi	14	25m 31.101s
15	**Alberto Moncayo**	SPA	23	Andalucia Banca Civica	Aprilia	14	25m 31.725s
16	Jakub Kornfeil	CZE	84	Ongetta-Centro Seta	Aprilia	14	25m 32.033s
17	Luigi Morciano	ITA	3	Team Italia FMI	Aprilia	14	25m 33.597s
18	Luca Gruenwald	GER	41	Freudenberg Racing Team	KTM	14	25m 36.514s
19	Giulian Pedone	SWI	30	Phonica Racing	Aprilia	14	25m 37.619s
20	Peter Sebestyen	HUN	56	Caretta Technology	KTM	14	25m 43.966s
21	Josep Rodriguez	SPA	28	Andalucia Banca Civica	Aprilia	14	25m 44.216s
22	Bryan Schouten	NED	51	Dutch Racing Team	Honda	14	25m 50.766s
23	Alessandro Tonucci	ITA	19	Team Italia FMI	Aprilia	14	25m 51.792s
24	Francesco Mauriello	ITA	43	WTR-Ten10 Racing	Aprilia	14	25m 52.051s
25	Harry Stafford	GBR	21	Ongetta-Centro Seta	Aprilia	14	25m 52.488s
26	Taylor Mackenzie	GBR	17	Phonica Racing	Aprilia	14	26m 08.109s
27	Joan Perello	SPA	36	Matteoni Racing	Aprilia	14	26m 10.494s
28	Thomas van Leeuwen	NED	75	RacingTeam Van Leeuwen	Honda	14	26m 14.550s
29	Jerry van de Bunt	NED	67	JerrysRacingTeam	Honda	14	26m 26.275s
30	Louis Rossi	FRA	96	Matteoni Racing	Aprilia	14	26m 27.210s
31	Sturla Fagerhaug	NOR	50	WTR-Ten10 Racing	Aprilia	14	26m 29.719s
32	Ernst Dubbink	NED	61	RV Racing Team	Honda	14	26m 37.581s
33	Adrian Martin	SPA	26	Bankia Aspar Team 125cc	Aprilia	11	25m 44.249s
	Jasper Iwema	NED	53	Ongetta-Abbink Metaal	Aprilia	12	DNF
	Niklas Ajo	FIN	31	TT Motion Events Racing	Aprilia	3	DNF

Fastest lap: Maverick Vinales, on lap 6, 1m 44.928s, 96.830mph/155.832km/h.
Lap record: Nicolas Terol, SPA (Aprilia), 1m 42.428s, 99.193mph/159.636km/h (2010).
Event best maximum speed: Efren Vasquez, 134.000mph/215.700km/h (race).

Qualifying: Dry
Air: 17° Humidity: 53% Ground: 24°

1	Vinales	1m 44.597s
2	Zarco	1m 44.785s
3	Cortese	1m 44.787s
4	Faubel	1m 44.963s
5	Salom	1m 45.235s
6	Vazquez	1m 45.338s
7	Folger	1m 45.859s
8	Terol	1m 45.983s
9	Gadea	1m 46.204s
10	Kent	1m 46.568s
11	Webb	1m 46.594s
12	Grotzkyj	1m 46.610s
13	Pedone	1m 46.668s
14	Schrotter	1m 46.819s
15	Morciano	1m 46.988s
16	Masbou	1m 47.091s
17	Fagerhaug	1m 47.438s
18	Kornfeil	1m 47.563s
19	Rossi	1m 47.819s
20	Moncayo	1m 47.973s
21	Stafford	1m 47.977s
22	Gruenwald	1m 47.996s
23	Martin	1m 48.003s
24	Ajo	1m 48.351s
25	Mackenzie	1m 48.883s
26	Schouten	1m 49.002s
27	Sebestyen	1m 49.118s
28	Tonucci	1m 49.377s
29	Van de Bunt	1m 49.625s
30	Rodriguez	1m 49.760s
31	Perello	1m 49.913s
32	Van Leeuwen	1m 50.020s
33	Iwema	1m 51.856s

Outside 107%

Dubbink	1m 52.054s
Mauriello	1m 57.548s
Khairuddin	No Time

Fastest race laps

1	Vinales	1m 44.928s
2	Gadea	1m 45.235s
3	Cortese	1m 45.372s
4	Kent	1m 45.471s
5	Folger	1m 45.495s
6	Faubel	1m 45.555s
7	Zarco	1m 45.621s
8	Vazquez	1m 45.652s
9	Salom	1m 45.654s
10	Masbou	1m 45.688s
11	Grotzkyj	1m 45.865s
12	Martin	1m 45.951s
13	Iwema	1m 46.259s
14	Schrotter	1m 46.310s
15	Stafford	1m 46.339s
16	Khairuddin	1m 46.359s
17	Moncayo	1m 46.576s
18	Fagerhaug	1m 46.663s
19	Gruenwald	1m 46.677s
20	Webb	1m 46.695s
21	Pedone	1m 47.107s
22	Kornfeil	1m 47.123s
23	Morciano	1m 47.167s
24	Rossi	1m 47.545s
25	Rodriguez	1m 47.703s
26	Schouten	1m 48.037s
27	Mackenzie	1m 48.238s
28	Sebestyen	1m 48.277s
29	Perello	1m 48.389s
30	Mauriello	1m 48.714s
31	Tonucci	1m 48.842s
32	Van Leeuwen	1m 49.245s
33	Dubbink	1m 50.350s
34	Van de Bunt	1m 51.332s

Championship Points

1	Terol	128
2	Folger	101
3	Cortese	94
4	Zarco	94
5	Vinales	90
6	Vazquez	77
7	Salom	55
8	Faubel	54
9	Gadea	52
10	Kent	38
11	Martin	30
12	Kornfeil	25
13	Oliveira	22
14	Moncayo	16
15	Grotzkyj	16
16	Mackenzie	15
17	Khairuddin	13
18	Rossi	13
19	Schrotter	10
20	Masbou	10
21	Ono	8
22	Webb	8
23	Ajo	5
24	Iwema	4
25	McPhee	1
26	Rodriguez	1

Constructor Points

1	Aprilia	175
2	Derbi	103
3	KTM	17
4	Mahindra	15

ITALIAN GRAND PRIX

MUGELLO CIRCUIT

Lorenzo is hoisted shoulder high by his ecstatic team. Crew chief Ramon Forcada (spectacles) is at his left shoulder.
Photo: Gold & Goose

MOST of the 83,746 fans who paid in advance had one thing in mind. They were there to watch Rossi's first home grand prix on a Ducati. Not only was it his favourite track, where his record (seven wins in ten attempts) is second to none, but also it was Ducati's test track. With a sea of red in the dedicated grandstands, what could possibly go wrong?

Optimism, however, had to discount all the omens, including that he had broken his leg here in 2010. More germane were the results so far, and the latest response – a new and effectively untested motorcycle. A risky strategy, which went sour early on when the weather played up once again. Friday afternoon's second free session was all but washed out, and qualifying also interrupted. And Vale lost most of the first free practice when one bike cooked a wire and the other suffered an electronic problem, preventing any meaningful laps.

And another factor: for the first time in his 189 premier-class starts, he was operating without crew chief Jeremy Burgess. The Australian was at home on urgent family business after his wife Claudine had been diagnosed with cancer. For this and the next race, crew chief duties were taken over by Ducati technical manager Max Bartolini.

The Rossi dream may have soured, but fans were rewarded with an extremely fine MotoGP race, with Lorenzo bucking the odds and beating the Hondas for his second win of the year. He had ridden every lap superbly, and executed two fine and daring overtakes: around the outside into the Casanova-Savelli corner combination. "I put everything I have on the track today," he said. "I have not much of any kind of energy left." Nor did he have any victory celebration planned.

As surprisingly, HRC's third wheel, Dovizioso, pushed early leader Stoner to third. He said later that being the first Italian home was a dream come true; beating his team-mate surely meant much more, even if left unsaid. The Australian was somewhat disgruntled, with an explanation about tyre pressures (they were too high, robbing him of contact patch: kept at that level on Bridgestone's advice, though he had wanted to run them lower), and awareness that Lorenzo had just reduced his points lead to less than a race, and that the Yamahas were becoming more of a threat.

Particularly since the day after the race was the second mid-season test. Days before, Yamaha had cancelled plans to give their 2012 1000cc prototype its first airing and the riders their first go. Rumours of engine problems in bench-testing were aired, but Spies spoke also for Lorenzo, saying it was "a blessing in disguise", since they could concentrate on getting more out of 2011's bike. As it turned out, like Honda, they didn't have much in the way of new parts to test.

Pedrosa was back, and wound up tight. He came face to face with Le Mans assailant Simoncelli as the riders assembled for the pre-event conference: the Italian loomed over him, hand outstretched, Pedrosa turned away petulantly, much to his neighbour Stoner's amusement. A clip of the incident appeared almost immediately on YouTube; for those in the conference room who hadn't seen it, Pedrosa gave a verbal blast, the choicest remark being, "He has nothing on his head but hair." He handed out similar short shrift to anyone who raised the question of whether his second collarbone surgery had been occasioned (as rumoured) by a training accident on a Supermotard bike. "Do you think I am stupid?" he snapped. Whatever the onlookers did think, over the following weeks Dani would prove that he certainly was tough, no matter what his prolonged absence might have suggested.

The 3.259-mile track in its picturesque Apennine setting had a treat for everybody. It had been completely resurfaced, the kerbs painted with the Italian Tricolore in celebration. Praise was universal, while the Ducati riders had already taken a sneaky peak, in testing the GP12. Lap times showed how much the smoothing of bumps and homogenising of the grip meant: new records in all classes, with that in MotoGP broken by better than a second, by Lorenzo. More so, Stoner's pole for the first time set a new best-ever lap, the first faster than that set by Rossi on a Yamaha in 2008, in the time of super-soft qualifying tyres.

Driven by Lorenzo to a rare show of solidarity, all MotoGP riders, with the understandable exception of Aoyama, had put their names to a letter indicating unwillingness to race at Motegi in October. This petition reputedly had a number of signatures also from the other classes, and it was presented to Dorna's Ezpeleta at the Friday evening Safety Commission, in a crowded room. By the time they had left, the riders had agreed to wait for an independent report, commissioned by Dorna and the FIM, and focused on Motegi in particular, promised by the end of July. At least, that's the way Ezpeleta saw it.

In the week since Assen, Bridgestone had come up with a fresh plan, changing their pre-allocation of tyres at Laguna Seca, Brno, Aragón and Motegi, by deleting the harder option and offering an even softer option than the current 'soft'. It was broadly welcomed, but would not be the final solution.

Capirossi was absent, nursing his Assen injuries; former GP rider Sylvain Guintoli was on hand to test the latest satellite Ducati the day after the race, to replace him at the next round. Those tests would prove interesting – not for the Frenchman, who was a long way off the pace, but for everybody as they watched the progress of Mika Kallio on the prototype CRT Suter BMW. Nobody was sure what to expect of a full litre bike in race trim, but nobody expected it would be quite so far off the pace. Kallio, in MotoGP in 2010, did manage to go seven-tenths faster than on a low-powered 600cc Moto2 bike the day before, but he was almost three seconds *slower* than on a Ducati MotoGP bike the year before, on the old bumpy track. As much to the point, his best test time in 63 laps of trying was an astonishing 6.3 seconds slower than Stoner's fastest on the same day, on his 800cc Honda. There were several reasons, many concerning the tyres, but the gap was so huge it sent a chill through the CRT believers.

MOTOGP RACE – 23 laps

Simoncelli was fastest in the first session, but when it mattered Stoner came through with a best-ever lap of the track. It was his fifth pole in eight races. Who knows who might have responded in the latter part of the hour, for rain that had threatened throughout began in earnest with 25 minutes to go. By then, Spies was second, four-tenths down, and earlier leader Simoncelli on the far end of the front row. Behind them, Dovizioso, Lorenzo and Edwards made up row two. Hayden, in ninth, was top Ducati, Rossi only the fourth in 12th, with Barbera and Abraham ahead.

The weather was sunny and glorious for the start of the race, and Stoner took a jet-pilot start to lead by nine-tenths after the first lap, Lorenzo heading the pursuit, from Dovizioso, Spies and Simoncelli. Hayden was closing behind, having got past fast-starter Elias. Then he ran off on the outside of turn one as they started lap two, followed a little distance behind by Elias. With Rossi 12th, behind Barbera, any Ducati threat was over.

Stoner's control seemed clear enough. At lap-record pace, he had a comfort zone of better than two seconds after only eight laps. On the same lap, Dovizioso had finally got the better of Lorenzo's Yamaha when he ran wide at the first corner; Simoncelli was closing steadily, Spies chasing hard behind.

Lorenzo was on his best form and fully determined. On lap 12, he pulled a daring move around the outside into the fast downhill right-left Casanova-Savelli. "I couldn't pass under brakes, but I found another place," he explained.

Now he was closing. Stoner was losing his edge. In the morning, he'd found the tyre grip was fading as they warmed up. "We wanted to change the pressure, but we were recommended not to," he said. Now with the tyres too hard, he was losing bite front and rear. Lorenzo could sense the weakness, and he set another new record as he closed rapidly on lap 17, pulling the same Casanova-Savelli move halfway around the next.

The factory Yamaha drew slowly clear. His final margin was almost a second, but it had been twice that the lap before. Stoner had his hands full with his junior team-mate. Dovi set him up on the second-last run down the front straight, passed with a masterful (and fiercely resisted) outbraking move at the end of the straight and held a jubilant second to the line.

Fourth was as bitterly disputed between Spies and Simoncelli, the latter trying to shrug off his accumulated disgrace and riding with a caution that diminished as the race wore on. But he couldn't prevent Spies' inexorable overtake on the inside of the final corner, the American holding an advantage of less than a tenth to the flag.

Much of the interest was concentrated on a lively battle for sixth. Rossi had found it surprisingly hard to pick his way through a gang of five, as surprisingly led for the first seven laps by Bautista's Suzuki. His first conquest was easy – Crutchlow, falling back in the group and pitting soon afterwards with his front tyre destroyed and his will to continue likewise. A verbal roasting from team chief Poncharal followed: he should have rejoined in the hope of picking up a point or two.

The hero of the crowd's next target was Edwards, dispatched on lap seven. Now he was tangled in a battle between old 250 adversaries Barbera and Bautista, and it took five more laps before he could get clear. He escaped from Barbera with only two laps to go.

Above: Moment of truth – Lorenzo has taken over the lead from Stoner.

Centre left: BMW engine in the Marc VDS Suter at post-race Mugello test.

Below far left: A chilly atmosphere as Pedrosa and Simoncelli meet for the first time since Le Mans. Simoncelli's apology was spurned.

Below centre left: Stoner lifts the rear under braking. Tyre troubles meant the Aussie had to settle for third place.

Below left: Barbera posted seventh for the Mapfre Aspar team.

Photos: Gold & Goose

Pedrosa was almost four seconds down, but could take comfort that he had been able to go the distance. He'd had clutch problems that dropped him to 13th on lap one and another place lower next time around. He'd passed Edwards on lap 11, but the veteran had stayed within a second or two all the way to the flag.

Hayden was next after his lap-two disaster, picking his way through from stone last. He was closing on Edwards at the end, but not fast enough to challenge. Aoyama was 11th, then Abraham. Bautista managed to fend off de Puniet in a distant battle: the Suzuki rider had lost his place in the mid-field group after running off on lap 16. Elias was even further behind, but with 15 finishers, Crutchlow's judgement turned out to have been right.

MOTO2 RACE – 21 laps

Marquez continued to rewrite the script, with a second pole of his class debut season and a second successive win. "Step by step, I am improving my feeling," he said. The win rewarded determination, aggression and a turn of speed down the long straight, after a five-bike battle had raged almost all race long. Bradl was inches behind, but behind nonetheless, with Smith on his back wheel.

Runaway early leader Bradl and upstart Marquez disputed the high ground in free practice, but in wet qualifying Marquez claimed a six-tenths advantage over second-placed de Angelis, with Bradl only seventh, to lead row three of a muddled grid. Smith was the third man up front, then Simeon, Krummenacher and Pol Espargaro.

The race started well, and got better. Marquez led away, chased by Smith and de Angelis, with Bradl pushing through to fifth behind fast-starting Simeon in an all-action first corner.

The German was past him next time around and Simeon would drop away. Over the next few laps, Bradl, Marquez and Smith gained a little advantage on de Angelis. At the same time, Iannone – starting from row five – had bullied his way through the next pack, Hernandez with him. The Colombian crashed out on lap eight; but now Iannone was about to join the leaders, and by half-distance they had closed up, first to fifth covered by one second.

Above: Pedrosa and Rossi found themselves scrapping among some unusual companions: Abraham (17), Aoyama (7) and de Puniet (14).

Left: Dovi was delighted with second: the first Italian home and ahead of team-mate Stoner on the same bike.

Below: Spies and Simoncelli had a titanic scrap for fourth.

Photos: Gold & Goose

Bradl had led from lap eight to ten, Marquez taking over again as fortunes see-sawed as the race wore on. De Angelis passed Bradl on lap 12 and held second for two laps, then a slip and slide consigned him to fourth. Soon he was dropping out of touch by a few tenths each lap.

The biggest sufferer, however, was Iannone, up to third soon after that, but from lap 16 fading even faster, while de Angelis rallied again.

Up at the front, the penultimate lap was hectic. Smith had mounted a powerful challenge to lead going on to the straight, but Marquez had powered past him. Bradl was poised and took advantage in the battle in the first corners. But he couldn't do anything about Marquez, and the order remained unchanged to the finish. It was Smith's third successive rostrum: good for a class rookie – but not as good as Marquez.

Corsi had qualified 23rd, finished lap one 21st and ridden forcefully through the huge gang. He was in what seemed a safe sixth soon after half-distance, after his pursuer Pol Espargaro had crashed – only to be mugged on the last lap by Luthi. The Swiss rider had an equally fruitful ride from 23rd on lap one, though it took him longer to get through the midfield madness.

Neukirchner was next, then Aleix Espargaro, with Sofuoglu tenth, team-mate Aegerter right behind. From 12th to 15th was covered by little over two seconds: Simeon, Krummenacher, Takahashi and Cluzel.

Raffaele de Rosa, the weekend's replacement for Simon, crashed out on the first lap; Pirro and Lorenzetti later on. Wilairot retired in pain: he had collided with Pons the day before, putting the Spaniard out of the race.

125cc RACE – 20 laps

Terol was back, but starting from row two after Zarco had taken pole with an early flier in treacherous wet-and-dry qualifying. Salom and Gadea were alongside up front; Vazquez and Cortese flanked Terol, Vinales led row three.

The varied race had a fascinating two-man tactical battle up front, with ever-larger groups forming up behind for that crucial final drafting battle down the long finishing straight.

Terol and Zarco were alone, but seldom more than a few centimetres apart. Terol led at first, then let the Frenchman through for the second half.

Terol's damaged right little finger was spoiling his braking, but he had reliably more speed down the straight. He waited until the very end of the last lap, taking a perfect exit line from the final corner and sweeping past to win by less than two-tenths.

Vinales outfoxed experienced rivals Vazquez and Faubel over the line for third; Salom had been part of this absorbing battle, but was 14 seconds behind by the end.

Folger came through from 21st to contend for seventh with Cortese and Gadea, moving past only to crash with three laps left. Gadea pipped Cortese to the line in spite of being roughly elbowed to one side, both within a second of Salom.

A huge gang fought over ninth, with returned Oliveira heading team-mate Moncayo, then Kornfeil and Schrotter on the Mahindra. His team-mate, Webb, retired with shoulder injuries from a morning warm-up crash.

After the chequered flag came the reshuffle: Cortese was penalised for elbowing Gadea, and an extra 20 seconds dropped him to 12th.

Above: Terol fends off Zarco over the line. The Frenchman seemed fated always to finish second, no matter how hard he tried.

Above left: Home favourite Alex de Angelis took fourth in Moto2.

Top: Scenic Mugello shot with Moto2 1-2-3 finishers Marquez leading Bradl and Smith.

Photos: Gold & Goose

AUTODROMO INTERNAZIONALE DEL MUGELLO

23 laps
Length: 5.245 km / 3,259 miles
Width: 14m

Key
96/60 kph/mph
⚙ Gear

Arrabbiata 2 156/97
Scarperia 109/68
Palagio 106/66
Correntaio 106/66
Biondetti 1 165/103
Biondetti 2 167/104
Bucine 114/71
Savelli 117/73
Materassi 119/74
San Donato 98/61
Arrabbiata 1 163/101
Cassanova 114/71
Luco 113/70
Borgo San Lorenzo 121/75
Poggio Seco 119/74

MotoGP

RACE DISTANCE: 23 laps, 74.959 miles/120.635km · RACE WEATHER: Dry (air 29°C, humidity 22%, track 54°C)

Pos.	Rider	Nat.	No.	Entrant	Machine	Tyres	Laps	Time & speed
1	Jorge Lorenzo	SPA	1	Yamaha Factory Racing	Yamaha	B	23	41m 50.089s 107.507mph/ 173.016km/h
2	Andrea Dovizioso	ITA	4	Repsol Honda Team	Honda	B	23	41m 51.086s
3	Casey Stoner	AUS	27	Repsol Honda Team	Honda	B	23	41m 51.232s
4	Ben Spies	USA	11	Yamaha Factory Racing	Yamaha	B	23	41m 59.069s
5	Marco Simoncelli	ITA	58	San Carlo Honda Gresini	Honda	B	23	41m 59.165s
6	Valentino Rossi	ITA	46	Ducati Team	Ducati	B	23	42m 16.539s
7	Hector Barbera	SPA	8	Mapfre Aspar Team MotoGP	Ducati	B	23	42m 18.834s
8	Dani Pedrosa	SPA	26	Repsol Honda Team	Honda	B	23	42m 22.132s
9	Colin Edwards	USA	5	Monster Yamaha Tech 3	Yamaha	B	23	42m 23.510s
10	Nicky Hayden	USA	69	Ducati Team	Ducati	B	23	42m 24.813s
11	Hiroshi Aoyama	JPN	7	San Carlo Honda Gresini	Honda	B	23	42m 27.448s
12	Karel Abraham	CZE	17	Cardion AB Motoracing	Ducati	B	23	42m 34.053s
13	Alvaro Bautista	SPA	19	Rizla Suzuki MotoGP	Suzuki	B	23	42m 37.743s
14	Randy de Puniet	FRA	14	Pramac Racing Team	Ducati	B	23	42m 38.929s
15	Toni Elias	SPA	24	LCR Honda MotoGP	Honda	B	23	43m 05.288s
	Cal Crutchlow	GBR	35	Monster Yamaha Tech 3	Yamaha	B	6	DNF

Fastest lap: Jorge Lorenzo, on lap 17, 1m 48.402s, 108.233mph/174.184km/h (record).

Previous lap record: Dani Pedrosa, SPA (Honda), 1m 49.531s, 107.118mph/172.389km/h (2010).

Event best maximum speed: Hector Barbera, 208.600mph/335.700km/h (race).

Qualifying

Weather: Wet
Air Temp: 21° Humidity: 44%
Track Temp: 28°

1	Stoner	1m 48.034s
2	Spies	1m 48.479s
3	Simoncelli	1m 48.485s
4	Dovizioso	1m 48.694s
5	Lorenzo	1m 48.756s
6	Edwards	1m 48.974s
7	Crutchlow	1m 49.021s
8	Pedrosa	1m 49.398s
9	Hayden	1m 49.509s
10	Barbera	1m 49.663s
11	Abraham	1m 49.678s
12	Rossi	1m 49.902s
13	Aoyama	1m 50.156s
14	Bautista	1m 50.460s
15	De Puniet	1m 50.651s
16	Elias	1m 50.742s

Fastest race laps

1	Lorenzo	1m 48.402s
2	Stoner	1m 48.577s
3	Spies	1m 48.647s
4	Dovizioso	1m 48.678s
5	Simoncelli	1m 48.833s
6	Pedrosa	1m 49.226s
7	Rossi	1m 49.301s
8	Bautista	1m 49.448s
9	Barbera	1m 49.468s
10	Hayden	1m 49.524s
11	Abraham	1m 49.731s
12	Aoyama	1m 49.791s
13	Edwards	1m 49.909s
14	Crutchlow	1m 50.117s
15	De Puniet	1m 50.342s
16	Elias	1m 51.271s

Championship Points

1	Stoner	152
2	Lorenzo	133
3	Dovizioso	119
4	Rossi	91
5	Hayden	77
6	Spies	74
7	Pedrosa	69
8	Aoyama	56
9	Edwards	53
10	Simoncelli	50
11	Barbera	44
12	Abraham	37
13	Elias	35
14	Crutchlow	32
15	Bautista	30
16	Capirossi	22
17	De Puniet	12
18	Hopkins	6
19	Akiyoshi	3

Team Points

1	Repsol Honda Team	227
2	Yamaha Factory Racing	207
3	Ducati Team	168
4	San Carlo Honda Gresini	101
5	Monster Yamaha Tech 3	85
6	Mapfre Aspar Team MotoGP	44
7	Cardion AB Motoracing	37
8	Rizla Suzuki MotoGP	36
9	LCR Honda MotoGP	35
10	Pramac Racing Team	34

Constructor Points

1	Honda	185
2	Yamaha	164
3	Ducati	99
4	Suzuki	36

Grid order	1	2	3	4	5	6	7	8	9	10	11	12	13	14	15	16	17	18	19	20	21	22	23	
27 STONER	27	27	27	27	27	27	27	27	27	27	27	27	27	27	27	27	27	1	1	1	1	1	1	1
11 SPIES	1	1	1	1	1	1	1	4	4	4	1	1	1	1	1	1	1	27	27	27	27	27	4	2
58 SIMONCELLI	4	4	4	4	4	4	4	1	1	1	1	4	4	4	4	4	4	4	4	4	4	4	27	3
4 DOVIZIOSO	11	58	58	58	58	58	58	58	58	58	58	58	58	58	11	11	11	58	58	58	58	58	11	4
1 LORENZO	58	11	11	11	11	11	11	11	11	11	11	11	11	11	58	58	58	11	11	11	11	11	58	5
5 EDWARDS	69	5	19	19	19	19	19	19	8	8	46	46	46	46	46	46	46	46	46	46	46	46		6
35 CRUTCHLOW	24	19	5	5	8	8	46	8	19	46	8	8	8	8	8	8	8	8	8	8	8	8		7
26 PEDROSA	5	35	35	8	5	5	8	46	46	19	19	19	19	19	26	26	26	26	26	26	26	26		8
69 HAYDEN	19	8	8	35	46	46	5	5	5	5	26	26	26	26	5	5	5	5	5	5	5	5		9
8 BARBERA	35	46	46	46	35	35	17	26	26	26	5	5	5	5	69	69	69	69	69	69	69	69		10
17 ABRAHAM	8	24	17	17	17	17	26	17	17	17	17	69	69	69	7	7	7	7	7	7	7	7		11
46 ROSSI	46	17	24	24	26	26	7	7	7	7	69	69	17	7	17	17	17	17	17	17	17	17		12
7 AOYAMA	26	7	7	7	7	7	69	69	69	69	7	7	7	17	19	19	19	19	19	19	19	19		13
19 BAUTISTA	17	26	26	26	69	69	14	14	14	14	14	14	14	14	14	14	14	14	14	14	14	14		14
14 DE PUNIET	7	14	14	14	24	24	24	24	24	24	24	24	24	24	24	24	24	24	24	24	24	24		15
24 ELIAS	14	69	69	69	14	14																		

35 Pit stop

Moto2

RACE DISTANCE: 21 laps, 68.441 miles/110.145km · **RACE WEATHER:** Dry (air 27°C, humidity 25%, track 46°C)

Pos.	Rider	Nat.	No.	Entrant	Machine	Laps	Time & Speed
1	**Marc Marquez**	SPA	93	Team CatalunyaCaixa Repsol	Suter	21	40m 02.941s 102.536mph/ 165.015km/h
2	**Stefan Bradl**	GER	65	Viessmann Kiefer Racing	Kalex	21	40m 03.012s
3	**Bradley Smith**	GBR	38	Tech 3 Racing	Tech 3	21	40m 03.360s
4	**Alex de Angelis**	RSM	15	JIR Moto2	Motobi	21	40m 05.032s
5	**Andrea Iannone**	ITA	29	Speed Master	Suter	21	40m 07.536s
6	**Thomas Luthi**	SWI	12	Interwetten Paddock Moto2	Suter	21	40m 15.962s
7	**Simone Corsi**	ITA	3	Ioda Racing Project	FTR	21	40m 16.033s
8	**Max Neukirchner**	GER	76	MZ Racing Team	MZ-RE Honda	21	40m 16.350s
9	**Aleix Espargaro**	SPA	40	Pons HP 40	Pons Kalex	21	40m 17.080s
10	**Kenan Sofuoglu**	TUR	54	Technomag-CIP	Suter	21	40m 17.360s
11	**Dominique Aegerter**	SWI	77	Technomag-CIP	Suter	21	40m 18.013s
12	**Xavier Simeon**	BEL	19	Tech 3 B	Tech 3	21	40m 20.937s
13	**Randy Krummenacher**	SWI	4	GP Team Switzerland Kiefer Racing	Kalex	21	40m 21.514s
14	**Yuki Takahashi**	JPN	72	Gresini Racing Moto2	Moriwaki	21	40m 22.661s
15	**Jules Cluzel**	FRA	16	NGM Forward Racing	Suter	21	40m 23.298s
16	Esteve Rabat	SPA	34	Blusens-STX	FTR	21	40m 25.149s
17	Mika Kallio	FIN	36	Marc VDS Racing Team	Suter	21	40m 25.361s
18	Valentin Debise	FRA	53	Speed Up	FTR	21	40m 27.238s
19	Jordi Torres	SPA	18	Mapfre Aspar Team Moto2	Suter	21	40m 31.620s
20	Mattia Pasini	ITA	75	Ioda Racing Project	FTR	21	40m 31.817s
21	Anthony West	AUS	13	MZ Racing Team	MZ-RE Honda	21	40m 33.719s
22	Ricard Cardus	SPA	88	QMMF Racing Team	Moriwaki	21	40m 36.025s
23	Claudio Corti	ITA	71	Italtrans Racing Team	Suter	21	40m 37.509s
24	Mike di Meglio	FRA	63	Tech 3 Racing	Tech 3	21	40m 38.941s
25	Carmelo Morales	SPA	31	Desguaces La Torre G22	Moriwaki	21	40m 39.135s
26	Robertino Pietri	VEN	39	Italtrans Racing Team	Suter	21	40m 39.136s
27	Scott Redding	GBR	45	Marc VDS Racing Team	Suter	21	40m 49.672s
28	Pol Espargaro	SPA	44	HP Tuenti Speed Up	FTR	21	40m 51.995s
29	Kenny Noyes	USA	9	Avintia-STX	FTR	21	40m 53.042s
30	Santiago Hernandez	COL	64	SAG Team	FTR	21	41m 11.498s
31	Mashel Al Naimi	QAT	95	QMMF Racing Team	Moriwaki	20	40m 04.370s
	Ratthapark Wilairot	THA	14	Thai Honda Singha SAG	FTR	14	DNF
	Alex Baldolini	ITA	25	NGM Forward Racing	Suter	11	DNF
	Mattia Tarozzi	ITA	70	Faenza Racing	Suter	11	DNF
	Yonny Hernandez	COL	68	Blusens-STX	FTR	7	DNF
	Tommaso Lorenzetti	ITA	24	Aeroport de Castello	FTR	6	DNF
	Michele Pirro	ITA	51	Gresini Racing Moto2	Moriwaki	3	DNF
	Raffaele de Rosa	ITA	35	Mapfre Aspar Team Moto2	Suter	0	DNF

Fastest lap: Stefan Bradl, on lap 21, 1m 53.362s, 103.497mph/166.563km/h (record).
Previous lap record: Andrea Iannone, ITA (Speed Up), 1m 55.647s, 101.453mph/163.272km/h (2010).
Event best maximum speed: Alex de Angelis, 178.800mph/287.800km/h (race).

Qualifying: Dry
Air: 19° Humidity: 61% Ground: 26°

1	Marquez	2m 05.312s
2	De Angelis	2m 05.897s
3	Smith	2m 06.617s
4	Simeon	2m 06.757s
5	Krummenacher	2m 06.941s
6	P. Espargaro	2m 06.963s
7	Bradl	2m 07.013s
8	Pasini	2m 07.023s
9	Kallio	2m 07.147s
10	West	2m 07.249s
11	Rabat	2m 07.549s
12	Pietri	2m 07.612s
13	Sofuoglu	2m 07.692s
14	Iannone	2m 07.728s
15	Takahashi	2m 07.780s
16	Y. Hernandez	2m 07.844s
17	Cardus	2m 07.864s
18	Torres	2m 07.919s
19	De Rosa	2m 08.118s
20	Neukirchner	2m 08.272s
21	Pirro	2m 08.289s
22	Noyes	2m 08.444s
23	Corsi	2m 08.562s
24	Luthi	2m 08.681s
25	Lorenzetti	2m 08.840s
26	Baldolini	2m 08.883s
27	Morales	2m 08.970s
28	Redding	2m 09.265s
29	Tarozzi	2m 09.409s
30	Aegerter	2m 09.616s
31	Corti	2m 09.911s
32	A. Espargaro	2m 09.974s
33	Cluzel	2m 10.420s
34	Wilairot	2m 10.436s
35	Di Meglio	2m 10.652s
36	S. Hernandez	2m 10.723s
37	Al Naimi	2m 13.596s
Outside 107%		
	Debise	2m 14.539s
	Pons	No Time

Fastest race laps

1	Bradl	1m 53.362s
2	Sofuoglu	1m 53.515s
3	Marquez	1m 53.518s
4	Smith	1m 53.540s
5	Iannone	1m 53.560s
6	Luthi	1m 53.623s
7	Neukirchner	1m 53.630s
8	A. Espargaro	1m 53.658s
9	De Angelis	1m 53.727s
10	Corsi	1m 53.862s
11	P. Espargaro	1m 53.877s
12	Y. Hernandez	1m 53.887s
13	Aegerter	1m 53.905s
14	Redding	1m 54.036s
15	Takahashi	1m 54.089s
16	Debise	1m 54.136s
17	Simeon	1m 54.178s
18	Rabat	1m 54.234s
19	Cluzel	1m 54.307s
20	Kallio	1m 54.326s
21	Krummenacher	1m 54.391s
22	Pasini	1m 54.433s
23	Torres	1m 54.501s
24	Di Meglio	1m 54.575s
25	Pietri	1m 54.637s
26	Cardus	1m 54.733s
27	Corti	1m 54.770s
28	Morales	1m 54.778s
29	Pirro	1m 54.802s
30	West	1m 54.991s
31	Noyes	1m 55.178s
32	Baldolini	1m 55.293s
33	Lorenzetti	1m 55.746s
34	Wilairot	1m 56.277s
35	S. Hernandez	1m 56.437s
36	Tarozzi	1m 58.101s
37	Al Naimi	1m 58.342s

Championship Points

1	Bradl	147
2	Marquez	95
3	Smith	79
4	Corsi	76
5	Luthi	66
6	De Angelis	66
7	Iannone	64
8	Takahashi	58
9	Simon	49
10	Krummenacher	39
11	A. Espargaro	38
12	Pirro	37
13	Rabat	37
14	Sofuoglu	34
15	Neukirchner	32
16	Aegerter	29
17	Cluzel	28
18	Y. Hernandez	23
19	West	18
20	Baldolini	18
21	Redding	16
22	Pasini	13
23	P. Espargaro	13
24	Coghlan	11
25	Kallio	8
26	Di Meglio	7
27	Corti	6
28	Simeon	6
29	Wilairot	4
30	Cardus	2
31	Pons	1

Constructor Points

1	Suter	173
2	Kalex	154
3	Tech 3	88
4	FTR	88
5	Moriwaki	76
6	Motobi	66
7	Pons Kalex	39
8	MZ-RE Honda	39

125cc

RACE DISTANCE: 20 laps, 65.182 miles/104.900km · **RACE WEATHER:** Dry (air 21°C, humidity 33%, track 40°C)

Pos.	Rider	Nat.	No.	Entrant	Machine	Laps	Time & Speed
1	**Nicolas Terol**	SPA	18	Bankia Aspar Team 125cc	Aprilia	20	39m 51.815s 98.107mph/ 157.888km/h
2	**Johann Zarco**	FRA	5	Avant-AirAsia-Ajo	Derbi	20	39m 51.982s
3	**Maverick Vinales**	SPA	25	Blusens by Paris Hilton Racing	Aprilia	20	40m 00.194s
4	**Efren Vazquez**	SPA	7	Avant-AirAsia-Ajo	Derbi	20	40m 00.306s
5	**Hector Faubel**	SPA	55	Bankia Aspar Team 125cc	Aprilia	20	40m 00.409s
6	**Luis Salom**	SPA	39	RW Racing GP	Aprilia	20	40m 14.723s
7	**Sergio Gadea**	SPA	33	Blusens by Paris Hilton Racing	Aprilia	20	40m 15.804s
8	**Miguel Oliveira**	POR	44	Andalucia Banca Civica	Aprilia	20	40m 31.953s
9	**Alberto Moncayo**	SPA	23	Andalucia Banca Civica	Aprilia	20	40m 32.582s
10	**Jakub Kornfeil**	CZE	84	Ongetta-Centro Seta	Aprilia	20	40m 33.013s
11	**Marcel Schrotter**	GER	77	Mahindra Racing	Mahindra	20	40m 33.070s
12	**Sandro Cortese**	GER	11	Intact-Racing Team Germany	Aprilia	20	40m 35.814s
13	**Simone Grotzkyj**	ITA	15	Phonica Racing	Aprilia	20	40m 37.987s
14	**Jasper Iwema**	NED	53	Ongetta-Abbink Metaal	Aprilia	20	40m 50.791s
15	**Danny Kent**	GBR	52	Red Bull Ajo MotorSport	Aprilia	20	40m 51.540s
16	Alexis Masbou	FRA	10	Caretta Technology	KTM	20	40m 51.942s
17	Taylor Mackenzie	GBR	17	Phonica Racing	Aprilia	20	40m 52.042s
18	Zulfahmi Khairuddin	MAL	63	Airasia-Sic-Ajo	Derbi	20	41m 00.060s
19	Miroslav Popov	CZE	95	Ellegi Racing	Aprilia	20	41m 02.408s
20	Alessandro Tonucci	ITA	19	Team Italia FMI	Aprilia	20	41m 05.477s
21	Francesco Mauriello	ITA	43	WTR-Ten10 Racing	Aprilia	20	41m 15.764s
22	Niklas Ajo	FIN	31	TT Motion Events Racing	Aprilia	20	41m 30.626s
23	Giulian Pedone	SWI	30	Phonica Racing	Aprilia	20	41m 44.959s
	Luigi Morciano	ITA	3	Team Italia FMI	Aprilia	19	DNF
	Kevin Calia	ITA	74	MGP Racing	Aprilia	19	DNF
	Jonas Folger	GER	94	Red Bull Ajo MotorSport	Aprilia	17	DNF
	Danny Webb	GBR	99	Mahindra Racing	Mahindra	9	DNF
	Peter Sebestyen	HUN	56	Caretta Technology	KTM	9	DNF
	Louis Rossi	FRA	96	Matteoni Racing	Aprilia	7	DNF
	Joan Perello	SPA	36	Matteoni Racing	Aprilia	7	DNF
	Sturla Fagerhaug	NOR	50	WTR-Ten10 Racing	Aprilia	7	DNF
	Massimo Parziani	ITA	88	Faenza Racing	Aprilia	6	DNF
	Adrian Martin	SPA	26	Bankia Aspar Team 125cc	Aprilia	1	DNF
	Harry Stafford	GBR	21	Ongetta-Centro Seta	Aprilia	1	DNF

Fastest lap: Johann Zarco, on lap 9, 1m 57.783s, 99.613mph/160.311km/h (record).
Previous lap record: Bradley Smith, GBR (Aprilia), 1m 58.009s, 99.422mph/160.004km/h (2010).
Event best maximum speed: Sergio Gadea, 147.900mph/238.100km/h (warm up).

Qualifying: Dry
Air: 22° Humidity: 38% Ground: 34°

1	Zarco	1m 58.988s
2	Salom	2m 00.620s
3	Gadea	2m 00.903s
4	Vazquez	2m 01.026s
5	Terol	2m 01.033s
6	Cortese	2m 01.093s
7	Vinales	2m 01.201s
8	Faubel	2m 01.351s
9	Martin	2m 01.679s
10	Rossi	2m 01.768s
11	Oliveira	2m 01.781s
12	Webb	2m 01.811s
13	Schrotter	2m 01.839s
14	Grotzkyj	2m 01.927s
15	Kornfeil	2m 01.976s
16	Moncayo	2m 02.153s
17	Stafford	2m 02.349s
18	Fagerhaug	2m 02.483s
19	Iwema	2m 02.745s
20	Masbou	2m 02.929s
21	Folger	2m 02.931s
22	Calia	2m 02.949s
23	Ajo	2m 02.965s
24	Morciano	2m 03.077s
25	Khairuddin	2m 03.375s
26	Kent	2m 03.482s
27	Popov	2m 03.684s
28	Mackenzie	2m 03.915s
29	Mauriello	2m 04.632s
30	Tonucci	2m 04.663s
31	Pedone	2m 04.860s
32	Sebestyen	2m 05.954s
33	Perello	2m 07.064s
Outside 107%		
	Parziani	2m 09.633s

Fastest race laps

1	Zarco	1m 57.783s
2	Terol	1m 57.816s
3	Vazquez	1m 58.490s
4	Faubel	1m 58.560s
5	Vinales	1m 58.574s
6	Salom	1m 58.963s
7	Gadea	1m 59.365s
8	Cortese	1m 59.466s
9	Folger	1m 59.623s
10	Kornfeil	1m 59.883s
11	Schrotter	2m 00.181s
12	Oliveira	2m 00.261s
13	Ajo	2m 00.287s
14	Popov	2m 00.372s
15	Moncayo	2m 00.391s
16	Fagerhaug	2m 00.510s
17	Morciano	2m 00.592s
18	Rossi	2m 00.640s
19	Grotzkyj	2m 00.709s
20	Calia	2m 00.747s
21	Webb	2m 00.775s
22	Kent	2m 00.807s
23	Mackenzie	2m 00.824s
24	Masbou	2m 01.047s
25	Iwema	2m 01.092s
26	Parziani	2m 01.497s
27	Khairuddin	2m 01.553s
28	Mauriello	2m 01.984s
29	Tonucci	2m 02.014s
30	Pedone	2m 02.936s
31	Sebestyen	2m 03.015s
32	Perello	2m 03.592s

Championship Points

1	Terol	153
2	Zarco	114
3	Vinales	106
4	Folger	101
5	Cortese	98
6	Vazquez	90
7	Salom	65
8	Faubel	65
9	Gadea	61
10	Kent	39
11	Kornfeil	31
12	Martin	30
13	Oliveira	30
14	Moncayo	23
15	Grotzkyj	19
16	Mackenzie	15
17	Schrotter	15
18	Khairuddin	13
19	Rossi	13
20	Masbou	10
21	Ono	8
22	Webb	8
23	Iwema	6
24	Ajo	5
25	McPhee	1
26	Rodriguez	1

Constructor Points

1	Aprilia	200
2	Derbi	123
3	Mahindra	20
4	KTM	17

GERMAN GRAND PRIX

SACHSENRING

Dead heat. In a first for the electronic era, Zarco (5) and Faubel (55) couldn't be distinguished by timing or video. Race lap times decided the issue, and Zarco was denied again.
Photo: Gold & Goose

THE ninth event of the season, marking the halfway stage, started disastrously and ended superbly. The MotoGP race was a classic, close-fought and tense, and culminating with a triumphant return to winning form for the convalescent Pedrosa.

The bad kick-off occurred in the first free practice, on another cool morning and at a track where a huge preponderance of left-handers exacerbated the problems of the slow-to-warm and easy-to-lose Bridgestones.

The trouble on the fast right-hander that follows almost half a lap of constant left turns began early and took in most of the big names.

Stoner, who had not even completed a fast lap, was the first to go, flicking high and slamming down hard in a vicious high-sider from which he was lucky to emerge merely heavily knocked about. His mistake, he said, had been to try to fight it when the front just caved in as he flicked it over; it would have been a simpler crash if he'd just let it go.

Then it was Rossi: much the same sort of crash, which sent him to the medical centre with a big abrasion on his forearm. Then Elias. And then the third 'alien', Pedrosa, who escaped without troubling his healing injury.

Clearly something was wrong, and later Stoner expressed surprise that the session had not been red-flagged. The culprit was no mystery: cold conditions combined with hard-to-warm tyres. Bridgestone responded as best they could, having already brought their softest available version of the dual-compound rear. It was the fronts that were letting go, however, and past experiments with dual-compound front tyres had been unproductive, since they made for queasy braking. By the end of the weekend, a rule change proposal had been accepted, to come into effect two races hence, at Brno: a third extra-soft option front would be available for days like today.

By Sunday, in better weather, all was forgotten, when the pocket-handkerchief circuit outside Chemnitz laid on a feast of close MotoGP racing for the 101,309 fans who packed the stands – a race that belatedly went some way to redeem the reputation of the unloved 800s. And of circuits that, on the face of it, are too small for proper MotoGP racing.

The radiation report from Motegi was still awaited, but Stoner pre-empted it by announcing at a pre-race Press conference: "I am not going to Motegi." With fellow dissenter Lorenzo alongside, they faced a poignant question from a Japanese journalist, who pointed out that their bikes carried stickers saying "With you Japan" and "this helped to give us a little courage". Was it not now inconsistent to refuse to support the GP? They defended themselves as best they could. A day later, the mood of the assembly was well reflected at another Press conference chaired by Dorna chief Ezpeleta, where IRTA president Hervé Poncharal earned an unprecedented round of applause when he described the refusenik riders as "lacking respect for Japan." This one would run and run.

The other continuing saga was over at Ducati. Rossi, in a second race without Burgess in the pit, was persisting with the new GP11.1, but to little avail. In his 250th GP start, it was his worst premier-class qualifying ever – 16th and second from last; and while the race was a bit better, he was not only beaten by team-mate Hayden, but also even by Bautista's Suzuki.

Hayden meanwhile had his own concerns. He did not have the option of the new bike, even though one was available and he was keen to put some miles on it before his home GP. It was, he explained rather ruefully, a matter of engine mileage and schedules. In any case, the bikes were only on hand for freight logistics: the paddock shipped out to the USA the very next day.

By the end of the weekend, behind forced smiles, team chiefs said they would decide during the evening which machines to take to the USA. In the end, they took them all, just in case.

A wistful note from Hayden came after qualifying, when an over-friendly journalist tried to comfort his third-row grid position by saying, "At least you're the fastest Ducati." Hayden grimaced: "I'm also the fastest rider from Kentucky, but it don't mean much."

At the other end of the Ducati spectrum, Capirossi was back and anxious to ride, after missing Mugello with his pre-race Assen injuries. "I hate to see someone else riding my bike," he explained. But the effort proved premature, and he had to put up with the sight of ex-GP racer Sylvain Guintoli wheeling the bike around, in a very fruitless break from his SBK commitments. Guintoli had tested the bike at Mugello after the last GP, but was still struggling to re-adapt by Sunday.

Officialdom was in full spate, handing out penalties galore. In Moto2, the villains were Redding and Marquez. The latter (who was getting a reputation for this sort of thing) had slowed suddenly in front of Redding on Saturday morning. At the next opportunity, the Englishman gave him a 'thank-you' punch; Marquez flipped the bird in return. The incident cost Redding 3,000 euros, and Marquez 1,000. Barbera gave Hayden the same gesture at the end of MotoGP qualifying and was also fined 1,000 euros. The weekend had begun with a less blatant infringement, from the race before. It was judged that 125 riders Masbou, Perello and Iwema had ridden "very slowly, being passed by the Safety Car, which is contrary to instructions". Five hundred euros each.

The 125 race ended in the second ever dead heat in GP history, and the outcome would rob French title challenger Johann Zarco of victory for the fourth time. He'd crossed the line first in Catalunya, but had been penalised. In England, he had been outpaced, in Italy outdrafted by inches. Now for a second time by Race Direction. With neither electronics nor photo finish able to decide, they gave the race to Hector Faubel by virtue of a faster race best lap, by almost three-tenths.

MOTOGP RACE – 30 laps

After his big crash, Stoner took almost until the end of qualifying to regain dominance, for his sixth pole in nine races. Pedrosa was alongside, a quarter of a second slower. But another all-Honda front row was spoiled in the closing minutes by Lorenzo, who slipped in his Yamaha to push Simoncelli to the head of row two.

Spies and Dovizioso were next, then Edwards, Hayden and de Puniet. Rossi was 16th, only the floundering Guintoli behind him. "It's lucky Loris is out, or I would be last," he grinned thinly.

It was business as usual from the flag, Pedrosa leading into the first corner, tailed by Stoner, Lorenzo and Simoncelli. But not as usual when Lorenzo pushed into second in the first twisty section, and then took the lead at the bottom of the 'waterfall' back straight.

By the end of the lap, Dovizioso was up to third, past a cautious Stoner, while Simoncelli had Spies and Hayden behind him.

Above: Suzuki showing strength at last: Bautista is sandwiched by the Ducatis of Hayden and Rossi. Edwards follows.

Far left, top: Ezpeleta had his hands full with the threat of a Japanese Grand Prix boycott.

Far left, bottom: Guintoli was on hand to replace Capirossi when the task proved too much.

Left: The board says it all. Rossi qualified in a lowly 16th place.

Photos: Gold & Goose

The front battle was long and absorbing. Dovizioso passed Pedrosa for second as they started lap three; two laps later, Stoner was also ahead of him, promptly diving for the lead as he tried to see if he could run away. It proved "a bit risky with a full tank", and all four stayed with him, Pedrosa up to third at the start of lap nine, and Simoncelli ahead of Dovi on the 13th.

The next change came on lap 14, when Lorenzo retook the lead from Stoner into the penultimate corner. Two laps later, Pedrosa outbraked Stoner into the first turn. By now, the first three were starting to move clear, by a full second when Dovizioso repassed Simoncelli on lap 18. The gap would grow to the end.

Pedrosa took the lead for the first time on the straight as they started lap 22. They all stayed glued together, with Stoner consigning Lorenzo to third at the first corner on lap 25. Now he started to try to attack Pedrosa, but it was too little too late, and gradually the gap between them grew larger.

Even so, it was not until the second-last lap that it was more than a second, and less than half a second larger at the finish.

Lorenzo gave Stoner warning as they began the final lap, getting ahead briefly over the line. Stoner passed him straight back under braking and seemed to gain a little advantage. But he had run out of grip on the left-hand side, and Lorenzo could sense the weakness.

The Yamaha was on his tail as they hit the crucial right-hander at the top of the waterfall. Stoner held it tight into the ensuing left, slowing his exit – and that gave Lorenzo his chance in the final bend. "I made a speed corner of the last one, like a 125. I played all my cards," he said. It took him over the finish line less than a tenth ahead.

Importantly for his morale, he also closed to within 15 points in the title battle.

The close action had run all the way down the field.

Old rivals Dovizioso and Simoncelli had battled on as they slowly lost touch. At the same time, Spies was gradually closing a gap that had been around 3.5 seconds at half-distance. As Simoncelli regained the advantage on lap 22, the Yamaha was just 1.8 seconds behind, and three-tenths faster. By the time Dovizioso outbraked his rival again on lap 28, the American was on them, and they fought to the end, Spies just getting between them on the run to the line. "I didn't speed up. They came back at me," he said. "I wish the race had been 31 laps long."

The next gang was as fierce. Early on Bautista and Hayden had been trading blows with Edwards. Rossi meanwhile had finished lap one 14th, and he picked his way through to tenth over the first four laps. He joined in, and though Edwards would drop away, the other three were at it to the end. It was quite a sight to see the blue Suzuki on such obviously equal terms with the two top Ducatis, and the relative rookie rider with two world champions.

They started the last lap with Hayden narrowly ahead of Rossi and Bautista, but it was the Spaniard who won the last-corner scramble from Hayden, with Rossi blocked behind them – later he said a glitch with his quick-shift gearbox had thwarted his plans.

De Puniet and Crutchlow had been dicing behind; then with six laps to go, Abraham and then Barbera caught up. At the end, it was Barbera, Abraham, de Puniet, Crutchlow, all within half a second.

Aoyama, Elias and Guintoli trailed in behind.

MOTO2 RACE – 29 laps

Fresh from two wins in a row, Marquez took a third pole, pushing home hero Bradl to second. Aleix Espargaro claimed his first front row; Pirro led row two from Simon and de Angelis. Smith was ninth, Redding 23rd and Iannone 25th. With the first 24 within one second of pole, positions were something of a lottery.

The battle for the lead looked more competitive than it was. In fact, as Marquez explained after the race, he knew

all along that he was faster than Bradl – but he didn't feel like leading all the way, so he let him past from laps 14 to 21. Then he took him quite easily and ran on to win by less than a second. Three in a row, and looking dangerous for Bradl.

The pair had company almost all the way, the pack staying close even though a couple of major crashes had removed some leading players.

The first was at the first corner, where returned injury victim Simon lost it under braking and fell spectacularly, taking three other riders out into the gravel as he spun to a halt. At the same time, Smith (Tech 3) missed his braking point and ran on; he rejoined at the back and climbed almost into the points before crashing out terminally on lap 16.

A second scary crash removed Aleix Espargaro and MZ-mounted Neukirchner, who were battling for sixth on lap five. Espargaro fell at speed and Neukirchner was unable to avoid running into his bike. Both were tangled with the machines, but luckily escaped serious injury.

Up front, Marquez and Bradl were narrowly ahead of de Angelis, with the San Marino rider getting in front of Marquez from laps 17 to 20. He was still just half a second behind at the end, and ecstatic.

The lead pack was still five strong at half-distance, with Hernandez at the back. He had fallen away by the finish, but his place was taken by a flying Krummenacher. Bullied back to 16th in the opening laps, he had sliced his way through and was the fastest on the track in the closing stages. He closed up rapidly to get ahead of Luthi on the penultimate lap and pull a second clear over the line.

Redding won a long battle for seventh with Corsi, while Cluzel brought Pirro and Sofuoglu up with him at the finish.

Dominique Aegerter had caught and passed the next big group on the final lap to claim 12th. Pol Espargaro, Iannone, Corti and di Meglio were almost alongside, all five covered by less than nine-tenths. Tight Moto2 racing at its finest – fraught and furious.

125cc RACE – 27 laps

The opening race was a thriller, with frequent changes of lead right up to the final dead heat.

Vinales took pole number three, from Faubel and Salom; Terol led row two from Gadea and Zarco.

It was Gadea ahead on lap one, followed by Faubel, Zarco, Terol, Salom and the gang, Vinales tenth, but soon picking his way forward.

Faubel took over at the front, then Vazquez from laps five to seven. By half-distance, he'd dropped to the middle of the lead group of ten when he ran off, rejoining a little way back before crashing out for good.

By lap 16, there were six left up front, and Vinales was leading. He stayed there until they started the last lap, by which time he had just two companions.

Vinales came off worst as they swapped to and fro, and into the last corner it looked as though Faubel had done enough. But Zarco had a smoother entry and a faster exit; he pulled alongside and eventually ahead as they crossed the line. It was just too late: at the crucial point, they were side by side.

Terol and Salom scrapped to the line to finish in that order; Gadea, in sixth, had lost touch.

Folger prevailed in the next trio, from Cortese and British rookie Danny Kent; Ajo narrowly won the battle for tenth, holding off Moncayo; wild-card Toni Finsterbusch led the following gang fighting over 12th, from Kornfeil and Webb; Iwema had dropped back from this group by the finish for the last point. Martin and Stafford had been ahead of Finsterbusch, but crashed out together on the last lap.

Left: Pedrosa, here heading Dovizioso and Simoncelli, dropped to third before taking a convincing come-back win.

Below left: Alex de Angelis took his first rostrum of the season.

Bottom left: Hector Faubel celebrates his dead-heat win.

Below: Marquez leads Bradl, de Angelis and the remainder of the Moto2 scramble.

Photos: Gold & Goose

eni MOTORRAD GRAND PRIX DEUTSCHLAND

15–17 JULY, 2011 · FIM WORLD CHAMPIONSHIP ROUND 9

SACHSENRING GP CIRCUIT

30 laps
Length: 3.671 km / 3,259 miles
Width: 12m

Key
96/60 kph/mph
2 Gear

Castrol Omega 90/51
Karthallen 155/96
Turn 9 145/90
Sternquell 128/80
Coca Cola Kurve 75/47
Turn 6 115/71
Turn 10 185/115
Queckenburg Kurve 100/62
Turn 11 146/90
Turn 12 210/130
Sachsen Kurve 115/71

MotoGP — RACE DISTANCE: 30 laps, 68.432 miles/110.130km · RACE WEATHER: Dry (air 21°C, humidity 49%, track 29°C)

Pos.	Rider	Nat.	No.	Entrant	Machine	Tyres	Laps	Time & speed
1	**Dani Pedrosa**	SPA	26	Repsol Honda Team	Honda	B	30	41m 12.482s 99.638mph/ 160.352km/h
2	**Jorge Lorenzo**	SPA	1	Yamaha Factory Racing	Yamaha	B	30	41m 13.959s
3	**Casey Stoner**	AUS	27	Repsol Honda Team	Honda	B	30	41m 14.050s
4	**Andrea Dovizioso**	ITA	4	Repsol Honda Team	Honda	B	30	41m 22.995s
5	**Ben Spies**	USA	11	Yamaha Factory Racing	Yamaha	B	30	41m 23.201s
6	**Marco Simoncelli**	ITA	58	San Carlo Honda Gresini	Honda	B	30	41m 23.405s
7	**Alvaro Bautista**	SPA	19	Rizla Suzuki MotoGP	Suzuki	B	30	41m 39.933s
8	**Nicky Hayden**	USA	69	Ducati Team	Ducati	B	30	41m 39.992s
9	**Valentino Rossi**	ITA	46	Ducati Team	Ducati	B	30	41m 40.058s
10	Colin Edwards	USA	5	Monster Yamaha Tech 3	Yamaha	B	30	41m 45.973s
11	**Hector Barbera**	SPA	8	Mapfre Aspar Team MotoGP	Ducati	B	30	41m 51.426s
12	**Karel Abraham**	CZE	17	Cardion AB Motoracing	Ducati	B	30	41m 51.630s
13	Randy de Puniet	FRA	14	Pramac Racing Team	Ducati	B	30	41m 51.897s
14	**Cal Crutchlow**	GBR	35	Monster Yamaha Tech 3	Yamaha	B	30	41m 51.959s
15	Hiroshi Aoyama	JPN	7	San Carlo Honda Gresini	Honda	B	30	42m 06.998s
16	Toni Elias	SPA	24	LCR Honda MotoGP	Honda	B	30	42m 24.817s
17	Sylvain Guintoli	FRA	50	Pramac Racing Team	Ducati	B	29	41m 28.441s

Fastest lap: Dani Pedrosa, on lap 20, 1m 21.846s, 100.332mph/161.469km/h (record).

Previous lap record: Dani Pedrosa, SPA (Honda), 1m 21.882s, 100.288mph/161.398km/h (2010).

Event best maximum speed: Casey Stoner, 176.700mph/284.400km/h (free practice 1).

Qualifying

Weather: Dry
Air Temp: 25° Humidity: 25%
Track Temp: 42°

1	Stoner	1m 21.681s
2	Pedrosa	1m 21.933s
3	Lorenzo	1m 21.944s
4	Simoncelli	1m 21.954s
5	Spies	1m 22.056s
6	Dovizioso	1m 22.157s
7	Edwards	1m 22.368s
8	Hayden	1m 22.388s
9	De Puniet	1m 22.503s
10	Bautista	1m 22.604s
11	Barbera	1m 22.676s
12	Crutchlow	1m 22.676s
13	Abraham	1m 23.164s
14	Elias	1m 23.201s
15	Aoyama	1m 23.248s
16	Rossi	1m 23.320s
17	Guintoli	1m 24.707s

Fastest race laps

1	Pedrosa	1m 21.846s
2	Lorenzo	1m 22.024s
3	Stoner	1m 22.070s
4	Simoncelli	1m 22.125s
5	Dovizioso	1m 22.218s
6	Spies	1m 22.406s
7	Barbera	1m 22.588s
8	Bautista	1m 22.780s
9	Hayden	1m 22.787s
10	Rossi	1m 22.802s
11	Abraham	1m 22.897s
12	Edwards	1m 22.923s
13	Crutchlow	1m 22.984s
14	De Puniet	1m 23.065s
15	Aoyama	1m 23.398s
16	Elias	1m 23.797s
17	Guintoli	1m 24.683s

Championship Points

1	Stoner	168
2	Lorenzo	153
3	Dovizioso	132
4	Rossi	98
5	Pedrosa	94
6	Spies	85
7	Hayden	85
8	Simoncelli	60
9	Edwards	59
10	Aoyama	57
11	Barbera	49
12	Abraham	41
13	Bautista	39
14	Elias	35
15	Crutchlow	34
16	Capirossi	22
17	De Puniet	15
18	Hopkins	6
19	Akiyoshi	3

Team Points

1	Repsol Honda Team	265
2	Yamaha Factory Racing	238
3	Ducati Team	183
4	San Carlo Honda Gresini	112
5	Monster Yamaha Tech 3	93
6	Mapfre Aspar Team MotoGP	49
7	Rizla Suzuki MotoGP	45
8	Cardion AB Motoracing	41
9	Pramac Racing Team	37
10	LCR Honda MotoGP	35

Constructor Points

1	Honda	210
2	Yamaha	184
3	Ducati	107
4	Suzuki	45

Grid Order

Grid Order	1	2	3	4	5	6	7	8	9	10	11	12	13	14	15	16	17	18	19	20	21	22	23	24	25	26	27	28	29	30	
27 STONER	1	1	1	1	27	27	27	27	27	27	27	27	27	1	1	1	1	1	1	1	26	26	26	26	26	26	26	26	26		1
26 PEDROSA	26	26	4	4	1	1	1	1	1	1	1	1	1	27	27	26	26	26	26	26	1	1	1	27	27	27	27	1	1		2
1 LORENZO	4	4	26	27	4	4	4	4	26	26	26	26	26	26	26	27	27	27	27	27	27	27	27	1	1	1	1	27	27		3
58 SIMONCELLI	27	27	27	26	26	26	26	26	4	4	4	4	58	58	58	58	58	4	4	4	58	58	58	58	58	58	58	4	4		4
11 SPIES	58	58	58	58	58	58	58	58	58	58	58	58	4	4	4	4	4	58	58	58	58	4	4	4	4	4	4	58	58	11	5
4 DOVIZIOSO	11	11	11	11	11	11	11	11	11	11	11	11	11	11	11	11	11	11	11	11	11	11	11	11	11	11	11	11	11	58	6
5 EDWARDS	69	69	69	19	19	19	19	19	19	69	69	19	19	19	69	69	69	69	69	69	19	19	69	69	69	69	69	69	19		7
69 HAYDEN	5	5	19	69	69	69	69	69	69	19	19	69	69	69	19	19	19	46	19	19	69	69	19	46	46	46	46	46	69		8
14 DE PUNIET	19	19	5	5	5	5	5	5	5	46	46	46	46	46	46	46	19	19	46	46	46	46	46	19	19	19	19	19	46		9
19 BAUTISTA	24	24	24	46	46	46	46	46	46	5	5	5	5	5	5	5	5	5	5	5	5	5	5	5	5	5	5	5	5		10
8 BARBERA	35	35	46	24	35	35	35	35	35	14	14	14	14	14	14	14	14	14	14	14	35	35	35	17	17	8	8	8	8		11
35 CRUTCHLOW	8	46	35	35	24	14	14	14	14	35	35	35	35	35	35	35	35	35	14	14	14	14	14	14	14	8	17	17	17		12
17 ABRAHAM	14	14	14	14	14	7	7	7	7	17	17	17	17	17	17	17	17	17	17	17	17	17	17	8	14	14	14	14	14		13
24 ELIAS	46	7	7	7	7	24	24	17	17	7	7	7	7	7	7	7	7	7	7	7	7	7	8	35	35	35	35	35	24		14
7 AOYAMA	7	17	17	17	17	17	17	24	24	24	8	8	8	8	8	8	8	8	8	8	8	8	7	7	7	7	7	7	7		15
46 ROSSI	17	50	50	50	50	8	8	8	8	24	24	24	24	24	24	24	24	24	24	24	24	24	24	24	24	24	24	24	24		
50 GUINTOLI	50	8	8	8	8	50	50	50	50	50	50	50	50	50	50	50	50	50	50	50	50	50	50	50	50	50	50	50	50		

50 Lapped rider

Moto2

RACE DISTANCE: 29 laps, 66.151 miles/106.459km · RACE WEATHER: Dry (air 23°C, humidity 43%, track 30°C)

Pos.	Rider	Nat.	No.	Entrant	Machine	Laps	Time & Speed
1	**Marc Marquez**	SPA	93	Team CatalunyaCaixa Repsol	Suter	29	41m 37.457s 95.354mph/ 153.457km/h
2	**Stefan Bradl**	GER	65	Viessmann Kiefer Racing	Kalex	29	41m 38.353s
3	**Alex de Angelis**	RSM	15	JIR Moto2	Motobi	29	41m 38.844s
4	**Randy Krummenacher**	SWI	4	GP Team Switzerland Kiefer Racing	Kalex	29	41m 40.870s
5	**Thomas Luthi**	SWI	12	Interwetten Paddock Moto2	Suter	29	41m 41.642s
6	**Yonny Hernandez**	COL	68	Blusens-STX	FTR	29	41m 45.148s
7	**Scott Redding**	GBR	45	Marc VDS Racing Team	Suter	29	41m 48.063s
8	**Simone Corsi**	ITA	3	Ioda Racing Project	FTR	29	41m 48.124s
9	**Jules Cluzel**	FRA	16	NGM Forward Racing	Suter	29	41m 49.536s
10	**Michele Pirro**	ITA	51	Gresini Racing Moto2	Moriwaki	29	41m 49.794s
11	**Kenan Sofuoglu**	TUR	54	Technomag-CIP	Suter	29	41m 50.654s
12	**Dominique Aegerter**	SWI	77	Technomag-CIP	Suter	29	41m 58.973s
13	**Pol Espargaro**	SPA	44	HP Tuenti Speed Up	FTR	29	41m 59.109s
14	**Andrea Iannone**	ITA	29	Speed Master	Suter	29	41m 59.284s
15	**Claudio Corti**	ITA	71	Italtrans Racing Team	Suter	29	41m 59.695s
16	Mike di Meglio	FRA	63	Tech 3 Racing	Tech 3	29	41m 59.816s
17	Alex Baldolini	ITA	25	NGM Forward Racing	Suter	29	42m 03.955s
18	Xavier Simeon	BEL	19	Tech 3 B	Tech 3	29	42m 07.594s
19	Mattia Pasini	ITA	75	Ioda Racing Project	FTR	29	42m 11.480s
20	Kenny Noyes	USA	9	Avintia-STX	FTR	29	42m 11.645s
21	Jordi Torres	SPA	18	Mapfre Aspar Team Moto2	Suter	29	42m 11.757s
22	Axel Pons	SPA	80	Pons HP 40	Pons Kalex	29	42m 12.406s
23	Anthony West	AUS	13	MZ Racing Team	MZ-RE Honda	29	42m 26.606s
24	Santiago Hernandez	COL	64	SAG Team	FTR	29	42m 27.359s
25	Ratthapark Wilairot	THA	14	Thai Honda Singha SAG	FTR	29	42m 30.637s
26	Robertino Pietri	VEN	39	Italtrans Racing Team	Suter	29	42m 35.130s
27	Steven Odendaal	RSA	97	MS Racing	Suter	29	42m 49.775s
28	Ricard Cardus	SPA	88	QMMF Racing Team	Moriwaki	29	42m 50.400s
29	Tommaso Lorenzetti	ITA	24	Aeroport de Castello	FTR	28	42m 15.062s
30	Mashel Al Naimi	QAT	95	QMMF Racing Team	Moriwaki	28	42m 17.363s
	Yuki Takahashi	JPN	72	Gresini Racing Moto2	Moriwaki	23	DNF
	Esteve Rabat	SPA	34	Blusens-STX	FTR	19	DNF
	Bradley Smith	GBR	38	Tech 3 Racing	Tech 3	15	DNF
	Aleix Espargaro	SPA	40	Pons HP 40	Pons Kalex	5	DNF
	Max Neukirchner	GER	76	MZ Racing Team	MZ-RE Honda	5	DNF
	Valentin Debise	FRA	53	Speed Up	FTR	2	DNF
	Julian Simon	SPA	60	Mapfre Aspar Team Moto2	Suter	0	DNF
	Mika Kallio	FIN	36	Marc VDS Racing Team	Suter	0	DNS

Fastest lap: Yonny Hernandez, on lap 4, 1m 25.255s, 96.320mph/155.012km/h (record).
Previous lap record: Andrea Iannone, ITA (Speed Up), 1m 25.629s, 95.899mph/154.335km/h (2010).
Event best maximum speed: Jules Cluzel, 154.600mph/248.800km/h (free practice 1).

Qualifying: Dry
Air: 25° Humidity: 24% Ground: 45°

1	Marquez	1m 24.733s
2	Bradl	1m 24.862s
3	A. Espargaro	1m 24.900s
4	Pirro	1m 25.085s
5	Simon	1m 25.189s
6	De Angelis	1m 25.223s
7	Simeon	1m 25.235s
8	Kallio	1m 25.271s
9	Smith	1m 25.304s
10	Y. Hernandez	1m 25.310s
11	Neukirchner	1m 25.379s
12	Luthi	1m 25.434s
13	Takahashi	1m 25.443s
14	P. Espargaro	1m 25.453s
15	Krummenacher	1m 25.456s
16	Torres	1m 25.465s
17	Cluzel	1m 25.495s
18	Rabat	1m 25.510s
19	Pons	1m 25.515s
20	Sofuoglu	1m 25.579s
21	Corsi	1m 25.613s
22	Di Meglio	1m 25.616s
23	Redding	1m 25.637s
24	Cardus	1m 25.723s
25	Iannone	1m 25.788s
26	Noyes	1m 25.806s
27	Corti	1m 25.851s
28	Aegerter	1m 25.870s
29	Baldolini	1m 25.872s
30	Debise	1m 25.900s
31	West	1m 26.130s
32	Wilairot	1m 26.211s
33	Pasini	1m 26.340s
34	Pietri	1m 26.482s
35	S. Hernandez	1m 27.166s
36	Odendaal	1m 27.591s
37	Lorenzetti	1m 27.816s
38	Al Naimi	1m 28.412s

Fastest race laps

1	Y. Hernandez	1m 25.255s
2	De Angelis	1m 25.314s
3	Corsi	1m 25.512s
4	Bradl	1m 25.528s
5	Marquez	1m 25.564s
6	Luthi	1m 25.566s
7	Smith	1m 25.595s
8	Redding	1m 25.653s
9	Takahashi	1m 25.663s
10	Krummenacher	1m 25.680s
11	Pirro	1m 25.753s
12	Sofuoglu	1m 25.764s
13	P. Espargaro	1m 25.829s
14	Iannone	1m 25.861s
15	Neukirchner	1m 25.882s
16	Rabat	1m 25.893s
17	Cluzel	1m 25.910s
18	A. Espargaro	1m 25.937s
19	Corti	1m 25.996s
20	Di Meglio	1m 26.006s
21	Baldolini	1m 26.070s
22	Aegerter	1m 26.112s
23	Torres	1m 26.228s
24	Simeon	1m 26.286s
25	Noyes	1m 26.303s
26	Pons	1m 26.352s
27	Pasini	1m 26.504s
28	West	1m 26.706s
29	Wilairot	1m 26.892s
30	Cardus	1m 26.900s
31	Pietri	1m 26.960s
32	S. Hernandez	1m 26.980s
33	Debise	1m 27.248s
34	Odendaal	1m 27.475s
35	Al Naimi	1m 28.264s
36	Lorenzetti	1m 28.970s

Championship Points

1	Bradl	167
2	Marquez	120
3	Corsi	84
4	De Angelis	82
5	Smith	79
6	Luthi	77
7	Iannone	66
8	Takahashi	58
9	Krummenacher	52
10	Simon	49
11	Pirro	43
12	Sofuoglu	39
13	A. Espargaro	38
14	Rabat	37
15	Cluzel	35
16	Aegerter	33
17	Y. Hernandez	33
18	Neukirchner	32
19	Redding	25
20	West	18
21	Baldolini	18
22	P. Espargaro	16
23	Pasini	13
24	Coghlan	11
25	Kallio	8
26	Di Meglio	7
27	Corti	7
28	Simeon	6
29	Wilairot	4
30	Cardus	2
31	Pons	1

Constructor Points

1	Suter	198
2	Kalex	174
3	FTR	98
4	Tech 3	88
5	Moriwaki	82
6	Motobi	82
7	Pons Kalex	39
8	MZ-RE Honda	39

125cc

RACE DISTANCE: 27 laps, 61.588 miles/99.117km · RACE WEATHER: Wet (air 24°C, humidity 34%, track 33°C)

Pos.	Rider	Nat.	No.	Entrant	Machine	Laps	Time & Speed
1	**Hector Faubel**	SPA	55	Bankia Aspar Team 125cc	Aprilia	27	39m 57.979s 92.460mph/ 148.800km/h
2	**Johann Zarco**	FRA	5	Avant-AirAsia-Ajo	Derbi	27	39m 57.979s
3	**Maverick Vinales**	SPA	25	Blusens by Paris Hilton Racing	Aprilia	27	39m 58.251s
4	**Nicolas Terol**	SPA	18	Bankia Aspar Team 125cc	Aprilia	27	39m 59.702s
5	**Luis Salom**	SPA	39	RW Racing GP	Aprilia	27	40m 00.763s
6	**Sergio Gadea**	SPA	33	Blusens by Paris Hilton Racing	Aprilia	27	40m 04.765s
7	**Jonas Folger**	GER	94	Red Bull Ajo MotorSport	Aprilia	27	40m 11.095s
8	**Sandro Cortese**	GER	11	Intact-Racing Team Germany	Aprilia	27	40m 11.393s
9	**Danny Kent**	GBR	52	Red Bull Ajo MotorSport	Aprilia	27	40m 11.689s
10	**Niklas Ajo**	FIN	31	TT Motion Events Racing	Aprilia	27	40m 27.069s
11	**Alberto Moncayo**	SPA	23	Andalucia Banca Civica	Aprilia	27	40m 27.320s
12	**Toni Finsterbusch**	GER	42	Freudenberg Racing Team	KTM	27	40m 31.462s
13	**Jakub Kornfeil**	CZE	84	Ongetta-Centro Seta	Aprilia	27	40m 32.336s
14	**Danny Webb**	GBR	99	Mahindra Racing	Mahindra	27	40m 32.384s
15	**Jasper Iwema**	NED	53	Ongetta-Abbink Metaal	Aprilia	27	40m 34.857s
16	Marcel Schrotter	GER	77	Mahindra Racing	Mahindra	27	40m 41.066s
17	Simone Grotzkyj	ITA	15	Phonica Racing	Aprilia	27	40m 41.102s
18	Louis Rossi	FRA	96	Matteoni Racing	Aprilia	27	40m 50.466s
19	Luigi Morciano	ITA	3	Team Italia FMI	Aprilia	27	40m 59.915s
20	Giulian Pedone	SWI	30	Phonica Racing	Aprilia	27	41m 02.473s
21	Sturla Fagerhaug	NOR	50	WTR-Ten10 Racing	Aprilia	27	41m 03.783s
22	Francesco Mauriello	ITA	43	WTR-Ten10 Racing	Aprilia	27	41m 03.879s
23	Joan Perello	SPA	36	Matteoni Racing	Aprilia	27	41m 22.184s
24	Zulfahmi Khairuddin	MAL	63	Airasia-Sic-Ajo	Derbi	27	41m 25.306s
25	Alessandro Tonucci	ITA	19	Team Italia FMI	Aprilia	27	41m 25.484s
26	Alexis Masbou	FRA	10	Caretta Technology	KTM	26	39m 59.744s
27	Felix Forstenhaeusler	GER	78	Schwaben Racing Team	Honda	26	40m 06.261s
	Adrian Martin	SPA	26	Bankia Aspar Team 125cc	Aprilia	26	DNF
	Harry Stafford	GBR	21	Ongetta-Centro Seta	Aprilia	26	DNF
	Luca Gruenwald	GER	41	Freudenberg Racing Team	KTM	23	DNF
	Efren Vazquez	SPA	7	Avant-AirAsia-Ajo	Derbi	20	DNF
	Peter Sebestyen	HUN	56	Caretta Technology	KTM	19	DNF
	Marvin Fritz	GER	70	LHF Project Racing	Honda	8	DNF
	Jack Miller	AUS	73	RZT Racing	Aprilia	3	DNF
	Miguel Oliveira	POR	44	Andalucia Banca Civica	Aprilia	2	DNF
	Taylor Mackenzie	GBR	17	Phonica Racing	Aprilia	2	DNF

Fastest lap: Hector Faubel, on lap 11, 1m 27.867s, 93.457mph/150.404km/h.
Lap record: Gabor Talmacsi, HUN (Aprilia), 1m 26.909s, 94.487mph/152.062km/h (2007).
Event best maximum speed: Nicolas Terol, 131.700mph/212.000km/h (race).

Qualifying: Dry
Air: 22° Humidity: 26% Ground: 38°

1	Vinales	1m 27.477s
2	Faubel	1m 27.808s
3	Salom	1m 27.992s
4	Terol	1m 27.992s
5	Gadea	1m 28.067s
6	Zarco	1m 28.178s
7	Vazquez	1m 28.316s
8	Moncayo	1m 28.344s
9	Folger	1m 28.390s
10	Kent	1m 28.626s
11	Oliveira	1m 28.651s
12	Martin	1m 28.704s
13	Schrotter	1m 28.721s
14	Ajo	1m 28.752s
15	Cortese	1m 28.778s
16	Webb	1m 28.822s
17	Khairuddin	1m 28.929s
18	Morciano	1m 29.062s
19	Grotzkyj	1m 29.171s
20	Stafford	1m 29.226s
21	Mackenzie	1m 29.307s
22	Masbou	1m 29.446s
23	Rossi	1m 29.450s
24	Iwema	1m 29.523s
25	Gruenwald	1m 29.628s
26	Miller	1m 29.680s
27	Fagerhaug	1m 29.725s
28	Finsterbusch	1m 29.739s
29	Pedone	1m 29.825s
30	Kornfeil	1m 29.905s
31	Mauriello	1m 30.227s
32	Sebestyen	1m 30.602s
33	Perello	1m 30.606s
34	Tonucci	1m 31.273s
35	Forstenhaeusle	1m 31.431s
36	Fritz	1m 31.655s

Fastest race laps

1	Faubel	1m 27.867s
2	Gadea	1m 28.085s
3	Salom	1m 28.114s
4	Zarco	1m 28.136s
5	Kent	1m 28.181s
6	Vinales	1m 28.184s
7	Terol	1m 28.205s
8	Vazquez	1m 28.287s
9	Cortese	1m 28.301s
10	Folger	1m 28.378s
11	Martin	1m 28.562s
12	Moncayo	1m 28.802s
13	Iwema	1m 28.987s
14	Finsterbusch	1m 28.992s
15	Stafford	1m 29.006s
16	Kornfeil	1m 29.043s
17	Ajo	1m 29.120s
18	Webb	1m 29.217s
19	Schrotter	1m 29.278s
20	Rossi	1m 29.310s
21	Oliveira	1m 29.506s
22	Gruenwald	1m 29.610s
23	Morciano	1m 29.634s
24	Grotzkyj	1m 29.716s
25	Pedone	1m 29.832s
26	Masbou	1m 29.946s
27	Mauriello	1m 30.129s
28	Perello	1m 30.148s
29	Mackenzie	1m 30.244s
30	Fagerhaug	1m 30.260s
31	Khairuddin	1m 30.297s
32	Sebestyen	1m 30.527s
33	Tonucci	1m 30.993s
34	Fritz	1m 31.050s
35	Forstenhaeusler	1m 31.112s
36	Miller	1m 31.901s

Championship Points

1	Terol	166
2	Zarco	134
3	Vinales	122
4	Folger	110
5	Cortese	106
6	Faubel	90
7	Vazquez	90
8	Salom	76
9	Gadea	71
10	Kent	46
11	Kornfeil	34
12	Martin	30
13	Oliveira	30
14	Moncayo	28
15	Grotzkyj	19
16	Mackenzie	15
17	Schrotter	15
18	Khairuddin	13
19	Rossi	13
20	Ajo	11
21	Webb	10
22	Masbou	10
23	Ono	8
24	Iwema	7
25	Finsterbusch	4
26	McPhee	1
27	Rodriguez	1

Constructor Points

1	Aprilia	225
2	Derbi	143
3	Mahindra	22
4	KTM	21

FIM WORLD CHAMPIONSHIP · ROUND 10

UNITED STATES GRAND PRIX

LAGUNA SECA CIRCUIT

Above: Hostage to his electronics, Lorenzo was lucky to emerge relatively unscathed from his slow-but-high flip in practice.

Right: Chasing shadows, Rossi still finished sixth.

Top right: Former double winner Hayden was just a second behind his team-mate.

Above right: Legendary pair Kel Carruthers and Kenny Roberts were re-united as Yamaha continued their 50th-anniversary celebrations.
Photos: Gold & Goose

ONCE the morning mists had lifted, clear blue skies and a Californian welcome accompanied a relatively tranquil running of this often-bumpy event. The only significant complaint was a continuing niggle about tyres, in spite of a special 'extra-soft' delivery from Bridgestone. It came mainly from Stoner, who reiterated his wish for softer and harder choices to be separated more widely.

By Sunday, in an echo of the weather, Stoner had nothing more about which to complain, after a victory that he soon adopted as "one of my best races". Appeasement, perhaps, for his signal defeat by Rossi here in 2008, but not revenge: his rival once again was nowhere near the front action.

Importantly, Stoner's victory closed a run of four races with four different winners, and reversed his shrinking points lead. With rostrums everywhere and no repeat winners, generally this had been improving, until Germany. But two of those wins had been by Yamahas. The timing of this one was a boost to his confidence.

His rival for the race was as for the title: Lorenzo, with a return from a crash that is becoming something of a Laguna trademark for the Spaniard. In 2009, he fell heavily after setting pole time; knocked about, but with nothing broken, he was a close third the next day. The 2011 spectacular high-side came on Saturday morning, and for a very new-century reason, hostage to his electronics. Impressively, he came back in the afternoon to claim pole.

The champion had stopped on the short straight before turn five (his lap-one nemesis, by the way, in 2008) to do a practice start. This, he explained later, is done with the traction control switched off, to give the rider better control. It switches on automatically at the first downshift. Trouble was, he kept it in second gear, rolled into the corner slowly, then just cracked the throttle. With no traction control, it threw him straight off.

The landing was heavy, the worrying part that "I could not feel my legs". Bit by bit, feeling and movement returned and he limped to the ambulance, beaten up, but – as he would show – ready for action the next day.

Lorenzo and factory team-mate Spies were in Yamaha's retro-colours for a second race, and as usual the US branch of the company made much of the race, releasing one of its spasmodic, and always amusing and well-received video clips, featuring a parade of champions (Roberts, Lawson, Rainey, Lorenzo from GP, Rossi otherwise engaged; Edwards and Crutchlow from the SBK world) travelling backwards and forwards in time, suitably bewigged for the sixties and the opposite for the future.

Lorenzo was far from the only victim of the technical and treacherous little circuit, shortest of the year (by 61 metres from the Sachsenring). Qualifying particularly was littered with scrape marks and bits and pieces, the list comprising Hayden, Bautista, Spies and de Puniet.

Only the last was hurt, much worse than he realised after walking away, with fractures to two vertebrae and his pelvis.

Not surprisingly, he was out of the race, and troubled for several more.

De Puniet's loss from the grid was compensated by the recruitment of a rare wild-card, in more than one sense. For one thing, Ben Bostrom was a racing veteran of 37; nobody could recall a first-timer of such advanced years, at least in the modern era. He was given Toni Elias' spare LCR bike, so just one each; and was moonlighting from his real job, riding a Jordan Suzuki Superbike in the AMA championship. Since there is a concurrent round, it meant that he was jumping from one bike to the other. This made considerably harder the job of adapting – to the tyres, the power, the size, but most especially the carbon brakes.

"It's such a strange alien of a bike, and it's not doing what I want it to do … but I've seen what the thing could do, because I had the boys come by me," he said. He qualified respectably enough, a second off his erstwhile team-mate, but ran off early in the race, then pulled in to retire, to stay fresh enough to take fifth in the 23-lap Superbike race later in the afternoon.

Motegi talk rumbled on, with the awaited independent report apparently in Ezpeleta's hands, but only in the original Italian. He was awaiting translations before distributing it. HRC chief Nakamoto called the Repsol trio to a meeting on Thursday evening. Dovizioso revealed that they'd been advised to await the findings of the report, and if favourable, "then they [Honda] will push". Stoner, the only open

refusenik, snapped at a US reporter who dared ask the question, and shortly afterwards the team Press minder requested no further questions on the topic.

Ducati, it transpired later, had commissioned its own report on Motegi, but had much more to worry about. The return of Burgess to Rossi's pit brought some relief, and now Rossi could "concentrate on the newer bike and improve our potential". Not to great avail, as it would turn out, as he finished just seven-tenths ahead of team-mate Hayden on the GP11 Mk2.

Nicky had the newer GP11.1 available, and had a gallop on it in first qualifying, returning to praise its potential and showing real enthusiasm for the seamless gearbox. But all the same, "right now I'm at Laguna, a track I love, and you don't want to be here testing." There was one unwelcome implication: wheeling out the 11.1 meant breaking out a new engine, with different fittings – and it was rather early in the season to be up to number five out of six.

There was a good crowd for the first of two MotoGP visits to the USA, with 52,670 claimed on the day. For the 13th GP at Laguna, the seventh consecutive since the return in 2005, things seemed to be settling down nicely. The current contract runs until the 2014 race, with organisers anxious to renew after that. But with the new circuit at Austin coming on stream – already pencilled in for 2013, and Indianapolis likewise seeking to renew, in future this might be the first of three US races. That's almost as many as Spain!

The swoop through the Corkscrew is just one feature that makes Laguna a good Yamaha track; another is the lack of high-speed corner exits and subsequent straights, where they struggle to stay with the Hondas. Spies put his on provisional pole with 15 minutes to go, but crashed out near the end trying to keep up with the final rush.

The other Yamaha, surprisingly considering the morning's slam-dunk, emerged at the front. It was Lorenzo's second pole of the year, and his first since far-off Portugal. Stoner was second, crediting a "one-lap wonder" as they still sought the right settings, but he added ominously, "There's no rules about when you have to be on the pace, until the race."

He'd pushed Dani to third at the last gasp; Spies now led row two from Simoncelli and Dovizioso.

Rossi's seventh was his best grid position since Catalunya, and he'd made big improvements over the four sessions. He led an all-Ducati third row from Barbera and Hayden.

The surge through turn one into the first slow loop is crucial, and Pedrosa's aptitude at starting saw him past Stoner into turn two. But it was Lorenzo in front, a white-and-red streak, and for the next seven laps with only Dani in close pursuit. Stoner was a full second adrift of Pedrosa at the end of lap two, but began closing up thereafter, although he didn't seem able to do a lot more.

The first three held their positions as the race wore on. Only by lap 17 did Lorenzo start to edge away from his countryman. This was Stoner's signal to move. A few weeks later, he would describe it as one of his best races. "It looked like I couldn't do anything, but I was thinking and planning all the way, more than any other race. I was struggling to turn the bike after the start, but I was patient and when the fuel went out, it just got better," he said.

His pass on Pedrosa was clean and hard, into the Corkscrew on lap 18. The gap to the leader at the end of that lap was almost a full second, but would not last. Steadily the Honda closed, and he was on Lorenzo's tail by the end of lap 22, with ten to go.

His attack was impressive: around the outside at the daunting turn one. Lorenzo said later that they had touched and that Stoner had apologised on the rostrum, but that seemed like wishful thinking, for it was a great move that not only put his title quest back on track, but also went some way to erasing the bitter memories of his defeat here at the hands of Rossi in 2008.

After that, by his own admission, Lorenzo threw in the towel. Pain from his big smash the day before was a factor. "I feel lucky to be second," he said; it was in itself a heroic feat.

Pedrosa fell away steadily in third, with his own pain problems at a highly physical track. By the end, he was four seconds behind Lorenzo, and almost ten behind Stoner, but safe from threat.

Early on, Dovizioso had been close to Stoner, with Simoncelli pushing hard behind him. They had lost touch by the fourth lap, and on the seventh Simoncelli went down, losing the front into the downhill Rainey Corner.

Spies had been swamped at the start, while Rossi got a flyer, behind Simoncelli, but immediately lost ground. Spies attacked at turn two at the start of lap three to begin a lonely pursuit of Dovizioso. The Honda man was slowing and Spies speeding up when they met with seven laps to go, and they battled furiously to the end, Spies pushing past into the last corner on the penultimate lap and staying there.

Hayden had been behind Spies at the start, and then Rossi, the factory Ducatis together all race, seldom more than half a second apart. They finished in the same order, Rossi just that little fraction too fast and too good for double Laguna winner Hayden.

Bautista had been stuck behind Barbera for the early laps. He reversed the positions on the seventh lap, and the pair of them caught the Ducatis, Barbera struggling to stay with the Suzuki. By the time Bautista crashed out on lap 14, his Spanish rival had lost touch, and a near crash and a slow lap gave Edwards the chance to get ahead next time around. He pulled comfortably away for a lonely eighth and was six seconds clear of Barbera by the end. The latter was almost ten ahead of the next pair.

Abraham had appeared safe in tenth, but lost pace at the end to fall victim to Aoyama on the last lap. Capirossi and Elias were a lap down. Crutchlow crashed out on lap four. Bostrom made a gear-shift muddle while lying last and ran into the gravel, and then retired after nine laps, preferring to concentrate on his AMA Superbike duties.

Stoner's return to the winner's spot was his first for four races. He stretched his shrinking points lead to 20. It was, for him, a turning point of the year.

Inset above: Blast from the past. Four-time 500cc champion Eddie Lawson took a lap of honour on a street Yamaha.

Main photo: Laguna and its Corkscrew were at their blue-sky best.

Inset right: Spies, here leading a Ducati trio, moved forwards to fourth.

Inset below centre: Superbike veteran Ben Bostrom was a surprise choice for a ride on a second LCR Honda.

Inset bottom: Dovi on the gas.

Photos: Gold & Goose

motoGP · TISSOT SWISS WATCHES SINCE 1853 · **OFFICIAL TIMEKEEPER**

LAGUNA SECA

32 laps
Length: 3.610 km / 2.243 miles
Width: 15m

Key
96/60 kph/mph
⚙ Gear

Turn 1 266/165
Andretti Hairpin 83/52
Turn 3 109/68
Turn 5 115/71
Turn 11 65/40
Turn 4 140/87
Turn 10 130/81
Turn 7 229/142
Rainey Curve 130/81
The Corkscrew 80/67
Turn 6 135/84

RED BULL U.S. GRAND PRIX

Mazda Raceway
Laguna Seca 2011

MotoGP — RACE DISTANCE: 32 laps, 71.781 miles/115.52km · RACE WEATHER: Dry (air 23°C, humidity 39%, track 44°C)

Pos.	Rider	Nat.	No.	Entrant	Machine	Tyres	Laps	Time & speed
1	**Casey Stoner**	AUS	27	Repsol Honda Team	Honda	B	32	43m 52.145s 98.175mph/ 157.997km/h
2	**Jorge Lorenzo**	SPA	1	Yamaha Factory Racing	Yamaha	B	32	43m 57.779s
3	**Dani Pedrosa**	SPA	26	Repsol Honda Team	Honda	B	32	44m 01.612s
4	**Ben Spies**	USA	11	Yamaha Factory Racing	Yamaha	B	32	44m 12.707s
5	**Andrea Dovizioso**	ITA	4	Repsol Honda Team	Honda	B	32	44m 13.030s
6	**Valentino Rossi**	ITA	46	Ducati Team	Ducati	B	32	44m 22.496s
7	**Nicky Hayden**	USA	69	Ducati Team	Ducati	B	32	44m 23.176s
8	**Colin Edwards**	USA	5	Monster Yamaha Tech 3	Yamaha	B	32	44m 37.647s
9	**Hector Barbera**	SPA	8	Mapfre Aspar Team MotoGP	Ducati	B	32	44m 43.694s
10	**Hiroshi Aoyama**	JPN	7	San Carlo Honda Gresini	Honda	B	32	45m 00.995s
11	**Karel Abraham**	CZE	17	Cardion AB Motoracing	Ducati	B	32	45m 01.277s
12	**Loris Capirossi**	ITA	65	Pramac Racing Team	Ducati	B	31	44m 05.129s
13	**Toni Elias**	SPA	24	LCR Honda MotoGP	Honda	B	31	44m 29.962s
	Alvaro Bautista	SPA	19	Rizla Suzuki MotoGP	Suzuki	B	13	DNF
	Ben Bostrom	USA	23	LCR Honda MotoGP	Honda	B	8	DNF
	Marco Simoncelli	ITA	58	San Carlo Honda Gresini	Honda	B	6	DNF
	Cal Crutchlow	GBR	35	Monster Yamaha Tech 3	Yamaha	B	3	DNF

Fastest lap: Casey Stoner, on lap 3, 1m 21.673s, 98.874mph/159.122km/h.

Lap record: Casey Stoner, AUS (Ducati), 1m 21.376s, 99.235mph/159.703km/h (2010).

Event best maximum speed: Casey Stoner, 165.000mph/265.600km/h (qualifying).

Qualifying

Weather: Dry
Air Temp: 22° Humidity: 43%
Track Temp: 41°

1	Lorenzo	1m 21.202s
2	Stoner	1m 21.274s
3	Pedrosa	1m 21.385s
4	Spies	1m 21.578s
5	Simoncelli	1m 21.696s
6	Dovizioso	1m 21.731s
7	Rossi	1m 22.235s
8	Barbera	1m 22.238s
9	Hayden	1m 22.271s
10	Crutchlow	1m 22.385s
11	Edwards	1m 22.520s
12	Bautista	1m 22.669s
13	Abraham	1m 22.893s
14	Aoyama	1m 22.937s
15	De Puniet	1m 22.961s
16	Capirossi	1m 23.876s
17	Elias	1m 24.156s
18	Bostrom	1m 25.291s

Fastest race laps

1	Stoner	1m 21.673s
2	Lorenzo	1m 21.692s
3	Pedrosa	1m 21.738s
4	Dovizioso	1m 21.913s
5	Simoncelli	1m 22.091s
6	Spies	1m 22.244s
7	Rossi	1m 22.520s
8	Bautista	1m 22.592s
9	Hayden	1m 22.704s
10	Barbera	1m 22.850s
11	Edwards	1m 22.952s
12	Crutchlow	1m 23.063s
13	Abraham	1m 23.131s
14	Aoyama	1m 23.518s
15	Capirossi	1m 23.661s
16	Bostrom	1m 24.091s
17	Elias	1m 24.200s

Championship Points

1	Stoner	193
2	Lorenzo	173
3	Dovizioso	143
4	Pedrosa	110
5	Rossi	108
6	Spies	98
7	Hayden	94
8	Edwards	67
9	Aoyama	63
10	Simoncelli	60
11	Barbera	56
12	Abraham	46
13	Bautista	39
14	Elias	38
15	Crutchlow	34
16	Capirossi	26
17	De Puniet	15
18	Hopkins	6
19	Akiyoshi	3

Team Points

1	Repsol Honda Team	301
2	Yamaha Factory Racing	271
3	Ducati Team	202
4	San Carlo Honda Gresini	118
5	Monster Yamaha Tech 3	101
6	Mapfre Aspar Team MotoGP	56
7	Cardion AB Motoracing	46
8	Rizla Suzuki MotoGP	45
9	Pramac Racing Team	41
10	LCR Honda MotoGP	38

Constructor Points

1	Honda	235
2	Yamaha	204
3	Ducati	117
4	Suzuki	45

Grid order	1	2	3	4	5	6	7	8	9	10	11	12	13	14	15	16	17	18	19	20	21	22	23	24	25	26	27	28	29	30	31	32	
1 LORENZO	1	1	1	1	1	1	1	1	1	1	1	1	1	1	1	1	1	1	1	1	1	1	1	1	1	1	27	27	27	27	27	27	1
27 STONER	26	26	26	26	26	26	26	26	26	26	26	26	26	26	26	26	27	27	27	27	27	27	27	27	27	27	1	1	1	1	1	1	2
26 PEDROSA	27	27	27	27	27	27	27	27	27	27	27	27	27	27	27	27	26	26	26	26	26	26	26	26	26	26	26	26	26	26	26	26	3
11 SPIES	4	4	4	4	4	4	4	4	4	4	4	4	4	4	4	4	4	4	4	4	4	4	4	4	4	4	4	4	4	11	11	11	4
58 SIMONCELLI	58	58	58	58	58	58	11	11	11	11	11	11	11	11	11	11	11	11	11	11	11	11	11	11	11	11	11	11	11	4	4	4	5
4 DOVIZIOSO	46	46	11	11	11	11	46	46	46	46	46	46	46	46	46	46	46	46	46	46	46	46	46	46	46	46	46	46	46	46	46	46	6
46 ROSSI	11	11	46	46	46	46	69	69	69	69	69	69	69	69	69	69	69	69	69	69	69	69	69	69	69	69	69	69	69	69	69	69	7
8 BARBERA	69	69	69	69	69	69	19	19	19	19	19	19	19	19	5	5	5	5	5	5	5	5	5	5	5	5	5	5	5	5	5	5	8
69 HAYDEN	8	8	8	8	8	8	8	8	8	8	8	8	8	8	8	8	8	8	8	8	8	8	8	8	8	8	8	8	8	8		8	9
35 CRUTCHLOW	35	19	19	19	19	19	5	5	5	5	5	5	17	17	17	17	17	17	17	17	17	17	17	17	17	17	17	17	17	7			10
5 EDWARDS	19	35	35	5	5	5	17	17	17	17	17	17	7	7	7	7	7	7	7	7	7	7	7	7	7	7	7	7	7	17			11
19 BAUTISTA	5	5	5	17	17	17	7	7	7	7	7	7	65	65	65	65	65	65	65	65	65	65	65	65	65	65	65	65	65				12
17 ABRAHAM	65	17	17	7	7	7	65	65	65	65	65	65	24	24	24	24	24	24	24	24	24	24	24	24	24	24	24	24	24				13
7 AOYAMA	17	65	65	65	65	65	24	24	24	24	24	24																					
65 CAPIROSSI	24	7	7	23	23	24	23	23																									
24 ELIAS	7	23	23	24	24	23																											
23 BOSTROM	23	24	24																														

23 Pit stop   65/24 Lapped rider

CZECH REPUBLIC GRAND PRIX

BRNO CIRCUIT

Casey Stoner was back in command
for an important win – and beaming
about it (*inset*).
Photos: Gold & Goose

THE Honda steamroller reached full speed at Brno. For the first time since 2006 – back when MotoGP bikes were the full 990cc – Hondas took all three places on the rostrum. They would have taken the first four had pole qualifier Dani Pedrosa not crashed out, one corner after taking the lead early in the race.

Brno's hillsides were heaving with a huge crowd of 155,400; they came from far and wide in spite of rising prices in the now thoroughly westernised old industrial city. Those same sweeping hills, and a well-designed and especially wide layout make this a fine circuit: one, Stoner said, of his top three. He wasn't talking about the race, which in the absence of Dani, he would dominate in his usual style, in spite of a crash when rain came good and proper on Saturday morning. He was looking forward to Monday, a rare test day, and a second chance for him to ride the 2012 1000cc RC213V. He'd ridden it at Jerez, but Brno is a circuit where the corners are faster and for once riders get a chance to hold the throttles open wide on the big bikes.

A second chance for him, a first for team-mate Pedrosa. Dovizioso was not on the test list, however, and it was becoming increasingly clear that his future as a Honda factory rider was closed.

It was the first go on a 1000 also for Yamaha's Lorenzo and Spies, both of whom would be pleasantly impressed by the power of the full-size, all-black M1 Yamaha. This was especially welcome a day after being thoroughly out-powered on the Brno hill-climb.

But no chance for the Ducati riders, with rumours now strengthening that Rossi was demanding an aluminium replacement chassis for his no-feel carbon box. The 2012 bike was on hold, Rossi continuing with his current GP11.1. His qualifying had improved – on the second row – while the finish was encouraging: still only sixth, but just 12.6 seconds adrift. He also overtook no-score Pedrosa for fourth in the championship, another small fillip in what would prove a short-lived dawn of new hope. It was Hayden's time also to become familiar with the new bike and its seamless gearshift, after a morning's acquaintance at Laguna Seca three weeks before.

The short summer break was over and the European season resumed, amid continuing controversy over Motegi. The report from the independent Italian agency ARPA had been released during the break: tests of food, water and ambient conditions at Motegi indicated that the radiation risks were "negligible", but this was still not enough to quell the doubts of some riders. Stoner revealed that at least he had a cogent (or at least emotionally understandable) reason for his flat refusal in Germany: he had recently learned that his wife Adriana had become pregnant. In the break, he'd had some

Above: Lorenzo is second, but Dovizioso and Simoncelli are on him. He will succumb.

Top right: John Hopkins' latest comeback was put on hold after a hand injury.

Above right: Sixth for Rossi, again – but at least he was a little closer.

Right: Pedrosa took the lead, then hit the gravel. He was baffled.

Photos: Gold & Goose

reassurance from "people I trust" in Australia (not to mention some wise words from within HRC). "I'm not saying I'm going, but I'm not saying I'm not going," he said.

Also on hold: the expected announcement of his future from the old man of the grid, Loris Capirossi. Likewise the restitution of the otherwise thoroughly reborn John Hopkins. Hopper was completing his third consecutive weekend of high-level racing – World Superbikes and BSB preceding – with a second wild-card ride on the Suzuki. It all went wrong on Saturday morning in the rain, when he fell at the same corner as Stoner. His misfortune was to trap his right hand under the sliding handlebar; the consequence was three broken fingers (the third finger badly enough to require surgery) and a disconsolate early withdrawal. The day before, he'd placed tenth, with a near-identical time to on-form teammate Bautista.

There was restitution: of Simoncelli, at last able to shed his hangdog expression with his first MotoGP rostrum. Gone also was his caution of the previous couple of races. Later he told *MOTOCOURSE*, "Sure, all the polemic that people said and the newspaper wrote conditioned me, and for some races I paid more attention. Sometimes when it was time to do an attack, I thought it was a little bit too much for me. After Brno, after I got the podium, I went back to my style … I follow more my instinct on the track."

Ben Spies had the distraction of a trapped nerve that made his left arm go numb; worse afflicted was 125 Silverstone winner Jonas Folger. The 17-year-old Austrian pulled out of the race with a mystery ailment – rumours ranged from a chlamydia infection to over-indulgence at Karel Abraham's pre-race party, while the team punished him for several races after his return by handing his RSA Aprilia to junior teammate Danny Kent, leaving Folger with the older RSW.

As for Abraham, whose bachelor pad stands adjacent to his family's grand villa, itself beside the back road to the circuit in which Abraham senior has a very major interest, his home race was the usual disaster. Wonderment at how his wealthy father had effectively bought his boy his own MotoGP team had been eroded through the season by the rider's honest hard work and far from shabby lap times and results, for a rookie on the hard-to-ride Ducati. After qualifying 17th and last, he crashed early in the race, rejoining a lap down only to retire with a smoky blow-up.

This was the first race under the new tyre regulations: an extra-soft front on top of the existing allocation of eight, and more freedom of choice for the rear. But temperatures were not low enough to make much of the extra tyre, and then it rained anyway on Saturday morning.

MOTOGP RACE – 22 laps

In the wet on Saturday morning, Stoner's name topped the time sheets as usual, but in every other session Pedrosa had been unbeatable, and he claimed his first pole of the season. Lorenzo worked hard on soft tyres to claim second, with Stoner third.

Spies led row two from Simoncelli and Rossi, with another small step in improved feel credited to revised triple clamps that changed rake and trail, and a simple change to the handlebar position.

Tyre choice was significant: all had the softer rear, while up front, all but two had the extra-hard. Bautista and Lorenzo had gone for the softer option.

Pedrosa led into the first corner, with Stoner, Lorenzo, Dovizioso and Spies behind. But this would be no procession. Lorenzo took second at turn three, then moved into the lead out of the stadium bowl, his tyre choice paying early dividends.

By the end of the lap, a still tentative Stoner had lost another place to Dovizioso, while Simoncelli had barged past Rossi, then Hayden for sixth.

Pedrosa followed Lorenzo for one more lap, then made his move at turn three, cutting cleanly past with a clear track in

front. At the same time, Stoner had repassed Dovi at the first turn and followed Dani past Lorenzo. He had a grandstand view as Pedrosa lost the front and slid into the gravel on the next corner. Dani was baffled: "I was not even pushing so hard. Maybe I leaned too much, maybe the tyre was not warm enough. I don't know, but I have wasted an important race."

Stoner now led and was getting down to business. He was still less than a second away when Dovizioso also passed Lorenzo's Yamaha on lap four and started to close. Any hopes of attacking faded on lap seven, however, when Dovi all but crashed, recovering without losing second, but now with Lorenzo and Simoncelli right behind him.

As Stoner stretched away to his assured victory, Dovi had his hands full, and Lorenzo got back ahead at the start of lap nine, passing into the first corner. Lorenzo held second for two more laps, but then both of the Hondas were ahead of him in one go and he began losing ground steadily.

Simoncelli continued to hound the factory bike for the next six laps, and by the 17th was in a position to mount an attack. At this point, Dovi upped his pace and two laps later was a second clear for his second runner-up spot of the year. Simoncelli was a safe third, in spite of Lorenzo closing again in the last laps.

Spies had been fifth from the first lap and would stay there to the end. But again, this was no cake-walk. Rossi had taken sixth off Hayden on lap two, and by lap seven was working on a gap of a second to the Yamaha ahead.

He never was quite close enough to challenge, but only because of the sterling efforts of the American, who overcame his painful problems to keep the gap, albeit narrowly at times. This brought him ever closer to Lorenzo, while by the end Rossi had slackened off to finish 2.4 seconds adrift.

Nor was Rossi free from pressure. An inspired Bautista had moved to seventh on the third lap, and by lap 12 was right on Rossi's back wheel and clearly looking for a way past. He never found it, but was still right up close when he slid off on lap 16.

Hayden was losing ground steadily, his earlier version of the Ducati lacking Rossi's front-end modifications. Edwards was hard behind him all the way, the gap still a second over the line.

Aoyama was a similar distance behind, pulling through after finishing lap one 14th and closing steadily on the American pair in the latter half. He'd been promoted one place on lap six when Crutchlow slid off, just in front of Barbera and Aoyama, a second successive crash.

Barbera finished lap one 13th and moved up to tenth two laps later. After Aoyama passed him on the ninth, he started to drop away, and on lap 20 was back in the clutches of a two-bike battle at the back, between Elias and de Puniet. Elias did get past on lap 20, but Barbera reversed the positions on the final lap. Capirossi had been with this battle early on, but by half-distance he was dropping back.

Abraham had started second last, only de Puniet behind, but dropped to last after slipping off on lap five. After remounting, he spluttered to a smoky stop on lap 13, soon after being lapped by the leaders.

MOTO2 RACE – 20 laps

Marquez was looking for a fourth win in succession and claimed his third pole in a row. Bradl, close to home and with his huge points lead rapidly crumbling, was alongside; de Angelis completed the front row. Iannone was in the middle of row two, a shade slower than Luthi. This marked a new accord with his Suter chassis: in the previous five races, he had qualified in the top 20 just once, and then only 14th.

Bradl was away first, then the young Spaniard, who added to his growing reputation for rough riding by colliding with the German at turn three. In the ensuing confusion, Luthi grabbed the first-lap lead from Bradl, de Angelis, Marquez and Iannone.

This quintet, locked in combat, soon moved clear of the pack. Bradl was back in front next time around, and would stay there until the 12th lap. But there was never anything in it, with positions changing frequently around the sweeps and swoops, and some desperate riding from all of them. Most especially Marquez, whose aggression saw him collide again with de Angelis and Iannone. He might have earned official censure had a crash resulted, but he got away with it.

Iannone took the lead for the first time on lap 13 and stayed there for the next two before ceding it again for one

lap to Bradl. Luthi was at the back and with four laps to go lost touch. The rest were hard at it to the end.

Marquez looked the likeliest and led for the first time over the line as they started the last lap. But Iannone had other ideas, while Bradl and de Angelis were also trying hard.

In the end, Iannone managed to get enough of a gap at the bottom of the final hill to avoid being passed by the lightweight Marquez on the way up it, and took a fine win. It was his second of the year, and it underlined a major return to form. Remarkably, while class rules dictate that riders should be nursing spent tyres home, Iannone set a new record on the last lap.

Marquez was second, then Bradl and de Angelis. The top four crossed the line in less than nine-tenths of a second, after an absorbing battle. And yet another doom-laden shrinkage of Bradl's points lead.

Luthi was three seconds adrift by the end, but safe from a five-bike battle of similar ferocity some 12 seconds behind. Rabat was leader for a long spell, but Aleix Espargaro pipped him to the flag, with Aegerter and Corsi right behind. Sofuoglu lost touch in the closing stages for tenth.

Randy Krummenacher crashed out early, as did Jules Cluzel and Bradley Smith. Max Neukirchner was also among the fallers.

125cc RACE – 19 laps

Cortese took a narrow first win in seven years of trying in the opening 125 race, outfumbling Zarco in the last corner after a race-long battle.

Terol led away from pole in familiar fashion, but this would be no easy runaway.

Next time around, Zarco was in front, and two laps later the pair of them, along with Cortese, were pulling clear for a three-man battle.

Terol was narrowly ahead again by lap five, but he couldn't get away. Then on the ninth lap, he suddenly slowed, touring disconsolately back to the pits as the race passed him by. It was engine failure, an event so rare that mechanics were still scratching their heads hours later before eventually blaming an electronic glitch.

The other two didn't slack. Zarco led from lap nine to 17, then Cortese. Last time up the hill, the German was in front. Zarco pushed inside into the last fast left-right. It looked like enough, but Cortese held the outside line and was just in front into the final bend. Zarco tried again, ran over the inside kerb and almost crashed, gesticulating angrily as he followed the German over the line, robbed once again of victory.

His consolation was to close to within 12 points of Terol.

Six bikes were to and fro over third, and then five when Vazquez crashed out with six laps to go. There were only four over the line, with Oliveira crashing out on the last corner. Team-mate Moncayo took third, then Faubel, Gadea and Vinales, all four over the line within seven-tenths.

Kornfeil was seventh, his earlier companion, Grotzkyj, dropping away and almost caught at the end by the next big group, led over the line by Khairuddin from Iwema.

Above: Seven-year itch. Cortese was a winner at last.

Left: Iannone regained form and was overjoyed by his second Moto2 win of the season.

Below left: Rider willing, bike not. Runaway 125cc points leader Terol suffered a rare breakdown.

Below: Cortese (11) took the 125cc win to frustrate eternal 2011 runner-up Zarco (5).

Photos: Gold & Goose

OFFICIAL TIMEKEEPER

AUTODROM BRNO

22 laps
Length: 5.403 km / 3.357 miles
Width: 15m

Key
96/60 kph/mph
⚙ Gear

Turn 5 115/71
Turn 9 95/59
Kevin Schwantz 105/65
Turn 4 115/71
Stadion 95/59
Turn 8 95/59
Turn 3 115/71
Turn 11 95/59
František Štasný 130/81
Turn 12 120/75
Horizont 105/65
Turn 14 135/84
280/174

MotoGP

RACE DISTANCE: 22 laps, 73.860 miles/118.866km · RACE WEATHER: Dry (air 24°C, humidity 37%, track 37°C)

Pos.	Rider	Nat.	No.	Entrant	Machine	Tyres	Laps	Time & speed
1	**Casey Stoner**	AUS	27	Repsol Honda Team	Honda	B	22	43m 16.796s
								102.393mph/
								164.786km/h
2	**Andrea Dovizioso**	ITA	4	Repsol Honda Team	Honda	B	22	43m 23.328s
3	**Marco Simoncelli**	ITA	58	San Carlo Honda Gresini	Honda	B	22	43m 24.588s
4	**Jorge Lorenzo**	SPA	1	Yamaha Factory Racing	Yamaha	B	22	43m 25.309s
5	**Ben Spies**	USA	11	Yamaha Factory Racing	Yamaha	B	22	43m 26.982s
6	**Valentino Rossi**	ITA	46	Ducati Team	Ducati	B	22	43m 29.428s
7	**Nicky Hayden**	USA	69	Ducati Team	Ducati	B	22	43m 39.833s
8	**Colin Edwards**	USA	5	Monster Yamaha Tech 3	Yamaha	B	22	43m 40.985s
9	**Hiroshi Aoyama**	JPN	7	San Carlo Honda Gresini	Honda	B	22	43m 41.998s
10	**Hector Barbera**	SPA	8	Mapfre Aspar Team MotoGP	Ducati	B	22	43m 53.362s
11	**Toni Elias**	SPA	24	LCR Honda MotoGP	Honda	B	22	43m 53.475s
12	**Randy de Puniet**	FRA	14	Pramac Racing Team	Ducati	B	22	43m 53.905s
13	**Loris Capirossi**	ITA	65	Pramac Racing Team	Ducati	B	22	44m 05.707s
	Alvaro Bautista	SPA	19	Rizla Suzuki MotoGP	Suzuki	B	16	DNF
	Karel Abraham	CZE	17	Cardion AB Motoracing	Ducati	B	12	DNF
	Cal Crutchlow	GBR	35	Monster Yamaha Tech 3	Yamaha	B	6	DNF
	Dani Pedrosa	SPA	26	Repsol Honda Team	Honda	B	2	DNF

Fastest lap: Casey Stoner, on lap 2, 1m 57.191s, 103.132mph/165.975km/h.

Lap record: Jorge Lorenzo, SPA (Yamaha), 1m 56.670s, 103.593mph/166.716km/h (2009).

Event best maximum speed: Dani Pedrosa, 187.0mph/301.0km/h (free practice 2).

Qualifying

Weather: Dry
Air Temp: 22° **Humidity:** 52%
Track Temp: 30°

1	Pedrosa	1m 56.591s
2	Lorenzo	1m 56.704s
3	Stoner	1m 56.860s
4	Spies	1m 57.178s
5	Simoncelli	1m 57.351s
6	Rossi	1m 57.367s
7	Dovizioso	1m 57.442s
8	Edwards	1m 57.676s
9	Hayden	1m 57.721s
10	Aoyama	1m 57.784s
11	Crutchlow	1m 57.797s
12	Elias	1m 58.245s
13	Barbera	1m 58.273s
14	Bautista	1m 58.274s
15	De Puniet	1m 58.889s
16	Capirossi	1m 58.938s
17	Abraham	1m 58.946s

Fastest race laps

1	Stoner	1m 57.191s
2	Dovizioso	1m 57.468s
3	Simoncelli	1m 57.497s
4	Pedrosa	1m 57.518s
5	Lorenzo	1m 57.636s
6	Spies	1m 57.726s
7	Bautista	1m 57.821s
8	Rossi	1m 57.844s
9	Hayden	1m 58.264s
10	Crutchlow	1m 58.362s
11	Aoyama	1m 58.484s
12	Edwards	1m 58.522s
13	Barbera	1m 58.687s
14	De Puniet	1m 58.775s
15	Elias	1m 58.971s
16	Abraham	1m 58.978s
17	Capirossi	1m 59.139s

Championship Points

1	Stoner	218
2	Lorenzo	186
3	Dovizioso	163
4	Rossi	118
5	Pedrosa	110
6	Spies	109
7	Hayden	103
8	Simoncelli	76
9	Edwards	75
10	Aoyama	70
11	Barbera	62
12	Abraham	46
13	Elias	43
14	Bautista	39
15	Crutchlow	34
16	Capirossi	29
17	De Puniet	19
18	Hopkins	6
19	Akiyoshi	3

Team Points

1	Repsol Honda Team	326
2	Yamaha Factory Racing	295
3	Ducati Team	221
4	San Carlo Honda Gresini	141
5	Monster Yamaha Tech 3	109
6	Mapfre Aspar Team MotoGP	62
7	Pramac Racing Team	48
8	Cardion AB Motoracing	46
9	Rizla Suzuki MotoGP	45
10	LCR Honda MotoGP	43

Constructor Points

1	Honda	260
2	Yamaha	217
3	Ducati	127
4	Suzuki	45

Grid order		1	2	3	4	5	6	7	8	9	10	11	12	13	14	15	16	17	18	19	20	21	22	
26	PEDROSA	1	1	27	27	27	27	27	27	27	27	27	27	27	27	27	27	27	27	27	27	27	27	1
1	LORENZO	26	26	1	1	4	4	4	4	1	1	1	4	4	4	4	4	4	4	4	4	4	4	2
27	STONER	4	27	4	4	1	1	1	1	4	4	4	58	58	58	58	58	58	58	58	58	58	58	3
11	SPIES	27	4	58	58	58	58	58	58	58	58	58	1	1	1	1	1	1	1	1	1	1	1	4
58	SIMONCELLI	11	11	11	11	11	11	11	11	11	11	11	11	11	11	11	11	11	11	11	11	11	11	5
46	ROSSI	58	58	46	46	46	46	46	46	46	46	46	46	46	46	46	46	46	46	46	46	46	46	6
4	DOVIZIOSO	69	46	69	19	19	19	19	19	19	19	19	19	19	19	19	69	69	69	69	69	69	69	7
5	EDWARDS	46	69	19	69	69	69	69	69	69	69	69	69	69	69	69	5	5	5	5	5	5	5	8
69	HAYDEN	5	19	5	5	5	5	5	5	5	5	5	5	5	5	5	7	7	7	7	7	7	7	9
7	AOYAMA	19	5	8	8	8	35	8	8	7	7	7	7	7	7	7	8	8	8	24	24	8		10
35	CRUTCHLOW	24	24	35	35	35	8	7	7	8	8	8	8	8	8	8	24	24	24	8	8	24		11
24	ELIAS	35	35	24	7	7	7	24	24	24	24	24	24	24	24	24	14	14	14	14	14	14		12
8	BARBERA	8	8	7	24	24	24	65	65	14	14	14	14	14	14	14	65	65	65	65	65	65		13
19	BAUTISTA	7	7	65	65	65	65	14	14	65	65	65	65	65	65	65	19							
14	DE PUNIET	65	65	17	17	14	14	17	17	17	17	17	17											
65	CAPIROSSI	17	17	14	14	17	17																	
17	ABRAHAM	14	14																					

19 Pitstop   17 Lapped rider

Moto2

RACE DISTANCE: 20 laps, 67.145 miles/108.060km · RACE WEATHER: Dry (air 24°C, humidity 40%, track 35°C)

Pos.	Rider	Nat.	No.	Entrant	Machine	Laps	Time & Speed
1	**Andrea Iannone**	ITA	29	Speed Master	Suter	20	41m 13.255s 97.735 mph/ 157.289km/h)
2	**Marc Marquez**	SPA	93	Team CatalunyaCaixa Repsol	Suter	20	41m 13.416s
3	**Stefan Bradl**	GER	65	Viessmann Kiefer Racing	Kalex	20	41m 13.662s
4	**Alex de Angelis**	RSM	15	JIR Moto2	Motobi	20	41m 14.125s
5	**Thomas Luthi**	SWI	12	Interwetten Paddock Moto2	Suter	20	41m 17.480s
6	**Aleix Espargaro**	SPA	40	Pons HP 40	Pons Kalex	20	41m 26.891s
7	**Esteve Rabat**	SPA	34	Blusens-STX	FTR	20	41m 26.902s
8	**Dominique Aegerter**	SWI	77	Technomag-CIP	Suter	20	41m 27.620s
9	**Simone Corsi**	ITA	3	Ioda Racing Project	FTR	20	41m 27.872s
10	**Kenan Sofuoglu**	TUR	54	Technomag-CIP	Suter	20	41m 34.638s
11	**Mattia Pasini**	ITA	75	Ioda Racing Project	FTR	20	41m 39.490s
12	**Yuki Takahashi**	JPN	72	Gresini Racing Moto2	Moriwaki	20	41m 42.981s
13	**Mika Kallio**	FIN	36	Marc VDS Racing Team	Suter	20	41m 43.301s
14	**Claudio Corti**	ITA	71	Italtrans Racing Team	Suter	20	41m 43.635s
15	**Mike di Meglio**	FRA	63	Tech 3 Racing	Tech 3	20	41m 43.714s
16	Pol Espargaro	SPA	44	HP Tuenti Speed Up	FTR	20	41m 44.946s
17	Ratthapark Wilairot	THA	14	Thai Honda Singha SAG	FTR	20	41m 45.007s
18	Michele Pirro	ITA	51	Gresini Racing Moto2	Moriwaki	20	41m 48.803s
19	Jordi Torres	SPA	18	Mapfre Aspar Team Moto2	Suter	20	41m 53.525s
20	Kenny Noyes	USA	9	Avintia-STX	FTR	20	41m 53.977s
21	Valentin Debise	FRA	53	Speed Up	FTR	20	41m 54.058s
22	Ricard Cardus	SPA	88	QMMF Racing Team	Moriwaki	20	41m 55.502s
23	Xavier Simeon	BEL	19	Tech 3 B	Tech 3	20	41m 55.540s
24	Axel Pons	SPA	80	Pons HP 40	Pons Kalex	20	41m 55.603s
25	Robertino Pietri	VEN	39	Italtrans Racing Team	Suter	20	42m 06.291s
26	Scott Redding	GBR	45	Marc VDS Racing Team	Suter	20	42m 06.299s
27	Santiago Hernandez	COL	64	SAG Team	FTR	20	42m 19.929s
28	Steven Odendaal	RSA	97	MS Racing	Suter	20	42m 21.190s
29	Anthony West	AUS	13	MZ Racing Team	MZ-RE Honda	20	42m 43.615s
30	Mashel Al Naimi	QAT	95	QMMF Racing Team	Moriwaki	20	42m 43.754s
	Tommaso Lorenzetti	ITA	24	Aeroport de Castello	FTR	19	DNF
	Alex Baldolini	ITA	25	NGM Forward Racing	Suter	11	DNF
	Jules Cluzel	FRA	16	NGM Forward Racing	Suter	11	DNF
	Max Neukirchner	GER	76	MZ Racing Team	MZ-RE Honda	7	DNF
	Carmelo Morales	SPA	31	Desguaces La Torre G22	Suter	3	DNF
	Bradley Smith	GBR	38	Tech 3 Racing	Tech 3	1	DNF
	Yonny Hernandez	COL	68	Blusens-STX	FTR	1	DNF
	Randy Krummenacher	SWI	4	GP Team Switzerland Kiefer Racing	Kalex	0	DNF

Fastest lap: Andrea Iannone, on lap 20, 2m 02.640s, 98.549mph/158.600km/h (record).

Previous lap record: Toni Elias, SPA (Moriwaki), 2m 04.315s, 97.222mph/156.463km/h (2010).

Event best maximum speed: Thomas Luthi, 160.900mph/259.000km/h (race).

Qualifying: Dry

Air: 23° Humidity: 43% Ground: 33°

1	Marquez	2m 02.493s
2	Bradl	2m 02.704s
3	De Angelis	2m 02.725s
4	Luthi	2m 02.848s
5	Iannone	2m 02.943s
6	A. Espargaro	2m 03.461s
7	Corsi	2m 03.497s
8	Pasini	2m 03.523s
9	Corti	2m 03.545s
10	Krummenacher	2m 03.606s
11	Cluzel	2m 03.627s
12	Aegerter	2m 03.662s
13	Sofuoglu	2m 03.702s
14	P. Espargaro	2m 03.715s
15	Neukirchner	2m 03.749s
16	Smith	2m 03.844s
17	Takahashi	2m 03.849s
18	Rabat	2m 03.898s
19	Debise	2m 04.005s
20	Redding	2m 04.025s
21	Wilairot	2m 04.082s
22	Pirro	2m 04.153s
23	Torres	2m 04.178s
24	Di Meglio	2m 04.320s
25	Pietri	2m 04.351s
26	Cardus	2m 04.488s
27	Pons	2m 04.574s
28	Morales	2m 04.586s
29	Y. Hernandez	2m 04.623s
30	Kallio	2m 04.823s
31	Baldolini	2m 04.915s
32	Noyes	2m 04.957s
33	Simeon	2m 05.220s
34	West	2m 05.713s
35	Odendaal	2m 05.991s
36	S. Hernandez	2m 06.349s
37	Al Naimi	2m 07.505s
38	Lorenzetti	2m 08.257s

Fastest race laps

1	Iannone	2m 02.640s
2	Marquez	2m 02.835s
3	Bradl	2m 02.873s
4	De Angelis	2m 02.988s
5	Luthi	2m 03.087s
6	A. Espargaro	2m 03.366s
7	Corsi	2m 03.415s
8	Rabat	2m 03.445s
9	Sofuoglu	2m 03.618s
10	Di Meglio	2m 03.638s
11	Aegerter	2m 03.762s
12	Pasini	2m 03.789s
13	Takahashi	2m 04.045s
14	P. Espargaro	2m 04.141s
15	Kallio	2m 04.227s
16	Pirro	2m 04.244s
17	Wilairot	2m 04.246s
18	Corti	2m 04.263s
19	Torres	2m 04.431s
20	Pons	2m 04.444s
21	Noyes	2m 04.638s
22	Pietri	2m 04.664s
23	Debise	2m 04.715s
24	Neukirchner	2m 04.728s
25	Redding	2m 04.773s
26	Simeon	2m 04.788s
27	Baldolini	2m 04.831s
28	Cardus	2m 04.854s
29	Morales	2m 05.054s
30	West	2m 05.535s
31	Cluzel	2m 05.711s
32	Odendaal	2m 05.774s
33	S. Hernandez	2m 05.793s
34	Lorenzetti	2m 06.432s
35	Al Naimi	2m 06.479s
36	Smith	2m 10.962s
37	Y. Hernandez	2m 14.342s

Championship Points

1	Bradl	183
2	Marquez	140
3	De Angelis	95
4	Iannone	91
5	Corsi	91
6	Luthi	88
7	Smith	79
8	Takahashi	62
9	Krummenacher	52
10	Simon	49
11	A. Espargaro	48
12	Rabat	46
13	Sofuoglu	45
14	Pirro	43
15	Aegerter	41
16	Cluzel	35
17	Y. Hernandez	33
18	Neukirchner	32
19	Redding	25
20	West	18
21	Pasini	18
22	Baldolini	18
23	P. Espargaro	16
24	Kallio	11
25	Coghlan	11
26	Corti	9
27	Di Meglio	8
28	Simeon	6
29	Wilairot	4
30	Cardus	2
31	Pons	1

Constructor Points

1	Suter	223
2	Kalex	190
3	FTR	107
4	Motobi	95
5	Tech 3	89
6	Moriwaki	86
7	Pons Kalex	49
8	MZ-RE Honda	39

125cc

RACE DISTANCE: 19 laps, 63.788 miles/102.657km · RACE WEATHER: Dry (air 24°C, humidity 44%, track 36°C)

Pos.	Rider	Nat.	No.	Entrant	Machine	Laps	Time & Speed
1	**Sandro Cortese**	GER	11	Intact-Racing Team Germany	Aprilia	19	40m 59.229s 93.377mph/ 150.276km/h)
2	**Johann Zarco**	FRA	5	Avant-AirAsia-Ajo	Derbi	19	40m 59.626s
3	**Alberto Moncayo**	SPA	23	Andalucia Banca Civica	Aprilia	19	41m 10.002s
4	**Hector Faubel**	SPA	55	Bankia Aspar Team 125cc	Aprilia	19	41m 10.023s
5	**Sergio Gadea**	SPA	33	Blusens by Paris Hilton Racing	Aprilia	19	41m 10.373s
6	**Maverick Vinales**	SPA	25	Blusens by Paris Hilton Racing	Aprilia	19	41m 10.702s
7	**Jakub Kornfeil**	CZE	84	Ongetta-Centro Seta	Aprilia	19	41m 23.949s
8	**Simone Grotzkyj**	ITA	15	Phonica Racing	Aprilia	19	41m 39.211s
9	**Zulfahmi Khairuddin**	MAL	63	Airasia-Sic-Ajo	Derbi	19	41m 42.116s
10	**Jasper Iwema**	NED	53	Ongetta-Abbink Metaal	Aprilia	19	41m 42.252s
11	**Luigi Morciano**	ITA	3	Team Italia FMI	Aprilia	19	41m 42.412s
12	**Danny Webb**	GBR	99	Mahindra Racing	Mahindra	19	41m 42.904s
13	**Harry Stafford**	GBR	21	Ongetta-Centro Seta	Aprilia	19	41m 42.993s
14	**Marcel Schrotter**	GER	77	Mahindra Racing	Mahindra	19	41m 43.305s
15	**Louis Rossi**	FRA	96	Matteoni Racing	Aprilia	19	41m 49.469s
16	Sturla Fagerhaug	NOR	50	WTR-Ten10 Racing	Aprilia	19	41m 49.526s
17	Miroslav Popov	CZE	95	Ellegi Racing	Aprilia	19	42m 06.036s
18	Luca Gruenwald	GER	41	Freudenberg Racing Team	KTM	19	42m 06.099s
19	Alessandro Tonucci	ITA	19	Team Italia FMI	Aprilia	19	42m 06.233s
20	Francesco Mauriello	ITA	43	WTR-Ten10 Racing	Aprilia	19	42m 06.361s
21	Taylor Mackenzie	GBR	17	Phonica Racing	Aprilia	19	42m 14.772s
22	Joan Perello	SPA	36	Matteoni Racing	Aprilia	19	42m 18.752s
23	Miguel Oliveira	POR	44	Andalucia Banca Civica	Aprilia	19	42m 19.114s
24	Giulian Pedone	SWI	30	Phonica Racing	Aprilia	19	42m 33.043s
25	Ladislav Chmelik	CZE	24	RJR Racing	Aprilia	19	42m 44.793s
26	Peter Sebestyen	HUN	56	Caretta Technology	KTM	19	43m 02.999s
	Manuel Tatasciore	ITA	60	Phonica Racing	Aprilia	16	DNF
	Efren Vazquez	SPA	7	Avant-AirAsia-Ajo	Derbi	13	DNF
	Nicolas Terol	SPA	18	Bankia Aspar Team 125cc	Aprilia	8	DNF
	Alexis Masbou	FRA	10	Caretta Technology	KTM	2	DNF
	Danny Kent	GBR	52	Red Bull Ajo MotorSport	Aprilia	1	DNF
	Adrian Martin	SPA	26	Bankia Aspar Team 125cc	Aprilia	1	DNF
	Niklas Ajo	FIN	31	TT Motion Events Racing	Aprilia	0	DNF

Fastest lap: Sandro Cortese, on lap 7, 2m 08.365s, 94.155mph/151.527km/h.

Lap record: Lucio Cecchinello, ITA (Aprilia), 2m 07.836s, 94.544mph/152.154km/h (2003).

Event best maximum speed: Maverick Vinales, 138.900mph/223.500km/h (race).

Qualifying: Dry

Air: 21° Humidity: 62% Ground: 27°

1	Terol	2m 08.118s
2	Zarco	2m 08.503s
3	Cortese	2m 08.638s
4	Faubel	2m 08.689s
5	Salom	2m 09.125s
6	Vazquez	2m 09.189s
7	Kent	2m 09.211s
8	Moncayo	2m 09.421s
9	Vinales	2m 09.458s
10	Grotzkyj	2m 09.590s
11	Gadea	2m 09.865s
12	Masbou	2m 10.197s
13	Martin	2m 10.200s
14	Ajo	2m 10.270s
15	Khairuddin	2m 10.372s
16	Iwema	2m 10.450s
17	Oliveira	2m 10.483s
18	Morciano	2m 10.771s
19	Rossi	2m 10.828s
20	Kornfeil	2m 10.985s
21	Fagerhaug	2m 11.189s
22	Webb	2m 11.253s
23	Schrotter	2m 11.255s
24	Mauriello	2m 11.628s
25	Tonucci	2m 11.740s
26	Gruenwald	2m 11.890s
27	Popov	2m 12.084s
28	Perello	2m 12.419s
29	Pedone	2m 12.602s
30	Mackenzie	2m 12.621s
31	Stafford	2m 12.637s
32	Tatasciore	2m 13.226s
33	Chmelik	2m 13.387s
34	Sebestyen	2m 16.447s
Outside 107%		
	Jantulik	2m 18.622s

Fastest race laps

1	Cortese	2m 08.365s
2	Terol	2m 08.374s
3	Zarco	2m 08.553s
4	Vinales	2m 08.626s
5	Oliveira	2m 08.626s
6	Vazquez	2m 08.635s
7	Gadea	2m 08.681s
8	Moncayo	2m 08.871s
9	Faubel	2m 08.910s
10	Kornfeil	2m 09.055s
11	Grotzkyj	2m 09.689s
12	Iwema	2m 10.237s
13	Khairuddin	2m 10.417s
14	Morciano	2m 10.609s
15	Stafford	2m 10.613s
16	Schrotter	2m 10.719s
17	Webb	2m 10.733s
18	Rossi	2m 10.756s
19	Popov	2m 10.909s
20	Fagerhaug	2m 11.007s
21	Mauriello	2m 11.469s
22	Tonucci	2m 11.486s
23	Gruenwald	2m 11.728s
24	Mackenzie	2m 12.136s
25	Perello	2m 12.225s
26	Pedone	2m 12.614s
27	Tatasciore	2m 12.871s
28	Chmelik	2m 13.651s
29	Sebestyen	2m 13.967s
30	Kent	2m 18.151s
31	Martin	2m 20.006s
32	Masbou	3m 02.102s

Championship Points

1	Terol	166
2	Zarco	154
3	Vinales	132
4	Cortese	131
5	Folger	110
6	Faubel	103
7	Vazquez	90
8	Gadea	82
9	Salom	76
10	Kent	46
11	Moncayo	44
12	Kornfeil	43
13	Martin	30
14	Oliveira	30
15	Grotzkyj	27
16	Khairuddin	20
17	Schrotter	17
18	Mackenzie	15
19	Webb	14
20	Rossi	14
21	Iwema	13
22	Ajo	11
23	Masbou	10
24	Ono	8
25	Morciano	5
26	Finsterbusch	4
27	Stafford	3
28	McPhee	1
29	Rodriguez	1

Constructor Points

1	Aprilia	250
2	Derbi	163
3	Mahindra	26
4	KTM	21

INDIANAPOLIS GRAND PRIX

INDIANAPOLIS CIRCUIT

Inset left: A job well done: Honda 'pardners' Stoner and Pedrosa congratulate each other.

Main photo: Even a decent crowd is lost in the vast Brickyard arena.
Photos: Gold & Goose

Above: Coming through: rostrum-bound, Spies has just dealt with Simoncelli and Dovizioso.

Top right: Bautista cheered Suzuki with sixth.

Above right: Steve Parrish prepares for his tribute lap on the late Gary Nixon's Daytona Triumph.

Above far right: Lucky lady. Suzuki 600 Supersport racer Elena Myers had a pre-race MotoGP gallop: reward for becoming the first female to win an AMA Pro road race.

Right: Hayden put on a show for his home fans – for as long as his tyres let him.

Photos: Gold & Goose

THE Indianapolis Motor Speedway is a major-league car track that only lately has begun messing around with motorbikes. In 2011, paradoxes abounded. The chief concerned the surface, which was simultaneously very slippery and very abrasive: more usually contradictory properties. This led to all sorts of problems as tyres slipped and spun, then overheated and grained up (like a cold night at Qatar after a sandstorm, said Bridgestone), but the situation gave Stoner the opportunity to show another facet of his talent. His tyres lasted the race. "It depended on how you managed them," he said.

The fourth visit to the infield circuit within the imposing Brickyard oval revealed that many problems of 2010 – centring on bumps and mixed surfaces – had been fully addressed. More than half the track had been resurfaced, from turns 5 to 16, a distance of 1.5 miles. Therein lay the problem. The infield circuit exists almost exclusively for MotoGP, and although completed and passed fit to race early in July, a lack of subsequent use meant that the surface was as green as new-laid turf, and had about as much grip.

"It's as though it is wet… It was better with the bumps," said Pedrosa, while Stoner dubbed it "the worst ever". This was after the first day; by the end of the second, the racing line had been rubbered in and his pole time was 4.7 seconds faster than on the first morning. But woe betide the rider who strayed off line, and the graining problem remained.

The resurfacing had been done to demonstrate a continued commitment to MotoGP. The Indy contract expired after this race, and with Laguna having recently signed a new contract and the new Texas track at Austin putatively on the calendar for 2013, there was a danger of the Brickyard being squeezed off the calendar. A fair crowd of just over 64,000 (swallowed by the huge grandstands) came along, and negotiations continued throughout the weekend. Soon afterwards, a new three-year deal was announced.

There'd been another two weekends off after Brno, time to digest the results of tests there. The Yamaha riders were predictably impressed with their first taste of 1000cc and had been fast. Pedrosa had merely matched his 800 time, opining that perhaps he had to change his style somewhat. Hayden was next fastest after Lorenzo and Spies, in his first real go at the GP11.1 with its seamless gearshift. Compared with what he had, he liked it.

Rossi meanwhile was testing a variety of different settings – "different geometries, weight distributions and settings that were a little strange". He was in and out of the pits, all under the gaze of Filippo Preziosi, who described "extreme set-up solutions – much bigger adjustments than normal" in the search for "guidance for the next-generation bikes." In retrospect, it indicated increasing desperation as they cast around for a solution. In turn, Indy showed how far they were from finding one: 14th wasn't quite Rossi's worst grid position – he'd been 16th in Germany. But tenth was his worst finish.

There was another kind of nadir for the waning star, when he assembled a MotoGP riders' meeting, seeking agreement for concerted action to boycott the Motegi race. Press reports after Brno quoted him as saying that he didn't want to go, but he failed to find any consensus among the riders, most of whom (especially those from Honda and Yamaha)

had been made aware of their contractual obligations. The meeting broke up without agreement, with Dovizioso among other riders still expressing mistrust of the findings of the ARPA radiation report. Only Pedrosa seemed to have his feet on the ground: "The situation is that the race is on, which means you can't choose to go or not. Honda expects all the riders to go. Unless something really goes wrong before the GP, then the thing should be to go."

Neither mid-West nor back East, Indianapolis lacks the charm of Laguna's Monterey peninsula, and the race meeting suffered an extra blow with the cancellation of the annual pilgrimage to the Indy Mile. The classic AMA event, always well attended by paddock folk, was off because of a tragic accident at the fairground two weeks before. A storm during a country music concert had brought down overhead stage rigging, killing five. The dirt track was strewn with debris and it had to stay put during the police investigation.

Two legendary figures were remembered. Cagiva founder Claudio Castiglioni had succumbed to cancer in the week after the Brno race and was honoured with a very fitting minute's silence on the grid. Castiglioni had been a major figure in the Italian motorcycle industry, reviver of MV Agusta and one-time rescuer of Ducati: his red Cagiva GP 500s were always beautiful and ultimately successful, with Eddie Lawson winning the marque's first race in 1992, and John Kocinski two more.

Gary Nixon was twice AMA Grand National champion in the mid-1960s, and road-race champion in the mid-1970s. Only politics denied him the FIM 750 World Championship. His remembrance took the form of BBC commentator, friend and former racer Steve Parrish taking a lap of honour on one of Nixon's Daytona Triumphs – done, dirt-track style, in reverse direction.

Another couple of laps of honour came before the weekend, when fast female Suzuki 600 Supersport racer Elena Myers finally got her long-awaited reward for becoming the first of her sex to win an AMA Pro road race. The 17-year-old Californian became the first woman to ride a MotoGP machine, with five laps on Bautista's RGV. Reporting that she had been "blown away", she added, "It does everything 20 times better than I would have ever imagined."

Marquez's march to domination increased in pace with his fifth win of the season, Bradl having to work hard for sixth. The points lead was now down to 28.

Folger was back, but chastened; his newer RSA Aprilia was now in the hands of team-mate Danny Kent. The British rookie made a good enough fist of it to hang on to the bike, but in the end Folger was avenged by finishing ahead in the race.

MOTOGP RACE – 28 laps

Practice had been less about polishing bike settings than cleaning the racing line. Lap times fell drastically throughout: Stoner's pole on Saturday afternoon was almost five seconds faster than his second-place time on Friday morning. It created a one-line track, and made nonsense of the finer points of electronic and suspension settings, to say nothing of gearing.

Spies, on pole here in 2010, led the first session, ending up second on the grid, half a second down on Stoner and a quarter ahead of his team-mate. Pedrosa led row two, a second off and far from hopeful. Rossi had been up to eighth in free practice, but had crashed early in qualifying, losing the use of his better bike and its tyres. Hayden took eighth; Rossi was 14th, on row five.

Many were the worries about tyre life, especially fronts. Thus Hayden's unique choice of the softer option was a massive gamble, or perhaps a (successful) bid for early-laps glory, and hang the consequences.

Stoner got away cleanly, but was visibly cautious into turn one. Pedrosa had flown off row two and took advantage, to lead the first six laps. Still feeling his way under braking with a full tank, Stoner lost another position to Lorenzo before the end of the lap.

Hayden's gamble had paid off, albeit briefly. From eighth, he was up to fourth on the first lap, and though Simoncelli and Dovizioso would both get ahead of him next time around, Nicky was still fighting, getting back ahead of the factory Honda from laps five to nine.

The big loser off the line was Spies. In the first corners, he collided with Dovi and almost took a tumble; off line, he was elbowed backwards to finish the first lap ninth, behind Bautista and Edwards. It was the start of a long and impres-

sive afternoon's climb to the rostrum, thinking hard to find overtaking moves.

Stoner regained second down the straight to start lap three and before long was menacing Pedrosa. The pass came at the end of lap six into the first corner, and from there Stoner simply motored away. By lap 18, his lead was more than four seconds. After that, "it was about staying consistent, trying hard not to make mistakes, and not to run out on to that greasy part of the track." His seventh win of the year, a landmark 30th in his career, was another significant step in the championship.

Especially so because Lorenzo was not only unable to challenge Pedrosa, but also was in trouble from an unexpected source. He'd managed to see off a lap-five challenge from Simoncelli, getting back ahead when the Italian had a moment on to the front straight; but as the race wore on, his tyres were graining badly.

His team-mate, by contrast, was gaining positions steadily. By lap 13, he was fourth, two seconds adrift, but lapping as fast as Stoner. Within two laps, he was on Lorenzo's back wheel. He stayed there for one more lap, then, thinking "there's no team orders at Yamaha", he proved it by firmly passing and drawing clear. The gap to Pedrosa was some seven seconds – Spies nibbled away at it, but it was still more than six at the flag. Given his pace, it might have been different had his first lap been smooth.

Hayden's race was effectively over before half-distance, his tyre shot. He was out of the top ten when he pitted on lap 23, for a safety inspection, going straight out again to cruise to the finish. He was two laps down, but guaranteed two points, because by then both Abraham and Capirossi had retired (also due to tyres).

Simoncelli was in the same boat, as he had predicted, and was losing pace drastically when Spies and then Dovizioso passed him on consecutive laps just before half-distance. The next to go by was Bautista for his best dry finish of the year, pulling away from Edwards by the end.

There was a rare old scrap for eighth, with a fine old-fashioned finish on the treacherous kerb-ramp out of the final corner. Barbera had it, only to crash, leaving de Puniet and Aoyama to cross the line three-tenths apart.

This promoted Rossi to the top ten after a dire race. His seamless-shift gearbox played up for the first time all weekend. "Six or seven times, it selected neutral on the downshifts," he explained, which caused him to run wide on to the marbles several times, and then right off the track on lap nine, rejoining last behind Abraham. "Sincerely, I wanted to stop, but I decided to do what I could do to get some points."

By the flag, he was ahead of Crutchlow, the troubled Simoncelli and Elias, with Hayden two laps behind.

MOTO2 RACE – 26 laps

Redding had regained some confidence and was fast in free practice; when it came to qualifying, though, it was Marquez again, claiming his fifth pole and fourth in a row. He was getting stronger and stronger. Bradl, by contrast, was in the doldrums: a crash in practice left him behind the game, and though he was only 1.3 seconds off the pace, it was enough in this class to drop him to 22nd.

So far, each had won four races. Marquez claimed his fifth, while Bradl did a good job of limiting the damage, pushing steadily through to an eventual sixth. But the balance had tipped, and the turning of the tide was all the more obvious.

Corsi and Iannone joined Marquez on the front row; Smith led the second from Luthi and Pasini. Sofuoglu was out, after a heavy crash in the first practice.

Smith burst through from row two to lead away, but by the end of the first lap, Corsi had taken over, and next time around Marquez was in second.

The young class rookie was content to sit behind Corsi for the first seven laps, while a forceful Iannone accompanied by an on-form Rabat (another Moto2 first-timer) also got ahead of Smith. Redding, through from row four, and Pol Espargaro were closing from behind.

Turn one was the most popular overtaking spot, since it did not entail running off line. Marquez chose it and moved serenely past. In increasingly familiar style, he proceeded to pull clear at better than a second a lap until he was five seconds ahead just after half-distance. He'd done the same in 2010 in 125s, only to fall, remount, then run off and rejoin in the wrong place, and be penalised as a result.

On lap ten, Corsi all but crashed. A miracle save dropped him to the back of the group and he would fade further, into the clutches of Pasini and Simon, and finally down to 14th.

The rest stayed close. First Iannone made the running, before he too faded rapidly on shot tyres. Then Rabat took over. But Espargaro had got ahead of both Britons, then closed on his countryman. With seven laps to go, he was ahead, and he managed to cling on to second to the finish. A third high-

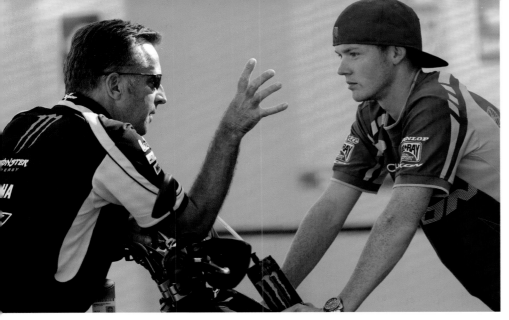

level ex-125 class rookie, Pol had finished on the rostrum at every visit to Indy.

Smith came out on top of the mid-race tussle with Redding and was better than two seconds clear at the end, and only one behind Rabat.

Bradl had been progressing rapidly throughout, finishing lap one 19th, up to tenth by the mid-point, and carrying on to an eventual sixth, three seconds down on Redding. Simon had followed along for a close seventh.

Pasini narrowly headed the next trio, from Kallio and Aleix Espargaro. The disheartened Iannone was now so slow that all three passed him on the last lap and left him trailing by two seconds. Aegerter was next, then Simeon, having done the same to Corsi. De Angelis wrestled the last point from Cluzel, with Luthi at the back.

Noyes, Baldolini and Wilairot were the only fallers.

125cc RACE – 23 laps

There were two 125 races at Indy. Nico Terol, claiming magnificent revenge on the technical gremlins that had taken him out at Brno, ran away from the start to command the race at his leisure. It was his sixth win, and valuable, with Zarco saving fifth after near disaster while battling at the front of a growing six-strong pursuit group.

Zarco had led at first from Vinales and Faubel. They'd been better than 2.5 seconds up on the next quartet: Vazquez, Gadea, Cortese and Danny Kent, in at the deep end.

Before half-distance, Kent had run off, rejoining near the back, while Cortese had taken over and brought the rest right up to join the battle for second.

Zarco's mistake – a near crash on the rampart kerbing on to the front straight – was crucial. It gave Vinales a little gap that he would stretch to almost two seconds. But Cortese was ready for a second charge, and with Gadea in his tracks, he closed again.

Vinales and Cortese changed places to and fro in the closing laps, but the audacious Spaniard was narrowly ahead at the flag; Gadea was close behind.

A little way back, a resurgent Zarco regained fifth from Vazquez, drafting past over the line.

Faubel had fallen away in seventh; behind him, rookie Oliveira won a race-long battle with Folger. Kent came back through to 13th, behind Kornfeil, Grotzkyj and Rossi, but ahead of Masbou and Morciano, who took the last points.

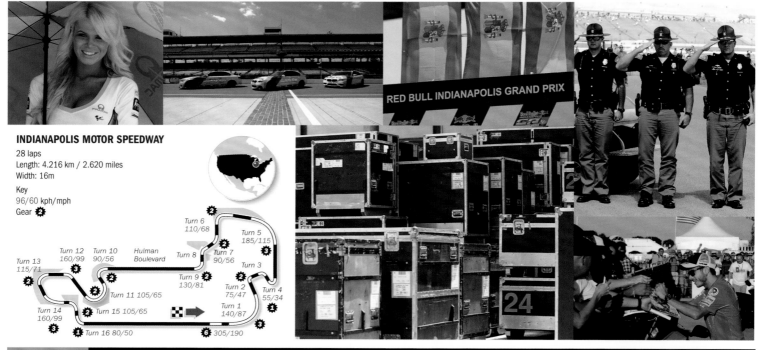

INDIANAPOLIS MOTOR SPEEDWAY

28 laps
Length: 4.216 km / 2.620 miles
Width: 16m

Key
96/60 kph/mph
Gear

Turn 6 110/68
Turn 5 185/115
Turn 12 160/99
Turn 10 90/56
Hulman Boulevard
Turn 8
Turn 7 90/56
Turn 13 115/71
Turn 9 130/81
Turn 3
Turn 11 105/65
Turn 2 75/47
Turn 4 55/34
Turn 14 160/99
Turn 15 105/65
Turn 1 140/87
Turn 16 80/50
305/190

MotoGP	RACE DISTANCE: 28 laps, 73.352 miles/118.048km · RACE WEATHER: Dry (air 27°C, humidity 34%, track 51°C)

Pos.	Rider	Nat.	No.	Entrant	Machine	Tyres	Laps	Time & speed
1	**Casey Stoner**	AUS	27	Repsol Honda Team	Honda	B	28	46m 52.786s 93.880mph/ 151.086km/h
2	**Dani Pedrosa**	SPA	26	Repsol Honda Team	Honda	B	28	46m 57.614s
3	**Ben Spies**	USA	11	Yamaha Factory Racing	Yamaha	B	28	47m 03.389s
4	**Jorge Lorenzo**	SPA	1	Yamaha Factory Racing	Yamaha	B	28	47m 09.362s
5	**Andrea Dovizioso**	ITA	4	Repsol Honda Team	Honda	B	28	47m 09.988s
6	**Alvaro Bautista**	SPA	19	Rizla Suzuki MotoGP	Suzuki	B	28	47m 23.233s
7	**Colin Edwards**	USA	5	Monster Yamaha Tech 3	Yamaha	B	28	47m 32.476s
8	**Randy de Puniet**	FRA	14	Pramac Racing Team	Ducati	B	28	47m 46.202s
9	**Hiroshi Aoyama**	JPN	7	San Carlo Honda Gresini	Honda	B	28	47m 46.576s
10	**Valentino Rossi**	ITA	46	Ducati Team	Ducati	B	28	47m 48.131s
11	**Cal Crutchlow**	GBR	35	Monster Yamaha Tech 3	Yamaha	B	28	47m 49.970s
12	**Marco Simoncelli**	ITA	58	San Carlo Honda Gresini	Honda	B	28	47m 52.927s
13	**Toni Elias**	SPA	24	LCR Honda MotoGP	Honda	B	28	47m 54.955s
14	**Nicky Hayden**	USA	69	Ducati Team	Ducati	B	26	47m 38.936s
	Hector Barbera	SPA	8	Mapfre Aspar Team MotoGP	Ducati	B	27	DNF
	Karel Abraham	CZE	17	Cardion AB Motoracing	Ducati	B	20	DNF
	Loris Capirossi	ITA	65	Pramac Racing Team	Ducati	B	16	DNF

Fastest lap: Casey Stoner, on lap 20, 1m 39.807s, 94.491mph/152.069km/h (record).

Previous Lap record: Jorge Lorenzo, SPA (Yamaha), 1m 40.152s, 103.593mph/151.545km/h (2009).

Event best maximum speed: Casey Stoner, 201.000mph/323.500km/h (qualifying practice).

Qualifying

Weather: Dry
Air Temp: 31° Humidity: 34%
Track Temp: 51°

1	Stoner	1m 38.850s
2	Spies	1m 39.373s
3	Lorenzo	1m 39.629s
4	Pedrosa	1m 39.947s
5	Dovizioso	1m 40.024s
6	Edwards	1m 40.098s
7	Simoncelli	1m 40.204s
8	Hayden	1m 40.244s
9	Bautista	1m 40.333s
10	Barbera	1m 40.360s
11	Crutchlow	1m 40.620s
12	De Puniet	1m 40.815s
13	Aoyama	1m 40.925s
14	Rossi	1m 40.975s
15	Elias	1m 41.030s
16	Abraham	1m 41.085s
17	Capirossi	1m 41.092s

Fastest race laps

1	Stoner	1m 39.807s
2	Spies	1m 39.874s
3	Pedrosa	1m 40.026s
4	Dovizioso	1m 40.108s
5	Lorenzo	1m 40.349s
6	Simoncelli	1m 40.470s
7	Hayden	1m 40.516s
8	Edwards	1m 40.521s
9	Aoyama	1m 40.608s
10	Bautista	1m 40.768s
11	De Puniet	1m 40.856s
12	Barbera	1m 40.892s
13	Crutchlow	1m 40.993s
14	Rossi	1m 41.189s
15	Elias	1m 41.739s
16	Capirossi	1m 41.799s
17	Abraham	1m 41.864s

Championship Points

1	Stoner	243
2	Lorenzo	199
3	Dovizioso	174
4	Pedrosa	130
5	Spies	125
6	Rossi	124
7	Hayden	105
8	Edwards	84
9	Simoncelli	80
10	Aoyama	77
11	Barbera	62
12	Bautista	49
13	Abraham	46
14	Elias	46
15	Crutchlow	39
16	Capirossi	29
17	De Puniet	27
18	Hopkins	6
19	Akiyoshi	3

Team Points

1	Repsol Honda Team	362
2	Yamaha Factory Racing	324
3	Ducati Team	229
4	San Carlo Honda Gresini	152
5	Monster Yamaha Tech 3	123
6	Mapfre Aspar Team MotoGP	62
7	Pramac Racing Team	56
8	Rizla Suzuki MotoGP	55
9	Cardion AB Motoracing	46
10	LCR Honda MotoGP	46

Grid order	1	2	3	4	5	6	7	8	9	10	11	12	13	14	15	16	17	18	19	20	21	22	23	24	25	26	27	28	
27 STONER	26	26	26	26	26	26	27	27	27	27	27	27	27	27	27	27	27	27	27	27	27	27	27	27	27	27	27	27	1
11 SPIES	1	27	27	27	27	27	26	26	26	26	26	26	26	26	26	26	26	26	26	26	26	26	26	26	26	26	26	26	2
1 LORENZO	27	1	1	1	1	1	1	1	1	1	1	1	1	1	1	1	11	11	11	11	11	11	11	11	11	11	11	11	3
26 PEDROSA	69	58	58	58	58	58	58	58	58	58	58	11	11	11	11	11	1	1	1	1	1	1	1	1	1	1	1	1	4
4 DOVIZIOSO	58	4	4	4	69	69	69	69	69	4	11	58	4	4	4	4	4	4	4	4	4	4	4	4	4	4	4	4	5
5 EDWARDS	4	69	69	69	4	4	4	4	4	11	4	4	58	58	58	19	19	19	19	19	19	19	19	19	19	19	19	19	6
58 SIMONCELLI	19	19	19	11	11	11	11	11	11	69	69	69	19	19	19	58	5	5	5	5	5	5	5	5	5	5	5	5	7
69 HAYDEN	5	5	11	19	19	19	19	19	19	19	19	19	69	5	5	5	58	58	58	58	58	58	58	58	58	8	8	14	8
19 BAUTISTA	11	11	5	5	5	5	5	5	5	5	5	5	69	69	69	69	69	69	69	8	8	8	8	14	14	7	7	9
8 BARBERA	46	46	46	8	8	8	8	8	8	8	8	8	8	8	8	8	8	8	8	14	14	14	14	8	14	7	46	10
35 CRUTCHLOW	8	8	8	46	46	46	46	46	24	14	14	14	14	14	14	14	14	14	14	69	7	7	7	7	7	46	35	11
14 DE PUNIET	35	35	35	24	24	24	24	24	14	24	7	7	7	7	7	7	7	7	7	7	69	46	46	46	46	58	58	12
7 AOYAMA	24	24	24	35	35	35	14	14	35	7	24	35	35	35	35	35	35	35	46	46	35	35	35	35	24	13
46 ROSSI	65	65	65	65	65	14	35	35	7	35	35	35	24	24	24	24	24	24	46	35	35	24	24	24	24	14
24 ELIAS	14	14	14	14	14	65	65	65	65	65	65	65	65	46	46	46	46	46	24	24	24	69	69	69	69	
17 ABRAHAM	17	17	17	7	7	7	7	7	17	17	17	17	17	46	17	17	17	17	17	17						
65 CAPIROSSI	7	7	7	17	17	17	17	17	46	46	46	46	46	17	65	65										

65/17/69 Pitstop   69 Lapped rider

Constructor Points

1	Honda	285
2	Yamaha	233
3	Ducati	135
4	Suzuki	55

Moto2

RACE DISTANCE: 26 laps, 68.112 miles/109.606km · **RACE WEATHER:** Dry (air 26°C, humidity 33%, track 45°C)

Pos.	Rider	Nat.	No.	Entrant	Machine	Laps	Time & Speed
1	**Marc Marquez**	SPA	93	Team CatalunyaCaixa Repsol	Suter	26	45m 50.601s 89.145mph/ 143.465km/h
2	**Pol Espargaro**	SPA	44	HP Tuenti Speed Up	FTR	26	45m 52.490s
3	**Esteve Rabat**	SPA	34	Blusens-STX	FTR	26	45m 52.911s
4	**Bradley Smith**	GBR	38	Tech 3 Racing	Tech 3	26	45m 53.990s
5	**Scott Redding**	GBR	45	Marc VDS Racing Team	Suter	26	45m 56.275s
6	**Stefan Bradl**	GER	65	Viessmann Kiefer Racing	Kalex	26	45m 59.735s
7	**Julian Simon**	SPA	60	Mapfre Aspar Team Moto2	Suter	26	45m 59.948s
8	**Mattia Pasini**	ITA	75	Ioda Racing Project	FTR	26	46m 05.611s
9	**Mika Kallio**	FIN	36	Marc VDS Racing Team	Suter	26	46m 05.632s
10	**Aleix Espargaro**	SPA	40	Pons HP 40	Pons Kalex	26	46m 05.940s
11	**Andrea Iannone**	ITA	29	Speed Master	Suter	26	46m 08.048s
12	**Dominique Aegerter**	SWI	77	Technomag-CIP	Suter	26	46m 12.328s
13	**Xavier Simeon**	BEL	19	Tech 3 B	Tech 3	26	46m 14.880s
14	**Simone Corsi**	ITA	3	Ioda Racing Project	FTR	26	46m 16.315s
15	**Alex de Angelis**	RSM	15	JIR Moto2	Motobi	26	46m 17.495s
16	Jules Cluzel	FRA	16	NGM Forward Racing	Suter	26	46m 17.976s
17	Thomas Luthi	SWI	12	Interwetten Paddock Moto2	Suter	26	46m 18.147s
18	Jordi Torres	SPA	18	Mapfre Aspar Team Moto2	Suter	26	46m 18.365s
19	Ricard Cardus	SPA	88	QMMF Racing Team	Moriwaki	26	46m 18.547s
20	Michele Pirro	ITA	51	Gresini Racing Moto2	Moriwaki	26	46m 19.963s
21	Randy Krummenacher	SWI	4	GP Team Switzerland Kiefer Racing	Kalex	26	46m 22.302s
22	Claudio Corti	ITA	71	Italtrans Racing Team	Suter	26	46m 22.631s
23	Raffaele de Rosa	ITA	35	NGM Forward Racing	Suter	26	46m 22.701s
24	Max Neukirchner	GER	76	MZ Racing Team	MZ-RE Honda	26	46m 25.988s
25	Yuki Takahashi	JPN	72	Gresini Racing Moto2	Moriwaki	26	46m 28.402s
26	Anthony West	AUS	13	MZ Racing Team	MZ-RE Honda	26	46m 32.747s
27	Mike di Meglio	FRA	63	Tech 3 Racing	Tech 3	26	46m 44.092s
28	Martin Cardenas	COL	10	Blusens-STX	FTR	26	46m 49.548s
29	JD Beach	USA	73	Aeroport de Castello	FTR	26	46m 54.935s
30	Valentin Debise	FRA	53	Speed Up	FTR	26	47m 02.831s
31	Jacob Gagne	USA	32	GPTech	FTR	26	47m 03.104s
32	Robertino Pietri	VEN	39	Italtrans Racing Team	Suter	26	47m 05.778s
33	Santiago Hernandez	COL	64	SAG Team	FTR	26	47m 06.500s
34	Alex Baldolini	ITA	25	Pons HP 40	Pons Kalex	26	47m 27.703s
35	Mashel Al Naimi	QAT	95	QMMF Racing Team	Moriwaki	25	46m 33.264s
	Ratthapark Wilairot	THA	14	Thai Honda Singha SAG	FTR	21	DNF
	Carmelo Morales	SPA	31	Desguaces La Torre G22	Moriwaki	15	DNF
	Kenny Noyes	USA	9	Avintia-STX	FTR	7	DNF

Fastest lap: Andrea Iannone, on lap 3, 1m 44.329s, 90.396mph/145.478km/h (record).
Previous lap record: Julian Simon, SPA (Suter), 1m 46.580s, 88.486mph/142.405km/h (2010).
Event best maximum speed: Pol Espargaro, 175.200mph/281.900km/h (free practice 2).

Qualifying: Dry
Air: 32° Humidity: 35% Ground: 54°

1	Marquez	1m 44.038s
2	Corsi	1m 44.039s
3	Iannone	1m 44.158s
4	Smith	1m 44.344s
5	Luthi	1m 44.623s
6	Pasini	1m 44.732s
7	P. Espargaro	1m 44.785s
8	Aegerter	1m 44.794s
9	Rabat	1m 44.859s
10	De Angelis	1m 44.864s
11	Redding	1m 44.865s
12	Cluzel	1m 45.043s
13	Pirro	1m 45.047s
14	Cardus	1m 45.060s
15	Simon	1m 45.062s
16	Neukirchner	1m 45.094s
17	A. Espargaro	1m 45.136s
18	Kallio	1m 45.160s
19	De Rosa	1m 45.173s
20	Takahashi	1m 45.184s
21	Torres	1m 45.369s
22	Bradl	1m 45.371s
23	Krummenacher	1m 45.448s
24	Simeon	1m 45.496s
25	Di Meglio	1m 45.534s
26	Corti	1m 45.682s
27	Wilairot	1m 45.889s
28	Morales	1m 46.059s
29	Noyes	1m 46.086s
30	West	1m 46.160s
31	Cardenas	1m 46.175s
32	Baldolini	1m 46.247s
33	Gagne	1m 46.594s
34	Debise	1m 46.953s
35	Beach	1m 47.219s
36	Al Naimi	1m 47.343s
37	Pietri	1m 47.439s
38	S. Hernandez	1m 48.170s

Fastest race laps

1	Iannone	1m 44.329s
2	Marquez	1m 44.579s
3	Rabat	1m 44.582s
4	Kallio	1m 44.634s
5	Corsi	1m 44.636s
6	Simon	1m 44.708s
7	Redding	1m 44.722s
8	Smith	1m 44.771s
9	De Angelis	1m 44.889s
10	P. Espargaro	1m 45.006s
11	A. Espargaro	1m 45.121s
12	Pasini	1m 45.151s
13	Bradl	1m 45.242s
14	Luthi	1m 45.261s
15	Aegerter	1m 45.335s
16	Cardus	1m 45.375s
17	Simeon	1m 45.473s
18	Wilairot	1m 45.542s
19	Takahashi	1m 45.633s
20	Pirro	1m 45.638s
21	Krummenacher	1m 45.710s
22	Neukirchner	1m 45.714s
23	De Rosa	1m 45.757s
24	Cluzel	1m 45.763s
25	Corti	1m 45.818s
26	Torres	1m 45.828s
27	Di Meglio	1m 46.020s
28	West	1m 46.047s
29	Baldolini	1m 46.095s
30	Morales	1m 46.399s
31	Beach	1m 46.458s
32	Cardenas	1m 46.520s
33	Gagne	1m 46.590s
34	Debise	1m 46.726s
35	S. Hernandez	1m 46.869s
36	Pietri	1m 46.900s
37	Noyes	1m 48.097s
38	Al Naimi	1m 48.994s

Championship Points

1	Bradl	193
2	Marquez	165
3	Iannone	96
4	De Angelis	96
5	Corsi	93
6	Smith	92
7	Luthi	88
8	Takahashi	62
9	Rabat	62
10	Simon	58
11	A. Espargaro	54
12	Krummenacher	52
13	Sofuoglu	45
14	Aegerter	45
15	Pirro	43
16	P. Espargaro	36
17	Redding	36
18	Cluzel	35
19	Hernandez	33
20	Neukirchner	32
21	Pasini	26
22	West	18
23	Kallio	18
24	Baldolini	18
25	Coghlan	11
26	Corti	9
27	Simeon	9
28	Di Meglio	8
29	Wilairot	4
30	Cardus	2
31	Pons	1

Constructor Points

1	Suter	248
2	Kalex	200
3	FTR	127
4	Tech 3	102
5	Motobi	96
6	Moriwaki	86
7	Pons Kalex	55
8	MZ-RE Honda	39

125cc

RACE DISTANCE: 23 laps, 60.253 miles/96.968km · **RACE WEATHER:** Dry (air 23°C, humidity 48%, track 36°C)

Pos.	Rider	Nat.	No.	Entrant	Machine	Laps	Time & Speed
1	**Nicolas Terol**	SPA	18	Bankia Aspar Team 125cc	Aprilia	23	42m 11.978s 85.668mph/ 137.870km/h
2	**Maverick Vinales**	SPA	25	Blusens by Paris Hilton Racing	Aprilia	23	42m 15.611s
3	**Sandro Cortese**	GER	11	Intact-Racing Team Germany	Aprilia	23	42m 15.715s
4	**Sergio Gadea**	SPA	33	Blusens by Paris Hilton Racing	Aprilia	23	42m 16.205s
5	**Johann Zarco**	FRA	5	Avant-AirAsia-Ajo	Derbi	23	42m 26.164s
6	**Efren Vazquez**	SPA	7	Avant-AirAsia-Ajo	Derbi	23	42m 26.178s
7	**Hector Faubel**	SPA	55	Bankia Aspar Team 125cc	Aprilia	23	42m 30.455s
8	**Miguel Oliveira**	POR	44	Andalucia Banca Civica	Aprilia	23	42m 35.970s
9	**Jonas Folger**	GER	94	Red Bull Ajo MotorSport	Aprilia	23	42m 36.217s
10	**Jakub Kornfeil**	CZE	84	Ongetta-Centro Seta	Aprilia	23	42m 50.726s
11	**Simone Grotzkyj**	ITA	15	Phonica Racing	Aprilia	23	42m 51.172s
12	**Louis Rossi**	FRA	96	Matteoni Racing	Aprilia	23	42m 52.181s
13	**Danny Kent**	GBR	52	Red Bull Ajo MotorSport	Aprilia	23	42m 56.066s
14	**Alexis Masbou**	FRA	10	Caretta Technology	KTM	23	42m 57.179s
15	**Luigi Morciano**	ITA	3	Team Italia FMI	Aprilia	23	42m 58.015s
16	Jasper Iwema	NED	53	Ongetta-Abbink Metaal	Aprilia	23	43m 10.429s
17	Brad Binder	RSA	14	RW Racing GP	Aprilia	23	43m 23.993s
18	Francesco Mauriello	ITA	43	WTR-Ten10 Racing	Aprilia	23	43m 24.876s
19	Zulfahmi Khairuddin	MAL	63	Airasia-Sic-Ajo	Derbi	23	43m 26.272s
20	Joan Perello	SPA	36	Matteoni Racing	Aprilia	23	43m 35.925s
21	Taylor Mackenzie	GBR	17	Phonica Racing	Aprilia	23	43m 41.347s
22	Peter Sebestyen	HUN	56	Caretta Technology	KTM	23	43m 41.791s
23	Alessandro Tonucci	ITA	19	Team Italia FMI	Aprilia	23	43m 46.274s
24	Giulian Pedone	SWI	30	Phonica Racing	Aprilia	21	43m 49.622s
	Marcel Schrotter	GER	77	Mahindra Racing	Mahindra	22	DNF
	Adrian Martin	SPA	26	Bankia Aspar Team 125cc	Aprilia	20	DNF
	Sturla Fagerhaug	NOR	50	WTR-Ten10 Racing	Aprilia	11	DNF
	Niklas Ajo	FIN	31	TT Motion Events Racing	Aprilia	7	DNF
	Harry Stafford	GBR	21	Ongetta-Centro Seta	Aprilia	7	DNF

Fastest lap: Nicolas Terol, on lap 6, 1m 48.380s, 87.017mph/140.040km/h (record).
Previous lap record: Marc Marquez, SPA (Derbi), 1m 48.672s, 86.783mph/139.664km/h (2010).
Event best maximum speed: Efren Vasquez, 144.800mph/233.100km/h (race).

Qualifying: Dry
Air: 28° Humidity: 39% Ground: 41°

1	Terol	1m 48.199s
2	Cortese	1m 48.919s
3	Zarco	1m 48.939s
4	Vinales	1m 48.991s
5	Kent	1m 49.256s
6	Faubel	1m 49.324s
7	Vazquez	1m 49.490s
8	Folger	1m 49.608s
9	Gadea	1m 49.919s
10	Masbou	1m 49.994s
11	Oliveira	1m 50.133s
12	Kornfeil	1m 50.345s
13	Grotzkyj	1m 50.549s
14	Martin	1m 50.600s
15	Ajo	1m 50.604s
16	Morciano	1m 50.859s
17	Schrotter	1m 50.906s
18	Rossi	1m 51.022s
19	Khairuddin	1m 51.232s
20	Mackenzie	1m 51.672s
21	Webb	1m 51.763s
22	Mauriello	1m 52.204s
23	Fagerhaug	1m 52.401s
24	Iwema	1m 52.498s
25	Tonucci	1m 52.661s
26	Perello	1m 53.291s
27	Binder	1m 53.447s
28	Pedone	1m 53.898s
29	Sebestyen	1m 53.992s
30	Stafford	1m 55.623s

Fastest race laps

1	Terol	1m 48.380s
2	Zarco	1m 49.038s
3	Vinales	1m 49.039s
4	Faubel	1m 49.123s
5	Vazquez	1m 49.223s
6	Cortese	1m 49.232s
7	Gadea	1m 49.434s
8	Oliveira	1m 49.687s
9	Kent	1m 49.767s
10	Folger	1m 50.103s
11	Martin	1m 50.220s
12	Grotzkyj	1m 50.258s
13	Morciano	1m 50.419s
14	Schrotter	1m 50.458s
15	Rossi	1m 50.617s
16	Ajo	1m 50.661s
17	Kornfeil	1m 50.685s
18	Masbou	1m 50.870s
19	Iwema	1m 51.229s
20	Fagerhaug	1m 51.522s
21	Binder	1m 51.636s
22	Mauriello	1m 51.735s
23	Khairuddin	1m 51.945s
24	Sebestyen	1m 52.144s
25	Perello	1m 52.157s
26	Mackenzie	1m 52.187s
27	Tonucci	1m 52.912s
28	Stafford	1m 53.050s
29	Pedone	1m 53.523s

Championship Points

1	Terol	191
2	Zarco	165
3	Vinales	152
4	Cortese	147
5	Folger	117
6	Faubel	112
7	Vazquez	100
8	Gadea	95
9	Salom	76
10	Kent	49
11	Kornfeil	49
12	Moncayo	44
13	Oliveira	38
14	Grotzkyj	32
15	Martin	30
16	Khairuddin	20
17	Rossi	18
18	Schrotter	17
19	Mackenzie	15
20	Webb	14
21	Iwema	13
22	Masbou	12
23	Ajo	11
24	Ono	8
25	Morciano	6
26	Finsterbusch	4
27	Stafford	3
28	McPhee	1
29	Rodriguez	1

Constructor Points

1	Aprilia	275
2	Derbi	174
3	Mahindra	26
4	KTM	23

Inset right: Lorenzo relished his second Italian win of the 2011 season.

Main photo: Victory put new life into his championship chances, with Stoner third.

Photos: Gold & Goose

FIM WORLD CHAMPIONSHIP · ROUND 13

SAN MARINO GRAND PRIX

MISANO CIRCUIT

Insets right and below: The top three laughed off the inevitable boos and catcalls in Rossi's backyard.
Photos: Gold & Goose

Above: Simoncelli and Dovizioso battled all the way. They finished less than half a second apart, Simoncelli being ahead.

Top right: Triple champion Wayne Rainey made a dignified and heart-warming return to Misano for the first time since his career-ending crash in 1993.

Top far right: Pioneers: Colin Edwards poses with Dorna's Ezpeleta, and Giovanni Cuzari and Stefano Nesi of his new Forward Racing CRT team.

Photos: Gold & Goose

NO country for old men? Something of the reverse at Misano. Old-timers of sundry stamp disported themselves in various ways – at least two of them tearful.

The most open weeping was at Loris Capirossi's announcement of his retirement, albeit only a brief succumbing to an understandable emotion. The tears at the return of Wayne Rainey to the track that had crippled him were deeper seated, and for the most part hidden behind smiles of welcome. The other old-timer outbreak was a revival, sort of: the announcement that Colin Edwards would not be quitting MotoGP after all, but would return again in 2012 with the first formally constituted CRT team to break water.

At 38 and five months, the oldest man on the grid, Capirossi's retirement was hardly unexpected. His career had been declining through three fruitless years with Suzuki; his move back to Ducati with the satellite Pramac team had been badly timed. The GP11 was a handful – "no feel at all," he said, cheerfully naming it as the worst bike he had ever raced. Even so, terminating a triple-title, 21-year career had caused him many sleepless nights.

Rainey's return, part of Yamaha's half-centenary celebrations, was the highlight of the weekend, certainly for those of us who had been in the paddock during his three-year reign, and its sudden termination here at the corner after the pits (leading the race and leading again on points) on 5th September, 1993. It was 18 years almost to the day since he had been helicoptered off with life-threatening spinal injuries. Misano had been struck off the calendar forthwith, returning in 2007 only after the direction had been reversed and safety thus (notionally at least) improved.

Ironically, this quite changed the aspect of the track that had made it Rainey's favourite: the three left-handers taken at increasing speed on to the back straight – an ex-dirt tracker's dream come true. "The last one was the only one on the calendar you could take flat out in sixth … at least for the first couple of laps until the tyres went off," he recalled.

Rainey was feted everywhere he went, and especially in a race-eve paddock presentation, where he spoke of how he

held no grudges against the track or against racing. There was no significance in choosing Misano for the visit, other than convenience. He had a new life now: "That's racing. It happens sometimes." He may not have had ghosts to lay, but he served that purpose for many others present.

Thirdly, Edwards, the second oldest racer by 11 months, and in 2012 the oldest. Negotiations to stay at Tech 3 had fallen short, but now another plan that he had been hinting at was revealed with a formal announcement that he would be joining the Italian Forward Racing on a CRT machine. The business side was applauded by Dorna CEO Ezpeleta, sitting at the conference table: "It is the first CRT team, but it will not be the last." For 2011, Forward fielded Cluzel and de Rosa in Moto2, and had the backing and the infrastructure. The only vagueness concerned hardware. Edwards expressed the hope that power would be by Yamaha, where his loyalty lay (not to mention the financial backing of Yamaha US). Over a month later, plans to use a Yamaha R1 motor were cancelled, the team choosing a Suter BMW instead.

Rossi is not yet in the 'old-timer' category, but at 32, he was the third oldest on the grid. Still ageless, of course, to the mainly banana-hued 53,140 crowd who packed the track close to his home, in spite of current setbacks. Which continued – qualifying 11th as second-best Ducati to Barbera, finishing a lone seventh after an admittedly bold and mildly encouraging race. His gearbox was troublesome again in practice, causing several run-offs. The army of fans invaded the track as usual for the rostrum ceremony, and – unused to not seeing Valentino there – greeted race winner Lorenzo with boos and catcalls. "They should be more respectful," said Rossi, before adding jauntily, "but this is Italy."

(Also, because Rossi was in Italy, his special helmet design was equally jaunty: a series of cartoon-style disaster icons – a black cat, a bomb, expostulations, etc – to indicate "what I am thinking when I ride the bike.")

The increasing pressure on Ducati's engineering guru, Filippo Preziosi, was plain to see at a special briefing, where he fielded questions most especially about whether Ducati

would build a Japanese-style full aluminium chassis. "We already built an aluminium chassis in 2009," he said. (A prototype of the carbon-fibre mini-chassis that was tested, but never raced.)

"But as I have said many times, I don't believe it is the material that makes the difference," he continued. He robustly denied that Ducati had approached other chassis builders (Suter and FTR had been named) to design a chassis. "The rumours are wrong. Our concept is to keep the design inside Ducati. Everything we do is conceived and designed in Ducati." But he did not rule out outside manufacture: previous steel chassis and current carbon chassis were produced by outside companies. Nor did he rule out a radical change. "We have no limit," he said. "As soon as we see something has an advantage, we will use it. But the thing for Ducati is to build knowledge, even if it means testing solutions that are not good. I am happy that the company gives me the freedom to do what we think is important."

"The ideal chassis does not exist," he added. "That is why Honda built eight different chassis in one year."

The waters were muddied the following week with a (suspiciously revealing) 'scoop' photo published in Britain's *MCN*. It clearly showed a CAD-CAM rendering of the rear section of a full aluminium chassis, casually held towards the camera by Ducati mechanics in the pits, against a backdrop of factory branding. It was thought to have originated from Britain's FTR concern. Steve Bones, a rather embarrassed FTR chief, was unable to confirm or deny anything.

MOTOGP RACE – 28 laps

Stoner's eighth pole followed a familiar pattern: fast throughout with a new track best lap, set on race tyres. The margin over Lorenzo was only 0.120 second, while Pedrosa was only six-hundredths slower. Spies narrowly led row two from Simoncelli, who had worries about fuel consumption. Dovi was three-hundredths down.

Although it wasn't actually raining when the race began,

the white flags came out as a precaution, which proved unnecessary. The conditions made the riders cautious – except for Rossi, who saw an opportunity.

Lorenzo flew off the line to lead into the first corner with Stoner, Pedrosa and Dovizioso in hot pursuit. Spies was fifth at the end of the lap, from Rossi and Simoncelli, but the Ducati sliced past him next time around, and then Simoncelli as well. Soon the American was more than a second adrift. In morning warm-up, he'd had "a disaster" with front-end changes; the bike had been significantly re-adjusted. "It worked, but it took a few laps to get confidence, as it was such a big change."

Up front, Lorenzo and Stoner gradually pulled away from Pedrosa by a few tenths a lap. By the eighth, he was more than a second adrift.

Stoner looked strong right up until lap 11. Then it quickly became clear that his challenge was over, in one of those moments of intermittent fragility that have shown from time to time. There was nothing wrong with the bike, he explained. It was only the rider who was not strong enough to make the most of it, suffering severely the after-effects of post-Indy jet lag and sleepless since returning to Europe. "I felt good at the start; quite confident, and being careful so Jorge could arrive at any wet points before me. As the race wore on, I got tired. I was running wide and struggling. I had to start braking earlier. I was losing chunks of energy."

Lorenzo continued at lap-record speed, setting his best lap on the 12th, while Dani took another ten laps to close on his team-mate, by a few tenths each lap. When he caught him, he was straight past under braking, Stoner making no attempt to resist the inevitable. In spite of it all, he was still on the rostrum.

By now, Lorenzo was almost seven seconds ahead, a gap he held to the finish for an immaculate third win of the year.

The next group had more action. Simoncelli moved to the front on lap eight, Dovi and Rossi right up behind. As half-distance approached, Spies was closing, and on lap 15 he outbraked Rossi for sixth.

Above: Silver Dream Racer. Alvaro Bautista's Rizla Suzuki boasted a new one-off paint job.

Above far left: Smiling through the tears, Capirossi announces the end of 21 years of GP racing.

Above left: Rossi produced a stark and angry home-track helmet design that reflected his current predicament.

Photos: Gold & Goose

He was leaning hard on Dovizioso, in turn saving his best to the end. It took a couple of goes to get ahead of Simoncelli, but he did so on lap 26. But he couldn't get away and Simoncelli kept attacking him back.

Their last lap was a classic. Dovi led at the start of it, Simoncelli at the end, with several changes of position on the way, and Spies getting between them, but only briefly.

Rossi had fallen away by six seconds, losing touch with slides in the closing stages. Nonetheless it had been a good race, after a fortuitous steering geometry change in the morning: "I could stay with my best time of yesterday for most of the race. This is a good target for us at the moment."

Edwards had been next for more than half the race before stricken with arm-pump that slowed him radically. "I never knew it could be so bad," he said. It struck as Bautista caught him, at his second attempt – the first had him off the track and back into the clutches of Crutchlow. He escaped on lap 14, and was ahead of the fast-fading Edwards three laps later.

Crutchlow was riding with an element of caution after crashing out of the previous two races, but had got clear of Aoyama. Barbera was coming through, however, after running wide on the second lap. On lap 12, he passed the Japanese rider, who stayed with him as he closed the two seconds to Crutchlow. He caught him with six laps to go and passed him two laps later. Aoyama also fancied his chances, but Crutchlow held him off.

Abraham had been gaining speed at the end and was less than a second adrift at the finish; Edwards was 13th, clear of de Puniet and a distant Elias. De Puniet had been struggling for grip all weekend, likewise team-mate Capirossi, who pitted, rejoined, then retired.

Hayden's race, at a gremlin track, lasted longer than ever before. He completed two laps in ninth before losing the front and crashing out.

MOTO2 RACE – 26 laps

While Marquez fell and bounced back to second, Bradl redeemed some pride with his first pole in five races. "We needed something from the bike for me to feel the limit, and we found it," he said. Takahashi completed the front row; Redding led the second from de Angelis and Smith, Iannone looming over his shoulder.

The race was always going to be a showdown between the title rivals, but they were far from alone, fighting hard in a pack that was eight- and then seven-strong for most of the race.

Bradl led away and until a big slide had him out of the saddle coming out of the last and tightest of the right-hander set, and he dropped to third. Marquez took over, but Redding was in blazing form, and as the former was mobbed and dropped to fourth after running wide, Redding even pulled a gap of better than a second by lap five.

By now, it was Iannone up to second, from Bradl, Marquez, Smith, Corsi, Takahashi and de Angelis.

Redding led until lap 12, and there would be three others up front. First Marquez took over, deposed after a handful of laps by Bradl, who swapped the lead with Iannone for the next few laps.

The move that mattered came six laps from the end, when Marquez pushed past Iannone to the front and little by little opened up enough of a gap that he could remain there to the end. Even so, he led over the line by no more than 0.619 second.

He explained why he had to wait. "The first laps with a full tank were difficult, and I almost lost the front ... but in the end, I could see from the TV that Bradl was close, so I pushed my best to get a small gap."

Bradl had to fight hard for second, Iannone pushing to the end and less than a tenth behind over the line.

Corsi had dropped out of the group before half-distance,

Above: Scott Redding pulled an early lead, ahead of Iannone, Bradl and Marquez: as usual, the Briton's size and weight told against him.

Left: Marquez took a second successive Moto2 win.

Far left: Valentino Rossi applauds the support of his fans after making the best of it for seventh.

Below left: Vazquez took a second rostrum with third in the 125cc race.

Bottom left: Loris Capirossi prepares for his last ever grand prix in Italy.

Bottom centre: Crestfallen again, Zarco clutches his runner-up trophy one more time.

Below: Not quite. With his fist clenched, Zarco looks around to see Terol snatch victory.

Photos: Gold & Goose

with Takahashi also fading mid-race with a big slide, catching up again, then losing touch once more.

The strong man was de Angelis, who pushed through to challenge Iannone, a second behind over the line in fourth. Redding managed to stay clear of Smith, Takahashi two seconds away.

Luthi had escaped from Pol Espargaro for eighth, closing by the end; Espargaro was left to battle with Corsi. He passed him with two laps to go, less than half a second ahead over the line.

Rabat was next, then Simon and Aegerter, a tenth apart, both having got the better of Pirro on the last lap. Another five seconds down, Kallio defeated di Meglio and Pasini for the last point.

In the first corner, a midfield crash eliminated Pietri, Baldolini, Simeon and Wilairot. There were worrying moments as the last-named was stretchered away, and the bearers dropped the stretcher. But the Thai rider escaped serious injury. Cluzel also crashed out; Morales, Aleix Espargaro and Neukirchner all retired.

125cc RACE – 23 laps

Zarco took pole, Terol third behind team-mate Faubel. Twenty-six points adrift, the Frenchman was optimistic: "Nico is fast everywhere ... but I have a little light in my head that tells me it is not impossible to catch him."

Sadly for Zarco, the fates again decreed otherwise.

Terol led away, with Cortese, Vazquez, Zarco and Kent (still on the Aprilia RSA) in pursuit. By lap two, Zarco was second, and there followed a fascinating pursuit. Accompanied at first by Vazquez, Zarco gradually reeled in the more experienced rider on the faster bike. By lap ten, he was with him, Vazquez now losing ground, but well clear of a five-bike battle behind him.

With five laps to go, Zarco attacked. The pair exchanged the lead several times, Terol ahead as they started the final lap. Zarco was faster in the twists, though, and led again early in the final lap. He rebuffed every attack and led into the last corner.

But, as he explained later, "I knew Terol was faster on to the straight." At the same time, the experienced Spaniard had taken a later line with a faster exit.

Zarco came out ahead, looked over his shoulder and then gestured as if to push his rival back. In vain, and he only made himself look foolish. Terol reached the line 0.022 second ahead.

Cortese finally won a big battle for fourth, with Faubel still close and Kent two seconds adrift, impressively fending off Vinales and Gadea. Team-mate Folger was almost ten seconds down in ninth.

MotoGP · TISSOT · OFFICIAL TIMEKEEPER

MISANO WORLD CIRCUIT

28 laps
Length: 4.226 km / 2.626 miles
Width: 12m

Key
96/60 kph/mph
Gear

Tramonto 75/47
Rio 75/47
Turn 5
Turn 9
Turn 6 120/75
Rimini 265/165
Quercia 80/50
Curvone 260/161
Turn 2
Turn 12
Misano 105/65
Variante del Parco 155/71
Turn 1 115/71
Turn 15 135/84
Carro 80/50
Turn 13

MotoGP

RACE DISTANCE: 28 laps, 73.526 miles/118.328km · **RACE WEATHER:** Dry (air 28°C, humidity 62%, track 35°C)

Pos.	Rider	Nat.	No.	Entrant	Machine	Tyres	Laps	Time & speed
1	Jorge Lorenzo	SPA	1	Yamaha Factory Racing	Yamaha	B	28	44m 11.877s / 99.813mph / 160.633km/h
2	Dani Pedrosa	SPA	26	Repsol Honda Team	Honda	B	28	44m 19.176s
3	Casey Stoner	AUS	27	Repsol Honda Team	Honda	B	28	44m 23.844s
4	Marco Simoncelli	ITA	58	San Carlo Honda Gresini	Honda	B	28	44m 29.230s
5	Andrea Dovizioso	ITA	4	Repsol Honda Team	Honda	B	28	44m 29.267s
6	Ben Spies	USA	11	Yamaha Factory Racing	Yamaha	B	28	44m 29.969s
7	Valentino Rossi	ITA	46	Ducati Team	Ducati	B	28	44m 35.580s
8	Alvaro Bautista	SPA	19	Rizla Suzuki MotoGP	Suzuki	B	28	44m 42.555s
9	Hector Barbera	SPA	8	Mapfre Aspar Team MotoGP	Ducati	B	28	44m 49.379s
10	Cal Crutchlow	GBR	35	Monster Yamaha Tech 3	Yamaha	B	28	44m 49.597s
11	Hiroshi Aoyama	JPN	7	San Carlo Honda Gresini	Honda	B	28	44m 51.425s
12	Karel Abraham	CZE	17	Cardion AB Motoracing	Ducati	B	28	44m 52.383s
13	Colin Edwards	USA	5	Monster Yamaha Tech 3	Yamaha	B	28	45m 05.226s
14	Randy de Puniet	FRA	14	Pramac Racing Team	Ducati	B	26	45m 14.243s
15	Toni Elias	SPA	24	LCR Honda MotoGP	Honda	B	27	45m 32.033s
	Loris Capirossi	ITA	65	Pramac Racing Team	Ducati	B	6	DNF
	Nicky Hayden	USA	69	Ducati Team	Ducati	B	2	DNF

Fastest lap: Jorge Lorenzo, on lap 12, 1m 33.906s, 100.667mph/162.008km/h (record).

Previous lap record: Dani Pedrosa, SPA (Honda), 1m 34.340s, 100.204mph/161.263km/h (2010).

Event best maximum speed: Dani Pedrosa, 173.600mph/279.400km/h (free practice 1).

Qualifying

Weather: Dry
Air Temp: 29° Humidity: 55%
Track Temp: 39°

1	Stoner	1m 33.138s
2	Lorenzo	1m 33.258s
3	Pedrosa	1m 33.318s
4	Spies	1m 33.947s
5	Simoncelli	1m 33.990s
6	Dovizioso	1m 34.026s
7	Edwards	1m 34.054s
8	Bautista	1m 34.360s
9	Barbera	1m 34.592s
10	Aoyama	1m 34.637s
11	Rossi	1m 34.676s
12	Abraham	1m 34.727s
13	Crutchlow	1m 34.791s
14	De Puniet	1m 34.870s
15	Hayden	1m 34.955s
16	Capirossi	1m 35.502s
17	Elias	1m 36.167s

Fastest race laps

1	Lorenzo	1m 33.906s
2	Stoner	1m 33.965s
3	Pedrosa	1m 34.224s
4	Spies	1m 34.518s
5	Simoncelli	1m 34.529s
6	Dovizioso	1m 34.581s
7	Rossi	1m 34.633s
8	Bautista	1m 34.737s
9	Edwards	1m 34.836s
10	Crutchlow	1m 34.920s
11	Barbera	1m 35.069s
12	Abraham	1m 35.352s
13	Aoyama	1m 35.375s
14	De Puniet	1m 35.623s
15	Elias	1m 36.338s
16	Hayden	1m 36.423s
17	Capirossi	1m 36.633s

Championship Points

1	Stoner	259
2	Lorenzo	224
3	Dovizioso	185
4	Pedrosa	150
5	Spies	135
6	Rossi	133
7	Hayden	105
8	Simoncelli	93
9	Edwards	87
10	Aoyama	82
11	Barbera	69
12	Bautista	57
13	Abraham	50
14	Elias	47
15	Crutchlow	45
16	De Puniet	29
17	Capirossi	29
18	Hopkins	6
19	Akiyoshi	3

Team Points

1	Repsol Honda Team	393
2	Yamaha Factory Racing	359
3	Ducati Team	238
4	San Carlo Honda Gresini	170
5	Monster Yamaha Tech 3	132
6	Mapfre Aspar Team MotoGP	69
7	Rizla Suzuki MotoGP	63
8	Pramac Racing Team	58
9	Cardion AB Motoracing	50
10	LCR Honda MotoGP	47

Constructor Points

1	Honda	305
2	Yamaha	258
3	Ducati	144
4	Suzuki	63

Grid order

Grid order	1	2	3	4	5	6	7	8	9	10	11	12	13	14	15	16	17	18	19	20	21	22	23	24	25	26	27	28	
27 STONER	1	1	1	1	1	1	1	1	1	1	1	1	1	1	1	1	1	1	1	1	1	1	1	1	1	1	1	1	1
1 LORENZO	27	27	27	27	27	27	27	27	27	27	27	27	27	27	27	27	27	27	27	27	27	26	26	26	26	26	26	26	2
26 PEDROSA	26	26	26	26	26	26	26	26	26	26	26	26	26	26	26	26	26	26	26	26	26	27	27	27	27	27	27	27	3
11 SPIES	4	4	4	4	4	4	4	58	58	58	58	58	58	58	58	58	58	58	58	58	58	58	58	58	4	4	58		4
58 SIMONCELLI	11	46	46	46	58	58	58	4	4	4	4	4	4	4	4	4	4	4	4	4	4	4	4	4	58	58	4		5
4 DOVIZIOSO	46	58	58	58	46	46	46	46	46	46	46	46	46	46	11	11	11	11	11	11	11	11	11	11	11	11	11		6
5 EDWARDS	58	11	11	11	11	11	11	11	11	11	11	11	11	11	46	46	46	46	46	46	46	46	46	46	46	46	47		7
19 BAUTISTA	5	5	5	5	5	5	5	5	5	5	5	5	5	5	19	19	19	19	19	19	19	19	19	19	19	19	9		8
8 BARBERA	69	69	19	19	19	19	19	19	19	19	19	19	19	19	5	5	5	5	5	35	35	35	35	8	8	8	8		9
7 AOYAMA	19	19	35	35	35	35	35	35	35	35	35	35	35	35	35	35	35	35	5	8	8	8	35	35	35	35			10
46 ROSSI	35	35	7	7	7	7	7	7	7	7	8	8	8	8	8	8	8	8	8	7	7	7	7	7	7	7	7		11
17 ABRAHAM	7	7	8	8	8	8	8	8	8	8	7	7	7	7	7	7	7	7	7	5	5	17	17	17	17	17	17		12
35 CRUTCHLOW	8	24	17	17	17	17	17	17	17	17	17	17	17	17	17	17	17	17	17	17	17	5	5	5	5	5	5		13
14 DE PUNIET	24	8	24	24	24	14	14	14	14	14	14	14	14	14	14	14	14	14	14	14	14	14	14	14	14	14	14		14
69 HAYDEN	17	17	14	14	14	24	24	24	24	24	24	24	24	24	24	24	24	24	24	24	24	24	24	24	24	24	24		15
65 CAPIROSSI	65	14	65	65	65	65	65	65																					
24 ELIAS	14	65																											

65 Pitstop   65 Lapped rider

Moto2 — RACE DISTANCE: 26 laps, 68.274 miles/109.876km · RACE WEATHER: Dry (air 27°C, humidity 55%, track 34°C)

Pos.	Rider	Nat.	No.	Entrant	Machine	Laps	Time & Speed
1	**Marc Marquez**	SPA	93	Team CatalunyaCaixa Repsol	Suter	26	43m 08.197s 94.964mph/ 152.829km/h
2	**Stefan Bradl**	GER	65	Viessmann Kiefer Racing	Kalex	26	43m 08.816s
3	**Andrea Iannone**	ITA	29	Speed Master	Suter	26	43m 08.910s
4	**Alex de Angelis**	RSM	15	JIR Moto2	Motobi	26	43m 09.831s
5	**Scott Redding**	GBR	45	Marc VDS Racing Team	Suter	26	43m 11.472s
6	**Bradley Smith**	GBR	38	Tech 3 Racing	Tech 3	26	43m 11.633s
7	**Yuki Takahashi**	JPN	72	Gresini Racing Moto2	Moriwaki	26	43m 13.452s
8	**Thomas Luthi**	SWI	12	Interwetten Paddock Moto2	Suter	26	43m 16.936s
9	**Pol Espargaro**	SPA	44	HP Tuenti Speed Up	FTR	26	43m 21.421s
10	**Simone Corsi**	ITA	3	Ioda Racing Project	FTR	26	43m 21.748s
11	**Esteve Rabat**	SPA	34	Blusens-STX	FTR	26	43m 25.730s
12	**Julian Simon**	SPA	60	Mapfre Aspar Team Moto2	Suter	26	43m 26.360s
13	**Dominique Aegerter**	SWI	77	Technomag-CIP	Suter	26	43m 26.451s
14	**Michele Pirro**	ITA	51	Gresini Racing Moto2	Moriwaki	26	43m 27.377s
15	**Mika Kallio**	FIN	36	Marc VDS Racing Team	Suter	26	43m 32.651s
16	Mike Di Meglio	FRA	63	Tech 3 Racing	Tech 3	26	43m 33.055s
17	Mattia Pasini	ITA	75	Ioda Racing Project	FTR	26	43m 33.189s
18	Claudio Corti	ITA	71	Italtrans Racing Team	Suter	26	43m 43.555s
19	Randy Krummenacher	SWI	4	GP Team Switzerland Kiefer Racing	Kalex	26	43m 43.997s
20	Tomoyoshi Koyama	JPN	7	Technomag-CIP	Suter	26	43m 45.568s
21	Ricard Cardus	SPA	88	QMMF Racing Team	Moriwaki	26	43m 45.681s
22	Raffaele de Rosa	ITA	35	NGM Forward Racing	Suter	26	43m 56.101s
23	Kenny Noyes	USA	9	Avintia-STX	FTR	26	43m 57.030s
24	Santiago Hernandez	COL	64	SAG Team	FTR	26	44m 05.055s
25	Valentin Debise	FRA	53	Speed Up	FTR	26	44m 14.968s
26	Joan Olive	SPA	6	Blusens-STX	FTR	26	44m 15.250s
27	Anthony West	AUS	13	MZ Racing Team	MZ-RE Honda	26	44m 21.575s
28	Jacob Gagne	USA	32	Aeroport de Castello	FTR	26	44m 29.938s
29	Alessandro Andreozzi	ITA	22	Andreozzi Reparto Corse	FTR	26	44m 38.841s
30	Mashel Al Naimi	QAT	95	QMMF Racing Team	Moriwaki	25	43m 55.412s
	Aleix Espargaro	SPA	40	Pons HP 40	Pons Kalex	13	DNF
	Max Neukirchner	GER	76	MZ Racing Team	MZ-RE Honda	13	DNF
	Carmelo Morales	SPA	31	Desguaces La Torre G22	Moriwaki	12	DNF
	Jules Cluzel	FRA	16	NGM Forward Racing	Suter	6	DNF
	Alex Baldolini	ITA	25	Pons HP 40	Pons Kalex	0	DNF
	Xavier Simeon	BEL	19	Tech 3 B	Tech 3	0	DNF
	Robertino Pietri	VEN	39	Italtrans Racing Team	Suter	0	DNF
	Ratthapark Wilairot	THA	14	Thai Honda Singha SAG	FTR	0	DNF

Fastest lap: Andrea Iannone, on lap 8, 1m 38.609s, 95.866mph/154.282km/h (record).
Previous lap record: Alex de Angelis, RSM (Motobi), 1m 39.430s, 95.075mph/153.008km/h (2010).
Event best maximum speed: Andrea Iannone, 149.400mph/240.400km/h (warm up).

Qualifying: Dry
Air: 31° Humidity: 41% Ground: 44°

1	Bradl	1m 37.828s
2	Marquez	1m 38.084s
3	Takahashi	1m 38.340s
4	Redding	1m 38.364s
5	De Angelis	1m 38.461s
6	Smith	1m 38.535s
7	Iannone	1m 38.544s
8	Pirro	1m 38.600s
9	P. Espargaro	1m 38.647s
10	Luthi	1m 38.657s
11	Cluzel	1m 38.730s
12	A. Espargaro	1m 38.785s
13	Pasini	1m 38.883s
14	Simon	1m 38.887s
15	Corsi	1m 39.005s
16	Rabat	1m 39.152s
17	Neukirchner	1m 39.166s
18	Di Meglio	1m 39.239s
19	Krummenacher	1m 39.411s
20	Corti	1m 39.432s
21	Baldolini	1m 39.436s
22	De Rosa	1m 39.440s
23	Simeon	1m 39.564s
24	West	1m 39.570s
25	Pietri	1m 39.685s
26	Kallio	1m 39.701s
27	Cardus	1m 39.726s
28	Koyama	1m 39.774s
29	Aegerter	1m 40.013s
30	Andreozzi	1m 40.363s
31	Olive	1m 40.459s
32	S. Hernandez	1m 40.474s
33	Debise	1m 40.538s
34	Wilairot	1m 40.606s
35	Morales	1m 40.607s
36	Torres	1m 40.821s
37	Noyes	1m 41.339s
38	Gagne	1m 41.540s
39	Al Naimi	1m 41.840s

Fastest race laps

1	Iannone	1m 38.609s
2	Marquez	1m 38.712s
3	De Angelis	1m 38.816s
4	Bradl	1m 38.831s
5	Redding	1m 38.866s
6	Smith	1m 38.915s
7	Luthi	1m 39.039s
8	Corsi	1m 39.058s
9	Takahashi	1m 39.064s
10	P. Espargaro	1m 39.088s
11	Rabat	1m 39.243s
12	A. Espargaro	1m 39.266s
13	Aegerter	1m 39.279s
14	Pirro	1m 39.280s
15	West	1m 39.304s
16	Cluzel	1m 39.390s
17	Neukirchner	1m 39.395s
18	Kallio	1m 39.407s
19	Simon	1m 39.432s
20	Di Meglio	1m 39.482s
21	Pasini	1m 39.497s
22	Corti	1m 39.917s
23	Cardus	1m 39.920s
24	Krummenacher	1m 39.995s
25	Koyama	1m 40.043s
26	De Rosa	1m 40.446s
27	Morales	1m 40.459s
28	Noyes	1m 40.528s
29	Olive	1m 40.696s
30	S. Hernandez	1m 40.714s
31	Debise	1m 40.832s
32	Gagne	1m 40.843s
33	Andreozzi	1m 40.896s
34	Al Naimi	1m 42.517s

Championship Points

1	Bradl	213
2	Marquez	190
3	Iannone	112
4	De Angelis	109
5	Smith	102
6	Corsi	99
7	Luthi	96
8	Takahashi	71
9	Rabat	67
10	Simon	62
11	A. Espargaro	54
12	Krummenacher	52
13	Aegerter	48
14	Redding	47
15	Sofuoglu	45
16	Pirro	45
17	P. Espargaro	43
18	Cluzel	35
19	Y. Hernandez	33
20	Neukirchner	32
21	Pasini	26
22	Kallio	19
23	West	18
24	Baldolini	18
25	Coghlan	11
26	Corti	9
27	Simeon	9
28	Di Meglio	8
29	Wilairot	4
30	Cardus	2
31	Pons	1

Constructor Points

1	Suter	273
2	Kalex	220
3	FTR	134
4	Tech 3	112
5	Motobi	109
6	Moriwaki	95
7	Pons Kalex	55
8	MZ-RE Honda	39

125cc — RACE DISTANCE: 23 laps, 60.396 miles/97.198km · RACE WEATHER: Dry (air 28°C, humidity 54%, track 31°C)

Pos.	Rider	Nat.	No.	Entrant	Machine	Laps	Time & Speed
1	**Nicolas Terol**	SPA	18	Bankia Aspar Team 125cc	Aprilia	23	40m 02.164s 90.506mph/ 145.655km/h
2	**Johann Zarco**	FRA	5	Avant-AirAsia-Ajo	Derbi	23	40m 02.186s
3	**Efren Vazquez**	SPA	7	Avant-AirAsia-Ajo	Derbi	23	40m 07.096s
4	**Sandro Cortese**	GER	11	Intact-Racing Team Germany	Aprilia	23	40m 11.486s
5	**Hector Faubel**	SPA	55	Bankia Aspar Team 125cc	Aprilia	23	40m 12.128s
6	**Danny Kent**	GBR	52	Red Bull Ajo MotorSport	Aprilia	23	40m 14.264s
7	**Maverick Vinales**	SPA	25	Blusens by Paris Hilton Racing	Aprilia	23	40m 14.488s
8	**Sergio Gadea**	SPA	33	Blusens by Paris Hilton Racing	Aprilia	23	40m 14.720s
9	**Jonas Folger**	GER	94	Red Bull Ajo MotorSport	Aprilia	23	40m 23.653s
10	**Miguel Oliveira**	POR	44	Andalucia Banca Civica	Aprilia	23	40m 32.842s
11	**Alberto Moncayo**	SPA	23	Andalucia Banca Civica	Aprilia	23	40m 33.485s
12	**Jakub Kornfeil**	CZE	84	Ongetta-Centro Seta	Aprilia	23	40m 33.716s
13	**Miroslav Popov**	CZE	95	Ellegi Racing	Aprilia	23	40m 34.801s
14	**Luigi Morciano**	ITA	3	Team Italia FMI	Aprilia	23	40m 54.706s
15	**Marcel Schrotter**	GER	77	Mahindra Racing	Mahindra	23	40m 56.014s
16	Kevin Calia	ITA	74	MGP Racing	Aprilia	23	40m 56.081s
17	Alessandro Tonucci	ITA	19	Team Italia FMI	Aprilia	23	41m 00.906s
18	Manuel Tatasciore	ITA	60	Phonica Racing	Aprilia	23	41m 05.887s
19	Alessandro Giorgi	ITA	27	VFT Racing	Aprilia	23	41m 06.277s
20	Alexis Masbou	FRA	10	Caretta Technology	KTM	23	41m 07.120s
21	Danny Webb	GBR	99	Mahindra Racing	Mahindra	23	41m 10.959s
22	Taylor Mackenzie	GBR	17	Phonica Racing	Aprilia	23	41m 11.010s
23	Giulian Pedone	SWI	30	Phonica Racing	Aprilia	23	41m 19.883s
24	Jack Miller	AUS	8	Caretta Technology	KTM	23	41m 20.916s
25	Joan Perello	SPA	36	Matteoni Racing	Aprilia	23	41m 39.114s
26	Adrian Martin	SPA	26	Bankia Aspar Team 125cc	Aprilia	21	41m 07.711s
27	Zulfahmi Khairuddin	MAL	63	Airasia-Sic-Ajo	Derbi	20	40m 28.067s
	Sturla Fagerhaug	NOR	50	WTR-Ten10 Racing	Aprilia	17	DNF
	Jasper Iwema	NED	53	Ongetta-Abbink Metaal	Aprilia	10	DNF
	Massimo Parziani	ITA	88	Faenza Racing	Aprilia	10	DNF
	Luis Salom	SPA	39	RW Racing GP	Aprilia	7	DNF
	Francesco Mauriello	ITA	43	WTR-Ten10 Racing	Aprilia	3	DNF
	Harry Stafford	GBR	21	Ongetta-Centro Seta	Aprilia	0	DNF
	Louis Rossi	FRA	96	Matteoni Racing	Aprilia	0	DNF

Fastest lap: Johann Zarco, on lap 8, 1m 43.379s, 91.443mph/147.163km/h.
Lap record: Marc Marquez, SPA (Derbi), 1m 43.195s, 91.606mph/147.425km/h (2010).
Event best maximum speed: Maverick Vinales, 125.800mph/202.400km/h (warm up).

Qualifying: Dry
Air: 28° Humidity: 60% Ground: 35°

1	Zarco	1m 43.247s
2	Faubel	1m 43.440s
3	Terol	1m 43.604s
4	Cortese	1m 43.605s
5	Kent	1m 44.240s
6	Popov	1m 44.255s
7	Folger	1m 44.266s
8	Salom	1m 44.275s
9	Oliveira	1m 44.327s
10	Vinales	1m 44.351s
11	Vazquez	1m 44.617s
12	Moncayo	1m 44.651s
13	Gadea	1m 44.740s
14	Morciano	1m 44.940s
15	Schrotter	1m 45.034s
16	Khairuddin	1m 45.102s
17	Kornfeil	1m 45.169s
18	Martin	1m 45.193s
19	Webb	1m 45.524s
20	Stafford	1m 45.527s
21	Iwema	1m 45.639s
22	Tonucci	1m 45.833s
23	Rossi	1m 45.840s
24	Parziani	1m 46.081s
25	Giorgi	1m 46.083s
26	Masbou	1m 46.256s
27	Tatasciore	1m 46.316s
28	Calia	1m 46.345s
29	Fagerhaug	1m 46.634s
30	Miller	1m 47.031s
31	Mauriello	1m 47.198s
32	Pedone	1m 47.625s
33	Perello	1m 48.376s
34	Mackenzie	1m 48.893s

Fastest race laps

1	Zarco	1m 43.379s
2	Vazquez	1m 43.410s
3	Terol	1m 43.417s
4	Faubel	1m 43.876s
5	Cortese	1m 43.967s
6	Kent	1m 44.005s
7	Vinales	1m 44.024s
8	Gadea	1m 44.143s
9	Salom	1m 44.565s
10	Kornfeil	1m 44.572s
11	Folger	1m 44.599s
12	Popov	1m 44.722s
13	Moncayo	1m 44.923s
14	Oliveira	1m 44.991s
15	Morciano	1m 45.211s
16	Calia	1m 45.392s
17	Iwema	1m 45.467s
18	Schrotter	1m 45.602s
19	Martin	1m 45.651s
20	Khairuddin	1m 45.660s
21	Masbou	1m 45.709s
22	Tatasciore	1m 45.778s
23	Tonucci	1m 45.875s
24	Giorgi	1m 45.877s
25	Webb	1m 45.983s
26	Mackenzie	1m 46.020s
27	Pedone	1m 46.283s
28	Miller	1m 46.525s
29	Parziani	1m 47.000s
30	Fagerhaug	1m 47.187s
31	Mauriello	1m 47.437s
32	Perello	1m 47.448s

Championship Points

1	Terol	216
2	Zarco	185
3	Vinales	161
4	Cortese	160
5	Folger	124
6	Faubel	123
7	Vazquez	116
8	Gadea	103
9	Salom	76
10	Kent	59
11	Kornfeil	53
12	Moncayo	49
13	Oliveira	44
14	Grotzkyj	32
15	Martin	30
16	Khairuddin	20
17	Schrotter	18
18	Rossi	18
19	Mackenzie	15
20	Webb	14
21	Iwema	13
22	Masbou	12
23	Ajo	11
24	Ono	8
25	Morciano	8
26	Finsterbusch	4
27	Popov	3
28	Stafford	3
29	McPhee	1
30	Rodriguez	1

Constructor Points

1	Aprilia	300
2	Derbi	194
3	Mahindra	27
4	KTM	23

ARAGON GRAND PRIX

ARAGON CIRCUIT

Main photo: The grid lines up while Rossi prepares to start from pit lane.

Inset: Implausibly orange, Stoner distances himself from Pedrosa and Lorenzo. That's how it went up front.

Photos: Gold & Goose

Above: Bautista found himself battling Hayden again, wheel to wheel. He won out for another good sixth.

Top right: The Repsol Hondas adopted a Playskool livery for the race. Some called it naive, others merely tragic.

Above right: Carbon out, aluminium in: the front of Rossi's new chassis.

Right: Hector Barbera enjoyed a good day for his Mapfre team.

Photos: Gold & Goose

REMOTE and isolated amid wide, dry vistas of empty countryside, the Aragon Motorland circuit is in every respect a fine state-of-the-art facility. Every respect, for a second year, except one – the provision of power. A transformer failure and signs of instability from a second transformer forced a complete shut-down just as the big class was about to go out for Friday afternoon's second free practice. Officials were fearful of the consequences of losing all on-track communications and CCTV should there be a second failure.

Replacements had to be brought in from Zaragoza, more than 100km away by road, and by the time they had been delivered and installed, a series of postponements had become cancellation of the second sessions for both MotoGP and Moto2 – the 125s, luckily, had finished before the problem struck.

Saturday morning sessions were extended forthwith: from 45 minutes to 70, but the loss of a session was a blow to tactics and set-up procedure. As Rossi explained, "If you lose a session, you cannot make adjustments for the next session; an extra half-hour is not the same."

The problem was especially acute in his case because he had a brand-new motorbike to get settled in and upon. No name was accorded to the machine, which went halfway to being the full aluminium chassis that had been rumoured, but that still (according to the rider) "followed the Ducati philosophy" (the swinging-arm pivoting directly from the engine casing). The outward sign was that the chassis member on each side extended back to the nose of the seat,

demonstrating a big change from the minimal airbox/chassis of the past.

Rossi had tested the latest bike in 1000cc-rules guise at Mugello and discerned some improvement in the elusive front-end feel. He had one of each in the pit on Friday morning, but didn't use the carbon chassis at all. Instead, a second aluminium 'GP12.minus-one' was decanted and prepared. Now fully in testing rather than racing mode, Rossi was resigned to accepting the penalty that came with it – a pit-lane start, ten seconds after the lights.

This was because the new chassis required modified engine casings for the altered mounting system. One engine had been pre-modified, but that for the second bike took him over the allocation of six. He was discarding engines that still had plenty of life in them, but as Burgess explained, "We kissed this season goodbye a long time ago. We're just testing Friday and Saturday, then going for a longer run with the other bikes on Sunday."

Rossi accepted the inevitable also, at last, on Motegi, just two weeks away. Finally he confirmed he would be going. This followed written confirmation the previous Monday from Yamaha that both Lorenzo and Spies would take part in the race. (Honda also announced two wild-card entries: Shinichi Ito and Kousuke Akiyoshi would be joining all their regular riders on the Japanese grid.) Stoner unaccountably fudged on Thursday. "I'm not saying I'm going, but I'm not saying I'm not going," he said, but he admitted during the weekend that he would be there. It had been feared that a refusal by Rossi (lacking the obligation to a Japanese employer) would set off

a snowball effect among non-factory teams in all classes, so his confirmation was a relief, if belated. There was still rebellion, however, with talk of dismissal of at least two mechanics from the Aspar and BQR teams for refusing to attend; the Mahindra 125 squad took a kinder view, giving their Italian pit crew a free choice. All elected to stay at home. There was also much relief that this embarrassing saga would soon be at an end.

With the title still in the balance, Ben Spies was happy to confirm that there were no team orders at Yamaha. "I'm not a team-orders type of guy," he would confirm later. This was added to a similar and earlier confirmation from Pedrosa that it was the same at Honda – every man for himself. Stoner was happy enough with that, as he returned to winning form while team-mate Pedrosa consigned Lorenzo to third. It was another inexorable step towards the championship.

The Moto2 title battle was approaching fever pitch, as Marquez added a third consecutive win from another pole, while Bradl had another dire weekend, finishing only eighth. There was at least a technical explanation for the radical shift in the balance of power between them. In the interim, Marquez had not only been testing again (with his rich team well able to afford it, he clocked up more than 20 days of testing during the season), but also doing so with the latest and best from Suter, including a new swinging-arm and revisions to the front of what was effectively a factory chassis.

Bradl had a technical explanation, too, after dropping from the leading group to eighth. His rear tyre had shifted on the rim and the resultant imbalance made it impossible to sustain the lap times.

There was another first in the class: Spanish girl racer Elena Roselli became the first female to qualify not just in Moto2, but also in the intermediate class since Katja Poensgen ran a 250 campaign in 2003. Roselli crashed out before qualifying when she substituted for Simon at Assen, but scraped in last, 5.5 seconds off pole, at a more familiar circuit. She finished 33rd and last, although still on the same lap as the leader.

The new calendar, also much belated, was announced at last, the major change being that the two US rounds would now be back to back, although separated by two dead weekends. Worryingly, three races were still to be confirmed: Jerez and the Sachsenring for financial/contract reasons, but Estoril wavering on the brink of extinction. With spare circuit Aragon already on, the loss of another race might be hard to replace.

MOTOGP RACE – 23 laps

Fatigue was forgotten as Stoner dominated practice and qualifying, with a new track best lap. Pedrosa was a close second, Spies was third: he and Stoner had both crashed, Casey baling out in the gravel to avoid running into the barrier, Ben rather faster, but unhurt.

Lorenzo was two-tenths slower, complaining of a shortage of speed on the long straight as well as poor traction. The speed trap backed him up: his best was 323.4km/h, Stoner's 327.5 (Aoyama, Rossi and Bautista were faster, with the satellite Honda recording 330.5). Dovizioso and Simoncelli were close alongside. Hayden outqualified Rossi, equalling his best of the season to lead row three; Abraham was alongside.

Rossi's qualifying went wrong when he crashed his new aluminium-chassis bike early on. "I was about one metre off line. The front slid, then the back … I have crashed many times this way this year," he said. Down in 13th, he decided to take a new engine to liberate a second aluminium chassis and start from the pit lane.

Race day was cooler and windier than practice, making tyres yet more marginal. "They were cooling down between corners," said Stoner. Once again, he showed his tyre management skills when every other rider ran into at least some degree of trouble.

Above: De Puniet (14) takes to the grass as Abraham cartwheels into the gravel on the opening lap.

Above right: Team-mates, but no team orders. Lorenzo finally takes third from Spies.

Top: Crutchlow wins the fight from Rossi and Aoyama – but it was for ninth place.

Opposite, from top: Marquez disposes of Iannone on his way to another win; Terol was out on his own again in the 125 class; Elena Roselli was the first woman to race in the middle class since 2003.

Right: Redding leads as the Moto2 field streams into turn one at the start of lap two. Marquez, Bradl and Simon lead the pursuit.

Photos: Gold & Goose

Pedrosa took his usual flier off the line, Stoner on his tail – then the Australian locked up the front under brakes and they almost collided. It put the Spaniard off line, letting Spies through to the lead.

It lasted only for the first few corners, as Stoner first disposed of Pedrosa, then simply powered past Spies down the long straight. By the end of the lap, Pedrosa was also ahead of the Yamaha. From there to the end, the two ultra-orange Hondas galloped away, getting ever further ahead and ever further apart. Stoner's return to winning form at a track he had also dominated on the Ducati was achieved in copybook fashion, and rewarded with a new lap record on lap four.

Lorenzo was fourth at the end of lap one and Hayden fifth, but Simoncelli passed the Ducati into the first corner, and a lap later Hayden was more than a second adrift.

Simoncelli was pushing hard, passing Lorenzo into turn one at the start of lap four and closing rapidly on Spies. He was stuck there for a bit, his size and leaner fuel settings robbing him of the top speed advantage that had served Stoner so well.

He finally made it into third on lap nine, but only stayed there for a little more than half a lap before running on to the paved run-off at the top of the hill. By the time he got back, both Yamahas had flashed past him again.

Simoncelli did close up on Spies once more, getting ahead and moving away on lap 17. By then, Lorenzo had also passed his fast-fading team-mate and was clear ahead in a lonely, but safe third. Spies' tyres had "dropped off real quickly", and he would struggle to the end.

Thus the top five. Behind them, Hayden also had tyre issues: "I was sliding going *into* the corners." As he slowed, Bautista and Barbera closed: on him by lap nine, Bautista ahead two laps later. Then Barbera also got by and Hayden ran off, losing a second. He caught the other Ducati again,

but Bautista was out of reach and he was left to exchange blows to the finish until Barbera ran wide on the last lap.

Rossi of course moved steadily forward, but he didn't slice through in his normal fashion. It took him seven laps to get up to ninth, passing Capirossi, Edwards, Aoyama, Elias and Crutchlow on the way. He got no further, and even then he had been helped by Elias, who led the gang for the first five laps and slowed them.

Edwards dropped back, Elias and Capirossi behind him and heading for their own collision on lap 16. Capirossi ran into the back of the Honda at the Esses before the straight, suffering a dislocated shoulder as punishment.

Aoyama and Crutchlow stuck with Rossi, until his pace dropped – also out of tyre grip – in the closing laps. First Crutchlow and then Aoyama got back ahead of him. Rossi managed to regain one place on the final lap, but Crutchlow stayed just out of reach, the trio crossing the line within less than four-tenths. How did it feel to beat Rossi? "It doesn't count, because he started from pit lane," said Crutchlow, preferring to enjoy instead a revival in his own confidence.

De Puniet had caught up, but another run-off cost him any chance of making a difference, and he was 15 seconds away in 12th, with Edwards another three seconds down.

MOTO2 RACE – 21 laps

More testing and new parts – a swing-arm and modified chassis from Suter – only added to Marquez's steamroller effect. He led throughout practice, finishing an astonishing six-tenths ahead of second-placed Simon. Redding claimed his second front row of the year, making it an all-Suter show.

Bradl was less than a tenth slower to lead row two from de Angelis and Aleix Espargaro. Iannone was tenth; Smith 15th, times as close as usual in the middle group.

The race was a thriller from the off, although this time the full field made it through the first corner without one of their trademark pile-ups.

Bradl and Marquez were up front and battling from the start, but it was Redding ahead over the line for the first two laps, before Marquez took over for the next two, and Bradl the next three.

There was nothing in it, places being changed at almost every corner, and the next one up front was Iannone, for three laps. By lap ten, the lead group was nine strong and covered by less than two seconds, with Corsi up to second, ahead of Marquez, de Angelis, Bradl and Redding.

As much as they could work together, the joint aim was to stop Marquez from getting away. The key moment came braking into the first corner as they started lap 15. Iannone almost hit Marquez and ran wide. It was the chance the Spaniard had been waiting for. He was better than a second clear at the end of that lap, setting a new record; and two seconds next time around. At the finish, his lead was still just 2.4 seconds, but it was as good as the proverbial country mile.

Iannone, Corsi and de Angelis fought to the flag. But on lap 16, Bradl was in trouble, more than a second adrift and looking down at his bike as he started to lose places. His rear tyre had spun on the rim, causing ruinous vibration.

This delayed the rest of the group, which had grown as more riders tagged on from behind. By the finish, fifth to 18th places were covered by less than five seconds.

Aleix Espargaro narrowly retained fifth from Smith, through from 16th on lap one. Luthi had come with him; Bradl was eighth, Aegerter and Kallio completing the top ten. It was a best-yet race for the MZ riders, with West 11th and team-mate Neukirchner 13th.

Redding was the biggest loser, his size and weight leading to all-too-familiar tyre problems. Having been fast enough to lead, he had to fight hard to save one point for 15th.

Pasini was an early retirement, likewise de Rosa and late in the race also Pirro; Cluzel crashed out – twice; Wilairot and Takahashi only once each.

After the British GP, Marquez was 82 points down. Now he was just six behind, and the luck was all going his way.

125cc RACE – 19 laps

Vinales looked set for a fourth pole until veteran Faubel shaded him by nine tiny thousandths. Team-mate Terol had to be content with the far end of the front row after missing much of the third free practice with mechanical problems; his title challenger, Zarco, led row two from the increasingly impressive Kent, again on the RSA machine.

Terol got the jump to lead into the first corner. From there, he drew steadily clear to win by 6.7 seconds. It was his third win in a row, his eighth of the season. "After my engine broke again in practice, I was worried, but today everything was perfect," he said.

Zarco was lucky to get second. All race long, he and Faubel were back and forth, and the tussle looked set to go to the flag. Before the last run down the straight, Faubel dived forcefully inside him out of the last fast corner – and immediately crashed out. It was a small miracle that Zarco didn't hit him.

Vinales had started off third, dropping to fourth when Zarco came by on lap five, and alone from there to the end, although promoted to the rostrum by Faubel's crash.

There was a fine battle behind, five riders locked in race-long close combat. Back and forth at almost every corner, it took a photo finish to establish the final order. Fourth went to Vazquez from Salom, Kent, Cortese and Moncayo.

Martin was a lone ninth; Folger came through in the latter half of the race for tenth, dropping Schrotter (Mahindra) to 11th. Second Mahindra rider Webb battled through to 15th after qualifying 23rd.

Iwema, Stafford, Louis Rossi, Mackenzie and Ajo joined Faubel on the crash list.

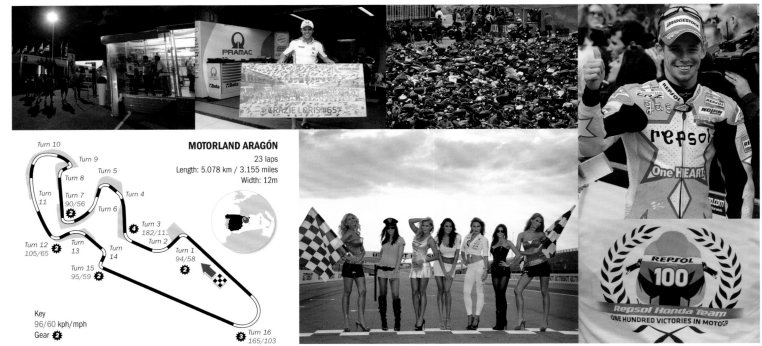

MOTORLAND ARAGÓN
23 laps
Length: 5.078 km / 3.155 miles
Width: 12m

Turn 10
Turn 9
Turn 8
Turn 5
Turn 7 90/56
Turn 11
Turn 4
Turn 6
Turn 3 182/113
Turn 2
Turn 12 105/65
Turn 13
Turn 14
Turn 1 94/58
Turn 15 95/59
Turn 16 165/103

Key
96/60 kph/mph
Gear

MotoGP

RACE DISTANCE: 23 laps, 72.572 miles/116.794km · RACE WEATHER: Dry (air 19°C, humidity 50%, track 26°C)

Pos.	Rider	Nat.	No.	Entrant	Machine	Tyres	Laps	Time & speed
1	**Casey Stoner**	AUS	27	Repsol Honda Team	Honda	B	23	42m 17.427s 102.962mph/ 165.702km/h
2	**Dani Pedrosa**	SPA	26	Repsol Honda Team	Honda	B	23	42m 25.589s
3	**Jorge Lorenzo**	SPA	1	Yamaha Factory Racing	Yamaha	B	23	42m 31.636s
4	**Marco Simoncelli**	ITA	58	San Carlo Honda Gresini	Honda	B	23	42m 38.073s
5	**Ben Spies**	USA	11	Yamaha Factory Racing	Yamaha	B	23	42m 45.166s
6	**Alvaro Bautista**	SPA	19	Rizla Suzuki MotoGP	Suzuki	B	23	42m 47.800s
7	**Nicky Hayden**	USA	69	Ducati Team	Ducati	B	23	42m 51.715s
8	**Hector Barbera**	SPA	8	Mapfre Aspar Team MotoGP	Ducati	B	23	42m 54.732s
9	**Cal Crutchlow**	GBR	35	Monster Yamaha Tech 3	Yamaha	B	23	42m 57.079s
10	**Valentino Rossi**	ITA	46	Ducati Team	Ducati	B	23	42m 57.259s
11	**Hiroshi Aoyama**	JPN	7	San Carlo Honda Gresini	Honda	B	23	42m 57.424s
12	**Randy de Puniet**	FRA	14	Pramac Racing Team	Ducati	B	23	43m 12.144s
13	**Colin Edwards**	USA	5	Monster Yamaha Tech 3	Yamaha	B	23	43m 15.857s
	Toni Elias	SPA	24	LCR Honda MotoGP	Honda	B	15	DNF
	Loris Capirossi	ITA	65	Pramac Racing Team	Ducati	B	15	DNF
	Andrea Dovizioso	ITA	4	Repsol Honda Team	Honda	B	0	DNF
	Karel Abraham	CZE	17	Cardion AB Motoracing	Ducati	B	0	DNF

Fastest lap: Casey Stoner, on lap 4, 1m 49.046s, 104.169mph/167.643km/h (record).
Previous lap record: Dani Pedrosa, SPA (Honda), 1m 49.521s, 103.716mph/166.915km/h (2010).
Event best maximum speed: Hiroshi Aoyama, 205.400mph/330.500km/h (race).

Qualifying
Weather: Dry
Air Temp: 28° Humidity: 49%
Track Temp: 41°

1	Stoner	1m 48.451s
2	Pedrosa	1m 48.747s
3	Spies	1m 49.155s
4	Lorenzo	1m 49.270s
5	Dovizioso	1m 49.372s
6	Simoncelli	1m 49.528s
7	Hayden	1m 49.752s
8	Abraham	1m 49.777s
9	Aoyama	1m 49.813s
10	De Puniet	1m 49.826s
11	Bautista	1m 49.883s
12	Crutchlow	1m 49.893s
13	Rossi	1m 49.960s
14	Barbera	1m 49.976s
15	Edwards	1m 50.105s
16	Capirossi	1m 50.752s
17	Elias	1m 51.073s

Fastest race laps

1	Stoner	1m 49.046s
2	Pedrosa	1m 49.454s
3	Spies	1m 49.593s
4	Simoncelli	1m 49.650s
5	Lorenzo	1m 50.056s
6	Bautista	1m 50.564s
7	Hayden	1m 50.685s
8	Rossi	1m 50.743s
9	Barbera	1m 50.807s
10	De Puniet	1m 51.029s
11	Crutchlow	1m 51.097s
12	Aoyama	1m 51.225s
13	Edwards	1m 51.600s
14	Capirossi	1m 51.627s
15	Elias	1m 51.863s

Championship Points

1	Stoner	284
2	Lorenzo	240
3	Dovizioso	185
4	Pedrosa	170
5	Spies	146
6	Rossi	139
7	Hayden	114
8	Simoncelli	106
9	Edwards	90
10	Aoyama	87
11	Barbera	77
12	Bautista	67
13	Crutchlow	52
14	Abraham	50
15	Elias	47
16	De Puniet	33
17	Capirossi	29
18	Hopkins	6
19	Akiyoshi	3

Team Points

1	Repsol Honda Team	418
2	Yamaha Factory Racing	386
3	Ducati Team	253
4	San Carlo Honda Gresini	188
5	Monster Yamaha Tech 3	142
6	Mapfre Aspar Team MotoGP	77
7	Rizla Suzuki MotoGP	73
8	Pramac Racing Team	62
9	Cardion AB Motoracing	50
10	LCR Honda MotoGP	47

Constructor Points

1	Honda	330
2	Yamaha	274
3	Ducati	153
4	Suzuki	73

	Grid order	1	2	3	4	5	6	7	8	9	10	11	12	13	14	15	16	17	18	19	20	21	22	23	
27	STONER	27	27	27	27	27	27	27	27	27	27	27	27	27	27	27	27	27	27	27	27	27	27	27	1
26	PEDROSA	26	26	26	26	26	26	26	26	26	26	26	26	26	26	26	26	26	26	26	26	26	26	26	2
11	SPIES	11	11	11	11	11	11	11	11	58	11	11	11	11	1	1	1	1	1	1	1	1	1	1	3
1	LORENZO	1	1	1	58	58	58	58	58	11	1	1	1	1	11	11	11	58	58	58	58	58	58	58	4
4	DOVIZIOSO	69	58	58	1	1	1	1	1	1	58	58	58	58	58	58	58	11	11	11	11	11	11	11	5
58	SIMONCELLI	58	69	69	69	69	69	69	69	69	69	19	19	19	19	19	19	19	19	19	19	19	19	19	6
69	HAYDEN	8	8	8	8	8	8	8	19	19	19	69	8	8	8	8	8	8	8	8	8	8	8	69	7
17	ABRAHAM	19	19	19	19	19	19	19	8	8	8	8	69	69	69	69	69	69	69	69	69	69	8		8
7	AOYAMA	24	24	24	24	24	35	46	46	46	46	46	46	46	46	46	46	35	35	35	35	35	35		9
14	DE PUNIET	7	7	7	7	35	24	35	35	7	7	7	7	7	7	7	46	46	46	7	7	46			10
19	BAUTISTA	5	5	5	35	7	46	7	7	35	35	35	35	35	35	35	35	7	7	46	46	7			11
35	CRUTCHLOW	35	35	35	5	46	7	24	24	5	5	5	5	5	14	14	14	14	14	14	14	14			12
8	BARBERA	65	65	65	65	5	5	5	24	24	24	14	14	14	5	5	5	5	5	5	5	5			13
5	EDWARDS	46	46	46	46	65	65	65	65	65	65	65	24	24	24	24									
65	CAPIROSSI	14	14	14	14	14	14	14	14	14	14	14	65	65	65	65									
24	ELIAS																								
46	ROSSI																								

Moto2

RACE DISTANCE: 21 laps, 66.262 miles/106.638km · RACE WEATHER: Dry (air 19°C, humidity 57%, track 24°C)

Pos.	Rider	Nat.	No.	Entrant	Machine	Laps	Time & Speed
1	**Marc Marquez**	SPA	93	Team CatalunyaCaixa Repsol	Suter	21	40m 20.575s / 98.548mph / 158.597km/h
2	**Andrea Iannone**	ITA	29	Speed Master	Suter	21	40m 23.041s
3	**Simone Corsi**	ITA	3	Ioda Racing Project	FTR	21	40m 23.149s
4	**Alex de Angelis**	RSM	15	JIR Moto2	Motobi	21	40m 23.629s
5	**Aleix Espargaro**	SPA	40	Pons HP 40	Pons Kalex	21	40m 31.406s
6	**Bradley Smith**	GBR	38	Tech 3 Racing	Tech 3	21	40m 31.445s
7	**Thomas Luthi**	SWI	12	Interwetten Paddock Moto2	Suter	21	40m 31.580s
8	**Stefan Bradl**	GER	65	Viessmann Kiefer Racing	Kalex	21	40m 31.787s
9	**Dominique Aegerter**	SWI	77	Technomag-CIP	Suter	21	40m 32.385s
10	**Mika Kallio**	FIN	36	Marc VDS Racing Team	Suter	21	40m 32.514s
11	**Anthony West**	AUS	13	MZ Racing Team	MZ-RE Honda	21	40m 32.683s
12	**Mike di Meglio**	FRA	63	Tech 3 Racing	Tech 3	21	40m 32.689s
13	**Max Neukirchner**	GER	76	MZ Racing Team	MZ-RE Honda	21	40m 32.755s
14	**Pol Espargaro**	SPA	44	HP Tuenti Speed Up	FTR	21	40m 33.483s
15	**Scott Redding**	GBR	45	Marc VDS Racing Team	Suter	21	40m 33.904s
16	Esteve Rabat	SPA	34	Blusens-STX	FTR	21	40m 34.450s
17	Julian Simon	SPA	60	Mapfre Aspar Team Moto2	Suter	21	40m 34.529s
18	Xavier Simeon	BEL	19	Tech 3 B	Tech 3	21	40m 35.826s
19	Claudio Corti	ITA	71	Italtrans Racing Team	Suter	21	40m 39.045s
20	Jordi Torres	SPA	18	Mapfre Aspar Team Moto2	Suter	21	40m 40.703s
21	Randy Krummenacher	SWI	4	GP Team Switzerland Kiefer Racing	Kalex	21	40m 59.549s
22	Alex Baldolini	ITA	25	Pons HP 40	Pons Kalex	21	40m 59.647s
23	Kenny Noyes	USA	9	Avintia-STX	FTR	21	40m 59.915s
24	Tomoyoshi Koyama	JPN	7	Technomag-CIP	Suter	21	41m 09.270s
25	Ricard Cardus	SPA	88	QMMF Racing Team	Moriwaki	21	41m 09.418s
26	Santiago Hernandez	COL	64	SAG Team	FTR	21	41m 23.245s
27	Sergio Gadea	SPA	33	Desguaces La Torre G22	Moriwaki	21	41m 26.208s
28	Joan Olive	SPA	6	Aeroport de Castello	FTR	21	41m 27.194s
29	Valentin Debise	FRA	53	Speed Up	FTR	21	41m 32.407s
30	Robertino Pietri	VEN	39	Italtrans Racing Team	Suter	21	41m 48.087s
31	Yuki Takahashi	JPN	72	Gresini Racing Moto2	Moriwaki	21	41m 51.977s
32	Mashel Al Naimi	QAT	95	QMMF Racing Team	Moriwaki	21	41m 54.300s
33	Elena Rosell	SPA	82	Mapfre Aspar Team Moto2	Suter	21	41m 57.123s
	Michele Pirro	ITA	51	Gresini Racing Moto2	Moriwaki	17	DNF
	Jules Cluzel	FRA	16	NGM Forward Racing	Suter	9	DNF
	Ratthapark Wilairot	THA	14	Thai Honda Singha SAG	FTR	9	DNF
	Raffaele De Rosa	ITA	35	NGM Forward Racing	Suter	9	DNF
	Mattia Pasini	ITA	75	Ioda Racing Project	FTR	3	DNF

Fastest lap: Marc Marquez, on lap 15, 1m 53.956s, 99.680mph/160.419km/h (record).
Previous lap record: Andrea Iannone, ITA (Speed Up), 1m 55.003s, 98.773mph/158.959km/h (2010).
Event best maximum speed: Aleix Espargaro, 176.000mph/283.200km/h (race).

Qualifying: Dry
Air: 29° Humidity: 46% Ground: 41°

1	Marquez	1m 53.296s
2	Simon	1m 53.980s
3	Redding	1m 54.004s
4	Bradl	1m 54.075s
5	De Angelis	1m 54.174s
6	A. Espargaro	1m 54.220s
7	Cluzel	1m 54.289s
8	P. Espargaro	1m 54.358s
9	Kallio	1m 54.385s
10	Iannone	1m 54.390s
11	Luthi	1m 54.413s
12	Corsi	1m 54.518s
13	Pirro	1m 54.574s
14	Takahashi	1m 54.599s
15	Smith	1m 54.619s
16	Corti	1m 54.625s
17	Neukirchner	1m 54.753s
18	Pasini	1m 54.793s
19	Di Meglio	1m 54.889s
20	Rabat	1m 54.946s
21	West	1m 55.047s
22	Torres	1m 55.084s
23	Aegerter	1m 55.175s
24	Simeon	1m 55.283s
25	Krummenacher	1m 55.324s
26	Cardus	1m 55.395s
27	Baldolini	1m 55.445s
28	Y. Hernandez	1m 55.560s
29	De Rosa	1m 55.593s
30	Koyama	1m 55.608s
31	Wilairot	1m 55.735s
32	S. Hernandez	1m 55.867s
33	Debise	1m 55.926s
34	Noyes	1m 55.948s
35	Olive	1m 56.613s
36	Gadea	1m 56.636s
37	Pietri	1m 56.691s
38	Al Naimi	1m 57.197s
39	Rosell	1m 58.806s

Fastest race laps

1	Marquez	1m 53.956s
2	Bradl	1m 54.033s
3	Corsi	1m 54.145s
4	Iannone	1m 54.150s
5	A. Espargaro	1m 54.630s
6	De Angelis	1m 54.672s
7	Neukirchner	1m 54.723s
8	Simon	1m 54.771s
9	Smith	1m 54.807s
10	Redding	1m 54.813s
11	Aegerter	1m 54.893s
12	Luthi	1m 54.914s
13	Di Meglio	1m 54.916s
14	Takahashi	1m 54.920s
15	Corti	1m 54.948s
16	Rabat	1m 54.976s
17	Kallio	1m 55.020s
18	West	1m 55.057s
19	Pirro	1m 55.100s
20	Simeon	1m 55.136s
21	P. Espargaro	1m 55.137s
22	Torres	1m 55.297s
23	Wilairot	1m 55.306s
24	Cluzel	1m 55.334s
25	Baldolini	1m 55.535s
26	De Rosa	1m 55.767s
27	Noyes	1m 56.031s
28	Pasini	1m 56.136s
29	Krummenacher	1m 56.167s
30	Koyama	1m 56.540s
31	Cardus	1m 56.590s
32	S. Hernandez	1m 56.637s
33	Debise	1m 56.812s
34	Gadea	1m 56.898s
35	Pietri	1m 56.985s
36	Olive	1m 57.114s
37	Al Naimi	1m 58.197s
38	Rosell	1m 58.886s

Championship Points

1	Bradl	221
2	Marquez	215
3	Iannone	132
4	De Angelis	122
5	Corsi	115
6	Smith	112
7	Luthi	105
8	Takahashi	71
9	Rabat	67
10	A. Espargaro	65
11	Simon	62
12	Aegerter	55
13	Krummenacher	52
14	Redding	48
15	P. Espargaro	45
16	Sofuoglu	45
17	Pirro	45
18	Cluzel	35
19	Neukirchner	35
20	Y. Hernandez	33
21	Pasini	26
22	Kallio	25
23	West	23
24	Baldolini	18
25	Di Meglio	12
26	Coghlan	11
27	Corti	9
28	Simeon	9
29	Wilairot	4
30	Cardus	2
31	Pons	1

Constructor Points

1	Suter	298
2	Kalex	228
3	FTR	150
4	Tech 3	122
5	Motobi	122
6	Moriwaki	95
7	Pons Kalex	66
8	MZ-RE Honda	44

125cc

RACE DISTANCE: 20 laps, 63.106 miles/101.560km · RACE WEATHER: Dry (air 19°, humidity 59%, track 23°)

Pos.	Rider	Nat.	No.	Entrant	Machine	Laps	Time & Speed
1	**Nicolas Terol**	SPA	18	Bankia Aspar Team 125cc	Aprilia	20	40m 26.726s / 93.617mph / 150.662km/h
2	**Johann Zarco**	FRA	5	Avant-AirAsia-Ajo	Derbi	20	40m 33.497s
3	**Maverick Vinales**	SPA	25	Blusens by Paris Hilton Racing	Aprilia	20	40m 45.655s
4	**Efren Vazquez**	SPA	7	Avant-AirAsia-Ajo	Derbi	20	40m 54.198s
5	**Luis Salom**	SPA	39	RW Racing GP	Aprilia	20	40m 54.195s
6	**Danny Kent**	GBR	52	Red Bull Ajo MotorSport	Aprilia	20	40m 54.476s
7	**Sandro Cortese**	GER	11	Intact-Racing Team Germany	Aprilia	20	40m 54.466s
8	**Alberto Moncayo**	SPA	23	Andalucia Banca Civica	Aprilia	20	40m 54.504s
9	**Adrian Martin**	SPA	26	Bankia Aspar Team 125cc	Aprilia	20	41m 09.735s
10	**Jonas Folger**	GER	94	Red Bull Ajo MotorSport	Aprilia	20	41m 15.816s
11	**Marcel Schrotter**	GER	77	Mahindra Racing	Mahindra	20	41m 20.602s
12	**Luigi Morciano**	ITA	3	Team Italia FMI	Aprilia	20	41m 23.121s
13	**Jakub Kornfeil**	CZE	84	Ongetta-Centro Seta	Aprilia	20	41m 24.239s
14	**Alessandro Tonucci**	ITA	19	Team Italia FMI	Aprilia	20	41m 33.941s
15	**Danny Webb**	GBR	99	Mahindra Racing	Mahindra	20	41m 41.632s
16	Sturla Fagerhaug	NOR	50	WTR-Ten10 Racing	Aprilia	20	41m 57.992s
17	Manuel Tatasciore	ITA	60	Phonica Racing	Aprilia	20	42m 03.597s
18	Giulian Pedone	SWI	30	Phonica Racing	Aprilia	20	42m 07.394s
19	Damien Raemy	SWI	90	Caretta Technology	KTM	20	42m 25.624s
20	Pedro Rodriguez	SPA	37	Turismo de Aragon - DVJ	Aprilia	19	41m 08.095s
	Hector Faubel	SPA	55	Bankia Aspar Team 125cc	Aprilia	19	DNF
	Zulfahmi Khairuddin	MAL	63	Airasia-Sic-Ajo	Derbi	18	DNF
	Harry Stafford	GBR	21	Ongetta-Centro Seta	Aprilia	16	DNF
	Josep Rodriguez	SPA	28	Blusens by Paris Hilton Racing	Aprilia	11	DNF
	Miguel Oliveira	POR	44	Andalucia Banca Civica	Aprilia	7	DNF
	Niklas Ajo	FIN	31	TT Motion Events Racing	Aprilia	7	DNF
	Francesco Mauriello	ITA	43	WTR-Ten10 Racing	Aprilia	7	DNF
	Taylor Mackenzie	GBR	17	Phonica Racing	Aprilia	6	DNF
	Louis Rossi	FRA	96	Matteoni Racing	Aprilia	5	DNF
	Kevin Hanus	GER	86	Team Hanusch	Honda	5	DNF
	Alexis Masbou	FRA	10	Caretta Technology	KTM	4	DNF
	Jasper Iwema	NED	53	Ongetta-Abbink Metaal	Aprilia	1	DNF
	Joan Perello	SPA	36	Matteoni Racing	Aprilia	0	DNF

Fastest lap: Maverick Vinales, on lap 4, 1m 59.835s, 94.790mph/152.549km/h.
Lap record: Pol Espargaro, SPA (Derbi), 1m 59.509s, 95.048mph/152.965km/h (2010).
Event best maximum speed: Sandro Cortese, 150.900mph/242.900km/h (race).

Qualifying: Dry
Air: 28° Humidity: 51% Ground: 42°

1	Faubel	1m 59.222s
2	Vinales	1m 59.231s
3	Terol	1m 59.365s
4	Zarco	1m 59.598s
5	Kent	1m 59.814s
6	Salom	1m 59.902s
7	Cortese	2m 00.011s
8	Moncayo	2m 00.316s
9	Vazquez	2m 00.432s
10	Folger	2m 00.447s
11	Martin	2m 00.697s
12	Rodriguez	2m 00.720s
13	Rossi	2m 00.786s
14	Kornfeil	2m 00.845s
15	Schrotter	2m 00.853s
16	Oliveira	2m 01.118s
17	Iwema	2m 01.492s
18	Ajo	2m 01.504s
19	Morciano	2m 02.064s
20	Masbou	2m 02.082s
21	Stafford	2m 02.119s
22	Tonucci	2m 02.375s
23	Webb	2m 02.400s
24	Pedone	2m 02.796s
25	Mauriello	2m 02.881s
26	Fagerhaug	2m 02.963s
27	Tatasciore	2m 03.153s
28	Mackenzie	2m 03.284s
29	Perello	2m 04.010s
30	Hanus	2m 04.653s
31	Khairuddin	2m 04.654s
32	Rodriguez	2m 04.886s
33	Raemy	2m 04.926s

Fastest race laps

1	Vinales	1m 59.835s
2	Zarco	1m 59.867s
3	Terol	1m 59.995s
4	Faubel	2m 00.037s
5	Salom	2m 01.256s
6	Rossi	2m 01.420s
7	Moncayo	2m 01.446s
8	Cortese	2m 01.470s
9	Kent	2m 01.485s
10	Vazquez	2m 01.514s
11	Oliveira	2m 01.948s
12	Folger	2m 02.052s
13	Kornfeil	2m 02.262s
14	Martin	2m 02.278s
15	Schrotter	2m 02.443s
16	Webb	2m 02.760s
17	Rodriguez	2m 02.782s
18	Mauriello	2m 02.817s
19	Mackenzie	2m 02.855s
20	Ajo	2m 02.996s
21	Morciano	2m 03.031s
22	Fagerhaug	2m 03.044s
23	Tonucci	2m 03.067s
24	Tatasciore	2m 03.287s
25	Stafford	2m 04.360s
26	Pedone	2m 04.927s
27	Masbou	2m 04.976s
28	Khairuddin	2m 05.740s
29	Raemy	2m 05.758s
30	Hanus	2m 06.539s
31	Rodriguez	2m 06.643s
32	Iwema	2m 13.187s

Championship Points

1	Terol	241
2	Zarco	205
3	Vinales	177
4	Cortese	170
5	Folger	130
6	Vazquez	127
7	Faubel	123
8	Gadea	103
9	Salom	89
10	Kent	68
11	Moncayo	57
12	Kornfeil	56
13	Oliveira	44
14	Martin	37
15	Grotzkyj	32
16	Schrotter	23
17	Khairuddin	20
18	Rossi	18
19	Mackenzie	15
20	Webb	15
21	Iwema	13
22	Morciano	12
23	Masbou	12
24	Ajo	11
25	Ono	8
26	Finsterbusch	4
27	Popov	3
28	Stafford	3
29	Tonucci	2
30	McPhee	1
31	Rodriguez	1

Constructor Points

1	Aprilia	325
2	Derbi	214
3	Mahindra	32
4	KTM	23

Main photo: "Thank you for coming." MotoGP winner Dani Pedrosa acknowledges the crowd's cheers.

Inset: Japanese officials and dignitaries are joined by (*from left*) riders Shinya Nakano and Hiro Aoyama, plus Carmelo Ezpeleta (Dorna) and Vito Ippolito (FIM) in a minute's silence for the victims of the March earthquake and tsunami.
Photos: Gold & Goose

JAPANESE GRAND PRIX

MOTEGI CIRCUIT

Top: A moment of horror as Rossi falls between the Yamahas of Lorenzo and Spies. He was lucky to escape largely unscathed.

Photos: Gold & Goose

Above: "I promise to stay out of the way." Veteran Shinichi Ito bolstered the grid on a works-backed Honda.

THE crowd at Honda's mountain racing retreat was relatively small – just 34,096. But the welcome at Motegi was palpable. To MotoGP fell the appropriate honour of being the first major international sporting event in Japan since the horrors of 11th March. Only by a week, though: F1 would be at Suzuka seven days later.

Any doubts about the value of the weekend over and above its importance as a GP were surely swept away. And how appropriate that it should be motorcycles, the most Japanese of all international industries, to pioneer attempts to return to the pre-disaster status quo.

After all the amateur dramatics, all but two riders showed up – not counting injury victims like Capirossi, who had been looking forward to a final gallop at a track where he had won twice. Abraham did turn up, only to find that he was still not race-fit after his bruising get-off at Aragón. One absentee was Moto2's Corti, replaced by Japanese Takaaki Nakagami; plus 125 rookie Francesco Mauriello. There were more absences in the pits: de Angelis had a skeleton staff with places taken by Japanese stand-ins, and there were more temps scattered here and there. Mahindra had found freelance Italian mechanics for their pit, with rider Danny Webb mischievously suggesting that his weekend had gone better than usual, though he was undermined when a cylinder-head stud failed in the race and put him out.

There were other absences (Spanish TV commentators Alex Criville and Angel Nieto were two). The only mass boycott was by the Italian media, with only one journalist instead of the usual dozen or so, and only a couple of photographers. Italian readers were regaled with stories written in absentia, such as *The Grand Prix of Fear*, which suggested that those who had attended were only there out of fear of losing jobs, contracts or championship points; and further castigated as cowards the current generation of riders for not having the courage to stand firm, as their predecessors had (nearly) done for the failed rebel World Series of 1980.

But the high moral ground belonged to those who did attend. These included FIM president Vito Ippolito and Honda Motor Company president Takanobu Ito, but not Ducati CEO Gabrielle del Torchio, as had been promised.

Ducati had brought its own pair of radiation experts to monitor the levels at the track all weekend. They found, as had Ben's mother, Mary Spies – who had one of several freelance Geiger counters – that levels were lower at Motegi than they had been in Florence before departure, and that the only time the readings had ever approached significant levels of background radiation (2.9) was at high altitude during the flight to Narita airport. "I was thinking this morning the batteries must be flat," she said.

All the same, many planned to leave their shoes behind, and in some cases even their clothes: one such was Dani Pedrosa, who smilingly agreed "it may be stupid". Lorenzo went further, admitting at the post-qualifying conference that he was eschewing the hotel shower and washing himself with bottled water. Talking of which, Gresini team rider Aoyama expressed wonderment at the amount – and the cost – of bottled water the Italian team had shipped in together with their motorbikes.

Pedrosa, all along the most matter-of-fact of top riders, redeemed himself further with the anti-panic faction when asked after the race how he now felt about the visit. While rostrum companions Stoner and Lorenzo prevaricated with "wait and see" comments, Dani said out straight, "Coming here was the right thing to do."

Honda had two grid-boosters: Kousuke Akiyoshi on the second LCR bike, and a factory wild-card bike for veteran ex-racer Shinichi Ito, who set a record for the new four-stroke era as, at 44, the oldest ever combatant. A contemporary of Doohan in the 1990s, he promised to "try to stay out of the way".

Talking of new-age records, Stoner garnered another for himself and Honda with his tenth pole of the season: still short of Mick Doohan's record 12 of 1997.

The Rossi-Ducati saga took another twist at a track where

the marque had claimed four wins in the previous six years, including Stoner's in 2010. Working with the new aluminium chassis, he qualified a relatively encouraging seventh, his first time back in the top ten (and as top Ducati) in four races, and with a decent improvement through four full dry sessions. "It is the happiest I have been on a Saturday evening," he said.

It all went badly wrong very quickly in the race. Well placed in the front pack roaring into the second corner, Rossi was first pushed hard from the left as Lorenzo came back across before hitting the brakes, and simultaneously squeezed from the right by Spies. He hit Lorenzo, then his brake lever caught on the American's Yamaha and locked his wheel, and he was down, luckily sliding out of harm's way as the rest came through. Spies, in turn, ran on to the gravel to fall at low speed, remounting directly to chase after his long-departed rivals.

Spies was already suffering such severe food poisoning that he had almost been refused permission to board his flight; he only managed five laps on Friday afternoon.

Simoncelli had a treat in store, as the first non-factory rider to try the 1000cc RC213V, in a special test on Monday. Again, Dovizioso had been bypassed, and his career choices came to a head at Motegi. He had an offer of a satellite-factory Honda with the LCR team or the option of turning his back on a full GP career with Honda to take his chances at Yamaha, in their satellite Tech 3 squad. In the break after the race, he took the second option.

At a race where goodwill was a theme, Honda showed it to Yamaha, celebrating 50 years of GP racing. In the hugely impressive Honda Collection Hall, a special section had been created for "Rivals". Five historic machines – Phil Read's 1968 RD05A, Kenny Roberts' 1978 YZR500, John Kocinski's 1990 YZR250, Wayne Rainey's 1993 YZR500 and Max Biaggi's 2001 M1 – were on display. And on race morning, the father of Japanese star Norick Abe rode one of his late son's YZR500s for two demonstration laps, in company

with three other historic Yamahas, including Jarno Saarinen's 500 from 1973 – the first successful two-stroke racer in the premier class. Smoky and unsilenced, the machine created a big impression.

Honda's other rival, for even longer than Yamaha, is Suzuki, and while the protracted uncertainty about their 2011 plans was in no way relieved at Motegi, there were encouraging signs. Factory tester Nobu Aoki was on hand and reporting that he had started track-testing a 1000cc MotoGP bike, although there were "still many problems".

MOTOGP RACE – 24 laps

The GP circuit had been damaged in the March earthquake and had been extensively resurfaced. Stoner hailed it as "a fantastic job" for the way the grip matched the sections of the old track, and all enjoyed the smooth new surface, but there were still rough patches, in particular some bumps on the back straight that would play a crucial part in his race.

Stoner, opining that his Honda had been "basically built for this circuit" added his own magic for a quarter-second advantage over Lorenzo in qualifying, with Dovi edging Pedrosa off the front row. He led the second, from Spies and Simoncelli; the somewhat rejuvenated Rossi headed the third from Bautista and Barbera, team-mate Hayden right behind. Abraham qualified 15th, but withdrew from the race. Last-minute Capirossi substitute Australian Damian Cudlin made a good fist of his first go on a MotoGP bike, a Ducati at that, slotting in 18th, between Japanese part-timers Akiyoshi and last qualifier Ito.

Honda had never won an 800cc MotoGP at their own circuit. It happened at last, but not quite how everybody had expected, in a race already disrupted twice.

The lights stayed on a fraction longer than the riders expected, and a twitch at the start by Dovizioso on the front row triggered the reflexes of those behind him – Simoncelli and Crutchlow. All three would incur ride-through penalties.

Above: Veteran Yamaha GP racers Akiyasu Motohashi, Hiroyuki Kawasaki and Shinya Nakano are joined by Norick Abe's father, Mitsuo (bike 17), for a race-day demonstration.

Top: The fans who did attend had a panoramic view.

Above left, from top: A warm handshake: Dani Pedrosa gains a fan for life; Marco Simoncelli exercises the team's Geiger counter; another Tissot watch for Stoner's tenth pole – a record in the four-stroke era.

Photos: Gold & Goose

Above: Lorenzo pressed Pedrosa, but settled for a safe second.

Top right: A resurgent Iannone ended Marquez's winning streak in Moto2.

Above centre right: Cudlin stood in for the injured Capirossi. His hat tells you where he's from.

Above far right: Zarco about to pounce on Terol. After a season of near misses, the Frenchman finally took his first 125 win.

Right: Cardus, De Rosa and Torres crash out in a scary tangle on the first lap of the Moto2 race.

Photos: Gold & Goose

Then came the Rossi-Yamaha sandwich on the second corner, removing two more potentially interesting combatants. Rossi was going for a move up to fifth place after his own good start.

Stoner had also started perfectly to beat Pedrosa into the first corner, Dovizioso behind and Lorenzo trying to run around the outside. Stoner was more than a second ahead of Pedrosa at the end of the first lap – and then Dovizioso, not yet aware of his penalty, took second off his team-mate into the second corner on lap two, and by lap four had closed back to within a second of Stoner, setting a new record in the process.

The leader was feeling the pressure. "I didn't want to push too hard early on, but I knew Andrea had the softer tyre," said Stoner. It was a tank-slapper over the earthquake bumps on the back straight that caught him out on lap five. "It's not one bump, there's a lot. As I came over, I had the slightest movement before the bigger bump, got some air on that one, and when the front came down it just shook. I almost lost hold of the handlebars."

By now, he was already in the hard braking zone, but the shaking had spread the pads and he had to pump the lever twice. Then they grabbed and almost locked. He had to pick the bike up and ran into the gravel, dropping from first to seventh in the process – though he would regain two places when Dovizioso and Simoncelli took their penalties. By half-distance, he had got back ahead of Hayden and Bautista on consecutive laps to regain third.

Dovi pitted from the lead, a depressing moment; Simoncelli followed him in. Crutchlow had survived a lap-four run-off that dropped him from ninth to 15th, and trailed them down the pit lane a little later.

Dani had also been promoted when Dovi pulled in. He stayed there to the end, lowering the lap record still further on the way. "I was lucky, but it feels great," he said. He still had to fight, because Lorenzo was on blazing form, overcoming his Yamaha's speed and acceleration disadvantages to hound him in the early stages. He even attempted a pass on lap ten, but it didn't work, and now he started to lose touch, preferring a safe second to further superhuman effort.

There was plenty of to and fro as the penalised riders moved back through, culminating in a fierce battle for fourth as Simoncelli caught Dovizioso. He got ahead on the penultimate lap, and managed to stay there in spite of Dovi's determined efforts.

Spies came steadily through to sixth, almost 15 seconds down, but getting the better of Hayden with two laps left to finish just a second ahead. Edwards was a lone eighth, followed by a well-spaced Aoyama, de Puniet, Crutchlow, and then Akiyoshi and Ito.

Bautista crashed out after managing to fend off a pressing Hayden for 13 laps: he was lying fourth at the time. Cudlin also fell, after shadowing Akiyoshi for 13 laps. Elias was another to crash unhurt, but Barbera suffered a heavy fall on the second lap and was stretchered away suffering from a broken collarbone.

MOTO2 RACE – 23 laps

With Marquez on pole again, by an impressive two-tenths from Luthi, and Bradl eighth, on row three, the scene was set for the see-saw to teeter over the point of balance. For Bradl, at this moment, it also looked like the point of no return.

Iannone completed the front row; Smith led the second from Takahashi and Corsi. Only then came Bradl and his Kalex, although still only seven-tenths off pole.

Rather surprisingly, given the nature of the course, all 33 riders made it through the first two hard-braking corners unscathed, although Cardus, de Rosa and Torres would crash out together a little further around.

Iannone won the first-lap scramble, staying in front of Marquez and the rest for the first six laps. Then Marquez

took over on the seventh. But his usual breakaway was not forthcoming, and two laps later Iannone took over again.

It took until two-thirds distance before the pair broke free from the front pack to make a race of their own, Iannone up front and Marquez his shadow. Then on lap 19 came an extraordinary turn of events. It appeared that Iannone deliberately slowed to let Marquez past, perhaps with the plan of enjoying passing him once more. He did get that pleasure, but it wasn't planned.

In fact, his Honda engine had suddenly slowed radically and he thought it had died. As suddenly, with Marquez past, it chimed in again at full steam. "I got quite scared when the engine turned off, but then it was back to normal and I was able to recover quite quickly," said Iannone.

To very good effect: by the end of the following lap, he was in front again and clearing off, to win by a convincing two seconds.

Marquez's first defeat in four races was not a total loss. He was safe in second, Luthi less so in third. He had gained control of a fearsome gang of four only in the last four laps after erstwhile leader Bradl had run wide and then lost another place to Corsi. He was ahead of the Italian again over the line, but not quite close enough to Luthi, while de Angelis was in ultra-close attendance throughout. Third to sixth was covered by just over one second.

The outcome was that Marquez took the title lead. It was only by one point, but the way things were going, it seemed impossible to stem the tide. The season, apparently, still had some surprises in store.

Smith caught and passed Aegerter for seventh with five laps to go; Rabat was a close ninth; the improving Kallio was not far off him. Improving form was also the case for Anthony West, ever since he had been joined in the MZ pit by experienced race engineer Warren Willing. He was 12th, behind Xavier Simeon.

Takahashi crashed out of his home GP on lap six while battling to get back into the top ten. He remounted for a dispirited 30th, second-last and one lap down. Pons and Santi Hernandez also tumbled out.

125cc RACE – 20 laps

Zarco's growing strength was underlined with his third pole of the year, ahead of the green Bankia bikes of Faubel and Terol. Vinales led row two, a couple of tenths down.

Terol led away, Zarco and Faubel going with him as they drew clear of the remainder. It was two against one. But when, on lap five, Faubel consigned Zarco to third, any hopes he might slow him to let his team-mate escape came to naught. One lap later, Zarco was in front again, and Faubel gradually lost touch.

The Frenchman was hounding Terol, but was the Spaniard keeping something for the final battle again? He never got the chance: Zarco took over firmly with six laps to go and stretched away to win by 5.9 seconds. His long-awaited and long-deferred first win was "a great step. I sometimes thought it would never happen."

Vinales provided the rest of the excitement in a stretched-out race. His chain broke just before the off and he had to start from the back of the grid. The talented teen had scythed through to eighth by half-distance.

Then he steadily picked through a group of four disputing fourth, seven seconds clear by the end. But for losing his grid position, he would surely have been in the battle for the lead on his first visit to the track.

Cortese was narrowly the strongest of the quartet, followed by Folger, Moncayo and Martin. Kent came through to snitch ninth; Kornfeil all but took tenth from Tonucci. His last previous victim had been Schrotter, whose Mahindra team-mate, Webb, had been in the top ten when he broke down.

Terol's points lead shrunk, but remained an impressive, if not impregnable, 31.

TWIN RING MOTEGI

24 laps
Length: 4.801 km / 2.983 miles
Width: 13m

Key
96/60 kph/mph
⚙ Gear

Victory Corner 85/53
90° Corner 78/49
Turn 1 98/61
Turn 3 96/60
V Corner 78/48
Turn 4 132/82
Turn 5 81/50
Turn 2 95/59
S Curve 126/78
130R 191/119
Hairpin 61/38

MotoGP

RACE DISTANCE: 24 laps, 71.597 miles/115.224km · RACE WEATHER: Dry (air 19°C, humidity 55%, track 29°C)

Pos.	Rider	Nat.	No.	Entrant	Machine	Tyres	Laps	Time & speed
1	**Dani Pedrosa**	SPA	26	Repsol Honda Team	Honda	B	24	42m 47.481s 100.389mph/ 161.561km/h
2	**Jorge Lorenzo**	SPA	1	Yamaha Factory Racing	Yamaha	B	24	42m 54.780s
3	**Casey Stoner**	AUS	27	Repsol Honda Team	Honda	B	24	43m 05.861s
4	**Marco Simoncelli**	ITA	58	San Carlo Honda Gresini	Honda	B	24	43m 11.031s
5	**Andrea Dovizioso**	ITA	4	Repsol Honda Team	Honda	B	24	43m 11.172s
6	**Ben Spies**	USA	11	Yamaha Factory Racing	Yamaha	B	24	43m 25.085s
7	**Nicky Hayden**	USA	69	Ducati Team	Ducati	B	24	43m 26.648s
8	**Colin Edwards**	USA	5	Monster Yamaha Tech 3	Yamaha	B	24	43m 32.504s
9	**Hiroshi Aoyama**	JPN	7	San Carlo Honda Gresini	Honda	B	24	43m 36.555s
10	**Randy de Puniet**	FRA	14	Pramac Racing Team	Ducati	B	24	43m 46.503s
11	**Cal Crutchlow**	GBR	35	Monster Yamaha Tech 3	Yamaha	B	24	44m 01.445s
12	**Kousuke Akiyoshi**	JPN	64	LCR Honda MotoGP	Honda	B	24	44m 09.190s
13	**Shinichi Ito**	JPN	72	Honda Racing Team	Honda	B	24	44m 13.862s
	Toni Elias	SPA	24	LCR Honda MotoGP	Honda	B	17	DNF
	Alvaro Bautista	SPA	19	Rizla Suzuki MotoGP	Suzuki	B	13	DNF
	Damian Cudlin	AUS	6	Pramac Racing Team	Ducati	B	13	DNF
	Hector Barbera	SPA	8	Mapfre Aspar Team MotoGP	Ducati	B	1	DNF
	Valentino Rossi	ITA	46	Ducati Team	Ducati	B	0	DNF

Fastest lap: Dani Pedrosa, on lap 11, 1m 46.090s, 101.230mph/162.914km/h (record).

Previous lap record: Casey Stoner, AUS (Ducati), 1m 47.091s, 100.284mph/161.391km/h (2008).

Event best maximum speed: Casey Stoner, 183.900mph/295.900km/h (free practice 3).

Qualifying

Weather: Dry
Air Temp: 22° Humidity: 50%
Track Temp: 32°

1	Stoner	1m 45.267s
2	Lorenzo	1m 45.523s
3	Dovizioso	1m 45.791s
4	Pedrosa	1m 45.966s
5	Spies	1m 46.042s
6	Simoncelli	1m 46.211s
7	Rossi	1m 46.467s
8	Bautista	1m 46.586s
9	Barbera	1m 46.694s
10	Hayden	1m 46.763s
11	Aoyama	1m 46.811s
12	Crutchlow	1m 46.818s
13	De Puniet	1m 46.917s
14	Edwards	1m 47.165s
15	Abraham	1m 47.922s
16	Elias	1m 48.169s
17	Akiyoshi	1m 48.367s
18	Cudlin	1m 48.962s
19	Ito	1m 49.971s

Fastest race laps

1	Pedrosa	1m 46.090s
2	Dovizioso	1m 46.114s
3	Stoner	1m 46.193s
4	Lorenzo	1m 46.398s
5	Simoncelli	1m 46.484s
6	Spies	1m 46.715s
7	Hayden	1m 47.098s
8	Bautista	1m 47.153s
9	Edwards	1m 47.434s
10	Crutchlow	1m 47.638s
11	Aoyama	1m 47.788s
12	Elias	1m 47.951s
13	De Puniet	1m 48.092s
14	Cudlin	1m 48.798s
15	Akiyoshi	1m 48.850s
16	Ito	1m 49.633s
17	Barbera	1m 57.120s

Championship Points

1	Stoner	300
2	Lorenzo	260
3	Dovizioso	196
4	Pedrosa	195
5	Spies	156
6	Rossi	139
7	Hayden	123
8	Simoncelli	119
9	Edwards	98
10	Aoyama	94
11	Barbera	77
12	Bautista	67
13	Crutchlow	57
14	Abraham	50
15	Elias	47
16	De Puniet	39
17	Capirossi	29
18	Akiyoshi	7
19	Hopkins	6
20	Ito	3

Team Points

1	Repsol Honda Team	454
2	Yamaha Factory Racing	416
3	Ducati Team	262
4	San Carlo Honda Gresini	208
5	Monster Yamaha Tech 3	155
6	Mapfre Aspar Team MotoGP	77
7	Rizla Suzuki MotoGP	73
8	Pramac Racing Team	68
9	Cardion AB Motoracing	50
10	LCR Honda MotoGP	47

Constructor Points

1	Honda	355
2	Yamaha	294
3	Ducati	162
4	Suzuki	73

Grid order		1	2	3	4	5	6	7	8	9	10	11	12	13	14	15	16	17	18	19	20	21	22	23	24	
27	STONER	27	27	27	27	4	26	26	26	26	26	26	26	26	26	26	26	26	26	26	26	26	26	26	26	1
1	LORENZO	26	4	4	4	26	1	1	1	1	1	1	1	1	1	1	1	1	1	1	1	1	1	1	1	2
4	DOVIZIOSO	4	26	26	26	1	19	19	19	19	19	19	27	27	27	27	27	27	27	27	27	27	27	27	27	3
26	PEDROSA	1	1	1	1	58	69	69	69	69	69	27	19	19	4	4	4	4	4	4	4	4	4	58	58	4
11	SPIES	58	58	58	58	19	27	27	27	27	27	69	4	4	58	58	58	58	58	58	58	58	58	4	4	5
58	SIMONCELLI	19	19	19	19	69	24	24	24	24	24	4	58	58	24	24	24	24	69	69	69	69	69	11	11	6
46	ROSSI	24	69	69	69	27	4	4	4	4	24	24	24	7	7	7	69	5	5	11	11	11	69	69	7
19	BAUTISTA	69	24	24	24	24	14	5	5	5	7	7	7	5	5	11	11	5	5	5	5	5	8
8	BARBERA	8	35	35	7	7	5	4	4	4	5	5	69	69	69	7	7	7	7	7	7	9
69	HAYDEN	7	7	7	14	14	4	58	58	58	58	58	69	69	11	11	11	14	14	14	14	14	14	10
7	AOYAMA	35	14	14	5	5	58	14	14	14	14	11	11	14	14	14	14	64	64	64	35	35	35	11
35	CRUTCHLOW	5	5	5	64	64	64	64	64	64	11	11	11	14	64	64	64	64	35	35	35	64	64	64	64	12
14	DE PUNIET	14	64	64	6	6	6	6	6	6	64	64	64	64	72	72	72	72	72	72	72	72	72	72	13
5	EDWARDS	64	6	6	72	72	72	72	11	11	6	6	6	35	35	35	35
24	ELIAS	6	72	72	35	35	11	11	72	72	72	72	72
64	AKIYOSHI	72	11	11	11	11	35	35	35	35	35	35	35
6	CUDLIN	11											
72	ITO												

4/58/35 Ride through penalties

Moto2

RACE DISTANCE: 23 laps, 68.614 miles/110.423km · RACE WEATHER: Dry (air 19°C, humidity 59%, track 29°C)

Pos.	Rider	Nat.	No.	Entrant	Machine	Laps	Time & Speed
1	**Andrea Iannone**	ITA	29	Speed Master	Suter	23	43m 25.007s 94.821mph/ 152.599km/h
2	**Marc Marquez**	SPA	93	Team CatalunyaCaixa Repsol	Suter	23	43m 27.006s
3	**Thomas Luthi**	SWI	12	Interwetten Paddock Moto2	Suter	23	43m 28.693s
4	**Stefan Bradl**	GER	65	Viessmann Kiefer Racing	Kalex	23	43m 29.320s
5	**Simone Corsi**	ITA	3	Ioda Racing Project	FTR	23	43m 29.654s
6	**Alex de Angelis**	RSM	15	JIR Moto2	Motobi	23	43m 29.820s
7	**Bradley Smith**	GBR	38	Tech 3 Racing	Tech 3	23	43m 35.527s
8	**Dominique Aegerter**	SWI	77	Technomag-CIP	Suter	23	43m 35.732s
9	**Esteve Rabat**	SPA	34	Blusens-STX	FTR	23	43m 36.394s
10	**Mika Kallio**	FIN	36	Marc VDS Racing Team	Suter	23	43m 37.810s
11	**Xavier Simeon**	BEL	19	Tech 3 B	Tech 3	23	43m 43.266s
12	**Anthony West**	AUS	13	MZ Racing Team	MZ-RE Honda	23	43m 45.822s
13	**Michele Pirro**	ITA	51	Gresini Racing Moto2	Moriwaki	23	43m 48.802s
14	**Mattia Pasini**	ITA	75	Ioda Racing Project	FTR	23	43m 49.395s
15	**Pol Espargaro**	SPA	44	HP Tuenti Speed Up	FTR	23	43m 59.078s
16	Jules Cluzel	FRA	16	NGM Forward Racing	Suter	23	44m 03.243s
17	Kenny Noyes	USA	9	Avintia-STX	FTR	23	44m 04.512s
18	Max Neukirchner	GER	76	MZ Racing Team	MZ-RE Honda	23	44m 04.616s
19	Kenan Sofuoglu	TUR	54	Technomag-CIP	Suter	23	44m 07.303s
20	Scott Redding	GBR	45	Marc VDS Racing Team	Suter	23	44m 09.169s
21	Valentin Debise	FRA	53	Speed Up	FTR	23	44m 11.669s
22	Ratthapark Wilairot	THA	14	Thai Honda Singha SAG	FTR	23	44m 11.957s
23	Yonny Hernandez	COL	68	Blusens-STX	FTR	23	44m 14.632s
24	Randy Krummenacher	SWI	4	GP Team Switzerland Kiefer Racing	Kalex	23	44m 15.597s
25	Robertino Pietri	VEN	39	Italtrans Racing Team	Suter	23	44m 17.051s
26	Joan Olive	SPA	6	Aeroport de Castello	FTR	23	44m 17.372s
27	Mike di Meglio	FRA	63	Tech 3 Racing	Tech 3	23	44m 27.880s
28	Tomoyoshi Koyama	JPN	7	CIP with TSR	TSR 6	23	45m 00.566s
29	Mashel Al Naimi	QAT	95	QMMF Racing Team	Moriwaki	23	45m 00.778s
30	Yuki Takahashi	JPN	72	Gresini Racing Moto2	Moriwaki	22	43m 30.959s
31	Aleix Espargaro	SPA	40	Pons HP 40	Pons Kalex	20	43m 53.990s
	Axel Pons	SPA	80	Pons HP 40	Pons Kalex	17	DNF
	Santiago Hernandez	COL	64	SAG Team	FTR	17	DNF
	Jordi Torres	SPA	18	Mapfre Aspar Team Moto2	Suter	0	DNF
	Raffaele de Rosa	ITA	35	NGM Forward Racing	Suter	0	DNF
	Ricard Cardus	SPA	88	QMMF Racing Team	Moriwaki	0	DNF

Fastest lap: Andrea Iannone, on lap 21, 1m 52.307s, 95.627mph/153.896km/h (record).
Previous lap record: Julian Simon, SPA (Suter), 1m 53.653s, 94.494mph/152.073km/h (2010).
Event best maximum speed: Thomas Luthi, 162.100mph/260.900km/h (qualifying practice).

Qualifying: Dry
Air: 21° Humidity: 55% Ground: 28°

1	Marquez	1m 52.067s
2	Luthi	1m 52.260s
3	Iannone	1m 52.423s
4	Smith	1m 52.645s
5	Takahashi	1m 52.694s
6	Corsi	1m 52.696s
7	De Angelis	1m 52.763s
8	Bradl	1m 52.789s
9	Aegerter	1m 52.799s
10	Pasini	1m 52.853s
11	Torres	1m 52.949s
12	Kallio	1m 53.082s
13	A. Espargaro	1m 53.135s
14	Pirro	1m 53.172s
15	Redding	1m 53.201s
16	Simeon	1m 53.210s
17	Rabat	1m 53.274s
18	Nakagami	1m 53.291s
19	Sofuoglu	1m 53.376s
20	De Rosa	1m 53.430s
21	P. Espargaro	1m 53.532s
22	Cardus	1m 53.638s
23	West	1m 53.715s
24	Pons	1m 53.755s
25	Di Meglio	1m 53.779s
26	Wilairot	1m 53.818s
27	Cluzel	1m 53.820s
28	Y. Hernandez	1m 53.966s
29	Neukirchner	1m 53.969s
30	Noyes	1m 54.161s
31	Debise	1m 54.341s
32	S. Hernandez	1m 54.375s
33	Koyama	1m 54.441s
34	Olive	1m 54.740s
35	Al Naimi	1m 54.744s
36	Pietri	1m 54.911s
37	Gadea	1m 55.558s
38	Krummenacher	No Time

Fastest race laps

1	Iannone	1m 52.307s
2	Marquez	1m 52.385s
3	Corsi	1m 52.415s
4	Bradl	1m 52.621s
5	Luthi	1m 52.642s
6	De Angelis	1m 52.749s
7	Takahashi	1m 52.793s
8	Kallio	1m 52.832s
9	Rabat	1m 52.909s
10	Smith	1m 52.918s
11	Aegerter	1m 52.959s
12	West	1m 53.040s
13	Simeon	1m 53.046s
14	P. Espargaro	1m 53.263s
15	Sofuoglu	1m 53.368s
16	Pasini	1m 53.423s
17	Pirro	1m 53.466s
18	Noyes	1m 53.777s
19	Pons	1m 53.789s
20	Neukirchner	1m 53.793s
21	Y. Hernandez	1m 53.892s
22	Redding	1m 53.916s
23	Cluzel	1m 53.933s
24	A. Espargaro	1m 53.960s
25	Di Meglio	1m 53.968s
26	Debise	1m 54.092s
27	Krummenacher	1m 54.189s
28	Pietri	1m 54.243s
29	Olive	1m 54.314s
30	Wilairot	1m 54.431s
31	S. Hernandez	1m 54.518s
32	Koyama	1m 55.314s
33	Al Naimi	1m 55.795s

Championship Points

1	Marquez	235
2	Bradl	234
3	Iannone	157
4	De Angelis	132
5	Corsi	126
6	Smith	121
7	Luthi	121
8	Rabat	74
9	Takahashi	71
10	A. Espargaro	65
11	Aegerter	63
12	Simon	62
13	Krummenacher	52
14	Pirro	48
15	Redding	48
16	P. Espargaro	46
17	Sofuoglu	45
18	Cluzel	35
19	Neukirchner	35
20	Y. Hernandez	33
21	Kallio	31
22	Pasini	28
23	West	27
24	Baldolini	18
25	Simeon	14
26	Di Meglio	12
27	Coghlan	11
28	Corti	9
29	Wilairot	4
30	Cardus	2
31	Pons	1

Constructor Points

1	Suter	323
2	Kalex	241
3	FTR	161
4	Motobi	132
5	Tech 3	131
6	Moriwaki	98
7	Pons Kalex	66
8	MZ-RE Honda	48

125cc

RACE DISTANCE: 20 laps, 59.664 miles/96.020km · RACE WEATHER: Dry (air 17°C, humidity 73%, track 25°C)

Pos.	Rider	Nat.	No.	Entrant	Machine	Laps	Time & Speed
1	**Johann Zarco**	FRA	5	Avant-AirAsia-Ajo	Derbi	20	39m 49.968s 89.871mph/ 144.634km/h
2	**Nicolas Terol**	SPA	18	Bankia Aspar Team 125cc	Aprilia	20	39m 55.868s
3	**Hector Faubel**	SPA	55	Bankia Aspar Team 125cc	Aprilia	20	40m 03.573s
4	**Maverick Vinales**	SPA	25	Blusens by Paris Hilton Racing	Aprilia	20	40m 06.159s
5	**Sandro Cortese**	GER	11	Intact-Racing Team Germany	Aprilia	20	40m 13.390s
6	**Jonas Folger**	GER	94	Red Bull Ajo MotorSport	Aprilia	20	40m 13.629s
7	**Alberto Moncayo**	SPA	23	Andalucia Banca Civica	Aprilia	20	40m 14.002s
8	**Adrian Martin**	SPA	26	Bankia Aspar Team 125cc	Aprilia	20	40m 14.139s
9	**Danny Kent**	GBR	52	Red Bull Ajo MotorSport	Aprilia	20	40m 39.086s
10	**Alessandro Tonucci**	ITA	19	Team Italia FMI	Aprilia	20	40m 41.361s
11	**Jakub Kornfeil**	CZE	84	Ongetta-Centro Seta	Aprilia	20	40m 41.861s
12	**Marcel Schrotter**	GER	77	Mahindra Racing	Mahindra	20	40m 51.011s
13	**Jasper Iwema**	NED	53	Ongetta-Abbink Metaal	Aprilia	20	40m 54.889s
14	**Harry Stafford**	GBR	21	Ongetta-Centro Seta	Aprilia	20	40m 55.574s
15	**Zulfahmi Khairuddin**	MAL	63	Airasia-Sic-Ajo	Derbi	20	40m 56.213s
16	Jack Miller	AUS	8	Caretta Technology	KTM	20	40m 57.621s
17	Hikari Ookubo	JPN	82	18 Garage Racing Team	Honda	20	40m 57.738s
18	Sturla Fagerhaug	NOR	50	WTR-Ten10 Racing	Aprilia	20	41m 01.020s
19	Giulian Pedone	SWI	30	Phonica Racing	Aprilia	20	41m 05.922s
20	Brad Binder	RSA	14	Andalucia Banca Civica	Aprilia	20	41m 06.195s
21	Syunya Mori	JPN	65	Phonica Racing	Aprilia	20	41m 06.697s
22	Joan Perello	SPA	36	Matteoni Racing	Aprilia	20	41m 07.482s
23	Luis Salom	SPA	39	RW Racing GP	Aprilia	20	41m 30.586s
24	Takehiro Yamamoto	JPN	79	Team Nobby	Honda	20	41m 31.804s
25	Luca Fabrizio	ITA	89	WTR-Ten10 Racing	Aprilia	19	39m 59.785s
	Taylor Mackenzie	GBR	17	Phonica Racing	Aprilia	17	DNF
	Alexis Masbou	FRA	10	Caretta Technology	KTM	13	DNF
	Hyuga Watanabe	JPN	81	Project u 7C Harc	Honda	10	DNF
	Danny Webb	GBR	99	Mahindra Racing	Mahindra	9	DNF
	Efren Vazquez	SPA	7	Avant-AirAsia-Ajo	Derbi	8	DNF
	Niklas Ajo	FIN	31	TT Motion Events Racing	Aprilia	1	DNF
	Luigi Morciano	ITA	3	Team Italia FMI	Aprilia	1	DNF
	Josep Rodriguez	SPA	28	Blusens by Paris Hilton Racing	Aprilia	1	DNF

Fastest lap: Johann Zarco, on lap 9, 1m 58.508s, 90.623mph/145.843km/h.
Lap record: Mika Kallio, FIN (KTM), 1m 57.666s, 91.271mph/146.886km/h (2006).
Event best maximum speed: Nicolas Terol, 137.800mph/221.800km/h (free practice 3).

Qualifying: Dry
Air: 22° Humidity: 50% Ground: 31°

1	Zarco	1m 57.888s
2	Faubel	1m 58.130s
3	Terol	1m 58.248s
4	Vinales	1m 58.458s
5	Moncayo	1m 58.937s
6	Vazquez	1m 59.002s
7	Cortese	1m 59.178s
8	Folger	1m 59.210s
9	Martin	1m 59.418s
10	Tonucci	1m 59.917s
11	Morciano	1m 59.977s
12	Salom	1m 59.978s
13	Kornfeil	2m 00.143s
14	Rodriguez	2m 00.164s
15	Iwema	2m 00.367s
16	Schrotter	2m 00.413s
17	Rossi	2m 00.510s
18	Kent	2m 00.514s
19	Webb	2m 00.781s
20	Pedone	2m 00.939s
21	Masbou	2m 01.003s
22	Ajo	2m 01.149s
23	Khairuddin	2m 01.234s
24	Stafford	2m 01.286s
25	Ookubo	2m 01.422s
26	Miller	2m 01.442s
27	Binder	2m 01.682s
28	Mackenzie	2m 01.914s
29	Perello	2m 01.939s
30	Fagerhaug	2m 02.141s
31	Watanabe	2m 02.234s
32	Mori	2m 02.247s
33	Yamamoto	2m 04.122s
34	Ohnishi	2m 04.551s
35	Fabrizio	2m 05.631s

Fastest race laps

1	Zarco	1m 58.508s
2	Faubel	1m 58.806s
3	Terol	1m 58.814s
4	Vinales	1m 59.062s
5	Folger	1m 59.629s
6	Cortese	1m 59.692s
7	Moncayo	1m 59.741s
8	Martin	1m 59.753s
9	Vazquez	1m 59.762s
10	Kornfeil	2m 00.204s
11	Kent	2m 00.606s
12	Tonucci	2m 00.755s
13	Salom	2m 00.939s
14	Webb	2m 01.088s
15	Khairuddin	2m 01.123s
16	Schrotter	2m 01.227s
17	Miller	2m 01.366s
18	Iwema	2m 01.441s
19	Stafford	2m 01.461s
20	Ookubo	2m 01.468s
21	Fagerhaug	2m 01.554s
22	Binder	2m 01.633s
23	Masbou	2m 01.646s
24	Mori	2m 01.937s
25	Perello	2m 01.961s
26	Pedone	2m 02.026s
27	Mackenzie	2m 02.098s
28	Yamamoto	2m 03.054s
29	Watanabe	2m 03.401s
30	Fabrizio	2m 04.345s
31	Ajo	2m 12.079s
32	Morciano	2m 12.434s
33	Rodriguez	3m 05.335s

Championship Points

1	Terol	261
2	Zarco	230
3	Vinales	190
4	Cortese	180
5	Folger	140
6	Faubel	139
7	Vazquez	129
8	Gadea	103
9	Salom	87
10	Kent	76
11	Moncayo	66
12	Kornfeil	61
13	Martin	45
14	Oliveira	44
15	Grotzkyj	32
16	Schrotter	27
17	Khairuddin	21
18	Rossi	18
19	Iwema	16
20	Mackenzie	15
21	Webb	15
22	Morciano	12
23	Masbou	12
24	Ajo	11
25	Ono	8
26	Tonucci	8
27	Stafford	5
28	Finsterbusch	4
29	Popov	3
30	McPhee	1
31	Rodriguez	1

Constructor Points

1	Aprilia	345
2	Derbi	239
3	Mahindra	36
4	KTM	23

AUSTRALIAN GRAND PRIX

PHILLIP ISLAND CIRCUIT

Main photo: Stoner put on a masterful display in front of his home crowd.

Inset: Birthday boy Stoner celebrates his championship with his family.

Photos: Gold & Goose

Above: Jorge Lorenzo's championship challenge was ended with his nasty hand injury.

Clockwise, from top right: The mighty fallen? Rossi pushed the envelope too far in his attempt to compensate for the Ducati's shortcomings; Suzuki's Paul Denning congratulates Alvaro Bautista on a great qualifying performance; Randy de Puniet posted a season-best sixth place for Pramac; Kung Fu Fighter? Damion Cudlin, stand-in for Mapfre's Barbera was sidelined after this crash.

Photos: Gold & Goose

EVERYTHING was as usual at Phillip Island – beautiful track, bitter weather and a highly partisan 43,800-strong race-day crowd rewarded with a fifth win in a row for Stoner plus another Australian world championship. On his 26th birthday, things couldn't have gone more right for him; he also secured Honda's 18th top-class constructors' title.

Yet it was here that things seemed to start unravelling, in a season that still had much in store, and not much of it very good.

With a best average of 180.598km/h (Stoner, of course), Phillip Island is the fastest track on the calendar, so it is not surprising that when accidents happen, they can hurt. There were several that did. One of these – a race-morning highside on the fast exit on to the front straight – accounted for Jorge Lorenzo. He suffered a grisly injury to the tip of the third finger on his left hand, and was out for this race and the next. This quite defused any lingering tension about the championship: all Stoner needed to do now was finish sixth.

It also caused the factory Yamaha team to shut up shop, for they soon afterwards lost the services of Spies. The American had crashed heavily on the fast third turn after hitting a bump and getting pushed off line early in qualifying. That was at 270km/h; he was not going much slower when he decided against trying to save the crash with the barrier so close, and baled out for a punishing head-over-heels through the gravel. He'd gone out later in that session, but had awoken next day feeling woozy and concussed. After attempting warm-up, he withdrew from the race.

Damian Cudlin was also *hors de combat*, after sustaining a severe laceration across his hip when he crashed on Saturday morning. The Australian was back for a second Ducati go in different colours, this time on the Aspar bike in place of Barbera, still recovering from his Motegi injury.

That left only 14 starters and, after an eventful race in typically challenging conditions, only ten finishers.

Thus something of a flurry of belated action among would-be CRT teams for 2012 was particularly welcome. The catalyst was the announcement during the break by Jorge 'Aspar' Martinez – that he had failed to find the backing he needed for the (reputedly higher) lease price of a factory Ducati and

had abandoned the notion in favour of the cheaper option of running not one, but two CRT bikes. With the Edwards/ Forward Racing Suter BMW in place, interest from Laglisse in running another BMW, two entries from BQR (soon to start track testing a Kawasaki), Gresini planning a Honda-powered entry, Speed Master and Ioda still on the list, and Paul Bird Racing putting together a new plan, fuller grids became a less distant prospect.

Another stumble for Rossi and Ducati followed a tough couple of weeks for his team-mate. Hayden had been home from Japan less than 24 hours before he had to leave again, called in to substitute for Rossi at another pre-planned GP12 (1000cc) test day at Jerez. An undiagnosed fracture from Rossi's Motegi misadventure had shown up on X-rays when he got home. It was Hayden's first go on the aluminium chassis that his team-mate had been racing since Aragón, and he dutifully recorded it as "a good step".

Rossi was not so sure. This is a favourite track, where he has won five times in a row, and never finished off the rostrum. But with no excuses, he could qualify no better than 13th, fourth out of five Ducatis. For the first time, there was a note of despair in his comments, as he admitted that in spite of all the work and changes, no progress had been made. "Maybe we don't modify the right things. A year has already passed, and Ducati has worked hard from many points of view, but the problem has remained the same. Probably we haven't understood what it is."

This was followed by a typically feisty race ended by a second successive race crash, when his hopes of exceeding the bike's limits in tricky half-damp conditions all came tumbling down.

Of all the many crashes in the weekend, one in particular had a nasty taste. And marked another unexpected change of balance in the increasingly tense Moto2 battle. It was at the end of Saturday morning's third free practice. Marquez had tumbled early on and spent most of the time in the pits, finally rolling out just before the end. He completed his out-lap only to find the chequered flag, but anxious for some more fast work, he sped on. As he came steaming around the Southern Loop, he was confronted by riders slowing to do a practice start. Unsighted, he ran straight into the back

of Ratthapark Wilairot, and both went flying.

In retrospect, it was foolish and immature, and he was punished with a minute's penalty to his qualifying time, plus a stitch over his left eye and a bruise under it; while his team had a massive job to assemble another 2012 Suter chassis for his bid from the back row. Wilairot paid a greater price: comprehensively battered, although mercifully without fractures and out for the next two races at least. Rear-end collisions have caused more deaths and serious injuries than any other sort of accident, and a frisson of fear had run through the paddock as TV images showed the heavy impact.

Riders who had been looking forward to the return to a great track faced some disappointment, mostly because it had gained a lot of bumps, prompting Stoner to remark, "I don't know what they've been racing here." The best the organisers could offer was a promise that it would be resurfaced in 2013, and there were more problems to come, when both ends of the event's uniquely large range of support races added a veneer of oil to long stretches, and not just once. A BMW Superbike was one culprit, and at least one classic racer, prompting rumblings in MotoGP circles that questioned the wisdom of mixing vintage and GP racing on the same weekend.

MOTOGP RACE – 27 laps

Stoner was lord of all he surveyed at his scenic seaside home track, bumps and all, and claimed pole by almost half a second from Lorenzo. Up alongside, back on the front row for the first time in seven races, Simoncelli was in exuberant form. He had denied Bautista his first-ever front row, but fourth was still best yet for the blue bike, and at a track where previously it had struggled. Dovizioso was next, then Hayden (still the lap record holder, even after this race), equalling his best of the season and almost 1.2 seconds faster than team-mate Rossi.

Spies, impressively, had come back out after his crash to claim seventh, ahead of Pedrosa, but didn't make the start line. Nor of course did Lorenzo, putting everyone one slot forward. Thus Bautista and the 800 Suzuki made the front row after all.

There was drama at the back of the grid when Crutchlow stalled. The bikes were held as a shove-and-bump attempt failed before mechanics came out with the starter ramp.

Stoner's idea of a top six finish was clear right away as he took the lead into the first corner, with Hayden bursting up into second from row two, then Simoncelli, Dovizioso, Bautista and Pedrosa. And in seventh? Rossi, with a flyer.

Simoncelli was ahead of Hayden next time around, but was no more capable of catching the flying Stoner. He rapidly built up a cushion, better than five seconds after seven laps. But on a freezing and only intermittently sunny day that had already seen several squalls, the weather was threatening.

On lap eight, spots of rain fell here and there. The 'wet race' flags came out and there was a cacophony in the pit lane as second bikes were warmed and readied. But though it became wet enough to cause serious worries and to contribute to Rossi's crash, the worst of the rain held off until the final four laps.

And it was real rain, wet enough to trigger a number of crashes, but too late to change bikes. Stoner, leading and thus the first to run into the wet, had a major moment, but managed to stay on. "I was the one having to test all the conditions. It wasn't the way I wanted to do this race." He slowed considerably, and a six-second lead on lap 24 had shrunk to 2.2 seconds at the end. But it was enough, perfectly judged, for his fifth home win in a row – every race in the 800cc era. It was important for another reason. He was world champion. "I don't think too many more things could happen today," he said.

Simoncelli had outdistanced a fierce orange-on-orange battle between uneasy team-mates Dovizioso and Pedrosa.

Above: Marco Simoncelli and Andrea Dovizioso were once again locked in combat.

Top centre right: Wrong choice. Adrian Martin gambled for wets at the start of the 125cc and led inially before being swallowed by the field.

Above right: A patched up Marquez was lucky to escape serious injury in practice.

Top far right: Alex de Angelis won a tense battle with Stefan Bradl to take the Moto 2 honours.

Right: The Mahindras of Danny Webb and Marcel Schrotter in convoy on their way to 10th and 11th places.

Bottom right: German rider Sandro Cortese mastered the conditions for a convincing 125cc win.

Photos: Gold & Goose

The San Carlo rider seemed to have it in the bag when the rain came, until a heart-stopping slide at the fast first corner.

By the time he'd gathered his wits, Dovi was on him again, and ahead as they started the last lap. Typically, Simoncelli was not for giving up. "I thought, 'I stayed ahead all race. I can't lose now.'" He seized his moment with a hard, but fair pass into MG Corner at the end of the lap, and held it over the line.

Pedrosa had fought back after Dovi had passed him, but by the end had settled for a safe fourth.

The muddle behind started on lap 14, shortly after Rossi fell. With the track on the edge of being wet, he fancied his chances, as at Jerez. He passed Hayden and Bautista in the same lap for fifth. The last pass was into MG, and it asked too much of the tyres. Rossi was down and out.

By the time the rain came on lap 24, Bautista had escaped from Hayden, only to be the first to crash as he came over the Lukey Heights, where the track was suddenly properly wet.

Hayden and Capirossi both pitted to change bikes – the field so spaced by then and whittled down by crashes that the American only lost two places – but he did hand fifth to Edwards, soldiering on with his slicks.

De Puniet in sixth was sole survivor of a fierce four-bike battle that lasted most of the race. Crutchlow and Aoyama also hit the wet and crashed together, as did Abraham a little further on, after playing a prominent role.

So Hayden claimed a distant seventh, ahead of the slow-coaches: Elias and Capirossi one lap down. Abraham secured tenth and six points after remounting, two laps adrift.

MOTO2 RACE – 25 laps

It was cold and bright for Moto2, a race that would see Marquez bounce back impressively from his penalty, while Bradl (who had also crashed at speed in practice) was not quite able to take the fullest advantage.

Qualifying was extraordinary: the track dried only in the last five minutes, and pole position was handed from one rider to the next as everyone went out and got quicker and quicker. At one point, Bradl was fastest, but as first one then another completed their laps on the fast-drying track, he was rapidly shuffled down to seventh, albeit barely three-tenths slower.

Pole changed hands five times *after* the flag had fallen.

De Angelis was the winner, from di Meglio (by far his best grid position) and Takahashi. Row two comprised Redding, Sofuoglu and Espargaro; then came Smith, Bradl and Luthi. Marquez had set a time good enough for 13th, but it hardly mattered: adding a minute put him right at the back.

Though the sun was out, it took Bradl a couple of laps to be confident in the conditions. In the meantime, Redding had seized the lead, disputed vigorously by Pol Espargaro. Bradl finished the first lap seventh; Marquez was already up to 16th.

Redding and Pol Espargaro disputed the lead over the first four laps, the Spaniard leading over the line once before running wide. Bradl had now come through to second, de Angelis with him. The German took the lead on lap five. Marquez was now up to tenth.

Bradl and de Angelis at once started to inch away from a nine-strong pack fighting over third. Marquez was part of it, riding right on the edge, but gaining positions with merciless efficiency. Smith was also well placed, and up to fourth on lap eight, only to slip off at low speed after running off; he rejoined 28th and charged back to an eventual 18th.

On lap 11, de Angelis took over, but Bradl came straight back and tried to escape. To no avail. "He had a good pace, so I stayed with him. I knew victory would be decided on the last lap," said de Angelis.

So it was. De Angelis swept past into turn one; Bradl came out stronger and was trying to nose inside into the next bend, but he was too far back. Instead he tagged de Angelis' back wheel and only narrowly avoided crashing.

Marquez had to spend time shaking off Pol Espargaro around half-distance, and when he got clear he still had an inspired Corti's Suter better than a second ahead. He caught him easily, but Corti battled all the way to the line. Marquez saved third by a tenth: "My rear tyre was completely finished … maybe I pushed too much," he said.

Espargaro won the battle for fifth, still five-strong, from Sofuoglu , Redding, Iannone and di Meglio. Takahashi managed to stay clear of Luthi; Aegerter was alone in 12th, then a gang disputed the last points, Aleix Espargaro just ahead of Pirro and Corsi, who took the last point by inches from Kallio and Cardus: 15th to 17th covered by four-hundredths of a second.

West was a victim at home, taken out on only the second corner by crashing rookie Torres. MZ team-mate Neukirchner was another victim, running off and falling at turn one after a very rough overtake by Marquez. Pasini, Cluzel, Rabat, Simeon and wild-card Kris McLaren also crashed out.

125cc RACE – 20 laps

Zarco claimed a second successive pole, with Cortese and Folger next. Terol was fourth, from Faubel. He needed to at least keep Zarco in sight to protect his 31-point advantage.

The 125s got the worst of the squally weather, with a drencher hitting the start. A 15-minute delay meant frantic debates about tyre choice. The race started on a wet track, but under clear skies.

Only Martin pitted for wet tyres, accepting a consequent back-of-the-grid start, and for a while he looked brilliant. After two laps, he had a lead of better than five seconds over Cortese, who was stretching away from briefly inspired KTM rider Masbou.

But the track was drying fast, and on lap six Cortese caught and passed the now rapidly fading Martin, who would pit later for another tyre change.

Cortese cleared off unchallenged for a second win of the year. "With the rain at the beginning … okay, I had to risk a little bit," he admitted.

Masbou dropped behind what would be a three-bike battle for the next few laps, with Zarco heading Salom and Faubel, who would soon start fading, replaced by Vazquez.

Luckily, Zarco had repassed Vazquez at the crucial moment; unluckily, he would be denied an end-of-race attack on Salom for second – after 21 of 23 scheduled laps, the rain returned and the race was red-flagged.

Terol, ultra-cautious at first, was 16th on lap four. As conditions improved, he got going and was through to sixth, still five seconds down on Moncayo, but ahead of obliging team-mate Faubel.

Vinales started slowly in 21st on lap one, but was through to eighth at the finish, taking Rossi with him past Mahindra pair Webb and Schrotter on the final lap. Tenth and 11th were the best yet for the Indian team.

Folger did not start after losing his engine in morning warm-up.

OFFICIAL TIMEKEEPER

PHILLIP ISLAND
27 laps
Length: 4.448 km / 2.764 miles
Width: 13m

Key
96/60 kph/mph
Gear

Southern Loop 105/65
Gardner Straight 313/195
Doohan 130/81
Swan Corner 135/84
Honda Hairpin 55/34
MG 72/45
Turn 3 255/158
Turn 11 129/80
Siberia 90/56
Turn 8 145/90
Turn 7 160/99
Lukey Hieghts 120/75

MotoGP · RACE DISTANCE: 27 laps, 74.624 miles/120.096km · RACE WEATHER: Dry/wet (air 14°C, humidity 72%, track 26°C)

Pos.	Rider	Nat.	No.	Entrant	Machine	Tyres	Laps	Time & speed
1	**Casey Stoner**	AUS	27	Repsol Honda Team	Honda	B	27	42m 02.425s
								106.503mph/
								171.400km/h
2	**Marco Simoncelli**	ITA	58	San Carlo Honda Gresini	Honda	B	27	42m 04.635s
3	**Andrea Dovizioso**	ITA	4	Repsol Honda Team	Honda	B	27	42m 04.879s
4	**Dani Pedrosa**	SPA	26	Repsol Honda Team	Honda	B	27	42m 15.585s
5	**Colin Edwards**	USA	5	Monster Yamaha Tech 3	Yamaha	B	27	42m 33.311s
6	**Randy de Puniet**	FRA	14	Pramac Racing Team	Ducati	B	27	42m 51.225s
7	**Nicky Hayden**	USA	69	Ducati Team	Ducati	B	27	43m 18.739s
8	**Toni Elias**	SPA	24	LCR Honda MotoGP	Honda	B	26	42m 05.177s
9	**Loris Capirossi**	ITA	65	Pramac Racing Team	Ducati	B	26	42m 09.187s
10	**Karel Abraham**	CZE	17	Cardion AB Motoracing	Ducati	B	25	42m 45.142s
	Alvaro Bautista	SPA	19	Rizla Suzuki MotoGP	Suzuki	B	23	DNF
	Hiroshi Aoyama	JPN	7	San Carlo Honda Gresini	Honda	B	23	DNF
	Cal Crutchlow	GBR	35	Monster Yamaha Tech 3	Yamaha	B	23	DNF
	Valentino Rossi	ITA	46	Ducati Team	Ducati	B	13	DNF
	Jorge Lorenzo	SPA	1	Yamaha Factory Racing	Yamaha	B	0	DNS
	Ben Spies	USA	11	Yamaha Factory Racing	Yamaha	B	0	DNS
	Damian Cudlin	AUS	6	Mapfre Aspar Team MotoGP	Ducati	B	0	DNS

Fastest lap: Casey Stoner, on lap 3, 1m 30.629s, 109.787mph/176.685km/h.

Lap record: Nicky Hayden, USA (Honda), 1m 30.059s, 110.482mph/177.803km/h (2008).

Event best maximum speed: Loris Capirossi, 202.500mph/325.900km/h (free practice 1).

Qualifying
Weather: Dry
Air Temp: 17° Humidity: 69%
Track Temp: 33°

1	Stoner	1m 29.975s
2	Lorenzo	1m 30.448s
3	Simoncelli	1m 30.599s
4	Bautista	1m 30.714s
5	Dovizioso	1m 30.780s
6	Hayden	1m 30.792s
7	Spies	1m 30.835s
8	Pedrosa	1m 30.871s
9	Edwards	1m 31.237s
10	Capirossi	1m 31.583s
11	De Puniet	1m 31.635s
12	Aoyama	1m 31.889s
13	Rossi	1m 31.980s
14	Crutchlow	1m 32.023s
15	Abraham	1m 32.054s
16	Elias	1m 32.503s

Outside 107%

17	Cudlin	1m 36.666s

Fastest race laps
1	Stoner	1m 30.629s
2	Pedrosa	1m 31.486s
3	Dovizioso	1m 31.501s
4	Simoncelli	1m 31.519s
5	Bautista	1m 31.619s
6	Hayden	1m 31.652s
7	Rossi	1m 31.965s
8	Edwards	1m 32.153s
9	De Puniet	1m 32.243s
10	Capirossi	1m 32.695s
11	Abraham	1m 32.866s
12	Crutchlow	1m 32.901s
13	Aoyama	1m 32.916s
14	Elias	1m 33.189s

Championship Points
1	Stoner	325
2	Lorenzo	260
3	Dovizioso	212
4	Pedrosa	208
5	Spies	156
6	Simoncelli	139
7	Rossi	139
8	Hayden	132
9	Edwards	109
10	Aoyama	94
11	Barbera	77
12	Bautista	67
13	Crutchlow	57
14	Abraham	56
15	Elias	55
16	De Puniet	49
17	Capirossi	36
18	Akiyoshi	7
19	Hopkins	6
20	Ito	3

Grid order	1	2	3	4	5	6	7	8	9	10	11	12	13	14	15	16	17	18	19	20	21	22	23	24	25	26	27	
27 STONER	27	27	27	27	27	27	27	27	27	27	27	27	27	27	27	27	27	27	27	27	27	27	27	27	27	27	27	1
58 SIMONCELLI	69	58	58	58	58	58	58	58	58	58	58	58	58	58	58	58	58	58	58	58	58	58	58	58	4	4	58	2
19 BAUTISTA	58	69	4	4	4	4	4	4	4	4	4	4	26	26	26	26	26	26	26	26	4	4	4	58	58	4		3
4 DOVIZIOSO	4	4	69	26	26	26	26	26	26	26	26	26	4	4	4	4	4	4	4	4	26	26	26	26	26	26		4
69 HAYDEN	19	19	19	69	69	69	69	69	69	69	19	19	19	19	19	19	19	19	19	19	19	19	19	5	5	5	5	5
26 PEDROSA	26	26	26	19	19	19	19	19	19	19	69	69	69	69	69	69	69	69	69	69	69	69	69	14	14	14	14	6
5 EDWARDS	46	46	46	46	46	46	46	46	46	46	46	46	46	5	5	5	5	5	5	5	5	5	5	69	69	69	69	7
65 CAPIROSSI	5	5	5	5	5	5	5	5	5	5	5	5	5	14	14	14	17	17	17	7	7	7	7	65	24	24		8
14 DE PUNIET	65	14	14	14	14	14	14	14	14	14	14	14	14	17	17	17	35	35	7	35	17	35	35	24	65	65		9
7 AOYAMA	14	65	17	17	17	17	17	7	7	7	7	17	17	7	35	35	7	7	35	17	35	17	14	14	17	17		10
46 ROSSI	17	17	65	65	35	35	35	17	17	17	17	7	7	35	7	7	14	14	14	14	14	17	65					
35 CRUTCHLOW	35	35	35	35	65	7	7	35	65	65	35	35	35	65	65	65	65	65	65	65	65	24						
17 ABRAHAM	7	7	7	7	7	65	65	65	35	35	65	65	65	24	24	24	24	24	24	24	24	17						
24 ELIAS	24	24	24	24	24	24	24	24	24	24	24	24	24															

69/65 Pit stop   17 Lapped rider

Team Points
1	Repsol Honda Team	492
2	Yamaha Factory Racing	416
3	Ducati Team	271
4	San Carlo Honda Gresini	228
5	Monster Yamaha Tech 3	166
6	Pramac Racing Team	85
7	Mapfre Aspar Team MotoGP	77
8	Rizla Suzuki MotoGP	73
9	Cardion AB Motoracing	56
10	LCR Honda MotoGP	55

Constructor Points
1	Honda	380
2	Yamaha	305
3	Ducati	172
4	Suzuki	73

Moto2 — RACE DISTANCE: 25 laps, 69.096 miles/111.200km · RACE WEATHER: Dry (air 16°C, humidity 54%, track 32°C)

Pos.	Rider	Nat.	No.	Entrant	Machine	Laps	Time & Speed
1	**Alex de Angelis**	RSM	15	JIR Moto2	Motobi	25	39m 44.774s 104.306mph/ 167.864km/h
2	**Stefan Bradl**	GER	65	Viessmann Kiefer Racing	Kalex	25	39m 46.132s
3	**Marc Marquez**	SPA	93	Team CatalunyaCaixa Repsol	Suter	25	39m 51.136s
4	**Claudio Corti**	ITA	71	Italtrans Racing Team	Suter	25	39m 51.249s
5	**Pol Espargaro**	SPA	44	HP Tuenti Speed Up	FTR	25	39m 59.589s
6	**Kenan Sofuoglu**	TUR	54	Technomag-CIP	Suter	25	39m 59.929s
7	**Scott Redding**	GBR	45	Marc VDS Racing Team	Suter	25	40m 00.035s
8	**Andrea Iannone**	ITA	29	Speed Master	Suter	25	40m 00.821s
9	**Mike di Meglio**	FRA	63	Tech 3 Racing	Tech 3	25	40m 01.105s
10	**Yuki Takahashi**	JPN	72	Gresini Racing Moto2	Moriwaki	25	40m 05.111s
11	**Thomas Luthi**	SWI	12	Interwetten Paddock Moto2	Suter	25	40m 06.855s
12	**Dominique Aegerter**	SWI	77	Technomag-CIP	Suter	25	40m 11.022s
13	**Aleix Espargaro**	SPA	40	Pons HP 40	Pons Kalex	25	40m 14.069s
14	**Michele Pirro**	ITA	51	Gresini Racing Moto2	Moriwaki	25	40m 14.977s
15	**Simone Corsi**	ITA	3	Ioda Racing Project	FTR	25	40m 15.519s
16	Mika Kallio	FIN	36	Marc VDS Racing Team	Suter	25	40m 15.550s
17	Ricard Cardus	SPA	88	QMMF Racing Team	Moriwaki	25	40m 15.558s
18	Bradley Smith	GBR	38	Tech 3 Racing	Tech 3	25	40m 28.294s
19	Axel Pons	SPA	80	Pons HP 40	Pons Kalex	25	40m 31.838s
20	Raffaele de Rosa	ITA	35	NGM Forward Racing	Suter	25	40m 35.131s
21	Randy Krummenacher	SWI	4	GP Team Switzerland Kiefer Racing	Kalex	25	40m 35.138s
22	Kenny Noyes	USA	9	Avintia-STX	FTR	25	40m 49.521s
23	Joan Olive	SPA	6	Aeroport de Castello	FTR	25	40m 49.681s
24	Yonny Hernandez	COL	68	Blusens-STX	FTR	25	41m 04.508s
25	Ivan Moreno	SPA	20	Mapfre Aspar Team Moto2	Suter	24	39m 49.997s
26	Santiago Hernandez	COL	64	SAG Team	FTR	24	39m 54.371s
27	Blake Leigh-Smith	AUS	56	BRP Racing	FTR	24	39m 56.099s
28	Mashel Al Naimi	QAT	95	QMMF Racing Team	Moriwaki	24	41m 13.556s
	Robertino Pietri	VEN	39	Italtrans Racing Team	Suter	20	DNF
	Valentin Debise	FRA	53	Speed Up	FTR	19	DNF
	Kris McLaren	AUS	43	BRP Racing	Suter	14	DNF
	Xavier Simeon	BEL	19	Tech 3 B	Tech 3	12	DNF
	Jules Cluzel	FRA	16	NGM Forward Racing	Suter	12	DNF
	Max Neukirchner	GER	76	MZ Racing Team	MZ-RE Honda	1	DNF
	Mattia Pasini	ITA	75	Ioda Racing Project	FTR	0	DNF
	Jordi Torres	SPA	18	Mapfre Aspar Team Moto2	Suter	0	DNF
	Esteve Rabat	SPA	34	Blusens-STX	FTR	0	DNF
	Anthony West	AUS	13	MZ Racing Team	MZ-RE Honda	0	DNF

Fastest lap: Alex de Angelis, on lap 6, 1m 34.549s, 105.235mph/169.359km/h (record).
Previous lap record: Andrea Iannone, ITA (Speed Up), 1m 34.771s, 104.989mph/168.963km/h (2010).
Event best maximum speed: Andrea Iannone, 178.600mph/287.500km/h (race).

Qualifying: Dry/wet
Air: 15° Humidity: 78% Ground: 25°

1	De Angelis	1m 34.574s
2	Di Meglio	1m 34.662s
3	Takahashi	1m 34.689s
4	Redding	1m 34.699s
5	Sofuoglu	1m 34.729s
6	P. Espargaro	1m 34.797s
7	Smith	1m 34.867s
8	Bradl	1m 34.902s
9	Luthi	1m 34.958s
10	Pasini	1m 35.092s
11	Neukirchner	1m 35.267s
12	Pirro	1m 35.281s
13	Aegerter	1m 35.399s
14	Torres	1m 35.519s
15	Kallio	1m 35.564s
16	Iannone	1m 35.647s
17	Rabat	1m 35.668s
18	West	1m 35.675s
19	De Rosa	1m 35.700s
20	Corti	1m 35.735s
21	Cluzel	1m 35.830s
22	Corsi	1m 35.912s
23	Simeon	1m 36.354s
24	A. Espargaro	1m 36.366s
25	Pons	1m 36.471s
26	Noyes	1m 36.539s
27	Cardus	1m 36.695s
28	Debise	1m 36.732s
29	Y. Hernandez	1m 37.145s
30	Olive	1m 37.187s
31	Moreno	1m 37.414s
32	McLaren	1m 37.600s
33	Krummenacher	1m 38.227s
34	S. Hernandez	1m 38.827s
35	Leigh-Smith	1m 38.902s
36	Pietri	1m 38.933s
37	Al Naimi	1m 39.658s
38	Marquez	*2m 35.298s

* Received 1-minute time penalty.

Fastest race laps

1	De Angelis	1m 34.549s
2	Corti	1m 34.550s
3	Bradl	1m 34.638s
4	Marquez	1m 34.688s
5	Iannone	1m 34.847s
6	P. Espargaro	1m 34.970s
7	Di Meglio	1m 34.971s
8	Smith	1m 35.053s
9	Sofuoglu	1m 35.069s
10	Luthi	1m 35.118s
11	Redding	1m 35.134s
12	Kallio	1m 35.339s
13	Takahashi	1m 35.365s
14	Aegerter	1m 35.400s
15	Corsi	1m 35.445s
16	Cardus	1m 35.629s
17	Pirro	1m 35.642s
18	A. Espargaro	1m 35.715s
19	Noyes	1m 36.206s
20	Pons	1m 36.361s
21	Simeon	1m 36.578s
22	De Rosa	1m 36.626s
23	Krummenacher	1m 36.627s
24	Olive	1m 36.885s
25	Y. Hernandez	1m 36.888s
26	Debise	1m 37.018s
27	Moreno	1m 37.111s
28	S. Hernandez	1m 37.477s
29	Cluzel	1m 37.734s
30	McLaren	1m 37.946s
31	Leigh-Smith	1m 38.141s
32	Pietri	1m 38.157s
33	Al Naimi	1m 41.066s
34	Neukirchner	1m 44.311s

Championship Points

1	Bradl	254
2	Marquez	251
3	Iannone	165
4	De Angelis	157
5	Corsi	127
6	Luthi	126
7	Smith	121
8	Takahashi	77
9	Rabat	74
10	A. Espargaro	68
11	Aegerter	67
12	Simon	62
13	P. Espargaro	57
14	Redding	57
15	Sofuoglu	55
16	Krummenacher	52
17	Pirro	50
18	Cluzel	35
19	Neukirchner	35
20	Y. Hernandez	33
21	Kallio	31
22	Pasini	28
23	West	27
24	Corti	22
25	Di Meglio	19
26	Baldolini	18
27	Simeon	14
28	Coghlan	11
29	Wilairot	4
30	Cardus	2
31	Pons	1

Constructor Points

1	Suter	339
2	Kalex	261
3	FTR	172
4	Motobi	157
5	Tech 3	138
6	Moriwaki	104
7	Pons Kalex	69
8	MZ-RE Honda	48

125cc — RACE DISTANCE: 20 laps, 55.277 miles/88.960km · RACE WEATHER: Wet/dry (air 14°C, humidity 61%, track 29°C)

Pos.	Rider	Nat.	No.	Entrant	Machine	Laps	Time & Speed
1	**Sandro Cortese**	GER	11	Intact-Racing Team Germany	Aprilia	20	34m 49.670s 95.229mph/ 153.256km/h
2	**Luis Salom**	SPA	39	RW Racing GP	Aprilia	20	35m 03.242s
3	**Johann Zarco**	FRA	5	Avant-AirAsia-Ajo	Derbi	20	35m 03.981s
4	**Efren Vazquez**	SPA	7	Avant-AirAsia-Ajo	Derbi	20	35m 04.596s
5	**Alberto Moncayo**	SPA	23	Andalucia Banca Civica	Aprilia	20	35m 11.998s
6	**Nicolas Terol**	SPA	18	Bankia Aspar Team 125cc	Aprilia	20	35m 16.359s
7	**Hector Faubel**	SPA	55	Bankia Aspar Team 125cc	Aprilia	20	35m 18.557s
8	**Maverick Vinales**	SPA	25	Blusens by Paris Hilton Racing	Aprilia	20	35m 25.305s
9	**Louis Rossi**	FRA	96	Matteoni Racing	Aprilia	20	35m 26.223s
10	**Danny Webb**	GBR	99	Mahindra Racing	Mahindra	20	35m 26.356s
11	**Marcel Schrotter**	GER	77	Mahindra Racing	Mahindra	20	35m 28.278s
12	**Luigi Morciano**	ITA	3	Team Italia FMI	Aprilia	20	35m 31.367s
13	**Jakub Kornfeil**	CZE	84	Ongetta-Centro Seta	Aprilia	20	35m 33.019s
14	**Alexis Masbou**	FRA	10	Caretta Technology	KTM	20	35m 37.566s
15	**Sturla Fagerhaug**	NOR	50	WTR-Ten10 Racing	Aprilia	20	35m 44.829s
16	Alessandro Tonucci	ITA	19	Team Italia FMI	Aprilia	20	35m 46.579s
17	Josep Rodriguez	SPA	28	Blusens by Paris Hilton Racing	Aprilia	20	35m 59.763s
18	Taylor Mackenzie	GBR	17	Phonica Racing	Aprilia	20	35m 59.907s
19	Manuel Tatasciore	ITA	60	Phonica Racing	Aprilia	20	36m 00.472s
20	Zulfahmi Khairuddin	MAL	63	Airasia-Sic-Ajo	Derbi	20	36m 00.514s
21	Brad Binder	RSA	14	Andalucia Banca Civica	Aprilia	20	36m 17.635s
22	Danny Kent	GBR	52	Red Bull Ajo MotorSport	Aprilia	20	36m 27.346s
23	Jack Miller	AUS	8	Caretta Technology	KTM	20	36m 29.985s
24	Marco Colandrea	SWI	40	WTR-Ten10 Racing	Aprilia	19	35m 13.181s
25	Giulian Pedone	SWI	30	Phonica Racing	Aprilia	19	35m 14.440s
26	Joshua Hook	AUS	46	Hook Racing.com	Aprilia	19	35m 38.587s
27	Adrian Martin	SPA	26	Bankia Aspar Team 125cc	Aprilia	19	36m 15.252s
	Niklas Ajo	FIN	31	TT Motion Events Racing	Aprilia	19	DNF
	Joan Perello	SPA	36	Matteoni Racing	Aprilia	12	DNF
	Jasper Iwema	NED	53	Ongetta-Abbink Metaal	Aprilia	9	DNF
	Nicky Diles	AUS	47	Aprilia RSW Racing	Aprilia	6	DNF
	Jonas Folger	GER	94	Red Bull Ajo MotorSport	Aprilia	0	DNS

Fastest lap: Sandro Cortese, on lap 14, 1m 40.276s, 99.225mph/159.687km/h.
Lap record: Alvaro Bautista, SPA (Aprilia), 1m 36.927s, 102.653mph/165.204km/h (2006).
Event best maximum speed: Nicolas Terol, 147.300mph/237.000km/h (free practice 3).

Qualifying: Dry
Air: 17° Humidity: 65% Ground: 33°

1	Zarco	1m 39.207s
2	Cortese	1m 39.558s
3	Folger	1m 39.610s
4	Terol	1m 39.702s
5	Faubel	1m 39.963s
6	Vazquez	1m 40.272s
7	Kent	1m 40.292s
8	Moncayo	1m 40.301s
9	Vinales	1m 40.334s
10	Salom	1m 40.424s
11	Morciano	1m 40.506s
12	Rossi	1m 40.672s
13	Kornfeil	1m 40.705s
14	Martin	1m 40.984s
15	Masbou	1m 41.018s
16	Tonucci	1m 41.066s
17	Ajo	1m 41.325s
18	Stafford	1m 41.380s
19	Webb	1m 41.517s
20	Schrotter	1m 41.543s
21	Rodriguez	1m 41.963s
22	Tatasciore	1m 42.084s
23	Fagerhaug	1m 42.172s
24	Pedone	1m 42.192s
25	Binder	1m 42.218s
26	Iwema	1m 42.304s
27	Khairuddin	1m 42.330s
28	Mackenzie	1m 42.713s
29	Miller	1m 42.833s
30	Perello	1m 44.312s
31	Colandrea	1m 44.618s
32	Diles	1m 45.176s

Outside 107%

33	Phillis	1m 46.200s
34	Hatton	1m 47.583s
35	Hook	No Time
36	Biddle	No Time

Fastest race laps

1	Cortese	1m 40.276s
2	Terol	1m 40.347s
3	Vinales	1m 40.474s
4	Zarco	1m 40.677s
5	Salom	1m 40.748s
6	Vazquez	1m 40.839s
7	Rossi	1m 40.852s
8	Moncayo	1m 40.964s
9	Morciano	1m 41.263s
10	Faubel	1m 41.343s
11	Ajo	1m 41.639s
12	Webb	1m 41.840s
13	Kent	1m 41.853s
14	Schrotter	1m 42.057s
15	Kornfeil	1m 42.067s
16	Tonucci	1m 42.461s
17	Khairuddin	1m 42.598s
18	Martin	1m 42.619s
19	Fagerhaug	1m 42.661s
20	Rodriguez	1m 42.846s
21	Masbou	1m 43.101s
22	Tatasciore	1m 43.172s
23	Mackenzie	1m 43.470s
24	Binder	1m 43.618s
25	Hook	1m 43.896s
26	Perello	1m 44.380s
27	Colandrea	1m 44.580s
28	Pedone	1m 44.862s
29	Iwema	1m 46.315s
30	Miller	1m 46.679s
31	Diles	2m 02.084s

Championship Points

1	Terol	271
2	Zarco	246
3	Cortese	205
4	Vinales	198
5	Faubel	148
6	Vazquez	142
7	Folger	140
8	Salom	107
9	Gadea	103
10	Moncayo	77
11	Kent	76
12	Kornfeil	64
13	Martin	45
14	Oliveira	44
15	Grotzkyj	32
16	Schrotter	32
17	Rossi	25
18	Khairuddin	21
19	Webb	21
20	Iwema	16
21	Morciano	16
22	Mackenzie	15
23	Masbou	14
24	Ajo	11
25	Ono	8
26	Tonucci	8
27	Stafford	5
28	Finsterbusch	4
29	Popov	3
30	Fagerhaug	1
31	McPhee	1
32	Rodriguez	1

Constructor Points

1	Aprilia	370
2	Derbi	255
3	Mahindra	42
4	KTM	25

FIM WORLD CHAMPIONSHIP · ROUND 17
MALAYSIAN GRAND PRIX
SEPANG CIRCUIT

THE Malaysian GP started badly and got worse, culminating in the saddest of Sundays. The opening gaffe came from marshals, who failed to warn Moto2 riders on their first out-lap of the weekend that one corner was drenched. The consequence would injure two riders and take all the steam out of the Moto2 championship. The finish was – well, nobody's fault, really, with consequences much more grave. A quirk of physics dealt MotoGP's rising Young Lion, Marco Simoncelli, the cruellest of blows. The 24-year-old Italian was scooped back across the track by his bike. The freak trajectory took him right under the wheels of Edwards and Rossi. Simoncelli suffered fatal injuries.

In the blackest day in racing that most in the paddock had ever experienced, the MotoGP race was cancelled. The dread atmosphere in the pit lane as everyone awaited news, which when it came seemed inevitable, was not improved by the angry baying of the record crowd of 67,000, many in the grandstands overlooking the pits. They'd been denied a race without having any real explanation of the reason.

Simoncelli's accident was the same kind of chance-in-a-million that had ended the life of Shoya Tomizawa just over a year previously. The kind of accident against which no protection can be offered. In fact, his helmet came off as he was hit by two MotoGP bikes at speed, but it made little difference: the greater cause of death was internal injuries.

The severity of the crash had nothing to do with the rider's often over-exuberant style, though that may have been why he lost control. Another reason may have been that his harder rear tyre had not yet fully warmed – only one other rider, de Puniet, had made the same choice. Bautista's on-board camera showed the Honda's back wheel scribing a black line as it spun and searched for grip, a split second before the bike slid away and Simoncelli slipped off the inside.

So far, it was just a normal crash. Similar to any number, both in his own experience and that of other riders in the course of a racing year. He would either continue to slide away, probably unhurt, or at worst the tyres would catch again and flick him over the high side on a similar outward-bound trajectory. Instead, as with Tomizawa, by some freak of momentum and angle, the tyres gripped, picked the bike up and carried it swerving back across the track, the rider half-trapped underneath.

Edwards and Rossi two places back didn't have a chance of missing him. Simoncelli didn't have a chance at all.

Simoncelli had been the most exciting competitor to appear in MotoGP for a few years: an attacking rider who broke the mould of follow-my-leader 800-class exponents, and he was starting to pose a serious threat to the status quo. Only a week before, he'd fought for a career-best second in Australia, his second rostrum after also claiming two poles. He had recently signed a contract for a factory Honda in 2012. Wins were surely soon to come. Much more than a young life was lost in the catastrophe. A potentially important racing spirit was also snuffed out prematurely.

Rossi somehow had stayed on his bike after the crash. He was desolate and left the track for the airport to catch the first flight home. Simoncelli, he said the next day, had been "like a little brother to me". Edwards had gone tumbling and flailing along with the wreckage, suffering a dislocated shoulder with some small fractures, which were relocated under anaesthetic at the track.

At first, the race was postponed, but while the announcement of cancellation was deferred for 30 minutes, the demeanour of Dorna CEO Ezpeleta as he toured the pits, speaking to riders and team chiefs, meant that it was not unexpected. Soon afterwards came confirmation that attempts to revive Simoncelli – including 45 minutes of CPR – had not been successful. In a numbed state of shock, mechanics started to pack up the freight, while riders and teams all paid tribute to the fallen hero.

After this, the remaining events of the weekend did not seem important.

The Moto2 incident on Saturday resulted in a fine of 15,000 euros for the organisers, because of the complete failure of marshals to flag an isolated, but sodden section of track, at the left-hand turn ten. Jules Cluzel hit it first and then fell; several others managed to avoid the puddle, then Marquez went flying, landing heavily and immobile in

the gravel trap. Even while he was being attended to, Bradley Smith did much the same, also landing hard, but then sliding at speed into Marquez's bike. The Briton was left with a damaged shoulder and coughing up blood, out for the weekend; Marquez had shoulder injuries as well as more bashes to his face. He went out next in qualifying, although probably shouldn't have, but there is no mechanism to stop such action. The next day he voluntarily ruled himself out of the race. Apart from the shoulder, he was suffering from blurred and double vision.

Marquez's absence gave Bradl the opportunity to secure the title with one race to spare. He needed to win, but he failed to do so, by a cruel twist of fate. He was poised in second and planning a last-lap lunge when the red flags came out, cutting the race by two laps and denying him the chance. He would need to race for it again at the final round. For Marquez, the loss of a maiden title was less catastrophic than it might have been: there will be another chance, for earlier in the weekend he had put an end to rumours of a MotoGP move for 2012, announcing that he would stay put. "I'm still learning something every race," he said.

Hopkins was back, but stricken with a hangover from his last wild-card ride at Brno, where serious finger damage had left him requiring surgery to rebuild a knuckle joint. Since the operation, he'd been racing almost every weekend, including losing the British Superbike title by a matter of inches. On top of this, the extra stress of a MotoGP bike, especially the braking, had the effect of dismantling the internal metalwork of the surgery. He awoke on Saturday morning with his finger swollen, immobile and painful. "I could feel the bits of metal moving around in there," he said. Still left hanging, along

with the whole Rizla Suzuki team, awaiting a firm decision on 2012, he was out of the race.

So too was Lorenzo, replaced by somewhat overawed factory tester Katsuyuki Nakasuga. And, once again only after qualifying, Ben Spies. After his battering and concussion at Phillip Island, another fall on Saturday morning left him too much the worse for wear. He qualified 16th, then withdrew later that evening.

It was a race anyone would have preferred to miss.

MOTOGP RACE – Cancelled

Hondas disputed the top slots in free practice, and qualifying meant the front row was a Repsol Honda lockout. All three had headed the time sheets at one stage, and they ended up Pedrosa, Stoner, Dovizioso. It was Dani's second pole of the season.

Yamaha's brightest hope was Edwards, who slotted in to fourth, ahead of Simoncelli and Hayden. Pedrosa fell during qualifying, as did Rossi – on the far end of row three, behind Aoyama and Bautista.

Tyre choice was tricky, and riders tight-lipped. As Pedrosa said, "I am able to go fast with both tyres. Obviously they are different. With the soft, you feel more grip; with the hard, you spin more, but still go quick. So it's not clear." In the event, all but Elias, Aoyama and Bautista chose the harder front, and all except Simoncelli and de Puniet the softer rear, in the marginally cooler conditions.

The sky was brooding and a tropical storm threatening as they lined up.

Stoner, for a second race, managed to beat Pedrosa off

Opening spread: Sepang's saddest Sunday: Marco Simoncelli awaits the start of his last race.

Left: Solemn faces at the formal announcement of the fatality. From left: Xavier Alonzo (Dorna), Franco Uncini (safety delegate), Dr Michele Macchiagodena, Paul Butler (race director) and Claude Danis (FIM).

Below left: A second wild-card ride for Hopkins was a second false start.

Bottom left: Dazed and confused? Ben Spies joined his compatriot on the sidelines.

Below: Rossi's nightmare season was about to take a turn for the worse.

Photos: Gold & Goose

Right: Dorna's Ezpeleta breaks the bad news to Dovizioso and Pedrosa.

Far right: Luthi leads Bradl and the pack on the first lap of the Moto2 race. By the end of the lap, Bradl was ahead.

Below right: Pol Espargaro claimed a second debut-season Moto2 podium with third.

Bottom centre: Vinales (25), Terol (18) and Cortese dispute the lead in the 125 race. Zarco and Faubel shadow them.

Bottom right: Joy unrestrained for Luthi, with his first Moto2 win.

Photos: Gold & Goose

the line into the first corner, with Simoncelli slotting into fourth behind Dovisioso, ahead of fast-starting Bautista and Hayden. By the time they were halfway around, Rossi was eighth behind Edwards, the biggest loser off the line.

Over the first lap, Stoner drew a little clear, while Simoncelli had his hands full with Bautista. The Suzuki passed him on the run to the last hairpin, only to go wide: Simoncelli dived back inside. Bautista passed him again before the first corner of lap two; Simoncelli dived straight back underneath under braking, and though a little slip meant he too ran wide, he was in position to stay ahead into the second, very tight left-hander.

Over the next half-lap, Simoncelli held the Suzuki at bay. He was still narrowly ahead through the left-right flick of turns nine and ten, and as they heeled it into the next right-hander. It was there that he slid out as Bautista and Hayden flashed past, and on the exit where his traitorous Honda suddenly veered back across the track.

As Edwards sat despairingly, looking over at the lifeless and helmetless figure of Simoncelli on the track, and as Rossi regained control on the grass before touring to the pits, broken fairing flapping, the red flags came out, and the race was over.

The last time a race had been cancelled due to a fatality was at Monza in 1973, after Jarno Saarinen and Renzo Pasolini died in a multiple first-lap crash in the 250 event. The subsequent 500 race was also cancelled. There were no parallels between that black day, when riders had been sent out to race even though there was an oil spill on the track, and this one, when all the safety measures in the world were of no consequence.

No parallels, except the tragic fact – a great talent had been lost.

MOTO2 RACE – 17 laps (shortened)

Bradl had regained the points lead a week before: now victory would give him the crown. But he was denied pole position by first-timer Luthi, gaining speed and confidence in the latter half of the year. Pirro was alongside in his best grid position; Takahashi led row two from the Espargaro brothers, Pol the faster. Redding was ninth; Smith and Marquez out.

Bradl took off up front, smooth and determined. Pacing it out, he set a new lap record on the fourth tour. Luthi went with him, and stayed within a second over the early laps as they drew away. From lap 13, he closed right up again. The challenge would come, but when? And how much did Bradl, still riding neatly, have to spare?

The pass came on lap 17 on the back straight and into the crucial final hairpin – and it resolved the race. Though Bradl stayed close and certainly would have made every attempt to win, that chance was denied him by the red flags. "I was a little bit unlucky today," he grimaced.

Third-placed Pol Espargaro had seen off a challenge from older brother Aleix, and in the end another from a storming de Angelis, who had finished lap one 15th.

Another couple of seconds down, Aegerter also battled

through, narrowly heading Kallio, Pirro, Aleix Espargaro and Iannone. Kallio had been with de Angelis, but ran wide on the last lap.

Redding had dropped back from this group, but saved tenth as he outpaced Rabat. Sofuoglu won a race-long dice with Cluzel and di Meglio for 12th. Takahashi and Pasini were among the crashers; so too Corsi and Corti, out together on lap four, after Corsi had caught the front group from tenth on lap one. Both MZs, Neukirchner and West, also crashed out, as did Krummenacher; Hernandez was black-flagged and excluded after pitting to retire, then rejoining the race.

The crash that stopped the race would have echoes later that afternoon, but luckily no such terminal consequences. Axel Pons, the forgotten victim of Sepang, crashed while disputing the final points. It was the son of a 250 champion's second fall of the weekend and the 20th of a crash-strewn year. Unfortunately, it was under the wheels of American Kenny Noyes, who could not avoid running over the Spaniard. Pons was left unconscious on the track and hospitalised with cerebral bleeding, but he was discharged and allowed to go home almost a week later.

The five points Bradl lost cost him the chance of securing the title with one race to spare, but the change in fortunes

remained extraordinary. He would go to the last race with a lead of 23 points. It was not quite over yet.

125cc RACE – 18 laps

The title battle stayed open in the smallest class, too, as Terol faltered in the final laps, dropping to fifth after leading much of the race. With rival Zarco securing third, the Spaniard would have to wait two more weeks.

Terol took a seventh pole of the year, while Zarco had a nightmare, qualifying only 15th on a hastily patched-up bike after crashing in the early stages.

Terol led away first, chased by Cortese, Vinales and Folger. Zarco had an amazing first lap and lay fifth.

Folger dropped away as Faubel joined in, the lead group of five up close for the first ten laps. By now, Vinales had led for three laps, with Cortese in second. On lap 13, Terol took over again and tried to break away.

No way. All four went with him and now he started to make the odd mistake. He blamed fading tyres, and on the last lap, as Cortese took to the front again, he almost crashed and ran on to the grass at the esses.

Vinales was in front after a desperate last lap, Cortese three-tenths down. By then, Zarco was a couple of seconds away and Faubel likewise. Only then did Terol cross the line. He didn't complete the slow-down lap, parking the bike, walking off and collapsing with heat exhaustion, to be revived at the medical centre.

Folger was a lone sixth; a long way back, Malaysian Zulfahmi Khairuddin thrilled home fans by defeating Kornfeil, Moncayo and Kent in a long fight for seventh. It equalled his best-ever result. Vazquez had started the last lap ahead of Folger, but slipped off, remounting to take 11th.

SEPANG INTERNATIONAL CIRCUIT

20 laps
Length: 5.548 km / 3.447 miles
Width: 25m

Key
96/60 kph/mph
Gear

Langkawi curve 90/56
Genting Curve 145/90
Turn 5 155/96
Turn 3 179/112
Hairpin 75/47
Turn 7 124/77
Pangkor Laut Chicane 65/40
KLIA Curve 130/81
Berjaya Tioman Corner 65/40
Sunway Lagoon Corner 90/56
Turn 12 155/96
Kenyir Lake 105/65

MotoGP   Race stopped and then cancelled due to a fatal accident involving Marco Simoncelli on lap 2.

Qualifying

Weather: Dry
Air Temp: 31°   **Humidity:** 61%
Track Temp: 46°

1	Pedrosa	2m 01.462s
2	Stoner	2m 01.491s
3	Dovizioso	2m 01.666s
4	Edwards	2m 02.010s
5	Simoncelli	2m 02.105s
6	Hayden	2m 02.172s
7	Aoyama	2m 02.254s
8	Bautista	2m 02.332s
9	Rossi	2m 02.395s
10	Crutchlow	2m 02.756s
11	De Puniet	2m 02.939s
12	Capirossi	2m 03.077s
13	Abraham	2m 03.438s
14	Barbera	2m 03.619s
15	Elias	2m 03.646s
16	Spies	2m 03.678s
17	Nakasuga	2m 04.072s

Championship Points

As at Round 16

1	Stoner	325
2	Lorenzo	260
3	Dovizioso	212
4	Pedrosa	208
5	Spies	156
6	Simoncelli	139
7	Rossi	139
8	Hayden	132
9	Edwards	109
10	Aoyama	94
11	Barbera	77
12	Bautista	67
13	Crutchlow	57
14	Abraham	56
15	Elias	55
16	De Puniet	49
17	Capirossi	36
18	Akiyoshi	7
19	Hopkins	6
20	Ito	3

Team Points

1	Repsol Honda Team	492
2	Yamaha Factory Racing	416
3	Ducati Team	271
4	San Carlo Honda Gresini	228
5	Monster Yamaha Tech 3	166
6	Pramac Racing Team	85
7	Mapfre Aspar Team MotoGP	77
8	Rizla Suzuki MotoGP	73
9	Cardion AB Motoracing	56
10	LCR Honda MotoGP	55

Constructor Points

1	Honda	380
2	Yamaha	305
3	Ducati	172
4	Suzuki	73

Moto2 — RACE DISTANCE: 17 laps, 58.605 miles/94.316km · RACE WEATHER: Dry (air 34°C, humidity 53%, track 48°C)

Pos.	Rider	Nat.	No.	Entrant	Machine	Laps	Time & Speed
1	**Thomas Luthi**	SWI	12	Interwetten Paddock Moto2	Suter	17	36m 35.114s 96.112mph/ 154.678km/h
2	**Stefan Bradl**	GER	65	Viessmann Kiefer Racing	Kalex	17	36m 35.301s
3	**Pol Espargaro**	SPA	44	HP Tuenti Speed Up	FTR	17	36m 42.579s
4	**Alex de Angelis**	RSM	15	JIR Moto2	Motobi	17	36m 44.241s
5	**Dominique Aegerter**	SWI	77	Technomag-CIP	Suter	17	36m 46.608s
6	**Mika Kallio**	FIN	36	Marc VDS Racing Team	Suter	17	36m 47.017s
7	**Michele Pirro**	ITA	51	Gresini Racing Moto2	Moriwaki	17	36m 47.682s
8	**Aleix Espargaro**	SPA	40	Pons HP 40	Pons Kalex	17	36m 48.077s
9	**Andrea Iannone**	ITA	29	Speed Master	Suter	17	36m 49.212s
10	**Scott Redding**	GBR	45	Marc VDS Racing Team	Suter	17	36m 51.811s
11	**Esteve Rabat**	SPA	34	Blusens-STX	FTR	17	36m 54.682s
12	**Kenan Sofuoglu**	TUR	54	Technomag-CIP	Suter	17	36m 59.999s
13	**Jules Cluzel**	FRA	16	NGM Forward Racing	Suter	17	37m 00.459s
14	**Mike di Meglio**	FRA	63	Tech 3 Racing	Tech 3	17	37m 01.810s
15	**Xavier Simeon**	BEL	19	Tech 3 B	Tech 3	17	37m 07.920s
16	Joan Olive	SPA	6	Aeroport de Castello	FTR	17	37m 11.611s
17	Jordi Torres	SPA	18	Mapfre Aspar Team Moto2	Suter	17	37m 15.683s
18	Mohamad Zamri Baba	MAL	87	Petronas Malaysia	Moriwaki	17	37m 31.870s
19	Ivan Moreno	SPA	20	Mapfre Aspar Team Moto2	Suter	17	37m 41.080s
20	Hafizh Syahrin	MAL	86	Petronas Malaysia	Moriwaki	17	37m 41.224s
21	Randy Krummenacher	SWI	4	GP Team Switzerland Kiefer Racing	Kalex	17	37m 52.197s
22	Robertino Pietri	VEN	39	Italtrans Racing Team	Suter	17	37m 54.529s
24	Mashel Al Naimi	QAT	95	QMMF Racing Team	Moriwaki	16	37m 29.730s
	Axel Pons	SPA	80	Pons HP 40	Pons Kalex	17	DNF
	Kenny Noyes	USA	9	Avintia-STX	FTR	17	DNF
	Raffaele de Rosa	ITA	35	NGM Forward Racing	Suter	12	DNF
	Mattia Pasini	ITA	75	Ioda Racing Project	FTR	8	DNF
	Santiago Hernandez	COL	64	SAG Team	FTR	7	DNF
	Apiwat Wongthananon	THA	23	Thai Honda Singha SAG	FTR	7	DNF
	Valentin Debise	FRA	53	Speed Up	FTR	6	DNF
	Yuki Takahashi	JPN	72	Gresini Racing Moto2	Moriwaki	5	DNF
	Claudio Corti	ITA	71	Italtrans Racing Team	Suter	3	DNF
	Simone Corsi	ITA	3	Ioda Racing Project	FTR	3	DNF
	Anthony West	AUS	13	MZ Racing Team	MZ-RE Honda	1	DNF
	Max Neukirchner	GER	76	MZ Racing Team	MZ-RE Honda	1	DNF
	Yonny Hernandez	COL	68	Blusens-STX	FTR	-	DSQ
	Marc Marquez	SPA	93	Team CatalunyaCaixa Repsol	Suter	0	DNS

Fastest lap: Stefan Bradl, on lap 4, 2m 8.220s, 96.790mph/155.769km/h (record).
Previous lap record: Julian Simon, SPA (Suter), 2m 8.691s, 96.436mph/155.199km/h (2010).
Event best maximum speed: Jules Cluzel, 166.200mph/267.500km/h (warm up).

Qualifying: Dry
Air: 33° Humidity: 49% Ground: 52°

1	Luthi	2m 07.512s
2	Bradl	2m 07.724s
3	Pirro	2m 08.004s
4	Takahashi	2m 08.069s
5	P. Espargaro	2m 08.107s
6	A. Espargaro	2m 08.154s
7	Kallio	2m 08.240s
8	Corti	2m 08.319s
9	Redding	2m 08.412s
10	Pasini	2m 08.414s
11	De Angelis	2m 08.417s
12	Rabat	2m 08.466s
13	Iannone	2m 08.520s
14	Corsi	2m 08.549s
15	Neukirchner	2m 08.620s
16	West	2m 08.714s
17	Di Meglio	2m 08.855s
18	Cluzel	2m 08.934s
19	Sofuoglu	2m 09.015s
20	Aegerter	2m 09.087s
21	Olive	2m 09.278s
22	De Rosa	2m 09.307s
23	Simeon	2m 09.315s
24	Debise	2m 09.382s
25	Pons	2m 09.472s
26	S. Hernandez	2m 09.625s
27	Torres	2m 09.686s
28	Zamri Baba	2m 09.822s
29	Krummenacher	2m 09.911s
30	Noyes	2m 10.319s
31	Pietri	2m 10.348s
32	Moreno	2m 10.875s
33	Y. Hernandez	2m 11.022s
34	Syahrin	2m 11.388s
35	Al Naimi	2m 12.180s
36	Marquez	2m 12.864s
37	Wongthananon	2m 13.201s

Fastest race laps

1	Bradl	2m 08.220s
2	Luthi	2m 08.240s
3	P. Espargaro	2m 08.332s
4	A. Espargaro	2m 08.559s
5	Kallio	2m 08.640s
6	Takahashi	2m 08.667s
7	Corsi	2m 08.674s
8	Pirro	2m 08.727s
9	Iannone	2m 08.753s
10	De Angelis	2m 08.758s
11	Corti	2m 08.816s
12	Aegerter	2m 08.920s
13	Rabat	2m 08.983s
14	Redding	2m 09.027s
15	Sofuoglu	2m 09.152s
16	Cluzel	2m 09.531s
17	Pasini	2m 09.585s
18	Pons	2m 09.613s
19	Zamri Baba	2m 09.668s
20	Simeon	2m 09.674s
21	Di Meglio	2m 09.741s
22	Noyes	2m 09.803s
23	Debise	2m 09.879s
24	Krummenacher	2m 09.904s
25	Olive	2m 09.985s
26	De Rosa	2m 09.986s
27	Torres	2m 10.090s
28	S. Hernandez	2m 10.214s
29	Y. Hernandez	2m 10.501s
30	Moreno	2m 11.759s
31	Syahrin	2m 11.791s
32	Pietri	2m 12.086s
33	Al Naimi	2m 12.474s
34	Wongthananon	2m 15.649s
35	West	2m 18.373s
36	Neukirchner	2m 18.435s

Championship Points

1	Bradl	274
2	Marquez	251
3	Iannone	172
4	De Angelis	170
5	Luthi	151
6	Corsi	127
7	Smith	121
8	Rabat	79
9	Aegerter	78
10	Takahashi	77
11	A. Espargaro	76
12	P. Espargaro	73
13	Redding	63
14	Simon	62
15	Sofuoglu	59
16	Pirro	59
17	Krummenacher	52
18	Kallio	41
19	Cluzel	38
20	Neukirchner	35
21	Y. Hernandez	33
22	Pasini	28
23	West	27
24	Corti	22
25	Di Meglio	21
26	Baldolini	18
27	Simeon	15
28	Coghlan	11
29	Wilairot	4
30	Cardus	2
31	Pons	1

Constructor Points

1	Suter	364
2	Kalex	281
3	FTR	188
4	Motobi	170
5	Tech 3	140
6	Moriwaki	113
7	Pons Kalex	77
8	MZ-RE Honda	48

125cc — RACE DISTANCE: 18 laps, 62.053 miles/99.864km · RACE WEATHER: Dry (air 34°C, humidity 49%, track 55°C)

Pos.	Rider	Nat.	No.	Entrant	Machine	Laps	Time & Speed
1	**Maverick Vinales**	SPA	25	Blusens by Paris Hilton Racing	Aprilia	18	40m 34.280s 91.768mph/ 147.686km/h
2	**Sandro Cortese**	GER	11	Intact-Racing Team Germany	Aprilia	18	40m 34.634s
3	**Johann Zarco**	FRA	5	Avant-AirAsia-Ajo	Derbi	18	40m 36.735s
4	**Hector Faubel**	SPA	55	Bankia Aspar Team 125cc	Aprilia	18	40m 37.201s
5	**Nicolas Terol**	SPA	18	Bankia Aspar Team 125cc	Aprilia	18	40m 44.329s
6	**Jonas Folger**	GER	94	Red Bull Ajo MotorSport	Aprilia	18	40m 52.244s
7	**Zulfahmi Khairuddin**	MAL	63	Airasia-Sic-Ajo	Derbi	18	41m 12.986s
8	**Jakub Kornfeil**	CZE	84	Ongetta-Centro Seta	Aprilia	18	41m 13.379s
9	**Alberto Moncayo**	SPA	23	Andalucia Banca Civica	Aprilia	18	41m 13.503s
10	**Danny Kent**	GBR	52	Red Bull Ajo MotorSport	Aprilia	18	41m 14.517s
11	**Efren Vazquez**	SPA	7	Avant-AirAsia-Ajo	Derbi	18	41m 29.086s
12	**Alexis Masbou**	FRA	10	Caretta Technology	KTM	18	41m 42.171s
13	**Danny Webb**	GBR	99	Mahindra Racing	Mahindra	18	41m 42.187s
14	**Josep Rodriguez**	SPA	28	Blusens by Paris Hilton Racing	Aprilia	18	41m 42.379s
15	**Alessandro Tonucci**	ITA	19	Team Italia FMI	Aprilia	18	41m 42.436s
16	Jack Miller	AUS	8	Caretta Technology	KTM	18	41m 49.510s
17	Giulian Pedone	SWI	30	Phonica Racing	Aprilia	18	41m 52.983s
18	Louis Rossi	FRA	96	Matteoni Racing	Aprilia	18	41m 53.193s
19	Sturla Fagerhaug	NOR	50	WTR-Ten10 Racing	Aprilia	18	42m 04.550s
20	Arthur Sissis	AUS	32	TT Motion Events Racing	Aprilia	18	42m 06.090s
21	Taylor Mackenzie	GBR	17	Phonica Racing	Aprilia	18	42m 07.530s
22	Manuel Tatasciore	ITA	60	Phonica Racing	Aprilia	18	42m 24.970s
23	Marco Colandrea	SWI	40	WTR-Ten10 Racing	Aprilia	18	42m 36.532s
24	Farid Badrul	MAL	64	AirAsia-Sic-Ajo	Derbi	18	42m 51.248s
	Brad Binder	RSA	14	Andalucia Banca Civica	Aprilia	16	DNF
	Adrian Martin	SPA	26	Bankia Aspar Team 125cc	Aprilia	10	DNF
	Luigi Morciano	ITA	3	Team Italia FMI	Aprilia	8	DNF
	Harry Stafford	GBR	21	Ongetta-Centro Seta	Aprilia	8	DNF
	Marcel Schrotter	GER	77	Mahindra Racing	Mahindra	5	DNF
	Luis Salom	SPA	39	RW Racing GP	Aprilia	0	DNF
	Jasper Iwema	NED	53	Ongetta-Abbink Metaal	Aprilia	0	DNF
	Joan Perello	SPA	36	Matteoni Racing	Aprilia	0	DNF

Fastest lap: Nicolas Terol, on lap 12, 2m 14.229s, 92.458mph/148.796km/h.
Lap record: Alvaro Bautista, SPA (Aprilia), 2m 13.118s, 93.229mph/150.038km/h (2006).
Event best maximum speed: Nicolas Terol, 139.900mph/225.200km/h (qualifying).

Qualifying: Dry
Air: 30° Humidity: 66% Ground: 46°

1	Terol	2m 13.579s
2	Faubel	2m 13.594s
3	Cortese	2m 13.954s
4	Vazquez	2m 14.581s
5	Salom	2m 14.682s
6	Folger	2m 14.776s
7	Vinales	2m 15.055s
8	Moncayo	2m 15.272s
9	Martin	2m 15.304s
10	Kent	2m 15.590s
11	Kornfeil	2m 15.888s
12	Webb	2m 15.892s
13	Khairuddin	2m 15.909s
14	Masbou	2m 15.965s
15	Zarco	2m 16.209s
16	Schrotter	2m 16.233s
17	Rossi	2m 16.373s
18	Pedone	2m 16.601s
19	Stafford	2m 16.638s
20	Iwema	2m 16.652s
21	Tonucci	2m 17.180s
22	Mackenzie	2m 17.230s
23	Perello	2m 17.443s
24	Rodriguez	2m 17.494s
25	Morciano	2m 17.530s
26	Miller	2m 17.550s
27	Binder	2m 17.867s
28	Fagerhaug	2m 17.941s
29	Tatasciore	2m 18.237s
30	Sissis	2m 19.203s
31	Badrul	2m 19.744s
32	Colandrea	2m 19.972s

Fastest race laps

1	Terol	2m 14.229s
2	Faubel	2m 14.437s
3	Vinales	2m 14.485s
4	Cortese	2m 14.528s
5	Zarco	2m 14.572s
6	Vazquez	2m 14.713s
7	Folger	2m 14.985s
8	Kornfeil	2m 15.847s
9	Kent	2m 16.162s
10	Moncayo	2m 16.253s
11	Khairuddin	2m 16.340s
12	Schrotter	2m 16.801s
13	Martin	2m 17.068s
14	Masbou	2m 17.302s
15	Binder	2m 17.364s
16	Rodriguez	2m 17.385s
17	Webb	2m 17.398s
18	Rossi	2m 17.558s
19	Morciano	2m 17.638s
20	Tonucci	2m 17.700s
21	Pedone	2m 17.924s
22	Miller	2m 17.939s
23	Stafford	2m 17.954s
24	Tatasciore	2m 18.167s
25	Mackenzie	2m 18.416s
26	Fagerhaug	2m 18.753s
27	Sissis	2m 19.133s
28	Colandrea	2m 20.167s
29	Badrul	2m 20.968s

Championship Points

1	Terol	282
2	Zarco	262
3	Cortese	225
4	Vinales	223
5	Faubel	161
6	Folger	150
7	Vazquez	147
8	Salom	107
9	Gadea	103
10	Moncayo	84
11	Kent	82
12	Kornfeil	72
13	Martin	45
14	Oliveira	44
15	Grotzkyj	32
16	Schrotter	32
17	Khairuddin	30
18	Rossi	25
19	Webb	24
20	Masbou	18
21	Iwema	16
22	Morciano	16
23	Mackenzie	15
24	Ajo	11
25	Tonucci	9
26	Ono	8
27	Stafford	5
28	Finsterbusch	4
29	Popov	3
30	Rodriguez	3
31	Fagerhaug	1
32	McPhee	1

Constructor Points

1	Aprilia	395
2	Derbi	271
3	Mahindra	45
4	KTM	29

Insets, left to right: Tributes and fresh memories were everywhere; Rossi, flanked by Gresini and Ezpeleta, leads his fellow riders in applause; specially bestickered, the MotoGP machines headed an 88-bike tribute; Simoncelli's towering farewell.

Main photo: Powerless to prevent it, Spies looks across as Stoner edges past over the line.
Photos: Gold & Goose

FIM WORLD CHAMPIONSHIP · ROUND 18

VALENCIA GRAND PRIX

VALENCIA CIRCUIT

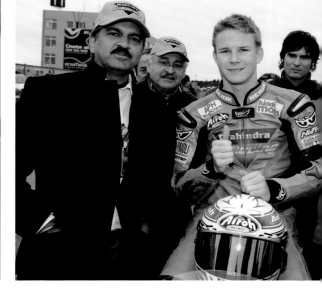

Above: "Intelligent tactics" – Dovizioso is poised to rough up Pedrosa once more.

Above right: Mahindra man and motorbike, with Danny Webb on pole.

Above far right: Cal Crutchlow took a best-yet fourth to secure Rookie of the Year.

Top: First-corner disaster. Note perpetrator Bautista (*bottom left*), Rossi to the right of his still-upright bike.

Right: Stefan Bradl, Moto2 champion after holding his breath for most of the year.

Far right: Josh Hayes (41) was an impressive bike, track and class novice, here battling with factory test rider Nakasuga.

Photos: Gold & Goose

IT was hardly surprising the mood at Valencia was drear. The weather matched, so too the size of the crowd – barely 75,000, and the hillsides and access roads relatively quiet. Both Lorenzo and Marquez were out of the races, which was bad enough. The far greater absence was of Marco Simoncelli.

He was also a towering presence, literally so in the form of a giant portrait that covered the control tower, looking down on a suitably unique post-warm-up ceremony to honour his memory – the "minute of noise and chaos" requested by his father. It was preceded by a slow lap comprising all 88 bikes from all the classes, following Marco's own Number 58 Honda RC212V, ridden by his hero and admirer, Kevin Schwantz.

Then the firecrackers. The *mascleta* is a speciality of the region, and was suitably deafening as well as oddly moving. And then everyone got back to the business of finishing off the season.

There wasn't a great deal to be decided. Just the last showdown between uneasy Repsol team-mates Dovizioso and Pedrosa. Dovi had an axe to grind with HRC and four points in hand; Dani wanted third, even though "it is not the real result because I missed so many races". This would liven up the first part of yet another race rendered the more dramatic by the onset of rain towards the end.

Stoner didn't need to do anything at all except ride around, and it would have been understandable if he had done little more. Since the crash, he said, he'd spent a lot of time

"thinking about what racing means to me". Then he went out to demonstrate what it meant – a second faster than anyone else in practice, a runaway race gallop and a final display of heroics after the rain hit for his tenth win of the year by less than two-thousandths.

The heat of the fiercest battle had been quenched when Marquez crashed on his out-lap in Malaysia. He was still suffering double vision ("I see too much.") and was clinging vainly to one doctor's opinion that the stretched-muscle problem in his right eye might correct itself suddenly. It hadn't done so by qualifying, and Stefan Bradl was able to start celebrating his championship even before the session was over. Germany's first world champion since Dirk Raudies (125) in 1993 could even laugh off a crash in the race: "I fall off every time at Valencia". He'd never regained his early-season form, but he'd ridden a workmanlike campaign. "In the end, I guess I was more consistent … because I am the champion," he said, before talking about how he had nearly quit racing back in 2006 after a career slump followed a bad injury. "But I thought that perhaps I had some talent, and I wanted to find out for myself."

The lingering chances of Zarco in the last ever 125 championship essentially depended on him winning and Terol suffering some disaster. The slender thread was cut on the third lap when he slipped off. Terol was champion, but with his real nemesis, Vinales, galloping away up front, he wasn't in any condition to celebrate it with the style of a Stoner.

Back to business included readjusting the rider market to the loss of Simoncelli. Fausto Gresini had been through agonies and contemplated not only missing this race, but also even quitting altogether. In the end, he felt it was not what Marco would have wanted. This meant a vacant Honda, possibly to the same factory spec as that allotted to the late Italian. At the same time, Suzuki had not yet made any factory decision, while LCR was looking for a rider. Barbera had switched to Pramac, but there was much yet to be decided, with Bautista torn three ways between a phantom Suzuki ride, an offer from LCR and the possibility of a higher-grade Gresini bike.

Eras were ending elsewhere. It was Loris Capirossi's last GP, finishing a career he had started with a debut 125 championship in 1990. Loris raced with Simoncelli's Number 58 on his bike. Race director Paul Butler was overseeing his last race, which happened to coincide with the more momentous occasion of the last ever 125 race, and the last smell and sound of two-stroke grand prix bikes. He celebrated by flagging the finish.

And eras beginning. There was much talk about the new CRT bikes, with Chris Vermeulen a paddock visitor looking to see if there were any vacant saddles, and even a couple of bikes ready for a first-ever joint public track test in the days after the GP. Other plans, including that from Paul Bird Racing, were still coming together and entries yet to be finalised, pending a decision from Suzuki that would determine the number of places on the grid.

Ezpeleta was in fighting form in his growing battle with the factories, suggesting in a radio interview that by 2013, MotoGP would be a production-based series, though he was rather more restrained when interviewed by *MOTOCOURSE* (See *State of Racing*, pages 18–20). In the days after the race, he also put his foot down with Suzuki, imposing a deadline of the following Friday for their decision.

At the far end of the paddock, similar things were happening in Moto3. Or rather more, with the launch of the 2012 Mahindra by the managing director of the huge Indian automotive group Anand Mahindra. An urbane figure, he promised that after a fairly low-key learning year, "Mahindra is here to stay," adding, before smashing a ceremonial coconut per national custom, "Ladies and gentlemen, watch out. The Indians are coming." Later that day, Danny Webb claimed the last ever 125 pole on the red-and-silver Mahindra, by far

his and the bike's best after a brave and canny late-session switch to slick tyres.

The new bike had an Oral Engineering motor (also launched at Valencia the day before) in an anachronistic steel multi-tube frame. This was for ease of development, explained Alberto Strazzari, chief of Mahindra-owned Italian Engines Engineering: "We can make a new steel chassis in a week; aluminium takes a month." A more modern-looking machine was on show at Ioda Racing, with its own engine, but the planned launch was deferred out of respect for Simoncelli, who had ridden for Ioda chief Giampiero Sacchi in the Gilera 250 team.

The final end-of-era found few mourners. It was the last 800cc MotoGP race, with the arrival of the 1000s in two day's time eagerly awaited. It started with a horrible multiple crash in the first corner, evoking deadly echoes of Sepang. Thankfully, none of the four involved – Rossi, Hayden, de Puniet and instigator Bautista – was badly hurt.

MOTOGP RACE – 30 laps

The race evoked gasps of horror only seconds after the start. As the 16-strong pack peeled into the first corner, a head-strong Bautista ran out of room, tagged Dovizioso's back wheel and fell. He took Rossi, Hayden and de Puniet down with him, bike Number 46 bizarrely regaining its wheels.

Bautista came within inches of being run over, but amazingly all four emerged from the tangle without major injury, although Hayden later discovered a fracture in his right wrist, which meant he missed post-race tests.

Stoner had claimed a four-stroke record 12th pole by a huge margin, with Pedrosa and Spies alongside; then de Puniet, Bautista and Rossi, equalling his best performance yet. The iffy conditions suited him, and he was full of hope for a strong final 800 Ducati race.

All lined up on dry tyres. Stoner once again got the drop from Pedrosa to lead him into the first corner, Spies and Dovizioso following closely. Mayhem erupted behind, however, eliminating the aforementioned riders. Crutchlow was a couple of seconds adrift at the end of lap one, in fifth, from Abraham and Elias.

Stoner's lead was already 1.6 seconds, and he took another 1.2 next time around, as Dovizioso lined up Pedrosa. Before half-distance, he had opened that up to better than

ten seconds, and settled down to maintain the gap and await developments.

The battle behind was absorbing. Dovizioso feared Pedrosa's faster pace at a track where he had always struggled: "I had to adopt an intelligent strategy: every time he got past me, I had to pass him back immediately." This doubtless helped Stoner's escape.

Spies was right with them, aware of the championship battle. He got ahead of Pedrosa briefly on lap three, but then he settled back: "I thought there might be some fireworks that I could capitalise on."

The Hondas swapped back and forth, sometimes twice a lap, but with Dovizioso always managing to stop the Spaniard from escaping. Only when the rain came did things change.

As in Australia, the race had already been declared wet, and spare bikes had been revving in the pit lane since lap 15. But it stayed marginally dry until lap 24.

Pedrosa lost a couple of seconds on lap 25. He was feeling stiff and uncomfortable on the treacherous surface, and would fade radically. But Spies was confident, poised to attack Dovizioso. He moved past cleanly next time around.

Stoner had also slowed dramatically, and on that same lap his lead was cut from 6.3 seconds to 2.5. It was just caution in the rain, and some battle fatigue through again being the one to test the conditions. "We've had too many races like this, and I've always been the one in front," he said.

On lap 28, he missed a down-shift and locked the rear when the bike hooked first at turn six, running wide as he recovered. It was all Spies needed. He nipped past, taking over the pathfinder role.

Stoner stayed with him, for his final devastating run out of the last corner, finding a drier line and using all his seamless-shift Honda's acceleration. Spies could do nothing as the Repsol bike came alongside as they approached the line. Stoner was grinningly apologetic, explaining, "With half a lap to go, I thought, 'I haven't taken any risks all season, but I'm going to do it now.'"

Dovi was more than five seconds away, but free from serious threat. Crutchlow crossed the line another three seconds back. Pedrosa had been in front of him as they began the last lap, but was half a second behind at the end. More important for the Briton had been another last-lap incident. In fact, he had followed Abraham past the factory Honda,

and now he swept past on the outside. Abraham touched his back wheel and fell off. Though he remounted to finish eighth, it firmly swung the balance of points in Crutchlow's favour to become top rookie.

Nakasuga was 15 seconds further behind. For much of the race, he and Hayes had been battling, but he moved clear as the rain came, soon after the pair had caught and passed Elias.

Hayes was another nine seconds down, a very creditable seventh on his debut, five ahead of the remounted Abraham. Capirossi and Elias trailed in, then miles behind came Barbera and a disheartened Aoyama.

The top championship positions remained unchanged, Stoner reinforcing his second title with 350 points. Lorenzo remained a safe second on 260; Dovizioso saved his third, 228 points to Pedrosa's 219. Spies was fifth on 176; Simoncelli and Rossi were equal on 139, but Marco sixth by virtue of his second place in Australia. "It is my tribute to him," said Rossi.

MOTO2 RACE – 27 laps

Moto2 qualifying was dry enough for lap times within a second of the race lap record, but was damp enough to shuffle the pack.

Ten days before, Gresini had contemplated pulling out of the race. It was a better tribute to their team companion that his riders Pirro and Takahashi took the first two positions on the grid. Kallio was alongside, continuing to find form at last. Champion Bradl led row two from de Angelis and Luthi; Smith was 12th and Redding 14th, Pol Espargaro sandwiched between. Iannone was at sea in 25th.

Aegerter jumped into the lead from row three, but by the end of lap two, Takahashi had taken it off him, and next time around Pirro followed him past. The white bikes gained a little gap, the Japanese a second ahead as they started lap six.

Then he pushed too hard on the iffy surface, triggering a massive high-side crash. He landed heavily on his back and rolled head over heels to end up motionless in the gravel. It was a worrying sight, especially for Gresini, but the race went on as he was stretchered away.

Pirro thus inherited the lead and didn't see another bike for the rest of the afternoon. His first pole position had turned

Above: Terol clinches the 125cc title.

Above left: Capirossi's last of 328 GPs was with Simoncelli's number.

Top centre: A weekend of mixed emotions for Fausto Gresini.

Above centre: Lorenzo was reduced to the role of spectator.

Top right: A fitting maiden Moto2 win for Gresini's rider, Pirro.

Right: Tucked-in teenager Vinales ran away from Faubel (55) and Terol to take his fourth win.

Photos: Gold & Goose

into a first win. Team boss Fausto, just back from the medical centre (where the news on Takahashi was good), watched his rider win from the pit wall and collapsed in floods of tears.

Bradl was seventh when he also fell victim to the conditions and crashed out on lap five. By then, Smith had already fallen out of the front group on lap two after a clash with Kallio, rejoining near the back. Two laps later, countryman Redding also slid off and got straight back on.

Aegerter was now behind Kallio and Yonny Hernandez, the pair locked in merciless combat almost all the way – until Hernandez ran off with three laps left, regaining the track in the middle of the next gang.

Now Aegerter closed again, but Kallio was able to fend him off for second by two-tenths over the line.

The next group of four had been all over one another for most of the race. Hernandez was in the middle of it as they swapped back and forth. By the end, experienced wet-weather expert West was inches ahead of American Kenny Noyes – a strong race at last after important changes in his pit. Then came Hernandez, di Meglio and Xavier Simeon, all five over the line within less than 1.5 seconds.

Neukirchner and Simon led the next group over the line, Iannone and de Angelis up close in a last-ditch battle for third overall. Jules Cluzel had been among them, but ran off, then came back, repassing Pol Espargaro and Corti for 13th. An out-of-sorts Luthi lost 16th to Krummenacher on the last lap.

Pasini, Baldolini and de Rosa also crashed out.

Bradl was already champion, finishing on 274 points to the absent Marquez's 251. Iannone saved third from de Angelis, 177 points to 174. Luthi was safe on 151 for fifth.

125cc RACE – 24 laps

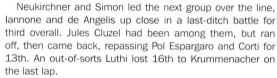

The last ever 125 race brought a fourth win to the discovery of the season, Vinales, but the last day of the two-strokes and the last ever 125 title belonged to Terol. He needed to finish only better than 13th if his last rival, Zarco, were to win. Instead the Frenchman crashed out of fifth on the third lap, triggering unseemly cheers and hugs in the Aspar pit.

The track was treacherously almost dry. Webb led the first lap from pole, then dropped back out of the top ten before slipping off.

Faubel was next up front and looked as though he might escape. But by half-distance, Vinales was with him, Terol close behind. Terol led for four laps, then Faubel for one more, but on the 19th Vinales tucked in and took off. By the finish, he was more than three seconds ahead.

It mattered little to Terol, with team-mate Faubel a similar distance behind him in third place. He cruised across the line as champion.

Folger had started well, but gradually lost touch. With seven laps to go, he was caught and passed by Vazquez, the Spaniard picking his way through from 13th.

Salom had been defending sixth in the last laps from a closing Martin. On the last lap they crashed out together, Salom remounting to save seventh, behind a lucky Moncayo, promoted to sixth.

Ajo narrowly defeated Marciano for eighth; Rossi was three seconds behind in tenth.

Terol had eight race wins to underline his season-long superiority, and a total of 302 points to one-race winner Zarco's 262. Vinales secured third on 248, ahead of Cortese (225) – the German crashed out while lying 11th on lap 16.

CIRCUITO DE LA COMUNITAT VALENCIANA

30 laps
Length: 4.005 km / 2.489 miles
Width: 12m

Key
96/60 kph/mph
⚙ Gear

Angel Nieto 95/59 ⚙

Afición 210/130 ⚙

Mick Doohan 80/50 ⚙

Turn 8 90/56 ⚙

Turn 11 80/50 ⚙

Turn 13 195/122 ⚙

Turn 5 105/65 ⚙

Turn 4 105/65 ⚙

Adrian Campos 90/56 ⚙

Champi Herreros 130/81 ⚙

Turn 1 135/84 ⚙

MotoGP · RACE DISTANCE: 30 laps, 74.658 miles/120.150km · RACE WEATHER: Wet (air 17°C, humidity 49%, track 16°C)

Pos.	Rider	Nat.	No.	Entrant	Machine	Tyres	Laps	Time & speed
1	**Casey Stoner**	AUS	27	Repsol Honda Team	Honda	B	30	48m 18.645s 92.722mph/ 149.221km/h
2	**Ben Spies**	USA	11	Yamaha Factory Racing	Yamaha	B	30	48m 18.660s
3	**Andrea Dovizioso**	ITA	4	Repsol Honda Team	Honda	B	30	48m 24.581s
4	**Cal Crutchlow**	GBR	35	Monster Yamaha Tech 3	Yamaha	B	30	48m 27.363s
5	**Dani Pedrosa**	SPA	26	Repsol Honda Team	Honda	B	30	48m 27.966s
6	**Katsuyuki Nakasuga**	JPN	89	Yamaha Factory Racing	Yamaha	B	30	48m 42.463s
7	**Josh Hayes**	USA	41	Monster Yamaha Tech 3	Yamaha	B	30	48m 51.763s
8	**Karel Abraham**	CZE	17	Cardion AB Motoracing	Ducati	B	30	48m 56.597s
9	**Loris Capirossi**	ITA	58	Pramac Racing Team	Ducati	B	30	49m 07.598s
10	**Toni Elias**	SPA	24	LCR Honda MotoGP	Honda	B	30	49m 11.146s
11	**Hector Barbera**	SPA	8	Mapfre Aspar Team MotoGP	Ducati	B	30	49m 25.164s
12	**Hiroshi Aoyama**	JPN	7	San Carlo Honda Gresini	Honda	B	30	49m 27.405s
	Randy de Puniet	FRA	14	Pramac Racing Team	Ducati	B	0	DNF
	Alvaro Bautista	SPA	19	Rizla Suzuki MotoGP	Suzuki	B	0	DNF
	Valentino Rossi	ITA	46	Ducati Team	Ducati	B	0	DNF
	Nicky Hayden	USA	69	Ducati Team	Ducati	B	0	DNF

Fastest lap: Andrea Dovizioso, on lap 14, 1m 34.167s, 95.138mph/153.110km/h.

Lap record: Casey Stoner, AUS (Ducati), 1m 32.582s, 96.767mph/155.732km/h (2008).

Event best maximum speed: Toni Elias, 194.600mph/313.200km/h (qualifying).

Qualifying

Weather: Dry
Air Temp: 17° Humidity: 51%
Track Temp: 16°

1	Stoner	1m 31.861s
2	Pedrosa	1m 32.875s
3	Spies	1m 33.057s
4	De Puniet	1m 33.118s
5	Bautista	1m 33.443s
6	Rossi	1m 33.478s
7	Hayden	1m 33.656s
8	Dovizioso	1m 33.824s
9	Barbera	1m 34.186s
10	Abraham	1m 34.265s
11	Crutchlow	1m 34.329s
12	Capirossi	1m 34.671s
13	Elias	1m 34.680s
14	Aoyama	1m 34.838s
15	Nakasuga	1m 35.999s
16	Hayes	1m 36.042s

Fastest race laps

1	Dovizioso	1m 34.167s
2	Pedrosa	1m 34.214s
3	Stoner	1m 34.259s
4	Spies	1m 34.442s
5	Abraham	1m 34.997s
6	Crutchlow	1m 35.015s
7	Aoyama	1m 35.142s
8	Barbera	1m 35.152s
9	Elias	1m 35.201s
10	Capirossi	1m 35.267s
11	Nakasuga	1m 35.668s
12	Hayes	1m 35.721s

Championship Points

1	Stoner	350
2	Lorenzo	260
3	Dovizioso	228
4	Pedrosa	219
5	Spies	176
6	Simoncelli	139
7	Rossi	139
8	Hayden	132
9	Edwards	109
10	Aoyama	98
11	Barbera	82
12	Crutchlow	70
13	Bautista	67
14	Abraham	64
15	Elias	61
16	De Puniet	49
17	Capirossi	43
18	Nakasuga	10
19	Hayes	9
20	Akiyoshi	7
21	Hopkins	6
22	Ito	3

Grid order

Grid order	1	2	3	4	5	6	7	8	9	10	11	12	13	14	15	16	17	18	19	20	21	22	23	24	25	26	27	28	29	30	
27 STONER	27	27	27	27	27	27	27	27	27	27	27	27	27	27	27	27	27	27	27	27	27	27	27	27	27	27	11	11	27		1
26 PEDROSA	26	26	4	4	4	26	4	4	4	4	4	26	26	26	4	4	4	4	4	4	4	4	4	4	11	11	27	27	11		2
11 SPIES	11	4	11	26	26	4	26	26	26	26	26	4	4	4	26	26	26	26	26	26	26	26	11	11	4	4	4	4	4		3
14 DE PUNIET	4	11	26	11	11	11	11	11	11	11	11	11	11	11	11	11	11	11	11	11	11	11	26	26	26	26	26	26	35		4
19 BAUTISTA	35	35	35	35	35	35	17	17	17	17	35	35	35	17	17	17	17	17	17	17	17	17	17	17	35	35	35	35	26		5
46 ROSSI	17	17	17	17	17	17	35	35	35	17	17	17	35	35	35	35	35	35	35	35	35	35	35	35	17	17	17	17	89		6
69 HAYDEN	24	24	24	24	58	58	58	58	58	58	58	58	58	58	58	58	58	58	58	58	58	58	58	58	58	58	58	89	41		7
4 DOVIZIOSO	89	89	89	58	24	24	24	24	24	24	24	24	24	24	24	24	24	24	24	24	24	24	24	89	89	89	41	17			8
8 BARBERA	58	58	58	89	89	89	89	89	89	89	41	41	41	41	89	89	89	89	89	89	89	89	89	24	41	41	58	58			9
17 ABRAHAM	41	41	41	41	41	41	41	41	41	89	89	89	89	41	41	41	41	41	41	41	41	41	41	41	24	24	24	24			10
35 CRUTCHLOW	8	8	7	7	8	8	8	8	8	8	8	8	8	8	8	8	8	8	8	8	8	8	8	8	8	8	8	8			11
58 CAPIROSSI	7	7	8	8	7	7	7	7	7	7	7	7	7	7	7	7	7	7	7	7	7	7	7	7	7	7	7	7			12
24 ELIAS																															
7 AOYAMA																															
89 NAKASUGA																															
41 HAYES																															

Team Points

1	Repsol Honda Team	528
2	Yamaha Factory Racing	446
3	Ducati Team	271
4	San Carlo Honda Gresini	232
5	Monster Yamaha Tech 3	188
6	Pramac Racing Team	92
7	Mapfre Aspar Team MotoGP	82
8	Rizla Suzuki MotoGP	73
9	Cardion AB Motoracing	64
10	LCR Honda MotoGP	61

Constructor Points

1	Honda	405
2	Yamaha	325
3	Ducati	180
4	Suzuki	73

Moto2

RACE DISTANCE: 27 laps, 67.192 miles/108.135km · RACE WEATHER: Dry (air 17°C, humidity 50%, track 16°C)

Pos.	Rider	Nat.	No.	Entrant	Machine	Laps	Time & Speed
1	**Michele Pirro**	ITA	51	Gresini Racing Moto2	Moriwaki	27	46m 22.205s 89.942mph/ 139.919 km/h
2	**Mika Kallio**	FIN	36	Marc VDS Racing Team	Suter	27	46m 28.355s
3	**Dominique Aegerter**	SWI	77	Technomag-CIP	Suter	27	46m 28.568s
4	**Anthony West**	AUS	13	MZ Racing Team	MZ-RE Honda	27	46m 31.048s
5	**Kenny Noyes**	USA	9	Avintia-STX	FTR	27	46m 31.434s
6	**Yonny Hernandez**	COL	68	Blusens-STX	FTR	27	46m 32.131s
7	**Mike di Meglio**	FRA	63	Tech 3 Racing	Tech 3	27	46m 32.320s
8	**Xavier Simeon**	BEL	19	Tech 3 B	Tech 3	27	46m 32.590s
9	**Max Neukirchner**	GER	76	MZ Racing Team	MZ-RE Honda	27	46m 35.223s
10	**Julian Simon**	SPA	60	Mapfre Aspar Team Moto2	Suter	27	46m 35.890s
11	**Andrea Iannone**	ITA	29	Speed Master	Suter	27	46m 36.891s
12	**Alex de Angelis**	RSM	15	JIR Moto2	Motobi	27	46m 37.405s
13	**Jules Cluzel**	FRA	16	NGM Forward Racing	Suter	27	46m 40.633s
14	**Pol Espargaro**	SPA	44	HP Tuenti Speed Up	FTR	27	46m 41.382s
15	**Claudio Corti**	ITA	71	Italtrans Racing Team	Suter	27	46m 42.561s
16	Randy Krummenacher	SWI	4	GP Team Switzerland Kiefer Racing	Kalex	27	46m 48.236s
17	Thomas Luthi	SWI	12	Interwetten Paddock Moto2	Suter	27	46m 49.365s
18	Jordi Torres	SPA	18	Mapfre Aspar Team Moto2	Suter	27	46m 56.018s
19	Alex Baldolini	ITA	25	Desguaces La Torre G22	Moriwaki	27	47m 08.208s
20	Kenan Sofuoglu	TUR	54	Technomag-CIP	Suter	27	47m 11.840s
21	Aleix Espargaro	SPA	40	Pons HP 40	Pons Kalex	27	47m 34.392s
22	Santiago Hernandez	COL	64	SAG Team	FTR	27	47m 36.772s
23	Bradley Smith	GBR	38	Tech 3 Racing	Tech 3	27	47m 37.599s
24	Robertino Pietri	VEN	39	Italtrans Racing Team	Suter	27	47m 38.972s
25	Elena Rosell	SPA	82	Mapfre Aspar Team Moto2	Suter	27	47m 42.098s
26	Joan Olive	SPA	6	Aeroport de Castello	FTR	27	47m 44.544s
27	Mashel Al Naimi	QAT	95	QMMF Racing Team	Moriwaki	26	46m 48.955s
28	Oscar Climent	SPA	61	Team Climent	MIR Racing	26	46m 50.707s
29	Nasser Hasan Al Malki	QAT	96	QMMF Racing Team	Moriwaki	26	47m 06.423s
30	Scott Redding	GBR	45	Marc VDS Racing Team	Suter	26	48m 06.787s
	Raffaele de Rosa	ITA	35	NGM Forward Racing	Suter	25	DNF
	Simone Corsi	ITA	3	Ioda Racing Project	FTR	25	DNF
	Valentin Debise	FRA	53	Speed Up	FTR	20	DNF
	Ratthapark Wilairot	THA	14	Thai Honda Singha SAG	FTR	13	DNF
	Mattia Pasini	ITA	75	Ioda Racing Project	FTR	10	DNF
	Esteve Rabat	SPA	34	Blusens-STX	FTR	6	DNF
	Yuki Takahashi	JPN	72	Gresini Racing Moto2	Moriwaki	5	DNF
	Stefan Bradl	GER	65	Viessmann Kiefer Racing	Kalex	4	DNF

Fastest lap: Andrea Iannone, on lap 21, 1m 39.730s, 89.832mph/144.570km/h.

Lap record: Karel Abraham, CZE (FTR), 1m 36.611s, 92.732mph/149.237km/h (2010).

Event best maximum speed: Stefan Bradl, 167.000mph/268.800km/h (free practice 3).

Qualifying: Dry/wet

Air: 15° Humidity 57% Ground: 14°

1	Pirro	1m 37.067s
2	Takahashi	1m 37.076s
3	Kallio	1m 37.477s
4	Bradl	1m 37.870s
5	De Angelis	1m 37.888s
6	Luthi	1m 37.963s
7	Aegerter	1m 38.095s
8	Simeon	1m 38.182s
9	Di Meglio	1m 38.496s
10	Corsi	1m 38.565s
11	A. Espargaro	1m 38.633s
12	Smith	1m 38.652s
13	P. Espargaro	1m 38.655s
14	Redding	1m 38.703s
15	Torres	1m 38.924s
16	Rabat	1m 38.936s
17	Pasini	1m 39.096s
18	Baldolini	1m 39.293s
19	Cluzel	1m 39.309s
20	Y. Hernandez	1m 39.316s
21	Simon	1m 39.403s
22	West	1m 39.442s
23	Noyes	1m 39.549s
24	Neukirchner	1m 39.671s
25	Iannone	1m 39.716s
26	Corti	1m 39.743s
27	Krummenacher	1m 39.818s
28	De Rosa	1m 39.849s
29	Sofuoglu	1m 40.277s
30	Debise	1m 40.368s
31	S. Hernandez	1m 40.441s
32	Olive	1m 40.512s
33	Pietri	1m 40.690s
34	Climent	1m 40.953s
35	Rosell	1m 42.006s
36	Wilairot	1m 42.317s
37	Al Naimi	1m 42.627s
38	Hasan Al Malki	1m 43.709s
	Pons	No Time
	Marquez	No Time

Fastest race laps

1	Iannone	1m 39.730s
2	Simon	1m 39.807s
3	Cluzel	1m 39.813s
4	Neukirchner	1m 39.898s
5	Di Meglio	1m 39.902s
6	P. Espargaro	1m 39.969s
7	West	1m 40.103s
8	De Angelis	1m 40.165s
9	Simeon	1m 40.241s
10	Aegerter	1m 40.243s
11	Baldolini	1m 40.279s
12	Corti	1m 40.345s
13	Noyes	1m 40.349s
14	De Rosa	1m 40.504s
15	Pirro	1m 40.509s
16	Luthi	1m 40.523s
17	Y. Hernandez	1m 40.573s
18	Kallio	1m 40.681s
19	Takahashi	1m 41.125s
20	Krummenacher	1m 41.182s
21	Smith	1m 41.471s
22	Torres	1m 41.661s
23	Sofuoglu	1m 41.953s
24	Redding	1m 42.118s
25	Pietri	1m 42.194s
26	Pasini	1m 42.376s
27	A. Espargaro	1m 42.710s
28	S. Hernandez	1m 42.733s
29	Olive	1m 42.765s
30	Rosell	1m 42.795s
31	Corsi	1m 42.801s
32	Bradl	1m 42.859s
33	Rabat	1m 43.514s
34	Al Naimi	1m 44.145s
35	Hasan Al Malki	1m 44.761s
36	Climent	1m 44.786s
37	Debise	1m 44.805s
38	Wilairot	1m 45.254s

Championship Points

1	Bradl	274
2	Marquez	251
3	Iannone	177
4	De Angelis	174
5	Luthi	151
6	Corsi	127
7	Smith	121
8	Aegerter	94
9	Pirro	84
10	Rabat	79
11	Takahashi	77
12	A. Espargaro	76
13	P. Espargaro	75
14	Simon	68
15	Redding	63
16	Kallio	61
17	Sofuoglu	59
18	Krummenacher	52
19	Y. Hernandez	43
20	Neukirchner	42
21	Cluzel	41
22	West	40
23	Di Meglio	30
24	Pasini	28
25	Corti	23
26	Simeon	23
27	Baldolini	18
28	Noyes	11
29	Coghlan	11
30	Wilairot	4
31	Cardus	2
32	Pons	1

Constructor Points

1	Suter	384
2	Kalex	281
3	FTR	199
4	Motobi	174
5	Tech 3	149
6	Moriwaki	138
7	Pons Kalex	77
8	MZ-RE Honda	61

125cc

RACE DISTANCE: 24 laps, 59.726 miles/96.120km · RACE WEATHER: Dry (air 17°C, humidity 47%, track 16°C)

Pos.	Rider	Nat.	No.	Entrant	Machine	Laps	Time & Speed
1	**Maverick Vinales**	SPA	25	Blusens by Paris Hilton Racing	Aprilia	24	41m 44.138s 85.864 mph/ 138.184 km/h
2	**Nicolas Terol**	SPA	18	Bankia Aspar Team 125cc	Aprilia	24	41m 47.354s
3	**Hector Faubel**	SPA	55	Bankia Aspar Team 125cc	Aprilia	24	41m 51.598s
4	**Efren Vazquez**	SPA	7	Avant-AirAsia-Ajo	Derbi	24	41m 58.698s
5	**Jonas Folger**	GER	94	Red Bull Ajo MotorSport	Aprilia	24	42m 02.589s
6	**Alberto Moncayo**	SPA	23	Andalucia Banca Civica	Aprilia	24	42m 20.610s
7	**Luis Salom**	SPA	39	RW Racing GP	Aprilia	24	42m 36.752s
8	**Niklas Ajo**	FIN	31	TT Motion Events Racing	Aprilia	24	42m 44.276s
9	**Luigi Morciano**	ITA	3	Team Italia FMI	Aprilia	24	42m 44.391s
10	**Louis Rossi**	FRA	96	Matteoni Racing	Aprilia	24	42m 47.396s
11	**Manuel Tatasciore**	ITA	60	Phonica Racing	Aprilia	24	42m 54.030s
12	**Marcel Schrotter**	GER	77	Mahindra Racing	Mahindra	24	42m 56.879s
13	**Alessandro Tonucci**	ITA	19	Team Italia FMI	Aprilia	24	43m 02.475s
14	**John McPhee**	GBR	71	Racing Steps Foundation KRP	Aprilia	24	43m 02.572s
15	**Giulian Pedone**	SWI	30	Phonica Racing	Aprilia	24	43m 04.718s
16	Sturla Fagerhaug	NOR	50	WTR-Ten10 Racing	Aprilia	24	43m 05.293s
17	Danny Kent	GBR	52	Red Bull Ajo MotorSport	Aprilia	24	43m 11.908s
18	Peter Sebestyen	HUN	56	Matteoni Racing	Aprilia	24	43m 17.544s
19	Daniel Ruiz	SPA	34	Larresport	Honda	24	43m 18.731s
20	Jasper Iwema	NED	53	Ongetta-Abbink Metaal	Aprilia	24	43m 18.970s
21	Marco Colandrea	SWI	40	WTR-Ten10 Racing	Aprilia	23	41m 53.491s
22	Alexis Masbou	FRA	10	Caretta Technology	KTM	23	42m 00.252s
23	Kevin Hanus	GER	86	Team Hanusch	Honda	23	42m 05.787s
24	Jakub Kornfeil	CZE	84	Ongetta-Centro Seta	Aprilia	23	42m 16.779s
25	Zulfahmi Khairuddin	MAL	63	Airasia-Sic-Ajo	Derbi	21	42m 01.106s
	Taylor Mackenzie	GBR	17	Phonica Racing	Aprilia	18	DNF
	Brad Binder	RSA	14	Andalucia Banca Civica	Aprilia	17	DNF
	Josep Rodriguez	SPA	28	Blusens by Paris Hilton Racing	Aprilia	15	DNF
	Sandro Cortese	GER	11	Intact-Racing Team Germany	Aprilia	11	DNF
	Danny Webb	GBR	99	Mahindra Racing	Mahindra	11	DNF
	Harry Stafford	GBR	21	Ongetta-Centro Seta	Aprilia	7	DNF
	Jack Miller	AUS	8	Caretta Technology	KTM	3	DNF
	Johann Zarco	FRA	5	Avant-AirAsia-Ajo	Derbi	2	DNF
	Adrian Martin	SPA	26	Bankia Aspar Team 125cc	Aprilia	24	Finished in pits

Fastest lap: Maverick Vinales, on lap 17, 1m 42.882s, 87.080mph/140.141km/h.

Lap record: Hector Faubel, SPA (Aprilia), 1m 39.380s, 90.148mph/145.079km/h (2007).

Event best maximum speed: Nicolas Terol, 140.300mph/225.800km/h (race).

Qualifying: Wet

Air: 15° Humidity 66% Ground: 14°

1	Webb	1m 45.898s
2	Rossi	1m 46.325s
3	Zarco	1m 48.028s
4	Salom	1m 48.264s
5	Masbou	1m 48.283s
6	Faubel	1m 48.288s
7	Cortese	1m 48.731s
8	Vinales	1m 48.756s
9	Terol	1m 48.920s
10	Folger	1m 49.438s
11	Martin	1m 49.456s
12	Miller	1m 49.721s
13	Vazquez	1m 49.726s
14	Moncayo	1m 49.779s
15	Khairuddin	1m 49.794s
16	Rodriguez	1m 50.178s
17	Tonucci	1m 50.345s
18	Kent	1m 50.382s
19	Ajo	1m 50.583s
20	Tatasciore	1m 51.023s
21	Fagerhaug	1m 51.088s
22	Morciano	1m 51.162s
23	Schrotter	1m 51.667s
24	Kornfeil	1m 51.953s
25	McPhee	1m 52.005s
26	Mackenzie	1m 52.699s
27	Iwema	1m 53.063s
Outside 107%		
29	Sebestyen	1m 53.313s
30	Stafford	1m 53.370s
31	Pedone	1m 53.556s
32	Ruiz	1m 54.437s
33	Guevara	1m 54.767s
34	Hanus	1m 55.262s
35	Petersen	1m 55.406s
36	Colandrea	1m 56.230s
37	Binder	1m 56.887s

Fastest race laps

1	Vinales	1m 42.882s
2	Faubel	1m 42.938s
3	Terol	1m 43.120s
4	Vazquez	1m 43.308s
5	Cortese	1m 43.424s
6	Salom	1m 43.634s
7	Folger	1m 43.912s
8	Martin	1m 44.234s
9	Kent	1m 44.502s
10	Moncayo	1m 44.599s
11	Rossi	1m 44.885s
12	Masbou	1m 45.115s
13	Tatasciore	1m 45.398s
14	Zarco	1m 45.457s
15	Tonucci	1m 45.565s
16	Morciano	1m 45.696s
17	McPhee	1m 45.697s
18	Ajo	1m 45.901s
19	Schrotter	1m 45.934s
20	Webb	1m 46.002s
21	Kornfeil	1m 46.031s
22	Pedone	1m 46.079s
23	Fagerhaug	1m 46.495s
24	Sebestyen	1m 46.527s
25	Binder	1m 46.702s
26	Mackenzie	1m 46.715s
27	Iwema	1m 46.748s
28	Ruiz	1m 46.954s
29	Rodriguez	1m 47.219s
30	Khairuddin	1m 47.300s
31	Colandrea	1m 47.714s
32	Miller	1m 47.909s
33	Hanus	1m 48.234s
34	Stafford	1m 48.626s

Championship Points

1	Terol	302
2	Zarco	262
3	Vinales	248
4	Cortese	225
5	Faubel	177
6	Folger	161
7	Vazquez	160
8	Salom	116
9	Gadea	103
10	Moncayo	94
11	Kent	82
12	Kornfeil	72
13	Martin	45
14	Oliveira	44
15	Schrotter	36
16	Grotzkyj	32
17	Rossi	31
18	Khairuddin	30
19	Webb	24
20	Morciano	23
21	Ajo	19
22	Masbou	18
23	Iwema	16
24	Mackenzie	15
25	Tonucci	12
26	Ono	8
27	Tatasciore	5
28	Stafford	5
29	Finsterbusch	4
30	Popov	3
31	McPhee	3
32	Rodriguez	3
33	Pedone	1
34	Fagerhaug	1

Constructor Points

1	Aprilia	420
2	Derbi	284
3	Mahindra	49
4	KTM	29

WORLD CHAMPIONSHIP POINTS 2011

Compiled by PETER McLAREN

Photo: Gold & Goose

MotoGP – Riders

Position	Rider	Nationality	Machine	Qatar	Spain	Portugal	France	Catalunya	Great Britain	Netherlands	Italy	Germany	United States	Czech Republic	Indianapolis	San Marino	Aragón	Japan	Australia	Malaysia	Valencia	Points total
1	Casey Stoner	AUS	Honda	25	–	16	25	25	25	20	16	16	25	25	25	16	25	16	25	–	25	**350**
2	Jorge Lorenzo	SPA	Yamaha	20	25	20	13	20	–	10	25	20	20	13	13	25	16	20	–	–	–	**260**
3	Andrea Dovizioso	ITA	Honda	13	4	13	20	13	20	16	20	13	11	20	11	11	–	11	16	–	16	**228**
4	Dani Pedrosa	SPA	Honda	16	20	25	–	–	–	–	8	25	16	–	20	20	20	25	13	–	11	**219**
5	Ben Spies	USA	Yamaha	10	–	–	10	16	–	25	13	11	13	11	16	10	11	10	–	–	20	**176**
6	Marco Simoncelli	ITA	Honda	11	–	–	11	10	–	7	11	10	–	16	4	13	13	13	20	–	–	**139**
7	Valentino Rossi	ITA	Ducati	9	11	11	16	11	10	13	10	7	10	10	6	9	6	–	–	–	–	**139**
8	Nicky Hayden	USA	Ducati	7	16	7	9	8	13	11	6	8	9	9	2	–	9	9	9	–	–	**132**
9	Colin Edwards	USA	Yamaha	8	–	10	3	–	16	9	7	6	8	8	9	3	3	8	11	–	–	**109**
10	Hiroshi Aoyama	JPN	Honda	6	13	9	8	–	7	8	5	1	6	7	7	5	5	7	–	–	4	**98**
11	Hector Barbera	SPA	Ducati	4	10	–	7	5	5	4	9	5	7	6	–	7	8	–	–	–	5	**82**
12	Cal Crutchlow	GBR	Yamaha	5	8	8	–	9	–	2	–	2	–	–	5	6	7	5	–	–	13	**70**
13	Alvaro Bautista	SPA	Suzuki	–	–	3	4	4	11	5	3	9	–	–	10	8	10	–	–	–	–	**67**
14	Karel Abraham	CZE	Ducati	3	9	–	6	6	9	–	4	4	5	–	4	–	–	6	–	–	8	**64**
15	Toni Elias	SPA	Honda	–	7	5	5	3	8	6	1	–	3	5	3	1	–	–	8	–	6	**61**
16	Randy de Puniet	FRA	Ducati	–	–	6	–	–	4	–	2	3	–	4	8	2	4	6	10	–	–	**49**
17	Loris Capirossi	ITA	Ducati	–	5	4	–	7	6	–	–	–	4	3	–	–	–	7	–	–	7	**43**
18	Katsuyuki Nakasuga	JPN	Yamaha	–	–	–	–	–	–	–	–	–	–	–	–	–	–	–	–	–	10	**10**
19	Josh Hayes	USA	Yamaha	–	–	–	–	–	–	–	–	–	–	–	–	–	–	–	–	–	9	**9**
20	Kousuke Akiyoshi	JPN	Honda	–	–	–	–	–	–	3	–	–	–	–	–	–	–	–	4	–	–	**7**
21	John Hopkins	USA	Suzuki	–	6	–	–	–	–	–	–	–	–	–	–	–	–	–	–	–	–	**6**
22	Shinichi Ito	JPN	Honda	–	–	–	–	–	–	–	–	–	–	–	–	–	–	3	–	–	–	**3**

MotoGP - Teams

Position	Team	Qatar	Spain	Portugal	France	Catalunya	Great Britain	Netherlands	Italy	Germany	United States	Czech Republic	Indianapolis	San Marino	Aragón	Japan	Australia	Malaysia	Valencia	Points total
1	Repsol Honda Team	38	20	38	25	25	25	28	28	38	36	25	36	31	25	36	38	–	36	**528**
2	Yamaha Factory Racing	30	25	20	23	36	–	35	38	31	33	24	29	35	27	30	–	–	30	**446**
3	Ducati Team	16	27	18	25	19	23	24	16	15	19	19	8	9	15	9	9	–	–	**271**
4	San Carlo Honda Gresini	17	13	9	19	10	7	10	16	11	6	23	11	18	18	20	20	–	4	**232**
5	Monster Yamaha Tech 3	13	8	18	3	9	16	11	7	8	8	8	14	9	10	13	11	–	22	**188**
6	Pramac Racing Team	–	5	10	–	7	10	–	2	3	4	7	8	2	4	6	17	–	7	**92**
7	Mapfre Aspar Team MotoGP	4	10	–	7	5	5	4	9	5	7	6	–	7	8	–	–	–	5	**82**
8	Rizla Suzuki MotoGP	–	6	3	4	4	11	5	3	9	–	–	10	8	10	–	–	–	–	**73**
9	Cardion AB Motoracing	3	9	–	6	6	9	–	4	4	5	–	4	–	–	6	–	–	8	**64**
10	LCR Honda MotoGP	–	7	5	5	3	8	6	1	–	3	5	3	1	–	–	8	–	6	**61**

Moto2

Position	Rider	Nationality	Machine	Qatar	Spain	Portugal	France	Catalunya	Great Britain	Netherlands	Italy	Germany	Czech Republic	Indianapolis	San Marino	Aragón	Japan	Australia	Malaysia	Valencia	Points total
1	Stefan Bradl	GER	Kalex	25	11	25	16	25	25	–	20	20	16	10	20	8	13	20	20	–	274
2	Marc Marquez	SPA	Suter	–	–	–	25	20	–	25	25	25	20	25	25	25	20	16	–	–	251
3	Andrea Iannone	ITA	Suter	20	25	3	–	1	–	4	11	2	25	5	16	20	25	8	7	5	177
4	Alex de Angelis	RSM	Motobi	13	9	4	6	10	–	11	13	16	13	1	13	13	10	25	13	4	174
5	Thomas Luthi	SWI	Suter	16	20	–	11	–	1	8	10	11	11	–	8	9	16	5	25	–	151
6	Simone Corsi	ITA	FTR	10	16	11	9	13	6	2	9	8	7	2	6	16	11	1	–	–	127
7	Bradley Smith	GBR	Tech 3	7	13	–	7	–	20	16	16	–	–	13	10	10	9	–	–	–	121
8	Dominique Aegerter	SWI	Suter	3	–	13	8	–	–	5	4	8	4	3	7	8	4	11	16	–	94
9	Michele Pirro	ITA	Moriwaki	8	7	–	2	4	16	–	6	–	–	2	–	3	2	9	–	25	84
10	Esteve Rabat	SPA	FTR	2	1	6	–	9	10	9	–	9	16	5	–	7	–	5	–	–	79
11	Yuki Takahashi	JPN	Moriwaki	11	–	16	20	–	9	–	2	–	4	–	9	–	–	6	–	–	77
12	Aleix Espargaro	SPA	Pons Kalex	5	–	–	10	16	–	–	7	–	10	6	–	11	–	3	8	–	76
13	Pol Espargaro	SPA	FTR	–	–	10	3	–	–	–	3	–	–	20	7	2	1	11	16	2	75
14	Julian Simon	SPA	Suter	6	10	20	13	–	–	–	–	–	9	4	–	–	–	–	–	6	68
15	Scott Redding	GBR	Suter	–	–	–	–	5	11	–	–	9	–	11	11	1	–	9	6	–	63
16	Mika Kallio	FIN	Suter	–	–	–	–	–	8	–	–	–	3	7	1	6	6	–	10	20	61
17	Kenan Sofuoglu	TUR	Suter	–	–	–	–	–	8	20	6	5	–	6	–	–	–	–	10	4	59
18	Randy Krummenacher	SWI	Kalex	–	–	9	4	11	5	7	3	13	–	–	–	–	–	–	–	–	52
19	Yonny Hernandez	COL	FTR	4	2	–	–	7	7	3	–	10	–	–	–	–	–	–	–	10	43
20	Max Neukirchner	GER	MZ–RE Honda	1	6	–	1	6	4	6	8	–	–	–	–	3	–	–	–	7	42
21	Jules Cluzel	FRA	Suter	9	–	–	5	–	13	–	1	7	–	–	–	–	–	–	3	3	41
22	Anthony West	AUS	MZ–RE Honda	–	5	–	–	–	–	13	–	–	–	–	–	5	4	–	–	13	40
23	Mike di Meglio	FRA	Tech 3	–	–	7	–	–	–	–	1	–	–	–	–	4	–	7	2	9	30
24	Mattia Pasini	ITA	FTR	–	3	–	–	–	–	–	10	–	5	8	–	–	2	–	–	–	28
25	Claudio Corti	ITA	Suter	–	–	–	5	–	–	–	1	–	1	2	–	–	13	–	–	1	23
26	Xavier Simeon	BEL	Tech 3	–	–	–	2	–	–	4	–	–	–	3	–	–	5	–	1	8	23
27	Alex Baldolini	ITA	Suter	–	–	–	8	3	2	5	–	–	–	–	–	–	–	–	–	–	18
28	Kenny Noyes	USA	FTR	–	–	–	–	–	–	–	–	–	–	–	–	–	–	–	11	–	11
29	Kev Coghlan	GBR	FTR	–	–	8	–	–	3	–	–	–	–	–	–	–	–	–	–	–	11
30	Ratthapark Wilairot	THA	FTR	–	4	–	–	–	–	–	–	–	–	–	–	–	–	–	–	–	4
31	Ricard Cardus	SPA	Moriwaki	–	2	–	–	–	–	–	–	–	–	–	–	–	–	–	–	–	2
32	Axel Pons	SPA	Pons Kalex	–	1	–	–	–	–	–	–	–	–	–	–	–	–	–	–	–	1

125cc

Position	Rider	Nationality	Machine	Qatar	Spain	Portugal	France	Catalunya	Great Britain	Netherlands	Italy	Germany	Czech Republic	Indianapolis	San Marino	Aragón	Japan	Australia	Malaysia	Valencia	Points total
1	Nicolas Terol	SPA	Aprilia	25	25	25	20	25	8	–	25	13	–	25	25	25	20	10	11	20	302
2	Johann Zarco	FRA	Derbi	10	16	16	11	10	20	11	20	20	20	11	20	20	25	16	16	–	262
3	Maverick Vinales	SPA	Aprilia	7	–	13	25	20	–	25	16	16	10	20	9	16	13	8	25	25	248
4	Sandro Cortese	GER	Aprilia	20	10	20	9	13	9	13	4	8	25	16	13	9	11	25	20	–	225
5	Hector Faubel	SPA	Aprilia	5	5	–	13	9	16	6	11	25	13	9	11	–	16	9	13	16	177
6	Jonas Folger	GER	Aprilia	11	20	11	10	16	25	8	–	9	–	7	7	6	10	–	10	11	161
7	Efren Vazquez	SPA	Derbi	13	7	10	16	11	11	9	13	–	–	16	13	–	13	5	13	–	160
8	Luis Salom	SPA	Aprilia	8	–	8	6	–	13	20	10	11	–	–	–	11	–	20	–	9	116
9	Sergio Gadea	SPA	Aprilia	16	–	4	8	8	–	16	9	10	11	13	8	–	–	–	–	–	103
10	Alberto Moncayo	SPA	Aprilia	9	–	–	5	1	–	1	7	5	16	–	5	8	9	11	7	10	94
11	Danny Kent	GBR	Aprilia	3	13	1	–	5	6	10	1	7	–	3	10	10	7	–	6	–	82
12	Jakub Kornfeil	CZE	Aprilia	–	9	3	–	6	7	–	6	3	9	6	4	3	5	3	8	–	72
13	Adrian Martin	SPA	Aprilia	–	4	7	2	7	10	–	–	–	–	–	–	7	8	–	–	–	45
14	Miguel Oliveira	POR	Aprilia	6	–	9	7	–	–	8	–	8	–	6	–	–	–	–	–	–	44
15	Marcel Schrotter	GER	Mahindra	–	3	–	–	–	–	7	5	–	2	–	5	–	–	–	–	4	36
16	Simone Grotzkyj	ITA	Aprilia	2	–	6	4	–	–	4	–	–	8	5	–	–	–	–	–	–	32
17	Louis Rossi	FRA	Aprilia	1	2	–	3	4	3	–	–	1	4	–	–	–	7	–	–	6	31
18	Zulfahmi Khairuddin	MAL	Derbi	–	6	5	–	–	–	2	–	–	7	–	–	1	–	–	9	–	30
19	Danny Webb	GBR	Mahindra	–	–	–	–	–	5	3	–	2	4	–	–	–	1	6	3	–	24
20	Luigi Morciano	ITA	Aprilia	–	–	–	–	–	–	–	–	5	1	2	4	–	4	–	–	7	23
21	Niklas Ajo	FIN	Aprilia	–	–	2	3	–	–	–	–	6	–	–	–	–	–	–	–	8	19
22	Alexis Masbou	FRA	KTM	–	–	1	2	2	5	–	–	–	2	–	–	–	2	4	–	–	18
23	Jasper Iwema	NED	Aprilia	4	–	–	–	–	–	2	1	6	–	–	–	–	3	–	–	–	16
24	Taylor Mackenzie	GBR	Aprilia	–	11	–	–	4	–	–	–	–	–	–	–	–	–	–	–	–	15
25	Alessandro Tonucci	ITA	Aprilia	–	–	–	–	–	–	–	–	–	–	–	–	2	6	–	1	3	12
26	Hiroki Ono	JPN	KTM	–	8	–	–	–	–	–	–	–	–	–	–	–	–	–	–	–	8
27	Manuel Tatasciore	ITA	Aprilia	–	–	–	–	–	–	–	–	–	–	–	–	–	–	–	5	–	5
28	Harry Stafford	GBR	Aprilia	–	–	–	–	–	–	–	–	–	–	3	–	–	–	2	–	–	5
29	Toni Finsterbusch	GER	KTM	–	–	–	–	–	–	–	–	4	–	–	–	–	–	–	–	–	4
30	Miroslav Popov	CZE	Aprilia	–	–	–	–	–	–	–	–	–	–	–	3	–	–	–	–	–	3
31	John McPhee	GBR	Aprilia	–	–	–	–	–	1	–	–	–	–	–	–	–	–	–	–	2	3
32	Josep Rodriguez	SPA	Aprilia	–	1	–	–	–	–	–	–	–	–	–	–	–	–	2	–	–	3
33	Giulian Pedone	SWI	Aprilia	–	–	–	–	–	–	–	–	–	–	–	–	–	–	–	–	1	1
34	Sturla Fagerhaug	NOR	Aprilia	–	–	–	–	–	–	–	–	–	–	–	–	–	–	1	–	–	1

SUPERBIKE WORLD CHAMPIONSHIP
REVIEW OF 2011
By GORDON RITCHIE

Photo: Gold & Goose

Results and statistics
By PETER McLAREN

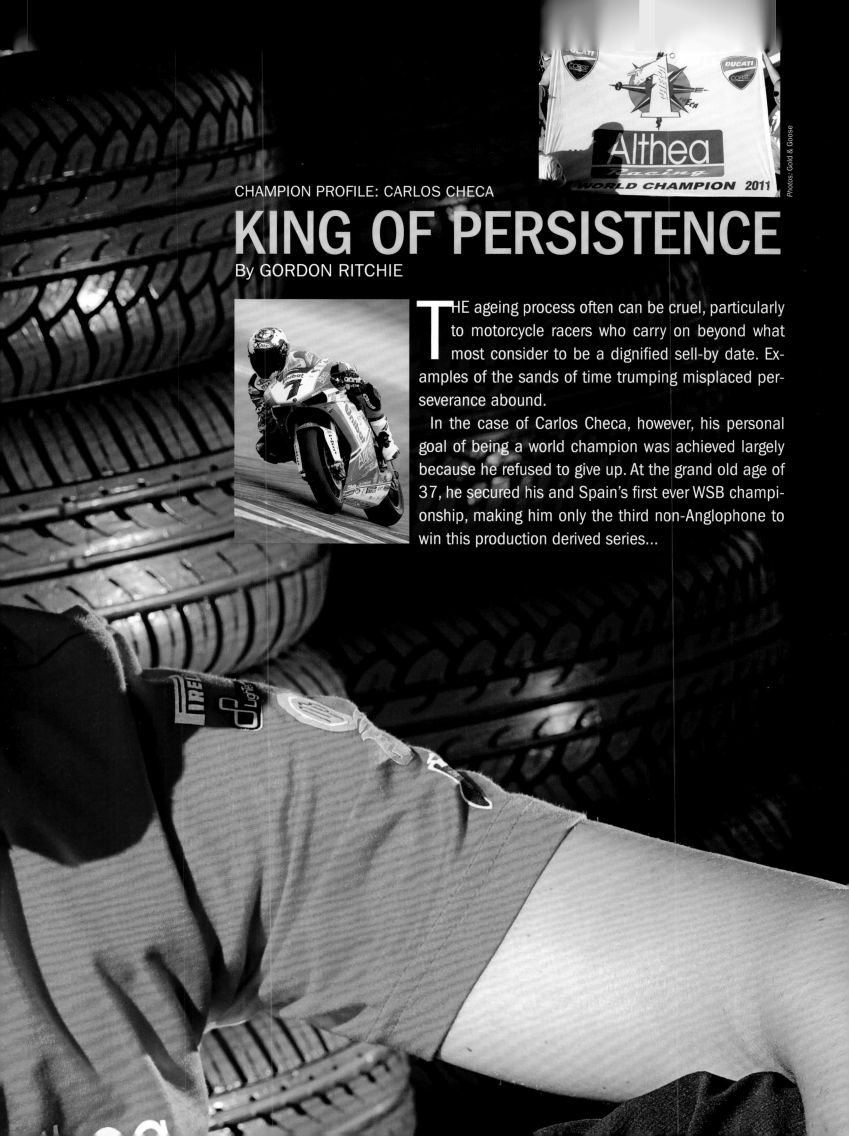

CHAMPION PROFILE: CARLOS CHECA

KING OF PERSISTENCE

By GORDON RITCHIE

THE ageing process often can be cruel, particularly to motorcycle racers who carry on beyond what most consider to be a dignified sell-by date. Examples of the sands of time trumping misplaced perseverance abound.

In the case of Carlos Checa, however, his personal goal of being a world champion was achieved largely because he refused to give up. At the grand old age of 37, he secured his and Spain's first ever WSB championship, making him only the third non-Anglophone to win this production derived series...

Above: Althea Racing's tight-knit crew exultant at Magny-Cours.

Right: Checa celebrates a double win at Silverstone. The Spaniard took 15 of the season's 26 races.

Photos: Gold & Goose

As a GP rider, Checa's nationality was seen by jealous outsiders as the passport to continued opportunities, even after the years when the results did not come so easily. To GP insiders, including Ducati, for whom he rode for a season, he was dependable and podium-fast. Not a potential number one perhaps, but a good second rider. A real grand prix pro.

Eventually, inevitably, Checa simply was not offered a ride that would allow him to continue in MotoGP. In fact, he wasn't sure if he wanted to stay, after one year on a bonsai 800.

Twice a 500cc GP race winner, he did not automatically turn up his nose at the prospect of WSB racing. He was convinced that it was possible to win in this peculiar championship, having seen Bayliss do it after he had been released from his personal GP shroud. Carlos had also seen James Toseland win the WSB championship on a Hannspree Ten Kate Honda in 2007. The prospect of a ride with the world's biggest manufacturer, in its lead WSB team, seemed more than just a means of extending his career.

It was not until some time in the latter part of his two-year stint that he realised he could not win the series, even on the best Honda. When offered a ride with the privateer Althea Racing Ducati team, he also realised that the perceived drop in status was actually a step up for his prospects. He had won three races for Honda in 2008, and in 2010 he also had won three for Ducati, making the official Ducati Xerox team look second best in the process.

With the bombshell that the Ducati factory would withdraw its omnipresent works effort in 2011, some riders may have been downcast. Checa was, presciently, the opposite. He realised that Ducati was still serious about WSB, but needed extra funds to point both its GP programme and road bikes in new directions.

Checa and Althea, a marriage made in heaven as we now know, managed to lift each other to new heights: sweet and impossible glories accrued for a team that was entirely private in set-up, but satellite or better in terms of technical support. It was almost a return to the true WSB ethos of the early years.

The symbiosis was three-fold: Ernesto Marinelli's 'skunk-works' low-key Superbike programme running from within MotoGP-centric Ducati Corse; the infrastructure and guiding hand of Althea Racing owner Genesio Bevilaqua's tight one-rider team; plus the speed and quiet brilliance of half missile/half metronome Checa. It led to more than just race wins.

The Italian civil war between 2010 champion Max Biaggi and another ex-GP star, Marco Melandri, proved a bonus for Checa, as Biaggi dropped points. Other potential contenders ran out of luck, experience or machine consistency at key times.

When Checa left Ducati's double-bogey track of Monza with a championship advantage of 27 points, his confidence gave way to true belief.

Question is, said some, how much was man and how much was machine in this championship win?

Well, Ducati is always a good choice in WSB, even if Checa's restricted V-twin was a moped in terms of top speed, and furthermore had been written off as incapable of a full-season challenge by the factory 1198 riders in 2010. Checa's stratospheric and consistent 2011 results – as a well-supported privateer, remember – made a mockery of that notion.

Rider number seven won because he found the sweet spots on his machine and tyres pretty much every session and then rode almost faultlessly, right on the edge between greatness and gravel trap. Plainly, Carlos Checa had improved with age.

He may not have become a MotoGP emperor, but earning the right to be the Superbike monarch is a special achievement for a rider who just never stopped believing in himself.

CARLOS CHECA

MAX BIAGGI

NORIYUKI HAGA

JAKUB SMRZ

LEON HASLAM

AYRTON BADOVINI

SYLVAIN GUINTOLI

TROY CORSER

LEON CAMIER

SUPERBIKE WORLD CHAMPIONSHIP

2011 TEAMS AND RIDERS

By GORDON RITCHIE

APRILIA

Aprilia Alitalia Racing

World champions in 2010, the top Aprilia team was the same as the year before, all a year older and some a year wiser. Max Biaggi (40) was forced to run the number-one plate, wanting to keep his number three, but he struggled to make even that many race wins in a difficult year, finally blighted by injury.

Leon Camier (25) was deemed worthy of a second year in the top team and scored podiums again, if not the wins Aprilia may have hoped for, particularly in Biaggi's absence.

Team PATA Racing Aprilia

Noriyuki Haga (36) soldiered on, fuelled by snack company money, and a desire to keep racing and remain living in Europe for as long as possible. And given the age of recent champions, he's got years in him still. The better his bike became, the better were his results.

BMW

BMW Motorrad Motorsport

The biggest wallets and ambitions in the paddock once more achieved less than their resources and workload deserved, prompting speculation of some fundamental error in approach since 2009. Troy Corser (39) battled on towards his twilight racing years, complaining that the bike has been doing some of the same things wrong since day one. Many new faces appeared over the winter.

Further proof came from the fact that Leon Haslam (28) blew into the squad full of motivation and proven brilliance on the relatively underfunded 2010 Suzuki,

only to find the Beemer far from co-operative, preventing him from challenging for wins. He had done that almost every weekend in 2010.

BMW Motorrad Italia SBK

Ayrton Badovini (25) brought his whole team up from Superstock and did brilliantly on occasion, proving that on a good bike he was well worth his new status. James Toseland (31) never got the chance to shine. After a career-threatening injury did its worst, he unwillingly called it quits.

He was replaced at various times by Barry Veneman (34), then Lorenzo Lanzi (29) and finally Javier Fores (26), all of whom put in a good effort on a satellite bike that made the factory effort look second-rate at times.

DUCATI

Althea Racing Ducati

The non-factory/factory one-man effort from Ducati and its privately owned partner, Althea Racing, looked good as championship challengers, while the focus and endless winning pace of Carlos Checa (38) saw off all comers, an incredible achievement no matter how you looked at it. One-off Imola rider Federico Sandi (22) bounced in to score points in each race, and then Althea's new Superstock champion, Davide Giugliano (21), was drafted in to serve at the final round.

Effenbert-Liberty Racing Ducati

A new team, built on the bones of the previous B&G combo, with some old PSG-1 engineering souls and a decent slab of Czech beer money to keep things afloat. And at a high-water mark, with Jakub Smrz (28) often fastest in tests and practice, but Sylvain Guin-

MARCO MELANDRI

JOAN LASCORZ

EUGENE LAVERTY

ROBERTO ROLFO

MAXIME BERGER

MARK AITCHISON

RUBEN XAUS

TOM SYKES

JONATHAN REA

MICHEL FABRIZIO

toli (29) the more consistent points plunderer. A very welcome sight for the IMS organisers, at it showed that real privateers like these could still come WSB racing and go podium fast in year one.

Supersonic Racing Team Ducati
The least extravagantly financed 1198 squad was still capable of putting aggressive rookie Maxime Berger (27) in the mix. A real heart-and-soul effort, they impressed many and often.

Wild-cards Matteo Baiocco (27) and Alessandro Polita (27) took their fluoro orange-and-white Barni Racing Team twins to a few WSB races and pestered some of the lower order regulars into submission, showing that wild-cards still have a valid place in WSB racing.

HONDA
. . . .

Castrol Honda
The same group of people from the north Netherlands town of Nieuwleusen, Ten Kate hooked a legendary sponsor for 2011 and became Castrol Honda. Supported by Honda Europe, their rollercoaster season was littered with rider injuries, regulars Jonathan Rea (24) and Ruben Xaus (33) both missing chunks of the year.
Fabrizio Lai (32), Alex Lowes (21), Makoto Tamada (34) and finally Karl Muggeridge (37) all stepped in, but the difficulty of making an instant impact proved too hard for them all.

One time WSB regulars Echo Sport Racing Company Honda also fielded Fabrizio Lai as a wild-card at one round, while Prop-tech Ltd Honda put Hungarian Viktor Kisaptaki (25) out as a wild-card at Brno.

KAWASAKI
. . . .

Kawasaki Racing Team
Despite having a new bike, both Chris Vermeulen (29) and Joan Lascorz (26) missed most of the pre-season due to injuries sustained in 2010. Vermeulen would never get a fair go thanks to an elbow injury that combined with his old knee woes to wreck his second season with the team. Lascorz was weak at the start of the year from his gigantic WSS smash at Silverstone in 2010, but stronger as the season went on, just like his new bike. Paul Bird Motorsport looked after the bikes and the garage again, with KHI providing tech support.

Kawasaki Racing Team Superbike
Kawasaki ran a third official bike because the Paul Bird Motorsport side of the garage insisted on it, and Tom Sykes (26) delivered some great rides, as well as solid development work in the winter and all through the year. His experience helped Lascorz immensely, and despite PBM being fired for 2012, in Germany, Sykes went out and won on the new bike.

Team Pedercini Kawasaki
Once a private Ducati team of variable results, the supported – but not official – Pedercini squad went another way from the factory in terms of engineering. Mark Aitchison (27) and Roberto Rolfo (31) occasionally found benefits in this arrangement. After being injured in a cycle accident at home, Rolfo was subbed at Portimao by Spain's Santiago Barragan Portilla (24). Bryan Staring (24) was a wild-card at Phillip Island, before heading off to his regular employment as one of Pedercini's Superstock hordes in European races.

SUZUKI
. . . .

Team Suzuki Alstare
Michel Fabrizio (27) was a lone gunman, who sometimes hit the target and shot himself in the foot at other times, to the dismay of team boss Francis Batta. Michel likes four-cylinders more than twins, but the forces ranged against him were often more consistent, if not always that much faster.

Yoshimura Suzuki Racing Team rider Joshua Waters (24) took three bites of the WSB fruit, the team not having the funds or support to go for a full-time effort. Their gorgeously prepared machines were welcomed at Phillip Island, Miller and Portimao.

Samsung Crescent Suzuki pairing John Hopkins (28) and Jon Kirkham (26) set pulses racing at Silverstone, as part of another left-field Suzuki effort that will go WSB racing full-time in 2012.

YAMAHA
. . . .

Yamaha Sterilgarda Team
Yet again, Yamaha rang the changes with not one, but two new riders. Marco Melandri (29) was a rookie with teeth, claws and a head on his shoulders, like every good ex-GP rider. He took little time to settle, won and always rode at the maximum.
Amazingly, Melandri was still outshone occasionally by his fellow WSB rookie team-mate, Eugene Laverty (25), who took a double win and was the only non-MotoGP veteran to fight for top-three ranking places all year. Some WSS riders really can make the switch after all. Team boss was Andrea Dosoli, another ex-GP figure.

THE BIKES OF 2011

BMW S1000RR

Kawasaki Ninja ZX-10R

Ducati 1198RS11

Suzuki GSX-R1000K11

Honda CBR1000RR

Yamaha YZF-R1

APRILIA RSV4R

The highly-adjustable and race-focused V4 Aprilia received a few new bits in 2011, but also lost some key old ones, most notably the crank-to-cam gear drive. This had been replaced by the original part-gear/part-chain-driven system found on the road bike.

The engine remained a compact and businesslike 999cc, 65-degree V4, narrow at the top to allow the twin-spar aluminium chassis to hug it tightly and to ensure a small frontal area. Bore and stroke stayed the same, at 78x52.3mm, and a compression ratio of 14.5:1 – already high – delivered over 220bhp at the same claimed 15,000rpm as in 2010. Many felt that actually it was a bit more, and the Aprilia was still the top-speed king.

The clutch was of Aprilia's own design and build; likewise electronics and engine management. With variable-height intake ducts, electronic injection running eight injectors and ride-by-wire throttle control, it was state of the art. Stock injectors caused few limitations for Aprilia, for whom power went up in 2011.

On the chassis side, an Aprilia swing-arm was the same as the final 2010 version. Brembo supplied the braking parts once more, with the T-shaped bobbins holding the brake rotor to the inside carrier.

Öhlins works material was adopted for the suspension front and rear, with 42mm TRVP25 front forks and RSP40 rear shock systems.

BMW S1000RR

The over-square, liquid-cooled transverse four pitched into its third year of development with the same 999cc, 80x49.7mm bore-and-stroke internal geometry. Fast to rev, the 2011 engine had a 14.5:1 compression ratio and punched out over 220bhp at 14,000 rpm, but did not develop enough of its epic engine power low down. A shortie under-engine exhaust used in the early rounds was short-lived.

The Dell'Orto throttles remained at 48mm, the ride-by-wire system taking orders from BMW's own RSM5 EFI control box. The electronics on the BMW were still all home-made, with smaller bike-sized connectors on the way for 2012.

Haslam brought Brembos and Corser went back to them as well, with both Evo and lithium aluminium types being used.

Öhlins TRSP25 front forks and Öhlins RSP40 rear shocks came with full tech support. Astounding as it may sound, the stock road-bike rear swing-arm was deemed better than the many race versions the team had tried in three years. Both OZ and Marchesini wheels were used in 2011.

The BMW weighed 165kg for 2011, just like the rest, but the main challenge was to get the weight moved back a bit to improve balance. There was also a new tank design, which pushed the riders' seats to the rear.

DUCATI 1198RS11

At the same 165kg and with over 20bhp less than its rivals, on paper it was hard to see where the Ducati could score over the others, especially as the bike was approaching senior-citizen status.

The latest 90-degree V-twin got its near 1200cc displacement from the same 106x67.9mm bore and stroke

as 2010, and Checa found his 2011 'privateer' bike the same as the factory one from 2010.

The Marvel 4 Marelli EFI unit, with IWP 162 + IWP 189 twin injectors per cylinder, was used again, in preference to the newer MHT Marelli system.

A supposed 200bhp at the crank, at 11,000rpm, seemed a bit low to some, as exhaust, mapping and electronics advances nudged the performance up through the season. Steel replaced titanium in some components, including the exhaust in places, as the new twin's weight limit was 3kg more than 2010.

Öhlins TRVP25 forks and RSP40 rear shocks held the bike off the ground.

Ducati continued with its own rear swing-arm. Brembo radial P4X34-38 calipers grabbed the 320mm front discs, which were connected to the disc carriers by round bobbins, not the more modern angular types.

HONDA CBR1000RR

The only real gap in the spec sheet seemed to be the lack of a full factory Öhlins suspension contract. By the first few races, this had to be rectified in some way, as the riders ran into chatter and had to ride too hard to make results, sometimes overstepping the mark.

Öhlins 43mm (not the more prevalent 42mm) front forks were used most often, and an RSP36 rear shock.

Near the end of the year, there was also a new Pectel PI ride-by-wire system, with software programming by Cosworth under the influence of Ten Kate's rider/team requests. The championship rules had to be changed mid-season to allow this add-on to a bike that did not feature it as a road model.

The 220bhp-plus Honda engine breathed with a bore and stroke of 76x55.1mm, but figures like peak revs and torque were not quoted. Lots of HRC race-kit components – airbox, clutch, pistons, conrods and gearbox – were used in 2011.

Stock injectors operated in conjunction with the 46mm throttle bodies.

All four bikes in the Castrol Honda garage had exquisite KR swing-arms in 2011, and the tyres again ran on PVM forged magnesium wheels.

Long-time partner Nissin continued to provide the brake calipers, with a new design of Yutaka discs being tried out as well as the existing models.

KAWASAKI NINJA ZX-10R

All new and the only one to be so in 2011, the Kawasaki caused a stir, if not a storm. The engine technology caught up with modern practice with a high clutch position and other refinements inside, but the engine's position in the chassis remained relatively conservative. The inline four's 76x55mm cylinders were claimed to make 215bhp at 15,500rpm.

Keihin 47mm throttle bodies and the latest MHT Marelli ignition provided the intake mixture.

A main change on the bike, which is still not Aprilia small, was to the rear end, with a horizontal back link rear suspension system adopted. This put the rear shock in an almost laid-down position, entirely above the underslung swing-arm, with the top/front end bolted directly to a horizontal chassis spar and the bottom/rear end to the rising-rate link, which was visible as a banana-shaped polished alloy item.

The advantages, technically, are that the shock can

run cooler and with a simpler link system, and the swing-arm has no massive hole for the shock in its centre, allowing for more freedom in swing-arm design. After lots of experimentation, one final design was found to suit the bike best, no matter who rode it.

The rear suspension body itself was the latest Showa T518-BFR, allied to beefy 47mm-diameter Showa Big Piston Forks up front, with 120mm of travel at the max. Brembo lithium aluminium brakes were used.

SUZUKI GSX-R1000K11

Much of the work on the 74.5x57.3mm bore-and-stroke Suzuki engine was done in Belgium in 2011, with the Alstare team claiming that their 14.8:1 compression ratio delivered 207bhp at 13,600rpm. Both revs and power were lower than claimed for 2010, but the average top-speed figures and podium abilities of the bike were still sometimes evident. Unusually, Alstare provided a torque figure: 118N/m at unspecified revs. The engine breathed out of two highly-sculpted Arrow silencers, as the original road bike has paired silencers.

Inside the engines there were two different philosophies at work, by necessity, as the supply of Suzuki spares was limited. Pankl and Suzuki conrods, plus Pankl and Suzuki pistons gave similar results, with sometimes Suzuki and sometimes Alstare engine specs pressed into service.

There was no new MHT Magneti Marelli EFI system for the one-rider team, but the same Marelli Marvel 4 with 2D acquisition, as that system is what Suzuki uses to analyse data in Japan. The GPS system was used solely for acquisition, unlike some other teams.

Brembo lithium aluminium calipers were employed, on Brembo floating discs. For suspension, Öhlins RSP40 rear shocks were adopted, with 42mm RSP forks preferred, again possibly because of budget constraints.

YAMAHA YZF-R1

The troublesome under-seat fuel tank was finally ditched and a vertical line running through the tank on the race bike separated the real fuel tank (behind and below the line) from the airbox and electronics area (under the dummy front tank cover). It all worked well for both new riders, with tyre wear improvements an instantly noticeable benefit.

The cross-plane crank now rotated for peak power at approximately 15,000rpm, and the output from the 78x52.2mm engine was an impressive 230bhp or so.

Helping control machine behaviour into and out of the corners, a MotoGP-inspired Magneti Marelli MHT EFI system was the hardware of the electronics package, the software settings inside supplied by the team themselves. An inertial platform was pressed into service, measuring all angles of pitch, lean and yaw, although such niceties as fuel saving algorithms were not needed in a class with no fuel limit.

A close relationship between Yamaha and Öhlins meant great performance from the new TRSP25 front forks, which gave more support and feedback to the riders mid-corner. The new slotted triple clamps also improved feel and flex while leaned over. Öhlins RSP40 rear shocks worked well on a new, more flexible swing-arm that appeared mid-season.

Brembo 320mm rotors were sometimes dropped in favour of 314mm ones.

PHILLIP ISLAND

Above: The first action of the 2011 season. Biaggi (1) leads Checa (7), Laverty (58) and a healthy field towards the awesome first turn.

Right: Tall boys Xaus (111) and Smrz (96) try to live high-speed life inside the bubble.

Centre right: A trio of Pedercini Kawasakis: Rolfo (44), Staring (67) and Aitchison (8) on the only all-new bike for 2011.

Right: Ex-WSS star Laverty leads Fabrizio in race one, making a quick impact in the biggest class.

Photos: Gold & Goose

Below: Wild-card 1: Yoshimura's local man, Waters, had a first go.

Below centre: Wild-card 2: Regular Pedercini Superstocker Staring had an early run on the full WSB version.

Below left: Corser power slides his official BMW at his favourite circuit.

Bottom: Race two top three: Biaggi, Checa and Melandri. Re-invigorated GP sprites would haunt the podiums all year.

Bottom right: Leon Haslam leads Marco Melandri; it was the Italian rider's first ever WSB race.

Photos: Gold & Goose

KICKING off a season in February, no matter what the continent, inevitably means that some parts for some race machines will not be fully proven beforehand. Hence the ideal preparation of an official pre-season test in the days running up to the Phillip Island race, which is now the norm.

Some machines, of course, needed less preparation than others, simply because they had been under development for WSB racing in one form or another since 1988. Like, maybe, the Ducati.

In an era free from factory team involvement, it was obvious from the outset that it was a case of little show, but all go for the Althea Racing Team. They immediately benefited from the developments the factory team had reserved for its own Pantah-based efforts in the most recent past

It was evident that talk over the winter of a blunted Ducati attack was misguided, as most twin-cylinder practice times were good, and from one rider in particular they were exceptional. Carlos Checa was dominant in testing, practice and then both races on Sunday.

He also won Superpole, in another new format with 16 riders in a three-stage knockout, instead of 20 riders as before.

Others had to look on, if not quite helplessly, then at least fretfully, as even the fire breathing Aprilia V4 of reigning champion Biaggi fell short. Twice he finished second to Checa in Australia, by an almost insulting 4.365 seconds in race one and then a still unchallenging, but closer, 1.188 seconds in race two. Checa said race two was harder, but to the casual observer, it simply looked less easy.

Third in race one was the official BMW of Leon Haslam, holding off Eugene Laverty, who almost took a podium in his first ever WSB race for the official Yamaha team. The man behind Laverty, Marco Melandri, would have to wait only two races to get his first top-three finish in this category of racing.

Checa, Biaggi and Melandri were less than 1.5 seconds apart after 22 laps of racing in the second leg, the old GP guard proving too strong for the existing and new WSB forces.

At Phillip Island, a fast track, although not in the same league as Monza, the fact that Biaggi's bike was 17km/h faster than Checa's was nullified because in every other department, the relatively forgiving and co-operative Ducati had enough of an advantage to allow Checa to ride at nearly 100 per cent.

Lap after impressive lap, Checa made the best of what he had, doling out lessons in how to ride a Superbike faster and faster, and keep the tyres working.

Unfortunately, fast qualifier Sylvain Guintoli fell heavily in race one, suffering foot and hand injuries that proved more problematic than they first appeared. He had been third in qualifying with his Effenbert-Liberty Racing Ducati. On 2010's factory 1198s, he and team-mate Jakub Smrz had showed that the twins were not dead for the midfield either.

Michel Fabrizio was a cool and relatively close sixth in race one, on an official Suzuki race bike Haslam had left behind because he had been given no assurances of ongoing factory involvement.

Leon Camier had his first up-and-down weekend as Biaggi's returning team-mate: sixth in race two, after a 13th in the opener.

Above: Haslam leads through Craner Curves in the opening leg.

Right: Camier battles with Melandri in race two, but he would have to yield.

Above right: A podium for Smrz was so nearly his first win.

Centre, top left: A chilly wait for Eugene Laverty on the grid.

Centre, bottom left: Race two winner Checa was increasingly inspired.

Centre, right: Melandri leads Midland maestro Haslam in race 1.

Far right: Mind that bike! Tom Sykes swaps stricken green machine for imaginary yellow flag.

Photos: Gold & Goose

DONINGTON WSB in 2011 almost never happened, because the track had nearly closed for good as a race venue the year before. An act of collective will, however, brought one of the most bike-friendly circuits back to life, although the hurried nature of the return meant that the only slot available for the Superbike calendar was at the end of March.

Many riders had deep misgivings after previous frozen outings at the circuit under the flight path of the nearby East Midlands Airport. Result? Shirt sleeves on Friday, thermal underwear on Sunday.

A lot of riders were intimately acquainted with the circuit layout, only the Esses having been changed significantly. The result was a faster lap and an overall design that should have suited reigning champion Max Biaggi just fine. Sadly, he left chastened, punished and clearly rattled.

The reason for his upset was his countryman, Melandri. Biaggi crossed his path on track in a rough manner, gently slapped his face in the pit lane and then completely lost all semblance of control to ignore a black-flag penalty for jump-starting in race two.

He was up in front of Race Direction twice during the weekend and could only finish seventh in race one, when he rode like an angry novice, not a five-times world champion. He left in a poor fourth place in the championship table, facing a real rebuild job before heading to the next round at Assen.

All the judicial jousting detracted from the fact that Melandri won his first WSB race in race one, Checa took the second, and privateer Jakub Smrz came close to his first win in this class, riding for a team that was only three races old in its current form – Effenbert-Liberty Racing Ducati.

Smrz was the star man in race one. Ultimately, though, he was outshone when his tyre had given its best and the remarkable Melandri had made up a gap that had seemed impossible to bridge.

Checa was a little emotional at winning race two at a circuit that had come close to claiming his life after a big crash there many years ago.

The final podium places went to Checa in race one and then local man Camier in the second, at least one of the top Aprilia runners having a day that ended with an upswing and not an upper-cut.

Battling a bike that seemed difficult to ride, BMW man Leon Haslam was full of fight, but only fourth on two occasions. He survived the near crash of the season in race two.

The new Kawasaki challenge had been battling against the usual developmental issues, but it was proving a brutally tough season for all of the seven manufacturers, the combined regulation qualifying session putting the top 14 inside the same second. Checa took pole eventually, from Haslam and Sykes. When Sykes' team-mate, Lascorz, scored fifth place in race two, 14 seconds behind the increasingly brilliant Checa, the new bike made an arrival of sorts.

Only the sheer desperation of Haslam gave the Englishman fourth in leg two. Sykes could not replicate his top practice form in the races, falling from a good position in race one, then going 12th in race two.

The top seven places in the second race went to seven different makes of machine (Rea sixth for Honda and Fabrizio seventh for Suzuki).

Few were disappointed to be back at Donington, despite the fact that it is still far from a modern race circuit and that tarmac temperature was only six degrees in race one.

ASSEN
ROUND 3 · HOLLAND

Above: Toreador Checa triumphed in race two.

Left: Biaggi's self-deprecating fuel tank sticker.

Far left: Rea and Ronald grin at their team's home win.

Main photo: Über-trier Rea leads race one from Biaggi, Checa and Sykes.

Photos: Gold & Goose

A SSEN in April: in theory, it should have pelted down with rain at some stage. In reality, it was dry, remaining so until the podium finishers uncorked the fizz on Sunday.

Jonathan Rea was sprayer-in-chief in race one, the tough rider from Northern Ireland taking his Castrol Honda to a win that had been prevented at Phillip Island and Donington by his many big falls. Going third in Assen's race two, Rea showed that he was back and ready to join what was becoming a game of hunt the bull for all the top competitors not in possession of a V-twin.

Rea had even been fastest in pre-Superpole qualifying, before giving way in Superpole to – guess who? – Checa.

The Spaniard played a cool game in race two and scored the race win, his fourth of six attempts, and once again he pulled away from the chasers in the rankings.

Momentum was maintained for Checa, resurrected for Biaggi.

After an ego- and reputation-bruising weekend at Donington, Biaggi showed why he had endured at the top of the results sheets for 20 years or so. Only sixth in Superpole, he was second in both races, 0.7 second behind Rea in race one, 0.5 second off Checa in race two. The podium in race one was Rea, Biaggi and Checa, then Checa, Biaggi and Rea. Three top men monopolised the podium this weekend, while one was on the slide, literally so in race two.

Melandri could not follow up on Donington. He was fourth in race one, over nine seconds off. Then he fell with six laps to go in the second.

The chances of Leon Haslam winning a race again anytime soon – on a BMW that was proving fast on the straights, but trickily erratic going into corners – were receding at an alarming rate. A depressing 12th in race one was followed by a climb back up to fifth in race two, but Haslam was having to exert too much for too little reward again.

Troy Corser, a double champion, was sixth on his BMW in race one, but a faller in race two. It was not going to plan for the biggest presence in the paddock, despite all the changes over the winter.

Only 14 of 21 riders finished race one, but only 20 started race two after Chris Vermeulen withdrew, still struggling with his old right knee injury. He also had technical issues in practice at his 'second home' race, held in the country of his grandparents' birth and his father's schooling.

Bizarrely, the top Kawasaki was a Pedercini bike, with rookie Mark Aitchison battling to tenth. That was not in the script: it was one thing to have an ongoing injury holding back Vermeulen, quite another that tyre gambles and lack of set-up consistency put riders like Sykes and Lascorz into the bottom half.

The return of not just form, but coolness and assuredness to the Biaggi effort was evident from day one, Max looking relaxed and even contrite enough to display a cartoon depicting himself as a supermarket chicken with the following caption: "Top Quality Chicken: 99% Italian; Born: Italy; Raised: Monte Carlo; Plucked: England; Cooked: Donington." At Assen, it was a case of a rebirth in racing ability and even a degree of humility. Cartoon stickers aside, to him it was as if Donington had never happened.

Above: Still work to do for BMW's official team.

Top: Smrz went down and put out Guintoli as race one fell flat for the Effenbert team-mates.

Right: Local rider Veneman subbed for Toseland in the BMW Italia squad.

Below: Vermeulen looks happy before race one, but had not recovered enough to race at his normal level.

Below right: Checa relegates Haga in race two; behind Biaggi gets ready to pounce.

Photos: Gold & Goose

Above: A podium in race two for local hero Fabrizio, as Alstare Suzuki drank champagne on a beer-money budget.

Left: James Toseland was sidelined with a broken wrist and hand, which eventually would force his retirement.

Far left: Laverty rode a self-propelled jet stream for Yamaha at the team's home round, winning both races at the historic track.

Bottom left: Corser made a great start to race one, leading Biaggi, Melandri, Haslam and co. The veteran double champion finished seventh.

Below left: Maxime Berger, a fast rookie on a Ducati, which was not suited to Monza's full-throttle sections.

Below centre left: Fabrizio Lai had another go at this WSB stuff.

Bottom: Kawasaki team-mates Lascorz and Sykes battle it out on the track as Biaggi re-emerges from the pit lane after taking his ride-through penalty.

Below right: Haslam and Rea were eliminated on the opening lap of race two, in the near-obligatory Monza chicane smack-up.

Photos: Gold & Goose

O NCE again, off-track tribulations threatened to overshadow the usual breathtakingly fast Monza track action, as once more a Yamaha rider would have his first ever WSB triumph overshadowed by controversy after the engines had been silenced.

Eugene Laverty's double victory at his team's home round at Monza normally would have been a reason for celebration all round, even if it had robbed theoretical crowd favourite Melandri of at least one clear chance of victory. As it was, recrimination abounded after Max Biaggi was given a ride-through penalty for crossing into a prohibited area of escape road at the infamous turn one, during race two.

The tarmac run-off is clearly marked in this area to provide a safe channel for riders who overshoot their braking to rejoin the track. However, Biaggi had strayed a little.

The penalties for entering the area had been explained by the organisers at a riders' meeting before the race weekend, but Biaggi had not been present, although his team manager had been.

Biaggi's latest controversy saw him drop a place, and the post-race Press conference, held as usual in the public area of the paddock, descended into a heckling match between Biaggi fans and the rest. In the midst of the fuss, bemused double race winner Laverty and erudite team-mate Melandri sat alongside the other podium finisher, Michel Fabrizio, high-water mark for the low-budget Suzuki so far.

Melandri stated that everybody knew the rules and Biaggi had broken them – no matter how inadvertently – so the result was as it stood.

Laverty, who had worked cleverly and well to hold off Biaggi in race one, with Haslam beating Melandri to third, said afterwards that he had never seen anything quite like it. Neither had anyone else, because this was easily the most disrupted, noisiest and potentially explosive conference in WSB history. At least it didn't end in a fight.

Biaggi would certainly have been in with a shout of a win, had he not been pulled in for a long ride down Monza's pit lane, which lost him a valuable chance to peg back Checa. The Spanish rider knew that Monza would hurt his points tally, and he was right, as he took only ninth and tenth. A certain sixth was lost in race two when wisps of oil smoke became evident and he slowed. The one weak spot of the Ducati twin was that its top speed was strangled by air restrictors and internal limits.

Monza is a place where the 200mph-plus four-cylinder machines can really fly, but not all the fours were able to deliver what their teams had hoped.

BMW had Haslam on the podium, but the cracks were still showing in the bike's overall balance and the Briton had to ride awfully hard to stay in the mix. He tangled with Rea and Smrz in a race-two crash that put them all out.

Corser was seventh and fifth, good results in the grand scheme. Rea, for Honda, was sixth in race one, 12 seconds off.

The satellite BMW squad, with more freedom to do as it pleases with the factory engines, was showing signs of a better mid-season approach than the factory team. The 2010 Superstock 1000 champion, Ayrton Badovini, was 11th in race one, but a vastly improved sixth in race two, and also ten seconds closer to the winner.

Kawasaki had a down day again, considering how much effort was being put into the development plan, with Sykes 13th in the opener and Lascorz ninth in race two. Tyre choice, performance and set-up were all ingredients that had yet to be blended into a homogenous whole.

Left: The circuit and bikes were dwarfed by the dramatic mountain backdrop, the late-May snowline descending almost to track level at one stage.

Below far left: Checa was perfect, except while celebrating his first race victory.

Below centre left: Tom Sykes took an encouraging sixth place for Kawasaki in race two.

Below left: Grid girls opted for leggings to fight the mountain chill.

Below: Second place for Smrz in race one was his second of the year.

Bottom: Post-race two burnout for Leon Camier. Second was cause for celebration with Checa on peerless form.

Bottom left: Privateers Guintoli and Smrz went podium bagging as MMP equated to Ducati heaven in race one.

Photos: Gold & Goose

IF asked to name a favourite circuit, undoubtedly Carlos Checa would choose Miller Motorsports Park. Even two potentially soul-destroying DNFs from easy leading positions in 2010 were not enough to stop him looking forward eagerly to 2011's WSB visit.

The circuit is nearly three miles long. It seems about three miles high for some engines, too, as the thin air at high altitude means less power.

For Checa and Ducati, 2011 was pure perfection that delivered two large pieces of silverware to check in as excess baggage on the way home.

Almost the entire weekend went well for Carlos, who was top of combined qualifying by 0.795 second, and who then headed Superpole by 0.075.

In the races, his margins of victory were 2.7 and 7.1 seconds, and he even shaved 24 seconds from his race-one time to prove that really he was only racing himself.

The only downsides for the Spanish star were two mechanical breakdowns in early practice, which had the whole Althea garage wondering, temporarily, if they were jinxed as far as their luck at Miller was concerned. On top of that, a comical topple-over in the sand, after some atrocious pre-race weather had turned the run-off areas into gritty clay swamps, saw even Checa joining in with this silliness.

With the Aprilia gasping for air and the in-line fours simply trounced, race one was a Ducati-fest as the Effenbert-Liberty duo of Smrz and Guintoli claimed second and third respectively. Guintoli's first ever podium was a relief, but the privateer Ducati riders' joint pace seemed set for the day, and they barely went faster in race two: this time Guintoli finished seventh and Smrz eighth.

Race two saw Leon Camier beat team-mate Max Biaggi for an Aprilia two-three. Camier had been fourth in race one, Biaggi a non-finisher after a tumble with Rea. Camier was lucky to have survived a run across the sodden gravel in race one to rejoin, and so high up. He was riding with a sore wrist after a big crash in practice.

Max blamed Rea for the race-one crash, revealing that the impact had been hard enough to crack his helmet.

Best of the Japanese bikes was the Yamaha of Eugene Laverty, who won a tussle with Fabrizio in race two for fourth; the latter was seven seconds up on Miller virgin Melandri. Tenth and sixth were the high points for one of the Checa-chasers-in-chief, despite qualifying impressively on the front row at this tricky circuit – it looks flat from a distance, but hides lots of elevation changes and blind-corner entries.

Kawasaki man Tom Sykes had a strong ride to sixth in race one, but was a second a lap slower than Checa.

Haslam was depressed to have qualified 12th and then be down in eighth in race one. He was almost in tears after riding his butt off in race two, only to finish 13th, some 37 seconds slower than Checa. It was a tough day for BMW's bigger names, but Ayrton Badovini took his Italian-run Beemer to seventh and ninth.

Rea and his Castrol Honda team had chosen MMP as their test track and had lapped as extensively as the unseasonably bad weather allowed. Nonetheless, it was all gloom on race day, as Rea finished 11th in race two. Victory at Assen in May seemed a long way back down a darkening tunnel.

James Toseland rode in America despite suffering from a nasty hand and wrist injury after crashing in testing at Aragón: he lasted just one race and earned one point. A minute's gap showed how difficult it had been.

Above, left to right: Giorgio Barbier (Pirelli), FIM President Vito Ippolito and Paolo Flammini (IMS CEO) on the grid.

Top: Checa the winner – a common occurrence in 2011.

Above right: Badovini impressed with a battling fourth in race two.

Right: Sykes on the Kawasaki leads at the start of race one.

Centre right: Melandri won the battle for third in race one, with Haslam and Sykes his co-combatants.

Far right: Checa takes the plaudits after another double win.

Photos: Gold & Goose

Italian wild-cards Matteo Baiocco (*top*) and Alessandro Polita (*above*). Both grabbed some points in one race and crashed into retirement in the other.

Above left: The unusually damp conditions saw Sykes take a confidence-boosting Kawasaki Superpole win.

Left: Race-one crasher Smrz came down to earth after his American high.

Below: A welcome return to the podium for privateer Haga in race two.

Photos: Gold & Goose

H UBRIS is not something of which you can accuse Carlos Checa. Despite having run away to a double at Miller, he had the good grace to say that he had never expected to repeat the feat at the very next round, Misano.

He had expected Biaggi to win a race or two, but the best Max could muster was second. Twice. It was close at one of Max's home tracks: less than a second in race one, then only 1.4 seconds in race two, which was run in two parts, but with only the second session counting.

After wet periods of practice, it was a weird weekend by the seaside for the many at Misano.

The reason for the race-two stoppage was that first Melandri and then Camier had fallen at the first chicane, and with Melandri's bike sliding back on the circuit, the red flag had appeared. Some thought the decision too quick, as there had been no red flag when Smrz had crashed in Tramonto corner during race one in arguably similar circumstances, but others were unequivocal that it was the right decision. Safety first is always the wise option in this sport.

Until that race-two fall, it had been proving a decent, but by no means great day for Melandri. He was third in race one, but the fact that he was 17 seconds from the leading duo proved his earlier assertion that he could not compete at this track on this weekend. He had been fourth after Superpole, but race set-up eluded him.

Number 33 had to work doubly hard in race one to head up wet-and-dry Superpole winner Sykes, the number 66 rider giving the new Kawasaki its first truly measurable success, albeit one that gained him no points.

Those had been saved for the first race, when a conventional in-line Kawasaki four had split the dominant forces of V-twin, V4 and cross-plane-crank, in-line four. Sykes was only 1.5 seconds from a podium. Laverty was just behind, then came Camier again a little further back.

The second race two was an intense contest, with only 14 finishers from 17 starters. In race one, 22 had started and only 15 had finished.

Jonathan Rea had made neither race, as a staggeringly fast warm-up crash had left him with a snapped tendon and a broken right wrist, injuries that would keep him out for some time. He had already been riding injured, having needed stitches in his arm the day before.

Guintoli couldn't match team-mate Smrz's third in qualifying, but made amends with eighth in race one, then seventh in race two.

Badovini posted a quite reasonable eighth in race one, but in the second he was ablaze, running hard and heroically with Haga, who finally took a privateer podium that sent his Italian Pata Aprilia team into paroxysms of joy. A podium for a privateer is great at any time, but for Haga it was particularly fortuitous. He had been in danger of disappearing in terms of profile and had qualified only 17th.

Badovini's ride to fourth was just as special, as it gave his Italian team their best result yet as the works BMW boys struggled with an inconsistent machine yet again.

Toseland had been replaced by Lorenzo Lanzi, as he needed to rest his injured and slowly healing hand. But Chris Vermeulen came back to action for Kawasaki, and despite falling early in his practice sessions (an electronics sensor went wrong, it was said) and suffering an elbow gash that would prove problematical, he still posted results of 14th and tenth.

Fabrizio fell and hurt his wrist in race one, but he recovered to take sixth in the second.

Above: Biaggi finally won a 2011 race, in WSB's first visit to the splendid Motorland circuit.

Right: The end of another dry spell. Melandri took an overdue second win in race one.

Above right: Fast learner Aitchison ponders life on a Kawasaki.

Centre right: Catalan Lascorz had two strong rides on the Kawasaki in Aragón.

Below centre right: Haga celebrated 300 World Superbike starts.

Below far right: Xaus struggled at the tail of the field on his Castrol Honda.

Photos: Gold & Goose

DESPITE some relatively heavy promotion for WSB's first visit to Aragon, few of Checa's countrymen came to cheer him. The claim was for 30,000 across the weekend, but they were real enthusiasts only. Motorland Aragón may well qualify as the most remote circuit imaginable, but it is still in Spain and is no further from the two-wheel heartland of Catalunya than Valencia. And Valencia did get a reasonable crowd for the most recent Superbike races.

The dismissive masses missed a rare and remarkable occurrence – a crash by championship leader Checa. He had been fastest after regular qualifying (and fourth in Superpole), and it looked like the awesome straight at Aragón was not going to be that much of a problem after all for his choked 1200cc twin. Under real race conditions, however, he realised that Melandri and Biaggi's unfettered fours were untouchable.

He tried to stay with them in any case, setting a new lap record on lap seven, but fell from contention on lap eight. The small, but loyal crowd groaned theatrically; the rest of the WSB world was stunned to learn that Clockwork Carlos had suddenly bust a psychological spring. Wound too tight at home, it seemed.

Any doubts were emphatically quashed in short order, though, as he recovered his composure to finish third in race two.

Fact was, however, Checa had to watch from a distance as Melandri showed true class to win race one by a second-and-a-half from Biaggi, with Camier third; then witness Biaggi winning his first race of the year by well over four seconds from Melandri.

The 2010 champ had led every lap, and the relief for him and his team was visible and audible. He became the fifth rider to have won at least a single race in WSB in 2011.

The impressive Aragón facility was four-cylinder friendly to most, as Laverty, Sykes, Haga, Lascorz, Badovini, Haslam and Corser followed the leaders home, but once again the BMW guys were in the relative doldrums.

In the second race, only Checa dented the four-cylinder dominance, as first-race faller Fabrizio gathered his wits and willpower to record an impressive fourth. There was still life in the old GSX-R dog yet, and plenty of fight in Fabrizio, hurting or not.

Lots of riders had chosen Aragón as their test track, including Joan Lascorz, but bad winter weather had wrecked a few teams' plans on that score.

By contrast, in June, the northern track had a good go at posting the highest asphalt temperatures of the year, with 53°C recorded for race two.

On home ground, Lascorz's fifth was a good reward for the rookie, but teammate Sykes fell in race two, as at Misano. For the other main Kawasaki rider, Vermeulen, Aragon was an effort, as he was still not fully fit. Twelfth in race one, he was 14th in the second running, but 49 seconds from the winner.

It was best not to ask Ruben Xaus about Aragon, as he was plainly stunned to be 16th in race one, his bike delivering so little grip that he went for a ride in the gravel in the opener and entered the pit lane twice in race two, the second time to park it. Afterwards, he looked like a man in shock, as his first Honda experiment appeared to be running out of repeatable data, never mind results.

Corser became the latest in a growing list of riders to be injured: he had run wide, returned towards the track, only to find that Maxime Berger had similar problems. They collided. Corser broke his left radius and ulna, but did not blame Berger.

Above: Biaggi leads Melandri, Checa and Laverty, with creaky communist-era backdrop unable to conceal the fact that the Brno circuit is a truly brilliant race venue.

Right: Badovini pushed on to sixth place in race two as he grew in Superbike stature again.

Below right: Laverty extracting the max from his Yamaha, although he could not stay with the imposing top three of Biaggi, Melandri and Checa.

Centre right: Melandri and Biaggi battle for victory in race one.

Photos: Gold & Goose

Above, top to bottom: Alex Lowes substituted for the injured Jonathan Rea at Castrol Honda; Hungarian wild-card Viktor Kipspataki took a point in race two; Corser was present, but was *hors de combat.*

Below right: Melandri and Biaggi celebrate after race one.

Photos: Gold & Goose

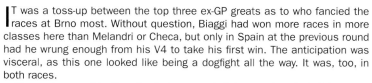

IT was a toss-up between the top three ex-GP greats as to who fancied the races at Brno most. Without question, Biaggi had won more races in more classes here than Melandri or Checa, but only in Spain at the previous round had he wrung enough from his V4 to take his first win. The anticipation was visceral, as this one looked like being a dogfight all the way. It was, too, in both races.

The motorway-wide Brno track is a wonderful example of what happens when nature and intelligent design are combined. It is a tutorial in tarmac for anyone attempting to build a 'modern' circuit: use the topography, make the chicanes flowing and provide endless passing opportunities. By and large, the riders love it, the spectators get great views wherever they sit, and it has a unique ex-Iron Curtain charm that is both dowdy and endearing.

After the (relative) quietness of the Aragón races, Brno brought fireworks and ferocity, and Checa would leave with more points trimmed from his lead.

It was even a close thing after Superpole, with Biaggi, Melandri and Checa the top three, joined by the man making the next biggest mark, Laverty.

As it turned out, we had the same top ranked riders in each Brno race, the only difference being that Melandri won race one, while Biaggi took race two.

Marco, Max and Carlos were covered by 0.436 second in race one, with Biaggi and Melandri swapping the lead all over. There was close action; there was even some rubbing it seemed, but none of the kicking and gouging we had seen at Donington.

Behind, some eight seconds back, at his absolute all-time best track, Fabrizio was fourth. Laverty, 11 seconds down, was well clear of Badovini, the latter's satellite bike gently toasting Haslam and his own temporary team-mate, Lanzi. Twice.

Corser was missing, unable to ride because of his forearm injury.

In race two, which even aced Aragón's sweatbox by sizzling the tarmac to 54°C, Biaggi got the better of Melandri by just 0.222 second. Checa was lucky to finish after losing power near the end, his big twin coming close to crying enough before lap 20 had been completed. Just as well he got his podium, because the battle between Italy's finest annexed large portions of his advantage once again: Biaggi left Brno only 30 points adrift.

Behind the contenders, Fabrizio put up the best fight in race two. Laverty was close, but just too far behind in fifth, then came Badovini, well off the pace, but well inside the top rankings.

One space behind, Haslam and Lascorz battled away, with Leon eighth and then ninth in the races; Joan was ninth and then eighth. Sykes had to give best to Lascorz by one place in race one, but changes to his machine in race two saw him lapping way slower than the leaders at the end, dropping off to finish 14th, 46 seconds adrift. He had been 'only' 22 seconds off in race one.

Local man Smrz enjoyed a lot of publicity and promise at Brno, especially after taking fifth in Superpole. The only problem was that he does not much like the track. Hence 11th in race one, then a turn-12 crash in race two were not exactly surprises.

Xaus' season went from bad at home to worse away: he qualified 17th, then crashed in race one, hard enough to miss race two. He would go on to miss Silverstone, too.

Vermeulen was another who had no race to run in the second outing. He had finished 18th in race one, but was forced to pull out of the second, still suffering. Alex Lowes replaced the recovering Rea at Brno, the rolling medical dramas becoming as much the story as the racing.

Above: Wild-card Hopkins showed his worth with fifth and seventh.

Above right: We meet again. Laverty, Checa and Melandri filled the podium positions in each race.

Right: Jon Kirkham also did a solid job for Crescent Suzuki.

Centre right: Melandri and Biaggi had a fine battle in race two.

Photos: Gold & Goose

Above left: Former WSB champions Hodgson (*left*) and Fogarty took on TV commentary roles.

Photo: Gold & Goose

Left: Hopkins grabbed Saturday glory with Superpole.

Photo: Clive Challinor Motorsport Photography

Far left: The field streams past the vast new Silverstone 'Wing' complex.

Below: Checa's race-one win was the 300th for Ducati in WSB. It would soon be 301.

Bottom: Laverty had the edge on team-mate Melandri this time around.

Photos: Gold & Goose

Below right: Castrol Honda substitutes Lowes and Lai did not really fly.

Photo: Clive Challinor Motorsport Photography

CHECA was nervous about Silverstone, pointing to his lowly performances there in 2010, on ostensibly the same bike as for the 2011 season. He was taking nothing for granted at this ever-improving bike venue.

Presented with a new pit lane and a new Silverstone 'Wing', Checa flew to the top four in Superpole, an overnight perch so high it was a surprise to some of his rivals.

Ahead of him, and everybody else, was a rider resurrecting his international career: John Hopkins was a wild-card on his BSB Samsung Crescent Suzuki, with which he is a regular front-runner, and he set a new track best lap before the race. Fast British (or even Anglo/American) wild-cards had been out of the mix in WSB for a while, but Hopkins tweaked the tails of the big dogs only temporarily. Fifth and then seventh would be his race rankings, 11 seconds down each time.

Down on Carlos Checa each time, as it transpired, his Ducati being as dominant at this track as at most others. His Aragón blip was wiped from memory, if not from history.

Speaking of history, Checa took Ducati's record win total to over 300, but with no official Ducati squad any more, the celebrations were of a more personal nature.

Each race was a mirror image in the final podium places, with Laverty leading from second on the grid each time, but then being forced to succumb to peerless overtaker Checa on lap six.

Checa felt that maybe the difference in 2011 was in his bike's ability to handle the bumps over race distance; he had made a considerable change to his set-up during the weekend. That and his experience made the difference, as he put in his consistent attacks just as Laverty's tyres began to go off, leaving the Yamaha rider two step changes to deal with.

Nonetheless, Laverty's big shows in front of many of his Irish and British fans would give him his first podiums since his rookie race wins at Monza, his Yamaha being happy enough around the fast curves and high-momentum sequences that characterise much of the new Silverstone.

That was underlined when Melandri finished third on each occasion, 4.7 seconds down on Checa in race one and then 3.6 down in race two. Haslam posted a fourth place and then an eighth after much effort.

Biaggi was 11th in race one after suffering clutch issues and bending his brake lever in a collision with Corser, then a greatly improved fourth in race two, just behind Melandri. The Italian duellists had a go at each other again, but a repeat of Donington it was not.

For other British riders, Silverstone was hard, with Xaus substitute Alex Lowes scoring one crash and one retirement; while series regular Sykes missed the race after a big crash in final free practice on Saturday afternoon cracked his ankle and knocked him unconscious. With Vermeulen missing still, Lascorz (19th off the grid) pitched in with a miracle and took seventh in race one.

It was another lost weekend for the Netherlands-based Ten Kate squad and Castrol Honda, pointless after Lowes' two no-scores and with Rea replacement Fabrizio Lai falling in race one, then 16th and last in the other. Once more, the true privateer club was wielded with greatest enthusiasm by Guintoli, who posted a pair of sixths and had the pleasure of overhauling Hopkins in race two.

Alstare Suzuki rider Fabrizio had no such luck, falling in race one, then struggling to ninth in race two.

Double race winner in 2010, Cal Crutchlow's lap record remained intact, with Biaggi coming closest in race two.

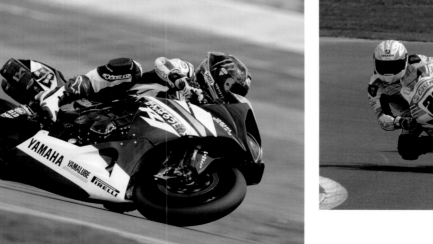

NÜRBURGRING
ROUND 10 · GERMANY

Above: Sykes and the Kawasaki squad celebrate their first win.

Above right: Melandri and Haga battle in race one.

Centre right: Checa cruised to another win in the opener.

Photos: Gold & Goose

Left: Privateer Haga was on sparkling form, taking third in race one.

Below left: Japanese star Tamada made a return as substitute for Xaus.

Far left: Horrible weather as the field faces up to the dramatic first hairpin in race two.

Below: Ducati jet-skier Guintoli took second place behind Sykes in race two.

Bottom: Rea was off and back on as the rains went from sustained to biblical and back again.

Below right: Race two fallers Haga and Camier were down and out before the red flag.

Photos: Gold & Goose

SUCH were the contrasts between a dry race one and an eventually fully wet race two that at one stage there was a real threat of cancellation. The deluge waxed and waned in race two, walls of water crashing down as threatening clouds met the nearby mountains.

Some of the riders were extremely irritated that the second race was not called earlier than the 13th lap of the proposed 20, but because it went this distance, Sykes and his Kawasaki Racing Team Superbike squad were awarded full points.

It was a field day for the statisticians: a first race victory for Sykes at this level, a first for the new Kawasaki Ninja ZX-10R, too. Sykes also became the sixth different race winner of the season so far, and Kawasaki the fifth different manufacturer to get the big trophy in 2011.

Most pleasingly for Sykes, he was once again quick in qualifying, the new bike getting closer to the top as a consistent package. Less pleasingly for the Paul Bird Motorsports element of the Kawasaki team, their contract was not renewed for 2012, shortly before Sykes won.

At their home circuit, BMW types were green with envy at Kawasaki's success, as they were nearly three years in with their 'new' bike and not a win to show for it.

Checa had no reason to feel anything but satisfaction, having taken pole again and a race-one victory ahead of Melandri and an experienced Aprilia rider who lives in Italy. Not, however, Max Biaggi, who claimed not to have missed a race in 19 years of competition – until now.

Full credit to satellite/privateer rider Noriyuki Haga, who took his Pata Racing RSV4 to third, 2.3 seconds from the win around a circuit where he had performed exceptionally well in the past, on a variety of engine configurations.

Biaggi missed both races, having been hit on the left foot by something flicked up from the track during practice, then having turned a large metatarsal crack into a full-blown fracture when stamping down the gears later in the weekend.

The dry first race saw Laverty fourth, Haslam fifth for the big Beemer team and the year's most consistently fast privateer, Guintoli, sixth.

The month off between Silverstone and Nürburgring obviously did Sykes the world of good, healing his ankle injury and allowing his head to clear well enough to keep it while many around him were losing theirs in the truncated splash-athon of race two. Fellow fast-thinkers Guintoli and Smrz navigated their Ducatis around to podium places, with the former closing in on Sykes, while the latter was 22 seconds off. Haga had led for ages, but fell at exactly the wrong moment, had he but known it.

Rea, in his comeback ride for Honda, had been down in tenth in race one, but finished fourth in race two. He even overtook Sykes at one time, but unfortunately he did so while separated from his machine, sliding at full speed into the dead-stop first hairpin. It was lucky that Sykes was just peeling into the corner by that time, the supine Rea and his bike sailing on past.

Rea continued his remarkable race two by extracting his bike from the air fence, getting back into action and finishing just off the podium.

Laverty, one of the early signallers for race control to call the race, was fifth, and Melandri sixth. Badovini was top BMW rider this time, seventh, but Checa's number seven was one place behind.

It had been some time since Checa had finished 50 seconds from the winner in this class, but he cared not a jot. One of his title challengers no-scored and the other still lost ground to him, despite finishing two places higher in race two.

Left: Toseland made a heartfelt retirement speech.

Below left: Biaggi was forced to miss the event with his foot injury.

Far left: Rea and Checa head into race one cheek by jowl.

Below: Althea Racing ran a second machine for Federico Sandi, who scored points on both outings.

Below far left: Badovini leads Guintoli and Smrz at the Variante Alta.

Bottom centre: Melandri's girlfriend exerted a magnetic force on Messrs Nikon and Canon all year.

Below right: An on-form Haga in pursuit of Rea in race one.
Photos: Gold & Goose

WHILE one top rider in WSB racing had to rule himself out of the Imola weekend, another proved that he really was back, and to full effect. The biggest star of the year, however, left Imola still not quite the new king, but only three points shy of lifting the championship trophy.

Biaggi had to sit out his final home race of the year, as he would the imminent race in France, due to his injured left foot.

Rea proved that he was really firing from the hip again after an up-and-down Nürburgring comeback the week before. He was second in Superpole (behind Checa, naturally) before making race one his own with a swashbuckling display, after breaking the early charge of Sykes.

Haga had another brilliant run on his satellite Aprilia, finishing only 0.111 second from Rea in race one. Checa was nine seconds back, in third, having got the better of a last-lap tussle with Sykes. Melandri, watching his championship chances go from slim to positively skinny, was eighth.

Race two was shaping up to be another big bang for Rea, but he broke down thanks to the original 50-cent part, a battery connector. Nonetheless, he had proved not only his prowess as a winning racer, but also that the new ride-by-wire system developed by Pectel PI and Cosworth was more than promising. In fact, it delivered first time out. Its appearance in Italy was only allowed by a swift change of tech rules shortly before Imola, as the stock Honda does not feature a ride-by-wire system.

With Rea out and a solitary Checa five seconds ahead, Haga took his second runner-up spot of the day, while lone factory Aprilia rider Camier had the joyful experience of scoring another podium – tempered by the fact that he was over ten seconds from Haga. The English rider had made some very rude passes on his rivals and then had run on, doing well to recover.

Haga may have benefited from some Biaggi parts, but in any case, two second places were great rewards for a Pata team that had been down as often as up in 2011.

Privateers had a good go at Imola all round, with Guintoli and Smrz sixth and seventh for the effervescent Effenbert-Liberty Racing team. Guintoli then took seventh in race two.

The wild-cards were out again at Imola, Polita and Baiocco pushing on for Barni racing Ducati, and there was even a second Althea Ducati Superbike, for Federico Sandi. He placed 13th and 12th, good results in this season. Race two saw only 14 finishers, with eight riders no-scoring.

Laverty won a race-two battle for fourth, only just in front of Haslam, while for Melandri finishing sixth was still just enough to stop Checa and company from celebrating the title win at home.

James Toseland had tethered both his world championship dreams to *terra firma* in France, in 2004 and 2007, but even getting to the penultimate round in 2011 proved impossible, never mind round 11 at Imola. At the previous German event, he had talked about returning fully fit in 2012, but a subsequent check showed that the injured bone in his hand had not recovered after all, and he had to accept inevitable retirement.

There were two public and innumerable private tributes to his career and character at Imola, one at the Paddock Show and one at the BMW hospitality unit, heartfelt for a rider who was a true product of WSS and WSB racing.

MAGNY-COURS
ROUND 12 · FRANCE

Main photo: Finally, the championship was won; the weather helped Checa celebrate.

Inset below: Checa gave it everything, despite his huge points lead.

Inset bottom: The first Spanish champion was an international favourite.

Photos: Gold & Goose

Above: Haslam engages elbows with Hard-man Haga.

Left: Joan Lascorz was top Kawasaki rider with eighth and seventh places.

Below: Guintoli shimmered on hot home asphalt.

Bottom: Two second places cemented Melandri's position as runner-up to Checa in the series.

Below right: Laverty worked hard to overhaul absent Biaggi's points total.

Photos: Gold & Goose

CONSIDERING the domination of Checa and his Althea team in 2011, it was almost a surprise that it took until the penultimate round for the championship to be finally awarded.

Checa was third in Superpole and then stole away at the front after following for a while in each 23-lap race. Margins of victory of 2.2 and 1.2 seconds did no justice to the way he held himself in check during the earlier laps, pushed on again as soon as riders in front showed signs of tyre squirm, then rode away as smoothly as if he were out for a sunny Sunday blast on an 1198 in the hills around Barcelona.

But he was in France, winning each race in style and, with his first victory, the title itself. Checa did not need to cover himself in all this glory to be champion, but his determination to win and win again spoke volumes about his approach to being a world champion for the first time in his long career.

Melandri also showed his class by scoring second each time, his package and experience of the Magny-Cours circuit not quite on a par with Checa's, but his willingness to fight absolutely clear. Ask his team-mate, Laverty, who unwillingly gave up second in race two, unable to contain Melandri's passing aggression.

Haslam (for a BMW first podium since Monza) and Camier finished ahead of Laverty in race one; Guintoli, once more the privateer *de jour*, was sixth and then fifth in race two. Haslam was fourth in race one, Camier sixth.

With no Biaggi, Melandri scored a guaranteed second in his first year of WSB competition, and even Laverty passed Max's static total by two points, setting up a belter of a final-round war for third.

Once more, Rea made himself a potential winning player on race day by taking only his second career Superpole win on the Saturday. He duffed his race-one start and fell trying to get back on terms, then encountered another silly electrical problem in race two; he left France pointless and frustrated.

Behind the leading lights, the early-season surge of riders on the grid had dwindled considerably. Javier Fores, who had taken over Toseland's BMW Motorrad Italia SBK ride at Imola, was 11th on two occasions in France, but he only had two riders behind him in race one, and only one in race two.

Chris Vermeulen was a no-show again – still not deemed fit to ride – and Xaus had fallen in the very first session in France and never got near the grid at all.

The result was 17 starters in race two, hardly a happy near-ending to a season, despite the strength in depth demonstrated by the fact that the last rider in race one was a 250cc GP race winner of yore – Rolfo. Berger, Superstock Championship runner up from 2010, was 12th and just 47 seconds behind the blur that was Checa in race two.

In race one, the top seven riders were within nine seconds; the top nine in race two were covered by 16, perhaps proving that the rules are not that bad as they stand.

Magny-Cours, which features a bit of everything, was well attended and the weather conditions contributed to the sunny disposition of most. In a way, it was almost the perfect place for Checa to be crowned, rather than in the overexcitement of Imola.

By the end of the weekend, Checa had scored double wins on five occasions during the year and had 14 race wins in total, with two more races to go. Not bad for a guy in his 38th year.

Above: Checa slips past Guintoli to take charge of race one.

Right: Hail and farewell. Yamaha riders Laverty and Melandri share their final podium as team-mates.

Centre right: Yamaha's last official in-house battle proved to be chemorable and meaningful.

Photos: Gold & Goose

Above, from the top: New and old blood was injected into the final weekend: Santiago Barragan, Davide Giugliano and Karl Muggeridge.

Above left: Rea leads the first lap of race one.

Left: So near, so far. Privateer of the year Guintoli nearly scored a win in race one.

Below right: The last race for Troy Corser, who had a special crocodile paint job on his BMW. He points to his WSB record: two times world champion – 1996, 2005; all-time championship points – 4000+; all-time most pole positions – 43; all-time podiums – 130; all-time most races – 377; victories – 33.

Photos: Gold & Goose

WITH the title wrapped up and even second place decided, the WSB riders came back for one last time in 2011 at a wonderfully warm, perfectly dry and perennially picturesque Parkalgar circuit.

Nobody was there for a holiday, evidently.

Even champion Checa and vice-champion Melandri were on a full war footing, both looking for wins that they finally achieved, Checa in race one and Melandri in race two.

Intrigue's best mate, Uncertainty, hovered over the final round, with who-goes-where stories abounding in these cash-strapped times, and all played a part in the fact that the last round was no go-as-you-please celebration.

There was also the small matter of overall third to be decided, as Biaggi came back from his enforced absence, determined to put the race number three back on his bike in 2012. Laverty, third by two points and loving it pre-race, was ready to defend. His effort would not be quite good enough, however, as 19th in race one, followed by a strong second in race two fell short when Biaggi posted a fourth and a seventh. With each rider tied on 303 points and also locked on two wins apiece in 2011, the second-place count-back was key, and Biaggi crossed the invisible line with nine to Laverty's three. Fourth was a superb rookie season for one of the year's six race winning riders.

Sylvain Guintoli almost made it a fairytale ending for his rookie Effenbert-Liberty team, but on a soft race-one rear tyre, his seemingly perfect display of front running dropped a notch when Checa finally caught up, on a harder rear that was better over all 22 laps.

Second again for Guintoli and sixth in the championship made his the best 'proper' privateer campaign, all done on a bike that was not quite Checa's and so did not have as much manufacturer support.

Third in each race was Jonathan Rea, with Superpole two weekends in a row. He led the first for two laps, but finished eight seconds down and three seconds up on the rapidly advancing Biaggi.

In race two, Rea was much closer to the Yamahas of Melandri and Laverty, only 1.3 down, and with traces of needle coming into the all-Ireland battle: a late attempted pass took all of Laverty's gumption and cross-plane grunt to see off.

Checa, having changed his rear tyre, paid the price for a rare error, although his season's almost perfect performance was exemplified by the fact that fourth place, only 2.268 seconds from the win, was his idea of a bad form.

The last outing for the WSB wild bunch in 2011 saw the top seven riders covered by 6.5 seconds. Numerous other strident battles for points (and 2012 contracts) played out all through a field that included Josh Waters on a Yoshimura Suzuki, Davide Giugliano on an Althea Ducati (a step up as a reward for winning the big Superstock class), Santiago Barragan (Pedercini Kawasaki) and Karl Muggeridge (Castrol Honda), who replaced the injured Roby Rolfo and Ruben Xaus respectively.

Of these, only Giugliano, on his Checa-replica 1198R, took points in a race day that saw 22 riders in each class, a small end-of-season boost.

Speaking of which, Checa would be back with Ducati and Althea after all, as an expectation that the manufacturer was not going to pay his 2012 salary or help the privateer Althea team was suddenly turned on its head shortly after race two. A happy story to end Checa's dream season as the winter loomed.

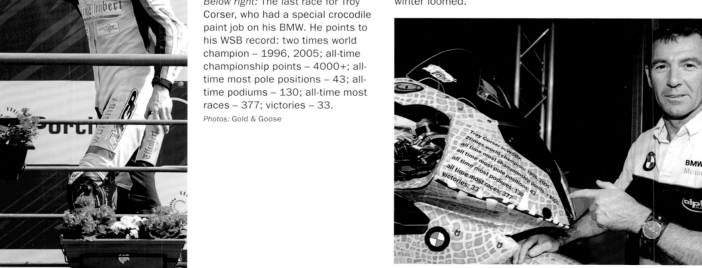

2011 WORLD SUPERBIKE CHAMPIONSHIP RESULTS

Compiled by Peter McLaren

| Round 1 | PHILLIP ISLAND, Australia · 27 February, 2011 · 2.762-mile/4.445km circuit · WEATHER: Race 1 · Dry · Track 23°C · Air 19°C; Race 2 · Dry · Track 37°C · Air 20°C |

Race 1: 22 laps, 60.764 miles/97.790km

Time of race: 34m 16.503s · **Average speed:** 106.370mph/171.186km/h

Pos.	Rider	Nat.	No.	Entrant	Machine	Tyres	Time & Gap	Laps
1	**Carlos Checa**	ESP	7	Althea Racing	Ducati 1098R	P		22
2	**Max Biaggi**	ITA	1	Aprilia Alitalia Racing Team	Aprilia RSV4 Factory	P	4.365s	22
3	**Leon Haslam**	GBR	91	BMW Motorrad Motorsport	BMW S1000 RR	P	10.719s	22
4	**Eugene Laverty**	IRL	58	Yamaha World Superbike Team	Yamaha YZF R1	P	11.266s	22
5	**Marco Melandri**	ITA	33	Yamaha World Superbike Team	Yamaha YZF R1	P	11.293s	22
6	**Michel Fabrizio**	ITA	84	Team Suzuki Alstare	Suzuki GSX-R1000	P	12.039s	22
7	**Jakub Smrz**	CZE	96	Team Effenbert-Liberty Racing	Ducati 1098R	P	20.294s	22
8	**Tom Sykes**	GBR	66	Kawasaki Racing Team	Kawasaki ZX-10R	P	20.742s	22
9	**Noriyuki Haga**	JPN	41	PATA Racing Team Aprilia	Aprilia RSV4 Factory	P	22.421s	22
10	**Troy Corser**	AUS	11	BMW Motorrad Motorsport	BMW S1000 RR	P	25.822s	22
11	**Roberto Rolfo**	ITA	44	Team Pedercini	Kawasaki ZX-10R	P	29.270s	22
12	**Jonathan Rea**	GBR	4	Castrol Honda	Honda CBR1000RR	P	31.059s	22
13	**Leon Camier**	GBR	2	Aprilia Alitalia Racing Team	Aprilia RSV4 Factory	P	31.721s	22
14	**Ayrton Badovini**	ITA	86	BMW Motorrad Italia SBK Team	BMW S1000 RR	P	36.389s	22
15	**Bryan Staring**	AUS	67	Team Pedercini	Kawasaki ZX-10R	P	36.470s	22
16	Ruben Xaus	ESP	111	Castrol Honda	Honda CBR1000RR	P	41.928s	22
17	James Toseland	GBR	52	BMW Motorrad Italia SBK Team	BMW S1000 RR	P	55.239s	22
18	Joshua Waters	AUS	12	Yoshimura Suzuki Racing Team	Suzuki GSX-R1000	P	1m 00.312s	22
19	Mark Aitchison	AUS	8	Team Pedercini	Kawasaki ZX-10R	P	1m 00.316s	22
20	Maxime Berger	FRA	121	Supersonic Racing Team	Ducati 1098R	P	1m 30.125s	22
	Joan Lascorz	ESP	17	Kawasaki Racing Team	Kawasaki ZX-10R	P	DNF	13
	Sylvain Guintoli	FRA	50	Team Effenbert-Liberty Racing	Ducati 1098R	P	DNF	6

Fastest race lap: Max Biaggi on lap 2, 1m 32.034s, 108.038mph/173.871km/h.

Race 2: 22 laps, 60.764 miles/97.790km

Time of race: 34m 15.041s · **Average speed:** 106.446mph/171.308km/h

Pos.	Rider	Time & Gap	Laps
1	**Carlos Checa**		22
2	**Max Biaggi**	1.188s	22
3	**Marco Melandri**	1.406s	22
4	**Jonathan Rea**	10.563s	22
5	**Leon Haslam**	10.885s	22
6	**Leon Camier**	16.914s	22
7	**Noriyuki Haga**	17.558s	22
8	**Michel Fabrizio**	17.679s	22
9	**Tom Sykes**	18.070s	22
10	**Ruben Xaus**	19.053s	22
11	**Jakub Smrz**	19.060s	22
12	**Roberto Rolfo**	23.771s	22
13	**Joshua Waters**	23.956s	22
14	**James Toseland**	28.713s	22
15	**Eugene Laverty**	32.673s	22
16	Mark Aitchison	33.226s	22
17	Bryan Staring	42.598s	22
18	Maxime Berger	51.819s	22
19	Troy Corser	55.738s	22
	Joan Lascorz	DNF	14
	Ayrton Badovini	DNF	0

Fastest race lap: Max Biaggi on lap 3, 1m 32.012s, 108.064mph/173.912km/h.
Lap record: Troy Corser, AUS (Yamaha), 1m 31.826s, 108.280mph/174.260km/h (2007).

Superpole			Points	
1	Checa	1m 30.882s	1	Checa	50
2	Biaggi	1m 30.895s	2	Biaggi	40
3	Guintoli	1m 31.293s	3	Melandri	27
4	Haslam	1m 31.429s	4	Haslam	27
5	Laverty	1m 31.858s	5	Fabrizio	18
6	Smrz	1m 31.980s	6	Rea	17
7	Corser	1m 32.182s	7	Haga	16
8	Melandri	1m 32.662s	8	Sykes	15
			9	Laverty	14
9	Fabrizio	1m 32.153s	10	Smrz	14
10	Sykes	1m 32.204s	11	Camier	13
11	Waters	1m 32.240s	12	Rolfo	9
12	Rea	1m 32.708s	13	Xaus	6
			14	Corser	6
13	Lascorz	1m 32.346s	15	Waters	3
14	Haga	1m 32.391s	16	Toseland	2
15	Toseland	1m 32.547s	17	Badovini	2
16	Xaus	1m 32.788s	18	Staring	1

Round 2 — DONINGTON PARK, Great Britain · 27 March, 2011 · 2.500-mile/4.023km circuit · WEATHER: Race 1 · Dry · Track 6°C · Air 7°C; Race 2 · Dry · Track 16°C · Air 10°C

Race 1: 23 laps, 57.495 miles/92.529km
Time of race: 34m 33.189s · Average speed: 99.837mph/160.672km/h

Pos.	Rider	Nat.	No.	Entrant	Machine	Tyres	Time & Gap	Laps
1	**Marco Melandri**	ITA	33	Yamaha World Superbike Team	Yamaha YZF R1	P		23
2	**Jakub Smrz**	CZE	96	Team Effenbert-Liberty Racing	Ducati 1098R	P	2.455s	23
3	**Carlos Checa**	ESP	7	Althea Racing	Ducati 1098R	P	5.839s	23
4	**Leon Haslam**	GBR	91	BMW Motorrad Motorsport	BMW S1000 RR	P	6.176s	23
5	**Jonathan Rea**	GBR	4	Castrol Honda	Honda CBR1000RR	P	9.039s	23
6	**Noriyuki Haga**	JPN	41	PATA Racing Team Aprilia	Aprilia RSV4 Factory	P	9.215s	23
7	**Max Biaggi**	ITA	1	Aprilia Alitalia Racing Team	Aprilia RSV4 Factory	P	9.960s	23
8	**Leon Camier**	GBR	2	Aprilia Alitalia Racing Team	Aprilia RSV4 Factory	P	14.860s	23
9	**Troy Corser**	AUS	11	BMW Motorrad Motorsport	BMW S1000 RR	P	14.877s	23
10	**Joan Lascorz**	ESP	17	Kawasaki Racing Team	Kawasaki ZX-10R	P	16.182s	23
11	**Sylvain Guintoli**	FRA	50	Team Effenbert-Liberty Racing	Ducati 1098R	P	25.820s	23
12	**Ruben Xaus**	ESP	111	Castrol Honda	Honda CBR1000RR	P	28.378s	23
13	**Ayrton Badovini**	ITA	86	BMW Motorrad Italia SBK Team	BMW S1000 RR	P	31.869s	23
14	**Roberto Rolfo**	ITA	44	Team Pedercini	Kawasaki ZX-10R	P	40.015s	23
15	**Mark Aitchison**	AUS	8	Team Pedercini	Kawasaki ZX-10R	P	1m 0.128s	23
	Tom Sykes	GBR	66	Kawasaki Racing Team	Kawasaki ZX-10R	P	DNF	17
	Michel Fabrizio	ITA	84	Team Suzuki Alstare	Suzuki GSX-R1000	P	DNF	14
	Maxime Berger	FRA	121	Supersonic Racing Team	Ducati 1098R	P	DNF	5
	Eugene Laverty	IRL	58	Yamaha World Superbike Team	Yamaha YZF R1	P	DNF	3

Fastest race lap: Noriyuki Haga on lap 3, 1m 29.137s, 100.959mph/162.478km/h.

Race 2: 23 laps, 57.495 miles/92.529km
Time of race: 34m 21.537s · Average speed: 100.402mph/161.581km/h

Pos.	Rider	Time & Gap	Laps
1	**Carlos Checa**		23
2	**Marco Melandri**	3.397s	23
3	**Leon Camier**	5.902s	23
4	**Leon Haslam**	13.842s	23
5	**Joan Lascorz**	14.253s	23
6	**Jonathan Rea**	19.413s	23
7	**Michel Fabrizio**	20.278s	23
8	**Jakub Smrz**	21.160s	23
9	**Ayrton Badovini**	24.298s	23
10	**Ruben Xaus**	24.907s	23
11	**Sylvain Guintoli**	32.440s	23
12	**Tom Sykes**	32.679s	23
13	**Troy Corser**	34.070s	23
14	**Eugene Laverty**	36.418s	23
15	**Roberto Rolfo**	44.037s	23
16	Mark Aitchison	52.412s	23
17	Noriyuki Haga	56.634s	23
	Maxime Berger	DNF	1
	Max Biaggi	DSQ	9

Superpole	
1 Checa	1m 28.099s
2 Haslam	1m 28.365s
3 Sykes	1m 28.556s
4 Smrz	1m 28.561s
5 Haga	1m 28.673s
6 Biaggi	1m 28.702s
7 Camier	1m 28.737s
8 Rea	1m 29.514s
9 Melandri	1m 28.803s
10 Corser	1m 28.836s
11 Fabrizio	1m 29.135s
12 Lascorz	1m 29.422s
13 Laverty	1m 29.312s
14 Guintoli	1m 29.879s
15 Berger	1m 30.002s
16 Xaus	1m 30.076s

Points	
1 Checa	91
2 Melandri	72
3 Haslam	53
4 Biaggi	49
5 Smrz	42
6 Rea	38
7 Camier	37
8 Fabrizio	27
9 Haga	26
10 Sykes	19
11 Lascorz	17
12 Laverty	16
13 Corser	16
14 Xaus	16
15 Badovini	12
16 Rolfo	12
17 Guintoli	10
18 Waters	3
19 Toseland	2
20 Aitchison	1
21 Staring	1

Fastest race lap: Carlos Checa on lap 8, 1m 28.988s, 101.128mph/162.750km/h (record).
Previous lap record: New circuit layout.

Round 3 — ASSEN, Holland · 17 April, 2011 · 2.822-mile/4.545km circuit · WEATHER: Race 1 · Dry · Track 17°C · Air 15°C; Race 2 · Dry · Track 26°C · Air 19°C

Race 1: 22 laps, 62.090 miles/99.924km
Time of race: 35m 46.486s · Average speed: 104.135mph/167.589km/h

Pos.	Rider	Nat.	No.	Entrant	Machine	Tyres	Time & Gap	Laps
1	**Jonathan Rea**	GBR	4	Castrol Honda	Honda CBR1000RR	P		22
2	**Max Biaggi**	ITA	1	Aprilia Alitalia Racing Team	Aprilia RSV4 Factory	P	0.739s	22
3	**Carlos Checa**	ESP	7	Althea Racing	Ducati 1098R	P	3.572s	22
4	**Marco Melandri**	ITA	33	Yamaha World Superbike Team	Yamaha YZF R1	P	9.508s	22
5	**Michel Fabrizio**	ITA	84	Team Suzuki Alstare	Suzuki GSX-R1000	P	9.892s	22
6	**Troy Corser**	AUS	11	BMW Motorrad Motorsport	BMW S1000 RR	P	11.120s	22
7	**Eugene Laverty**	IRL	58	Yamaha World Superbike Team	Yamaha YZF R1	P	15.235s	22
8	**Ruben Xaus**	ESP	111	Castrol Honda	Honda CBR1000RR	P	30.081s	22
9	**Ayrton Badovini**	ITA	86	BMW Motorrad Italia SBK Team	BMW S1000 RR	P	32.071s	22
10	**Mark Aitchison**	AUS	8	Team Pedercini	Kawasaki ZX-10R	P	35.000s	22
11	**Joan Lascorz**	ESP	17	Kawasaki Racing Team	Kawasaki ZX-10R	P	43.287s	22
12	**Leon Haslam**	GBR	91	BMW Motorrad Motorsport	BMW S1000 RR	P	45.289s	22
13	**Barry Veneman**	NED	37	BMW Motorrad Italia SBK Team	BMW S1000 RR	P	45.298s	22
14	**Tom Sykes**	GBR	66	Kawasaki Racing Team	Kawasaki ZX-10R	P	50.764s	22
	Jakub Smrz	CZE	96	Team Effenbert-Liberty Racing	Ducati 1098R	P	DNF	18
	Sylvain Guintoli	FRA	50	Team Effenbert-Liberty Racing	Ducati 1098R	P	DNF	18
	Leon Camier	GBR	2	Aprilia Alitalia Racing Team	Aprilia RSV4 Factory	P	DNF	17
	Maxime Berger	FRA	121	Supersonic Racing Team	Ducati 1098R	P	DNF	10
	Chris Vermeulen	AUS	77	Kawasaki Racing Team	Kawasaki ZX-10R	P	DNF	8
	Noriyuki Haga	JPN	41	PATA Racing Team Aprilia	Aprilia RSV4 Factory	P	DNF	6
	Roberto Rolfo	ITA	44	Team Pedercini	Kawasaki ZX-10R	P	DNF	3

Fastest race lap: Tom Sykes on lap 3, 1m 36.660s, 105.112mph/169.162km/h.

Race 2: 22 laps, 62.090 miles/99.924km
Time of race: 35m 38.693s · Average speed: 104.514mph/168.199km/h

Pos.	Rider	Time & Gap	Laps
1	**Carlos Checa**		22
2	**Max Biaggi**	0.524s	22
3	**Jonathan Rea**	3.584s	22
4	**Leon Camier**	5.913s	22
5	**Leon Haslam**	16.916s	22
6	**Eugene Laverty**	17.375s	22
7	**Michel Fabrizio**	17.740s	22
8	**Noriyuki Haga**	18.329s	22
9	**Jakub Smrz**	18.378s	22
10	**Sylvain Guintoli**	18.404s	22
11	**Tom Sykes**	26.284s	22
12	**Joan Lascorz**	27.053s	22
13	**Maxime Berger**	38.614s	22
14	**Ruben Xaus**	40.824s	22
15	**Ayrton Badovini**	40.953s	22
16	Roberto Rolfo	40.982s	22
17	Barry Veneman	45.423s	22
18	Mark Aitchison	3 laps	19
	Marco Melandri	DNF	16
	Troy Corser	DNF	7

Superpole	
1 Checa	1m 35.292s
2 Smrz	1m 35.560s
3 Laverty	1m 35.580s
4 Haga	1m 35.920s
5 Rea	1m 36.138s
6 Biaggi	1m 36.302s
7 Sykes	1m 36.351s
8 Melandri	1m 37.036s
9 Camier	1m 35.903s
10 Corser	1m 35.954s
11 Lascorz	1m 35.983s
12 Haslam	1m 36.089s
13 Fabrizio	1m 36.148s
14 Xaus	1m 36.260s
15 Guintoli	1m 36.361s
16 Badovini	1m 36.920s

Points	
1 Checa	132
2 Biaggi	89
3 Melandri	85
4 Rea	79
5 Haslam	68
6 Camier	50
7 Smrz	49
8 Fabrizio	47
9 Laverty	35
10 Haga	34
11 Lascorz	26
12 Corser	26
13 Sykes	26
14 Xaus	26
15 Badovini	20
16 Guintoli	16
17 Rolfo	12
18 Aitchison	7
19 Berger	3
20 Veneman	3
21 Waters	3
22 Toseland	2
23 Staring	1

Fastest race lap: Leon Camier on lap 3, 1m 36.476s, 105.313mph/169.485km/h.
Lap record: Jonathan Rea, GBR (Honda), 1m 36.312s, 105.492mph/169.773km/h (2010).

Round 4 **MONZA, Italy** · 8 May, 2011 · 3.590-mile/5.777km circuit · WEATHER: Race 1 · Dry · Track 40°C · Air 24°C; Race 2 · Dry · Track 45°C · Air 30°C

Race 1: 18 laps, 64.614m/103.986km
Time of race: 31m 09.584s · **Average speed:** 124.418mph/200.231km/h

Pos.	Rider	Nat.	No.	Entrant	Machine	Tyres	Time & Gap	Laps
1	**Eugene Laverty**	IRL	58	Yamaha World Superbike Team	Yamaha YZF R1	P		18
2	**Max Biaggi**	ITA	1	Aprilia Alitalia Racing Team	Aprilia RSV4 Factory	P	1.575s	18
3	**Leon Haslam**	GBR	91	BMW Motorrad Motorsport	BMW S1000 RR	P	3.078s	18
4	**Marco Melandri**	ITA	33	Yamaha World Superbike Team	Yamaha YZF R1	P	3.255s	18
5	**Michel Fabrizio**	ITA	84	Team Suzuki Alstare	Suzuki GSX-R1000	P	11.812s	18
6	**Jonathan Rea**	GBR	4	Castrol Honda	Honda CBR1000RR	P	12.371s	18
7	**Troy Corser**	AUS	11	BMW Motorrad Motorsport	BMW S1000 RR	P	13.280s	18
8	**Leon Camier**	GBR	2	Aprilia Alitalia Racing Team	Aprilia RSV4 Factory	P	17.419s	18
9	**Carlos Checa**	ESP	7	Althea Racing	Ducati 1098R	P	17.569s	18
10	**Jakub Smrz**	CZE	96	Team Effenbert-Liberty Racing	Ducati 1098R	P	18.420s	18
11	**Ayrton Badovini**	ITA	86	BMW Motorrad Italia SBK Team	BMW S1000 RR	P	20.031s	18
12	**Sylvain Guintoli**	FRA	50	Team Effenbert-Liberty Racing	Ducati 1098R	P	20.405s	18
13	**Tom Sykes**	GBR	66	Kawasaki Racing Team	Kawasaki ZX-10R	P	26.693s	18
14	**Maxime Berger**	FRA	121	Supersonic Racing Team	Ducati 1098R	P	38.429s	18
15	**Ruben Xaus**	ESP	111	Castrol Honda	Honda CBR1000RR	P	40.164s	1
16	Noriyuki Haga	JPN	41	PATA Racing Team Aprilia	Aprilia RSV4 Factory	P	49.081s	18
17	Mark Aitchison	AUS	8	Team Pedercini	Kawasaki ZX-10R	P	57.930s	18
18	Fabrizio Lai	ITA	32	Echo Sport Racing Company	Honda CBR1000RR	P	1m 03.039s	18
	Joan Lascorz	ESP	17	Kawasaki Racing Team	Kawasaki ZX-10R	P	DNF	9
	Roberto Rolfo	ITA	44	Team Pedercini	Kawasaki ZX-10R	P	DNF	6

Race 2: 18 laps, 64.614 miles/103.986km
Time of race: : 31m 19.948s · **Average speed:** 123.732mph/199.128km/h

Pos.	Rider	Time & Gap	Laps
1	**Eugene Laverty**		18
2	**Marco Melandri**	0.327s	18
3	**Michel Fabrizio**	2.466s	18
4	**Noriyuki Haga**	2.583s	18
5	**Troy Corser**	4.502s	18
6	**Ayrton Badovini**	10.865s	18
7	**Sylvain Guintoli**	11.038s	18
8	**Max Biaggi**	18.724s	18
9	**Joan Lascorz**	20.093s	18
10	**Carlos Checa**	20.376s	18
11	**Tom Sykes**	21.111s	18
12	**Ruben Xaus**	28.608s	18
13	**Roberto Rolfo**	33.459s	18
14	**Mark Aitchison**	42.810s	18
15	**Fabrizio Lai**	55.759s	18
	Maxime Berger	DNF	13
	Leon Camier	DNF	7
	Jakub Smrz	DNF	0
	Leon Haslam	DNF	0
	Jonathan Rea	DNF	0

Superpole		
1	Biaggi	1m 41.745s
2	Laverty	1m 42.393s
3	Rea	1m 42.614s
4	Corser	1m 42.688s
5	Melandri	1m 42.714s
6	Haslam	1m 42.723s
7	Fabrizio	1m 42.954s
8	Haga	1m 43.043s
9	Badovini	1m 42.886s
10	Camier	1m 42.995s
11	Checa	1m 43.116s
12	Guintoli	1m 43.146s
13	Lascorz	1m 43.090s
14	Sykes	1m 43.437s
15	Smrz	1m 43.993s
16	Berger	1m 44.005s

Points		
1	Checa	145
2	Melandri	118
3	Biaggi	117
4	Rea	89
5	Laverty	85
6	Haslam	84
7	Fabrizio	74
8	Camier	58
9	Smrz	55
10	Haga	47
11	Corser	46
12	Badovini	35
13	Sykes	34
14	Lascorz	33
15	Xaus	31
16	Guintoli	29
17	Rolfo	15
18	Aitchison	9
19	Berger	5
20	Veneman	3
21	Waters	3
22	Toseland	2
23	Lai	1
24	Staring	1

Fastest race lap: Michel Fabrizio on lap 3, 1m 43.275s, 125.130mph/201.377km/h.

Fastest race lap: Max Biaggi on lap 4, 1m 43.023s, 125.452mph/201.869km/h.
Lap record: Cal Crutchlow, GBR (Yamaha), 1m 42.937s, 125.542mph/202.040km/h (2010).

Round 5 **MILLER, USA** · 30 May, 2011 · 3.049-mile/4.907km circuit · WEATHER: Race 1 · Dry · Track 24°C · Air 14°C; Race 2 · Dry · Track 20°C · Air 13°C

Race 1: 21 laps, 64.030 miles/103.047km
Time of race: 38m 46.915s · **Average speed:** 99.062mph/159.425km/h

Pos.	Rider	Nat.	No.	Entrant	Machine	Tyres	Time & Gap	Laps
1	**Carlos Checa**	ESP	7	Althea Racing	Ducati 1098R	P		21
2	**Jakub Smrz**	CZE	96	Team Effenbert-Liberty Racing	Ducati 1098R	P	2.766s	21
3	**Sylvain Guintoli**	FRA	50	Team Effenbert-Liberty Racing	Ducati 1098R	P	4.093s	21
4	**Leon Camier**	GBR	2	Aprilia Alitalia Racing Team	Aprilia RSV4 Factory	P	8.885s	21
5	**Eugene Laverty**	IRL	58	Yamaha World Superbike Team	Yamaha YZF R1	P	15.718s	21
6	**Tom Sykes**	GBR	66	Kawasaki Racing Team	Kawasaki ZX-10R	P	20.477s	21
7	**Ayrton Badovini**	ITA	86	BMW Motorrad Italia SBK Team	BMW S1000 RR	P	22.170s	21
8	**Leon Haslam**	GBR	91	BMW Motorrad Motorsport	BMW S1000 RR	P	22.267s	21
9	**Noriyuki Haga**	JPN	41	PATA Racing Team Aprilia	Aprilia RSV4 Factory	P	24.087s	21
10	**Marco Melandri**	ITA	33	Yamaha World Superbike Team	Yamaha YZF R1	P	27.150s	21
11	**Maxime Berger**	FRA	121	Supersonic Racing Team	Ducati 1098R	P	29.422s	21
12	**Joshua Waters**	AUS	12	Yoshimura Suzuki Racing Team	Suzuki GSX-R1000	P	33.428s	21
13	**Troy Corser**	AUS	11	BMW Motorrad Motorsport	BMW S1000 RR	P	36.573s	21
14	**Joan Lascorz**	ESP	17	Kawasaki Racing Team	Kawasaki ZX-10R	P	1m 05.369s	21
15	**James Toseland**	GBR	52	BMW Motorrad Italia SBK Team	BMW S1000 RR	P	1m 14.382s	21
16	Mark Aitchison	AUS	8	Team Pedercini	Kawasaki ZX-10R	P	1m 14.736s	21
17	Roberto Rolfo	ITA	44	Team Pedercini	Kawasaki ZX-10R	P	2 laps	19
	Michel Fabrizio	ITA	84	Team Suzuki Alstare	Suzuki GSX-R1000	P	DNF	3
	Ruben Xaus	ESP	111	Castrol Honda	Honda CBR1000RR	P	DNF	3
	Jonathan Rea	GBR	4	Castrol Honda	Honda CBR1000RR	P	DNF	0
	Max Biaggi	ITA	1	Aprilia Alitalia Racing Team	Aprilia RSV4 Factory	P	DNF	0

Race 2: 21 laps, 64.030 miles/103.047km
Time of race: 38m 22.082s · **Average speed:** 100.131mph/161.145km/h

Pos.	Rider	Time & Gap	Laps
1	**Carlos Checa**		21
2	**Leon Camier**	7.194s	21
3	**Max Biaggi**	8.734s	21
4	**Eugene Laverty**	14.214s	21
5	**Michel Fabrizio**	14.750s	21
6	**Marco Melandri**	21.634s	21
7	**Sylvain Guintoli**	24.079s	21
8	**Jakub Smrz**	25.688s	21
9	**Ayrton Badovini**	29.621s	21
10	**Tom Sykes**	30.681s	21
11	**Jonathan Rea**	31.033s	21
12	**Joan Lascorz**	37.063s	21
13	**Leon Haslam**	37.455s	21
14	**Maxime Berger**	40.509s	21
15	**Joshua Waters**	40.894s	21
16	Roberto Rolfo	48.989s	21
17	Mark Aitchison	52.388s	21
18	Ruben Xaus	1m 18.485s	21
	Noriyuki Haga	DNF	2
	Troy Corser	DNF	2

Superpole		
1	Checa	1m 58.315s
2	Smrz	1m 58.390s
3	Melandri	1m 58.609s
4	Laverty	1m 58.860s
5	Guintoli	1m 59.069s
6	Corser	1m 59.262s
7	Biaggi	1m 59.736s
8	Badovini	1m 59.827s
9	Haga	2m 00.303s
10	Sykes	2m 00.477s
11	Camier	2m 00.643s
12	Haslam	2m 01.127s
13	Rea	2m 03.232s
14	Xaus	2m 03.382s
15	Fabrizio	2m 03.397s
16	Waters	2m 04.156s

Points		
1	Checa	195
2	Melandri	134
3	Biaggi	133
4	Laverty	109
5	Haslam	95
6	Rea	94
7	Camier	91
8	Fabrizio	85
9	Smrz	83
10	Guintoli	54
11	Haga	54
12	Badovini	51
13	Sykes	50
14	Corser	49
15	Lascorz	39
16	Xaus	31
17	Rolfo	15
18	Berger	12
19	Aitchison	9
20	Waters	8
21	Veneman	3
22	Toseland	3
23	Lai	1
24	Staring	1

Fastest race lap: Carlos Checa on lap 7, 1m 49.779s, 99.989mph/160.916km/h.

Fastest race lap: Carlos Checa on lap 4, 1m 48.827s, 100.863mph/162.324km/h.
Lap record: Carlos Checa, SPA (Ducati) 1m 48.045s, 101.594mph/163.500km/h (2010).

OFFICIAL TIMEKEEPER

Round 6 · MISANO, Italy · 12 June, 2011 · 2.626-mile/4.226km circuit · WEATHER: Race 1 · Dry · Track 37°C · Air 25°C; Race 2 · Dry · Track 44°C · Air 24°C

Race 1: 24 laps, 63.022 miles/101.424km
Time of race: 39m 03.132s · **Average speed:** 96.827mph/155.828km/h

Pos.	Rider	Nat.	No.	Entrant	Machine	Tyres	Time & Gap	Laps
1	**Carlos Checa**	ESP	7	Althea Racing	Ducati 1098R	P		24
2	**Max Biaggi**	ITA	1	Aprilia Alitalia Racing Team	Aprilia RSV4 Factory	P	0.984s	24
3	**Marco Melandri**	ITA	33	Yamaha World Superbike Team	Yamaha YZF R1	P	17.124s	24
4	**Tom Sykes**	GBR	66	Kawasaki Racing Team Superbike	Kawasaki ZX-10R	P	18.652s	24
5	**Eugene Laverty**	IRL	58	Yamaha World Superbike Team	Yamaha YZF R1	P	18.929s	24
6	**Leon Camier**	GBR	2	Aprilia Alitalia Racing Team	Aprilia RSV4 Factory	P	21.003s	24
7	**Sylvain Guintoli**	FRA	50	Team Effenbert-Liberty Racing	Ducati 1098R	P	22.942s	24
8	**Ayrton Badovini**	ITA	86	BMW Motorrad Italia SBK Team	BMW S1000 RR	P	23.117s	24
9	**Joan Lascorz**	ESP	17	Kawasaki Racing Team	Kawasaki ZX-10R	P	31.729s	24
10	**Maxime Berger**	FRA	121	Supersonic Racing Team	Ducati 1098R	P	34.466s	24
11	**Ruben Xaus**	ESP	111	Castrol Honda	Honda CBR1000RR	P	36.683s	24
12	**Matteo Baiocco**	ITA	15	Barni Racing Team S.N.C.	Ducati 1098R	P	37.692s	24
13	**Alessandro Polita**	ITA	53	Barni Racing Team S.N.C.	Ducati 1098R	P	37.984s	24
14	**Chris Vermeulen**	AUS	77	Kawasaki Racing Team	Kawasaki ZX-10R	P	41.016s	24
15	**Lorenzo Lanzi**	ITA	57	BMW Motorrad Italia SBK Team	BMW S1000 RR	P	43.514s	24
	Mark Aitchison	AUS	8	Team Pedercini	Kawasaki ZX-10R	P	DNF	20
	Roberto Rolfo	ITA	44	Team Pedercini	Kawasaki ZX-10R	P	DNF	14
	Leon Haslam	GBR	91	BMW Motorrad Motorsport	BMW S1000 RR	P	DNF	9
	Troy Corser	AUS	11	BMW Motorrad Motorsport	BMW S1000 RR	P	DNF	5
	Noriyuki Haga	JPN	41	PATA Racing Team Aprilia	Aprilia RSV4 Factory	P	DNF	4
	Jakub Smrz	CZE	96	Team Effenbert-Liberty Racing	Ducati 1098R	P	DNF	3
	Michel Fabrizio	ITA	84	Team Suzuki Alstare	Suzuki GSX-R1000	P	DNF	1

Fastest race lap: Carlos Checa on lap 5, 1m 36.660s, 97.799mph/157.393km/h.

Race 2 (part 2): 14 laps, 36.763 miles/59.164km
Time of race: 22m 44.117s · **Average speed:** 97.020mph/156.138km/h

Pos.	Rider	Time & Gap	Laps
1	**Carlos Checa**		14
2	**Max Biaggi**	1.484s	14
3	**Noriyuki Haga**	7.772s	14
4	**Ayrton Badovini**	7.856s	14
5	**Leon Haslam**	9.714s	14
6	**Michel Fabrizio**	10.777s	14
7	**Sylvain Guintoli**	10.875s	14
8	**Ruben Xaus**	13.483s	14
9	**Joan Lascorz**	13.576s	14
10	**Chris Vermeulen**	17.962s	14
11	**Lorenzo Lanzi**	22.768s	14
12	**Roberto Rolfo**	24.535s	14
13	**Eugene Laverty**	51.895s	14
14	**Tom Sykes**	1m 04.134s	14
	Maxime Berger	DNF	8
	Jakub Smrz	DNF	5
	Matteo Baiocco	DNF	3

Fastest race lap: Max Biaggi on lap 5 (of part 1), 1m 36.344s, 98.120mph/157.909km/h (record).
Previous lap record: Cal Crutchlow, GBR (Yamaha), 1m 36.546s, 97.915mph/157.580km/h (2010).

Superpole

1	Sykes	1m 55.197s	9	Badovini	1m 57.374s
2	Checa	1m 55.373s	10	Laverty	1m 57.454s
3	Smrz	1m 55.745s	11	Rea	1m 57.831s
4	Melandri	1m 55.768s	12	Lascorz	1m 58.509s
5	Haslam	1m 56.034s	13	Fabrizio	2m 02.235s
6	Corser	1m 56.285s	14	Berger	2m 02.440s
7	Biaggi	1m 56.480s	15	Xaus	No Time
8	Guintoli	1m 57.054s	16	Camier	No Time

Points

1	Checa	245
2	Biaggi	173
3	Melandri	150
4	Laverty	123
5	Haslam	106
6	Camier	101
7	Fabrizio	95
8	Rea	94
9	Smrz	83
10	Guintoli	72
11	Badovini	72
12	Haga	70
13	Sykes	65
14	Lascorz	53
15	Corser	49
16	Xaus	44
17	Rolfo	19
18	Berger	18
19	Aitchison	9
20	Vermeulen	8
21	Waters	8
22	Lanzi	6
23	Baiocco	4
24	Polita	3
25	Veneman	3
26	Toseland	3
27	Lai	1
28	Staring	1

Round 7 · ARAGÓN, Spain · 19 June, 2011 · 3.321-mile/5.344km circuit · WEATHER: Race 1 · Dry · Track 40°C · Air 20°C; Race 2 · Dry · Track 53°C · Air 27°C

Race 1: 20 laps, 66.412 miles/106.880km
Time of race: 40m 01.968s · **Average speed:** 99.537mph/160.189km/h

Pos.	Rider	Nat.	No.	Entrant	Machine	Tyres	Time & Gap	Laps
1	**Marco Melandri**	ITA	33	Yamaha World Superbike Team	Yamaha YZF R1	P		20
2	**Max Biaggi**	ITA	1	Aprilia Alitalia Racing Team	Aprilia RSV4 Factory	P	1.572s	20
3	**Leon Camier**	GBR	2	Aprilia Alitalia Racing Team	Aprilia RSV4 Factory	P	2.432s	20
4	**Eugene Laverty**	IRL	58	Yamaha World Superbike Team	Yamaha YZF R1	P	10.799s	20
5	**Tom Sykes**	GBR	66	Kawasaki Racing Team	Kawasaki ZX-10R	P	10.847s	20
6	**Noriyuki Haga**	JPN	41	PATA Racing Team Aprilia	Aprilia RSV4 Factory	P	11.931s	20
7	**Joan Lascorz**	ESP	17	Kawasaki Racing Team	Kawasaki ZX-10R	P	12.591s	20
8	**Ayrton Badovini**	ITA	86	BMW Motorrad Italia SBK Team	BMW S1000 RR	P	16.954s	20
9	**Leon Haslam**	GBR	91	BMW Motorrad Motorsport	BMW S1000 RR	P	24.205s	20
10	**Troy Corser**	AUS	11	BMW Motorrad Motorsport	BMW S1000 RR	P	24.694s	20
11	**Sylvain Guintoli**	FRA	50	Team Effenbert-Liberty Racing	Ducati 1098R	P	24.731s	20
12	**Chris Vermeulen**	AUS	77	Kawasaki Racing Team	Kawasaki ZX-10R	P	30.407s	20
13	**Maxime Berger**	FRA	121	Supersonic Racing Team	Ducati 1098R	P	34.107s	20
14	**Roberto Rolfo**	ITA	44	Team Pedercini	Kawasaki ZX-10R	P	37.233s	20
15	**Mark Aitchison**	AUS	8	Team Pedercini	Kawasaki ZX-10R	P	43.004s	20
16	Ruben Xaus	ESP	111	Castrol Honda	Honda CBR1000RR	P	3 Laps	17
	Michel Fabrizio	ITA	84	Team Suzuki Alstare	Suzuki GSX-R1000	P	DNF	9
	Carlos Checa	ESP	7	Althea Racing	Ducati 1098R	P	DNF	7
	Jakub Smrz	CZE	96	Team Effenbert-Liberty Racing	Ducati 1098R	P	DNF	5
	Lorenzo Lanzi	ITA	57	BMW Motorrad Italia SBK Team	BMW S1000 RR	P	DNF	2

Fastest race lap: Carlos Checa on lap 7, 1m 58.862s, 100.572mph/161.855km/h (record).

Race 2: 20 laps, 66.412 miles/106.880km
Time of race: 40m 04.407s · **Average speed:** 99.436mph/160.026km/h

Pos.	Rider	Time & Gap	Laps
1	**Max Biaggi**		20
2	**Marco Melandri**	4.809s	20
3	**Carlos Checa**	6.944s	20
4	**Michel Fabrizio**	9.001s	20
5	**Joan Lascorz**	11.562s	20
6	**Eugene Laverty**	14.288s	20
7	**Noriyuki Haga**	15.138s	20
8	**Leon Camier**	17.660s	20
9	**Leon Haslam**	24.184s	20
10	**Ayrton Badovini**	24.676s	20
11	**Sylvain Guintoli**	29.300s	20
12	**Mark Aitchison**	33.163s	20
13	**Roberto Rolfo**	38.080s	20
14	**Chris Vermeulen**	49.042s	20
15	**Lorenzo Lanzi**	53.156s	20
	Ruben Xaus	DNF	10
	Tom Sykes	DNF	6
	Jakub Smrz	DNF	4
	Maxime Berger	DNF	0
	Troy Corser	DNF	0

Fastest race lap: Marco Melandri on lap 3, 1m 59.159s, 100.322mph/161.452km/h.
Previous lap record: New circuit.

Superpole

1	Melandri	1m 57.634s	9	Haga	1m 58.566s
2	Biaggi	1m 57.790s	10	Guintoli	1m 58.640s
3	Camier	1m 58.279s	11	Fabrizio	1m 58.950s
4	Checa	1m 58.472s	12	Aitchison	1m 59.680s
5	Sykes	1m 58.641s	13	Smrz	1m 59.355s
6	Laverty	1m 58.756s	14	Haslam	1m 59.367s
7	Lascorz	1m 59.194s	15	Berger	1m 59.507s
8	Badovini	1m 59.591s	16	Corser	1m 59.565s

Points

1	Checa	261
2	Biaggi	218
3	Melandri	195
4	Laverty	146
5	Camier	125
6	Haslam	120
7	Fabrizio	108
8	Rea	94
9	Haga	89
10	Badovini	86
11	Smrz	83
12	Guintoli	82
13	Sykes	76
14	Lascorz	73
15	Corser	55
16	Xaus	44
17	Rolfo	24
18	Berger	21
19	Vermeulen	14
20	Aitchison	14
21	Waters	8
22	Lanzi	7
23	Baiocco	4
24	Polita	3
25	Veneman	3
26	Toseland	3
27	Lai	1
28	Staring	1

Round 8 · BRNO, Czech Republic · 10 July, 2011 · 3.357-mile/5.403km circuit · WEATHER: Race 1 · Dry · Track 44°C · Air 28°C; Race 2 · Dry · Track 54°C · Air 28°C

Race 1: 20 laps, 67.145 miles/108.060km
Time of race: 40m 23.699s · Average speed: 99.733mph/160.505km/h

Pos.	Rider	Nat.	No.	Entrant	Machine	Tyres	Time & Gap	Laps
1	Marco Melandri	ITA	33	Yamaha World Superbike Team	Yamaha YZF R1	P		20
2	Max Biaggi	ITA	1	Aprilia Alitalia Racing Team	Aprilia RSV4 Factory	P	0.241s	20
3	Carlos Checa	ESP	7	Althea Racing	Ducati 1098R	P	0.436s	20
4	Michel Fabrizio	ITA	84	Team Suzuki Alstare	Suzuki GSX-R1000	P	8.448s	20
5	Eugene Laverty	IRL	58	Yamaha World Superbike Team	Yamaha YZF R1	P	11.863s	20
6	Ayrton Badovini	ITA	86	BMW Motorrad Italia SBK Team	BMW S1000 RR	P	16.374s	20
7	Leon Camier	GBR	2	Aprilia Alitalia Racing Team	Aprilia RSV4 Factory	P	20.075s	20
8	Leon Haslam	GBR	91	BMW Motorrad Motorsport	BMW S1000 RR	P	21.399s	20
9	Joan Lascorz	ESP	17	Kawasaki Racing Team	Kawasaki ZX-10R	P	21.555s	20
10	Tom Sykes	GBR	66	Kawasaki Racing Team	Kawasaki ZX-10R	P	22.330s	20
11	Jakub Smrz	CZE	96	Team Effenbert-Liberty Racing	Ducati 1098R	P	22.494s	20
12	Noriyuki Haga	JPN	41	PATA Racing Team Aprilia	Aprilia RSV4 Factory	P	24.710s	20
13	Maxime Berger	FRA	121	Supersonic Racing Team	Ducati 1098R	P	27.958s	20
14	Roberto Rolfo	ITA	44	Team Pedercini	Kawasaki ZX-10R	P	31.724s	20
15	Alex Lowes	GBR	22	Castrol Honda	Honda CBR1000RR	P	31.998s	20
16	Mark Aitchison	AUS	8	Team Pedercini	Kawasaki ZX-10R	P	34.771s	20
17	Lorenzo Lanzi	ITA	57	BMW Motorrad Italia SBK Team	BMW S1000 RR	P	36.582s	20
18	Chris Vermeulen	AUS	77	Kawasaki Racing Team	Kawasaki ZX-10R	P	45.690s	20
19	Viktor Kispataki	HUN	13	Prop-tech ltd.	Honda CBR1000RR	P	1m 28.907s	20
20	Sylvain Guintoli	FRA	50	Team Effenbert-Liberty Racing	Ducati 1098R	P	1 Lap	19
	Matteo Baiocco	ITA	15	Barni Racing Team	Ducati 1098R	P	DNF	12
	Ruben Xaus	ESP	111	Castrol Honda	Honda CBR1000RR	P	DNF	0

Race 2: 20 laps, 67.145 miles/108.060km
Time of race: 40m 21.646s · Average speed: 99.818mph/160.641km/h

Pos.	Rider	Time & Gap	Laps
1	Max Biaggi		20
2	Marco Melandri	0.222s	20
3	Carlos Checa	3.558s	20
4	Michel Fabrizio	7.863s	20
5	Eugene Laverty	8.534s	20
6	Ayrton Badovini	18.085s	20
7	Leon Haslam	21.650s	20
8	Joan Lascorz	21.862s	20
9	Sylvain Guintoli	25.306s	20
10	Noriyuki Haga	27.366s	20
11	Roberto Rolfo	33.716s	20
12	Mark Aitchison	36.549s	20
13	Lorenzo Lanzi	37.468s	20
14	Tom Sykes	46.878s	20
15	Viktor Kispataki	1m 38.074s	20
	Maxime Berger	DNF	15
	Leon Camier	DNF	14
	Jakub Smrz	DNF	12
	Matteo Baiocco	DNF	9
	Alex Lowes	DNF	5
	Chris Vermeulen	DNS	0

Superpole		
1	Biaggi	1m 58.580s
2	Melandri	1m 58.801s
3	Checa	1m 58.908s
4	Laverty	1m 59.055s
5	Smrz	1m 59.541s
6	Fabrizio	1m 59.908s
7	Camier	1m 59.925s
8	Sykes	2m 00.303s
9	Badovini	1m 59.684s
10	Guintoli	1m 59.800s
11	Aitchison	2m 00.362s
12	Berger	2m 01.011s
13	Haslam	2m 00.252s
14	Haga	2m 00.374s
15	Lanzi	2m 00.619s
16	Baiocco	2m 00.864s

Points		
1	Checa	293
2	Biaggi	263
3	Melandri	240
4	Laverty	168
5	Haslam	137
6	Camier	134
7	Fabrizio	134
8	Badovini	106
9	Haga	99
10	Rea	94
11	Guintoli	89
12	Smrz	88
13	Lascorz	88
14	Sykes	84
15	Corser	55
16	Xaus	44
17	Rolfo	31
18	Berger	24
19	Aitchison	18
20	Vermeulen	14
21	Lanzi	10
22	Waters	8
23	Baiocco	4
24	Polita	3
25	Veneman	3
26	Toseland	3
27	Kispataki	1
28	Lowes	1
29	Lai	1
30	Staring	1

Fastest race lap: Marco Melandri on lap 3, 2m 0.118s, 100.619mph/161.931km/h.

Fastest race lap: Marco Melandri on lap 2, 2m 0.058s, 100.670mph/162.012km/h.
Lap record: Cal Crutchlow, GBR (Yamaha) 1m 59.291s, 101.316mph/163.053km/h (2010).

Round 9 · SILVERSTONE, Great Britain · 31 July, 2011 · 3.667-mile/5.902km circuit · WEATHER: Race 1 · Dry · Track 31°C · Air 20°C; Race 2 · Dry · Track 38°C · Air 23°C

Race 1: 18 laps, 66.012 miles/106.236km
Time of race: 38m 06.477s · Average speed: 103.934mph/167.266km/h

Pos.	Rider	Nat.	No.	Entrant	Machine	Tyres	Time & Gap	Laps
1	Carlos Checa	ESP	7	Althea Racing	Ducati 1098R	P		18
2	Eugene Laverty	IRL	58	Yamaha World Superbike Team	Yamaha YZF R1	P	3.304s	18
3	Marco Melandri	ITA	33	Yamaha World Superbike Team	Yamaha YZF R1	P	4.782s	18
4	Leon Haslam	GBR	91	BMW Motorrad Motorsport	BMW S1000 RR	P	7.116s	18
5	John Hopkins	USA	211	Samsung Crescent Racing	Suzuki GSX-R1000	P	11.057s	18
6	Sylvain Guintoli	FRA	50	Team Effenbert-Liberty Racing	Ducati 1098R	P	21.899s	18
7	Joan Lascorz	ESP	17	Kawasaki Racing Team	Kawasaki ZX-10R	P	22.308s	18
8	Maxime Berger	FRA	121	Supersonic Racing Team	Ducati 1098R	P	22.734s	18
9	Troy Corser	AUS	11	BMW Motorrad Motorsport	BMW S1000 RR	P	25.491s	1
10	Ayrton Badovini	ITA	86	BMW Motorrad Italia SBK Team	BMW S1000 RR	P	25.725s	18
11	Max Biaggi	ITA	1	Aprilia Alitalia Racing Team	Aprilia RSV4 Factory	P	25.844s	18
12	James Toseland	GBR	52	BMW Motorrad Italia SBK Team	BMW S1000 RR	P	45.578s	18
13	Roberto Rolfo	ITA	44	Team Pedercini	Kawasaki ZX-10R	P	51.650s	18
14	Jon Kirkham	GBR	10	Samsung Crescent Racing	Suzuki GSX-R1000	P	57.310s	1
15	Leon Camier	GBR	2	Aprilia Alitalia Racing Team	Aprilia RSV4 Factory	P	1m 36.457s	18
	Fabrizio Lai	ITA	32	Castrol Honda	Honda CBR1000RR	P	DNF	12
	Mark Aitchison	AUS	8	Team Pedercini	Kawasaki ZX-10R	P	DNF	10
	Noriyuki Haga	JPN	41	PATA Racing Team Aprilia	Aprilia RSV4 Factory	P	DNF	9
	Jakub Smrz	CZE	96	Team Effenbert-Liberty Racing	Ducati 1098R	P	DNF	6
	Alex Lowes	GBR	22	Castrol Honda	Honda CBR1000RR	P	DNF	5
	Michel Fabrizio	ITA	84	Team Suzuki Alstare	Suzuki GSX-R1000	P	DNF	0

Race 2: 18 laps, 66.012 miles/106.236km
Time of race: 38m 03.361s · Average speed: 104.076mph/167.494km/h

Pos.	Rider	Time & Gap	Laps
1	Carlos Checa		18
2	Eugene Laverty	2.274s	18
3	Marco Melandri	3.675s	18
4	Max Biaggi	3.960s	18
5	Leon Camier	4.405s	18
6	Sylvain Guintoli	10.958s	18
7	John Hopkins	11.387s	18
8	Leon Haslam	11.496s	18
9	Michel Fabrizio	12.247s	18
10	Ayrton Badovini	19.705s	18
11	Jakub Smrz	19.753s	18
12	Maxime Berger	21.582s	18
13	James Toseland	27.235s	18
14	Mark Aitchison	30.702s	18
15	Jon Kirkham	42.579s	18
16	Fabrizio Lai	43.420s	18
	Roberto Rolfo	DNF	16
	Troy Corser	DNF	12
	Alex Lowes	DNF	7
	Joan Lascorz	DNF	6
	Noriyuki Haga	DNF	4

Superpole		
1	Hopkins	2m 04.041s
2	Laverty	2m 04.068s
3	Camier	2m 04.303s
4	Checa	2m 04.362s
5	Guintoli	2m 05.456s
6	Melandri	2m 05.639s
7	Fabrizio	2m 05.997s
8	Haga	No Time
9	Haslam	2m 05.091s
10	Badovini	2m 05.115s
11	Biaggi	2m 05.184s
12	Aitchison	2m 06.238s
13	Smrz	2m 05.400s
14	Toseland	2m 05.403s
15	Berger	2m 05.709s
16	Sykes	No Time

Points		
1	Checa	343
2	Biaggi	281
3	Melandri	272
4	Laverty	208
5	Haslam	158
6	Camier	146
7	Fabrizio	141
8	Badovini	118
9	Guintoli	109
10	Haga	99
11	Lascorz	97
12	Rea	94
13	Smrz	93
14	Sykes	84
15	Corser	62
16	Xaus	44
17	Berger	36
18	Rolfo	34
19	Hopkins	20
20	Aitchison	20
21	Vermeulen	14
22	Lanzi	10
23	Toseland	10
24	Waters	8
25	Baiocco	4
26	Polita	3
27	Veneman	3
28	Kirkham	3
29	Kispataki	1
30	Lowes	1
31	Lai	1
32	Staring	1

Fastest race lap: Carlos Checa on lap 5, 2m 06.045s, 104.743mph/168.568km/h.

Fastest race lap: Max Biaggi on lap 2, 2m 05.525s, 105.178mph/169.267km/h.
Lap record: Cal Crutchlow, GBR (Yamaha) 2m 05.259s, 105.401mph/169.626km/h (2010).

motogp / **T+ TISSOT** SWISS WATCHES SINCE 1853 / **OFFICIAL TIMEKEEPER**

Round 10 · NÜRBURGRING, Germany · 4 September, 2011 · 3.192-mile/5.137km circuit · WEATHER: Race 1 · Dry · Track 25°C · Air 20°C; Race 2 · Wet · Track 29°C · Air 21°C

Race 1: 20 laps, 63.840 miles/102.740km
Time of race: 38m 59.779s · **Average speed:** 98.224mph/158.076km/h

Pos.	Rider	Nat.	No.	Entrant	Machine	Tyres	Time & Gap	Laps
1	**Carlos Checa**	ESP	7	Althea Racing	Ducati 1098R	P		20
2	**Marco Melandri**	ITA	33	Yamaha World Superbike Team	Yamaha YZF R1	P	1.855s	20
3	**Noriyuki Haga**	JPN	41	PATA Racing Team Aprilia	Aprilia RSV4 Factory	P	2.322s	20
4	**Eugene Laverty**	IRL	58	Yamaha World Superbike Team	Yamaha YZF R1	P	7.789s	20
5	**Leon Haslam**	GBR	91	BMW Motorrad Motorsport	BMW S1000 RR	P	9.727s	20
6	**Sylvain Guintoli**	FRA	50	Team Effenbert-Liberty Racing	Ducati 1098R	P	10.113s	20
7	**Joan Lascorz**	ESP	17	Kawasaki Racing Team	Kawasaki ZX-10R	P	17.226s	20
8	**Leon Camier**	GBR	2	Aprilia Alitalia Racing Team	Aprilia RSV4 Factory	P	17.228s	20
9	**Ayrton Badovini**	ITA	86	BMW Motorrad Italia SBK Team	BMW S1000 RR	P	18.166s	20
10	**Jonathan Rea**	GBR	4	Castrol Honda	Honda CBR1000RR	P	19.457s	20
11	**Tom Sykes**	GBR	66	Kawasaki Racing Team	Kawasaki ZX-10R	P	22.136s	20
12	**Mark Aitchison**	AUS	8	Team Pedercini	Kawasaki ZX-10R	P	25.346s	20
13	**James Toseland**	GBR	52	BMW Motorrad Italia SBK Team	BMW S1000 RR	P	31.617s	20
14	**Roberto Rolfo**	ITA	44	Team Pedercini	Kawasaki ZX-10R	P	31.796s	20
15	**Troy Corser**	AUS	11	BMW Motorrad Motorsport	BMW S1000 RR	P	33.320s	20
16	Michel Fabrizio	ITA	84	Team Suzuki Alstare	Suzuki GSX-R1000	P	38.149s	20
17	Makoto Tamada	JPN	100	Castrol Honda	Honda CBR1000RR	P	1m 16.143s	20
	Jakub Smrz	CZE	96	Team Effenbert-Liberty Racing	Ducati 1098R	P	DNF	12
	Maxime Berger	FRA	121	Supersonic Racing Team	Ducati 1098R	P	DNF	4
	Max Biaggi	ITA	1	Aprilia Alitalia Racing Team	Aprilia RSV4 Factory	P	DNS	0

Fastest race lap: Carlo Checa on lap 4, 1m 55.971s, 99.086mph/159.464km/h.

Race 2: 13 laps, 41.496 miles/66.781km
Time of race: 29m 49.337s · **Average speed:** 83.486mph/234.358km/h

Pos.	Rider	Time & Gap	Laps
1	**Tom Sykes**		13
2	**Sylvain Guintoli**	4.063s	13
3	**Jakub Smrz**	22.759s	13
4	**Jonathan Rea**	28.497s	13
5	**Eugene Laverty**	38.374s	13
6	**Marco Melandri**	45.326s	13
7	**Ayrton Badovini**	47.030s	13
8	**Carlos Checa**	50.032s	13
9	**Leon Haslam**	53.586s	13
10	**Maxime Berger**	55.261s	13
11	**Joan Lascorz**	1m 12.805s	13
12	**Troy Corser**	1m 15.468s	13
13	**Roberto Rolfo**	1m 40.323s	13
	Noriyuki Haga	DNF	12
	Makoto Tamada	DNF	12
	Leon Camier	DNF	11
	Mark Aitchison	DNF	10
	James Toseland	DNF	8
	Michel Fabrizio	DNF	5
	Max Biaggi	DNS	0

Superpole	
1 Checa	1m 54.144s
2 Laverty	1m 54.512s
3 Biaggi	1m 54.743s
4 Melandri	1m 54.818s
5 Haga	1m 55.113s
6 Sykes	1m 55.223s
7 Haslam	1m 55.237s
8 Guintoli	1m 55.249s
9 Rea	1m 55.321s
10 Smrz	1m 55.598s
11 Aitchison	1m 55.625s
12 Fabrizio	1m 56.177s
13 Camier	1m 55.633s
14 Berger	1m 55.811s
15 Badovini	1m 56.101s
16 Lascorz	1m 56.162s

Points	
1 Checa	376
2 Melandri	302
3 Biaggi	281
4 Laverty	232
5 Haslam	176
6 Camier	154
7 Fabrizio	141
8 Guintoli	139
9 Badovini	134
10 Haga	115
11 Sykes	114
12 Rea	113
13 Lascorz	111
14 Smrz	109
15 Corser	67
16 Xaus	44
17 Berger	42
18 Rolfo	39
19 Aitchison	24
20 Hopkins	20
21 Vermeulen	14
22 Toseland	13
23 Lanzi	10
24 Waters	8
25 Baiocco	4
26 Polita	3
27 Veneman	3
28 Kirkham	3
29 Kispataki	1
30 Lowes	1
31 Lai	1
32 Staring	1

Fastest race lap: Noriyuki Haga on lap 7, 2m 14.619s, 85.360mph/137.374km/h.
Lap record: Jonathan Rea, GBR (Honda) 1m 55.392s, 99.583mph/160.264km/h (2010).

Round 11 · IMOLA, Italy · 25 September, 2011 · 3.067-mile/4.936km circuit · WEATHER: Race 1 · Dry · Track 36°C · Air 25°C; Race 2 · Dry · Track 44°C · Air 28°C

Race 1: 21 laps, 64.409 miles/103.656km
Time of race: 38m 03.396s · **Average speed:** 101.547mph/163.424km/h

Pos.	Rider	Nat.	No.	Entrant	Machine	Tyres	Time & Gap	Laps
1	**Jonathan Rea**	GBR	4	Castrol Honda	Honda CBR1000RR	P		21
2	**Noriyuki Haga**	JPN	41	PATA Racing Team Aprilia	Aprilia RSV4 Factory	P	0.111s	21
3	**Carlos Checa**	ESP	7	Althea Racing	Ducati 1098R	P	9.449s	21
4	**Tom Sykes**	GBR	66	Kawasaki Racing Team	Kawasaki ZX-10R	P	9.792s	21
5	**Eugene Laverty**	IRL	58	Yamaha World Superbike Team	Yamaha YZF R1	P	14.699s	21
6	**Sylvain Guintoli**	FRA	50	Team Effenbert-Liberty Racing	Ducati 1098R	P	16.820s	21
7	**Jakub Smrz**	CZE	96	Team Effenbert-Liberty Racing	Ducati 1098R	P	24.227s	21
8	**Marco Melandri**	ITA	33	Yamaha World Superbike Team	Yamaha YZF R1	P	24.935s	21
9	**Ayrton Badovini**	ITA	86	BMW Motorrad Italia SBK Team	BMW S1000 RR	P	25.224s	21
10	**Joan Lascorz**	ESP	17	Kawasaki Racing Team	Kawasaki ZX-10R	P	25.487s	21
11	**Mark Aitchison**	AUS	8	Team Pedercini	Kawasaki ZX-10R	P	26.148s	21
12	**Troy Corser**	AUS	11	BMW Motorrad Motorsport	BMW S1000 RR	P	26.444s	21
13	**Federico Sandi**	ITA	23	Althea Racing	Ducati 1098R	P	29.761s	21
14	**Alessandro Polita**	ITA	53	Barni Racing Team S.N.C.	Ducati 1098R	P	30.083s	21
15	**Leon Camier**	GBR	2	Aprilia Alitalia Racing Team	Aprilia RSV4 Factory	P	34.862s	21
16	Matteo Baiocco	ITA	15	Barni Racing Team	Ducati 1098R	P	40.331s	21
17	Ruben Xaus	ESP	111	Castrol Honda	Honda CBR1000RR	P	44.547s	21
18	Roberto Rolfo	ITA	44	Team Pedercini	Kawasaki ZX-10R	P	50.241s	21
	Leon Haslam	GBR	91	BMW Motorrad Motorsport	BMW S1000 RR	P	DNF	8
	Javier Fores	ESP	112	BMW Motorrad Italia SBK Team	BMW S1000 RR	P	DNF	6
	Michel Fabrizio	ITA	84	Team Suzuki Alstare	Suzuki GSX-R1000	P	DNF	1
	Maxime Berger	FRA	121	Supersonic Racing Team	Ducati 1098R	P	DNF	1

Fastest race lap: Noriyuki Haga on lap 12, 1m 47.960s, 102.274mph/164.594km/h.

Race 2: 21 laps, 64.409 miles/103,656km
Time of race: 38m 04.538s · **Average speed:** 101.496mph/163.342km/h

Pos.	Rider	Time & Gap	Laps
1	**Carlos Checa**		21
2	**Noriyuki Haga**	4.631s	21
3	**Leon Camier**	15.159s	21
4	**Eugene Laverty**	17.195s	21
5	**Leon Haslam**	17.388s	21
6	**Marco Melandri**	18.533s	21
7	**Sylvain Guintoli**	19.615s	21
8	**Joan Lascorz**	20.063s	21
9	**Mark Aitchison**	24.194s	21
10	**Ayrton Badovini**	28.485s	21
11	**Ruben Xaus**	28.600s	21
12	**Federico Sandi**	41.802s	21
13	**Maxime Berger**	54.750s	21
14	**Javier Fores**	1m 12.281s	21
	Alessandro Polita	DNF	19
	Jonathan Rea	DNF	17
	Michel Fabrizio	DNF	10
	Matteo Baiocco	DNF	9
	Troy Corser	DNF	9
	Tom Sykes	DNF	7
	Roberto Rolfo	DNF	2
	Jakub Smrz	DNF	1

Superpole	
1 Checa	1m 47.196s
2 Rea	1m 47.274s
3 Haga	1m 47.442s
4 Sykes	1m 47.468s
5 Laverty	1m 47.929s
6 Haslam	1m 48.081s
7 Badovini	1m 48.234s
8 Guintoli	1m 48.416s
9 Melandri	1m 47.781s
10 Camier	1m 47.858s
11 Fabrizio	1m 48.126s
12 Berger	1m 48.334s
13 Smrz	1m 48.741s
14 Sandi	1m 48.812s
15 Corser	1m 48.894s
16 Polita	1m 49.091s

Points	
1 Checa	417
2 Melandri	320
3 Biaggi	281
4 Laverty	256
5 Haslam	187
6 Camier	171
7 Guintoli	158
8 Haga	155
9 Badovini	147
10 Fabrizio	141
11 Rea	138
12 Sykes	127
13 Lascorz	125
14 Smrz	118
15 Corser	71
16 Xaus	49
17 Berger	45
18 Rolfo	39
19 Aitchison	36
20 Hopkins	20
21 Vermeulen	14
22 Toseland	13
23 Lanzi	10
24 Waters	8
25 Sandi	7
26 Polita	5
27 Baiocco	4
28 Veneman	3
29 Kirkham	3
30 Fores	2
31 Kispataki	1
32 Lowes	1
33 Lai	1
34 Staring	1

Fastest race lap: Carlos Checa on lap 13, 1m 47.934s, 102.299mph/164.634km/h (record).
Previous lap record: Carlos Checa, SPA (Ducati) 1m 48.877s, 101.413mph/163.208km/h (2010).

OFFICIAL TIMEKEEPER

Round 12 — MAGNY=COURS, France · 2 October, 2011 · 2.741-mile/4.411km circuit · WEATHER: Race 1 · Dry · Track 21°C · Air 21°C; Race 2 · Dry · Track 40°C · Air 27°C

Race 1: 23 laps, 63.040 miles/101.453km
Time of race: 38m 16.465s · Average speed: 98.823mph/159.040km/h

Pos.	Rider	Nat.	No.	Entrant	Machine	Tyres	Time & Gap	Laps
1	**Carlos Checa**	ESP	7	Althea Racing	Ducati 1098R	P		23
2	**Marco Melandri**	ITA	33	Yamaha World Superbike Team	Yamaha YZF R1	P	2.201s	23
3	**Leon Haslam**	GBR	91	BMW Motorrad Motorsport	BMW S1000 RR	P	3.218s	23
4	**Leon Camier**	GBR	2	Aprilia Alitalia Racing Team	Aprilia RSV4 Factory	P	3.796s	23
5	**Eugene Laverty**	IRL	58	Yamaha World Superbike Team	Yamaha YZF R1	P	5.602s	23
6	**Sylvain Guintoli**	FRA	50	Team Effenbert-Liberty Racing	Ducati 1098R	P	9.634s	23
7	**Noriyuki Haga**	JPN	41	PATA Racing Team Aprilia	Aprilia RSV4 Factory	P	9.814s	23
8	**Joan Lascorz**	ESP	17	Kawasaki Racing Team	Kawasaki ZX-10R	P	11.387s	23
9	**Troy Corser**	AUS	11	BMW Motorrad Motorsport	BMW S1000 RR	P	17.143s	23
10	**Tom Sykes**	GBR	66	Kawasaki Racing Team	Kawasaki ZX-10R	P	24.523s	23
11	**Javier Fores**	ESP	112	BMW Motorrad Italia SBK Team	BMW S1000 RR	P	34.532s	23
12	**Michel Fabrizio**	ITA	84	Team Suzuki Alstare	Suzuki GSX-R1000	P	1m 19.742s	23
13	**Roberto Rolfo**	ITA	44	Team Pedercini	Kawasaki ZX-10R	P	1 lap	22
	Maxime Berger	FRA	121	Supersonic Racing Team	Ducati 1098R	P	DNF	10
	Jonathan Rea	GBR	4	Castrol Honda	Honda CBR1000RR	P	DNF	4
	Ayrton Badovini	ITA	86	BMW Motorrad Italia SBK Team	BMW S1000 RR	P	DNF	4
	Jakub Smrz	CZE	96	Team Effenbert-Liberty Racing	Ducati 1098R	P	DNF	2
	Mark Aitchison	AUS	8	Team Pedercini	Kawasaki ZX-10R	P	DNF	0

Fastest race lap: Carlos Checa on lap 4, 1m 38.643s, 100.029mph/160.981km/h.

Race 2: 23 laps, 63.040 miles/101.453km
Time of race: 38m 17.851s · Average speed: 98.764mph/158.945km/h

Pos.	Rider	Time & Gap	Laps
1	**Carlos Checa**		23
2	**Marco Melandri**	1.267s	23
3	**Eugene Laverty**	2.043s	23
4	**Leon Haslam**	6.506s	23
5	**Sylvain Guintoli**	7.843s	23
6	**Leon Camier**	8.360s	23
7	**Joan Lascorz**	15.285s	23
8	**Ayrton Badovini**	15.549s	23
9	**Troy Corser**	16.278s	23
10	**Noriyuki Haga**	22.996s	23
11	**Javier Fores**	43.132s	23
12	**Maxime Berger**	47.846s	23
	Roberto Rolfo	DNF	19
	Jonathan Rea	DNF	13
	Mark Aitchison	DNF	4
	Michel Fabrizio	DNF	2
	Tom Sykes	DNF	0

Superpole		
1	Rea	1m 37.490s
2	Laverty	1m 37.600s
3	Checa	1m 37.932s
4	Camier	1m 38.006s
5	Guintoli	1m 38.094s
6	Sykes	1m 38.094s
7	Haslam	1m 38.382s
8	Melandri	1m 38.562s
9	Haga	1m 38.137s
10	Lascorz	1m 38.204s
11	Berger	1m 38.347s
12	Corser	1m 38.516s
13	Smrz	1m 38.524s
14	Fabrizio	1m 38.565s
15	Aitchison	1m 38.623s
16	Badovini	1m 38.687s

Points		
1	Checa	467
2	Melandri	360
3	Laverty	283
4	Biaggi	281
5	Haslam	216
6	Camier	194
7	Guintoli	179
8	Haga	170
9	Badovini	155
10	Fabrizio	145
11	Lascorz	142
12	Rea	138
13	Sykes	133
14	Smrz	118
15	Corser	85
16	Xaus	49
17	Berger	49
18	Rolfo	42
19	Aitchison	36
20	Hopkins	20
21	Vermeulen	14
22	Toseland	13
23	Fores	12
24	Lanzi	10
25	Waters	8
26	Sandi	7
27	Polita	5
28	Baiocco	4
29	Veneman	3
30	Kirkham	3
31	Kispataki	1
32	Lowes	1
33	Lai	1
34	Staring	1

Fastest race lap: Carlos Checa on lap 2, 1m 39.136s, 99.531mph/160.180km/h.
Lap record: Noriyuki Haga, JPN (Ducati), 1m 38.619s, 100.053mph/161.020km/h (2009).

Round 13 — PORTIMAO, Portugal · 16 October, 2011 · 2.853-mile/4.592km circuit · WEATHER: Race 1 · Dry · Track 32°C · Air 26°C; Race 2 · Dry · Track 39°C · Air 30°C

Race 1: 22 laps, 62.773 miles/101.024km
Time of race: 38m 13.293s · Average speed: 98.541mph/158.587km/h

Pos.	Rider	Nat.	No.	Entrant	Machine	Tyres	Time & Gap	Laps
1	**Carlos Checa**	ESP	7	Althea Racing	Ducati 1098R	P		22
2	**Sylvain Guintoli**	FRA	50	Team Effenbert-Liberty Racing	Ducati 1098R	P	2.860s	22
3	**Jonathan Rea**	GBR	4	Castrol Honda	Honda CBR1000RR	P	8.481s	22
4	**Max Biaggi**	ITA	1	Aprilia Alitalia Racing Team	Aprilia RSV4 Factory	P	11.963s	22
5	**Joan Lascorz**	ESP	17	Kawasaki Racing Team	Kawasaki ZX-10R	P	13.333s	22
6	**Marco Melandri**	ITA	33	Yamaha World Superbike Team	Yamaha YZF R1	P	18.960s	22
7	**Maxime Berger**	FRA	121	Supersonic Racing Team	Ducati 1098R	P	20.489s	22
8	**Tom Sykes**	GBR	66	Kawasaki Racing Team	Kawasaki ZX-10R	P	25.320s	22
9	**Leon Haslam**	GBR	91	BMW Motorrad Motorsport	BMW S1000 RR	P	26.695s	22
10	**Jakub Smrz**	CZE	96	Team Effenbert-Liberty Racing	Ducati 1098R	P	26.801s	22
11	**Michel Fabrizio**	ITA	84	Team Suzuki Alstare	Suzuki GSX-R1000	P	27.115s	22
12	**Leon Camier**	GBR	2	Aprilia Alitalia Racing Team	Aprilia RSV4 Factory	P	28.563s	22
13	**Ayrton Badovini**	ITA	86	BMW Motorrad Italia SBK Team	BMW S1000 RR	P	31.765s	22
14	**Troy Corser**	AUS	11	BMW Motorrad Motorsport	BMW S1000 RR	P	31.822s	22
15	**Noriyuki Haga**	JPN	41	PATA Racing Team Aprilia	Aprilia RSV4 Factory	P	31.866s	22
16	Davide Giugliano	ITA	34	Althea Racing	Ducati 1098R	P	47.694s	22
17	Mark Aitchison	AUS	8	Team Pedercini	Kawasaki ZX-10R	P	47.737s	22
18	Karl Muggeridge	AUS	31	Castrol Honda	Honda CBR1000RR	P	1m 6.213s	22
19	Eugene Laverty	IRL	58	Yamaha World Superbike Team	Yamaha YZF R1	P	2 laps	20
20	Santiago Barragan	ESP	51	Team Pedercini	Kawasaki ZX-10R	P	3 laps	19
21	Joshua Waters	AUS	12	Yoshimura Suzuki Racing Team	Suzuki GSX-R1000	P	4 laps	18
	Javier Fores	ESP	112	BMW Motorrad Italia SBK Team	BMW S1000 RR	P	DNF	15

Fastest race lap: Sylvain Guintoli on lap 3, 1m 43.453s, 99.291mph/159.794km/h.

Race 2: 22 laps, 62.773 miles/101.024km
Time of race: 38m 11.326s · Average speed: 98.626mph/158.723km/h

Pos.	Rider	Time & Gap	Laps
1	**Marco Melandri**		22
2	**Eugene Laverty**	1.075s	22
3	**Jonathan Rea**	1.363s	22
4	**Carlos Checa**	2.648s	22
5	**Sylvain Guintoli**	3.355s	22
6	**Leon Camier**	4.709s	22
7	**Max Biaggi**	6.514s	22
8	**Joan Lascorz**	14.441s	22
9	**Ayrton Badovini**	19.128s	22
10	**Maxime Berger**	25.527s	22
11	**Noriyuki Haga**	26.400s	22
12	**Davide Giugliano**	26.646s	22
13	**Jakub Smrz**	26.963s	22
14	**Michel Fabrizio**	30.209s	22
15	**Leon Haslam**	30.951s	22
16	Troy Corser	31.057s	22
17	Karl Muggeridge	57.941s	22
18	Joshua Waters	58.577s	22
19	Javier Fores	1m 04.011s	22
20	Mark Aitchison	1m 04.397s	22
	Tom Sykes	DNF	17
	Santiago Barragan	DNF	9

Superpole		
1	Rea	1m 41.712s
2	Checa	1m 41.951s
3	Laverty	1m 42.173s
4	Melandri	1m 42.259s
5	Guintoli	1m 42.627s
6	Smrz	1m 42.710s
7	Lascorz	1m 43.282s
8	Haga	1m 43.307s
9	Badovini	1m 42.645s
10	Sykes	1m 42.740s
11	Haslam	1m 42.879s
12	Camier	1m 43.012s
13	Berger	1m 43.306s
14	Fabrizio	1m 43.661s
15	Giugliano	1m 43.683s
16	Aitchison	1m 44.078s

Points		
1	Checa	505
2	Melandri	395
3	Biaggi	303
4	Laverty	303
5	Haslam	224
6	Guintoli	210
7	Camier	208
8	Haga	176
9	Rea	170
10	Badovini	165
11	Lascorz	161
12	Fabrizio	152
13	Sykes	141
14	Smrz	127
15	Corser	87
16	Berger	64
17	Xaus	49
18	Rolfo	42
19	Aitchison	36
20	Hopkins	20
21	Vermeulen	14
22	Toseland	13
23	Fores	12
24	Lanzi	10
25	Waters	8
26	Sandi	7
27	Polita	5
28	Giugliano	4
29	Baiocco	4
30	Veneman	3
31	Kirkham	3
32	Kispataki	1
33	Lowes	1
34	Lai	1
35	Staring	1

Fastest race lap: Joan Lascorz on lap 2, 1m 43.553s, 99.196mph/159.640km/h.
Lap record: Max Biaggi, ITA (Aprilia) 1m 42.774s, 99.948mph/160.850km/h (2010).

2011 POINTS TABLE

Position	Rider	Nationality	Machine	Phillip Island/1	Phillip Island/1	Donington/1	Donington/2	Assen/1	Assen/2	Monza/1	Monza/2	Utah/1	Utah/2	Misano/1	Misano/2	Aragón/1	Aragón/2	Brno/1	Brno/2	Silverstone/1	Silverstone/2	Nürburgring/1	Nürburgring/2	Imola/1	Imola/2	Magny-Cours/1	Magny-Cours/2	Portimao/1	Portimao/1	Total Points
1	**Carlos Checa**	ESP	Ducati	25	25	16	25	16	25	7	6	25	25	25	25	–	16	16	16	25	25	25	8	16	25	25	25	25	13	**505**
2	**Marco Melandri**	ITA	Yamaha	11	16	25	20	13	–	13	20	6	10	16	–	25	20	25	20	16	16	20	10	10	20	20	20	10	25	**395**
3	**Max Biaggi**	ITA	Aprilia	20	20	9	–	20	20	20	8	–	16	20	20	20	25	20	25	5	13	–	–	–	–	–	–	13	9	**303**
4	**Eugene Laverty**	IRL	Yamaha	13	1	–	2	9	10	25	25	11	13	11	3	13	10	11	11	20	20	13	11	11	13	11	16	–	20	**303**
5	**Leon Haslam**	GBR	BMW	16	11	13	13	4	11	16	–	8	3	–	11	7	7	8	9	13	8	11	7	–	11	16	13	7	1	**224**
6	**Sylvain Guintoli**	FRA	Ducati	–	–	5	5	–	6	4	9	16	9	9	9	5	5	–	7	10	10	10	20	10	9	10	11	20	11	**210**
7	**Leon Camier**	GBR	Aprilia	3	10	8	16	–	13	8	–	13	20	10	–	16	8	9	–	1	11	8	–	1	16	13	10	4	10	**208**
8	**Noriyuki Haga**	JPN	Aprilia	7	9	10	–	–	8	–	13	7	–	–	16	10	9	4	6	–	–	16	–	20	20	9	6	1	5	**176**
9	**Jonathan Rea**	GBR	Honda	4	13	11	10	25	16	10	–	–	5	–	–	–	–	–	–	6	13	25	–	–	–	–	–	16	16	**170**
10	**Ayrton Badovini**	ITA	BMW	2	–	3	7	7	1	5	10	9	7	8	13	8	6	10	10	6	6	7	9	7	6	–	8	3	7	**165**
11	**Joan Lascorz**	ESP	Kawasaki	–	–	6	11	5	4	–	7	2	4	7	7	9	11	7	8	9	–	9	5	6	8	9	8	11	8	**161**
12	**Michel Fabrizio**	ITA	Suzuki	10	8	–	9	11	9	11	16	–	11	–	10	–	13	13	13	–	7	–	–	–	–	4	–	5	2	**152**
13	**Tom Sykes**	GBR	Kawasaki	8	7	–	4	2	5	3	5	10	6	13	2	11	–	6	2	–	–	5	25	13	–	6	–	8	–	**141**
14	**Jakub Smrz**	CZE	Ducati	9	5	20	8	–	7	6	–	20	8	–	–	–	–	5	–	–	5	–	16	9	–	–	–	6	3	**127**
15	**Troy Corser**	AUS	BMW	6	–	7	3	10	–	9	11	3	–	–	6	–	–	7	–	1	4	4	–	7	7	2	–	–	–	**87**
16	**Maxime Berger**	FRA	Ducati	–	–	–	–	3	2	–	5	2	6	–	3	–	3	–	8	4	–	6	–	3	–	4	9	6	–	**64**
17	**Ruben Xaus**	ESP	Honda	–	6	4	6	8	2	1	4	–	–	5	8	–	–	–	–	–	–	–	–	–	5	–	–	–	–	**49**
18	**Roberto Rolfo**	ITA	Kawasaki	5	4	2	1	–	–	–	3	–	–	4	2	3	2	5	3	–	2	3	–	–	3	–	–	–	–	**42**
19	**Mark Aitchison**	AUS	Kawasaki	–	–	1	–	6	–	–	2	–	–	1	4	–	4	–	2	4	–	5	7	–	–	–	–	–	–	**36**
20	**John Hopkins**	USA	Suzuki	–	–	–	–	–	–	–	–	–	–	–	–	–	–	11	9	–	–	–	–	–	–	–	–	–	–	**20**
21	**Chris Vermeulen**	AUS	Kawasaki	–	–	–	–	–	–	–	–	–	–	2	6	2	4	–	–	–	–	–	–	–	–	–	–	–	–	**14**
22	**James Toseland**	GBR	BMW	–	2	–	–	–	–	1	–	–	–	–	–	–	–	–	–	4	3	3	–	–	–	–	–	–	–	**13**
23	**Javier Fores**	ESP	BMW	–	–	–	–	–	–	–	–	–	–	–	–	–	–	–	–	–	–	–	–	–	–	–	2	5	5	**12**
24	**Lorenzo Lanzi**	ITA	BMW	–	–	–	–	–	–	–	–	1	5	–	–	–	1	3	–	–	–	–	–	–	–	–	–	–	–	**10**
25	**Joshua Waters**	AUS	Suzuki	–	3	–	–	–	–	–	–	4	1	–	–	–	–	–	–	–	–	–	–	–	–	–	–	–	–	**8**
26	**Federico Sandi**	ITA	Ducati	–	–	–	–	–	–	–	–	–	–	–	–	–	–	–	–	–	–	–	–	–	–	3	4	–	–	**7**
27	**Alessandro Polita**	ITA	Ducati	–	–	–	–	–	–	–	–	–	–	3	–	–	–	–	–	–	–	–	–	–	–	–	2	–	–	**5**
28	**Davide Giugliano**	ITA	Ducati	–	–	–	–	–	–	–	–	–	–	–	–	–	–	–	–	–	–	–	–	–	–	–	–	4	–	**4**
29	**Matteo Baiocco**	ITA	Ducati	–	–	–	–	–	–	–	–	–	–	–	4	–	–	–	–	–	–	–	–	–	–	–	–	–	–	**4**
30	**Barry Veneman**	NED	BMW	–	–	–	–	3	–	–	–	–	–	–	–	–	–	–	–	–	–	–	–	–	–	–	–	–	–	**3**
31	**Jon Kirkham**	GBR	Suzuki	–	–	–	–	–	–	–	–	–	–	–	–	–	–	–	–	2	1	–	–	–	–	–	–	–	–	**3**
32	**Viktor Kispataki**	HUN	Honda	–	–	–	–	–	–	–	–	–	–	–	–	–	–	–	1	–	–	–	–	–	–	–	–	–	–	**1**
33	**Alex Lowes**	GBR	Honda	–	–	–	–	–	–	–	–	–	–	–	–	–	–	1	–	–	–	–	–	–	–	–	–	–	–	**1**
34	**Fabrizio Lai**	ITA	Honda	–	–	–	–	–	–	–	1	–	–	–	–	–	–	–	–	–	–	–	–	–	–	–	–	–	–	**1**
35	**Bryan Staring**	AUS	Kawasaki	1	–	–	–	–	–	–	–	–	–	–	–	–	–	–	–	–	–	–	–	–	–	–	–	–	–	**1**

FROM TRIUMPHS TO TRIUMPH

By GORDON RITCHIE

Inset above: The Yamaha ParkinGO Team and family celebrate the title at Magny-Cours.

Inset top: Enjoying the plaudits after a home win at Silverstone.

Main photo: Chaz on the gas, a state of being he often experienced on his way to six race victories.

Photos: Gold & Goose

Above: David Salom was second overall thanks to unerring consistency and three podiums.

Top right: Luca Scassa – what might have been?

Above right: James Ellison enjoyed a strong return to action after an injury-hit 2010 season.

Right: Fabien Foret: a bad start due to injury held back the former champion.

Below right: Broc Parkes: three DNFs halted his title challenge.

Photos: Gold & Goose

AFTER the big three – Kenan Sofuoglu, Eugene Laverty and Joan Lascorz – moved on in the winter of 2010, surely it was reasonable to assume that the next best rider in World Supersport, Welshman Chaz Davies, would become the man to beat in 2011.

And that's the way it ended up, although at the beginning of the 12-round championship, things looked quite promising for Davies' new team-mate, Luca Scassa (Yamaha ParkinGO Team).

The R6 pairing rode the same bikes that Cal Crutchlow had used to win the title in 2009, which had been in warm storage ever since, awaiting an opportunity to spring into action. When Triumph BE-1 Racing team boss Giuliano Rovelli felt the British manufacturer had pulled the plug with a lowly 2011 offer, there was a last-second change, and it was R6s not Daytona 675s in the ParkinGO garage.

Scassa, an ex-Superbike rider, won the first round in Australia in yet another of those classic WSS encounters that the middleweight class serves up with such regularity in Oz. He took the victory from Broc Parkes (Kawasaki Provec Motocard.com) and red-hot rookie Sam Lowes (Parkalgar Honda), who was filling Laverty's shoes as BSS champion. Leading out of the final corner, the latter was passed twice on the straight, but still clambered on to the podium first time out. The top three were covered by only 0.033 second, with Scassa a tyre ply ahead of Parkes – 0.009 second.

Even fourth-placed David Salom (Provec Motocard.com Kawasaki) was only 0.272 second from his first ever win in this category. This Spanish rider had just joined a Spanish-based team. He started from pole, and would do so again at Silverstone and Portimao.

Paddock enthusiasm about such a fantastic battle in the new single-bike era was tempered by the fact that several riders suffered terminal tyre issues, including blistering that eventually caused punctures for some, among them Davies and another pre-season championship tip, Fabien Foret (Hannspree Ten Kate Honda). The latter was riding injured after hurting his hand during a fall in practice, but had to retire for rubber reasons in P1, as did Kawasaki Lorenzini by Leoni rider Massimo Roccoli.

The next round at Donington Park was a coldie, but goody, as team-mates Scassa and Davies slugged it out over 22 laps, pole man Scassa winning by a mere 0.270 second. For the others, the writing was already on the wall, as Gino Rea (Step Racing Honda) scored a podium in third, but was over 20 seconds from the 1-2 R6 fight.

Robbin Harms (Harms Benjan Racing) was having a great season start, and was top Honda at this stage after scoring fourth in the UK, where Lowes dropped out with a technical issue. Harms' year would drift away in five consecutive no-scores at the end, triggered by mechanical and electrical woes as he ran out of budget.

At Assen, it started to go wrong for pole man Scassa, as he collided with fast and precocious teenager Florian Marino (Hannspree Ten Kate Honda) and each no-scored, just as Davies put in his first WSS race win. That came in a shortened event because of a red flag when Sam Lowes crashed hard in the first attempt. Foret, the 2002 champion, was sufficiently recovered to post second at his team's home round, heading up a great fight with Parkes, Harms, Salom and Roccoli.

The *autostrada*-like, ultra-high-speed track at Monza was the scene of Davies' first and only pole. It was also where he scored his second race win, team-mate Scassa being four seconds back and Foret another three behind. Parkes was fourth, the recovering Lowes fifth and strong privateer rider Roberto Tamburini (Bike Service RT Yamaha) sixth; he would finish ninth overall in the season.

There was no WSS race at Miller Motorsports Park in the USA, so the first of two substantial breaks was ended with the Misano race weekend.

Finally, the Yamaha victory hegemony was broken, by Parkes' Kawasaki 1.9 seconds ahead of Foret and Lowes. Davies was sixth, but Scassa was not there at all – he was serving a ban for riding at his race school at Misano, which was not his team's designated test track. That blunder effectively ended his push while the others mustered strength.

Lowes scored his first pole, while race day saw a purposeful wild-card, ex-Superstocker Ilario Dionisi (Honda Italia), take fifth.

Six rounds in, and at the new track of Motorland Aragón. Parkes' hard-won championship lead disappeared when he fell while under pressure, allowing Davies to take his third win in four races. Lowes piled in with second, only 0.6 behind, but for Salom it was home sweet home as he scored his first podium by crossing the line four seconds away. Yamaha, Honda and Kawasaki on the podium – there were a few races where all three main manufacturers would shuffle their order, but share the top three spots.

Parkes would soon no-score again, this time in Brno, where he fell at turn nine, dropping further back in the points.

Rea won his team's home race to huge acclaim all round, even though it had been abbreviated to 15 laps after a red flag. He was only 0.4 second in front of Foret, and 0.8 ahead of Davies. Rea's season would start to go off the rails as thinning budgets were hit hard as big crashes took their toll, and he would push too hard to make up for it.

We did not know it at the time, but the finish at Silverstone, shortly before the regular summer break, would mimic the end-of-season top three, with Davies, Salom and Foret separated by 2.4 seconds.

Back at the scene of a big smash between himself and Joan Lascorz in 2010, Tamburini appeared unaffected by the memory and maybe even spurred on, as he slotted in fourth. Roccoli beat Parkes on his semi-official Kawasaki, as the Aussie ran into issues with set-up, having qualified a lowly (by his standards) seventh. No such problems for Salom: first on the grid, second in the race and growing in stature as the only top rider to have finished each race – a record that he would sustain.

In Germany, after a long few weeks of nothing much, Foret took pole, but managed only sixth in the race. Salom was in a worse state: eighth on the grid and in the race. Davies' rivals needed to step it up to stop him winning now, as he took another full pointer in Germany, though he had to work some blocking magic on the suddenly resurgent James Ellison (Bogdanka PTR Honda). Ellison had started well, but had suffered technical issues that led to a fallow mid-season. He

CHAZ DAVIES

DAVID SALOM

FABIEN FORET

BROC PARKES

LUCA SCASSA

SAM LOWES

JAMES ELLISON

FLORIAN MARINO

ROBERTO TAMBURINI

MASSIMO ROCCOLI

GINO REA

ROBIN HARMS

Photos: Gold & Goose

Above: SSTK600 Champion Jed Metcher worked hard and well enough to win in his first full season.

Top: SSTK1000 Champion Davide Giugliano was convincing all the way.

Above right: Frenchman Florian Marino heads Gino Rea (4), Broc Parkes, and Sam Lowes (11) at Imola.

Right: Sam Lowes: no race wins, but a real threat already.

Photos: Gold & Goose

appeared ready to attack the admittedly desperate Davies, but looking at a definite second or a possible no-pointer, he opted for one try only, and lost by just 0.091 second.

Over three seconds back, Lowes was third; six seconds behind, Scassa claimed fourth, his best result for some time.

Entering the Imola weekend, Davies had a commanding 59-point lead over Salom, with Foret and Parkes not far behind the Spaniard. A good race in Italy would seal it, and all he had to do was make sure none of his rivals got too far ahead. Parkes was back, sitting on pole and looking like a man with one more throw of the dice to go. Davies was impossible to hold back in the race, however, hitting the front and running clear, his many rivals distant in his wake.

Only misfortune could stop Davies and, sure enough, on lap 15 his engine let go; neither he nor Scassa would score points. Foret, an old hand, seized control and won, with Lowes second by only 0.188 second and Parkes beating whippersnapper Marino to fourth. Broc was now too far behind for even miracles to intervene.

Foret and Salom, on the other hand, still had a chance, if very slim.

Hope was proved false only one week later, however, when Davies rode a sensible race to sixth in France to take his first world championship. Team-mate Scassa won, putting himself back in the team's good books.

Lowes was second in a battle with pole man Parkes and Salom. Foret, at home in Magny-Cours, but hating the track as usual, was eighth. Worse was to come.

Going for overall second was Foret's final task, but he was beaten to it in Portugal where Salom scored pole position

and then finished second, earning the runner-up spot on his 27th birthday. Foret was a dejected 12th, again not finding the right set-up. He had qualified seventh and, like many others in the hot October temperatures, could not get his tyres to last.

Ellison ended his season on a high, in third, but the main glut of glory on the final day belonged to the man who by that time had been champion for two weeks, Chaz Davies.

Rescued almost from the scrapheap by a team that took him from Triumph podiums to triumph in the table, Davies was a worthy champion, who no doubt would have had more than six wins – a 50-per cent ratio – had he not had occasional tyre and bike problems. He even had to get used to Bitubo suspension on the Yamaha, as team boss Rovelli insisted on using the Italian units, despite all of Yamaha's available data from its Öhlins season with Crutchlow. A good, and highly individual championship winning effort, the paddock mavericks having played the best hands all season long. With Scassa winning three races, it was nine from 12 for Rovelli's team and Yamaha's bike.

In the manufacturers' championship, Chaz's final win put Yamaha in the top slot, while ParkinGO won the team award.

In the Superstock 1000 FIM Cup class, fast Ducatis usurped the BMW dominance shown in 2010, and it took Checa's junior team stable-mate, Davide Giugliano (Althea Racing Ducati), only nine races to score the championship win. He notched four race wins, as did eventual second-place rider Danilo Petrucci (Barni Racing Ducati), who gained the last one in the absence of Giugliano, who had been given a leg up to the Superbike class at the final round in Portimao.

Sylvain Barrier (BMW Motorrad Italia STK) and his team-mate, Lorenzo Zanetti, each won a single round.

In the final analysis, Giugliano scored 171 (declared), Petrucci 169, Zanetti 148 and Barrier 132.

The only title fight to go to the wire was the Superstock 600 European Championship, which could have had three possible winners, depending on just how bizarrely the last race turned out. Aussie rider Jed Metcher (MTM-RT Motorsports Yamaha) had a 19-point advantage over American Joshua Day (Revolution Racedays Kawasaki) and a 25-point gap on Dutchman Michael van der Mark (Ten Kate Junior Team Honda).

When the Honda rider crossed the line to win his fourth of the year and all 25 points, it was possible he would be champion, as Metcher had only one race win. Just 3.8 seconds later, however, Day crossed the line for second and 20 points, passing van der Mark by one point and still in with a chance of being champion. But when Metcher survived a few crashes around him, and some close encounters with wild-card riders, to take fourth, it was all over. He was the champion. Three different bikes fought for the win in the end, and there were no fewer than six different winners in ten rounds.

TOUGH TO CALL...

Some riders were injured, others had switched teams, and the outcome of the 2011 TT was anybody's guess. Then the red flags came out... MARK FORSYTH reports from the Island.

THE 2011 TT was always going to be tough to predict. There were so many unknowns, so many spurious factors and so much pre-event hype – including a cinema release – that every class became a bookmaker's nightmare.

In 2010, one rider and one manufacturer owned the event. Honda-mounted Ian Hutchinson smashed Philip Mc-Callen's four-wins-in-a-week record with victories in all five of the races he entered. Being any more dominant was a physical impossibility.

But Hutchinson's fierce determination would not be a threat at 2011's event. The quietly-spoken Yorkshireman had come close to losing his left leg in a horrific accident during a Supersport 600 short-circuit race at Silverstone in September, 2010. After extensive and at times pioneering surgery, doctors saved his lower leg, but he faced a very long battle to regain fitness and strength.

In a press release announcing Hutchinson's absence from the TT, his surgeon issued the following statement:

"Ian Hutchinson is an incredibly determined young man. When I first saw him I advised him that I thought he should prepare himself for protracted rehabilitation before he could even walk without any aid. His courage and determination to win this 'race' is setting new standards in orthopaedic trauma surgery. To get as close as he has to competing at the TT races less than a year after his accident at Silverstone is nothing less than remarkable and I am sure he will win many more races in future."

Connor Cummins was another determined rider. Fast and fearless at the 2010 event, he had been riding the crest of a confidence tsunami. His purple McAdoo Kawasakis were quick and he posed a real threat in every race – until the last one of the week, the Senior.

He crashed heavily at the ultra-quick, four-apex Verandah corner near the top of Snaefell mountain, where the gravel traps look more like dry stone walls, and barbed-wire fences and the drops are severe. It was such a horrific accident that the TV footage was considered too gruesome to broadcast.

Connor survived, but his injuries were extensive. Unlike Hutchy, however, the Manxman announced his participation in the 2011 event, a decision that commanded huge respect, but also an understanding that he would not be fit enough to fight for the wins. The 21-year-old also had some demons to exorcise.

There had been some saddle swapping in the closed season, too. Perhaps somewhat optimistically, Hutchinson had announced from his hospital bed that he would be riding for Shaun Muir's Swan Yamaha team. Guy Martin had left his one-rider Wilson Craig Honda team to sign for the more corporate Relentless Suzuki by TAS squad. Talented Aussie Cameron Donald had filled Martin's vacant seat at Wilson Craig, which became a two-rider team with William Dunlop on the extra machine.

It didn't stop there either. Bruce Anstey had replaced Hutchinson at Padgetts Honda, while Keith Amor had joined John McGuinness at the massively experienced HM Plant Honda squad. Another previous winner, Michael Dunlop, hedged his bets with a WSB-spec Kawasaki for the two Superbike races and an R6 Yamaha for the Supersport races. The ascendant Gary Johnson plumped for Honda power in all classes.

But the biggest unknown was caused by the abandonment of the first big road race of the year, the NorthWest 200. Held in mid-May, the NW offers TT riders the chance to shake down their bikes while they chase a set-up for the monumentally high speeds and mechanical punishment of riding on public roads.

The 2011 NW200 was hit by catastrophic rainfall, a huge oil spill and even the absurdity of a hoax terrorist threat. Some riders didn't even turn a wheel.

So the first practice session of the 2011 TT was expected to begin answering some questions. However, it was held on Monday night in patchy weather conditions, so it looked like those questions might have to remain unanswered. With damp patches and rain in the west and northwest of the circuit, riders were making up for a lack of road miles and gradually getting up to speed.

McGuinness explained: "It was a bit greasy out there tonight, dusty and windy in places too, so I just had a bit of a cruise round on the opening lap to see where it was bad and where it wasn't. It was a shame we couldn't get a whole session in, but two laps on the big bike were definitely valuable. Having done all the endurance racing, I feel really race sharp and the bike's feeling a million dollars, so I'm glad we're all up and running now and can look forward to the rest of practice week in a good frame of mind."

Cruising or not, McGuinness posted the fastest lap of the evening at 122.838mph, with team-mate Amor right behind him on the timesheets. Donald, Martin and Johnson were also all in the 120s.

McGuinness upped the ante during the following evening's session. Making it clear that he should never be underestimated, he raised the bar with a lap at 129.041mph. But Guy Martin appeared to be in determined mood, perhaps thinking that 2011 was the year he could take his first win. He lapped at 128.261 on his big Suzuki to place second.

Gary Johnson raised eyebrows with his 127.717mph lap from a standing start, and so did newcomer Simon Andrews on only his second night of practice – 116.276mph will have done nothing to steady his friends' and family's nerves. All riders were reporting an abundance of wildlife on the track, with small birds and much larger ones, like geese, being spotted – and hit – all around the circuit.

Wednesday saw a number of riders suffering technical problems, including McGuinness with clutch slip on his Superstock bike and a misfire on his 600. Ryan Farquhar was also in the wars, becoming stranded on the wrong side of the circuit and unable to get back in time to ride any of his other bikes. Michael Dunlop had handling trouble with his Kawasaki Superbike as he battled to set it up for road use. But poor Keith Amor injured his shoulder in a low-speed spill at Quarter Bridge, the Scot being advised by doctors to rest his damaged AC joint until Friday.

With Thursday's practice sessions cancelled due to an oil spill after a road accident adjacent to the course, Friday evening offered the last ray of hope for those who had been blighted by troubles.

The last practice session got off to a delayed start after another road accident, this time on the course itself at Ginger Hall. Sunshine and good grip levels saw the times tumble. Anstey took the practice fight to McGuinness with a near-record 131.431mph lap to top the leaderboard. Michael Dunlop, clearly one of the fastest riders on 600 and Superstock machines, topped 125mph on his R6 Yamaha. Simon Andrews finished his week of learning with an astonishing 121.039mph lap. Poor, luckless Ryan Farquhar spent the night in hospital, however, with soft tissue injuries after he tipped off at Keppel Gate.

The sidecars grabbed the final practice slot. In the late evening sunshine, it was Tim Reeves and Greg Cluzel quickest, with 113.321mph, but the fastest practice lap of the week belonged to Klaus Klaffenbock and Dan Sayle from Wednesday evening. John Holden and Andy Winkle were also obvious challengers.

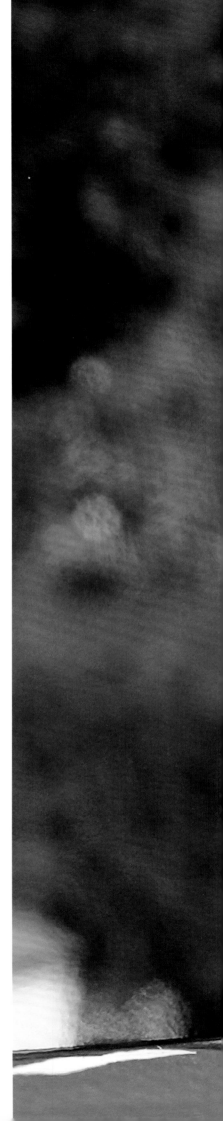

Isle of Man master-class. Focused, economical and fast, John McGuinness took the Senior TT on his Padgetts Honda.
Photo: David Collister/photocycles.com

SUPERBIKE

The first showdown of the week, Saturday's Dainese Super-bike race, saw Anstey start where he had finished practice. The Padgetts Honda-mounted Kiwi pushed hard from the start to pile the pressure on McGuinness' slender lead. Gary Johnson and Guy Martin matched the 130mph laps of the leaders to place third and fourth at the end of the first lap.

Anstey moved ahead, taking a second-and-a-half lead over McGuinness by Glen Helen on the second lap. By the time they stopped for fuel at the end of that lap, the gap in the battle for the lead had see-sawed from as much as 3.1 seconds at the Bungalow to 0.9 second at the pit entrance.

The Padgett Honda team suffered an unusually slow pit stop, HM Plant Honda the opposite. As they raced down Glencrutchery Road with their tanks brimmed, McGuinness held a 12-second advantage over Anstey. Despite the prob-lems in the pit lane, Anstey held on to second, with Martin now up to third and Johnson fourth.

By Quarry Bends on the fast run up to Sulby Straight, An-stey had retired with technical problems, giving second to Guy Martin. While Martin, Johnson and Donald squabbled over the lower orders, McGuinness kept up the pressure, stretching his lead relentlessly. By the end of lap four, as they came in for the second and final pit stop, the Morecambe missile commanded a healthy 20-second lead.

After another textbook stop by the HM Plant Honda squad, McGuinness was away for the final 75.5 miles with an even healthier lead. What had been a very close scrap between Guy Martin and Gary Johnson for third became a nightmare for the latter when he picked up a time penalty for speeding in the pit lane – one of ten riders to be caught out – on his East Coast Racing Fireblade. This promoted Cameron Donald to third while Johnson now languished 40 seconds back – an eternity – in fourth.

On lap five, Martin started applying the pressure to chip away at McGuinness' commanding lead, but it would be short lived, as he coasted to a halt at Hillberry. Donald now moved to second, with Johnson still third.

Johnson was obviously annoyed by his penalty and was pushing hard. The Yorkshireman recorded 177.1mph as he flashed over the line to start his final lap – some feat when you consider that the visibility is atrocious and the start/finish straight is actually a very ballsy, bumpy corner.

By the start of lap six – electrical gremlins allowing – there was little doubt that McGuinness had the win in the bag. By Ramsey, at the start of his final mountain ascent, his lead was over a minute, but he knew he'd have to coax it over Snaefell to ensure enough fuel to finish the lap.

Johnson's hard riding had narrowed the gap between him and second-placed Donald to under ten seconds. Also charging hard was Michael Dunlop. After his disastrous first pit stop, he'd upped the pace on his Street Sweep Kawasaki to record the fastest lap on lap four and again on lap six; by the flag, he was up to fifth – quite an achievement.

McGuinness crossed the line to secure his 16th TT victory. He'd done just enough, and this time luck was with him. A delighted Donald finished second, with Gary Johnson taking the last podium step.

On his pit-lane speeding incident, Johnson alluded to Guy Martin's reaction in 2010, when he said, tongue firmly in cheek, "I'm going to have a protest, stamp my feet, and go and sit in my van."

For McGuinness, the first win of the week was a confi-dence booster. A new generation of challengers had applied extra pressure, and this burden had shown on his face and in his statements. But the message on Saturday afternoon was crystal clear: McGuinness and his HM Plant Superbike were the team to beat.

SUPERSPORT 600 – Race One

Perfect, dry and sunny conditions greeted the start of the Mon-ster Energy 600 Supersport race on the Monday of race week. The majority of riders had suffered a lack of saddle time due to the interruptions of practice week, while most of the top con-tenders had been concentrating on their Superbike and Super-stock bikes.

The screaming 600cc Supersport bikes spend over 75 per cent of a TT lap at full throttle, and are lighter, smaller and

Above: Guy Martin switched to the Relentless Suzuki in his still incomplete quest for a first win.

Photo: David Collister/photocycles.com

Left: Rostrum-bound, Keith Amor gets ready for action.

Far left: Cameron Donald took second place in the Superbike race.

Photos: Gavan Caldwell

easier to manhandle – or womanhandle, if your name's Jenny Tinmouth. But with dizzying red lines of around 17,000rpm, four laps of the TT circuit are a tough test for these small-capacity screamers.

And so it proved.

Michael Dunlop had been fast or fastest every time he went out on his 600 Yamaha in practice, and by the time the leading riders had reached Glen Helen on lap one, it was pretty clear that his practice times were no fluke. Dunlop trailed fast-starting Cameron Donald by just one second, with Gary Johnson pressing hard in third.

By Ballaugh, the gap was down to 0.6 second, and as an indication of how competitive the class is, just 14 seconds covered the top 15. By Ramsey, the tables had turned and Dunlop commanded a half-second lead, but just a mile-and-a-half later his efforts were undone as he coasted to a halt at the Gooseneck. The luck of the Irish?

Dunlop's misfortune gave Cameron Donald the lead and a nine-second gap back to Johnson in second. A battered and bruised Keith Amor held third, with McGuinness in fourth.

By the time the top riders peeled into Signpost, Guy Martin had disappeared, having fallen foul of the tyre wall on the exit of Creg ny Baa. Martin's accident became a YouTube hit after an amateur cameraman captured and posted his neat somersault dismount.

By lap two, Donald appeared to be in control at the front. His ultra-fast Wilson Craig Honda clearly had the speed, clocking 172.5mph through the Sulby Straight speed trap. By Glen Helen, Donald had forged himself a 17-second gap to second, which now belonged to Amor, with Johnson demoted to third.

On lap two, however, the red flags came out, signalling an immediate stoppage. Thirty-four-year-old Derek Brien from County Meath in Ireland had crashed at Gorse Lea, suffering fatal injuries. The competitors were chaperoned back to the pits by travelling marshals.

SUPERSPORT 600 – Race One (part 2)

Under very subdued circumstances, the three-lap restart allowed Michael Dunlop and Guy Martin another opportunity to take part. But with the bikes only capable of two laps on a full tank, the three-lap format threw in another permutation: pit after the first lap or at the end of the second? Everyone, it appeared, had different strategies.

From the start of the three-lap sprint, it was the same suspects. Dunlop held a narrow margin from Donald, but the fuel stops were about to re-shuffle the pack. Most stopped at the end of the first lap for a splash and dash, presumably on the assumption that half a tank of fuel doesn't take as long to brim as a full one. But with Donald, Anstey and McGuinness in the pits, Dunlop flew past to take advantage of a clear road and a flying lap. Again, however, his bike expired, this time at Ballig Bridge on the run to Glen Helen.

Clearly the race was going to be a commentator's nightmare. Working out who had pitted for fuel and who hadn't meant that until the first 15 or 20 riders on the road had gone through a checkpoint, the top five couldn't be calculated. Johnson was in the lead by 34 seconds at the start of the second lap.

As they approached the end of the second lap, Johnson finally pitted for fuel, giving the lead back to Donald. Then

Above: Anstey inherited victory in the re-started Supersport race one.

Photo: Dave Purves

with less than 20 miles to the chequered flag, Donald's engine blew on the charge through Kirk Michael village, and he almost collected Guy Martin, who was slipstreaming him at the time. "That nearly ended in tears for both of us. I had to use the kerbs," said Martin.

With the leader out, Anstey, Amor and Martin were now 1-2-3, positions they held to the flag.

The 42-year-old Anstey was clearly pleased, as too was Amor. "I was in hospital three days ago and on the podium today. That can't be bad," said the Scot.

Anstey was far more self-deprecating in the post-race interviews: "I thought I rode like a bit of a wuss in that one," he said.

Two stunning Supersport rides are also worthy of note. Manxman Dan Kneen in sixth and Ben Wylie in eighth proved that more young talent is emerging.

1000cc SUPERSTOCK

It's hard to fathom why magazines still do 1000cc sports bike group tests when the Superstock TT exists. Speed, handling, braking, stability, fuel range and reliability are all tested to the limits for four laps of the 37.75-mile circuit – by the best road riders on the planet.

With only an exhaust system, a Dynojet Power Commander, suspension, tyres and brake mods allowed, these 'race' bikes are as close to showroom models as possible. So on Tuesday afternoon, the greatest Superbike group test got under way.

Michael Dunlop, on the fearsomely fast Kawasaki ZX-10, was on a mission from the word go, and by Ballaugh Bridge on the first lap, he was leading. On the run to Ramsey, Dunlop was clocked at 186.4mph before the braking zone for Sulby Bridge – faster than most Superbikes.

At Ramsey hairpin, it was clear that Dunlop wasn't in for an easy race. Guy Martin was snapping at his heels, just half

a second back, with McGuinness, Johnson and William Dunlop all pushing hard. Pre-race favourite Anstey was clearly out of the reckoning – he'd slipped back to 13th, and his machine troubles would see him pit and retire at the end of lap one. Martin kept the pressure on over the mountain, and by the start of the second lap, he'd claimed the leading spot.

Martin's lead was short lived, though. Michael Dunlop, clearly just getting into his stride, was three-and-a-half seconds ahead by Glen Helen, six seconds by Ballaugh, nine by Ramsey and eleven by the Bungalow. It was positively electrifying listening to this information on the local radio station. Dunlop had pulled the pin.

McGuinness was having a good second lap as well. He'd been pinching fractions of a second from Martin in almost every sector, and their dispute over second looked like running for the rest of the race, their pace being so evenly matched.

On the third lap, after a less-than-perfect pit stop for McGuinness, when his Fireblade didn't fire into life immediately, the HM plant rider was clearly getting into his groove as well. By Ramsey hairpin, he was ahead of Martin and closing down Michael Dunlop, taking a second out of his lead. Dunlop still had a big lead, though, and despite some fearsome riding from McGuinness, he held a cushion of 17.27 seconds at the Bungalow.

By the start of the fourth and final lap, it was pretty clear that Dunlop had checked out, extending his lead to 19 seconds at Glen Helen. McGuinness was still pushing and had worked a four-second gap between himself and third-placed Martin, who was locked in his own private battle with Keith Amor in fourth.

Unpressured and untroubled, Dunlop crossed the line to win by an incredible 19 seconds, with McGuinness second and Guy Martin third, again the bridesmaid.

Want to know the fastest stock Superbike? Paul Shoesmith's Ice Valley S1000RR BMW delivered a superbike-humbling 188mph through the Sulby trap. Amazing.

SPORTMAX GP RACER D211

WE RACE, YOU WIN

DERIVED FROM THE RACE DOMINATING D211 GP, THE GP RACER D211
SETS A NEW REFERENCE FOR TRACK DAY TYRES *

SPORTMAX GP RACER D211

/ NTEC SYSTEM ALLOWS RIDERS TO LOWER TYRE PRESSURES FOR ULTIMATE GRIP IN TRACK DAY CONDITIONS

/ MULTI-TREAD (MT) COMPOUND GUARANTEES RAPID WARM-UP, HIGH STABILITY UNDER BRAKING AND TOTALLY FOCUSED FEEDBACK OVER A HIGH MILEAGE IN ALL CONDITIONS

/ BELT-TO-CARCASS ANGLES ARE ENGINEERED TO STABILISE SIDEWALLS FOR SMOOTH, RESPONSIVE TRANSITIONS BETWEEN MAXIMUM LEAN ANGLES

/ NYLON BREAKER BELTS AND CONTINUOUSLY-WOUND ARAMID-FIBRE TREAD BELT ELIMINATE CIRCUMFERENTIAL GROWTH FOR COOLER RUNNING AND PREDICTABLE PERFORMANCE UNDER HEAVY USE

MT MULTI TREAD COMPOUND TECHNOLOGY

NTec JLB

WWW.DUNLOPMOTORCYCLE.EU

DUNLOP

RIDE WITH CONFIDENCE

* IN 2010 DUNLOP D211 GP RACE TYRES AND NTEC SLICKS DELIVERED A CLEAN SWEEP
OF FIVE RACE WINS, TEN PODIUM FINISHES AND TWO LAP RECORDS AT THE I.O.M TT.

Above: Runaway Superstock winner Michael Dunlop climbs the Mountain. His 1000cc Kawasaki ZX-10 street bike set a higher top speed than the 750 Superbikes.

Photo: David Collister/photocycles.com

Right: Supersport 2 race winner Gary Johnston passes the Kirk Michael grocery store at 160mph in a timeless classic TT photo.

Photo: Gavan Caldwell

SUPERSPORT – Race Two

If you believe in omens, the second Supersport race had all the hallmarks of trouble before it had even started.

A rain shower had left the track in a perilously dangerous condition, neither fully wet nor fully dry. The tyre companies and the riders were clearly very concerned about racing between the walls and hedges at insane speeds when grip levels were so hard to call.

McGuinness, the most experienced TT rider, obviously wasn't happy. With a glum face, he said, "Dunlop don't want us to race. They've got a tyre for the wet and a tyre for the dry, but nothing to cope with wet and dry at race pace."

Amor was audibly angry: "You could be doing 140 round a corner and there's a damp patch, and that's it, game over." His pre-race sound bite would prove prophetic.

After a riders' near mutiny, the race eventually got under way with the 'lack of adhesion' flags being displayed around the circuit. Commentator Charlie Lambert echoed everyone's thoughts when he said, "Let's just hope Michael [Dunlop] doesn't overcook it, bearing in mind the doubtful conditions." It was far from a slur on Dunlop, rather an acknowledgement of his bravery and determination, two attributes that tend not to mix very well with unpredictable conditions and an unforgiving course.

By Ballaugh on the opening lap, the courage of both Dunlop brothers was quite apparent: Michael was leading while William was in second place. McGuinness, ever the pragmatist, was treating the lap as a recce and had dropped down the order to 12th as he tested the conditions cautiously. Donald lay third.

The start of lap two was the beginning of the end for Supersport 2. It had started to rain, quite hard in some places, and as the leading bunch flicked left into what they thought was a dry and grippy Union Mills, Keith Amor crashed, thankfully unscathed. He wasn't the only rider to have a moment there, but the others were luckier and stayed on.

Heavier rain was also reported at Glen Helen and Ramsey,

and as the leading riders slowed to a crawl, the race was eventually red-flagged, but not until Mark Parrot had slid off at Laurel Bank and suffered an ankle injury.

SUPERSPORT TT – Race Two (part 2)

The omens appeared to be better for the restarted 600 race. Good weather, a dry track and calm winds provided the ideal racing backdrop.

Gary Johnson set the pace from the start, leading by three seconds among the trees of Glen Helen, six by the humpback bridge of Ballaugh and nine seconds at the slippery, off-camber hairpin at Ramsey. Michael Dunlop was gone, having retired with mechanical problems at Ballacraine.

McGuinness was in hot pursuit of Johnson to hold second, with Martin pressing hard in third.

Johnson seemed comfortable up front on his East Coast Racing Honda. On lap two, with a lighter fuel load, he stretched his lead over McGuinness from ten seconds at Glen Helen to 15 by Cronk ny Mona near the end of the lap.

But as Johnson pitted for fuel in Douglas, red flags were being shown at Ramsey. Several riders stopped at Ramsey hairpin before being told that it was a mistake and they should continue. The commentators were at a loss, even comparing notes from section to section. Guy Martin spotted a red flag at Union Mills and, in his own words, "cruised for three or four miles. I saw a bird on the track, a feathered one, not one in a skirt, and thought that must have been what the flags were for."

The erroneous red flags – the result of miscommunication – ruined what was left of the race. Taking nothing away from Gary Johnson's peerless performance at the front (like McGuinness, he didn't see a red flag), the remainder of the positions were thrown into chaos by the stoppage.

Johnson took his first ever win in fine style, an impressive feat considering he'd only been competing since 2007. Post race, he said, "I made a break from the start and tried to hold it. Full credit to the East Coast team. I was a bit mardy

with meself after the Superbike race. I'd like to win a big race now, but we're not going to push it."

Second-placed McGuinness had different problems to contend with, and they weren't red flags. Fresh from his 50th finish on the TT course and his 32nd podium, he said, "It was just another thoroughly enjoyable race on this little 600. I was a bit rusty on the bike and learned a load off Keith in the first race. Fair play to Gary. I had no problems. I've had three starts on my Padgett's bikes and three finishes, but when I hit the bottom of Bray Hill my foreskin came back and I had a bit of chafage for an hour-and-a-quarter. I'll maybe get Becky to check it out for me later. I didn't see a red flag. Maybe they just missed me. Strange that race: I never saw another bike and I didn't clobber a bird, either."

Guy Martin took his third third of the week, and Ben Wylie a commendable seventh.

SENIOR TT

· ·

As a rider, an hour's delay to the race start time can rattle your nerves a bit. You start getting ready, going through your routines – zipping zips, buckling buckles, strapping straps. And then, this being the Isle of Man, the weather gets in the way and the mental processes have to be reversed, adding to the stress and worry. Heavy rain – and hail – in Ramsey at lunchtime didn't bode well for the running of the last and most prestigious event of the week..

With the organisers mindful of the second Supersport race debacle, Friday's weather created much head scratching and cloud watching. It would be an excruciating five-hour delay before the Poker Stars Senior race got under way, and that, in itself, would prove to be a real test of mental strength.

Guy Martin, desperate for his first win, set off like a scalded cat to lead with Johnson, Anstey, McGuinness and Dunlop in close pursuit. Anstey had bullied his way into second by Ramsey, and McGuinness was still holding fourth, but clearly finding his rhythm as he chipped away the deficit.

By the Bungalow, Martin had stretched his lead to seven seconds and was clearly on a mission, but McGuinness had moved up to third and was building speed. As they flashed over the line for the start of the second lap, Martin's standing-start average speed was an impressive 131.038mph.

Martin appeared to have the job in hand on the second lap until they reached the Mountain Climb, where Anstey and McGuinness began to claw back his advantage. Michael Dunlop was also getting into his stride, deposing Amor for fourth as they rattled over Snaefell towards their first pit stop.

The HM Plant Honda team turned McGuinness around faultlessly in the pits. That slick pit work and a lap at 131.788mph were enough to propel the Lancastrian into second place, just two seconds down on leader Martin. By Glen Helen, the gap was two seconds; by Ballaugh, nearer a second; and by Ramsey, the HM Plant Honda was leading the race by the narrowest of margins, 0.0006 second.

Martin's problems were not just McGuinness-shaped: Anstey was charging as well, two seconds adrift and gaining ground. Michael Dunlop held fourth, but 33 seconds back. Lap three saw Dan Stewart retire at Ballacrye after a bird strike broke his finger.

McGuinness kept on the pressure for his third lap, and by the time he reached the pits for his final fuel stop, he'd managed to lap seven seconds faster than his two nearest rivals to pull a 12-second gap as he entered the pits. A hard ride over the mountain placed Anstey second, demoting Guy Martin to third. Michael Dunlop, clearly trying hard, slipped to sixth after overshooting the Ballacraine braking area.

For the last two laps, McGuinness showed his experience, reacting to his pit boards around the circuit to control his lead. Guy Martin pipped Bruce Anstey for second place, but the battle for fourth and fifth, between Amor and Donald, went all the way to the line, with Donald getting the better of the Scot by just one second. Simon Andrews finished in 11th spot with a 125mph lap, the second fastest newcomer lap in the history of the event.

McGuinness' victory, his 17th overall and second of the week, added the coveted Joey Dunlop Trophy to his already impressive silver haul.

SES ZERO TT

With a £5,000 university bounty and a £10,000 payout for the first 100mph Zero TT lap, the stakes were attractive.

From the electric bikes' practice sessions, the race itself looked like being a two-, possibly three-horse race, between the slick Segway Motoczysz team riders of American Mark Miller and the experienced Michael Rutter. Flashes of brilliance and speed were also being shown by Irish rider John Burrows on the American Lightning Motorcycles machine.

Rutter had notched more than 138mph on Sulby Straight in practice, and his average speed of 106mph from the start line to Ballaugh hinted at the possibility of a big pay packet for the Midlander.

From nine starters (only five reached the finish line), Rutter stamped his mark on the one-lap race with team-mate Miller in close contention.

Clocking nearly 150mph on Sulby Straight, Rutter used all his course experience to maintain momentum. But, somewhat cruelly, he was denied his big bonus by just 0.3mph – his race winning average lap speed was 99.6mph. Team-mate Miller finished a close second, with Kingston University's George Spence third.

Rutter, dry and sardonic at the best of times, did his best to put on a brave face: "99.6mph: that's the story of my life. I tried to conserve battery life and stay smooth. It's a totally different way of riding, but I really enjoyed it. We only saw the bike on Wednesday, so I think if we had more time, there would be more to come set-up wise."

Better luck for 2012, Michael.

SIDECAR – Race A

Klaus Klaffenbock and passenger Dan Sayle made it three wins in a row when they took victory in the first Sure Sidecar race from John Holden and Andy Winkle.

The Austrian/Manx pair gained the lead at Glen Helen on the opening lap and were never headed, catching Holden on the road and circulating together in high-speed formation. Lapping at just under 115mph, the two outfits were well clear of the rest of the field, with Conrad Harrison and Mike Aylott overhauling Tim Reeves and Gregory Cluzel on the final lap for third.

SIDECAR – Race B

John Holden and Andy Winkle won their first TT when they took the second three-lap Sidecar race after long-time leaders Klaus Klaffenbock and Dan Sayle suffered a loose water pipe clip on the final lap, which forced them to nurse their overheating machine home.

The Austrian ex-world champion held a dominant 17-second lead starting the third and final lap, but Holden and Winkle took full advantage when the pairing slowed on the approach to Ramsey. After five runner-up spots, it was a dream TT win, 45 seconds clear of Conrad Harrison and Mike Aylott, who claimed a best-ever second. Tony Elmer and Darren Marshall took a debut TT podium with a fine third.

NORTH WEST 200 & ULSTER GRAND PRIX

BUMPS ALONG THE WAY

By OLLIE BARSTOW

Main photo: Guy Martin gained a popular win in the second Superbike Ulster race.

Insets, from left: Michael Dunlop scored wins in Supersport and Superstock at the Ulster; Michael Rutter shrugs as the North West 200 Superbike race is cancelled; oil and water combined to halt proceedings.

Photos: Gavan Caldwell

Above: Alastair Seeley battles with Cameron Donald in the Supersport race, the only one to be completed at the problem-beset North West 200.

Top: Ulsterman Michael Dunlop leads Australian Cameron Donald in the second Ulster Supersport race.

Above right: New Zealander Bruce Anstey took the honours in the first Ulster Superbike race, denying Guy Martin a first win.

Photos: Gavan Caldwell

FEW could have envisaged the drama that would afflict the 2011 running of the Relentless International North West 200, one of the world's premier road races, but incidents and misfortune culminated in much of race day being cancelled.

An event that has grown in status over the years, the North West 200 attracts a healthy entry list, often a blend of riders who are either warming up for the blue-riband Isle of Man TT or taking their first steps into road racing before tackling the fearsome Mountain course on the Manx isle.

Indeed, the 2011 event would see an interesting mix of notable road racers, such as Guy Martin, Cameron Donald and Martin Dunlop, sharing the spotlight with short-circuit regulars Michael Rutter, Martin Jessopp, Stuart Easton and Gary Mason. If anything, the influx of British Superbike riders, who included Simon Andrews and James Hillier, was enough to put it on a par with the TT in terms of recognisable stars.

Even so, no matter how impressive the names and how dedicated the crowd, no one could have been prepared for the ensuing day of disruptions, which included a security threat, inclement weather and a critical oil spill. Though probably manageable situations in isolation, together they would ensure that just one race would be completed before the decision was taken to stop the event altogether.

Practice and provisional qualifying began with Fuchs-Silkolene British Supersport racer – and 2010 North West 200 winner – Alastair Seeley assuming the early pace, the Relentless by TAS rider topping the timesheets in both Superbike and Superstock free practice, before going second behind Cameron Donald in the Supersport class.

The Ulsterman went on to secure pole position in the Superstock and Supersport categories, but his hopes of making

it a clean sweep were scuppered by mechanical problems on his GSX-R1000 Superbike during the second qualifying session. However, his performance in Q1 ensured he would start the Superbike race from seventh.

Instead, it was a Rapid-Bathams Ducati 1-2, Rutter leading his British Superbike team-mate, Jessopp, by six-tenths of a second, the twin-cylinder 1198R proving well suited to the crests and troughs of the challenging 8.9-mile layout.

Just a handful of seconds adrift, Michael Dunlop was third fastest on the Street Sweep Kawasaki, ahead of Wilson Craig Honda's Cameron Donald and East Coast Honda's Gary Johnson.

However, the day's activities were marred by an accident involving MSS Colchester Kawasaki team-mates Stuart Easton and Gary Mason, the latter having broken down in the path of the Scot and being struck at high-speed.

Although Mason escaped unhurt from the horrific smash, Easton – who at this stage was classified third in the BSB standings – was admitted to hospital with serious injuries to his femur, pelvis and hands. Necessitating a stay in hospital of almost a month, the accident would curtail what was shaping up to be a promising season for Easton.

As dawn broke on race day, persistent rain was already causing havoc for the organisers, who took the decision to amend the schedule, allowing the Supersport race to start before the Superbike race, in the hope that the lower-powered machines would disperse some of the standing water on the treacherous course.

From pole position, Seeley fended off the attentions of Cameron Donald to win by less than a second for the first of what he hoped would be a trio of wins. Bruce Anstey completed the podium on the Padgetts Honda in a lonely third

place, with Michael Dunlop, Gary Johnson and William Dunlop finishing the five-lap race in fourth, fifth and sixth.

However, just as the Superbikes were set to venture out on course, the day took a dramatic turn when a security alert forced police to evacuate the paddock. Although the threat turned out to be a hoax, it put the programme well behind schedule and the organisers under extra pressure.

The stressful situation was further exacerbated by the constant rain and unseasonal cool conditions that had continued into the afternoon. Indeed, when the Superbikes did eventually make it on to the grid, they formed up without the front-row pairing of Rutter and Jessopp, the BSB riders having decided the conditions were too tricky.

Even so, the race did get under way, with Seeley moving into an early lead, only for the red flags to be deployed after Ryan Farquhar's KMR Kawasaki expired in dramatic fashion at the Juniper chicane and dumped a significant amount of oil on the track.

During another lengthy delay as marshals attempted to clear the corner, riders and organisers embarked on a series of meetings to discuss whether it was safe to continue racing. With a handful of riders going out on course to ascertain the state of the conditions, the general consensus was that visibility and the surface were poor, particularly at the affected Juniper chicane.

As a result, the decision was taken reluctantly to cancel the event on safety grounds, a bitter disappointment for the sizeable crowd, who had spent much of the day waiting patiently in the rain. Nonetheless, despite the setbacks, it would take more than such unforeseen circumstances to tarnish Northern Ireland's most popular racing event, and plans were soon afoot to make amends in 2012.

ULSTER GRAND PRIX

No such drama would afflict the 2011 Ulster Grand Prix, which saw a thrilling exchange between the year's road racing standouts in each of the scheduled events..

The two Superbike races were disputed by Bruce Anstey and Guy Martin, an intense tussle that had the added element of a chase after the pair were split into two different racing groups. It meant that, while Martin was the first past the chequered flag, all eyes were on the timing screens to determine Anstey's pace in the second group, which proved enough for the Kiwi to be classified the race winner.

It was a particular frustration for Martin, who had shown pace with new team Relentless by TAS Suzuki without posting any wins as yet. However, he struck back to deny Padgett Honda's Anstey in the second race, culminating his road racing season in impressive style.

In the Supersport class, it was all about the brothers Dunlop as Michael and William, sons of Robert and nephews of Joey, disputed glory on their respective Yamaha and Honda machines. Victory would go the way of Michael on the Street Sweep YZF-R6; William, riding the Wilson Craig CBR600RR, extended the Dunlop dynasty's success on the roads by following his brother in second place on both occasions.

Michael Dunlop went on to make it a hat trick of Ulster Grand Prix triumphs with success in the Superstock class, this time aboard a Kawasaki ZX-6R, ahead of Martin and Gary Johnson. In the 250cc/Supertwins class, Ian Lougher rode to success, ahead of Denver Robb and Jamie Coward.

BRITISH SUPERBIKE REVIEW

LICENSED TO THRILL

By OLLIE BARSTOW

Above: On the comeback trail, ex-GP star John Hopkins was a serious force on the Crescent Suzuki.
Photo: Gold & Goose

Top right: Hopkins brought a welcome international flavour to the series and very nearly took the title at his first attempt.

Above right: Ryuichi Kiyonari, 2010's champion, had a downbeat year on the HM Plant Honda.
Photos: Clive Challinor Motorsport Photography

Right: Shane Byrne returned to winning ways after an undistinguished spell in World Superbikes.
Photo: Gold & Goose

THE 2011 MCE British Superbike Championship may have been contested over 12 rounds, 26 races and 487 laps, but it was only one round, one race and one lap that would decide the outcome of a thrilling season.

Indeed, while Tommy Hill was always confident of becoming BSB champion for the first time, even after injuring his shoulder in an early-season crash and even as he entered the final race two points behind John Hopkins, there was little to predict that he would triumph by a mere 0.006 second.

As ever, 2011 signalled change at the top, with new faces appearing in new places. Indeed, the off-season had been busy as contracts and negotiations developed into an enticing entry list of 30-plus riders, seven manufacturers and ten former race winners.

Reigning champions HM Plant Honda headed up the grid with arguably its strongest line-up yet in Ryuichi Kiyonari, who returned to defend his crown, and Shane Byrne, who was back on the national scene after two fairly nondescript years in World Superbike. With five BSB titles achieved over the previous eight seasons between them, this was a dream pairing for the factory-backed Honda team.

Byrne's arrival would see HM Plant's 2010 runner-up, Josh Brookes, defect to Relentless by TAS Suzuki, the Irish team slimming to one Superbike, but gaining Suzuki GB backing from counterparts Crescent Racing.

Having sat out 2010, despite dominating in 2009, Yamaha returned in an official capacity by teaming with former Honda outfit Shaun Muir Racing, the Swan backed team signing Hill and Michael Laverty as its new pairing.

With its factory support, title sponsor and lead rider all elsewhere for 2011, Crescent Racing could have been forgiven for feeling apprehensive about the new season. Yet Jack Valentine's popular squad returned with a bold new sponsor in electronics giant Samsung, and a rider pairing of National Superstock champion Jon Kirkham and exciting acquisition John Hopkins. Personal issues and persistent injury woes may have called into question the wisdom behind Hop-

kins' approach, but at his best, he had been a force in a field that had included Valentino Rossi, Casey Stoner and Dani Pedrosa. A season in BSB was an opportunity to shine again.

Elsewhere, MSS Colchester Kawasaki had the much anticipated new ZX-10R, which was alluring enough for Stuart Easton to join Gary Mason in the team with which he had made his BSB debut in 2008. Michael Rutter and Martin Jessopp were back on the Bathams Ducati 1198R, now backed by Rapid Solicitors.

Having marked its BSB debut in 2010 with a successful run at the inaugural EVO title, BMW stepped up to the championship class in 2011 with Buildbase, who retained John Laverty and secured 2009 top-five finisher Ian Lowry. EVO rivals Splitlath Aprilia and Hudson Kennaugh also graduated, but while the team made column inches with its signing of Jenny Tinmouth – the first woman to race at BSB level – that relationship would sour after just two rounds.

As ever, a bevy of impressive privateer teams did their utmost to bother the established order, with Tyco Racing (née Quay Garage) entering Tommy Bridewell and Peter Hickman on the 2010 title-winning Hondas; Motorpoint Yamaha pairing Frenchman Loris Baz with British Supersport runner-up James Westmoreland; Sorrymate.com SMT Honda signing Dan Linfoot; and Chris Walker riding a Kawasaki for the newly-formed Pr1mo Racing.

Finally, the success of the first EVO sub-series attracted some impressive names for 2011, most notably Team WFR, which entered three Hondas for the experienced Glen Richards and Supersport front-runners Graeme Gowland and Alex Lowes.

Brands Hatch played host to the season opener once more, the traditional Easter bank holiday curtain raiser providing a more conclusive indication of who would emerge the front-runners in 2011 than testing ever could.

First blood went to HM Plant Honda and Swan Yamaha, Byrne and Hill scoring a win apiece, forging a rivalry that would set the tone for the season.

Byrne's success in the first race came after surviving a chaotic three laps at the mid-point that eliminated his fiercest competition, Michael Laverty high-siding out of the lead going on to the start-finish straight and very nearly wiping out the top three. Fortunately, Laverty was unhurt in the accident, despite receiving a fairly hefty blow from team-mate Hill as he went down. The accident split the leading pack, with Byrne recovering in second and Hill, having trundled through the gravel trap, rejoining outside the top ten.

Byrne quickly relieved Kawasaki's Easton of first, while a challenge from Josh Brookes, up to second after qualifying poorly on his debut for Relentless by TAS Suzuki, ended with a spectacular somersault through the Paddock Hill Bend gravel trap.

As a result, Byrne completed a fairly comfortable victory. Hill battled through the order for a satisfying second, a fight back that, unbeknown to him, would prove critical at the same circuit eight months later, while Tommy Bridewell's last-corner pass on Easton brought his and Tyco Racing's first-ever BSB podium.

Hill resumed his authority in race two with a maiden win for SMR in its Swan Yamaha iteration, ahead of Kiyonari, Byrne, Laverty – who bounced back from his dramatic first-race exit – and Hopkins, whose fairly quiet BSB debut saw him end the weekend with fifth, having fallen and remounted out of the points in race one.

Having edged into an early lead overall, Hill threatened to extend that advantage in the second round at Oulton Park, where he dominated each practice session and qualified on pole. However, his season was thrown into jeopardy when a nasty warm-up crash, caused by slipping on oil deposited by Loris Baz's broken Yamaha, left him with a torn tendon in his shoulder. That ruled him out at Oulton Park, and the doctors weren't optimistic for a swift recovery.

As it happened, Hill toughed it out at the very next Croft event, where he placed his faith in the six-way BSB Title Showdown format. Introduced to mixed opinion in 2010, the format was retained for 2011, with Hill becoming a significant beneficiary after he switched his focus from attempting to lead from the front to that of reaching the top six.

With Hill out of the running, Kiyonari evoked memories of his third title glory at the Lancashire circuit by posting his first win of the season, the Japanese rider methodically working his way up the order to finish ahead of Hopkins and Easton.

In race two, Hopkins upgraded his maiden podium into a maiden victory after prevailing in an entertaining tussle with Easton, Byrne, Kiyonari and Laverty. He was the first American race winner in BSB and passed his initiation into British panel-bashing with flying colours.

Having hosted one of the Showdown rounds in 2010, Croft appeared earlier in the schedule than usual, the demandingly twisty circuit always likely to take its toll on the injured Hill. Consequently, Byrne and tentative title contenders Hopkins and Easton had ample opportunity to stretch their advantage, but it was not an easy first race for the trio: mechanical problems sidelined long-time leader Byrne, Hopkins lost out in second and Easton came home sixth.

Instead, victory went the way of Kirkham, who not only celebrated his first success in 112 attempts, but also did so with a run from 16th position on the grid. Taking advantage of the unpredictable weather conditions and a mid-race safety-car period, necessitated to clear the remnants of Byrne's expired Honda engine, Kirkham moved into the lead fight. Having taken on Hopkins and won, it was a well-deserved first triumph for the younger rider.

Behind the Samsung Crescent Suzuki 1-2, Gary Mason was also a happy man in third place, his first BSB podium in almost 200 races.

Byrne made amends in race two, winning comfortably, ahead of Easton and Hopkins, while Brookes, Baz and a brave Hill completed the top six positions. Kirkham was bundled out on the opening lap after an altercation with Laverty.

With three rounds down – already a quarter of the season

– Byrne led the way from the increasingly prominent Hopkins and Easton, who had given Kawasaki its most convincing BSB start in several years. Sadly, any hopes of a title challenge disappeared before round four when a horrific accident in the North West 200 road race landed the Scot in hospital with terrible injuries. As a consequence, his season was over.

His elimination promoted the first of several rider shuffles, as is often the case in BSB, as Lowes assumed Easton's place. Ironically, he was seeking new employment after parting from WFR Honda, the youngster refusing to commit his long-term future to the burgeoning outfit after winning five of six EVO races, finishing fifth overall at Croft and even leading a race outright at Oulton Park.

Lowes rewarded his new employers, MSS Colchester Kawasaki, with a sensational pole position straight away at Thruxton, seeming to assure his status as Britain's latest motorcycling talent. As it turned out, he couldn't convert it into anything better than seventh, which remarkably proved his best finish for the remainder of the year, the youngster's form dwindling as his evident speed was tempered by frustrating incidents. A stint on the World Superbike Castrol Honda, followed by a late-season switch to Motorpoint Yamaha was indicative of his stuttering campaign, which promised much, but didn't quite deliver.

Instead, Laverty would come away with his first win for Swan Yamaha after a measured ride to victory in slippery conditions, the Ulsterman finishing comfortably ahead of Rutter and Byrne, who put in a stellar ride to third from the back of a 33-strong field after crashing in qualifying.

Earning himself a spot at the opposite end of the grid for race two, Byrne made the most of his advantageous position to claim a third victory of the season, one that helped him edge further ahead in the standings. He was followed by an inspired Hickman, who became the fifth new BSB podium winner of the season with an excellent run to second aboard the 2010 title-winning HM Plant Honda. Hopkins rounded out the podium, while Hill gave a glimpse of his return to form with a run to fourth.

Indeed, Thruxton proved a warm-up for Hill's return to prominence, as he proceeded to dominate across the Scottish border at Knockhill. A clean sweep of pole position, fastest lap and victory in both races, it was a crushing display that laid out his title credentials for all to see.

Byrne kept Hill honest with podiums in both races, although Hopkins, having finished runner-up in the first encounter, suffered a costly fall in the second at Duffers Dip following tyre problems.

A new challenge awaited the BSB field at Snetterton, the Norfolk circuit having undergone modifications, including a track extension, over the winter, but the usual suspects rose to the front, Byrne, Hopkins and Hill disputing the honours – with mixed results.

Maiden pole-sitter Hopkins emerged victorious in race one after engaging in a race-long battle with Hill, which was settled on the final lap when the American got the jump on his rival. Byrne, meanwhile, rounded out the podium, ahead of Laverty and Kiyonari. Hopkins looked set for a win in race two as he sprinted into an early lead, his cause being aided when Hill crashed out at turn two after getting crossed up on Kiyonari's rear wheel. However, a mid-race stoppage – prompted after a horrific crash involving Steve Brogan and Simon Andrews, the latter sustaining season-ending leg injuries – would wipe out his lead.

With a nine-lap sprint to decide the race, Hopkins held firm until the penultimate revolution, when Byrne dived through into the lead at Coram. Not to be denied, Hopkins attempted a last-gasp pass on his rival, but an ill-timed dive at Oggie's merely sent them both across the grass. An apologetic Hopkins collected himself for third, while a disgruntled Byrne lost further ground in fourth place. The lead and victory were assumed instead by Kiyonari, who ended a dismal run of form, which at times had seen him finishing outside the points, to claim a second win of the season.

A second visit to Oulton Park beckoned next, with Hill eager to finish what he had started before his first 2011 appearance had ended in the medical centre. Even so, he had to contend with an increasingly confident Hopkins, who got the edge in qualifying with his second straight pole.

However, the rain-lashed race signalled disappointment for Hopkins who, having moved to the front on lap four, promptly slid out of the lead. His demise allowed Hill to come through for a fourth victory of the year to further strengthen his title hopes.

To Hopkins' frustration, he didn't get the chance to respond in race two, as inclement weather forced the organisers to call an early halt to the event, the race eventually being rescheduled as part of the Cadwell Park meeting.

Before that, the GP circuit at Brands Hatch hosted a pivotal triple-header, with Byrne, Hopkins and Hill all booking their places in the Title Showdown with one event to spare.

Even so, the weekend didn't begin terribly well for the title protagonists, with changeable weather and tricky track conditions prompting tyre gambles – some clever, some erroneous – throughout the field. Among those to fall into the latter category were Hill, Byrne, Kiyonari and both World Superbike Kawasaki riders, Joan Lascorz and Broc Parkes, the Paul Bird Motorsport team making its annual BSB jaunt, albeit without injured local hero Tom Sykes. Opting for wet-weather tyres on a drying circuit, they were among a handful of riders forced into the pit lane, putting themselves out of victory contention.

Consequently, Brookes assumed the lead, the Australian's gamble on intermediate rubber paying dividends as he took control of the race from lap three, having started down in 13th. Hopkins held second place initially, only to be usurped by Mason and Rutter.

Indeed, Rutter had gone one step further in his gamble by opting for a slick rear tyre, a move that allowed him to make rapid progress in the closing stages as the circuit dried, the Ducati man peaking in second position behind Brookes, who completed his first win for Relentless by TAS Suzuki. Mason rounded out the podium, with Hopkins fourth and Chris Walker taking a season's-best fifth.

Byrne and Hill, meanwhile, could not recover to the points, but at least had done enough to secure good grid positions for race two after a controversial, but rule-abiding decision to pit for slick tyres had been to their benefit over those racing to the finish on tired intermediate rubber.

From pole position, Hill got in front early, but was reeled in by Byrne, the Kent rider unleashing his impressive form on his local circuit to claim a fourth victory of the season, and his first since Thruxton. Hill finished second, ahead of Hopkins, but the Swan rider turned it around in the third race by beating the American for his fifth win of the season, while Byrne settled for third.

Crucially, Brands Hatch saw all three riders firm their places in the upcoming Title Showdown one round and three races in advance, an advantageous position that proved a determining factor in Hopkins' decision to skip Cadwell Park

altogether. Indeed, he chose to play it safe after an accident during his MotoGP wild-card appearance with Rizla Suzuki at Brno left him nursing a nasty finger injury.

As a result, attention turned to Hill and Byrne in their quest to rack up as many podium credits as possible, and the dispute over the three available Showdown entry spots, at this point held by Laverty, Brookes and Kiyonari.

A second victory of the season for Laverty in the first race of the weekend secured his place, although controversy reigned behind when an incident involving Brookes and Rutter eliminated the latter from the Showdown. His four straight top-five finishes had put him on the cusp of overhauling the out-of-form Kiyonari to reach the shootout for the second year in succession, but the collision with Brookes, for which the Australian was disqualified, left him nursing broken ribs. Even worse, not only was Rutter out of Showdown contention, but also he would miss the next two rounds altogether.

Despite the exclusion, Brookes did enough in the remaining two races to reach the Showdown, while Kiyonari held his patchy form long enough to be offered a second shot at the title, denying a devastated Rutter, Kirkham and Mason.

Back at the front, Swan Yamaha completed its dominance at Cadwell Park when Hill won the two remaining races to end the first phase of the season with seven wins, compared to Byrne's four and Hopkins' two.

Consequently, while Byrne led on total points, with the top six equalised and the podium credits tallied, Hill was promoted to the top of the leader board with 529 points, while Byrne and Hopkins followed on 522 and 518. Not to be discounted, Laverty, Brookes and Kiyonari started the three-round shootout on 510, 509 and 508 respectively.

Following its hiatus in 2010, Donington Park's return to the schedules earned it billing as the first of the Showdown rounds, and the popular Leicestershire circuit didn't disappoint. Appropriately, victory was disputed by the four leading title fighters, with Hill, Byrne, Hopkins and Laverty all enjoying spells in the lead over the course of the opening race.

Four would become two when Hill's misjudged pass on leader Byrne at the final corner sent them both wide, allowing Laverty and Hopkins out front. From here, Hopkins – still nursing his finger injury – pounced with three laps remaining to notch up a third win of the season that put him just two points adrift of Hill, who finished third.

Hopkins went on to turn around the deficit in the second race by completing an impressive double triumph, Hill unable to do anything about his rival and playing runner-up from lap five onwards. Byrne and Laverty, meanwhile, saw their title hopes take a knock after colliding at the opening bend, the former losing significant ground despite recovering to eighth, while the latter fared even worse in 14th. Kirkham took the final spot on the podium, his first rostrum since his Croft win, while Rapid Ducati's Jessopp posted his best-ever BSB result in fourth after getting the better of Brookes.

Boosted by his newly acquired lead, Hopkins carried his momentum to the penultimate Silverstone round as he notched up a third victory in a row. Back at the scene of his tremendous World Superbike wild-card pole position two months earlier, he fended off the attentions of Laverty and Hill, while Brookes and Byrne completed the top five.

If the first race was absorbing, the second race was nothing less than heart-stopping as Hopkins, Hill, Laverty, Byrne and Brookes fought wheel to wheel from start to finish, the quintet well aware that one slip would almost certainly signal the end of their title dreams.

As it happened, each stayed upright, although it was slightly surprising that the rider with the least to lose, Brookes, emerged victorious after a feisty charge in the latter stages saw him get the better of Hill, who in turn clawed back some ground on third-placed Hopkins by holding on to second.

The pair would go into the final round, a three-race shootout at Brands Hatch, split by eight points in the American rider's favour. Brookes' win lifted him to third, although he was 41 points adrift of the leaders, while Laverty and Byrne – tied in fourth – had also all but conceded their hopes.

Although the 2011 MCE British Superbike Championship went down to the final round, one championship was decided at Silverstone, as former British Supersport champion Glen Richards wrapped up the EVO series. The Australian, riding for newcomers WFR Honda, was a model of consistency in 2011, reaching the podium on 20 occasions, even if he only stood atop it three times.

By contrast, team-mate Graeme Gowland tasted the winner's champagne 13 times after a stunning second half of the season, when he not only dominated the EVO reckoning, but also was a regular top-ten finisher on sub-Superbike machinery. Sadly, an early-season injury left him with too much

Above: Shane Byrne (67) and Josh Brookes (2) head the pack going into Druids hairpin at the Brands Hatch season opener.
Photo: Gavan Caldwell

Left: Airtime at Cadwell Park – Michael Laverty's Yamaha was a high flier.
Photo: Clive Challinor Motorsport Photography

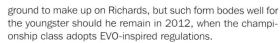

ground to make up on Richards, but such form bodes well for the youngster should he remain in 2012, when the championship class adopts EVO-inspired regulations.

Elsewhere, Barry Burrell, who won twice on the Buildbase BMW, secured third, ahead of Tyco Honda's Patric Muff and Moto Rapido Ducati's Scott Smart.

Heading to Brands Hatch, five of the six riders who began the Showdown had a shot at the title, Kiyonari having been eliminated at Silverstone. Even so, attention zoned in on Hopkins and Hill, the former getting the edge in qualifying by going third compared to his rival's fourth. The pair started behind pole-sitter Brookes and Laverty.

Hill's hopes took an early knock, however, when a tardy getaway left him in sixth place, behind Hopkins. Nonetheless, eventually he fought his way past Rutter and Ellison before chasing down Hopkins and even passing him on the penultimate lap, although the Suzuki rider coolly re-passed to finish ahead and eke out his advantage to 11 points.

Nonetheless, just as the pendulum appeared to be swinging in Hopkins' favour, a dramatic twist saw it swing back in Hill's direction during a tension-filled penultimate race.

With his two DNFs at Knockhill and Oulton Park attributed to crashes, Hopkins could be sure that his Samsung Crescent Suzuki had been reliable in 2011, so it was a surprise when it slowed on the opening lap. Eventually, the cause was traced to an electrical glitch, but the sight of Hopkins stricken on the grass immediately slashed Hill's odds of taking title – until the American, far from giving up, fired up the bike and got going again.

Even so, the initiative was firmly with Hill, who benefited further when Laverty and Brookes crashed out ahead of him, caught out by damp patches on an otherwise dry circuit.

Indeed, the attrition rate proved unusually high, enabling a flying Hopkins to get back into the points with a run to 12th, netting him four. Hill's failure to fully capitalise on the situation, having been demoted to fourth by winner Byrne, second-placed Kirkham and third-placed Ellison, the latter scoring Sorrymate.com SMT Honda's first-ever BSB podium, meant that Hopkins maintained a slim two-point lead heading into the final race.

It would be a straight fight between Hopkins and Hill, the pair acknowledging that whoever finished ahead of the other would likely be crowned champion.

Even so, few could have predicted the eventual outcome

of a championship that, for more than three-quarters of the race, looked to be going the way of Hopkins as he held down a comfortable third, ahead of Hill, who struggled initially to stay in touch.

Nonetheless, with Hopkins playing it safe behind second-placed Ellison, who in turn was doing his utmost to stay in front, Hill forged his way back into the reckoning. His charge came on lap 17 of 20, when he overtook Hopkins and, crucially, swiftly dispatched Ellison for second.

Sparked into action, Hopkins followed Hill past Ellison to size up his rival heading into what would become an epic final lap. Shadowing Hill over the first part of the lap, Hopkins dived through for the first time into Surtees, but a wider line allowed his adversary to get a better drive out of the bend, the Yamaha man sliding back up the inside at Hawthorne's.

However, an untidy exit allowed Hopkins to strike up the inside of Westfield, giving him the edge with just three corners remaining. Undeterred, Hill came straight back past with a daring move at Dingle Dell, setting the pair up for a grandstand finish around the very final bend at Clark Curve.

Naturally, Hopkins dived for the inside, but aware of this, Hill hung back slightly to switch to the inside as they entered the steep curve on to the finishing straight.

Hill nosed ahead, but Hopkins' momentum on the outside carried him forward, sending them across the line almost side by side. As both riders searched for an indication as to who had won, the stopwatch confirmed Hill ahead by just 0.006 second, heartbreaking for Hopkins, who surely would have overtaken – to win the title – had the finish line been just a few extra metres away.

It was jubilation for Hill, Yamaha and SMR, which in turn would celebrate its first BSB title – a fitting end to one of the most exciting seasons in BSB history.

Although Hill's joy was juxtaposed by the disappointment shared by Hopkins and Crescent, which had lost out on the title at the final hurdle for the second season in a row – ironically beaten by its former rider – the American was a hugely worthy runner-up and a credit to BSB.

Almost forgotten in the drama behind him, Byrne reeled off his second win of the weekend to finish his comeback season in third place. Even so, the former champion, who had dropped too much ground when it mattered, did point out that in terms of points scored over the whole season, he would have been champion under the previous format.

Above: Tommy Hill, champion by just thousandths, receives a bubbly shower from defeated rival Hopkins.

Top left: Suzuki's John Kirkham was a little overshadowed by his American team-mate, but won at Croft.

Above left: Australian veteran Glen Richards was the Mirror.co.uk EVO champion on his Honda.

Right: Kyle Ryde, aged just 14, showed his huge potential to win the 125cc championship.

Below right: All-action Harley-Davidson XR1200 Trophy champion James Webb, brother of 125 GP racer Danny, took a maiden title.

Photos: Clive Challinor Motorsport Photography

Laverty finished his year in fourth place for the second season in a row, ahead of Brookes and Kiyonari, who couldn't grasp the second shot at the title and promptly confirmed he wouldn't return to the series in 2012.

Outside the top six, Kirkham sealed the BSB Riders' Cup in seventh, ahead of Rutter, who returned in time to finish his 16th BSB season in eighth position overall, while Hickman enjoyed his best-ever campaign by cracking the top ten on 16 occasions in 2011.

Mason rounded out the top ten after spending the final rounds focusing on development for 2012, when BSB will go back to basics by enforcing an EVO-inspired regulations package. Notable changes will include the adoption of a standard ECU, where traction control and launch control will be outlawed.

The move is just the latest step in BSB's evolution, while the quality of the racing and calibre of riders in 2011 have rightly confirmed its premier billing in the motorcycle world.

Sunoco 125GP Championship

As ever, the MCE British Superbike Championship benefited from a fine support package in 2011, as manufacturers, riders and teams took advantage of an impressive publicity platform and reasonable budget requirements to hone their talents and keep the crowds entertained throughout the year.

Primarily a breeding ground for the next generation of rac-

ers, it is no surprise to find that many of the current top BSB riders, plus many more competing at an international level, cut their teeth in such series as the Sunoco 125GP Championship, where young and precocious talent is often first discovered.

This was no less apparent in 2011, when the title battle came down to a final-round, three-way fight between two of the youngest riders in Kyle Ryde (14) and Wayne Ryan (15), plus Rob Guiver, runner-up for the previous two seasons.

Of the trio, RS Honda rider Ryde had been the most prolific race winner, with successes at Knockhill, Brands Hatch, Cadwell Park, Donington Park and Silverstone, giving him the edge into the Brands Hatch finale. Although Ryan did his utmost to heap on the pressure with his second win of the season at the critical moment, Ryde's third-place finish was enough to see him crowned champion, two points ahead of Ryan and 12 up on Guiver.

Rapid Solicitors Ducati 848 Challenge

New for 2011, the one-make Rapid Solicitors Ducati 848 Challenge brought greater exposure for the legendary Italian manufacturer, supporting six BSB rounds and adding fly-away rounds at Assen and Monza.

Enlisting WSB legend Carl Fogarty as its ambassador, the Ducati 848 Challenge certainly had status, and it contributed to impressive grid sizes throughout the year.

With a four-time world champion to impress, JHP Buildbase's Leon Morris emerged as the series' most eye-catching standout, the 25-year-old taking nine wins from 17 races to finish 72 points clear of MSKWorks.com rider Mike Edwards.

Ducati Manchester's Robbie Brown and AOR rider Kenny Gilbertson won three races apiece to seal their eventual third- and fourth-place finishes overall, while Morris' teammate, Darren Fry, completed the top five.

Triumph Triple Challenge

Headlined by the impressive prize of a guaranteed ride in the 2012 British Supersport Cup Championship with T3 Triumph Racing, the Triumph Triple Challenge certainly gave the field something to fight for in 2011, although it was a dominant Luke Jones who would emerge victorious.

Having joined the Triumph series after a handful of outings aboard a Yamaha in BSB, Jones was in imperious form throughout 2011, winning 12 races and finishing outside the top two just twice during the season's duration.

Peter Ward gave a good fight with three wins, including a double at Croft, but he still found himself 102 points behind Jones at the season's end. Tommy Dale scored one win, the last of the year at Brands Hatch, to seal third overall, ahead of Ashley Beech, who finished outside the top three, but at least had the distinction of winning the blue-riband Silverstone round in support of the MotoGP British Grand Prix.

Harley-Davidson XR1200 Trophy

Having debuted in 2010, the dealer-supported Harley-Davidson XR1200 Trophy was an intriguing addition to the BSB support package, bringing the famed American brand into the British racing arena. With former grand prix rider Jeremy McWilliams standing as its inaugural champion, attention was focused on who would replace him in 2011.

The final-round shootout was between James Webb and Peter Ward, and the pair came into the Donington Park event split by 12 points. Ward – a winner at Knockhill – called upon his best form to win both races, but with his rival following him home on each occasion, it was Webb who was crowned champion by a mere two points.

Behind them, Dijon Compton ended the season in third place with a win at Oulton Park, while Alex Gault was another winner at Knockhill to end his year in fourth.

BRITISH SUPERSPORT REVIEW
TUG-OF-WAR
By OLLIE BARSTOW

Above: Relentless. Alastair Seeley took the Supersport honour after a closely fought battle with his pursuer Ben Wilson.

Photo: Gavan Caldwell

THE Fuchs-Silkolene British Supersport Championship may be billed as a support act to the main British Superbike event, but Alastair Seeley and Ben Wilson's intense tug-of-war over the course of the season would often earn it headline status in 2011.

Indeed, having been dominated by Sam Lowes and GNS Honda in 2010, both of whom were absent for the new season – the former graduating to the world stage and the latter disappearing because of the economic downturn – British Supersport 2011 was definitely all about two men, two teams and two manufacturers. It is fitting then that this epic battle would come down to just one race and one point.

The premise certainly created a pre-season buzz, particularly the return of former champions Relentless by TAS Suzuki, who came back with Suzuki GB backing, the brand-new GSX-R600 and its BSB race winner, Seeley. On paper, combinations don't come more formidable at this level.

If Seeley and Relentless by TAS were the Supersport Goliath, then Gearlink Kawasaki and Ben Wilson were the consequent David.

However, perhaps such a description does a disservice to a team and rider that had grown into a winning combination in 2009 and 2010, and there was certainly nothing 'underdog' about the way they began their title campaign, Wilson firing out of the blocks to win five of the first six races.

Crucially for the shape Seeley's challenge, save for a DNF in the season-opener at Brands Hatch, he kept Wilson honest, despite his early-season rout on the ZX-6R.

Indeed, Seeley gave a hint of what would come from the ever-improving GSX-R600 by winning the second race at Brands Hatch, a consequence of the new regulations that made each British Supersport round a double-header.

Even so, Wilson's double victories at Oulton Park and Croft, coupled to Seeley's two second places, a fourth and a fifth, saw them split by 49 points at this relatively early stage.

After six races, Seeley actually held down third overall, ten points adrift of Jack Kennedy on the Colin Appleyard Yamaha R6, the Irishman having notched up five podiums, while 2009 champion Steve Plater was only 17 points behind in fourth on the Padgetts Honda CBR600RR. However, round four at Thruxton ruled Kennedy and Plater out of any equation after separate accidents – coincidentally on the same lap – on the high-speed circuit left them with injuries that necessitated periods on the sidelines.

Ironically, Thruxton signalled a quiet weekend for the title protagonists, Wilson taking a third and fourth, while Seeley had a sole second place after technical issues scuppered a quest for victory in race two. Instead, Oxford TAG Triumph celebrated a double win, with Australian pair Billy McConnell and Paul Young sharing the spoils on their Daytona 675s.

A trip across the Scottish border brought Wilson a sixth victory at Knockhill; combined with a third and Seeley's two second places, this enabled him to eke out his lead to a sizeable 59 points with almost half of the season completed.

Far from all bets being off, Seeley nibbled the gap down with his first double victory at Snetterton, although Wilson would minimise the damage by standing alongside him on the podium.

From here, honours were kept even at Brands Hatch and Cadwell Park, Seeley doubling up at the former after prevailing in a breathtaking duel with his adversary, before Wilson fought back with a dominant double at the latter.

Wilson commanded a 53-point margin with three rounds and seven races remaining, a daunting prospect for Seeley even without considering his rival's unwavering consistency, which had seen him off the podium just twice in 17 races. Nonetheless, Seeley maintained the pressure by winning both races at Donington Park to slice a 17-point chunk from Wilson's lead.

Silverstone became the scene of the season's defining

Below: Superstock 600cc Champion Keith Farmer was one of the finds of the season.

Photo: Gavan Caldwell

Above: Alastair Seeley, Ben Wilson and Billy McConnell on the podium at Cadwell Park.

Photo: Gold & Goose

Left: Gearlink Kawasaki's Ben Wilson was just one point behind Seeley in the final Supersport standings.

Right: Richard Cooper took the honours in the Metzler National Superstock series.

Photos: Clive Challinor Motorsport Photography

Right: Cooper (47) leads the pack on his Buildbase BMW took the honours in the Metzler National Superstock 1000 BMW.

Photo: Gavan Caldwell

moment when, having become increasingly close as their intense rivalry escalated, the pair came together in the first of two races, Wilson subsequently crashing out. Although he was visibly aggrieved by the collision, officials deemed it to have been a racing incident, clearing the way for Seeley to wipe 25 points out of that lead.

When Wilson suffered an unprecedented mechanical failure in race two, the pendulum suddenly swung towards double winner Seeley, the Ulsterman leading for the first time by 14 points heading to a Brands Hatch showdown that few had envisaged just two rounds earlier.

With three races to determine the outcome of the championship, Seeley certainly appeared to hold the upper hand at the circuit where he had won earlier in the season; he could even call himself a British Superbike race winner at the Kent venue.

Few could have predicted that he would crash out of the lead in race one, however, gifting both the win and the series lead back to Wilson with two races remaining. With tricky weather conditions throwing an added element into an already tense situation, a braver Seeley clawed back ground with a run to second in race two, compared to Wilson's cautious fourth.

Such a result would prove crucial, the pair split by four points in Wilson's favour as they headed into the final race of the 2011 season. With perfect conditions and little doubt that the two would resume a head-to-head battle for victory, there was a 'winner-takes-all' billing for the crunch race.

The early stages saw Wilson signal his intentions by pushing ahead of Seeley. However, the latter soon began applying pressure and was past the Kawasaki with just over half of the

race remaining, the 'Wee Wizard' keeping his cool to take the win and the title.

Scoring the five additional points he required, Seeley secured the Fuchs-Silkolene British Supersport crown by a mere point, a fitting reflection of a season in which both riders were in a class of their own all year. A second national title for Seeley, who had won the 2009 National Superstock 1000 series, it was also a return to the top for 2007 winners Relentless by TAS Suzuki.

It was a heartbreaking result for Wilson and Gearlink, as success would have seen Kawasaki win its first British Supersport title since 1990. Nonetheless, they ended their breakthrough season with a greater number of victories.

While Seeley and Wilson occupied the headlines – and the lion's share of the race wins – there was still notable success further down the field, with McConnell securing third place overall after becoming the only other rider to win more than one race in 2011, the Australian adding to his tally at Oulton Park. His team-mate, Young, completed his best-ever Supersport season in a comfortable fourth place overall, ahead of top Yamaha rider Sam Warren, who scored both his and Seton-Interceptor's first victory at Knockhill.

Former BSB rider Christian Iddon endured a slow start on the third Oxford TAG Triumph, but a storming second half of the year saw him finish each of the final nine races inside the top four, while Kennedy marked his full recovery from injury by winning for the first time at the Brands Hatch season finale and snatching seventh overall.

Luke Mossey, Daniel Cooper and Luke Stapleford completed the top ten in the final standings, while John Simpson was the dominant winner of the British Supersport Cup.

NATIONAL SUPERSTOCK REVIEW
By OLLIE BARSTOW

Metzeler National Superstock 1000

Despite being a star turn on both the World Superbike and British Superbike stages in 2009, Richard Cooper's ascension to Metzeler National Superstock 1000 champion in 2011 was fairly steady.

A BMW ambassador, status that earned him a one-off outing for the factory BMW Motorrad team in the World Superbike Championship at the Nürburgring in 2009, Cooper was an obvious choice to ride the Jentin prepared, stock-specification S1000RR in the national SSTK series in 2010, but a sole win and ninth in the standings were not representative of his ability.

Nonetheless, a switch to Buildbase, which had defected from Kawasaki to BMW machinery, in 2011 would prove a more successful match, Cooper establishing himself as a front-runner from the outset.

Even so, his title odds remained fairly long during the early rounds, as victories were shared between MSS Colchester rookie Danny Buchan, who gave the new stock Kawasaki ZX-10R a magnificent debut with a win at Brands Hatch, and Tristan Palmer, Cooper's former Jentin team-mate, who tasted success at Oulton Park and Croft on the GBmoto Honda.

In fact, after three rounds, Cooper trailed Palmer, Buchan and HM Plant Honda's Jason O'Halloran, but he began to turn things around with wins in two of the following three races, at Thruxton and Snetterton, while his second place at Knockhill helped haul him back into the title fight.

Cooper's title credentials would receive a welcome boost mid-season, however, when Palmer was deducted 50 points – the equivalent of his two wins – after technical inspectors found the GBmoto Honda CBR1000RR to be in breach of the regulations. That ruled Palmer out of the title equation, and with O'Halloran also facing a lengthy spell on the sidelines after injuring himself at Knockhill, the battle for honours appeared to be down to Buchan and Cooper, the former holding a slim advantage over his more experienced rival.

Cooper closed again with a fourth place at Oulton Park before moving in front for the first time with a second at Brands Hatch, where Buchan could only manage ninth.

It was an advantage that Cooper would hammer home at the following pivotal rounds, with wins at Cadwell Park and Donington Park. Coupled with a disappointing run of form for Buchan, these gave him 'match point' at the penultimate Silverstone event.

Buchan needed a win combined with Cooper finishing outside the top ten, but the Buildbase man's run to sixth was more than enough to ensure that he would be crowned Metzeler National Superstock 1000 champion for the first time. A second success for BMW in only its sophomore year at Superstock level, it was also Cooper's first-ever title victory.

When the final event at Brands Hatch was cancelled after a serious accident necessitated a long delay, the standings after Silverstone decided the final finishing positions and Buchan sealed an impressive runner-up spot, the 18-year-old showing great speed and tenacity in his maiden season.

Formwise, Astro BMW's Luke Quigley notched up a win at Silverstone – and four podiums in the final four races – to secure third overall, ahead of Palmer, who probably would have been in the title hunt were it not for the penalty handed to GBmoto. Buchan's team-mate, Howie Mainwaring, completed the top five, having also tasted victory at Brands Hatch.

Metzeler Superstock 600

In the Superstock 600 class, Keith Farmer took the honours on his eponymous Farmer Racing Yamaha, his four wins in the opening five races going a long way to seeing off the opposition, which included Glenn Irwin. The latter pushed his rival all the way, but could not make up the margin Farmer had gained so impressively in the early stages.

In all, Farmer recorded six wins in 12 races to end up 48 points clear of CN Kawasaki's Irwin, who won three times, and third-place man Conor Behan, who showed consistency, but didn't stand atop the podium in 2011.

Other Superstock 600 race winners over the season included Ben Burke at the Brands Hatch season opener and Freddie Russo at Cadwell Park, although that event was tainted by the tragic death of Benjamin Gautrey, who succumbed to injuries sustained in an accident there.

SIDECAR WORLD CHAMPIONSHIP
TWO-TIMERS
By JOHN McKENZIE

Above: Six wins and two seconds in eight races gave Finn Paivarinta and passenger Haenni a second successive sidecar championship.

Photo: Mark Walters

WHILE the Sidecar World Championship may have slipped down the billing somewhat in recent years, no one could argue that a championship that can attract well over 20 teams from ten countries, employing four engine manufacturers, is in danger of further decline.

The 2011 series comprised eight races at five venues, although perhaps Germany, hosting three rounds, has become the natural home. Outings at the Sachsenring MotoGP and Le Mans 24-hour races continued to provide exposure to potential fans, but a round in the UK would be welcomed by many, and surely could be accommodated at some point on the British sporting calendar.

Experience counts in sidecar racing, proved once again by Pekka Paivarinta and his ageless passenger, Adolf Haenni, holding on to the championship they had won in 2010. Although almost always fastest in practice, the Birchall brothers couldn't quite translate that into enough race wins, and a crash in the second race at Schleiz knocked a big hole in their aspirations early on. Former triple world champion Tim Reeves had a troublesome season, with only two rostrums, which pushed him down to fourth in the final table, despite his dominance on the domestic scene in England.

Round 1 – 14/15 May, Schleiz, Germany

The season opened on a warm, sunny Saturday afternoon with an 11-lap Sprint race on the spectacular 3.805km Schleizer Dreieck. From pole position, the Birchall brothers, passenger Tom having recovered fully from pre-season testing crash injuries, were caught napping. Within two laps, however, they had tucked their Yamaha R1-powered LCR in behind race leaders Paivarinta and Haenni's Team Finland Suzuki outfit.

Paivarinta managed to hold off Birchall until the tenth lap, when the Worksop-based brothers finally forced a way through on the main straight to take the flag by half a second. Experienced Swiss ace Markus Schlosser, partnered by Tom Hofer, made up the rostrum. Three-time champion Tim Reeves struggled home to take fifth place after suffering engine problems

The win put the Birchalls in confident mood for Sunday's 22-lap Gold race, but fate had another plan.

Schlosser shot away at the start, with Birchall and Paivar-

inta in the slipstream. By lap four, Birchall had taken the lead, with Paivarinta needing another two laps to manoeuvre into second. With almost a third of the race gone, it looked as though Birchall was in control, having a three-second lead. But on the ninth lap, Janez Remse and Paul Knapton flipped their outfit. In the mayhem, Birchall collided heavily with the slowing BEM Racing Team machine. Paivarinta avoided the wreckage, but Schlosser also crashed out. Both Birchalls were hospitalised, but were released to return to the UK on the Monday, detouring via chassis constructor Louis Christen's LCR factory in Rorschach, Switzerland to make repairs to the extensively damaged machine.

The red flags had come out, and it was an hour before the track was cleared to allow the remaining 13 laps to be run, albeit with only nine outfits able to make it on to the new grid. Paivarinta was left with little opposition and took a comfortable win by 7.6 seconds from Kurt Hock. Mike Roscher was third, his best result for five years, and the first Sidecar World Championship rostrum for a BMW-powered machine since the 1970s. Devoid of any real opposition after the stoppage, Paivarinta and Haenni left Schleiz holding a 22-point lead in the table, which, it turned out, they would never relinquish.

Round 2 – 25/26 June, Rijeka, Croatia

After a busy month that involved an extensive rebuild and a two-week sojourn at the Isle of Man TT, the Birchall brothers returned to qualify fastest with another pole position, just under half a second faster than Paivarinta. Taking full advantage, they were first into the first corner in Saturday's ten-lap Sprint race, with Paivarinta and Reeves close behind. The lead chopped and changed in a race-long battle between Birchall and Paivarinta, but it was the Finn who finally wrested the honours, just 0.41 second in front of Reeves – second being his best result of 2011 – in turn just 0.325 second ahead of Birchall.

With temperatures reaching the high twenties on Sunday, the 18-lap Gold race was going to be long and hot, with tyre wear a big concern for all.

"The tyres and their durability will be decisive. After yesterday's Sprint race, our rear was finished," said Yokohama-shod Paivarinta before the race.

Hock steered his LCR Suzuki into an early lead from Birchall, with Paivarinta and Reeves biting at their rear tyres. Hock had seemed to establish some control, but the anticipated tyre wear issues came to the fore.

After six laps, Hock dropped back to third, leaving Paivarinta and Birchall at the front once again, with the latter desperately looking for a gap. With a lap to go, he found it, but on the last corner, with the two outfits side by side and exchanging paint, Paivarinta managed to hold the line and pass on the inside to win by 0.9 second.

Hock took third, 23 seconds back; fourth-placed Reeves, suffering from a lack of grip, was a further 14 seconds adrift.

Two wins for the reigning champions lifted them to a 33-point lead after just four races.

Round 3 – 17 July, Sachsenring, Germany

Against the glamorous backdrop of MotoGP, pole and a win for the Birchalls gave renewed hope for their title ambitions, but not until after Reeves and Cluze had set the early pace in the 22-lapper. It took until mid-race for the Birchalls to fight their way to the front. Once there and with a clear track, they dominated, pulling away to record a trouble-free win with a very comfortable 7.6-second gap.

"We've clawed points back and moved into second place in the table, but there are still 75 points to race for, so it's not over yet," said Ben Birchall after the win.

Paivarinta and Haenni had an uncharacteristic poor start, and it wasn't until only two laps remained that they got through to second, after battling with Reeves and Hock.

Round 4 – 18 August, Oschersleben, Germany

The two-race format returned at the 3.667km Oschersleben circuit in northern Germany, where the first rain of the year fell during practice. It was the Birchalls' first visit to the track, and a fuel leak further hampered their practice efforts. Paivarinta's experience of the course, however, gave him his first pole of the season by two seconds. With only three rounds to go, the Finnish/Swiss pair needed 46 points to take the title.

"All of our rivals had some kind of problem during the timed practice, but we had none and everything went just fine. We want to win at least one of the races tomorrow," said Paivarinta after qualifying.

Ominously for the rest of the field, the next morning he was able to throw down the gauntlet with a new record in warm-up. With both Sprint and Gold races on the same day, and with a fair chance of the title being settled, the season had reached a crucial point. Today would be the day.

Despite an early lead from Birchall, ten laps of the Sprint race were dominated by Paivarinta, culminating in a 9.5-second lead to give the pair their fourth win in six races.

"We went into the first race with the knowledge that we didn't have the pace to match Pekka. He's competed here a few times, and we of course had no track experience, but we finished second, so I am happy enough with the result," said Birchall.

Reeves had a tough battle from the last row of the grid through to the third rostrum place.

But all Paivarinta and Haenni needed now was a third from the Gold race to claim the title. Early leaders Hock and Enrico Becker were followed by Paivarinta on the first lap, with the Birchalls also challenging. But the Team Suzuki Finland's pilot was just too quick on a track he knew well, and rather than settling for that safe third place, he and veteran Haenni scorched away to win the race by nine seconds, crushing any remaining hopes among their rivals and retaining their world championship. Five wins in seven races had given them 165 points to take the title with a race in hand.

The Birchalls had a lonely race for the runner-up spot, but were still some 12 seconds up on third-placed Mike Roscher.

It was Paivarinta's third title, and his second with Haenni as passenger. A year before, Haenni had entered the record books as the oldest world champion. Now 56, he cemented that unlikely record. Pipe and slippers? No chance!

Round 5 – 24 September, Le Mans, France

With the Birchalls back on pole, almost a second in front of the new champions, it augured well for the Mitchell's of Mansfield sponsored pair for the final race, even if the main business had been settled.

Although the title was safe, however, Paivarinta was keen to display his skills and in no mood for playing around: he took an immediate lead. The Birchalls were caught up in fourth place, which was enough to allow Paivarinta to get away. Although they fought through to second, a mysterious misfire that had surfaced in practice continued to dog them, and Paivarinta was able to motor away, signing off with a nine-second winning margin.

The result gave the Birchalls their second runner-up spot in the championship. Hock and Becker took their fifth rostrum of the season to clinch third overall in the standings, one up from their 2010 placing.

For Paivarinta and Haenni, six wins and two seconds in eight races underlined their brilliance, but the Birchalls could take heart from their four pole positions, and from knowing they had time on their side to mount a challenge to regain the title they had won in 2009.

Below: Passenger Enrico Becker hangs off the Rolf Erdmann outfit piloted by Kurt Hock.

Bottom: Ben and Tom Birchall at Le Mans, where they secured second in the race and in the points standing.

Photos: Mark Walters

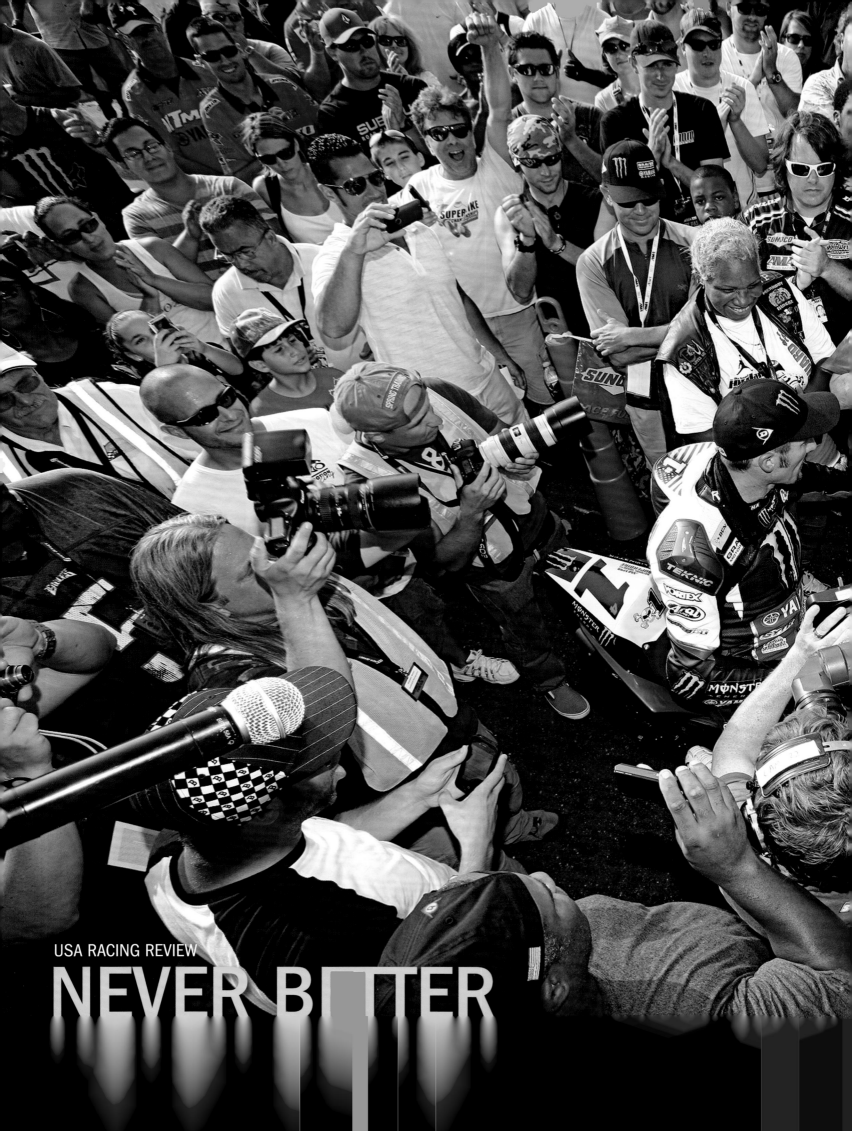

USA RACING REVIEW

NEVER BITTER

FAILING economy be damned. It all boils down to the fact that American road racing in 2011 should be remembered not for the negative impact of a spiralling economy, but for a spirited duel to the AMA Superbike Championship by two men hell-bent on being champion. Those two men were Josh Hayes and Blake Young, and their battle went to the very last lap of the very last race.

One man (Young) had won the most races (six) heading into the series finale; the other (Hayes) had kept himself in contention by winning two races and stockpiling the bonus points the AMA pays out for pole positions and leading the most laps. And it all went to a climactic finale in New Jersey – at the recently bankrupt New Jersey Motorsports Park.

Young vs Hayes. Rockstar Makita Suzuki vs Monster Graves Motorsports Yamaha. GSX-R1000 vs R1. Virtual upstart vs veteran.

Going in, Young led by five points. By the time the first of the double-headers rolled around, that margin was four as Hayes once again took pole. In the first race on Saturday afternoon, Young's inexperience in these situations showed as Hayes proudly put up a fight to retain his Superbike title. Hayes' win number three came after a battle with Michael Jordan Motorsports' Ben Bostrom while making certain he led the most laps; Young, meanwhile, floundered and finished nearly 16 seconds behind Hayes in fourth. Complete turn-around. Suddenly the margin was 11 points – in favour of Hayes.

All he needed to do on Sunday was finish third if Young were to win. Based on what happened a day earlier, no one thought a Young victory was remotely possible

Somewhat embarrassed by his Saturday performance, Young woke up a changed man, however, and rode with heart and plenty of gusto on Sunday. He led the most laps and on the final lap looked to be headed to the Superbike title.

Young led the Suzukis of Bostrom and Roger Lee Hayden, with Hayes a chasing fourth. But early on the last goaround, Young started a chain reaction that ended up putting Bostrom off the track while third and Hayes in a position to win. With the defending champion not certain of Bostrom's whereabouts, he kept his head down and passed Hayden – very nearly getting Young as well. And the title was his – by just five points, even though Young had won his seventh race of the season.

For the 35-year-old Hayes, who splits his time between his home in Gulfport, Mississippi and his winter training base in Oceanside, California, it marked a second successive AMA Superbike Championship after an 11-year battle to get to this point in his career. For the 24-year-old Young, a 'cheesehead' from Wisconsin, it was a tantalising taste of the success many had predicted for the man groomed for the job by Kevin Schwantz – success that had been derailed a year earlier when he suffered a broken back in a testing crash.

It was a classic battle to the very end, and while many believe Young was the victim of an AMA points system that rewards consistency (he did, after all, win seven races and his worst finish was that fifth in New Jersey), that's really not the case. If you add it all up using the same points system as in MotoGP (which means throwing away all of the pole position and laps-led points that Hayes accumulated), Hayes still would have won the title by ten points, 277–267.

The bottom line: it was a 14-race championship (the penultimate round scheduled for Virginia was cancelled at the 11th hour, resulting in a he-said/she-said controversy between the promoter and the AMA) that neither deserved to lose: Hayes won three races and added ten more podiums; Young won seven with podiums in five more.

Only two other men won races in 2011: Young's veteran team-mate on the Rockstar Makita team, Tommy Hayden (three times); and Team M4 Suzuki's Martin Cardenas (once), a rookie in the AMA Superbike ranks.

Things started where they always do in AMA racing – at Daytona International Speedway. And Young couldn't have had a better beginning. He won both races, starting with a race-long battle that featured five riders and came down to a typical Daytona drafting war out of the final chicane. He beat Tommy Hayden by just 0.026 second. It was Hayden's third straight second place at Daytona. Hayes was third, with Ben Bostrom fourth, besting team-mate Roger Lee Hayden and the National Guard GSX-R1000 that also runs out of the Jordan fold.

The following day, Hayes led 14 laps of the 15-lap race. But Young led the one that counted for a clean sweep of the Daytona double-header by a combined 0.097 second. Tommy Hayden was a shadow in third.

Cardenas had a big slide on the 13th lap that cost him dearly. He lost the draft and ultimately finished fourth. Still it was a solid AMA Superbike debut weekend for the non-defending AMA Daytona SportBike champion.

Young naysayers who pointed to the fact that Jake Zemke had won both races at Daytona the year before and never won again were given some ammunition at the next round at Infineon Raceway, where he could manage no better than fourth and third – and was never on pace with Hayes and Tommy Hayden.

Above: Blake Young and Josh Hayes congratulate each other after the dramatic finale of the AMA Superbike series in New Jersey.

Far left: Tommy Hayden took three wins and third overall.

Centre left: Despite scoring seven wins, Young finished just five points shy of the more consistent Hayes.

Left: One-time winner and class rookie Martin Cardenas impressed on the M4 Suzuki.

Opening spread: Champion again. Veteran Josh Hayes engulfed after confirming he will keep the Number 1 plate.

Photos: AMA Pro Series

Above: All-out action as Hayes leads Young, Tommy Hayden and Cardenas at Road America.

Top right: Hayes celebrates his second title in a row.

Above right: Veteran Larry Pegram did a solid job on the BMW, but never threatened to win a race.

Right: Ben Bostrom was an occasional visitor to the podium on the Jordan Suzuki.

Photos: AMA Pro Series

The win was Hayes' first of the year (15th in his career, tying him with Freddie Spencer in seventh on the all-time list) and it put him atop the series standings by three points. Tommy Hayden finished second in the first of the two races in Northern California's wine country, but he was over seven seconds behind.

Third went to Cardenas, edging Young by just 0.068 second. Chris Peris rode his San Diego BMW-sponsored BMW to fifth, after getting the better of a race-long scrap with Foremost Insurance Pegram Racing's Larry Pegram and the third BMW ridden by Steve Rapp.

Young would improve to third on Sunday, but it was team-mate Hayden who turned heads as he hounded Hayes for 17 laps before taking the lead and flat out beating the Yamaha factory rider. His first win of the season, sixth in his career, moved him to second overall, trailing Hayes by just six points.

Cardenas' troubles started at Infineon, the rookie crashing his GSX-R1000 in morning warm-up and dislocating his shoulder. He started the race from the front row, only to crash again early. Fortunately for him, a red flag was thrown and he was able to restart on his back-up bike, riding cautiously to eighth.

He crashed out of the next race at Miller Motorsports Park – a support race to the World Superbike round. He would finish fourth in the next two races before earning his first Superbike victory in round five at Barber Motorsports Park.

The win came in a race that had started dry, but ended wet (with a red flag thrown in between), with Cardenas becoming the first non-Anglophone non-native to win a Superbike race since Italian Alessandro Gramigni at Brainerd on 14th July, 1996. He followed with third the next day, but his progress slowed, as he ended the year with a pair of fifths, a pair of eighths and a fourth in the season finale. Still, he was the best of the non-big three (Hayes, Young and Tommy Hayden), as he finished fourth in the title chase. His performance over the year proved that he was a Superbike-calibre rider, but it was more than likely that his team would go back to the Daytona SportBike class in 2012, robbing him of a chance to take another step forward.

If you doubted Young after his performance at Infineon, you were made to look silly at the next round at Miller Motorsports Park. He showed his newly acquired racecraft by taking a tactical, last-lap victory over Hayes. Tommy Hayden was third.

After five races, Hayes led with 133 points to 129 for Young and 122 for Hayden.

Hayden's younger brother, Roger Lee, finished fourth, his best so far. It would take another five races to match that, but he would finish the season strong with two thirds and three fourths in the final five races. That put him sixth overall at the end of the season – good enough to earn a second term on the Jordan team for 2012.

Roger Lee's team-mate, Ben Bostrom, finished second in the second race at Barber, the ever-popular former World Superbike race winner having an up-and-down year that saw him finish fifth in the final standings. He would also likely retain his ride for 2012 with the team after running with Hayes at New Jersey Motorsports Park and finishing his season strongly.

With really only three men in the running for the title, the series went to Road America in America's heartland of Wisconsin for the next two races, and it was advantage

Young – at least it was supposed to be. After all, he was at home. Young beat Hayes in race one on the four-mile track, with Hayden third. But Hayes won on Sunday, with Hayden beating Young for second. Hayes led homeboy Young by ten points as they departed Wisconsin.

The riders love Barber Motorsports Park, and for good reason: the track is pristine and the facilities top-notch. But the weather can throw a curveball, and it did in 2011. Cardenas took advantage of iffy conditions to win his first national on Saturday, with Bostrom second and Young barely beating Hayes for third. Hayden's miserable Barber weekend started with a seventh-place finish, and the next day it would only get worse, as a blown motor took him out of the race while he was leading. It was the end of his championship hopes, although some of his best performances would come after the Alabama round.

On Sunday, it was all Young, snapping out of his funk to beat Hayes, with Cardenas wrapping up his best weekend as a Superbike rider with a third.

With the championship hotting up – Young was now just two points behind – so did the talk, the pair starting to sling barbs at each other off the track as well as on it. At the Mid-Ohio Sports Car Course, Young got the better of Hayes on Saturday and took the points lead for the first time since his two wins at Daytona. On Sunday, Hayden won it, beating Young and Roger Lee. Hayes was fourth, having been swamped by the three Suzukis. And Young was critical of Hayes' riding after Sunday's race: "I felt like he was maybe taking a little bit more of a risk than he should have been."

Hayes countered: "I didn't think it was any different than what Blake's done to me at Road America, Miller or anywhere else that we've raced."

The points chase had Young on top, 290–270. The game was definitely on.

The two championship rivals took a back seat at Laguna Seca to Tommy Hayden. Although his championship aspirations were far fetched, the senior member of the Hayden clan was on top form, with the entire family in attendance (middle brother Nicky was racing in the US Grand Prix). Hayden won a thrilling final over Hayes in a race that totally overshadowed the grand prix in terms of on-track action. Three passes for the lead on the opening lap and four passes for the lead on the final lap trumped anything MotoGP could do, and it was Hayden crossing the line first for his second win in a row and third of the season. Young, meanwhile, barely beat Roger Lee for third.

It all set up the aforementioned New Jersey finale, with Young leading Hayes by five points and the title going to Hayes by just five points.

DAYTONA SPORTBIKE

In 2010, Danny Eslick and Josh Herrin spent so much time in the season's finale trying to ruin each other's races that Martin Cardenas came up and stole the AMA Daytona Sport-Bike Championship.

In 2011, Cardenas had moved up, but Eslick and Herrin remained. And those two would fight for the title again, although all of it was above the table and the racing was clean. Well, as clean as it can be on 600cc Supersport bikes.

The series started with a Daytona 200 that was a bit of a debacle. The main issue was tyres. The spec Dunlop Sport-Max GP211 fronts started to fail, and Dunlop actually had to ask the AMA to stop the race so they could force everyone to change fronts. After a two-hour delay, the race was reduced to a 15-lap sprint, only to be red-flagged once more after a crash in turn two. Finally, the race was run, and it was Jason DiSalvo who took the win on his Ducati – but only after more controversy.

A big crash at the chequered flag caused the chaos, with some riders being taken to Victory Lane and then removed when the results were further resolved. There was much talk,

Above: Typically close Daytona Sport-bike action at Laguna Seca: Herrin leads Eslick, Aquino and Beaubier.

Right: Intense concentration from ex-Red Bull Rookie Cameron Beaubier.
Photos: Tom Hnatiw/Flick of the Wrist

Above right: Josh Herrin took five Sportbike wins to Eslick's three.

Above far right: Stylish youngster Chris Fillmore took the Harley XR1200 Championship crown.

Far right: Eslick ahead again en route to the Sportbike crown on his Suzuki GSX-R600.
Photos: AMA Pro Series

Left: Youngster Tommy Aquino ended up third in the points on the Pat Clark Graves Yamaha.
Photo: AMA Pro Series

but no protests, and when all was said and done, DiSalvo had given Ducati its first win in the 200. But he'd done so after using two engines. Say what?

The lap before the red flag came out, DiSalvo's 848 EVO motor went sour. He limped it home and put it behind the pit wall, thinking his day was done. But when the start kept being delayed – when it was mandated that everyone was not only to start on a new tyre, but also that it was to be put on warmers for 40 minutes – DiSalvo's team decided to change engines. The rulebook said this could be done under AMA control – and it was. DiSalvo made the restart and the rest is history.

Cory West was second on a Suzuki, with Jake Zemke third in a one-off ride on a privateer Project 1 Yamaha.

Of the two who would fight for the title, Herrin would fare better at Daytona. At least for the moment. Eslick, meanwhile, was one of the crashers, the tough kid from Oklahoma sliding down the Daytona Tri-Oval on his back at 150mph, but escaping uninjured.

Herrin was nailed with a one-race suspension for rough riding at Daytona after AMA Pro Racing decided he'd caused the finish-line fracas in the 200. Thus he was forced to sit out the first race at Infineon Raceway while DiSalvo again romped to two victories on the Ducati. Jake Holden was second on another Ducati, but it was the beginning of a dismal year for the rider from Washington State.

The AMA also didn't like what they saw, so they slapped a weight penalty on DiSalvo's V-twin.

Eslick, meanwhile, came away from Infineon with a third

and a second, while Herrin finished in third place in his return on Sunday.

Herrin would bounce back in a big way, taking victory in the lone race at Miller Motorsports Park and then sweeping both races at Road America. With DiSalvo suffering a string of crashes, Herrin was suddenly in the points lead.

It wasn't until the seventh race of the year that Eslick got his first win, the Geico Insurance-backed Suzuki rider taking race one at Barber and finishing second in the second. That result, combined with Herrin's nightmare first race, put Eslick in the points lead for the first time. Herrin's engine blew up on Saturday, allowing Eslick to gain 32 points on him, but he bounced back to win on Sunday. Still, he left Barber trailing Eslick by 24 points.

Herrin finished second and fifth at Mid-Ohio, while Eslick ended up third in the first race before winning race two.

Even though his chances of catching Eslick were slim when the Virginia round was cancelled, Herrin still held hope going into Laguna Seca. That hope turned to horror when his Yamaha R6 failed him again, the Monster Energy Graves rider being forced to watch from the pit lane while Eslick stormed to victory.

It was game over at that point.

Eslick did what he needed to do, finishing sixth and fifth in the two races at New Jersey. Herrin wasn't perfect, but he was close, finishing second on Saturday before winning his class-leading fifth race on Sunday. He'd lost the title by 19 points, but he'd given away three races – one to suspension and two to engine failures. He was left with a laundry list of what-ifs, but was rewarded by Yamaha with a factory Superbike for 2012.

Tommy Aquino ended up third in the championship after a strong late-season run that included his first career win in the class. DiSalvo, with his three early-season wins, was fourth in the final standings. The only other winner, Team M4 Suzuki's Dane Westby, ended up seventh overall.

HARLEY XR1200

Former Supermoto Champion Chris Fillmore won the upstart Vance & Hines Harley-Davidson XR1200 spec class, the 24-year-old from Michigan winning five times to beat veteran Steve Rapp by 29 points in a hard-fought championship. Tyler O'Hara ended up third. O'Hara and Kyle Wyman each won a race apiece to join Fillmore and Rapp (two wins) as the stars of the new series.

THE FUTURE

While there is hope for growth in the AMA series in 2012, with more races promised and a single promoter for some of those events, there's also the harsh reality of a racing economy that isn't improving as quickly as many believed.

There's some good news on the horizon, though, with KTM expected to join the series, after Chris Filmore showed the bike's capability in a few rides; Larry Pegram is expecting to bring back his BMW team in a large market for the German factory; and Josh Herrin will make a move to the Superbike class, giving Yamaha the two-man team of the two Joshes – Hayes and Herrin.

But the bad follows the good. Is Kawasaki likely to be back? Doubtful. There was still no sign of a Honda return, and Suzuki was cutting back to one rider – Young. The second bike would be a pay-for ride, with Chris Clark (eighth in the 2011 championship) getting the seat thanks to a father with deep pockets. That means, at press time, Tommy Hayden was rideless, although Pegram was trying to persuade BMW into financing him as a second rider for his team.

Only time will tell if the smaller teams and riders can survive the current economy, but there was no question that on the racetrack, AMA racing had really never been better than in 2011.

MAJOR RESULTS

OTHER CHAMPIONSHIP RACING SERIES WORLDWIDE

Compiled by PETER McLAREN

AMA Championship Road Race Series (Superbike)

DAYTONA INTERNATIONAL SPEEDWAY, Daytona Beach, Florida, 11–12 March, 44.300 miles/70.006km
Race 1
1 Blake Young (Suzuki); **2** Tommy Hayden (Suzuki); **3** Josh Hayes (Yamaha); **4** Ben Bostrom (Suzuki); **5** Roger Lee Hayden (Suzuki); **6** Martin Cardenas (Suzuki); **7** Larry Pegram (BMW); **8** Jeremy Toye (BMW); **9** Chris Ulrich (Suzuki); **10** David Anthony (Suzuki)

Race 2
1 Blake Young (Suzuki); **2** Josh Hayes (Yamaha); **3** Tommy Hayden (Suzuki); **4** Martin Cardenas (Suzuki); **5** Ben Bostrom (Suzuki); **6** Larry Pegram (BMW); **7** Chris Clark (Yamaha); **8** Eric Bostrom (Kawasaki); **9** David Anthony (Suzuki); **10** Chris Peris (BMW)

INFINEON RACEWAY, Sonoma, California, 14–15 May, 51.040 miles/82.141km
Race 1
1 Josh Hayes (Yamaha); **2** Tommy Hayden (Suzuki); **3** Martin Cardenas (Suzuki); **4** Blake Young (Suzuki); **5** Chris Peris (BMW); **6** Steve Rapp (BMW); **7** Larry Pegram (BMW); **8** Geoff May (Buell); **9** JD Beach (Kawasaki); **10** Chris Ulrich (Suzuki).

Race 2
1 Tommy Hayden (Suzuki); **2** Josh Hayes (Yamaha); **3** Blake Young (Suzuki); **4** Steve Rapp (BMW); **5** Larry Pegram (BMW); **6** Ben Bostrom (Suzuki); **7** Roger Lee Hayden (Suzuki); **8** Martin Cardenas (Suzuki); **9** Chris Peris (BMW); **10** Chris Clark (Yamaha).

MILLER MOTORSPORTS PARK, Tooele, Utah, 30 May, 48.780 miles/78.400km
1 Blake Young (Suzuki); **2** Josh Hayes (Yamaha); **3** Tommy Hayden (Suzuki); **4** Roger Lee Hayden (Suzuki); **5** Steve Rapp (BMW); **6** Chris Clark (Yamaha); **7** Geoff May (Buell); **8** Ben Bostrom (Suzuki) **9** David Anthony (Suzuki); **10** Jeremy Toye (BMW).

ROAD AMERICA, Elkhart Lake, Wisconsin, 4–5 June, 52.000 miles/83.686km
Race 1
1 Blake Young (Suzuki); **2** Josh Hayes (Yamaha); **3** Tommy Hayden (Suzuki); **4** Martin Cardenas (Suzuki); **5** Larry Pegram (BMW); **6** Roger Lee Hayden (Suzuki); **7** Ben Bostrom (Suzuki); **8** Chris Clark (Yamaha); **9** Jason Farrell (Kawasaki); **10** Geoff May (Buell).

Race 2
1 Josh Hayes (Yamaha); **2** Tommy Hayden (Suzuki); **3** Blake Young (Suzuki); **4** Martin Cardenas (Suzuki); **5** Roger Lee Hayden (Suzuki); **6** Steve Rapp (BMW); **7** Larry Pegram (BMW); **8** Chris Peris (BMW); **9** Chris Clark (Yamaha); **10** Ben Bostrom (Suzuki).

BARBER MOTORSPORTS PARK, Birmingham, Alabama, 18–19 June, 49.890 miles/80.435km
Race 1
1 Martin Cardenas (Suzuki); **2** Ben Bostrom (Suzuki); **3** Blake Young (Suzuki); **4** Josh Hayes (Yamaha); **5** Larry Pegram (BMW); **6** Roger Lee Hayden (Suzuki); **7** Tommy Hayden (Suzuki); **8** JD Beach (Kawasaki); 9. Trent Gibson (Suzuki); **10** Jeremy Toye (BMW).

Race 2
1 Blake Young (Suzuki); **2** Josh Hayes (Yamaha); **3** Martin Cardenas (Suzuki); **4** Steve Rapp (BMW); **5** Ben Bostrom (Suzuki); **6** Larry Pegram (BMW); **7** Geoff May (Buell); **8** Chris Clark (Yamaha); **9** Chris Peris (BMW); **10** JD Beach (Kawasaki).

MID-OHIO SPORTS CAR COURSE, Lexington, Ohio, 9–10 July, 50.400 miles/81.100km
Race 1
1 Blake Young (Suzuki); **2** Josh Hayes (Yamaha); **3** Tommy Hayden (Suzuki); **4** Roger Lee Hayden (Suzuki); **5** Martin Cardenas (Suzuki); **6** Larry Pegram (BMW); **7** Chris Fillmore (KTM); **8** Steve Rapp (BMW); **9** David Anthony (Suzuki); **10** JD Beach (Kawasaki).

Race 2
1 Tommy Hayden (Suzuki); **2** Blake Young (Suzuki); **3** Roger Lee Hayden (Suzuki); **4** Josh Hayes (Yamaha); **5** Martin Cardenas (Suzuki); **6** Ben Bostrom (Suzuki); **7** Larry Pegram (BMW); **8** JD Beach (Kawasaki); **9** Chris Fillmore (KTM); **10** Geoff May (Buell).

MAZDA RACEWAY LAGUNA SECA, Monterey, California, 24 July, 41.400 miles/66.627km
1 Tommy Hayden (Suzuki); **2** Josh Hayes (Yamaha); **3** Blake Young (Suzuki); **4** Roger Lee Hayden (Suzuki); **5** Ben Bostrom (Suzuki); **6** Larry Pegram (BMW); **7** Steve Rapp (BMW); **8** Martin Cardenas (Suzuki); **9** Chris Clark (Yamaha); **10** Geoff May (Buell).

NEW JERSEY MOTORSPORTS PARK, Millville, New Jersey, 3-4 September, 51.750 miles/82.284km
Race 1
1 Josh Hayes (Yamaha); **2** Ben Bostrom (Suzuki); **3** Tommy Hayden (Suzuki); **4** Roger Lee Hayden (Suzuki); **5** Blake Young (Suzuki); **6** Steve Rapp (Kawasaki); **7** Larry Pegram (BMW); **8** Martin Cardenas (Suzuki); **9** Chris Clark (Yamaha); **10** Brett McCormick (BMW).

Race 2
1 Blake Young (Suzuki); **2** Josh Hayes (Yamaha); **3** Roger Lee Hayden (Suzuki); **4** Martin Cardenas (Suzuki); **5** Ben Bostrom (Suzuki); **6** Geoff May (Buell); **7** Taylor Knapp (Buell); **8** Chris Clark (Yamaha); **9** Jeremy Toye (BMW); **10** JD Beach (Kawasaki).

Final Championship Points

1	Josh Hayes	363
2	Blake Young	358
3	Tommy Hayden	288
4	Martin Cardenas	231
5	Ben Bostrom	209
6	Roger Lee Hayden	202

7 Larry Pegram, 190; **8** Chris Clark, 157; **9** Steve Rapp, 139; **10** Geoff May, 139.

Endurance World Championship

24 HOURS BOL D'OR, Magny-Cours, France, 16–17 April.
QTEL FIM Endurance World Championship, Round 1.
814 laps of the 2.741-mile/4.411km circuit, 2,231.200 miles/3,590.700km
1 Suzuki Endurance Racing Team, FRA: Philippe/Foray/Delhalle (Suzuki), 24h 0m 18.152s, 92.94mph/149.57km/h.
2 Team SRC Kawasaki, FRA: Da Costa/Leblanc/Four (Kawasaki), 808 laps; **3** BMW Motorrad France 99, BEL: Gimbert/Cudlin/Nigon (BMW), 803 laps; **4** Bolliger Team Switzerland, SUI: Saiger/Stamm/Tangre (Kawasaki), 802 laps; **5** Honda TT Legends, GBR: Plater/McGuinness/Amor (Honda), 796 laps; **6** National Motos, FRA: Jonchiere/De Carolis/Masson (Honda), 794 laps; **7** YMES Folch Endurance, ESP: Ribalta/Vallcaneras/Luis Rita (Yamaha), 789 laps; **8** Yamaha Racing France GMT 94 Ipone, FRA: Checa/Foray/Lagrive (Yamaha), 785 laps; **9** Metiss JLC Moto, FRA: Michel/Fissette/Cheron (Metiss), 781 laps; **10** Team Motors Events Bodyguard AMT, FRA: Gines/Bocquet/Humeau (Suzuki), 779 laps; **11** TRT 27 City Bike, FRA: Hardt/Hedelin/Houssin (Suzuki), 776 laps; **12** Atomic MotoSport, FRA: Muteau/Lalevee/Lussiana (Suzuki), 776 laps; **13** Van Zon Boenig Motorsportschool Penz13 RT, GER: Filla/Daemen/Seidel (BMW), 776 laps; **14** MCP Starteam 67, FRA: Lucas/Prulhiere/Keller (Suzuki), 776 laps; **15** Infini Team Power Bike, FRA: Cuzin/Holub/Bernon (Kawasaki), 775 laps.
Fastest lap: BMW Motorrad France 99, 1m 41.177s, 97.520mph/156.948km/h (lap N/A).
Endurance World Championship (EWC) points: 1 Suzuki Endurance Racing Team, 35; **2** Team SRC Kawasaki, 28; **3** BMW Motorrad France 99, 22; **4** Bolliger Team Switzerland, 18; **5** Honda TT Legends, 15; **6** National Motos, 14.

8 HOURS OF ALBACETE, Albacete, Spain, 21 May.
QTEL FIM Endurance World Championship, Round 2.
306 laps of the 2.199-mile/3.539km circuit, 672.900 miles/1,082.900km
1 BMW Motorrad France 99, BEL: Gimbert/Nigon/Marchand (BMW), 8h 1m 29.512s, 83.85mph/134.95km/h.
2 Yamaha Racing France GMT 94 Ipone, FRA: Checa/Foray/Lagrive (Yamaha), 306 laps; **3** Suzuki Endurance Racing Team, FRA: Philippe/Foray/Sakai (Suzuki), 305 laps; **4** Monster Yamaha YART, AUT: Jerman/Martin/Giabbani (Yamaha), 302 laps; **5** Maco Racing Team, SVK: Pridmore/Junod/Black (Yamaha), 301 laps; **6** YMES Folch Endurance, SPA: Ribalta/Vallcaneras/Luis Rita (Yamaha), 299 laps; **7** Van Zon Boenig Motorsportschool Penz13 RT, GER: Daemen/Fastre/Filla (BMW), 296 laps; **8** Team Motors Events Bodyguard AMT, FRA: Gines/Bocquet/Humeau (Suzuki), 295 laps; **9** No Limits Motor Team, ITA: Casas/Aldrovandi/Tizón (Suzuki), 294 laps; **10** MCS Racing Ipone, ITA: Prosenik/Molero/Saseta (Suzuki), 292 laps; **11** Atomic MotoSport, FRA: Muteau/Lalevee/Lussiana (Suzuki), 291 laps; **12** AM Moto Racing Compétition, FRA: Auger/Loiseau/Denis (Suzuki), 291 laps; **13** Team Endurance Moto 45, FRA: Lagrive/Ganfornina/Benichou (Suzuki), 290 laps; **14** Team R2CL, FRA: Chausse/Baratin/Capela (Suzuki), 287 laps; **15** Rodi Circuit Alcarras, SPA: Sola/Moreno/Martinez (Yamaha), 286 laps.
Fastest lap: Monster Yamaha YART, 1m 31.609s, 86.42mph/139.07km/h, on lap 124.
Endurance World Championship (EWC) points: 1 Suzuki Endurance Racing Team, 54; **2** BMW Motorrad France 99, 52; **3** Yamaha Racing France GMT 94 Ipone, 35; **4** Team SRC Kawasaki, 28; **5** YMES Folch Endurance, 25; **6** National Motos, 22.

8 HOURS OF SUZUKA, Suzuka, Japan, 31 July.
QTEL FIM Endurance World Championship, Round 3.
217 laps of the 3.618-mile/5.821km circuit, 785.100 miles/1,263.500km
1 FCC TSR Honda, JPN: Akiyoshi/Ito/Kiyonari (Honda), 8h 0m 50.922s, 97.94mph/157.62km/h.
2 Yoshimura Suzuki Racing Team, JPN: Kagayama/Waters/Aoki (Suzuki), 217 laps; **3** Musashi Rt Harc-Pro, JPN: Takahashi/Tamada/Okada (Honda), 217 laps; **4** BMW Motorrad France 99, BEL: Gimbert/Nigon/Cudlin (BMW), 212 laps; **5** Eva Rt Trickstar, JPN: Deguchi/Serizawa/Takeishi (Kawasaki), 211 laps; **6** Crown Keibihosyou Racing, JPN: Hamaguchi/Kitaguchi/Watanabe (Honda), 210 laps; **7** Yamaha Racing France Gmt94 Ipone, FRA: Checa/Lagrive/Foray (Yamaha), 210 laps; **8** Teluru Honey Bee Racing, JPN: Iwata/Sekiguchi/Noda (Honda), 210 laps; **9** Suzuki Endurance Racing Team, FRA: Philippe/Delhalle/Sakai (Suzuki), 208 laps; **10** Toho Racing Hiroshima Desmo, JPN: Yamahguchi/Kunikawa/Eguchi (Ducati), 206 laps; **11** Honda Escargot, JPN: Kuboyama/Nakatsuhara/ (Honda), 205 laps; **12** Ridez & Panolin, JPN: Sato/Igarashi/Shimizu (Honda), 205 laps; **13** Honda Suzuka Racing Team, JPN: Yasuda/Tokudome/ (Honda), 205 laps; **14** Team Shinsuke, JPN: Nakaki/Tsuda/Suzuki (Honda), 204 laps; **15** Team Tras BMW S1000Rr, JPN: Takada/Teramoto/Katahira (BMW), 204 laps.
Fastest lap: FCC TSR Honda, 2m 8.634s, 101.23mph/162.91km/h, on lap 110.
Endurance World Championship (EWC) points: 1 BMW Motorrad France 99, 68; **2** Suzuki Endurance Racing Team, 62; **3** Yamaha Racing France GMT 94 Ipone, 46; **4** FCC TSR Honda, 30; **5** Team SRC Kawasaki, 28; **6** YMES Folch Endurance, 25.

24 HEURES DU MANS, Le Mans Bugatti Circuit, France, 24–25 September.
QTEL FIM Endurance World Championship, Round 4.
834 laps of the 2.600-mile/4.185km circuit, 2,168.800 miles/3,490.300km
1 Team SRC Kawasaki, FRA: Da Costa/Leblanc/Four (Kawasaki), 24h 00m 39.331s, 90.32mph/145.36km/h.
2 Suzuki Endurance Racing Team, FRA: Delhalle/Sakai/Guittet (Suzuki), 833 laps; **3** Monster Yamaha YART, AUT: Jerman/Martin/Baz (Yamaha), 826 laps; **4** Bolliger Team Switzerland, SUI: Saiger/Stamm/Tangre (Kawasaki), 823 laps; **5** Honda TT Legends, GBR: McGuinness/Amor/Donald (Honda), 819 laps; **6** YMES Folch Endurance, ESP: Ribalta/Vallcaneras/Luis Rita (Yamaha), 817 laps; **7** BMW Motorrad France 99, BEL: Gimbert/Nigon/Cudlin (BMW), 817 laps; **8** Team Motors Events Bodyguard AMT, FRA: Bocquet/Grarre/Gines (Suzuki), 813 laps; **9** Maccio Racing, FRA: Maurin/Richier/Moreira (Kawasaki), 811 laps; **10** TRT 27 City Bike, FRA: Hedelin/Varesco/Houssin (Suzuki), 810 laps; **11** Suzuki Junior Team LMS, FRA: Tangre/Enjolras/Napoleone (Suzuki), 809 laps; **12** Metiss JLC Moto, FRA: Michel/Huvier/Cheron (Metiss), 807 laps; **13** Atomic MotoSport, FRA: Muteau/Lalevee/Jond (Suzuki), 804 laps; **14** Team Endurance Moto 45, FRA: Diguet/Ganfornina/Lagrive (Suzuki), 803 laps; **15** MCP Starteam 67, FRA: Lucas/Hardt/Bertin (Suzuki), 802 laps.
Fastest lap: Team SRC Kawasaki, 1m 38.640s, 94.906mph/152.737km/h, on lap 105.
Endurance World Championship (EWC) points: 1 Suzuki Endurance Racing Team, 90; **2** BMW Motorrad France 99, 81; **3** Team SRC Kawasaki, 63; **4** Yamaha Racing France GMT 94 Ipone, 46; **5** YMES Folch Endurance, 39; **6** Monster Yamaha YART, 38.

8 HOURS OF DOHA, Losail, Qatar, 12 November.
QTEL FIM Endurance World Championship, Round 5.
231 laps of the 3.343-mile/5.380km circuit, 772.200 miles/1,242.700km
1 Yamaha Racing France GMT 94 Ipone, FRA: Checa/Foray/Lagrive (Yamaha), 231 laps, 8h 1m 49.279s, 96.16mph/154.76km/h.
2 BMW Motorrad France 99, BEL: Gimbert/Nigon/Cudlin (BMW), 231 laps; **3** Suzuki Endurance Racing Team, FRA: Philippe/Delhalle (Suzuki), 231 laps; **4** Monster Yamaha YART, AUT: Jerman/Martin/Nakasuga (Yamaha), 230 laps; **5** Honda TT Legends, GBR: McGuinness/Amor/Richards (Honda), 227 laps; **6** YMES Folch Endurance, ESP: Ribalta/Vallcaneras/Luis (Yamaha), 227 laps; **7** DG Sport, BEL: Marchand/Monge/Schouten (Yamaha), 225 laps; **8** Team Motors Events Bodyguard AMT, FRA: Gines/Bocquet/Grarre (Suzuki), 224 laps; **9** Qatar Endurance Racing Team, QAT: Cudlin/Al Malki/Al Mannai (Suzuki), 223 laps; **10** MCS Racing Ipone, ITA: Prosenik/Savary/Bellucci (Suzuki), 222 laps; **11** Maco Racing Team, SVK: Pridmore/Junod/Black (Yamaha), 222 laps; **12** Motobox Kremer By Shell Advance, GER: Gaziello/Scherrer/Moser (Suzuki), 221 laps; **13** Team FMA Assurances, FRA: Dumain/Morin/Mackels (Honda), 221 laps; **14** Team R2CL, FRA: Briere/Lefort/Capela (Suzuki), 221 laps; **15** Team Endurance Moto 45, FRA: Diguet/Ganfornina/Lagrive (Suzuki), 220 laps.
Fastest lap: BMW Motorrad France 99, 2m 0.347s, 100.00mph/160.94km/h, on lap 224.

Final Endurance World Championship (EWC) points:

1	Suzuki Endurance Racing Team, FRA	109
2	BMW Motorrad France 99, BEL	105
3	Yamaha Racing France GMT 94 Ipone, FRA	76
4	Team SRC Kawasaki, FRA	63
5	Monster Yamaha YART, AUT	54
6	YMES Folch Endurance, ESP	51

7 Honda TT Legends, GBR 43; **8** Bolliger Team Switzerland, SUI 42; **9** Maco Racing Team, SVK 34; **10** FCC TSR Honda, JPN 30; **11** Yoshimura Suzuki Racing Team, JPN 24; **12** Team R2CL, FRA 24; **13** National Motos, FRA 22; **14** TRT 27 City Bike, FRA 21; **15** Motobox Kremer by Shell Advance, GER 20.

Isle of Man Tourist Trophy Races

ISLE OF MAN TOURIST TROPHY COURSE, 4–10 June, 37.730-mile/60.720km circuit.
Dainese Superbike TT (6 laps, 226.380 miles/364.320km)
1 John McGuinness (999cc Honda), 1h 46m 13.40s, 127.870mph/205.787km/h.

2 Cameron Donald (1000cc Honda), 1h 47m 10.30s; 3 Gary Johnson (1000cc Honda), 1h 47m 19.97s; 4 Keith Amor (999cc Honda), 1h 48m 3.36s; 5 Michael Dunlop (1000cc Kawasaki), 1h 49m 1.53s; 6 Daniel Stewart (1000cc Honda), 1h 49m 3.50s; 7 William Dunlop (1000cc Honda), 1h 49m 5.34s; 8 James Hillier (1000cc Kawasaki), 1h 50m 11.01s; 9 Adrian Archibald (1000cc BMW), 1h 50m 26.81s; 10 Ian Mackman (1000cc Suzuki), 1h 51m 48.31s; 11 John Burrows (1000cc Suzuki), 1h 52m 17.42s; 12 Steve Mercer (1000cc BMW), 1h 52m 24.73s; 13 Mark Buckley (1000cc Kawasaki), 1h 52m 59.41s; 14 Stefano Bonetti (1000cc Kawasaki), 1h 53m 7.59s; 15 Paul Shoesmith (1000cc BMW), 1h 53m 16.17s.
Fastest lap: Bruce Anstey (999cc Honda), 17m 13.88s, 131.378mph/211.432km/h, on lap 2.
Superbike TT lap record: Conor Cummins (1000cc Kawasaki), 17m 12.83s, 131.511mph/211.646km/h (2010).

Sure Sidecar Race 1 (3 laps, 113.190 miles/182.160km)
1 Klaus Klaffenbock/Dan Sayle (600cc Honda), 59m 26.21s, 114.262mph/183.887km/h.
2 John Holden/Andrew Winkle (599cc LCR), 59m 37.87s; 3 Conrad Harrison/Mike Aylott (600cc Shelbourne), 1hr 0m 29.41s; 4 Tim Reeves/Gregory Cluze (600cc Honda), 1hr 0m 41.74s; 5 Tony Elmer/Darren Marshall (600cc Yamaha), 1hr 0m 54.91s; 6 Gary Bryan/Jamie Winn (600cc Baker), 1hr 1m 20.93s; 7 Ben Birchall/Tom Birchall (600cc LCR), 1hr 2m 2.56s; 8 Douglas Wright/Martin Hull (600cc Baker), 1hr 2m 7.19s; 9 Gregory Lambert/Aaron Galligan (600cc Honda), 1hr 2m 21.13s; 10 Carl Fenwick/Mark Sayers (600cc Shelbourne), 1hr 3m 21.17s; 11 Tony Baker/Fiona Baker-Milligan (600cc Suzuki), 1hr 3m 26.42s; 12 Roy Hanks/Dave Wells (599cc Molyneux), 1hr 3m 43.49s; 13 Karl Bennett/Lee Cain (600cc Honda), 1hr 3m 54.98s; 14 Gordon Shand/Lee Barrett (599cc Shand), 1hr 4m 4.15s; 15 Tony Thirkell/Nigel Barlow (600cc Equipe), 1hr 4m 17.07s.
Fastest lap: Holden/Winkle, 19m 42.55s, 114.861mph/184.851km/h, on lap 2.
Sidecar lap record: Nick Crowe/Dan Sayle (600cc LCR Honda), 19m 24.24s, 116.667mph/187.757km/h (2007).

Monster Energy Supersport TT Race 1 (3 laps, 113.190 miles/182.160km)
1 Bruce Anstey (599cc Honda), 54m 40.01s, 124.232mph/199.932km/h.
2 Keith Amor (599cc Honda), 54m 48.40s; 3 Guy Martin (599cc Suzuki), 54m 56.06s; 4 Gary Johnson (600cc Honda), 54m 57.24s; 5 John McGuinness (599cc Honda), 54m 58.45s; 6 Dan Kneen (600cc Yamaha), 55m 15.52s; 7 Ian Lougher (600cc Kawasaki), 56m 10.74s; 8 Ben Wylie (600cc Yamaha), 57m 0.35s; 9 Ian Mackman (675cc Triumph), 57m 16.07s; 10 Daniel Stewart (600cc Honda), 57m 25.17s; 11 Mark Buckley (600cc Kawasaki), 57m 27.89s; 12 James Hillier (599cc Kawasaki), 57m 28.57s; 13 Roy Richardson (599cc Yamaha), 57m 29.83s; 14 Adrian Archibald (600cc Yamaha), 57m 42.84s; 15 Robert Barber (600cc Suzuki), 57m 44.35s.
Fastest lap: Anstey, 17m 52.94s, 126.595mph/203.735km/h, on lap 3.
Supersport lap record: M. Dunlop (600cc Yamaha), 17m 42.52s, 127.836mph/205.732km/h (2010).

Royal London 360 Superstock TT (4 laps, 150.92 miles/242.88 km)
1 Michael Dunlop (1000cc Kawasaki), 1h 11m 13.69s, 127.129mph/204.594km/h.
2 John McGuinness (999cc Honda), 1h 11m 32.32s; 3 Guy Martin (999cc Suzuki), 1h 11m 36.59s; 4 Keith Amor (1000cc Honda), 1h 11m 44.79s; 5 William Dunlop (1000cc Honda), 1h 12m 16.10s; 6 Cameron Donald (1000cc Honda), 1h 12m 16.58s; 7 Dan Kneen (1000cc Kawasaki), 1h 12m 27.28s; 8 Michael Rutter (1200cc Ducati), 1h 13m 4.52s; 9 Adrian Archibald (1000cc BMW), 1h 13m 13.00s; 10 James Hillier (1000cc Kawasaki), 1h 13m 30.54s; 11 Simon Andrews (1000cc BMW), 1h 14m 6.50s; 12 Conor Cummins (1000cc Kawasaki), 1h 14m 14.60s; 13 Luis Carreira (1000cc Kawasaki), 1h 14m 16.06s; 14 Ian Lougher (1000cc Kawasaki), 1h 14m 32.76s; 15 Ian Mackman (1000cc Suzuki), 1h 14m 38.93s.
Fastest lap: M. Dunlop, 17m 27.17s, 129.709mph/208.746km/h, on lap 2.
Superstock lap record: Ian Hutchinson (1000cc Honda), 17m 18.91s, 130.741mph/210.407km/h (2010).

Monster Energy Supersport TT Race 2 (4 laps, 150.92 miles/242.88 km)
1 Gary Johnson (600cc Honda), 1h 13m 7.95s, 123.819mph/199.267km/h.
2 John McGuinness (599cc Honda), 1h 13m 16.35s; 3 Guy Martin (599cc Suzuki), 1h 13m 29.28s; 4 Keith Amor (599cc Honda), 1h 13m 37.67s; 5 Bruce Anstey (599cc Honda), 1h 13m 43.85s; 6 Conor Cummins (600cc Kawasaki), 1h 15m 24.68s; 7 Ben Wylie (600cc Yamaha), 1h 15m 33.25s; 8 Roy Richardson (599cc Yamaha), 1h 15m 56.04s; 9 James Hillier (599cc Kawasaki), 1h 16m 3.09s; 10 Mark Buckley (600cc Kawasaki), 1h 16m 27.92s; 11 Russ Mountford (599cc Yamaha), 1h 16m 31.79s; 12 Dean Harrison (600cc Yamaha), 1h 16m 56.19s; 13 Paul Owen (600cc Yamaha), 1h 17m 4.89s; 14 Roger Maher (600cc Yamaha), 1h 17m 20.96s; 15 Robert Barber (600cc Suzuki), 1h 17m 31.88s.
Fastest lap: Johnson, 17m 58.92s, 125.892mph/202.604km/h, on lap 2.
Supersport lap record: M. Dunlop (600cc Yamaha), 17m 42.52s, 127.836mph/205.732km/h (2010).

Sure Sidecar Race 2 (3 laps, 113.190 miles/182.160km)
1 John Holden/Andrew Winkle (599cc LCR), 59m 51.15s, 113.469mph/182.611km/h.
2 Conrad Harrison/Mike Aylott (600cc Shelbourne), 1hr 0m 36.23s; 3 Tony Elmer/Darren Marshall (600cc Yamaha), 1hr 1m 4.02s; 4 Tim Reeves/Gregory Cluze (600cc Honda), 1hr 1m 4.83s; 5 Ben Birchall/Tom Birchall (600cc LCR), 1hr 1m 11.98s; 6 Klaus Klaffenbock/Dan Sayle (600cc Honda), 1hr 1m 22.10s; 7 Gary Bryan/Jamie Winn (600cc Baker), 1hr 1m 47.97s; 8 Douglas Wright/Martin Hull (600cc Baker), 1hr 2m 12.21s; 9 Robert Handcock/Ken Edwards (600cc Honda), 1hr 3m 15.50s; 10 Carl Fenwick/Mark Sayers (600cc Shelbourne), 1hr 3m 35.15s; 11 Tony Baker/Fiona Baker-Milligan (600cc Suzuki), 1hr 3m 51.54s; 12 Gordon Shand/Lee Barrett (599cc Shand), 1hr 4m 20.47s; 13 Tony Thirkell/Nigel Barlow (600cc Equipe), 1hr 4m 20.87s; 14 Howard Baker/Mike Killingsworth (600cc Honda), 1hr 4m 22.04s; 15 Kenny Howles/Pete Alton (600cc Suzuki), 1hr 5m 37.76s.
Fastest lap: Klaffenbock/Sayle, 19m 44.50s, 114.672mph/184.547km/h, on lap 2.
Sidecar lap record: Nick Crowe/Dan Sayle (600cc LCR Honda), 19m 24.24s, 116.667mph/187.757km/h (2007).

SES TT Zero (1 lap, 37.730 miles/60.720km)
1 Michael Rutter (2011 MotoCzysz E1PC), 22m 43.68s, 99.604mph/160.297km/h (record).
2 Mark Miller (2011 MotoCzysz E1PC), 23m 1.93s; 3 George Spence (ION HORSE 2011), 25m 35.90s; 4 Allan Brew (BMW), 28m 35.81s; 5 Yoshinari Matsushita (Prozza TT Zero-11), h 32m 23.81s;
Previous lap record: Mark Miller (MotoCzysz E1PC), 23m 22.89s, 96.820mph/155.817km/h (2010).

PokerStars Senior TT (6 laps, 226.380 miles/364.320km)
1 John McGuinness (999cc Honda), 1h 45m 45.80s, 128.426mph/206.682km/h.
2 Guy Martin (1000cc Suzuki), 1h 45m 53.00s; 3 Bruce Anstey (999cc Honda), 1h 46m 1.50s; 4 Cameron Donald (1000cc Honda), 1h 46m 54.00s; 5 Keith Amor (999cc Honda), 1h 46m 55.06s; 6 Michael Dunlop (1000cc Kawasaki), 1h 47m 27.35s; 7 Gary Johnson (1000cc Honda), 1h 48m 26.21s; 8 William Dunlop (1000cc Honda), 1h 49m 9.17s; 9 James Hillier (1000cc Kawasaki), 1h 49m 36.47s; 10 Michael Rutter (1200cc Ducati), 1h 49m 51.87s; 11 Simon Andrews* (1000cc BMW), 1h 50m 32.17s; 12 Dan Kneen (1000cc Kawasaki), 1h 51m 0.91s; 13 Ryan Farquhar (1000cc Kawasaki), 1h 51m 37.89s; 14 Ian Mackman (1000cc Suzuki), 1h 51m 46.11s; 15 Paul Shoesmith (1000cc BMW), 1h 52m 27.76s.
Fastest lap: McGuinness, 17m 14.89s, 131.248mph/211.223km/h, on lap 4.
Senior TT and Outright lap record: John McGuinness (1000cc Honda), 17m 12.30s, 131.578mph/211.754km/h (2009).

British Championships

BRANDS HATCH INDY, 25 April, 1.208-mile/1.944km circuit.
MCE Insurance British Superbike Championship, Rounds 1 and 2 (2 x 30 laps, 36.240 miles/58.323km)
Race 1
1 Shane Byrne (Honda), 23m 47.412s, 91.39mph/147.08km/h.
2 Tommy Hill (Yamaha); 3 Thomas Bridewell (Honda); 4 Stuart Easton (Kawasaki); 5 Jon Kirkham (Suzuki); 6 Michael Rutter (Ducati); 7 Loris Baz (Yamaha); 8 Dan Linfoot (Honda); 9 Martin Jessopp (Ducati); 10 Chris Walker (Kawasaki); 11 Glen Richards (Honda); 12 Alex Lowes (Honda); 13 Peter Hickman (Honda); 14 Steve Brogan (Honda); 15 Simon Andrews (Kawasaki).
Fastest lap: Hill, 45.674s, 95.20mph/153.22km/h.

Race 2
1 Tommy Hill (Yamaha), 23m 3.483s, 94.29mph/151.75km/h.
2 Ryuichi Kiyonari (Honda); 3 Shane Byrne (Honda); 4 Michael Laverty (Yamaha); 5 John Hopkins (Suzuki); 6 Stuart Easton (Kawasaki); 7 Michael Rutter (Ducati); 8 Dan Linfoot (Honda); 9 Peter Hickman (Honda); 10 Gary Mason (Kawasaki); 11 Chris Walker (Kawasaki); 12 Alex Lowes (Honda); 13 Loris Baz (Yamaha); 14 Glen Richards (Honda); 15 Martin Jessopp (Ducati).
Fastest lap: M. Laverty, 45.679s, 95.19mph/153.20km/h.
Championship points: 1 Hill, 45; 2 Byrne, 41; 3 Easton, 23; 4 Kiyonari, 20; 5 Rutter, 19; 6 Bridewell, 16.

Fuchs-Silkolene British Supersport Championship, Rounds 1 and 2
Race 1 (18 laps, 21.744 miles/34.994km)
1 Ben Wilson (Kawasaki), 14m 19.462s, 91.07mph/146.56km/h.
2 Paul Young (Triumph); 3 Jack Kennedy (Yamaha); 4 Lee Johnston (Honda); 5 Steve Plater (Honda); 6 Allann Jon Venter (Triumph); 7 Luke Mossey (Triumph); 8 Jimmy Hill (Triumph); 9 Matthew Whitman (Triumph); 10 Gary Johnson (Honda); 11 Daniel Cooper (Triumph); 12 Jesse Trayler (Kawasaki); 13 Billy McConnell (Triumph); 14 Luke Stapleford (Kawasaki); 15 Sam Warren (Yamaha).
Fastest lap: Wilson, 47.128s, 92.27mph/148.49km/h.

Race 2 (26 laps, 31.408 miles/50.546km)
1 Alastair Seeley (Suzuki), 20m 37.275s, 91.38mph/147.06km/h.
2 Jack Kennedy (Yamaha); 3 Steve Plater (Honda); 4 Ben Wilson (Kawasaki); 5 Dean Hipwell (Yamaha); 6 Lee Johnston (Honda); 7 Jimmy Hill (Triumph); 8 Luke Mossey (Triumph); 9 Sam Warren (Yamaha); 10 Daniel Cooper (Triumph); 11 Gary Johnson (Honda); 12 Allann Jon Venter (Triumph); 13 Marty Nutt (Yamaha); 14 Jesse Trayler (Kawasaki); 15 Billy McConnell (Triumph).
Fastest lap: Johnston, 47.000s, 92.52mph/148.90km/h.
Championship points: 1 Wilson, 38; 2 Kennedy, 36; 3 Plater, 27; 4 Seeley, 25; 5 Johnston, 23; 6 Young, 20.

SUNOCO British 125GP Championship, Round 1 (19 laps, 22.952 miles/36.938km)
1 Luke Hedger (Honda), 16m 11.480s, 85.04mph/136.86km/h.
2 Ryan Watson (Seel); 3 Harry Hartley (Honda); 4 Matt Davies (Honda); 5 Tarran Mackenzie (Honda); 6 Philip Wakefield (Seel); 7 Callan Cooper (Honda); 8 Wayne Ryan (Honda); 9 Robert English (Honda); 10 Andrew Reid (Aztec); 11 Catherine Green (Honda); 12 Tom Carne (Honda); 13 Lee Jackson (Honda); 14 Jon Vincent (Honda); 15 Joe Irving (Honda).
Fastest lap: Ryde, 49.920s, 87.11mph/140.19km/h.
Championship points: 1 Hedger, 25; 2 Watson, 20; 3 Hartley, 16; 4 Davies, 13; 5 Mackenzie, 11; 6 Wakefield, 10.

OULTON PARK, 2 May, 2.692-mile/4.332km circuit.
MCE Insurance British Superbike Championship, Rounds 3 and 4 (2 x 18 laps, 48.456 miles/77.976km)
Race 1
1 Ryuichi Kiyonari (Honda), 29m 6.776s, 99.86mph/160.71km/h.
2 John Hopkins (Suzuki); 3 Stuart Easton (Kawasaki); 4 Shane Byrne (Honda); 5 Michael Laverty (Yamaha); 6 Josh Brookes (Suzuki); 7 Jon Kirkham (Suzuki); 8 Loris Baz (Yamaha); 9 Gary Mason (Kawasaki); 10 Dan Linfoot (Honda); 11 Michael Rutter (Ducati); 12 Alex Lowes (Honda); 13 Peter Hickman (Honda); 14 James Westmoreland (Yamaha); 15 Martin Jessopp (Ducati).
Fastest lap: Kiyonari, 1m 36.041s, 100.90mph/162.39km/h.

Race 2
1 John Hopkins (Suzuki), 30m 13.082s, 96.21mph/154.84km/h.
2 Stuart Easton (Kawasaki); 3 Shane Byrne (Honda); 4 Ryuichi Kiyonari (Honda); 5 Michael Laverty (Yamaha); 6 Michael Rutter (Ducati); 7 Jon Kirkham (Suzuki); 8 Peter Hickman (Honda); 9 Loris Baz (Yamaha); 10 Gary Mason (Kawasaki); 11 Chris Walker (Kawasaki); 12 Martin Jessopp (Ducati); 13 James Westmoreland (Yamaha); 14 Alex Lowes (Honda); 15 Dan Linfoot (Honda).
Fastest lap: Kirkham, 1m 36.049s, 100.89mph/162.38km/h.
Championship points: 1 Byrne, 70; 2 Easton, 59; 3 Kiyonari, 58; 4 Hopkins, 56; 5 Hill, 45; 6 Laverty, 35.

Fuchs-Silkolene British Supersport Championship, Rounds 3 and 4
Race 1 (12 laps, 32.304 miles/51.988km)
1 Ben Wilson (Kawasaki), 19m 57.585s, 97.10mph/156.27km/h.
2 Alastair Seeley (Suzuki); 3 Jack Kennedy (Yamaha); 4 Paul Young (Triumph); 5 Lee Johnston (Honda); 6 Luke Mossey (Triumph); 7 Steve Plater (Honda); 8 Daniel Cooper (Triumph); 9 Billy McConnell (Triumph); 10 Gary Johnson (Honda); 11 Matthew Whitman (Triumph); 12 Marty Nutt (Suzuki); 13 Sam Warren (Yamaha); 14 Dean Hipwell (Yamaha); 15 Allann Jon Venter (Triumph).
Fastest lap: Wilson, 1m 39.108s, 97.78mph/157.37km/h.

Race 2 (16 laps, 43.072 miles/69.318km)
1 Ben Wilson (Kawasaki), 26m 30.972s, 97.46mph/156.85km/h.
2 Alastair Seeley (Suzuki); 3 Jack Kennedy (Yamaha); 4 Luke Mossey (Triumph); 5 Billy McConnell (Triumph); 6 Paul Young (Triumph); 7 Daniel Cooper (Triumph); 8 Gary Johnson (Honda); 9 Sam Warren (Yamaha); 10 Max Hunt (Honda); 11 Allann Jon Venter (Triumph); 12 Pauli Pekkanen (Triumph); 13 Dean Hipwell (Yamaha); 14 Luke Stapleford (Kawasaki); 15 Marty Nutt (Suzuki).
Fastest lap: Seeley, 1m 38.791s, 98.09mph/157.87km/h.
Championship points: 1 Wilson, 88; 2 Kennedy, 68; 3 Seeley, 65; 4 Young, 43; 5 Mossey, 40; 6 Plater, 36.

SUNOCO British 125GP Championship, Round 2 (12 laps, 32.304 miles/51.988km)
1 Rob Guiver (Honda), 21m 47.360s, 88.95mph/143.15km/h.
2 Kyle Ryde (Honda); 3 Matt Davies (Honda); 4 Philip Wakefield (Seel); 5 Lee Jackson (Honda); 6 Harry Hartley (Honda); 7 Jordan Weaving (Honda); 8 Joe Irving (Honda); 9 Jon Vincent (Honda); 10 Catherine Green (Honda); 11 Bradley Hughes (Honda); 12 Richard Ferguson (Honda); 13 Bradley Ray (Honda); 14 Chrissy Rouse (Honda); 15 Sam Burman (Honda).

Fastest lap: Hedger, 1m 47.289s, 90.32mph/145.37km/h.
Championship points: 1 Davies, 29; **2** Hartley, 26; **3** Hedger, 25; **4** Guiver, 25; **5** Wakefield, 23; **6** Watson, 20.

CROFT, 15 May, 2.125-mile/3.420km circuit.
MCE Insurance British Superbike Championship, Rounds 5 and 6
Race 1 (18 laps, 38.250 miles/61.557km)
1 Jon Kirkham (Suzuki), 26m 41.827s, 85.96mph/138.34km/h.
2 John Hopkins (Suzuki); **3** Gary Mason (Kawasaki); **4** Loris Baz (Yamaha); **5** Alex Lowes (Honda); **6** Stuart Easton (Kawasaki); **7** Peter Hickman (Honda); **8** Josh Brookes (Suzuki); **9** Glen Richards (Honda); **10** Tommy Bridewell (Honda); **11** Hudson Kennaugh (Aprilia); **12** James Westmoreland (Yamaha); **13** John Laverty (BMW); **14** Tommy Hill (Yamaha); **15** Tom Tunstall (BMW).
Fastest lap: Kirkham, 1m 23.860s, 91.22mph/146.81km/h.

Race 2 (20 laps, 42.500 miles/68.400 km)
1 Shane Byrne (Honda), 27m 46.928s, 91.78mph/147.71km/h.
2 Stuart Easton (Kawasaki); **3** John Hopkins (Suzuki); **4** Josh Brookes (Suzuki); **5** Loris Baz (Yamaha); **6** Tommy Hill (Yamaha); **7** Gary Mason (Kawasaki); **8** Michael Rutter (Ducati); **9** Peter Hickman (Honda); **10** Tommy Bridewell (Honda); **11** Alex Lowes (Honda); **12** James Westmoreland (Yamaha); **13** Chris Walker (Kawasaki); **14** Ian Lowry (BMW); **15** Ryuichi Kiyonari (Honda).
Fastest lap: Byrne, 1m 20.394s, 95.15mph/153.14km/h.
Championship points: 1 Byrne, 95; **2** Hopkins, 92; **3** Easton, 89; **4** Kiyonari, 59; **5** Hill, 57; **6** Kirkham, 54.

Fuchs-Silkolene British Supersport Championship, Rounds 5 and 6
Race 1 (10 laps, 21.250 miles/34.199km)
1 Ben Wilson (Kawasaki), 13m 55.467s, 91.56mph/147.35km/h.
2 Jack Kennedy (Yamaha); **3** Steve Plater (Honda); **4** Billy McConnell (Triumph); **5** Alastair Seeley (Suzuki); **6** Gary Johnson (Honda); **7** Daniel Cooper (Triumph); **8** Paul Young (Triumph); **9** Sam Warren (Yamaha); **10** Lee Johnston (Honda); **11** Allann Jon Venter (Triumph); **12** Luke Stapleford (Kawasaki); **13** Luke Mossey (Triumph); **14** Marty Nutt (Suzuki); **15** Christian Iddon (Triumph).
Fastest lap: Plater, 1m 22.186s, 93.08mph/149.80km/h.

Race 2 (15 laps, 31.875 miles/51.298 km)
1 Ben Wilson (Kawasaki), 20m 46.965s, 92.02mph/148.09km/h.
2 Steve Plater (Honda); **3** Billy McConnell (Triumph); **4** Alastair Seeley (Suzuki); **5** Jack Kennedy (Yamaha); **6** Gary Johnson (Honda); **7** Lee Johnston (Honda); **8** Dean Hipwell (Yamaha); **9** Sam Warren (Yamaha); **10** Daniel Cooper (Triumph); **11** Allann Jon Venter (Triumph); **12** Pauli Pekkanen (Triumph); **13** David Jones (Triumph); **14** Christian Iddon (Triumph); **15** Jesse Trayler (Kawasaki).
Fastest lap: McConnell, 1m 22.220s, 93.04mph/149.74km/h.
Championship points: 1 Wilson, 138; **2** Kennedy, 99; **3** Seeley, 89; **4** Plater, 72; **5** Young, 51; **6** McConnell, 51.

SUNOCO British 125GP Championship, Round 3 (14 laps, 29.750 miles/47.878km)
1 Rob Guiver (Honda), 20m 45.136s, 86.01mph/138.42km/h.
2 Kyle Ryde (Honda); **3** Luke Hedger (Honda); **4** Lee Jackson (Honda); **5** Wayne Ryan (Honda); **6** Tarran Mackenzie (Honda); **7** Jordan Weaving (Honda); **8** Philip Wakefield (Seel); **9** Robert English (Honda); **10** Nigel Percy (Honda); **11** Bradley Ray (Honda); **12** Harry Hartley (Honda); **13** Ryan Watson (Seel); **14** Josh Corner (Honda); **15** Richard Ferguson (Honda).
Fastest lap: Ryde, 1m 27.722s, 87.20mph/140.34km/h.
Championship points: 1 Guiver, 50; **2** Hedger, 41; **3** Ryde, 40; **4** Wakefield, 31; **5** Hartley, 30; **6** Davies, 29.

THRUXTON, 30 May, 2.356-mile/3.792km circuit.
MCE Insurance British Superbike Championship, Rounds 7 and 8 (2 x 15 laps, 35.340 miles/56.874km)
Race 1
1 Michael Laverty (Yamaha), 20m 42.995s, 102.35mph/164.72km/h.
2 Michael Rutter (Ducati); **3** Shane Byrne (Honda); **4** John Hopkins (Suzuki); **5** Peter Hickman (Honda); **6** Dan Linfoot (Honda); **7** Alex Lowes (Kawasaki); **8** Chris Walker (Kawasaki); **9** Josh Brookes (Suzuki); **10** Ryuichi Kiyonari (Honda); **11** Steve Brogan (Honda); **12** Martin Jessopp (Ducati); **13** Barry Burrell (BMW); **14** Glen Richards (Honda); **15** Patric Muff (Honda).
Fastest lap: Byrne, 1m 21.012s, 104.69mph/168.49km/h.

Race 2
1 Shane Byrne (Honda), 20m 7.763s, 105.33mph/169.51km/h.
2 Peter Hickman (Honda); **3** John Hopkins (Suzuki); **4** Tommy Hill (Yamaha); **5** Dan Linfoot (Honda); **6** Josh Brookes (Suzuki); **7** Michael Laverty (Yamaha); **8** Chris Walker (Kawasaki); **9** Jon Kirkham (Suzuki); **10** Martin Jessopp (Ducati); **11** Loris Baz (Yamaha); **12** James Westmoreland (Yamaha); **13** John Laverty (BMW); **14** Gary Mason (Kawasaki); **15** Steve Brogan (Honda).
Fastest lap: Byrne, 1m 19.617s, 106.52mph/171.44km/h.
Championship points: 1 Byrne, 136; **2** Hopkins, 121; **3** Easton, 89; **4** Hill, 70; **5** Laverty, 69; **6** Hickman, 68.

Fuchs-Silkolene British Supersport Championship, Rounds 7 and 8 (2 x 12 laps, 28.272 miles/45.499km)
Race 1
1 Billy McConnell (Triumph), 15m 39.066s, 108.38mph/174.42km/h.
2 Alastair Seeley (Suzuki); **3** Ben Wilson (Kawasaki); **4** Sam Warren (Yamaha); **5** Dean Hipwell (Yamaha); **6** Paul Young (Triumph); **7** Christian Iddon (Triumph); **8** Steve Plater (Honda); **9** Luke Mossey (Triumph); **10** Daniel Cooper (Triumph); **11** Matthew Whitman (Triumph); **12** Marty Nutt (Suzuki); **13** Luke Stapleford (Kawasaki); **14** Allann Jon Venter (Triumph); **15** Max Hunt (Honda).
Fastest lap: Kennedy, 1m 17.136s, 109.95mph/176.95km/h.

Race 2
1 Paul Young (Triumph), 16m 42.530s, 101.52mph/163.38km/h.
2 Sam Warren (Yamaha); **3** Daniel Cooper (Triumph); **4** Ben Wilson (Kawasaki); **5** Billy McConnell (Triumph); **6** Marty Nutt (Suzuki); **7** Luke Mossey (Triumph); **8** Luke Stapleford (Kawasaki); **9** Pauli Pekkanen (Triumph); **10** Jesse Trayler (Kawasaki); **11** Allann Jon Venter (Triumph); **12** Max Hunt (Honda); **13** Josh Caygill (Triumph); **14** David Paton (Yamaha); **15** Jonny Buckley (Yamaha).
Fastest lap: Seeley, 1m 21.791s, 103.69mph/166.88km/h.
Championship points: 1 Wilson, 167; **2** Seeley, 109; **3** Kennedy, 99; **4** McConnell, 87; **5** Young, 86; **6** Plater, 80.

SUNOCO British 125GP Championship, Round 4 (12 laps, 28.272 miles/45.499km)
1 Rob Guiver (Honda), 17m 57.539s, 94.45mph/152.00km/h.
2 Andrew Reid (Aztec); **3** Wayne Ryan (Honda); **4** Bradley Ray (Honda); **5** Joe Irving (Honda); **6** Tom Carne (Honda); **7** Nigel Percy (Honda); **8** Lee Jackson (Honda); **9** Chrissy Rouse (Honda); **10** Luke Hedger (Honda); **11** Ryan Watson (Seel); **12** Tommy Philp (Honda); **13** Tarran Mackenzie (Honda); **14** Sam Burman (Honda); **15** Jamie Edwards (Aprilia).
Fastest lap: Guiver, 1m 28.311s, 96.04mph/154.56km/h.
Championship points: 1 Guiver, 75; **2** Hedger, 47; **3** Ryde, 40; **4** Jackson, 35; **5** Ryan, 35; **6** Wakefield, 31.

KNOCKHILL, 19 June, 1.271-mile/2.046km circuit.
MCE Insurance British Superbike Championship, Rounds 9 and 10 (2 x 30 laps, 38.130 miles/61.364km)
Race 1
1 Tommy Hill (Yamaha), 24m 35.133s, 93.07mph/149.78km/h.
2 John Hopkins (Suzuki); **3** Shane Byrne (Honda); **4** Gary Mason (Kawasaki); **5** Josh Brookes (Suzuki); **6** Michael Laverty (Yamaha); **7** James Westmoreland (Yamaha); **8** Jon Kirkham (Suzuki); **9** Loris Baz (Yamaha); **10** Ryuichi Kiyonari (Honda); **11** Tommy Bridewell (Honda); **12** Glen Richards (Honda); **13** Peter Hickman (Honda); **14** Chris Walker (Kawasaki); **15** Simon Andrews (Kawasaki).
Fastest lap: Hill, 48.730s, 93.97mph/151.23km/h.

Race 2
1 Tommy Hill (Yamaha), 26m 12.073s, 87.33mph/140.54km/h.
2 Shane Byrne (Honda); **3** Michael Laverty (Yamaha); **4** Ryuichi Kiyonari (Honda); **5** James Westmoreland (Yamaha); **6** Gary Mason (Kawasaki); **7** Chris Walker (Kawasaki); **8** Peter Hickman (Honda); **9** Michael Rutter (Ducati); **10** Simon Andrews (Kawasaki); **11** Jon Kirkham (Suzuki); **12** Martin Jessopp (Ducati); **13** Josh Brookes (Suzuki); **14** Scott Smart (Ducati); **15** Dan Linfoot (Honda).
Fastest lap: Hill, 48.510s, 94.34mph/151.83km/h.
Championship points: 1 Byrne, 172; **2** Hopkins, 141; **3** Hill, 120; **4** Laverty, 95; **5** Easton, 89; **6** Kiyonari, 84.

Fuchs-Silkolene British Supersport Championship, Rounds 9 and 10
Race 1 (18 laps, 22.878 miles/36.819km)
1 Sam Warren (Yamaha), 16m 37.479s, 82.59mph/132.92km/h.
2 Alastair Seeley (Suzuki); **3** Ben Wilson (Kawasaki); **4** Luke Stapleford (Kawasaki); **5** Luke Mossey (Triumph); **6** Daniel Cooper (Triumph); **7** Gary Johnson (Honda); **8** Marty Nutt (Suzuki); **9** Billy McConnell (Triumph); **10** Christian Iddon (Triumph); **11** David Paton (Yamaha); **12** Sam Hornsey (Triumph); **13** Pauli Pekkanen (Triumph); **14** Josh Caygill (Triumph); **15** Jonny Buckley (Yamaha).
Fastest lap: Warren, 54.590s, 83.83mph/134.92km/h.

Race 2 (20 laps, 25.420 miles/10.910km)
1 Ben Wilson (Kawasaki), 16m 59.821s, 89.75mph/144.44km/h.
2 Alastair Seeley (Suzuki); **3** Christian Iddon (Triumph); **4** Luke Stapleford (Kawasaki); **5** Paul Young (Triumph); **6** Jesse Trayler (Kawasaki); **7** Luke Mossey (Triumph); **8** Marty Nutt (Suzuki); **9** Daniel Cooper (Triumph); **10** Gary Johnson (Honda); **11** Allann Jon Venter (Triumph); **12** Sam Hornsey (Triumph); **13** Billy McConnell (Triumph); **14** Max Hunt (Honda); **15** John Simpson (Triumph).
Fastest lap: Wilson, 50.025s, 91.48mph/147.23km/h.
Championship points: 1 Wilson, 208; **2** Seeley, 149; **3** Kennedy, 99; **4** McConnell, 97; **5** Young, 97; **6** Warren, 90.

SUNOCO British 125GP Championship, Round 5 (15 laps, 19.065 miles/30.682km)
1 Kyle Ryde (Honda), 14m 2.465s, 81.48mph/131.13km/h.
2 Joe Irving (Honda); **3** Luke Hedger (Honda); **4** Tarran Mackenzie (Honda); **5** Wayne Ryan (Honda); **6** Chrissy Rouse (Honda); **7** Bradley Ray (Honda); **8** Jordan Weaving (Honda); **9** Callum Bey (Honda); **10** Robert English (Honda); **11** Ryan Watson (Seel); **12** Jason Douglas (Honda); **13** Sammi Tasker (Honda); **14** Tom Carne (Honda); **15** Neil Durham (Aprilia).
Fastest lap: Ryde, 55.162s, 82.96mph/133.52km/h.
Championship points: 1 Guiver, 75; **2** Ryde, 65; **3** Hedger, 63; **4** Ryan, 46; **5** Irving, 40; **6** Mackenzie, 37.

SNETTERTON, 3 July, 2.969-mile/4.778km circuit.
MCE Insurance British Superbike Championship, Rounds 11 and 12
Race 1 (17 laps, 50.473 miles/81.228km)
1 John Hopkins (Suzuki), 31m 59.427s, 94.66mph/152.34km/h.
2 Tommy Hill (Yamaha); **3** Shane Byrne (Honda); **4** Michael Laverty (Yamaha); **5** Ryuichi Kiyonari (Honda); **6** Jon Kirkham (Suzuki); **7** Josh Brookes (Suzuki); **8** Chris Walker (Kawasaki); **9** Loris Baz (Yamaha); **10** Peter Hickman (Honda); **11** Gary Mason (Kawasaki); **12** Martin Jessopp (Ducati); **13** Michael Rutter (Ducati); **14** James Westmoreland (Yamaha); **15** Graeme Gowland (Honda).
Fastest lap: Kiyonari, 1m 48.496s, 98.51mph/158.53km/h.

Race 2 (9 laps, 26.721 miles/43.003km)
1 Ryuichi Kiyonari (Honda), 16m 24.190s, 97.73mph/157.28km/h.
2 Josh Brookes (Suzuki); **3** John Hopkins (Suzuki); **4** Shane Byrne (Honda); **5** Michael Laverty (Yamaha); **6** Martin Jessopp (Ducati); **7** Loris Baz (Yamaha); **8** Chris Walker (Kawasaki); **9** Ian Lowry (BMW); **10** Jake Zemke (Honda); **11** Gary Mason (Kawasaki); **12** Dan Linfoot (Honda); **13** Glen Richards (Honda); **14** Barry Burrell (BMW); **15** Patric Muff (Honda).
Fastest lap: Byrne, 1m 48.023s, 98.94mph/159.23km/h.
Championship points: 1 Byrne, 201; **2** Hopkins, 182; **3** Hill, 140; **4** Kiyonari, 120; **5** Laverty, 119; **6** Brookes, 91.

Fuchs-Silkolene British Supersport Championship, Rounds 11 and 12
Race 1 (10 laps, 29.690 miles/47.780 km)
1 Alastair Seeley (Suzuki), 18m 46.382s, 94.88mph/152.70km/h.
2 Ben Wilson (Kawasaki); **3** Luke Mossey (Triumph); **4** Lee Johnston (Honda); **5** Billy McConnell (Triumph); **6** Sam Warren (Yamaha); **7** Allann Jon Venter (Triumph); **8** Paul Young (Triumph); **9** Matthew Whitman (Triumph); **10** Gary Johnson (Honda); **11** Christian Iddon (Triumph); **12** Dean Hipwell (Yamaha); **13** Daniel Cooper (Triumph); **14** Pauli Pekkanen (Triumph); **15** Jesse Trayler (Kawasaki).
Fastest lap: Seeley, 1m 51.579s, 95.78mph/154.15km/h.

Race 2 (15 laps, 44.535 miles/71.672km)
1 Alastair Seeley (Suzuki), 28m 11.261s, 94.79mph/152.77km/h.
2 Ben Wilson (Kawasaki); **3** Luke Mossey (Triumph); **4** Sam Warren (Yamaha); **5** Daniel Cooper (Triumph); **6** Allann Jon Venter (Triumph); **7** Matthew Whitman (Triumph); **8** Lee Johnston (Honda); **9** Paul Young (Triumph); **10** Jesse Trayler (Kawasaki); **11** Luke Stapleford (Kawasaki); **12** Max Hunt (Honda); **13** Billy McConnell (Triumph); **14** John Simpson (Triumph); **15** Matthew Hoyle (Kawasaki).
Fastest lap: Seeley, 1m 51.776s, 95.62mph/153.88km/h.
Championship points: 1 Wilson, 248; **2** Seeley, 199; **3** Warren, 113; **4** Young, 112; **5** McConnell, 111; **6** Mossey, 111.

SUNOCO British 125GP Championship, Round 6 (12 laps, 35.628 miles/57.338km)
1 Wayne Ryan (Honda), 24m 39.475s, 86.69mph/139.51km/h.
2 Rob Guiver (Honda); **3** Ryan Watson (Seel); **4** Lee Jackson (Honda); **5** Luke Hedger (Honda); **6** Kyle Ryde (Honda); **7** Nathan Westwood (Honda); **8** Callum Bey (Honda); **9** Jordan Weaving (Honda); **10** Tom Carne (Honda); **11** Harry Hartley (Honda); **12** Andrew Reid (Aztec); **13** Ian Raybon (Honda); **14** Nigel Percy (Honda); **15** Joe Irving (Honda).
Fastest lap: Ryan, 2m 1.811s, 87.74mph/141.20km/h.
Championship points: 1 Guiver, 95; **2** Ryde, 75; **3** Hedger, 74; **4** Ryan, 71; **5** Watson, 49; **6** Jackson, 48.

OULTON PARK, 17 July, 2.692-mile/4.332km circuit.
MCE Insurance British Superbike Championship, Round 13
Race 1 (15 laps, 43.380 miles/64.985km)
1 Tommy Hill (Yamaha), 28m 36.674s, 84.68mph/136.28km/h.
2 Josh Brookes (Suzuki); **3** Michael Rutter (Ducati); **4** Shane Byrne (Honda); **5** Gary Mason (Kawasaki); **6** Michael Laverty (Yamaha); **7** Loris Baz (Yamaha); **8** James Westmoreland (Yamaha); **9** Jon Kirkham (Suzuki); **10** Scott Smart (Ducati); **11** James Ellison (Honda); **12** Glen Richards (Honda); **13** Alex Lowes (Kawasaki); **14** Chris Walker (Kawasaki); **15** Ryuichi Kiyonari (Honda).
Fastest lap: Hill, 1m 47.622s, 90.04mph/144.92km/h.
Championship points: 1 Byrne, 214; **2** Hopkins, 182; **3** Hill, 165; **4** Laverty, 129; **5** Kiyonari, 121; **6** Brookes, 111.

Race 2
Postponed until Cadwell Park due to weather conditions.

Fuchs-Silkolene British Supersport Championship, Round 13
Race 1 (10 laps, 26.920 miles/43.320km)
1 Billy McConnell (Triumph), 16m 44.494s, 96.47mph/155.25km/h.
2 Ben Wilson (Kawasaki); **3** Alastair Seeley (Suzuki); **4** Paul Young (Triumph); **5** Sam Warren (Yamaha); **6** Daniel Cooper (Triumph); **7** Luke Mossey (Triumph); **8** Matthew Whitman (Triumph); **9** Lee Johnston (Honda); **10** Luke Stapleford (Kawasaki); **11** Christian Iddon (Triumph); **12** Jimmy Hill (Triumph); **13** Allann Jon Venter (Triumph); **14** Pauli Pekkanen (Triumph); **15** Dean Hipwell (Yamaha).
Fastest lap: Wilson, 1m 38.859s, 98.03mph/157.76km/h.
Championship points: 1 Wilson, 268; **2** Seeley, 215; **3** McConnell, 137; **4** Young, 125; **5** Warren, 124; **6** Mossey, 120.

Race 2
Postponed until the Brands Hatch GP season finale due to weather conditions.

SUNOCO British 125GP Championship, Round 7 (8 laps, 21.536 miles/34.659km)
1 Matt Davies (Honda), 16m 53.305s, 76.51mph/123.13km/h.
2 Wayne Ryan (Honda); **3** Rob Guiver (Honda); **4** Jason Douglas (Honda); **5** Ian Raybon (Honda); **6** Joe Irving (Honda); **7** Bradley Ray (Aztec); **8** Lee Jackson (Honda); **9** Luke Hedger (Honda); **10** Jordan Weaving (Honda); **11** Tom Carne (Honda); **12** Bryn Owen (Honda); **13** Ryan Watson (Seel); **14** Robert English (Honda); **15** Tommy Philp (Honda).

Fastest lap: Davies, 2m 2.783s, 78.93mph/127.02km/h.
Championship points: **1** Guiver, 111; **2** Ryan, 91; **3** Hedger, 81; **4** Ryde, 75; **5** Jackson, 56; **6** Davies, 54.

BRANDS HATCH GP, 6–7 August, 2.433-mile/3.916km circuit.
MCE Insurance British Superbike Championship, Rounds 14, 15 and 16 Race 1 (15 laps, 36.495 miles/58.733km)
1 Josh Brookes (Suzuki), 22m 53.718s, 95.65mph/153.93km/h.
2 Michael Rutter (Ducati); **3** Gary Mason (Kawasaki); **4** John Hopkins (Suzuki); **5** Chris Walker (Kawasaki); **6** James Westmoreland (Yamaha); **7** Graeme Gowland (Honda); **8** Michael Laverty (Yamaha); **9** Jon Kirkham (Suzuki); **10** Glen Richards (Honda); **11** Ian Lowry (BMW); **12** Patric Muff (Honda); **13** Dan Kneen (Kawasaki); **14** Jake Zemke (Honda); **15** Barry Burrell (BMW).
Fastest lap: Hill, 1m 26.459s, 101.31mph/163.05km/h.

Race 2 (20 laps, 48.660 miles/78.311km)
1 Shane Byrne (Honda), 29m 1.030s, 100.62mph/161.93km/h.
2 Tommy Hill (Yamaha); **3** John Hopkins (Suzuki); **4** Michael Laverty (Yamaha); **5** Michael Rutter (Ducati); **6** Josh Brookes (Suzuki); **7** Joan Lascorz (Kawasaki); **8** Jon Kirkham (Suzuki); **9** Martin Jessopp (Ducati); **10** Peter Hickman (Honda); **11** Graeme Gowland (Honda); **12** Ryuichi Kiyonari (Honda); **13** Broc Parkes (Kawasaki); **14** Glen Richards (Honda); **15** Chris Walker (Kawasaki).
Fastest lap: Hill, 1m 26.460s, 101.31mph/163.05km/h.

Race 3 (20 laps, 48.660 miles/78.311km)
1 Tommy Hill (Yamaha), 28m 55.830s, 100.92mph/162.42km/h.
2 John Hopkins (Suzuki); **3** Shane Byrne (Honda); **4** Michael Laverty (Yamaha); **5** Michael Rutter (Ducati); **6** Ryuichi Kiyonari (Honda); **7** Gary Mason (Kawasaki); **8** Joan Lascorz (Kawasaki); **9** Peter Hickman (Honda); **10** Jon Kirkham (Suzuki); **11** Graeme Gowland (Honda); **12** Broc Parkes (Kawasaki); **13** James Ellison (Honda); **14** James Westmoreland (Yamaha); **15** Chris Walker (Kawasaki).
Fastest lap: Hopkins, 1m 26.163s, 101.66mph/163.61km/h.
Championship points: **1** Byrne, 255; **2** Hopkins, 231; **3** Hill, 210; **4** Laverty, 163; **5** Brookes, 146; **6** Kiyonari, 135.

Fuchs-Silkolene British Supersport Championship, Rounds 14 and 15
Race 1 (10 laps, 24.330 miles/39.155km)
1 Alastair Seeley (Suzuki), 15m 29.311s, 94.26mph/151.70km/h.
2 Ben Wilson (Kawasaki); **3** Sam Warren (Yamaha); **4** Jimmy Hill (Triumph); **5** Billy McConnell (Triumph); **6** Luke Mossey (Triumph); **7** Daniel Cooper (Triumph); **8** Matthew Whitman (Triumph); **9** Jack Kennedy (Yamaha); **10** Pauli Pekkanen (Triumph); **11** Paul Young (Triumph); **12** Max Hunt (Honda); **13** Lee Johnston (Honda); **14** Allann Jon Venter (Triumph); **15** John Simpson (Triumph).
Fastest lap: Wilson, 1m 28.464s, 99.02mph/159.35km/h.

Race 2 (12 laps, 29.196 miles/46.986km)
1 Alastair Seeley (Suzuki), 17m 56.450s, 97.65mph/157.15km/h.
2 Ben Wilson (Kawasaki); **3** Matthew Whitman (Triumph); **4** Jack Kennedy (Yamaha); **5** Paul Young (Triumph); **6** Christian Iddon (Triumph); **7** Pauli Pekkanen (Triumph); **8** Allann Jon Venter (Triumph); **9** Luke Stapleford (Kawasaki); **10** Marty Nutt (Suzuki); **11** John Simpson (Triumph); **12** Sam Hornsey (Suzuki); **13** Adam Blacklock (Yamaha); **14** David Paton (Yamaha); **15** Jenny Tinmouth (Honda).
Fastest lap: Seeley, 1m 28.901s, 98.53mph/158.57km/h.
Championship points: **1** Wilson, 308; **2** Seeley, 265; **3** McConnell, 148; **4** Young, 141; **5** Warren, 140; **6** Mossey, 130.

SUNOCO British 125GP Championship, Round 8 (11 laps, 26.763 miles/43.071km)
1 Kyle Ryde (Honda), 17m 43.881s, 90.57mph/145.76km/h.
2 Wayne Ryan (Honda); **3** Rob Guiver (Honda); **4** Luke Hedger (Honda); **5** Lee Jackson (Honda); **6** Joe Irving (Honda); **7** Jordan Weaving (Honda); **8** Callum Bey (Honda); **9** Chrissy Rouse (Honda); **10** Harry Hartley (Honda); **11** Nathan Westwood (Honda); **12** Callan Cooper (Honda); **13** Robert English (Honda); **14** Ian Raybon (Honda); **15** Josh Corner (Honda).
Fastest lap: Ryde, 1m 35.634s, 91.59mph/147.41km/h.
Championship points: **1** Guiver, 127; **2** Ryan, 111; **3** Ryde, 100; **4** Hedger, 94; **5** Jackson, 67; **6** Irving, 61.

CADWELL PARK, 28–29 August, 2.180-mile/3.508km circuit.
MCE Insurance British Superbike Championship, Rounds 17, 18 and 19
Race 1 (11 laps, 23.980 miles/38.592km)
1 Michael Laverty (Yamaha), 16m 13.225s, 88.70mph/142.75km/h.
2 Tommy Hill (Yamaha); **3** Shane Byrne (Honda); **4** Jon Kirkham (Suzuki); **5** Ryuichi Kiyonari (Honda); **6** Gary Mason (Kawasaki); **7** Martin Jessopp (Ducati); **8** Peter Hickman (Honda); **9** Glen Richards (Honda); **10** Chris Walker (Kawasaki); **11** Graeme Gowland (Honda); **12** Alex Lowes (Kawasaki); **13** James Ellison (Honda); **14** Scott Smart (Ducati); **15** Karl Harris (Aprilia).
Fastest lap: Hill, 1m 27.670s, 89.51mph/144.06km/h.

Race 2 (18 laps, 39.240 miles/63.144 km)
1 Tommy Hill (Yamaha), 26m 23.316s, 89.22mph/143.59km/h.
2 Michael Laverty (Yamaha); **3** Shane Byrne (Honda); **4** Josh Brookes (Suzuki); **5** Peter Hickman (Honda); **6** Jon Kirkham (Suzuki); **7** Martin Jessopp (Ducati); **8** Graeme Gowland (Honda); **9** Ryuichi Kiyonari (Honda); **10** Gary Mason (Kawasaki); **11** James Ellison (Honda); **12** Scott Smart (Ducati); **13** Glen Richards (Honda); **14** Karl Harris (Aprilia); **15** Barry Burrell (BMW).
Fastest lap: Laverty, 1m 27.221s, 89.97mph/144.80km/h.

Race 3 (15 laps, 32.700 miles/52.626km)
1 Tommy Hill (Yamaha), 22m 0.965s, 89.11mph/143.41km/h.
2 Josh Brookes (Suzuki); **3** Michael Laverty (Yamaha); **4** Shane Byrne (Honda); **5** Peter Hickman (Honda); **6** Jon Kirkham (Suzuki); **7** Ryuichi Kiyonari (Honda); **8** Martin Jessopp (Ducati); **9** Graeme Gowland (Honda); **10** James Ellison (Honda); **11** Tommy Bridewell (Yamaha); **12** Gary Mason (Kawasaki); **13** Scott Smart (Ducati); **14** Glen Richards (Honda); **15** Karl Harris (Aprilia).
Fastest lap: Hill, 1m 27.166s, 90.03mph/144.89km/h.

The top six BSB riders in points after Cadwell Park qualified for The Showdown, to decide the championship over the last three rounds. These six Title Fighters had their points equalised at 500 and then individual podium credits added (3 points for each 1st place, 2 points for 2nd, 1 point for 3rd).

Championship points for start of Showdown: **1** Hill, 529; **2** Byrne, 522; **3** Hopkins, 518; **4** Laverty, 510; **5** Brookes, 509; **6** Kiyonari, 508.

Fuchs-Silkolene British Supersport Championship, Rounds 16 and 17
Race 1 (12 laps, 26.160 miles/42.100km)
1 Ben Wilson (Kawasaki), 18m 9.262s, 86.45mph/139.13km/h.
2 Alastair Seeley (Suzuki); **3** Billy McConnell (Triumph); **4** Christian Iddon (Triumph); **5** Sam Warren (Yamaha); **6** Allann Jon Venter (Triumph); **7** Gary Johnson (Honda); **8** Luke Stapleford (Kawasaki); **9** Jimmy Hill (Triumph); **10** Pauli Pekkanen (Triumph); **11** Paul Young (Triumph); **12** Anthony Rogers (Yamaha); **13** John Simpson (Triumph); **14** Marty Nutt (Suzuki); **15** David Jones (Kawasaki).
Fastest lap: Wilson, 1m 29.569s, 87.62mph/141.01km/h.

Race 2 (14 laps, 30.520 miles/49.117km)
1 Ben Wilson (Kawasaki), 21m 0.762s, 87.14mph/140.24km/h.
2 Alastair Seeley (Suzuki); **3** Billy McConnell (Triumph); **4** Christian Iddon (Triumph); **5** Gary Johnson (Honda); **6** Jimmy Hill (Triumph); **7** Jack Kennedy (Yamaha); **8** Allann Jon Venter (Triumph); **9** Marty Nutt (Suzuki); **10** Paul Young (Triumph); **11** Luke Stapleford (Kawasaki); **12** Josh Day (Triumph); **13** Anthony Rogers (Yamaha); **14** Shaun Winfield (Triumph); **15** Adam Blacklock (Yamaha).
Fastest lap: Wilson, 1m 29.437s, 87.74mph/141.21km/h.
Championship points: **1** Wilson, 358; **2** Seeley, 305; **3** McConnell, 180; **4** Young, 152; **5** Warren, 151; **6** Mossey, 130.

SUNOCO British 125GP Championship, Round 9 (12 laps, 26.160 miles/42.100km)
1 Kyle Ryde (Honda), 18m 58.519s, 82.71mph/133.11km/h.
2 Wayne Ryan (Honda); **3** Ryan Watson (Seel); **4** Lee Jackson (Honda); **5** Tom Carne (Honda); **6** Bradley Ray (Honda); **7** Philip Wakefield (Seel); **8** Callan Cooper (Honda); **9** Nathan Westwood (Honda); **10** Joe Irving (Honda); **11** Nigel Percy (Honda); **12** Bradley Hughes (Honda); **13** Catherine Green (Honda); **14** Jordan Weaving (Honda); **15** Callum Bey (Honda).
Fastest lap: Ryde, 1m 34.270s, 83.25mph/133.97km/h.
Championship points: **1** Ryan, 131; **2** Guiver, 127; **3** Ryde, 125; **4** Hedger, 94; **5** Jackson, 80; **6** Watson, 68.

DONINGTON PARK, 11 September, 2.487-mile/3.508km circuit.
MCE Insurance British Superbike Championship, Rounds 20 and 21 (2 x 20 laps, 49.740 miles/80.049km)
Race 1
1 John Hopkins (Suzuki), 30m 17.023s, 98.56mph/158.62km/h.
2 Michael Laverty (Yamaha); **3** Tommy Hill (Yamaha); **4** Shane Byrne (Honda); **5** Jon Kirkham (Suzuki); **6** Josh Brookes (Suzuki); **7** Peter Hickman (Honda); **8** James Ellison (Honda); **9** Martin Jessopp (Ducati); **10** Graeme Gowland (Honda); **11** James Westmoreland (Honda); **12** Ian Lowry (Kawasaki); **13** Glen Richards (Honda); **14** Tommy Bridewell (Yamaha); **15** Barry Burrell (BMW).
Fastest lap: Hopkins, 1m 30.109s, 99.37mph/159.92km/h.

Race 2
1 John Hopkins (Suzuki), 30m 15.777s, 98.62mph/158.71km/h.
2 Tommy Hill (Yamaha); **3** Jon Kirkham (Suzuki); **4** Martin Jessopp (Ducati); **5** Josh Brookes (Suzuki); **6** Ryuichi Kiyonari (Honda); **7** James Ellison (Honda); **8** Shane Byrne (Honda); **9** Chris Walker (Kawasaki); **10** Graeme Gowland (Honda); **11** Tommy Bridewell (Yamaha); **12** James Westmoreland (Honda); **13** Barry Burrell (BMW); **14** Michael Laverty (Yamaha); **15** Glen Richards (Honda).
Fastest lap: M. Laverty, 1m 29.680s, 99.84mph/160.69km/h.
Championship points: **1** Hopkins, 568; **2** Hill, 565; **3** Byrne, 543; **4** Laverty, 532; **5** Brookes, 530; **6** Kiyonari, 518.

Fuchs-Silkolene British Supersport Championship, Rounds 18 and 19
Race 1 (12 laps, 29.844 miles/48.029km)
1 Alastair Seeley (Suzuki), 18m 44.449s, 95.56mph/153.79km/h.
2 Ben Wilson (Kawasaki); **3** Christian Iddon (Triumph); **4** Paul Young (Triumph); **5** Jack Kennedy (Yamaha); **6** Jimmy Hill (Triumph); **7** Billy McConnell (Triumph); **8** Luke Stapleford (Kawasaki); **9** Josh Day (Triumph); **10** Gary Johnson (Honda); **11** David Paton (Yamaha); **12** John Simpson (Triumph); **13** Jenny Tinmouth (Honda); **14** Marty Nutt (Suzuki); **15** Allann Jon Venter (Triumph).
Fastest lap: Seeley, 1m 32.750s, 96.54mph/155.37km/h.

Race 2 (4 laps, 9.948 miles/16.010km)
1 Alastair Seeley (Suzuki), 6m 15.486s, 95.39mph/153.52km/h.
2 Christian Iddon (Triumph); **3** Paul Young (Triumph); **4** Ben Wilson (Kawasaki); **5** Billy McConnell (Triumph); **6** Jimmy Hill (Triumph); **7** Pauli Pekkanen (Triumph); **8** Luke Stapleford (Kawasaki); **9** Allann Jon Venter (Triumph); **10** Gary Johnson (Honda); **11** Jenny Tinmouth (Honda); **12** Sam Hornsey (Suzuki); **13** Josh Day (Triumph); **14** John Simpson (Triumph); **15** David Jones (Kawasaki).
Fastest lap: Seeley, 1m 32.682s, 96.61mph/155.48km/h.
Championship points: **1** Wilson, 391; **2** Seeley, 355; **3** McConnell, 200; **4** Young, 181; **5** Warren, 151; **6** Kennedy, 139.

SUNOCO British 125GP Championship, Round 10 (14 laps, 34.818 miles/56.034km)
1 Kyle Ryde (Honda), 23m 39.650s, 88.30mph/142.11km/h.
2 Bradley Ray (Honda); **3** Rob Guiver (Honda); **4** Wayne Ryan (Honda); **5** Luke Hedger (Honda); **6** Jordan Weaving (Honda); **7** Lee Jackson (Honda); **8** Philip Wakefield (Seel); **9** Callum Bey (Honda); **10** Ryan Watson (Seel); **11** Robert English (Honda); **12** Chrissy Rouse (Honda); **13** Tarran Mackenzie (Honda); **14** Tom Carne (Honda); **15** Nathan Westwood (Honda).
Fastest lap: Ryde, 1m 40.122s, 89.43mph/143.93km/h.
Championship points: **1** Ryde, 150; **2** Ryan, 144; **3** Guiver, 143; **4** Hedger, 105; **5** Jackson, 89; **6** Watson, 74.

SILVERSTONE, 25 September, 3.667-mile/5.902km circuit.
MCE Insurance British Superbike Championship, Rounds 22 and 23
Race 1 (14 laps, 51.338 miles/82.621km)
1 John Hopkins (Suzuki), 29m 46.200s, 103.47mph/166.52km/h.
2 Michael Laverty (Yamaha); **3** Tommy Hill (Yamaha); **4** Josh Brookes (Suzuki); **5** Shane Byrne (Honda); **6** Graeme Gowland (Honda); **7** Alex Lowes (Yamaha); **8** Michael Rutter (Ducati); **9** Martin Jessopp (Ducati); **10** Tommy Bridewell (Yamaha); **11** Ian Lowry (Kawasaki); **12** James Westmoreland (Honda); **13** Glen Richards (Honda); **14** Gary Mason (Kawasaki); **15** Dan Linfoot (Honda).
Fastest lap: Brookes, 2m 6.253s, 104.57mph/168.29km/h.

Race 2 (13 laps, 47.671 miles/76.719km)
1 Josh Brookes (Suzuki), 27m 44.338s, 103.12mph/165.96km/h.
2 Tommy Hill (Yamaha); **3** John Hopkins (Suzuki); **4** Michael Laverty (Yamaha); **5** Shane Byrne (Honda); **6** Jon Kirkham (Suzuki); **7** Peter Hickman (Honda); **8** Michael Rutter (Ducati); **9** Tommy Bridewell (Yamaha); **10** Dan Linfoot (Honda); **11** Graeme Gowland (Honda); **12** Alex Lowes (Yamaha); **13** Ryuichi Kiyonari (Honda); **14** Gary Mason (Kawasaki); **15** Ian Lowry (Kawasaki).
Fastest lap: Brookes, 2m 6.698s, 104.20mph/167.69km/h.
Championship points: **1** Hopkins, 609; **2** Hill, 601; **3** Brookes, 568; **4** Byrne, 565; **5** Laverty, 565; **6** Kiyonari, 521.

Fuchs-Silkolene British Supersport Championship, Round 20 and 21
Race 1 (9 laps, 33.003 miles/53.113km)
1 Alastair Seeley (Suzuki), 19m 49.381s, 99.90mph/160.77km/h.
2 Luke Mossey (Triumph); **3** Sam Warren (Yamaha); **4** Christian Iddon (Triumph); **5** Paul Young (Triumph); **6** Billy McConnell (Triumph); **7** Jack Kennedy (Yamaha); **8** Matthew Whitman (Triumph); **9** Allann Jon Venter (Triumph); **10** Josh Day (Triumph); **11** Luke Stapleford (Kawasaki); **12** Marty Nutt (Honda); **13** Jimmy Hill (Triumph); **14** John Simpson (Triumph); **15** Jenny Tinmouth (Honda).
Fastest lap: Young, 2m 11.273s, 100.57mph/161.85km/h.

Race 2 (12 laps, 44.004 miles/70.818km)
1 Alastair Seeley (Suzuki), 26m 26.349s, 99.87mph/160.73km/h.
2 Christian Iddon (Triumph); **3** Paul Young (Triumph); **4** Luke Mossey (Triumph); **5** Matthew Whitman (Triumph); **6** Billy McConnell (Triumph); **7** Luke Stapleford (Kawasaki); **8** Jimmy Hill (Triumph); **9** Allann Jon Venter (Triumph); **10** John Simpson (Triumph); **11** Gary Johnson (Honda); **12** Jenny Tinmouth (Honda); **13** David Jones (Kawasaki); **14** Sam Hornsey (Suzuki); **15** James Webb (Kawasaki).
Fastest lap: Warren, 2m 11.436s, 100.44mph/161.65km/h.
Championship points: **1** Seeley, 405; **2** Wilson, 391; **3** McConnell, 220; **4** Young, 208; **5** Warren, 167; **6** Mossey, 163.

SUNOCO British 125GP Championship, Round 11 (10 laps, 36.670 miles/59.015km)
1 Kyle Ryde (Honda), 23m 22.837s, 94.11mph/151.46km/h.
2 Wayne Ryan (Aprilia); **3** Rob Guiver (Honda); **4** Philip Wakefield (Seel); **5** Luke Hedger (Honda); **6** Bradley Ray (Honda); **7** Tom Carne (Honda); **8** Jordan Weaving (Honda); **9** Chrissy Rouse (Honda); **10** Nathan Westwood (Honda); **11** Callan Cooper (Honda); **12** Tarran Mackenzie (Honda); **13** Ryan Watson (Seel); **14** Elliot Lodge (Honda); **15** Arnie Shelton (Honda).
Fastest lap: Ryan, 2m 19.170s, 94.86mph/152.67km/h.
Championship points: **1** Ryde, 175; **2** Ryan, 164; **3** Guiver, 159; **4** Hedger, 116; **5** Jackson, 89; **6** Ray, 79.

BRANDS HATCH GP, 8–9 October, 2.433-mile/3.9126km circuit.
MCE Insurance British Superbike Championship, Rounds 24, 25 and 26 Race 1 (16 laps, 38.928 miles/62.649km)
1 Michael Laverty (Yamaha), 22m 58.539s, 101.67mph/163.62km/h.
2 Josh Brookes (Suzuki); **3** John Hopkins (Suzuki); **4** Tommy Hill (Yamaha); **5** James Ellison (Honda); **6** Shane Byrne (Honda); **7** Michael Rutter (Ducati); **8** Jon Kirkham (Suzuki); **9** Graeme Gowland (Honda); **10** Martin Jessopp (Ducati); **11** Tommy Bridewell (Yamaha); **12** Chris Walker (Kawasaki); **13** Ian Lowry (Kawasaki); **14** James Westmoreland (Honda); **15** Alex Lowes (Yamaha).
Fastest lap: Brookes, 1m 25.426s, 102.54mph/165.02km/h.

Race 2 (20 laps, 48.660 miles/78.311km)
1 Shane Byrne (Honda), 29m 33.994s, 98.75mph/158.92km/h.
2 Jon Kirkham (Suzuki); **3** James Ellison (Honda); **4** Tommy Hill (Yamaha); **5** Chris Walker

(Kawasaki); **6** Graeme Gowland (Honda); **7** Tommy Bridewell (Yamaha); **8** James Westmoreland (Honda); **9** Dan Linfoot (Honda); **10** Karl Harris (Aprilia); **11** Patric Muff (Honda); **12** John Hopkins (Suzuki); **13** Scott Smart (Ducati); **14** Peter Hickman (Honda); **15** James Hillier (Kawasaki).
Fastest lap: Byrne, 1m 27.107s, 100.56mph/161.84km/h.

Race 3 (20 laps, 48.660 miles/78.311km)
1 Shane Byrne (Honda), 29m 0.123s, 100.68mph/162.03km/h.
2 Tommy Hill (Yamaha); **3** John Hopkins (Suzuki); **4** James Ellison (Honda); **5** Michael Laverty (Yamaha); **6** Josh Brookes (Suzuki); **7** Michael Rutter (Ducati); **8** Graeme Gowland (Honda); **9** Peter Hickman (Honda); **10** James Westmoreland (Honda); **11** Ryuichi Kiyonari (Honda); **12** Tommy Bridewell (Yamaha); **13** Martin Jessopp (Ducati); **14** Barry Burrell (BMW); **15** Scott Smart (Ducati).
Fastest lap: Brookes, 1m 26.163s, 101.66mph/163.61km/h.

Fuchs-Silkolene British Supersport Championship, Rounds 22, 23 and 24
Race 1 (10 laps, 24.330 miles/39.155km)
1 Ben Wilson (Kawasaki), 14m 59.162s, 97.42mph/156.78km/h.
2 Sam Warren (Yamaha); **3** Billy McConnell (Triumph); **4** Christian Iddon (Triumph); **5** Paul Young (Triumph); **6** Luke Mossey (Triumph); **7** Pauli Pekkanen (Triumph); **8** Matthew Whitman (Triumph); **9** Jimmy Hill (Triumph); **10** Allann Jon Venter (Triumph); **11** Marty Nutt (Honda); **12** Luke Stapleford (Kawasaki); **13** David Paton (Yamaha); **14** Paul Curran (Triumph); **15** Sam Hornsey (Suzuki).
Fastest lap: Seeley, 1m 28.085s, 99.44mph/160.04km/h.

Race 2 (12 laps, 29.196 miles/46.986km)
1 Jack Kennedy (Yamaha), 19m 6.061s, 91.72mph/147.61km/h.
2 Alastair Seeley (Suzuki); **3** Christian Iddon (Triumph); **4** Ben Wilson (Kawasaki); **5** Paul Young (Triumph); **6** Daniel Cooper (Triumph); **7** Billy McConnell (Triumph); **8** Luke Stapleford (Kawasaki); **9** Josh Day (Triumph); **10** Marty Nutt (Honda); **11** Matthew Whitman (Triumph); **12** Jenny Tinmouth (Honda); **13** Jess Trayler (Suzuki); **14** Pauli Pekkanen (Triumph); **15** David Paton (Yamaha).
Fastest lap: Iddon, 1m 31.669s, 95.55mph/153.78km/h.

Race 3 (12 laps, 29.196 miles/46.986km)
1 Alastair Seeley (Suzuki), 17m 52.915s, 97.97mph/157.67km/h.
2 Ben Wilson (Kawasaki); **3** Jack Kennedy (Yamaha); **4** Christian Iddon (Triumph); **5** Luke Stapleford (Kawasaki); **6** Pauli Pekkanen (Triumph); **7** Billy McConnell (Triumph); **8** Matthew Whitman (Triumph); **9** Paul Young (Triumph); **10** Daniel Cooper (Triumph); **11** Luke Mossey (Triumph); **12** Sam Warren (Yamaha); **13** Marty Nutt (Honda); **14** Allann Jon Venter (Triumph); **15** Jess Trayler (Suzuki).
Fastest lap: Seeley, 1m 28.213s, 99.30mph/159.81km/h.

SUNOCO British 125GP Championship, Round 12 (9 laps, 21.897 miles/35.240km)
1 Wayne Ryan (Aprilia), 14m 35.485s, 90.05mph/144.92km/h.
2 Rob Guiver (Honda); **3** Kyle Ryde (Honda); **4** Luke Hedger (Honda); **5** Bradley Ray (Honda); **6** Ryan Watson (Seel); **7** Philip Wakefield (Seel); **8** Joe Irving (Honda); **9** Jordan Weaving (Honda); **10** Callum Bey (Honda); **11** Lee Jackson (Honda); **12** Callan Cooper (Honda); **13** Nathan Westwood (Honda); **14** Catherine Green (Honda); **15** Josh Corner (Honda).
Fastest lap: Ryan, 1m 35.725s, 91.51mph/147.27km/h.

Final British Superbike Championship points:

1	Tommy Hill	647
2	John Hopkins	645
3	Shane Byrne	625
4	Michael Laverty	601
5	Josh Brookes	598
6	Ryuichi Kiyonari	526

7 Jon Kirkham, 210; **8** Michael Rutter, 164; **9** Peter Hickman, 155; **10** Gary Mason, 139; **11** Martin Jessopp, 110; **12** Chris Walker, 105; **13** Graeme Gowland, 92; **14** Loris Baz, 88; **15** James Westmoreland, 88.

Final British Supersport Championship points:

1	Alastair Seeley	450
2	Ben Wilson	449
3	Billy McConnell	254
4	Paul Young	237
5	Sam Warren	191
6	Christian Iddon	191

7 Jack Kennedy, 189; **8** Luke Mossey, 178; **9** Daniel Cooper, 131; **10** Luke Stapleford, 129; **11** Allann Jon Venter, 123; **12** Matthew Whitman, 105; **13** Gary Johnson, 103; **14** Jimmy Hill, 89; **15** Steve Plater, 80.

Final British 125GP Championship points:

1	Kyle Ryde	191
2	Wayne Ryan	189
3	Rob Guiver	179
4	Luke Hedger	129
5	Lee Jackson	94
6	Bradley Ray	90

7 Ryan Watson, 87; **8** Joe Irving, 75; **9** Jordan Weaving, 75; **10** Philip Wakefield, 70; **11** Matt Davies, 54; **12** Tom Carne, 49; **13** Tarran Mackenzie, 44; **14** Harry Hartley, 41; **15** Chrissy Rouse, 37.

Supersport World Championship

PHILLIP ISLAND, Australia, 27 February, 2.762-mile/4.445km circuit.
Supersport World Championship, Round 1 (21 laps, 58.002 miles/93.345km)
1 Luca Scassa, ITA (Yamaha), 33m 34.739s, 103.640mph/166.792km/h.
2 Broc Parkes, AUS (Kawasaki); **3** Sam Lowes, GBR (Honda); **4** David Salom, ESP (Kawasaki); **5** Robbin Harms, DEN (Honda); **6** James Ellison, GBR (Honda); **7** Florian Marino, FRA (Honda); **8** Vittorio Iannuzzo, ITA (Kawasaki); **9** Alexander Lundh, SWE (Honda); **10** Danilo Dell'Omo, ITA (Triumph); **11** Ronan Quarmby, RSA (Triumph); **12** Ondrej Jezek, CZE (Honda); **13** Bastien Chesaux, SUI (Honda); **14** Balazs Nemeth, HUN (Honda); **15** Imre Toth, HUN (Honda).
Fastest lap: Fabien Foret, FRA (Honda), 1m 34.941s, 104.730mph/168.547km/h (record).
Championship points: **1** Scassa, 25; **2** Parkes, 20; **3** Lowes, 16; **4** Salom, 13; **5** Harms, 11; **6** Ellison, 10.

DONINGTON PARK, Great Britain, 27 March, 2.500-mile/4.023km circuit.
Supersport World Championship, Round 2 (22 laps, 54.995 miles/88.506km)
1 Luca Scassa, ITA (Yamaha), 33m 40.762s, 97.974mph/157.674km/h.
2 Chaz Davies, GBR (Yamaha); **3** Gino Rea, GBR (Honda); **4** Robbin Harms, DEN (Honda); **5** Broc Parkes, AUS (Kawasaki); **6** David Salom, ESP (Kawasaki); **7** Massimo Roccoli, ITA (Kawasaki); **8** Florian Marino, FRA (Honda); **9** Vittorio Iannuzzo, ITA (Kawasaki); **10** Alexander Lundh, SWE (Honda); **11** Miguel Praia, POR (Honda); **12** Roberto Tamburini, ITA (Yamaha); **13** Ondrej Jezek, CZE (Honda); **14** Balazs Nemeth, HUN (Honda); **15** Marko Jerman, SLO (Triumph).
Fastest lap: Sam Lowes, GBR (Honda), 1m 31.094s, 98.790mph/158.987km/h (record).
Championship points: **1** Scassa, 50; **2** Parkes, 31; **3** Harms, 24; **4** Salom, 23; **5** Davies, 20; **6** Marino, 17.

ASSEN, Holland, 17 April, 2.822-mile/4.542km circuit.
Supersport World Championship, Round 3 (16 laps, 45.156 miles/72.672km)
1 Chaz Davies, GBR (Yamaha), 26m 37.029s, 101.791mph/163.816km/h.
2 Fabien Foret, FRA (Honda); **3** Broc Parkes, AUS (Kawasaki); **4** Robbin Harms, DEN (Honda); **5** David Salom, ESP (Kawasaki); **6** Massimo Roccoli, ITA (Kawasaki); **7** James Ellison, GBR (Honda); **8** Miguel Praia, POR (Honda); **9** Vladimir Ivanov, UKR (Honda); **10** Balazs Nemeth, HUN (Honda); **11** Imre Toth, HUN (Honda); **12** Pawel Szkopek, POL (Honda); **13** Bastien Chesaux, SUI (Honda); **14** Danilo Dell'Omo, ITA (Triumph); **15** Robert Muresan, ROU (Honda).
Fastest lap: Luca Scassa, ITA (Yamaha), 1m 39.019s, 102.608mph/165.132km/h.
Championship points: **1** Scassa, 50; 2 Parkes, 47; **3** Davies, 45; **4** Harms, 37; **5** Salom, 34; **6** Foret, 20.

MONZA, Italy, 8 May, 3.590-mile/5.777km circuit.
Supersport World Championship, Round 4 (16 laps, 57.435 miles/92.432km)
1 Chaz Davies, GBR (Yamaha), 29m 5.363s, 118.465mph/190.651km/h.
2 Luca Scassa, ITA (Yamaha); **3** Fabien Foret, FRA (Honda); **4** Broc Parkes, AUS (Kawasaki); **5** Sam Lowes, GBR (Honda); **6** Roberto Tamburini, ITA (Yamaha); **7** Florian Marino, FRA (Honda); **8** David Salom, ESP (Kawasaki); **9** Massimo Roccoli, ITA (Kawasaki); **10** Robbin Harms, DEN (Honda); **11** Danilo Dell'Omo, ITA (Triumph); **12** Mirko Giansanti, ITA (Kawasaki); **13** Marko Jerman, SLO (Triumph); **14** Balazs Nemeth, HUN (Honda); **15** Luca Marconi, ITA (Yamaha).
Fastest lap: Chaz Davies, GBR (Yamaha), 1m 48.526s, 119.075mph/191.633km/h.
Championship points: **1** Davies, 70; 2 Scassa, 70; **3** Parkes, 60; **4** Harms, 43; **5** Salom, 42; **6** Foret, 36.

MISANO, Italy, 12 June, 2.623-mile/4.226km circuit.
Supersport World Championship, Round 5 (22 laps, 57.770 miles/92.972km)
1 Broc Parkes, AUS (Kawasaki), 37m 0.851s, 93.646mph/150.708km/h.
2 Fabien Foret, FRA (Honda); **3** Sam Lowes, GBR (Honda); **4** David Salom, ESP (Kawasaki); **5** Ilario Dionisi, ITA (Honda); **6** Chaz Davies, GBR (Yamaha); **7** James Ellison, GBR (Honda); **8** Robbin Harms, DEN (Honda); **9** Roberto Tamburini, ITA (Yamaha); **10** Gino Rea, GBR (Honda); **11** Florian Marino, FRA (Honda); **12** Miguel Praia, POR (Honda); **13** Alessio Velini, ITA (Honda); **14** Roman Stamm, SUI (Honda); **15** Alexander Lundh, SWE (Honda).
Fastest lap: Fabien Foret, FRA (Honda), 1m 40.054s, 94.482mph/152.054km/h.
Championship points: **1** Parkes, 85; **2** Davies, 80; **3** Scassa, 70; **4** Foret, 56; **5** Salom, 55; **6** Harms, 51.

ARAGON, Spain, 19 June, 3.321-mile/5.344km circuit.
Supersport World Championship, Round 6 (18 laps, 59.771 miles/96.192km)
1 Chaz Davies, GBR (Yamaha), 37m 6.751s, 96.632mph/155.514km/h.
2 Sam Lowes, GBR (Honda); **3** David Salom, ESP (Kawasaki); **4** Massimo Roccoli, ITA (Kawasaki); **5** Roberto Tamburini, ITA (Yamaha); **6** Gino Rea, GBR (Honda); **7** Fabien Foret, FRA (Honda); **8** Robbin Harms, DEN (Honda); **9** Miguel Praia, POR (Honda); **10** Florian Marino, FRA (Honda); **11** Vladimir Ivanov, UKR (Honda); **12** Balazs Nemeth, HUN (Honda); **13** Pawel Szkopek, POL (Honda); **14** Danilo Dell'Omo, ITA (Triumph); **15** Imre Toth, HUN (Honda).
Fastest lap: Sam Lowes, GBR (Honda), 2m 2.785s, 97.359mph/156.684km/h (record).
Championship points: **1** Davies, 105; **2** Parkes, 85; **3** Salom, 71; **4** Scassa, 70; **5** Foret, 65; **6** Lowes, 63.

BRNO, Czech Republic, 10 July, 3.357-mile/5.403km circuit.
Supersport World Championship, Round 7 (15 laps, 50.359 miles/81.045km)
1 Gino Rea, GBR (Honda), 31m 21.642s, 96.348mph/155.057km/h.
2 Fabien Foret, FRA (Honda); **3** Chaz Davies, GBR (Yamaha); **4** David Salom, ESP (Kawasaki); **5** Roberto Tamburini, ITA (Yamaha); **6** Sam Lowes, GBR (Honda); **7** Luca Scassa, ITA (Yamaha); **8** James Ellison, GBR (Honda); **9** Florian Marino, FRA (Honda); **10** Vittorio Iannuzzo, ITA (Kawasaki); **11** Danilo Dell'Omo, ITA (Triumph); **12** Alexander Lundh, SWE (Honda); **13** Imre Toth, HUN (Honda); **14** Luca Marconi, ITA (Yamaha); **15** Massimo Roccoli, ITA (Kawasaki).
Fastest lap: Gino Rea, GBR (Honda), 2m 4.352s, 97.193mph/156.417km/h.
Championship points: **1** Davies, 121; **2** Parkes, 85; **3** Foret, 85; **4** Salom, 84; **5** Scassa, 79; **6** Lowes, 73.

SILVERSTONE, Great Britain, 31 July, 3.667-mile/5.902km circuit.
Supersport World Championship, Round 8 (16 laps, 58.677 miles/94.432km)
1 Chaz Davies, GBR (Yamaha), 34m 55.198s, 100.820mph/162.254km/h.
2 David Salom, ESP (Kawasaki); **3** Fabien Foret, FRA (Honda); **4** Roberto Tamburini, ITA (Yamaha); **5** Massimo Roccoli, ITA (Kawasaki); **6** Broc Parkes, AUS (Kawasaki); **7** Balazs Nemeth, HUN (Honda); **8** Miguel Praia, POR (Honda); **9** Florian Marino, FRA (Honda); **10** James Ellison, GBR (Honda); **11** Gino Rea, GBR (Honda); **12** Luca Scassa, ITA (Yamaha); **13** Alexander Lundh, SWE (Honda); **14** Ronan Quarmby, RSA (Triumph); **15** Vittorio Iannuzzo, ITA (Kawasaki).
Fastest lap: Robbin Harms, DEN (Honda), 2m 09.771s, 101.736mph/163.728km/h.
Championship points: **1** Davies, 146; **2** Salom, 104; **3** Foret, 101; **4** Parkes, 95; **5** Scassa, 83; **6** Lowes, 73.

NÜRBURGRING, Germany, 4 September, 3.192-mile/5.137km circuit.
Supersport World Championship, Round 9 (19 laps, 60.648 miles/97.603km)
1 Chaz Davies, GBR (Yamaha), 38m 10.466s, 95.322mph/153.406km/h.
2 James Ellison, GBR (Honda); **3** Sam Lowes, GBR (Honda); **4** Luca Scassa, ITA (Yamaha); **5** Massimo Roccoli, ITA (Kawasaki); **6** Fabien Foret, FRA (Honda); **7** Broc Parkes, AUS (Kawasaki); **8** David Salom, ESP (Kawasaki); **9** Florian Marino, FRA (Honda); **10** Balazs Nemeth, HUN (Honda); **11** Roberto Tamburini, ITA (Yamaha); **12** Vittorio Iannuzzo, ITA (Kawasaki); **13** Alexander Lundh, SWE (Honda); **14** Imre Toth, HUN (Honda); **15** Ronan Quarmby, RSA (Triumph).
Fastest lap: James Ellison, GBR (Honda), 1m 59.795s, 95.924mph/154.374km/h.
Championship points: **1** Davies, 171; **2** Salom, 112; **3** Foret, 111; **4** Parkes, 104; **5** Scassa, 96; **6** Lowes, 89.

IMOLA, Italy, 25 September, 3.067-mile/4.936km circuit.
Supersport World Championship, Round 10 (19 laps, 58.275 miles/93.784km)
1 Fabien Foret, FRA (Honda), 35m 56.214s, 97.295mph/156.581km/h.
2 Sam Lowes, GBR (Honda); **3** Broc Parkes, AUS (Kawasaki); **4** Florian Marino, FRA (Honda); **5** David Salom, ESP (Kawasaki); **6** James Ellison, GBR (Honda); **7** Vittorio Iannuzzo, ITA (Kawasaki); **8** Miguel Praia, POR (Honda); **9** Stefano Cruciani, ITA (Kawasaki); **10** Danilo Dell'Omo, ITA (Triumph); **11** Gino Rea, GBR (Honda); **12** Pawel Szkopek, POL (Honda); **13** Patrik Vostárek, CZE (Honda); **14** Ondrej Jezek, CZE (Honda); **15** Imre Toth, HUN (Honda).
Fastest lap: Fabien Foret, FRA (Honda), 1m 52.059s, 98.533mph/158.574km/h (record).
Championship points: **1** Davies, 171; **2** Foret, 136; **3** Salom, 123; **4** Parkes, 120; **5** Lowes, 109; **6** Scassa, 96.

MAGNY-COURS, France, 2 October, 2.741-mile/4.411km circuit.
Supersport World Championship, Round 11 (22 laps, 60.299 miles/97.042km)
1 Luca Scassa, ITA (Yamaha), 37m 48.052s, 95.710mph/154.031km/h.
2 Sam Lowes, GBR (Honda); **3** Broc Parkes, AUS (Kawasaki); **4** David Salom, ESP (Kawasaki); **5** James Ellison, GBR (Honda); **6** Chaz Davies, GBR (Yamaha); **7** Roberto Tamburini, ITA (Yamaha); **8** Fabien Foret, FRA (Honda); **9** Florian Marino, FRA (Honda); **10** Ronan Quarmby, RSA (Triumph); **11** Balazs Nemeth, HUN (Honda); **12** Vittorio Iannuzzo, ITA (Kawasaki); **13** Miguel Praia, POR (Honda); **14** Alexander Lundh, SWE (Honda); **15** Louis Bulle, FRA (Yamaha).
Fastest lap: Massimo Roccoli, ITA (Kawasaki), 1m 42.507s, 96.258mph/154.912km/h.
Championship points: **1** Davies, 181; **2** Foret, 144; **3** Parkes, 136; **4** Salom, 136; **5** Lowes, 129; **6** Scassa, 121.

PORTIMAO, Portugal, 16 October, 2.853-mile/4.592km circuit.
Supersport World Championship, Round 12 (20 laps, 57.067 miles/91.840km)
1 Chaz Davies, GBR (Yamaha), 35m 31.062s, 96.403mph/155.145km/h.
2 David Salom, ESP (Kawasaki); **3** James Ellison, GBR (Honda); **4** Luca Scassa, ITA (Yamaha); **5** Florian Marino, FRA (Honda); **6** Roberto Tamburini, ITA (Yamaha); **7** Massimo Roccoli, ITA (Kawasaki); **8** Miguel Praia, POR (Honda); **9** Vladimir Leonov, RUS (Yamaha); **10** Balazs Nemeth, HUN (Honda); **11** Vittorio Iannuzzo, ITA (Kawasaki); **12** Fabien Foret, FRA (Honda); **13** Alexander Lundh, SWE (Honda); **14** Gino Rea, GBR (Honda); **15** Pawel Szkopek, POL (Honda).
Fastest lap: James Ellison, GBR (Honda), 1m 45.638s, 97.238mph/156.489km/h.

Final World Supersport Championship points:

1	Chaz Davies, GBR	206
2	David Salom, ESP	156
3	Fabien Foret, FRA	148
4	Broc Parkes, AUS	136
5	Luca Scassa, ITA	134
6	Sam Lowes, GBR	129

7 James Ellison, GBR, 99; **8** Florian Marino, FRA, 89; **9** Roberto Tamburini, ITA, 80; **10** Massimo Roccoli, ITA, 71; **11** Gino Rea, GBR, 69; **12** Robbin Harms, DEN, 59; **13** Miguel Praia, POR, 51; **14** Vittorio Iannuzzo, ITA, 44; **15** Balazs Nemeth, HUN, 42.